ISBN 978-1-333-05040-5
PIBN 10459176

This book is a reproduction of an important historical work. Forgotten Books uses
state-of-the-art technology to digitally reconstruct the work, preserving the original format
whilst repairing imperfections present in the aged copy. In rare cases, an imperfection in
the original, such as a blemish or missing page, may be replicated in our edition. We do,
however, repair the vast majority of imperfections successfully; any imperfections that
remain are intentionally left to preserve the state of such historical works.

English
Français
Deutsche
Italiano
Español
Português

www.forgottenbooks.com

Mythology Photography **Fiction**
Fishing Christianity **Art** Cooking
Essays Buddhism Freemasonry
Medicine **Biology** Music **Ancient**
Egypt Evolution Carpentry Physics
Dance Geology **Mathematics** Fitness
Shakespeare **Folklore** Yoga Marketing
Confidence Immortality Biographies
Poetry **Psychology** Witchcraft
Electronics Chemistry History **Law**
Accounting **Philosophy** Anthropology
Alchemy Drama Quantum Mechanics
Atheism Sexual Health **Ancient History**
Entrepreneurship Languages Sport
Paleontology Needlework Islam
Metaphysics Investment Archaeology
Parenting Statistics Criminology
Motivational

SCHOOL
LAWS

OF THE

STATE OF OHIO

WITH CITATIONS
AND BLANK FORMS

1915

FRANK W. MILLER
SUPERINTENDENT OF PUBLIC INSTRUCTION

Ohio. Laws, statutes, etc.

"OHIO

SCHOOL LAWS

BLANK FORMS AND DIRECTIONS TO SERVE AS
A GUIDE FOR SCHOOL OFFICERS
AND TEACHERS.

COMPILED UNDER THE DIRECTION OF

FRANK W. MILLER,

SUPERINTENDENT OF PUBLIC INSTRUCTION.

COLUMBUS, OHIO:
THE F. J. HEER PRINTING CO.
1915

Oh' 45s

PREFACE.

This edition of the Ohio School Laws is issued in accordance with Section 356 of the General Code of Ohio.

It is the desire of the State Department of Public Instruction to issue a sufficient number of copies that not only the Boards of Education may have them but that all others sufficiently interested may be supplied.

September 8, 1915.

FRANK W. MILLER,
Superintendent of Public Instruction.

3

CONSTITUTION OF OHIO

PUBLIC SCHOOLS.

ARTICLE I.

SECTION 7. All men have a natural and indefeasible right to worship Almighty God according to the dictates of their own conscience. No person shall be compelled to attend, erect, or support any place of worship, or maintain any form of worship, against his consent; and no preference shall be given, by law, to any religious society; nor shall any interference with the rights of conscience be permitted. No religious test shall be required, as a qualification for office, nor shall any person be incompetent to be a witness on account of his religious belief; but nothing herein shall be construed to dispense with oaths and affirmations. Religion, morality, and knowledge, however, being essential to good government, it shall be the duty of the General Assembly to pass suitable laws to protect every religious denomination in the peaceable enjoyment of its own mode of public worship, and to encourage schools, and the means of instruction.

"The system of public education in Ohio is the creature of the Constitution and statutory laws of the state. It is left to the discretion of the general assembly, in the exercise of the general legislative power conferred upon it (Art II, § 1), to determine what laws are 'suitable' to secure the organization and management of the contemplated system of common schools, without express restriction, except that 'no religious or other sect or sects shall ever have any exclusive right to, or control of, any part of the school funds of this state.'" 21 O. S., 198-205; Day, J.

The compulsory education law comes within this section. 5 C. C., 645.

Under article 15, section 4 of the constitution, a woman may not be elected to or appointed to any office in this state. Under article 6, section 2 and article 1, section 7 of the constitution, however, through the powers therein conferred upon the general assembly to secure a thorough and efficient system of common schools and to encourage schools and the means of instruction, the provisions of section 4862, General Code, permitting a woman to serve as member of a board of education and to vote for members thereof, is held to be valid and constitutional.

Since, therefore, women may serve on the board of education and since, furthermore, section 4747, General Code, provides that in any district other than the township school district, a member of a board of education may be elected clerk of the board, a woman in this district may be so elected clerk, under authority of this statute.

The statutes do not confer the right, however, of a woman to serve as clerk of a township, and since the statutes require such clerk to act as clerk to the school board, a woman may not serve in the latter capacity. The statutes, furthermore, have not made provision for service as treasurer of a school board by a woman and she may, therefore, not serve in that capacity.—*Attorney General*, 1913, p. 466.

ARTICLE II.

SECTION 26. All laws, of a general nature, shall have a uniform operation throughout the state; nor, shall any act, except such as relates to public schools, be passed, to take effect upon the approval of any other authority than the General Assembly, except, as otherwise provided in this constitution.

To permit state fines to be paid into city treasury would violate Article II, Section 26 of the constitution providing against special legislation, by its interference with respect to disposition of state fines and with reference to common school funds, poor funds, and law library associations. As there is furthermore, no apparent reason for the sacrifice of state fines to the city, the ambiguity must be construed in favor of the latter language of Section 30 aforesaid, and the clerk of the municipal court given the duties which formerly devolved on the former police clerk of paying a certain portion of state fines to the law library association.—*Attorney General*, 1912, p. 270.

ARTICLE VI.

EDUCATION.

SECTION 1. The principal of all funds, arising from the sale, or other disposition of lands, or other property, granted or entrusted to this state for educational and religious purposes, shall forever be preserved inviolate, and undiminished; and, the income arising therefrom, shall be faithfully applied to the specific objects of the original grants, or appropriations.

SECTION 2. The General Assembly shall make such provisions, by taxation, or otherwise, as, with the income arising from the school trust fund, will secure a thorough and efficient system of common schools throughout the state; but no religious or other sect, or sects, shall ever have any exclusive right to, or control of, any part of the school funds of this state.

As the tuition fund is in the nature of a trust fund, for the benefit of each individual youth in the state, transfers from said fund, in the treasury of a school district to a building fund cannot be made except under provision and conditions provided for in Section 5655 General Code for the purpose of reducing tax levy estimates at the annual meeting of the board.

The common pleas court has powers, under Sections 2296-2302, General Code, to permit transfers "when no injury will result therefrom" but in view of the peculiar nature of the tuition fund, such action would be a rare possibility.—*Attorney General*, 1912, p. 1206.

Under Section 4696, General Code, the funds and indebtedness of the township school district should be equitably apportioned between the township and village district as therein provided.

The statutes do not provide specifically for the disposition of the school building situated in the village but the decisions endorse the reasonability of permitting the newly created district to take title to school property within its limits and which was designed for its use, and such is to be deemed the policy of the law.—*Attorney General*, 1912, p. 1282.

Since repeals by implication are not admitted unless the latter act is clearly inconsistent with the former, and since both constitutional and legislative provision is made for "thorough and efficient schools," the State Aid law for weak school districts has not been repealed by the Smith Law, and the Auditor is still authorized under the proper circumstances to issue his warrant for State Aid as provided in Section 7959 General Code.

Such warrant shall only be issued when the maximum levy for school board purposes, (three-fourths of which has been made for tuition purposes) is insufficient to enable the Board to pay $40.00 per month for its teachers for eight months of the year.

The "maximum levy" provided for in the State Aid law which was formerly restricted by the twelve mill limitation, is now, by reason of the Smith Law, subject to the four limitations provided for therein. It, therefore, follows that what the Budget Commission determines to be the "maximum legal school levy for the district" shall be the maximum levy for the purpose of the State Aid Law.

When, therefore, the Board has properly certified a sufficient sum to the Auditor to provide sufficiently for payment of its teachers, and the Budget Commission has reduced the allowance to such an extent that teachers cannot be paid $40.00 per month for eight months in the year under the restrictions of Section 7959 General Code and three-fourths of such allowance is made for tuition purposes, the State Auditor may issue his State Aid Warrant. — *Attorney General,* 1912, p. 89.

SECTION 3. Provision shall be made by law for the organization, administration and control of the public school system of the state supported by public funds: provided, that each school district embraced wholly or in part within any city shall have the power by referendum vote to determine for itself the number of members and the organization of the district board of education, and provision shall be made by law for the exercise of this power by such school districts.

SECTION 4. A superintendent of public instruction to replace the state commissioner of common schools, shall be included as one of the officers of the executive department to be appointed by the governor, for the term of four years, with the powers and duties now exercised by the state commissioner of common schools until otherwise provided by law, and with such other powers as may be provided by law.

1. The expenses of a teacher, appointed by the board of education as delegate to the educational congress at Columbus, December 5, 1913, may not legally be paid out of the township, village, or special school district treasury.

2. When a teacher is appointed by a board of education of a city district, such expense may not be paid from the school treasury, nor can the expenses of members of a board of education to such convention be paid out of the city fund. The expenses of persons not members of a board of education or teachers, incurred in attending the above named congress, may not be paid from the school fund. Before such expenses can be paid, an appropriation for this purpose must be made by the legislature. — *Attorney General,* 1913, p. 416.

A school district receiving permission, prior to 1913, to maintain a school for the deaf, is entitled, without further permission, to maintain such school and to receive from the state treasury the sum of one hundred and fifty $150.00) dollars for each deaf pupil taught in such school during the year ending August, 1914. — *Attorney General,* Opinion No. 8, Jan. 16, 1915.

ARTICLE XII.

SECTION 2. Laws shall be passed, taxing by a uniform rule, all moneys, credits, investments in bonds, stocks, joint stock companies, or otherwise; and also all real and personal property according to its true value in money, excepting all bonds at present outstanding of the state of Ohio or of any city, village, hamlet, county, or township in this state or which have been issued in behalf of the public schools in Ohio and the means of instruction in connection therewith, which bonds so at present outstanding shall be exempt from taxation; but burying grounds, public school houses, houses used exclusively for public worship, institutions used exclusively for charitable purposes, public property used exclusively for any public purpose, and personal property, to an amount not exceeding in value five hundred dollars, for each individual, may, by general laws, be exempted from taxation; but all such laws shall be subject to alteration or repeal; and the value of all property, so exempted, shall, from time to time, be ascertained and published as may be directed by law.

School property is not liable to assessment for street improvement; nor can a judgement be rendered against the board of education for the payment of the assessment out of its contingent fund. 48 O. S., 83.

Sidewalk — School property not assessable for. 48 O. S., 87.

The provision of the statutes providing for exemption from taxation of institutions of purely public charity, is intended to apply to private institutions as distinguished from an official or public agency. Inasmuch as the board of trustees of a teachers' pension fund constitutes a public agency rather than a private corporation, pension funds may not be exempted from taxation under this head.

Under article 12, section 2, of the constitution, the legislature would be empowered to exempt such funds under the provisions for the exemption of "public property used exclusively for any public purpose." Not having done so, however, such pension funds must be held to be technically subject to taxation. — *Attorney General*, 1913, p. 470.

Section 16 of school lands in Marion township was vested in the state in trust for school purposes, by act of congress. There is no special statutory provision making such lands amenable to assessments for pike improvements and such an assessment would furthermore be a violation of the trust defined by agreement between the state and the United States.

Nor are the trustees of said section authorized or given any power to consent to such an assessment. — *Attorney General*, 1911-12, p. 1034.

Oberlin College being conducted without a view to individual pecuniary gain is, therefore, a public college within the meaning of section 5349, General Code. The further requirement of section 5349 referring to "lands not used with a view to profit" comprehends a profit for the institution itself.

Therefore, land owned by Oberlin College and so used and also "all buildings connected therewith," such as dormitories from which a rental is charged and devoted to the aims of the institution, are exempt from taxation.

The endowment fund of Oberlin College, under section 2732, Revised Statutes, was exempt under the phase "moneys and credits appropriated solely to sustain and belonging exclusively to said institutions," and now, under said section as codified, i. e., section 5353, General Code, such fund is consistently exempt by virtue of the phrase "property belonging to institutions of public charity only." — *Attorney General*, 1911-12, p. 1298.

The question as to the constitutionality of the state highway department law was before the supreme court in the case of Link v. Karb. The decision of the court in that case constitutes the constitutionality of the law *res adjudicata*. — *Attorney General*, Opinion No. 724, Jan. 29, 1914.

Under Article XII, Section 11 of the Constitution, as amended, serial bonds may be issued, and provision for the annual levy of taxes for the retirement of the indebtedness so incurred considered as a unit, the levies being equal in amount and distribution over the entire number of years between the incurring of the indebtedness and the date of maturity of the last series, would be a sufficient compliance with the constitutional requirement that provision be made for the annual levy of an amount sufficient to provide a sinking fund, although the series might so mature as practically to preclude any accumulation of a technical fund and to require the principal to be expended in the retirement of the maturing bonds as fast as it is levied. The phrase "annual levy * * * of taxes * * * sufficient to provide * * * a sinking fund" is interpreted as requiring that the burden of taxation on account of a debt incurred at a given time shall be evenly distributed during the life of the indebtedness, considered as a unit; and not as requiring the accumulation of a "sinking fund" in the strict and technical sense. — *Attorney General*, Opinion No. 1151, Sept. 12, 1914.

The following is the correct wording of an ordinance or resolution under Article XII, Section 11 of the constitution on an issuing of bonds:

"There shall be levied and collected, by taxation, annually, during the period for which said bonds are to run, an amount sufficient to pay the interest on said bonds as herein provided for, and to provide a sinking fund for their final redemption at maturity." — *Attorney General*, Opinion No. 861, April 24, 1914.

On authority of Rabe v. Board of Education, 88 O. S., 403, Section 7629, General Code, providing for the issuance of bonds under certain circumstances, by boards of education, is still in effect. This opinion discusses the present operation under the Smith Law and Article XII, Section 11 of the Constitution. — *Attorney General*, Opinion No. 1088, Aug. 3, 1914.

Where a man holds four one thousand dollar non-taxable bonds and these bonds are due and payable on April 1, 1913, but were not presented for payment until April 16th, this date being after the second Monday of April when money. becomes subject to listing for taxation, such bonds do not lose their character, as such, by reason of their being overdue, and being non-taxable before maturity continue to be so thereafter. — *Attorney General,* Opinion 732, Feb. 2, 1914.

A board of education may borrow money under Section 5656, G. C., for the purpose of paying unpaid installments of teachers' salaries.

Bonds may not be issued under this section, however, unless within the limitations of the law interest and sinking fund levies sufficient to retire them may be made during the years for which they are to run. Such interest and sinking fund levies being preferred to current levies by the Act found in 104 O. L., 12, the board should anticipate its needs for current purposes and its needs for interest and sinking fund purposes and so apportion its indebtedness as not to impair its future revenues for either purpose. — *Attorney General,* Opinion 178, March 27, 1915.

ARTICLE XV.

MISCELLANEOUS.

SECTION 7. Every person chosen or appointed to any office under this state, before entering upon the discharge of its duties, shall take an oath or affirmation, to support the Constitution of the United States. and of this state, and also an oath of office.

PART FIRST

POLITICAL.

11

PRELIMINARY.

CHAPTER I.

GENERAL PROVISIONS.

SECTION 10. When an elective office becomes vacant, and is filled by appointment, such appointee shall hold the office until his successor is elected and qualified. Unless otherwise provided by law, such successor shall be elected for the unexpired term at the first general election for the office which is vacant that occurs more than thirty days after the vacancy shall have occurred. This section shall not be construed to postpone the time for such election beyond that at which it would have been held had no such vacancy occurred, nor to affect the official term, or the time for the commencement thereof, of any person elected to such office before the occurrence of such vacancy. (Revised statistics of 1880.) *[Term of appointee to elective office.]*

In the case of vacancies in a school board filled by appointment Section 10, General Code, provides that a successor shall be elected for the unexpired term at the first general election for such office if such vacancy occurs more than thirty days before any election.

Such appointee, however, has the same right as an elective officer to hold over until his successor is elected and qualified.

Where at an election, five positions were to be filled, two for four years and three for approximately two years and there was no designation upon the ballot to determine who were the candidates for the long term and who were the candidates for the short term, the terms were not definitely settled and there was no valid election. — *Attorney General*, 1912, p. 1102.

For the manner of filling Vacancies in office, see the provisions of law relating to the same under each office.

Vacancy does not exist by reason of death of an officer before his term begins, until the time for the commencement of such term: State, ex rel., v. Metcalf, 80 O. S. 244.

No Vacancy exists where the successful candidate dies on election day before the polls are closed, until the commencement of the term for which he was a candidate: State, ex rel., v. Speidel, 62 O. S. 156.

The election must be one at which such officers are regularly and properly elected: State, ex rel., v. Nash, 66 O. S. 612.

It must be at least thirty days after the vacancy occurs: State, ex rel., v. Dahl, 55 O. S. 195.

A prospective Vacancy cannot be filled: State, ex rel., v. Metcalf. 80 O. S. 244.

If a successor is not appointed at such election. the appointee hold office until his successor is elected and qualified: State, ex rel., v. Metcalf, 80 O. S. 244.

SECTION 19. The state, a county, township, municipal corporation, or school board. shall not be precluded by the illegal loan or deposit of an officer or agent of public money, funds, bond. securities. or assets. belonging to it, from suing for and recovering the same. Such suit shall *[Illegal loans or deposits in public officers.]*

13

not be held to be an adoption or satisfaction of such illegal transaction. (60 v. 64.)

A so-called deposit of canal funds with an insurance company to be repaid in two years is, in legal effect, a loan, and prior to the present statute, the state could not recover such authorized loan, except by ratifying the transaction and relieving the agents of liability for their misconduct: *State v. Buttles*, 3 O. S. 309.

Held not to apply to an action by a village to recover land which it has bought from A and has donated to B to induce him to establish a factory in such village: *Markley* v. *Mineral City*, 58 O. S. 430.

Sales and leases of state lands shall reserve all oil, gas, coal and other minerals.
SECTION 23-1. All sales and leases of public or other state lands, except canal lands other than reservoirs and lands appurtenant and adjacent to reservoirs, shall exclude all oil, gas, coal or other minerals on or under such lands, except lands specifically leased for such purposes separate and apart from surface leases, and all deeds for such lands executed and delivered by the state shall expressly reserve to the state all gas, oil, coal and other minerals on or under such lands with the right of entry in and upon said premises for the purpose of selling or leasing the same, or prosecuting, developing or operating the same and this provision shall affect and apply to pending actions. (106 l. 245.)

Interpretation of certain words.
SECTION 27. In the interpretation of parts first and second, unless the context shows that another sense was intended, the word "bond" includes and "undertaking," and the word "undertaking" includes a "bond;" "and" may be read "or," and "or" read "and," if the sense requires it; words of the present include a future tense, in the masculine, include the feminine and neuter genders, and in the plural include the singular and in the singular include the plural number; but this enumeration shall not be construed to require a strict construction of other words in such parts, or in this code. (Revised statutes of 1880.)

FLAG, EMBLEM, COAT OF ARMS.

Official flag of state.
SECTION 28. The flag of the state of Ohio shall be pennant shaped. It shall have three red and two white horizontal stripes; the union of the flag shall be seventeen five-pointed stars, white in a blue triangular field, the base of which shall be the staff end or vertical edge of the flag. and the apex of which shall be the center of the middle red stripe. The stars shall be grouped around a red disc superimposed upon a white circular "O". The proportional dimensions of the flag and of its various parts shall be according to the official design thereof on file in the office of the secretary of state. One state flag of uniform dimensions shall be furnished to each company of the Ohio National Guard. (106 v. 341.)

As to displaying the United States flag on schoolhouses, see G. C., Sec. 7621.

As to displaying foreign flags on public buildings, see G. C. Sec. 12395.

Floral emblem of the state.
SECTION 29. The scarlet carnation is hereby adopted as the state flower of Ohio as a token of love and reverence for the memory of William McKinley. (97 v. 631.)

SECTION 30. The coat of arms of the state of Ohio shall consist of the following device: A shield, in form, a circle; on it, in the foreground, on the right, a sheaf of wheat; on the left a bundle of seventeen arrows, both standing erect; in the background, and rising above the sheaf and arrows, a mountain range, over which shall appear a rising sun. (65 v. 175.)

Device of coat of arms of the state.

SECTION 286. A report of the examination shall be made in triplicate, one copy thereof filed in the office of the auditor of state, and one copy filed in the auditing department of the taxing district reported upon, and one in the office of the legal officer of the taxing district or in the case of village having no solicitor or legal counsel, with the mayor thereof. If the report discloses malfeasance, misfeasance, or neglect of duty on the part of an officer or an employe, upon the receipt of such copy of said report it shall be the duty of the proper legal officer and he is hereby authorized and required, to institute in the proper court within ninety days from the receipt thereof civil actions in behalf of the state or the political divisions thereof to which the right of action has accrued, and promptly prosecute the same to final determination to recover any fees or public funds misappropriated or to otherwise determine the rights of the parties in the premises. He shall notify the attorney-general of the filing of such actions, keep him fully advised of the progress therefor, and before or after such civil action is commenced it shall not be lawful for the county commissioners or any board or officer to make a settlement or compromise of any claim, such civil action or controversy arising out of such malfeasance, misfeasance or neglect of duty so reported upon, nor for any court to enter any compromise or settlement of such civil action, without first giving notice thereof to the attorney-general and allowing him to be heard in the matter. Upon the refusal or neglect of the proper legal officer to take action as herein provided, the auditor of state shall direct the attorney-general to institute and prosecute the action to a final determination of the rights of the parties in the premises, and he is hereby authorized and required to do the same. (101 v. 382.)

Triplicate report of examination.

A city school district is not authorized to pay for publication in a newspaper of a statement of receipts and expenditures for the year.

When such action is performed.

1. The newspaper cannot be held, as the payment was voluntary.

2. The members of the board of education who voted for the move are guilty of a misfeasance and are subject under the terms of 286, G. C., to civil action by the proper legal officer for a recovery.

3. The president, clerk and treasurer, acting in good faith, in their respective capacities performed merely ministerial acts and are therefore not liable. — *Attorney General*, 1911-12, p. 272.

TITLE III. EXECUTIVE.

APPOINTIVE STATE OFFICERS.

CHAPTER 6.

SUPERINTENDENT OF PUBLIC INSTRUCTION.

Duties.

Employment of counsel, see G. C. 333.
School books to be submitted to, before purchase by board of education, see G. C. 7711.

SECTION 333. The attorney-general shall be the chief law officer for the state and all its departments. No state officer, board, or the head of a department or institution of the state shall employ, or be represented by, other counsel or attorneys-at-law. The attorney-general shall appear for the state in the trial and argument of all civil and criminal causes in the supreme court in which the state may be directly or indirectly interested. When required by the governor or the general assembly, he shall appear for the state in any court or tribunal in a cause in which the state is a party, or in which the state is directly interested. Upon the written request of the governor, he shall prosecute any person indicted for a crime. (97 v. 59.)

Superintendent of public instruction; appointment and term.

SECTION 352. There shall be a superintendent of public instruction, who shall be appointed by the Governor. He shall hold his office for a term of four years, and until his successor is appointed and qualified, such term commencing on the second Monday of July. He shall have an office in or near the state house, in which the books and papers pertaining to his office shall be kept. (104 v. 225.)

As to the appointment of state board of examiners by the state superintendent of public instruction, see G. C. 7805.

When the law requires that the state school commissioner will commence his term on Monday, July 10, the term of his predecessor expires on Sunday, July 9, at midnight, and Monday, July 10, belongs to the administration of the elected commissioner. — *Attorney General*, 1911-1912, p. 533.

Who eligible as superintendent.

SECTION 352-1. No one who is interested financially or otherwise in any book publishing or book selling company, firm or corporation, shall be eligible to appointment

16

as superintendent of public instruction. If any superintendent of public instruction becomes interested financially or otherwise, in any book publishing or book selling company, firm or corporation said superintendent of public instruction shall forthwith be removed from office by the governor. (104 v. 225.)

SECTION 353. Before entering upon the discharge of the duties of his office, the superintendent of public instruction shall give a bond to the state in the sum of five thousand dollars, with two or more sureties approved by the secretary of state, conditioned for the faithful discharge of the duties of his office. Such bond, with the approval of the secretary of state and the oath of office indorsed thereon, shall be deposited with secretary of state and kept in his office. (103 v. 528.)

Bond of superintendent, where filed.

SECTION 353-1. The superintendent of public instruction may employ such clerks, stenographers and assistants as will enable him to properly care for the duties of his office. The compensation of such appointees shall be fixed by the superintendent of public instruction, with the approval of the governor. (104 v. 225.)

Employment of clerks and assistants.

SECTIION 360. The superintendent of public instruction while holding such office shall not perform the duties of teacher or superintendent of a public or private school, or be employed as teacher in a college or hold any other office or position of employment. He may visit and inspect schools and attend educational gatherings either within or without the state, and deliver lectures on topics calculated to subserve the interests of popular education, and his necessary and actual expenses therefor when properly verified shall be paid by the state. (104 v. 225.)

Duties of Superintendent.

SECTION 355. The superintendent of public instruction shall have such supervision of the school funds of the state as is necessary to secure their safety and distribution as provided by law. He may require of auditors and treasurers of counties, boards of education, teachers, clerks and treasurers of such boards, and other local school officers, copies of all reports made by them in pursuance of law. He may also require of such officers any other information he deems proper in relation to the condition and management of schools and school funds. (104 v. 225.)

Supervision of school funds and reports.

SECTION 356. The superintendent of public instruction shall collate the laws relating to schools and teachers' institutes, and provide an appendix of forms and instructions for their execution. He may revise such collation and appendix as often as changes therein are in his opinion necessary. (106 v. 508.)

Collate school laws and forms.

Any notes which the superintendent of public instruction may insert in his book of school laws are in the nature of advice to school officers, and are of great force and weight, although not a judicial interpretation of the law: State, ex rel., v. Treasurer, 2 O. C. 363, 1 C. D. 532.

Forms and regulations for reports and proceedings.

SECTION 357. The superintendent of public instruction shall prescribe suitable forms and regulations for the reports and other proceedings required by the school laws, with such instructions for the organization and government of schools as he deems necessary, and transmit them to the local school officers, who shall be governed thereby in the performance of their duties. (104 v. 225.)

Publication and distribution of Arbor Day manual.

SECTION 358. The superintendent of public instruction shall issue each year a manual for arbor day exercises. The manual shall contain matters relating to forestry and birds, including a copy of such laws relating to the protection of song and insectivorous birds as he deems proper. He shall transmit copies of the manual to the superintendent of city, village, and rural schools and to the clerks of boards of education, who shall cause them to be distributed among the teachers of the schools under their charge. On arbor day, and other days when convenient, the teachers shall cause such laws to be read to the scholars of their respective schools and shall encourage them to aid in the protection of such birds. (104 v. 225.)

Reports from private schools.

SECTION 359. Each year the superintendent of public instruction shall require a report of the president, manager or principal of each seminary, academy or private school. The report shall be made upon blanks furnished by the superintendent and contain a statement of such facts as he prescribes. The president, manager or principal shall fill up and return the blanks within a time fixed by the superintendent of public instruction. (104 v. 225.)

Annual report of superintendent to governor.

SECTION 360. The superintendent fo public instruction shall make an annual report to the governor, which shall contain a statement of the amount and condition of the funds and property appropriated for purposes of education; the number of common schools in the state, the number of scholars attending such schools, their sex and the branches taught; the number of private or select schools in the state so far as can be obtained, the number of scholars attending such schools, their sex and the branches taught; the number of teachers' institutes, the number of teachers attending them, the number of instructors and lecturers employed therein and the amount paid to each; the estimate and accounts of expenditures of the public school fund, plans for the management and improvement of common schools, and such other information relative to the educational interests of the state as the superintendent deems important. (104 v. 225.)

As to the duty of county auditors in transmitting abstracts of school statistics to State Superintendent of Public Instruction, see C. C. Sec. 7789.

Complaint of fraudulent use of school funds.

SECTION 361. When three or more resident taxpayers of a school district have reason to believe that any portion of the school funds of the district has been unlawfully expended or misapplied by the officers thereof, or that fraudulent entries have have been made by an officer in the books, accounts, vouchers, or settlement sheets of the district, or that an officer has not made settlement of his account as required by law, they may make complaint thereof in writing, verify it by the affidavits of at least three such taxpayers, with the certificate of the auditor of the county that they are taxpayers attached, and file such complaint with the superintendent of public instruction. (104 v. 225.)

Cited by mistake in Commissioners v. Pennsylvania Co., 1 O. C. C. (N. S.) 409, 14 O. C. D. 550.

SECTION 362. Upon the filing of complaint, or when for other cause he deems it necessary, the superintendent of public instruction shall request the auditor of state to detail an examiner of his department to investigate the condition of the school funds of a district. The examiner shall be trustworthy and competent accountant and shall have authority to summon witnesses before him forthwith upon written notice and examine them under oath administered by him. He shall be sworn by a person authorized by law to administer oaths, and shall forthwith visit the school district, take possession of the books, papers, vouchers and accounts thereof and begin such investigation. (104 v. 225.) Examiner to investigate condition of funds.

Cited by mistake in Commissioners v. Pennsylvania Co., 1 O. C. C. (N. S.) 409, 14 O. C. D. 550.

SECTION 363. On application of the examiner, the officers of the school district shall immediately place in his passession the books, accounts, contracts, vouchers and other papers relating to the receipts and expenditures of the school funds. The auditor and treasurer of the county shall afford the examiner free access to the records, books, papers, vouchers and accounts of their respective offices relating to the subject of the investigation. (94 v. 313.) Duty of certain officers in case of examination.

SECTION 364. After completing an investigation, the examiner shall make a report in writing in duplicate showing the condition of the books, vouchers and accounts of the district, the amount of school funds received for all purposes and from what sources, the amount thereof expended and for what purposes and the amount in the treasury. The examiner shall file one copy of the report with the president of the county board of education of the county in which the district is located, and transmit the other to the superintendent of public instruction. (104 v. 225.) Report of examiner.

SECTION 365. With the written consent of the prosecuting attorney or a judge of the court of common pleas of the county in which the school district is located, the examiner may require the services of the official court stenographer of the county to aid him in making such examination; but the stenographer shall receive no compensation for such service in addition to the compensation provided for him by law. (94 v. 312.) Stenographer for examiner.

Cited by mistake in Commissioners v. Pennsylvania Co., 1 O. C. C. (N. S.) 409, 14 O. C. D. 550.

Compensation and mileage of examiner.

SECTION 366. The examiner shall receive five dollars for each day necessarily engaged in the performance of his duties and five cents for each mile of necessary travel not exceeding the distance from the seat of government to the school district. The compensation and mileage of the examiner shall be paid from the county treasurer upon the warrant of the county auditor. If the complaint or other cause be sustained, the amount so paid shall be assessed by the county auditor upon the taxable property of the school district and collected as other taxes. (94 v. 313.)

See court of common pleas, G. C. 11215, 13425.
See prosecuting attorney, G. C. 2909, et seq.
See grand jury, G. C. 13554, et seq.

Duty of judge and prosecuting attorney.

SECTION 367. A judge of the court of common pleas of the proper county shall examine the report of the examiner filed with the clerk, and, if it appear therefrom that any part of the school funds has been unlawfully used or misapplied, or that there has been fraud in the entries, accounts, vouchers, contracts or settlements, or that the settlements have not been made as required by law; or, if it appear thereform that there has been defalcation or embezzlement by an officer of such district, he shall give the reports specially in charge to the grand jury at the term of court following the filing of the report. The prosecuting attorney of the county shall forthwith prosecute such proceedings, civil or criminal, or both, as are authorized by law, against the delinquent officer or officers. (72 v. 82.)

This section neither expressly nor by implication confers upon the prosecuting attorney power to bring suit to enjoin the board of education from applying money, arising from taxes levied to build a schoolhouse, to the purpose of repaying money borrowed by such board in anticipation of such taxes: State, ex rel., v. Board of Education, 11 O. C. C. 41, 5 O. C. D. 447.

TITLE IV. JUDICIAL.

CHAPTER 8.

JUVENILE COURT.

SECTION 1639. Courts of common pleas, probate courts, and insolvency courts and superior courts, where established shall have and exercise, concurrently, the powers and jurisdiction conferred in this chapter. The judges of such courts in each county, at such times as they determine, shall designate one of their number to transact the business arising under such jurisdiction. When the term of the judge so designated expires, or his office terminates, another designation shall be made in like manner. *Courts having powers and jurisdiction under this chapter.*

The words, juvenile court when used in the statutes of Ohio shall be understood as meaning the court in which the judge so designated may be sitting while exercising such jurisdiction, and the words "judge of the juvenile court" or "juvenile judge" as meaning such judge while exercising such jurisdiction. *Juvenile court defined.*

The foregoing provisions shall not apply to Hamilton county, in which county the powers and jurisdiction conferred in this chapter shall be exercised by the court of common pleas, and in 1914 and every sixth year thereafter, one of the common pleas judges to be elected at said times shall be elected as a judge of the court of common pleas. *Provisions do not apply to Hamilton county; division of domestic relation and juvenile work.*

21

division of domestic relation. To him shall be assigned all juvenile court work arising under this chapter, and all divorce and alimony cases, and whenever said judge of the court of common pleas, division of domestic relations, shall be sick, absent or unable to perform his duties, the presiding judge of the common pleas court shall assign another common pleas judge to perform his duties during his illness, absence or indisposition. (104 v. 176.)

The federal court cannot adjudge that the juvenile act, (Gen. Code Ohio, Sec. 1629-1683) regulating the treatment and control of delinquent children, and giving the juvenile court jurisdiction over delinquent children, is invalid because it does not provide for a jury trial, since the privileges and immunities of a citizen do not include the right to a jury trial in a state court. 196 F. 125.

This act is constitutional; and the probate judge may be designated to act as judge of the juvenile court: Travis v. State, 12 O. C. C. (N. S.) 874, 21 O. C. D. 492.

1. The act of April 16, 1906, establishing juvenile courts and establishing procedure therein, does not contravene any of the provisions of the state Constitution.

2. In counties where three or more common pleas judges regularly hold court concurrently it is competent under section 548-361 that the probate judge should be designated to perform all the duties pertaining to the office of judge of the juvenile court. 12 O. C. C. (IV. S.) 374.

Sec. 548-361 cited in 12 O. C. C. above was repealed in 99 v. 192 and in substance re-enacted as Sec. 1639.

The only costs chargeable under the Mother's Pension Act are those incident to the hearing motion provided for under Section 1683-8, General Code.

The fees in such proceedings as are provided by law for services in the court, the Judge of which is exercising the juvenile jurisdiction at the time, may be taxed as costs in such proceedings. Such costs cannot be paid out of the county treasury. In the event that they are not paid by the contestor, as provided in Section 1683-8, they must go unpaid. — *Attorney General*, Opinion No. 1063, July 20, 1914.

Seal.

SECTION 1640. The seal of the court, the judge of which is designated to transact such business, shall be attached to all writs and processes. (99 v. 192.)

Appearance docket and journal.

SECTION 1641. The clerk of the court of the judge exercising the jurisdiction shall keep an appearance docket and a journal, in the former of which shall be entered the style of the case and a minute of each proceeding and in the latter of which shall be entered all orders, judgments and findings of the court. (99 v. 192.)

Jurisdiction.

SECTION 1642. Such courts of common pleas, probate courts, insolvency courts and superior courts within the provisions of this chapter shall have jurisdiction over and with respect to delinquent, neglected and dependent minors, under the age of eighteen years, not inmates of a state institution, or any institution incorporated under the laws of the state for the care and correction of delinquent neglected and dependent children, and their parents, guardians, or any person, persons, corporation or agent of a corporation, responsible for, or guilty of causing encouraging, aiding, abetting or contributing toward the deliquency, neglect or dependency of such minor, and such courts shall have jurisdiction to hear and determine any charge or prosecution against any person, persons, corporations, or their agents, for the commission of any misdemeanor involving the care, protection, education or comfort of any such minor under the age of eighteen years. (103 v. 864.)

The jurisdiction of the juvenile court extends to delinquent and dependent children who are inmates of all institutions except state institutions and incorporated institutions.

Jurisdiction of the juvenile court, when once acquired, continues until said child reaches its majority, unless said court commits it to a state institution, in which case control of the child is transferred to the respective state authorities.

When a child inmate which has been committed to an institution other than. those above excepted, becomes incorrigible or delinquent, the juvenile court has power in renewed proceedings or probably in the exercise of its continuing jurisdiction, to commit said child to another institution, state or otherwise.

If, in the judgment of the court, the care betsowed upon an inmate by any institution other than a state institution is deficient or detrimental to the child, said court may recommit said child to another institution.

In accordance with the above principles, the court, after having committed a dependent child to a city house of refuge, may when such child develops incorrigibility, commit him to the boys' industrial home. — *Attorney General*, 1912, p. 926.

SECTION 1643. When a child under the age of eighteen years comes into the custody of the court under the provisions of this chapter, such child shall continue for all necessary purposes of discipline and protection, a ward of the court, until he or she attain the age of twenty-one years. The power of the court over such child shall continue until the child attains such age. (103 v. 864.) When jurisdiction terminates.

n a prosecution of a minor under 17 years for being a "delinquent child" Iand "guilty of immoral conduct" as described by General Code 1644, evidence that complainant has a bad reputation or has been guilty of immoral conduct is not admissible, the purpose of the law being reformatory rather than retaliatory: State v. Hawkins, 56 Bull. 166.

"Delinquent child" was defined with sufficient accuracy under a former statute (98 v. 814): Travis v. State, 12 O. C. C. (N. S.) 374, 21 O. C. D. 492. See Section 1642 for attorney general opinion.

As .the statutes do not go · further than to authorize the probate courts to commit juvenile delinquents to institutions or reputable citizens within . this state, a probation officer may not be allowed his expenses for transporting a minor under direction of probate court to a home outside of the state. — *Attorney General*, 1911-1912, p. 1181.

The statutes do not authorize the payment from the county treasury of the expenses of transporting juvenile delinquents to relatives outside of the state.

Section 1682 authorizing expenses in such cases is confined to the transportation of such children to institutions or citizens within this state. *Attorney General*, 1911-1912, p. 1003.

1. The trustees of the county children's home cannot refuse to receive a child committed by the juvenile court to such home, unless such child so presented for admission is afflicted' with an infectious or contagious disease.

2. The trustees of a children's home have the right to accept through arrangement with parents children for temporary care and custody.

3. In the commitment of a child to the children's home by the juvenile court, the trustees of the institution are immediately vested with the guardianship and control of the child subject to the continuing jurisdiction of the juvenile court for the purpose of discipline and protection.

4. A dependent child of parents resident of the county, both of which parents have died, is eligible for admission to the county children's home, although such child is not yet one year of age. Section 3089, General Code, providing that the child should have resided in the county not less than one year not being one made for the purpose of placing a limitation upon the age of the child, but for the purpose of establishing residence.

5. The board of trustees have the legal right, to enter into a contract with proper families to board and care for a child of tender years, when such children's home is not properly equipped to care for such children. — *Attorney General*, Opinion No. 969, June 6, 1914.

The juvenile court can, at its pleasure, recall a child previously committed by it to a children's home, without any specific instructions as to future disposition of such child.

The juvenile court which has committed a child to the children's home, can recall such child after it has been placed in a foster home by the trustees, under Section 3100, General Code.

The trustees of county children's homes may remove a child from a foster home without giving any cause for such removal to the foster parents. — *Attorney General*, Opinion No. 1345, December 30, 1914.

"Delinquent Child" defined.

SECTION 1644. For the purpose of this chapter, the words "Delinquent child" includes any child under eighteen years of age who violates a law of this state, or a city or village ordinance, or who is incorrigible; or who knowingly associates with thieves, vicious or immoral persons; or who is growing up in idleness or crime; or who knowingly visits or enters a house of ill repute; or who knowingly patronizes or visits a policy shop or place where any gambling device or gambling scheme is, or shall be, operated or conducted; or who patronizes or visits a saloon or dram shop where intoxicating liquors are sold; or who patronizes or visits a public pool or billiard room or bucket shop; or who wanders about the streets in the night time; or who wanders about railroad yards or tracks, or jumps or catches on to a moving train, traction or street car, or enters a car or engine without lawful authority, or who uses vile, obscene, vulgar, profane or indecent language, or who is guilty of immoral conduct; or who uses cigarettes, cigarette wrapper or substitute for either, or cigars, or tabacco; or who visits or frequents any theater, gallery, penny arcade or moving picture show where lewd, vulgar or indecent pictures, exhibitions or performances are displayed, exhibited or given, or who is an habitual truant; or who uses any injurious or narcotic drug. A child committing any of the acts herein mentioned shall be deemed a juvenile delinquent person, and be proceeding against in the manner hereinafter provided. (106 v. 458.)

1. The trustees of the county children's home cannot refuse to receive a child committed by the juvenile court to such home, unless such child so presented for admission is afflicted with an infectious or contagious disease.

2. The trustees of a children's home have the right to accept through arrangement with parents children for temporary care and custody.

3. In the commitment of a child to the children's home by the juvenile court, the trustees of the institution are immediately

vested with the guardianship and control of the child subject to the continuing jurisdiction of the juvenile court for the purpose of discipline and protection.

4. A dependent child of parents resident of the county, both of which parents have died, is eligible for admission to the county children's home, although such child is not yet one year of age. Section 3089, General Code, providing that the child should have resided in the county not less than one year not being one made for the purpose of placing a limitation upon the age of the child, but for the purpose of establishing residence.

5. The board of trustees have the legal right, to enter into a contract with proper families to board and care for a child of tender years, when such children's home is not properly equipped to care for such children. — *Attorney General*, Opinion No. 969, June 6, 1914.

Charging accused with unlawfully aiding, encouraging and contributing to the delinquency of a female minor child and stating acts, means and methods of causing delinquency, states offense: Fisher v. State, 84 O. S. 360.

Evidence of complainant's immoral conduct inadmissible in prosecution against delinquent: State v. Hawkins, 56 Bull. 166.

"Dependent child" defined with sufficient accuracy under the former statute: Travis v. State, 12 O. C. C. (N. S.) 374, 21 O. C. D. 492.

In prosecution of a minor under seventeen, as prescribed by this section, evidence of complainant's bad reputation or immoral conduct is not admissible: State v. Hawkins, 56 Bull. No. 166.

SECTION 1645. For the purpose of this chapter, the words "dependent child" shall mean any child under eighteen years of age who is dependent upon the public for support; or who is destitute, homeless or abandoned; or who has not proper parental care or guardianship; or who begs or receives alms; or who is given away or disposed of in any employment, service, exhibition, occupation or vocation contrary to any law of this state; who is found living in a house of ill fame, or with any vicious or disreputable persons or whose home, by reason of neglect, cruelty or depravity on the part of its parent; step-parent guardian or other person in whose care it may be, is an unfit place for such child; or who is prevented from receiving proper education because of the conduct or neglect of its parent, step-parent, guardian or other person in whose care it may be; or whose environment is such as to warrant the state, in the interest of the child, in assuming its guardianship. (106 v. 458.)

"Dependent Child" defined.

SECTION 1646. A child within the provisions of this chapter whose parents, step-parents or guardian permits it to use or become addicted to the use of tobacco, or intoxicating liquors as a beverage and not for medicinal purposes, or any injurious or narcotic drug, or whose parents or guardian rears, keeps or permits it in or about a saloon or place where intoxicating liquors are sold, or a gambling house or place where gambling is practiced or carried on, or a house of ill fame, or ill repute, shall be deemed to be without proper parental care or guardianship. The word "child" or "children" may mean one or more children and includes males and females. The word "parent" may mean one or both parents or step-parents when consistent with the intent of this chapter. The word "minor" means child. (103 v. 864.)

"Proper parental care" defined.

Who may file
complaint.

SECTION 1647. Any person having knowledge of a minor under the age of eighteen years who appears to be either a delinquent, neglected or dependent child, may file with such juvenile court a complaint, sworn to, which may be upon information and belief, and for that purpose such complaint shall be sufficiently definite by using the word delinquent, or dependent, as the facts may be. (103 v. 864.)

Citation, war-
rant, con-
tempt

SECTION 1648. Upon filing of the the complaint, a citation shall issue, requiring such minor to appear, and the parents or guardian or other person, if any, having custody or control of the child or with whom it may be, to appear with the minor at a time and place to be stated in the citation; or the judge may in the first instance, issue a warrant for the arrest of such minor or for any person named in the complaint and charged therein with having abused or abandoned, or charged therein with neglect of or being responsible for or having encouraged, aided or abetted the delinquency or dependency of such child, or having acted in a way tending to cause delinquency in such child. A parent, step-parent, guardian or other person not cited may be subpœnaed to appear and testify at the hearing. Any one cited or subpœnaed to appear who fails to do so, may be punished as in other cases in the common pleas court for contempt of court. Whenever it shall appear from affidavit that a parent or guardian or other person having the custody of such child resides or has gone out of the state or that his or her place of residence is unknown so that such citation cannot be served on him or her, the clerk shall cause such citation to be published once in a newspaper of general circulation throughout the county, and published in the county, if there be one so published. The citation shall state the nature of the complaint, and the time and place of the hearing, which shall be held at least two weeks later than the date of the publication; and a copy of such citation shall be sent by mail to the last known address of such parent, guardian or other person having custody of such child, unless said affidavit, shows that a reasonable effort has been made without success to ascertain such address. The certificate of the clerk that such publication has been made or such citation mailed shall be sufficient evidence thereof. Until the time for the hearing arrives, the court shall make such temporary disposition of such child as it may deem best. When said period of two weeks from the time of publication shall have elapsed, said court shall have full jurisdiction to deal with such child as provided by this chapter. When a person charged with violating a provision of this chapter shall have fled from justice in this state, such judge shall have all the powers of a magistrate under the laws of this state relating to fugitives from justice. (103 v. 864.)

In publishing citations for non-resident parents that come into juvenile court as provided in Section 1648, General Code, the language of the statute should be followed and the citation rather than an abstract of its contents, and the time and place of the hearing should be published. — *Attorney General*, 1913, p. 1711.

SECTION 1648-1. In any case where a child under the age of eighteen years is arrested with or without a warrant, in order to avoid the incarceration of such child, if practicable, the officer so arresting, unless otherwise ordered by the court, shall accept the written promise of the parent, guardian or other person with whom such child resides, or any other reputable person, to be responsible for the presence of said child in the proper court at the time and place when such child is to appear, and at any other time to which the hearing in the case may be continued or adjourned by the court. Nothing herein contained shall be construed to prevent the admitting of such child to bail, in accordance with the general provisions of the crimes act. (103 v. 864.) *(margin: Provision to avoid incarceration.)*

SECTION 1649. The county commissioners shall provide a special room not used for the trial of criminal cases, when avoidable, for the hearing of juvenile cases. (99 v. 194.) *(margin: Special room for juvenile court.)*

SECTION 1650. On the day named in the citation or upon the return of the warrant of arrest, or as soon thereafter as may be, the judge shall proceed, in a summary manner to hear and dispose of the case, and the person arrested or cited to appear may be punished in the manner hereinafter provided. (99 v. 194.) *(margin: Hearing.)*

SECTION 1651. Any person charged with violating any of the provisions of this chapter or being responsible for or with causing, aiding or contributing to the delinquency, dependency or neglect of a child, or with acting in a way tending to cause delinquency in a child, arrested or cited to appear before such court, at any time before hearing, may demand a trial by jury, or the judge upon his own motion may call a jury. The statutes relating to the drawing and impaneling of jurors in criminal cases in the court of common pleas, other than in capital cases, shall apply to such jury trial. The compensation of jurors and costs of the clerk and sheriff shall be taxed and paid as in criminal cases in the court of common plea. (103 v. 864.) *(margin: Jury trial; costs.)*

SECTION 1652. In case of a delinquent child the judge may continue the hearing from time to time, and may commit the child to the care or custody of a probation officer, and may allow such child to remain at its own home, subject to the visitation of the probation officer or otherwise, as the court may direct, and subject to be returned to the judge for further or other proceedings whenever such action may appear to be necessary; or the judge may cause the child to be placed in a suitable family home subject to the friendly supervision of a probation officer, and the fur- *(margin: Commitment.)*

ther order of the judge, or he may authorize the child to be boarded in some suitable family home in case provision be made by voluntary contribution or otherwise for the payment of the board of such child, until suitable provision be made for it in a home without such payment; or the judge may commit such child, if a boy, to a training school for boys, or, if a girl, to an industrial school for girls, or commit the child to any institution within the county that may care for delinquent children, or be provided by a city or county suitable for the care of such children. In no case shall a child, committed to such institutions, be confined under such commitment after attaining the age of twenty-one years; or the judge may commit the child to the care and custody of an association that will receive it, embracing in its objects, the care of neglected or dependent children, if duly approved by the board of state charities, as provided by law. Where it appears at the hearing of a male delinquent child, that he is 16 years of age, or over, and has committed a felony, the juvenile ocurt may commit such child to the Ohio state reformatory. (103 v. 864.)

The juvenile court can, at its pleasure, recall a child previously committed by it to a children's home, without any specific instructions as to future disposition of such child.

The juvenile court which has committed a child to the children's home, can recall such child after it has been placed in a foster home by the trustees, under Section 3100, General Code.

The trustees of county children's homes may remove a child from a foster home without giving any cause for such removal to the foster parents. — Attorney General, Opinion No. 1345, Dec. 30, 1914.

1. The trustees of the county children's home cannot refuse to receive a child committed by the juvenile court to such home, unless such child so presented for admission is afflicted with an infectious or contagious disease.

2. The trustees of a children's home have the right to accept through arrangement with parents children for temporary care and custody.

3. In the committment of a child to the children's home by the juvenile court, the trustees of the institution are immediately vested with the guardianship and control of the child subject to the continuing jurisdiction of the juvenile court for the purpose of discipline and protection.

4. A dependent child of parent resident of the county, both of which parents have died, is eligible for admission to the county children's home, although such child is not yet one year of age. Section 3089, General Code, providing that the child should have resided in the county not less than one year not being one made for the purpose of placing a limitation upon the age of the child, but for the purpose of establishing residence.

5. The board of trustees have the legal right, to enter into a contract with proper families to board and care for a child of tender years, when such children's home is not properly equipped to care for such children. — Attorney General, Opinion No. 969, June 6, 1914.

When a boy is committed to the Boy's Industrial School by the juvenile court, the jurisdiction of the juvenile court ceases and such boy can only be released from the Industrial School by the Board of Administration, upon the recommendation of the superintendent.

If the juvenile court desires to grant a rehearing in the case of a boy committed to the Boys' Industrial School, it must do so within the time laid down by the rule of the court provided the same is within the term at which the boy was committed. — *Attorey General,* Opinion No. 1377, Jan. 6, 1915.

SECTION 1652-1. Every child coming within the provisions of this chapter, and by virtue of its provisions is committed to any institution, may be subjected to a physical and mental examination by a competent physician, or physicians, to be appointed by the juvenile court, and the physician so appointed shall certify the condition in which he finds such child, a copy of which certificate shall be sent to the institution, or person to whom it is committed. The boys' industrial school, the girls' industrial school and other penal institutions of the state shall provide separate quarters for any such child so certified as having a contagious or infectious disease. The juvenile court shall tax as part of the costs, a reasonable fee for such examination. (103 v. 864.)

Examination by competent physician.

SECTION 1653. When a minor under the age of eighteen years, or any ward of the court under this chapter, is found to be dependent or neglected, the judge may make an order commiting such child to the care of the children's home if there be one in the county where such court is held, if not, to such a home in another county, if willing to receive such child, for which the county commissioners of the county in which it has a settlement, shall pay reasonable board; or he may commit such child to the board of state charities or to some suitable state or county institution, or to the care of some reputable citizen of good moral character, or to the care of some training school or an industrial school, as provided by law, or to the care of some association willing to receive it, which embraces within its objects the purposes of caring for or obtaining homes for dependent, neglected or delinquent children or any of them, and which has been approved by the board of state charities as provided by law. When the health or condition of the child shall require it, the judge may cause the child to be placed in a public hospital or institution for treatment or special care, or in a private hospital or institution which will receive it for like purposes without charge. The court may make an examination regarding the income of the parents or guardian of a minor committed as provided by this section and may then order that such parent or guardian pay the institution or board to which the minor has been committed reasonable board for such minor, which order, if disobeyed, may be enforced by attachment as for contempt. (103 v. 864.)

Commitment to institution or suitable person.

As the statutes do not go further than to authorize the probate courts to commit juvenile delinquents to institutions or reputable citizens within this state, a probation officer may not be allowed his expenses for transporting a minor under direction of probate court to a home outside of the state. — *Attorney General,* 1911-1912, p. 1181.

The statutes do not authorize the payment from the county treasury of the expenses of transporting juvenile delinquents to relatives outside of the state.

Section 1682 authorizing expenses in such cases is confined to the transportation of such children to institutions or citizens within this state. — *Attorney General,* 1911-1912, p. 1003.

The jurisdiction of the juvenile court extends to delinquent and dependent children who are inmates of all institutions except state institutions and incorporated institutions.

Jurisdiction of the juvenile court, when once acquired, continues until said child reaches its majority, unless said court commits it to a state institution, in which case control of the child is transferred to the respective state authorities.

When a child inmate which has been committed to an institution other than those above excepted, becomes incorrigible or delinquent, the juvenile court has power in renewed proceedings or probably in the exercise of its continuing jurisdiction, to commit said child to another institution, state or otherwise.

If, in the judgment of the court, the care bestowed upon an inmate by any institution other than a state institution is deficient or detrimental to the child said court may recommit said child to another institution.

In accordance with the above principles, the court, after having committed a dependent child to a city house of refuge, may, when such child develops incorrigibility, commit him to the boys' industrial home. — *Attorney General,* 1912, p. 926.

Age limitations.

SECTION 1653-1. The provisions of section 1652 shall not apply to the girls' industrial school or the boys' industrial school, so far as the same allows the commitment of a child under ten years or over eighteen years of age to such institution. In no case shall a child found to be a dependent or neglected child be committed to such institution, nor shall any child under ten years or over eighteen years of age, be committed to such schools except as provided in section 2111 of the General Code. (103 v. 864.)

Penalty for abuse or aiding and abetting delinquency.

SECTION 1654. Whoever abuses a child or aids, abets, induces, causes, encourages or contributes toward the dependency, neglect or delinquency, as herein defined, of a minor under the age of eighteen years, or acts in a way tending to cause delinquency in such minor, shall be fined not less than ten dollars, nor more than one thousand dollars or imprisoned not less than ten days nor more than one year, or both. Each day of such contribution to such dependency, neglect or delinquency, shall be deemed a separate offense. If in his judgment it is for the best interest of a delinquent minor, under the age of eighteen years, the judge may impose a fine upon such delinquent not exceeding ten dollars, and he may order such person to stand committed until fine and costs are paid. (103 v. 864.)

An affidavit charging that F. on or about the 1st day of March, 1909, and at divers other days and times between that date and the 1st day of April, 1910, did unlawfully, aid, abet, induce, cause, encourage and contribute to the delinquency of L. S., a female, minor child, and further stating the acts, means and methods by which he contributed to such delinquency, states an offense under the provisions of this section, and is not bad for duplicity: Fisher v. State, 84 O. S. 360.

Delinquency must be an existing condition, to which all persons aiding or contributing may be held amenable under this section: State v. Hawkins, 56 Bull. 166.

The crime as charged in this affidavit is in its nature a continuing one. It is predicated upon the fact that S. is a "delinquent child", and that fact is the first one necessary to be proven, for it is only when she, by his aid, inducement, and encouragement has become a "delinquent" within the meaning of Sec. 1644, Gen. Code, that the crime of contributing to her delinquency is complete. * * * This defendant might have committed numerous acts that would tend to contribute to her delinquency, yet if these *facts* failed in their purpose, he would not be guilty of an offense within the prohibition of Section 1644, Gen. Code. It is only when by his aid, inducement and encouragement she has become a "delinquent" within the meaning of the statute that the crime of contributing to her delinquency is complete. (Ibid.)

Delinquency for which a minor under seventeen years may be prosecuted must be an existing condition, to which all persons aiding, abetting or contributing may be held amenable under General Code 1654 there being no limitation on account of age, sex or moral condition: State v. Hawkins, 56 Bull. 166.

·SECTION 1655. Whoever is charged by law with the care, support, maintenance or education of a minor under the age of eighteen years, and is able to support or contribute toward the support or education of such minor, fails, neglects, or refuses so to do, or who abandons such minor, or who unlawfully beats, injures, or otherwise ill treats such minor, or causes or allows him or her to engage in common begging, upon complaint filed in the juvenile court, as provided in this chapter, shall be fined not less than ten dollars, nor more than five hundred dollars, or imprisoned not less than ten days nor more than one year, or both. Such neglect, non-support, or abandonment shall be deemed to have been committed in the county in which such minor may be at the time of such neglect, non-support, or abandonment. Each day of such failure, neglect, or refusal shall constitute a separate offense, and the judge may order that such person stand committed until such fines and costs are paid. (103 v. 864.) [Failure or neglect to support; penalty.]

Under a former statute (94 O. L. 105, Bates, No. 1340-2) a non-resident parent was not within its provisions: State v. Ewers, without report, 76 O. S. 563.
Under the act in its present form (see also G. C. 13011) a non-resident parent may be prosecuted for non-support: State v. Sanner, 81 O. S. 393.

SECTION 1656. When a person is convicted and sentenced under this chapter for the abandonment of, or for the neglect of, or failure to maintain or support a minor, to imprisonment in a workhouse, the county from which such prisoner is so sentenced, shall pay from the general revenue fund fifty cents, for each day such prisoner is so confined. to the chief probation officer of such county, to be by him expended, under the direction of the judge, for the maintenance of the dependent minors of such prisoner, of which expenditure such officer shall make monthly reports to the judge. The county commissioners of such county shall make the allowances herein provided for, which shall be paid by the county treasurer from the county treasury upon the warrant of the county auditor in favor of such probation officer. (103 v. 864.) [Provisions in case of workhouse sentence.]

SECTION 1657. Pending final disposition of a case. the judge may commit any person arrested or cited to appear, except the minor under fourteen years of age, to the county jail until the case is disposed of. but such trial shall be commenced within four days of such commitment unless upon the request of the defendant. Pending final dispo- [Commitment to county jail, etc.]

sition, the judge may direct that the minor in question be
left in the possession of the person having charge of him,
or that he be kept in some suitable place provided by the
county or city authorities. (99 v. 196 § 17.)

Citation or ar-
rest ordered
after hearing. SECTION 1658. If it appear upon the hearing that any
person not cited to appear, has probably abused or has
aided, induced, caused, encouraged, or contributed to the
dependency, neglect or delinquency of a minor under the
age of eighteen years, or acted in a way tending to cause
delinquency in such minor, or that a person, charged by
law, with the care, support, education and maintenance of
any minor, has abandoned, failed, refused, or neglected,
being able to do so, to support, or sufficiently contribute
toward the support, education and maintenance of such
minor, the judge may order such person to be cited to appear at a subsequent day, or may issue a warrant to arrest
such person as hereinbefore provided, and upon citation,
warrant and hearing the same proceedings may be had as
in the first instance. (103 v. 864.)

Transfer of
case to ju-
venile court. SECTION 1659. When a minor under the age of eighteen years is arrested, such child, instead of being taken before a justice of the peace or police judge, shall be taken
directly before such juvenile judge; or, if 'the child is
taken before a justice of the peace or a judge of the police
court, it shall be the duty of such justice of the peace or
such judge of the police court, to transfer the case to the
judge exercising the jurisdiction herein provided. The
officers having such child in charge shall take it before such
judge, who shall proceed to hear and dispose of the case
in the same manner as if the child had been brought before
the judge in the first instance. (103 v. 864.)

Writs, to
whom issued. SECTION 1660. The summons; warrants, citations,
subpœnas and other writs of such judge may issue to a probation officer of any such court or to the sheriff of any
county, and the provisions of law relating to the subpœna-
ing of witnesses in criminal cases shall apply in so far as
they are applicable. (103 v. 864.)

Expense: how
paid. SECTION 1661. When a summons or warrant is issued to any such officer, the expense in pursuing and bringing the person named therein, before such judge, shall be
paid by the county in the manner prescribed by law for the
payment of deputies, assistants and other employes of
county officers. (103 v. 864.)

Probation offi-
cers; appoint-
ment, com-
pensation. SECTION 1662. The judge designated to exercise
jurisdiction may appoint one or more discreet persons of
good moral character, one or more of whom may be
women, to serve as probation officers, during the pleasure
of the judge. One of such officers shall be known as chief
probation officer and there may be first, second and third
assistants. Such chief probation officer and the first, sec-

ond and third assistants shall receive such compensation as
the judge appointing them may designate at the time of
the appointment, but the compensation of the chief probation officer shall not exceed twenty-five hundred dollars
per annum, that of the first assistant shall not exceed
twelve hundred dollars per annum, and of the second and
third shall not exceed one thousand dollars per annum, each
payable monthly. ' The judge may appoint other probation
officers, with or without compensation, but the entire compensation of all probation officers in any county shall not
exceed the sum of forty dollars for each full thousand inhabitants of the county at the last preceding federal census.
The compensation of the probation officers shall be paid
by the county treasurer from the county treasury upon the
warrant of the county auditor, which shall be issued upon
itemized vouchers sworn to by the probation officers and
certified to by the judge of the juvenile court. The county
auditor shall issue his warrant upon the treasury and the
treasurer shall honor and pay the same, for all salaries,
compensation and expenses provided for in this act, in
the order in which proper vouchers therefor are presented
to him. (103 v. 864.)

A humane society agent may also be appointed to act as
probation officer of the juvenile court. — *Attorney General,* Opinion
No. 818, March 23, 1914.

The appointment of John Weinig as special court constable
in the juvenile court, Hamilton County, Ohio, as evidenced by the
records of the entries filed and entered in the court of common
pleas of Hamilton County, Ohio, was in all respects valid, and
all questions with reference to the particular services to be
rendered by the appointee should be determined by the court
itself. — *Attorney General,* Opinion No. 823, March 18, 1914.

SECTION 1663. When a complaint is made or filed
against a minor, the probation officer shall inquire into and
make examination and investigation into the facts and
circumstances surrounding the alleged delinquency, neglect,
or dependency, the parentage and surroundings of such
minor, his exact age, habits, school record, and every fact
that will tend to throw light upon his life and character.
He shall be present in court to represent the interests of
the child when the case is heard, furnish to the judge
such information and assistance as he may require, and
take charge of any child before and after the trial as the
judge may direct. He shall serve the warrants and other
process of the court within or without the county, and in
that respect is hereby clothed with the powers and authority
of sheriffs. He may make arrests without warrant upon
reasonable information or upon view of the violation of
any of the provisions of this chapter, detain the person so
arrested pending the issuance of a warrant, and perform
such other duties, incident to their offices, as the judge
directs. All sheriffs, deputy sheriffs, constables, marshals
and police officers shall render assistance to probation

Duties and powers of probation officers.

3 S. L.

officers, in the perf... rmance of their duties, when requested so to do. (99 v. 198 § 23.)

A humane society agent may also be appointed to act as probation officer of the juvenile court. — *Attorney General*, Opinion No. 818, March 23, 1914.

Prosecuting attorney, duty of.   SECTION 1664. On the request of the judge exercising such jurisdiction, the prosecuting attorney of the county shall prosecute all persons charged with violating any of the provisions of this chapter. (99 v. 198 § 24.)

Bail.   SECTION 1665. The provisions of law relating to bail in criminal cases in the common pleas court shall apply to persons committed or held under the provisions of this chapter so far as they are applicable. (99 v. 198 § 25.)

Suspension of sentence.   SECTION 1666. In every case of conviction and where imprisonment is imposed as part of the punishment, such judge may suspend sentence upon such condition as he imposes. (99 v. 198 § 26.)

Forfeit of bond.   SECTION 1667. When, as a condition of suspension of sentence, bond is required and given, upon the failure of a person giving such bond to comply with the terms and conditions thereof, such bond may be forfeited, the suspension terminated by the judge, the original sentence executed as though it had not been suspended, and the term of any jail or workhouse sentence imposed in such case shall commence from the date of imprisonment of such person after such forfeiture and termination of suspension. Any part of such sentence which may theretofore have been served, shall be deducted from any such period of imprisonment. (99 v. 198 § 27.)

Error proceedings.   SECTION 1668. The provisions of the law relating to error proceedings from the court of common pleas, including the allowance and signing of bills of exceptions shall apply to prosecutions of persons over eighteen years of age under this chapter, and from the judgment of a judge of the court of common pleas in such prosecutions error may be prosecuted to the circuit court of the county under laws governing prosecution of proceedings in error in other criminal cases to such circuit court; and from the judgment of a judge of the probate court in such prosecution, error may be prosecuted to the common pleas court of the county under the laws governing prosecution of proceedings in error from the probate court to the court of common pleas. A petition in error shall not be filed either in the circuit court or court of common pleas except upon good cause shown, upon motion and notice to the prosecuting attorney, as in civil cases, or unless such motion is allowed by such courts. (103 v. 864.)

Findings, not lawful evidence.   SECTION 1669. The disposition of, or any order, judgment, or finding against a child under this chapter, or any evidence, given in any proceeding thereunder, shall not in any civil, criminal or other cause or proceeding whatever in any court, be lawful or proper evidence against such child for any purpose whatever, except in subsequent cases herein against the same child. (99 v. 199 § 29.)

SECTION 1670. Upon the advice and recommendation of the judge exercising the jurisdiction provided herein, the county commissioners shall provide by purchase or lease, a place to be known as a "detention home" within a convenient distance of the court house, not used for the confinement of adult persons charged with criminal offenses, where delinquent, dependent or neglected minors under the age of eighteen years may be detained until final disposition, which place shall be maintained by the county as in other like cases. In counties having a population in excess of forty thousand, the judge may appoint a superintendent and matron who shall have charge of said home, and of the delinquent, dependent and neglected minors detained therein. Such superintendent and matron shall be suitable and discreet persons; qualified as teachers of children. Such home shall be furnished in a comfortable manner as nearly as may be as a family home. So far as possible delinquent children shall be kept separate from dependent children in such home. The compensation of the superintendent and matron shall be fixed by the county commissioners. Such compensation and the expense of maintaining the home shall be paid from the county treasury upon the warrant of the county auditor, which shall be issued upon the itemized voucher, sworn to by the superintendent and certified by the judge. In all such homes the sexes shall be kept separate, so far as practicable. (103 v. 864.)

Detention home, how established and conducted.

SECTION 1671. When such detention home is provided by the county commissioners, and upon such home being recommended by the judge, the commissioners shall enter an order on their journal transferring to the proper fund from any other fund or funds of the county, in their discretion, such sums as may be necessary to purchase or lease such home and properly furnish and conduct it and pay the compensation of the superintendent and matron. The commissioners shall likewise upon the appointment of probation officers, transfer to the proper fund from any other fund or funds of the county, in their discretion, such sums as may be necessary to pay them, and such transfers shall be made upon the authority of this chapter. At the next tax levying period, provision shall be made for the expenses of the court. (99 v. 199 § 30.)

Expenses of detention home.

SECTION 1672. If the court awards a child to the care of an association, corporation or individual, in accordance with these provisions, unless otherwise ordered, the child shall become a ward, and be subject to the guardianship of such association, corporation or individual. Such association, corporation or individual may place such child in

When child becomes a ward.

a family home and shall be made party to any proceedings for the legal adoption of the child, and if the court when making such award so orders, may appear in any court where such proceedings are pending, and assent to such adoption. Such assent shall be sufficient to authorize the judge to enter the proper order or decree of adoption, and upon such order being made, all jurisdiction of the juvenile court over such child under section 1643 of the General Code, shall cease and determine. Such guardianship shall not include the guardianship of any estate of the child. (103 v. 864.)

1. The trustees of the county children's home cannot refuse to receive a child committed by the juvenile court to such home, unless such child so presented for admission is afflicted with an infectious or contagious disease.

2. The trustees of a children's home have the right to accept through arrangement with parents children for temporary care and custody.

3. In the commitment of a child to the children's home by the juvenile court, the trustees of the institution are immediately vested with the guardianship and control of the child subject to the continuing jurisdiction of the juvenile court for the purpose of discipline and protection.

4. A dependent child of parent resident of the county, both of which parents have died, is eligible for admission to the county children's home, although such child is not yet one year of age. Section 3089, General Code, providing that the child should have resided in the county not less than one year not being one made for the purpose of placing a limitation upon the age of the child, but for the purpose of establishing residence.

5. The board of trustees have the legal right, to enter into a contract with proper families to board and care for a child of tender years, when such children's home is not properly equipped to care for such children. — *Attorney General,* Opinion No. 969, June 6, 1914.

Agreement with incorporated institution for care of child.

SECTION 1673. The parents, parent, guardian or other person or persons having the right to dispose of a dependent or neglected child may enter into an agreement with any association or institution, incorporated under any law of this state which has been approved by the board of state charities as provided by law, for the purpose of aiding, caring for or placing in homes such children, or for the surrender of such child to such association or institution, to be taken and cared for by such association or institution, or put into a family home. Such agreement may contain any and all proper stipulations to that end, and may authorize the association or institution, to appear in any proceeding, for the legal adoption of such child, and consent to its adoption. The order of the judge made upon such consent shall be binding upon the child and its parents, guardian or other person, as if such persons were personally in court and consented thereto, whether made party to the proceeding or not. (103 v. 864.)

Agent of certain institutions; duties of.

SECTION 1674. The chief officer of the boys' industrial school, and of the girls' industrial school, and the manager of any other institution to which juvenile delinquents may be committed, shall, each, maintain agents of such institution, who shall examine the homes of children paroled for the purpose of reporting to such chief officer or manager, whether they are suitable homes, and assist children paroled or discharged from such institution in finding suitable employment, and maintain a friendly supervision over paroled inmates. Such agents shall hold office subject to the pleasure of the chief officer or manager making the appointment and shall receive such compensation as the Ohio board of administration may determine. (103 v. 864.)

Compensation.

SECTION 1675. At any time the judge may require from an association receiving or desiring so to receive children, such reports, information and statements as he deems proper and necessary. He may at any time require from an association or institution, reports, information or statements concerning any child or children committed to it by him, under the provisions of this chapter. (103 v. 864.)

Judge may require report from institution.

SECTION 1352-2. No association whose object may embrace the care of dependent, neglected or delinquent children or the placing of such children in private homes shall hereafter be incorporated unless the proposed articles of incorporation shall have been submitted first to the board of state charities. The secretary of state shall not issue a certificate of incorporation unless there shall first be filed in his office the certificate of the board of state charities that it has examined the articles of incorporation, and that in its judgment the incorporators are reputable and respectable persons, and that the proposed work is needed, and the incorporation of such association is desirable and for the public good. Amendments proposed to the articles of incorporation of any such association shall be submitted in like manner to the board of state charities, and the secretary of state shall not record such amendment or issue his certificate therefor unless there shall first be filed in his office the certificate of the board of state charities that it has examined such amendment, that the association in question is, in its judgment, performing in good faith, the work undertaken by it, and that such amendment is, in its judgment, a proper one, and for the public good. Section 1676 (repealed 103 v. 864.) Re-enacted as section 1352-2. (103 v. 864.)

Certificate required before filing articles of incorporation.

SECTION 1677. No association of another state, incorporated or otherwise, shall place a child in a family home within the boundaries of this state, either with or without indenture or for adoption, unless such association shall have furnished the board of state charities with such guaranty as it may require that no child having a contagious disease, deformity, feeble mind or vicious character, shall be brought into this state by such association or its agents, and that such association will promptly receive and remove from the state, a child brought into the state by its agents, which shall become a public charge within the period of five years thereafter. (103 v. 864.)

Associations of other states.

Penalty.

SECTION 1678. Whoever violates any of the provisions of section 1677 shall be imprisoned in the county jail not more than thirty days, or fined not less than five dollars or more than one hundred dollars, or both, in the discretion of the judge. (103 v. 864.)

Religious be-
lief.

SECTION 1679. The judge in committing children shall place them, so far as practicable, in the care and custody of an individual holding the same religious belief as such child or its parents, or with some association which is controlled by persons of like religious faith as such child or its parents. (99 v. 202 § 37.)

How chapter
constructed as
to industrial
schools.

SECTION 1680. Nothing herein shall be construed to repeal any provision of law relating to the boys' industrial school or the girls' industrial school. (103 v. 864.)

When child is
charged with
felony.

SECTION 1681. When any information or complaint shall be filed against a delinquent child under these provisions, charging him with a felony, the judge may order such child to enter into a recognizance, with good and sufficient surety, in such amount as he deems reasonable, for his appearance before the court of common pleas at the next term thereof. The same proceedings shall be had thereafter upon such complaint as now authoried by law for the indictment, trial, judgment and sentence of any other person charged with a felony. (99 v. 202 § 39.)

Fees and
costs, how
paid.

SECTION 1682. Fees and costs in all such cases with such sums as are necessary for the incidental expenses of the court and its officers, and the costs of transportation of children to places to which they have been committed, shall be paid from the county treasury upon itemized vouchers, certified to by the judge of the court. (99 v. 202 § 40.)

As the statutes do not go further than to authorize the probate courts to commit juvenile delinquents to institutions or reputable citizens within this state, a probation officer may not be allowed his expenses for transporting a minor under direction of probate court to a home outside of the state. — *Attorney General,* 1911-1912, p. 1181.

Chapter to be
liberally con-
strued.

SECTION 1683. This chapter shall be liberally construed to the end that proper guardianship may be provided for the child, in order that it may be educated and cared for, as far as practicable in such manner as best subserves its moral and physical welfare, and that, as far as practicable in proper cases, the parent, parents, or guardian of such child may be compelled to perform their moral and legal duty in the interest of the child. (99 v. 202 § 40.)

Jurisdiction.

SECTION 1683-1. The judge designated to transact the business arising under the jurisdiction conferred in this chapter shall have jurisdiction of all misdemeanors against minors, and of offenses prescribed in sections nine hundred and twenty-eight, six thousand three hundred and forty-four, six thousand three hundred and forty-five, six thousand three hundred and seventy-three, twelve thousand six hundred and sixty-four, twelve thousand six hundred and sixty-six, twelve thousand seven hundred and eighty-seven, thirteen thousand and thirty-one, thirteen thousand and thirty-five, and thirteen thousand and thirty-eight. In all such cases any person may file with the clerk of the judge exercising the jurisdiction an affidavit, setting forth briefly, in plain and ordinary language, the charges against the accused, and he shall be tried thereon, and in such prosecutions an indictment by the grand jury or information by the prosecuting attorney shall not be required. The judge shall forthwith issue his warrant for the arrest of the accused, who, when arrested, shall be taken before said judge, and tried according to the provisions of this chapter, and, if found guilty, shall be punished in the manner provided for by law. (102 v. 425.)

SECTION 1683-2. For the partial support of women whose husbands are dead, or become permanently disabled by reasons of physical or mental infirmity, or whose husbands are prisoners or whose husbands have deserted, and such desertion has continued for a period of three years, when such women are poor, and are the mothers of children not entitled to receive age and schooling certificate, and such mothers and children have a legal residence in any county of the state for two years, the juvenile court may make an allowance to each of such women, as follows. Not to exceed fifteen dollars a month, when she has but one child not entitled to an age and schooling certificate, and if she has more than one child not entitled to an age and schooling certificate, it shall not exceed fifteen dollars a month for the first child and seven dollars a month for each of the other children not entitled to an age and schooling certificate. The order making such allowance shall not be effective for a longer period than six months, but upon the expiration of such period, said court may from time to time, extend such allowance for a period of six months, or less. Such homes shall be visited from time to time by a probation officer, the agent of an associated charities organization, or of a humane society as the court may direct, or in the absence of such probation officer, society or organization in any county, the sheriff of said county shall make such visits as directed by the probate court; provided that the person, other than the sheriff, who actually makes such visits, shall be thoroughly trained in charitable relief work, and the report or reports of such visiting agent shall be considered by the court in making such order for relief. (106 v. 436.) *[marginal note: Mother's pension, who entitled to. / Visitation of homes and report.]*

SECTION 1683-3. Such allowance may be made by the juvenile court, only upon the following conditions: First, the child or children for whose benefit the allowance is made, must be living with the mother of such child or children; Second, the allowance shall be made only when in *[marginal note: Conditions of allowance.]*

the absence of such allowance, the mother would be required to work regularly away from her home and children, and when by means of such allowance she will be able to remain at home with her children, except that she may be absent for work for such time as the court deems advisable; Third, the mother must, in the judgment of the juvenile court, be a proper person, morally, physically and mentally, for the bringing up of her children; Fourth, such allowance shall in the judgment of the court be necessary to save the child or children from neglect and to avoid the breaking up of the home of such woman; Fifth, it must appear to be for the benefit of the child to remain with such mother; Sixth, a careful preliminary examination of the home of such mother must first have been made under the direction of the court by the probation officer, the agent of an associated charities organization or humane society, or in the absence of such probation officer, society or organization in any county, the sheriff of such county shall make such investigations as the court may direct, and a written report of the result of such examination or investigation shall be filed with the juvenile court, for the guidance of the court in making or withholding such allowance. (106 v. 436.)

When allowance shall cease. SECTION 1683-4. Whenever any child shall reach the age for legal employment, any allowance made to the mother of such child for the benefit of such child shall cease. The juvenile court may, in its discretion, at any time before such child reaches such age, discontinue or modify the allowance to any mother and for any child. (103 v. 864.)

Disposal of fund when amount insufficient. SECTION 1683-5. Should the fund at the disposal of the court for this purpose be sufficient to permit an allowance to only part of the persons coming within the provisions of this act, the juvenile court shall select those cases in most urgent need of such allowance. (103 v. 864.)

To whom act does not apply. SECTION 1683-6. The provisions of this act shall not apply to any woman who, while her husband is imprisoned receives sufficient of his wages to support the child or children. (103 v. 864.)

Attempt to obtain allowance by fraud; penalty. SECTION 1683-7. Any person or persons fraudulently attempting to obtain any allowance for a person not entitled thereto, shall be deemed guilty of a misdemeanor and on conviction thereof, shall be punished by a fine of not less than five nor more than fifty dollars, or imprisoned in the county jail, for a period of not less than two months, or both. (103 v. 864.)

Record of proceedings. SECTION 1683-8. In each case where an allowance is made to any woman under the provisions of this act, a record shall be kept of the proceedings, and any citizen of the county may, at any time, file a motion to set aside, or vacate of modify such judgment and on such motion said juvenile court shall hear evidence, and may make a new order sustaining the former allowance, modify or vacate the same, and from such order, error may be prosecuted, or an appeal may be taken as in civil action. If the judgment be not appealed from, or error prosecuted, or if appealed or error prosecuted, and the judgment of the juvenile court be sustained or affirmed, the person filing such motion shall pay all the costs incident to the hearing of such motion. (103 v. 864.)

Appeal; error.

SECTION 1683-9. It is hereby made the duty of the county commissioners to provide out of the money in the county treasury such sum each year thereafter as will meet the requirements of the court in these proceedings. To provide the same they shall levy a tax not to exceed one-tenth of a mill on the dollar valuation of the taxable property of the county. Such levy shall be subject to all the limitations provided by law upon the aggregate amount, rate, maximum rate and combined maximum rate of taxation. The county auditor shall issue a warrant upon the county treasurer for the payment of such allowance as may be ordered by the juvenile judge. (103 v. 864.)

Tax levy.

SECTION 1683-10. For the purpose of providing a sum which will meet the requirements of the juvenile court until the proceeds of the tax required to be levied under the provisions of section 1683-9 of the General Code, shall become available, any board of county commissioners may transfer from any surplus moneys in the county treasury to the credit of any fund therein to a fund for the use of the juvenile court under the provisions of section 1683-2 to 1683-9, inclusive, of the General Code, the creation of which for such purpose is hereby authorized. The moneys so transferred shall be paid as provided in section 1683-9 of the General Code, upon the order of the juvenile judge, under allowances made either before or after this act shall become effective. (104 v. 199.)

County commissioners may transfer surplus to meet requirements of juvenile court.

TITLE XI. TOWNSHIPS.

CHAPTER 2.

SCHOOL AND MINISTERIAL LANDS.

LEASING.

Trustees shall lay out and lease lands.

SECTION 3194. When either the ministerial or school section belonging to an original township or fractional township requires division, the trustees shall employ a surveyor to assist them, and lay out such section or sections into lots of not less than eighty acres, nor more than one-quarter of a section. Except when otherwise provided by law, the trustees shall lease out such section, after giving at least thirty days' notice, by advertisement, set up in four of the most public places in the township, mentioning the time and place where proposals will be received, and when they will meet to execute the lease giving a preference to those who, in their opinion, make the most advantageous proposals. The trustees may require the lessees of such lands, at the date of the leasing thereof, to execute their notes for the payment of the rents, with security to the approval of the trustees. (82 v. 256.)

To whom to be leased; terms of lease.

SECTION 3195. The trustees shall not lease more than one lot to any one person, and the lessee shall be bound not to waste or destroy the sugar trees or other timber,

42

further than is neessary. for improving thereon, and to make such improvements as the trustees think proper. The trustees shall examine the premises and see that they are left in good repair, and that the lease has been punctually complied with, and shall proceed again to give leases, as provided by the preecding section, giving preference to the original lessee if he has complied with his former lease. (29 v. 490.)

SECTIION 3196. Unimproved lots may be leased for any term, not exceeding seven years, for making such improvements thereon as the trustees think advisable. They may be leased for any term not exceeding fourteen years, but a cash rent shall be reserved in the lease at least after the first seven years. Improved lots may be leased for any term not exceeding ten years. All rents shall be payable on the first Monday of December, annually. (82 v. 256.) *Length of term for lease of improved and unimproved lots.*

SECTION 3197. The trustees may provide for improvements on the school lands in the lease or leases by which they are rented, or they may make such improvements directly. Where such improvements are made directly by the trustees, when in their judgment they are necessary, and the estimate or probable cost thereof exceeds one hundred dollars, they shall advertise for bids for the period of at least twenty days, by posting notices in four of the most public places in the township, and the contract for making such improvement shall be awarded to, and made with the person or persons who offer to make such improvement at the lowest price. But a good and sufficient bond shall be executed and delivered to the trustees, as such trustees, conditioned for the honest and faithful performance of such improvement. (82 v. 256.) *Improvements by the trustees.*

Lands in School Section 16 which have been sold or are held under a permanent lease subject to revaluation as unimproved land every thirty-three years may be assessed under the rule of benefits to pay a proportionate part of the cost and expense of establishing a county ditch through said lands. — *Attorney General, Opinion No. 143, 1915.*

SECTION 3198. The trustees shall lease section or fractional section twenty-nine, granted for religious purposes, within the Ohio company's and John Cleves Symmes' purchase, except such as have been heretofore leased or provided for by special acts, in lots of not less than eighty. acres nor more than one-quarter section, for the term of ninety-nine years, renewable forever, to be valued by three disinterested freeholders of the county previous to it being leased, and such valuation shall in no case be less than one dollar per acre. Ministerial lands so leased shall be subject to a revaluation every fifteen years without taking into view the improvements thereon, except at the first valuation, and six per cent on the valuation or revaluation of all ministerial lands shall be the rent required. (29 v. 490.) *Section twenty-nine in Ohio company's and Symme's purchase; how leased.*

SECTION 3199. When it becomes necessary by the terms of any lease, or by the law authorizing the leasing of either section sixteen or twenty-nine, or any part or lot of either, the trustees shall apply to the court of common pleas by petition setting forth therein the facts showing the necessity of such appraisement, and shall give each of the lessees or assignees at least twenty days' notice in writing of the pendency of such petition. The court on being satisfied of the truth of the petition and that such notice has been given, shall make an order appointing three disinterested citizens of the county, who, within twenty days shall appraise such tract, or lot, or part of a lot of land, on oath and an actual view thereof, without reference to the improvements thereon, under such lease, and within five days thereafter make a report of such appraisement and deliver it with such order of court to the clerk of the township in which such land is situated. The court shall make such further order, as to the payment and taxation of costs, as seems just and equitable. (54 v. 88.)

SECTION 3200. All rents arising from school or ministerial lands as they become due shall be paid by the lessee or lessees to the treasurer. On failure of such paymnt or for non-compliance with the conditions of the lease, when so directed by the trustees, the treasurer shall bring suit in the name of the trustees before any court having competent jurisdiction, and to the judgment rendered in such action no stay of execution shall be allowed. On final process, if goods and chattels cannot be found whereby colletcion can be made, or of mesne process cannot be served, upon the return thereof, the trustees may re-enter upon the lands of the delinquent and sell at public vendue his or their right and title in such lease or leases, to satisfy such rent, damages and costs. (85 v. 256.)

SECTION 3201. The trustees shall give twenty days' previous notice of the time and place when such lease or leases will be sold, by advertisement in three public places, or by insertion in a newspaper published within the county, subjecting the purchaser to the conditions contained in the lease of the delinquent. In case such lease or leases sell for more than the rent, damages and costs, the surplus shall be paid to the delinquent. Where secured notes are taken for payment of such rents, on failure of such payment when due, according to the terms thereof, the trustees may order the treasurer to bring suit in their name on such note or notes, and to the judgment rendered in such action no stay of execution shall be allowed. (85 v. 256.)

SECTION 3202. The treasurer shall keep a book with full and accurate entries of moneys received and of disbursements, and carefully file and preserve the vouchers relating thereto, which book and papers shall at all times be subject to the inspection of the trustees. No money shall be paid out by the treasurer except upon the written order of the trustees. For receiving, safekeeping, and paying out moneys belonging to the township treasury, the treasurer shall be allowed one per cent thereof as his fees. (82 v. 256.)

SECTION 3203. When, after the payment of just claims and necessary expenses, there is money in the hands of the treasurer arising from the rents of school lands, at least once a year, the trustees shall meet at the office or residence of the treasurer, and make a dividend thereof among the several school districts, or parts of districts within the original township, on the basis of thirty dollars for each teacher, and the balance according to the average daily attendance in the schools of such districts, and upon the order of the trustees, the treasurer shall pay out such money. (104 v. 158.) {.marginal Annual division of rents of school lands.}

SECTION 3204. The clerk of the board of education of any district which, in whole or in part, is composed of territory within the bounds of an original township incorporated as herein provided, shall, on demand of the clerk of such township, furnish him a certified copy of the report of the number of teachers employed and the average daily attendance of pupils in the schools within the bounds of such original township in such school districts, and the dividend shall be made on the basis of such certified report. (104 y. 158.) {.marginal Clerk of board shall furnish certified report of number of teachers and average daily attendance.}

SECTION 3205. When there is money in the hands of the treasurer arising from the rents or profits of ministerial lands, the trustees shall meet at his office or residence on the fourth Monday of April, each year, and make a dividend thereof to each religious society, as provided by the next following section. Such money shall thereupon be paid by the treasurer according to the order of the trustees in making such dividend. (59 v. 30.) {.marginal Dividend of ministerial funds.}

SECTION 3206. Each denomination of religious societies having members residing in such township shall be entitled to participate in such ministerial fund. After assuming a name each of them shall appoint an agent to receive its proper proportion, who shall produce to the trustees a sworn certificate, containing a list of the names of the members enrolled in the records of such society residing in such township, but no person shall be considered a member who is under fifteen years of age. At such annual meeting the trustees shall distribute such funds to the several societies applying by their agents and producing such certificates, in proportion to the number of their members residing in such township, without regard to the township in which any such society regularly assembles for public worship. (61 v. 74.) {.marginal Who entitled to participate in ministerial fund; proportion.}

Officers of civil township shall perform duties of officers of original township.

SECTION 3207. When either such school or ministerial section is in an original township where there are not four electors, the trustees and treasurer of the civil township in which such section is situated, shall perform the duties in this chapter prescribed for the officers of the original township. (29 v. 490.)

Certain leases of school lands made valid.

SECTION 3208. All leases of school lands made by the trustees of the original surveyed townships or by the county commissioners of any county, before the first day of June, in the year one thousand eight hundred and thirty-one, although not acknowledged before any officer authorized to take the acknowledgement of deeds or other instruments in writing for the conveyance, lease or incumbrance of lands, shall, between the lessors and lessees, their grantees, heirs and assigns, be held valid to the same extent and for the same purposes that they would have been, had they been so acknowledged. (80 v. 218.)

Duties of county auditor when lessees or trustees delinquent.

SECTION 3209. When it comes to his knowledge that a lessee of school or ministerial lands has failed to pay the rent he is bound to pay by the provisions of the lease thereon or that the trustees have failed to cause such lands to be reappraised according to the provisions of such lease, the county auditor shall immediately notify the lessee in writing of his delinquency. Upon receiving such notice, the lessee shall make full compliance with the provisions of his lease or the law, wherein he is delinquent, in default of which the auditor shall, in thirty days after notifying such lessee, immediately notify the trustees of such township of the delinquency, who shall proceed immediately to collect the rent or cause the reappraisement according to law. (69 v. 76.)

Auditor of State authorized to lease unsold portions of sections 16 and 29 and other land in lieu thereof for oil, gas or other minerals.

SECTION 3209-1. The auditor of state is hereby authorized to lease for oil, gas, coal, or other minerals, any unsold portions of Section Sixteen and Section Twenty-nine, or other lands granted in lieu thereof, of the original surveyed townships, for the support of schools and religion, to any person, persons, partnership or corporation, upon such terms and for such time as will be for the best interest of the beneficiaries thereof, but nothing herein shall be construed so as to require the auditor to so lease; and the auditor of state in such lease is empowered to grant to such lessee the right to use so much of the surface of such land as may be reasonably necessary to carry on the work of prospecting for, extracting, piping, storing and removing all oil, or gas, or prospecting for and producing coal or other minerals, and for sinking shafts, depositing waste material and maintaining such buildings and constructions as may be reasonably necessary for the mining, handling and removal of such coal or other minerals; provided, however, that such lease shall require the lessee to pay all damage to the holder of the lease holding under a lease from the trustees of the original township.

Should the lessee of the gas, oil, coal, or other minerals be unable to agree with the lessee holding under lease from the trustees of the original township, upon the damages sustained by the latter by reason of such occupancy of the surface, then the determination of the damages shall be submitted to the arbitrament or umpirage of a commission of three consisting of one person selected by each of the lessees, and one person selected by the attorney general. Such commission shall hear evidence, shall have the powers given to arbitrators under the provisions of Chapter 1, Division 9, Title 4, of the General Code, and shall make an award in writing, signed by a majority of them. Such award shall be filed with the auditor of state and shall be binding upon all parties.

When question of damages submitted to arbitration; where award shall be filed.

Should the lessee of the oil, gas, coal, or other minerals, fail to pay the damages so awarded, the auditor of state shall file a certified copy of the award in the court of common pleas of the county in which the lands, or the greater part of the lands, may be located, and proceedings thereon may be had as provided for awards of arbitrators by sections 12155, 12156, 12158, of the General Code.

Proceedings on failure to pay damages awarded.

In the event of any productive oil or gas wells having been drilled on any of said lands or coal or other minerals taken therefrom prior to obtaining a lease therefor, said auditor of state is hereby authorized to settle, adjust and compromise with the person, persons, firm or corporation, drilling such wells or removing other minerals upon such terms as may be just and equitable to such persons, and for the best interest of the beneficiaries of said lands. Provided that before any such lease, settlement, adjustment or compromise shall be binding, or in any manner affect existing rights or claims, the same shall be presented to and approved by the governor and attorney general, and providing further, that all moneys arising from any such lease, settlement, adjustment or compromise shall be paid to the treasurer of state monthly, to be disposed of in the same manner as is provided by law for the proceeds of sale of said section.

Settlement for minerals taken from lands prior to lease; approval by Governor and Attorney General.

And further provided, that, if, in such cases, a satisfactory settlement cannot be secured, then upon ten days' notice upon the persons sought to be dispossessed the auditor of state by and with the consent of the attorney general and Governor is authorized to re-enter upon such lands, to hold such oil or gas wells or coal or mineral developments with all the appurtenances thereunto belonging, and to either lease the same under the provisions of this act, or to operate such producing wells, or developments and dispose of the proceeds upon the market, and also to pay the net proceeds arising therefrom into the state treasury to the credit of the irreducible debt of the state, to be held and disbursed as other monies derived from sales of school and ministerial lands, and he shall also file a detailed statement of all receipts and expenditures covering such operation and sale.

Re-entry and further procedure when satisfactory settlement cannot be secured.

When facts shall be submitted to board of arbitration.

If it should be made to appear to the auditor, attorney general and governor that the occupancy of such lands so re-entered, and the making of improvements thereon in the development of such gas or oil wells, or coal or other minerals, was in good faith, there shall be submitted all the facts to a board of arbitration, one member of which shall be appointed by the Governor, one by the auditor of state and one by the trespasser, and such board of arbitration shall determine what just and equitable settlements shall be made with such trespasser for such improvements and the auditor of state is authorized and directed to make a settlement with such trespasser in accordance with the finding of such arbitration board. (105 v. 7.)

School lands may be sold; sales shall reserve to the state all oil, gas and other minerals.

SECTION 3210. Section Sixteen and all lands instead thereof, granted for school purposes, may be sold, and such sales shall be according to the regulations hereinafter prescribed. The proceedings for the sale of such lands for which a deed has been duly executed and delivered by the state to the purchaser thereof at such sale, or his assigns, shall be conclusively presumed to be regular and according to law, but this provision shall not apply to, or affect, pending litigation. Provided, that such sales shall exclude all oil, gas, coal, or other minerals on or under such lands, and all deeds executed and delivered by the state shall expressly reserve to the state all gas, oil, coal, or other minerals, on or under such lands, with the right of entry in and upon said premises for the purpose of selling or leasing the same, or prospecting, developing or operating the same, and this latter provision shall affect and apply to pending actions. (105 v. 8.)

Proceedings when vote has not been taken; subsequent vote.

SECTION 3211. Where no vote has been taken for the sale of any such land, the trustees of the township to which such lands belong, at least thirty days prior to the taking of such vote, shall cause not less than eight notices to be posted in as many of the most public places of the township, notifying the voters resident therein to meet at a convenient place and time therein specified, and cast their ballots for or against the sale of such lands. If the vote results in a refusal to sell such lands, the trustees, in the same manner, may authorize the taking of a subsequent vote as often as they deem proper, but no subsequent vote shall be taken until one year has elapsed since the last preceding vote. (70 v. 195.)

Notice to Auditor when vote is to be taken.

SECTION 3211-1. Whenever a vote is caused to be taken pursuant to sections 3211-3223 of the General Code, the trustees shall mail a certified notice thereof to the auditor of state at least thirty days prior to the taking of such vote. (105 v. 9.)

Trustees shall preside at election; poll-book shall be deposited with auditor.

SECTION 3212. The trustees of the township shall preside at the taking of such ballots and shall appoint two clerks, who shall keep two poll-books, containing the names of the voters and the result of the ballot, which poll-books must be signed by the trustees and clerks. If such ballots result in favor of a sale, within ten days after such election, the trustees shall deposit one of such poll-book with the auditor of the county within which such lands or the greater portion thereof are situated, with a copy of the notice given, and the affidavit of one or more of the trustees, stating the manner of giving such notices, and the time and place of posting them, which notices, affidavit, and poll-book shall be by such auditor copied into a book for that purpose to be provided, and when so recorded, such record shall be proof of the facts therein stated. (70 v. 195.)

SECTION 3213. When such record has been made, the *Trustees shall petition court of common pleas.* trustees of the township to which such lands belong, shall file a petition in the court of common pleas of the county within which such lands or the greater portion of them are situated, setting forth the giving of such notice, the taking of the ballot, the result thereof, the filling and recording of such papers in the office of the auditor of the proper county, and asking the court to appoint three disinterested freeholders, not resident of the township in which the land is situated, to divide and value it in money. (70 v. 195.)

SECTION 3214. If the court is satisfied that the statements of the petition are true, it shall appoint three persons to divide and appraise the lands according to the prayer of such petition. After being duly sworn before an officer authorized to administer oaths, and taking to their aid, if they think necessary, the county surveyor, such appraisers shall proceed to divide such lands into such parcels or tracts as, in their opinion, will be best for the sale thereof, and return in writing such divisions, suitably numbered and described, to the court with a just valuation of each separate division in money. *Appraisement of lands; existence of minerals excluded.*

In making such valuation the apraisers shall exclude from their consideration the existence or possible existence of oil, gas, coal, or other minerals upon such lands. (105 v. 8.)

SECTION 3215. When such return is made, the court shall examine it, and, if found in all things regular, just, *Returns shall be recorded.* and fair, shall certify it, and order it to be entered of record, together with the petition and all the proceedings had therein. The trustees shall cause a copy of each record to be filed in the office of the auditor of the proper county, who shall copy it into the book containing the notice, affidavit, and poll-book, and immediately following them. (70 v. 195.)

SECTION 3216. On the recording of such proceedings, the auditor of the county shall forthwith cause a notice to be published in a newspaper of general circulation in the county, for five consecutive weeks before the day of sale, *School lands; proceedings for sale.*

and, at the same time, by posting copies of such notice in
six of the most public places in the county, two of which
shall be in the township where the lands are situated, and
one at the court house. Such notices shall contain a description of the lots or lands to be sold, the valuation
thereof, and the time when they will be offered at public
auction by the auditor, at the door of the court house, at
not less than the appraised value thereof, one-third of the
purchase money to be paid at the time of sale, and the
balance in two annual installments of equal amount, with
interest payable annually thereon. At such time and place
the auditor shall proceed to offer them to the highest bidder
on the terms stated in the notice. If the principal value
of such school land consists in the timber growing thereon,
on the request of the trustees, or a majority of them, the
auditor who sells such school lands shall require the whole
of the purchase money to be paid at the time of sale. (81
v. 132.)

How lands
may be
offered again.
SECTION 3217. If such lands, or any part thereof,
are not sold as herein provided, on the application in writing of the trustees of the township to which they belong,
the auditor may continue to offer them at any future time
or times until they are sold, having first given like notices
as herein provided to be given on the first offer of sale.
No sale shall be had on any valuation made more than
two years prior to the day of sale. (85 v. 141.)

Action to re-
appraise.
SECTION 3218. When from any cause the value of
such lands or any part thereof, as fixed by the appraisers,
has decreased the trustees at any time after the land has
been once offered and remains unsold, may file a petition
in the court wherein the former petition was filed, setting
out in substance the filing of such petition and the subse-.
quent proceedings thereto, that the land has been offered
and remains unsold, and the facts and circumstances which
have decreased the value of such lands and asking for
a re-apraisement of them. (85 v. 141.)

Reappraisers
appointed by
court.
SECTION 3219. If the court is satisfied that the statements made in the petition are true, and that such lands by
reason thereof have decreased in value, it may order another appraisement, and thereupon the court shall appoint
three disinterested freeholders, having the same qualifications as original appraisers, and the same proceedings
shall be had as under the original petition. After such
appraisement is made the auditor shall again offer such
lands for sale, as provided in the preceding sections. (85
v. 141.)

Reappraise-
ment.
SECTION 3220. On such petition of the trustees setting forth the former appraisement and the subsequent
proceedings thereto, and that two years have elapsed and
the land remains unsold, the court shall direct a new valuation of them to be made in the manner hereinbefore di-

rected, unless such court, on testimony, shall be satisfied that the former appraisement is a just and fair valuation of such lands, in which case the court shall make an entry of the fact, which entry shall be certified to and recorded by the auditor in the same manner, and shall have the same effect as the new appraisement. (70 v. 195.)

SECTION 3221. If such lands are held under permanent leases, or leases for ninety-nine years, the legal or equitable holder of any such lease, who wishes to surrender it, and purchase the fee of such premises, with the consent of the trustees of the original township to which such lands belong, may file his petition in the court of common pleas of the county in which the largest portion of such lands are situated, setting forth a description of the premises so held, the date of his lease or his title thereto, that he is desirous of surrendering such lease and becoming the owner of the premises in fee, and asking the court to appoint tthree disinterested freeholders of the county and not resident of the township wherein such lands are situated to value them. (70 v. 195.) *Reappraisement of permanent leases.*

SECTION 3222. On being satisfied of the truth of the facts set forth in such petition, the court shall appoint such appraisers who shall proceed under oath to make a just valuation of the premises in money without reference to the improvements made thereon under and by reason of such lease, or to any gas, oil, coal, or other minerals that may be upon such lands, and shall return such valuation in writing to the court. If satisfied that the valuation is just, the court shall confirm it, and order it, with the petition and other proceedings therein to be recorded. (105 v. 8.) *Appraisers of such leases and how valuation shall be made.*

SECTION 3223. Before the trustees of any township consent to the surrender of a lease, as provided herein, they shall cause the proposition to be submitted to the electors of the township, at an election to be held and conducted in conformity with the provisions herein for the sale of section sixteen and lands in place thereof. If at such election a majority of the electors vote for such surrender, then, and not otherwise, the trustees shall consent to the surrender as herein provided. (70 v. 195.) *Must be submitted to vote.*

SECTION 3224. On producing to the auditor of the proper county, within one year after the making thereof, a certified copy of such petition, appraisement and confirmation, such lessee shall be permitted by indorsement thereon, attested by the auditor, to release to the state all his interest, title and claim in and to such lease, for the benefit of the township, to which it belongs, which certified copy of such record and release shall be recorded in a book for that purpose. (70 v. 195.) *How release of lease to be made.*

SECTION 3225. The purchaser of such lands at an auditor's sale, or the lessee of land held under such lease, on executing such release, shall each forthwith pay to the *Payments to county treasurers.*

treasury of the county, one-third of the purchase money in the first case, and one-third of the valuation in the second, and take the treasurer's receipt therefor. On receiving the treasurer's receipt for such first installment, the auditor shall give to the purchaser or lessee a certificate, containing the name of the purchaser or lessee, a description of the premises, the number, amount, and the time of payment of the subsequent installments, and such purchaser or lessee, his heirs or assigns, on the punctual payment of the sums still due, with annual interest up to the time of payment, shall be entitled to receive a final certificate from the auditor, but such lessee shall produce to the auditor the certifcate of the proper officer, that all rents due on such premises have been paid up to the time of surrendering the lease. (70 v. 195.)

How payments made.

SECTION 3226. A person wishing to pay any money under the provisions of this chapter in part or full payment of such lands shall first obtain the certificate of the auditor of the amount due or to be paid, and on presentation thereof, the treasurer may receive the amount therein specified, and shall give to the person presenting it a certificate, directed to the auditor, of the payment of such sum of money, and the auditor on the presentation of such certificate, shall give to such person a receipt therefor, credit him with the amount in his books and charge the treasurer therewith. (70 v. 195.)

Report of sales to auditor of state.

SECTION 3227. The county auditor shall keep an account with the county treasurer of all sales made and leases surrendered and moneys paid thereon by each purchaser or lessee, and on the first day of February, May, August, and November, in each year, make a report thereof to the auditor of state, which report shall distinguish between the amount paid in as principal and the amount paid in as interest. From the time of such report the state shall be liable to pay interest on all such sums of principal so reported as paid. On receiving a certified copy of such account from the auditor of state, the treasurer of state may immediately draw the money paid in as principal, from the county treasury. The amount so reported as interest shall be retained in the county treasury, and apportioned to the several civil townships and parts of civil townships, in the original surveyed townships or fractional townships to which such lands belong. (70 v. 195.)

Enforcing payment by sale.

SECTION 3228. If the purchaser or lessee of any tract of section sixteen, or lands granted in place thereof for the support of common schools, fails to make any payment on any tract of such land for the space of twelve months after the time it becomes due and payable, the auditor of the county wherein the land is situated shall forthwith proceed to sell such tract, with all the improvements thereon, at the door of the court house, to the highest and best bidder therefor, in cash, having first given notice of the time and place of such sale, containing a description of the land and the money due and to become due thereon, by publishing such notice in a newspaper of general circulation in such county for six consecutive weeks before the day of sale. (88 v. 321.)

SECTION 3229. On such sale no bid shall be entertained for a sum which will not be sufficient to pay all the purchase money due to the state, and all expenses incident to the sale. In case the premises cannot be sold for that amount, they shall revert to the state in trust for the township to which the lands belong to be sold in the manner provided for the sale of such lands not under permanent leases, or leases for ninety-nine years. In any such case, in addition to any other remedy provided by law for enforcing payment for such tract of land, the county auditor may institute suit by civil action in the court of common pleas of the county in which the land is situated, in his own name for the use of the proper township, against the purchaser or lessee and all other parties who have or claim an interest in the land, or are in any manner affected by such suit, and shall prosecute the action to final judgment, and he may have an order for the sale of, and have the premises sold, with all improvements thereon as upon execution at law, for the satisfaction of such judgment. The sheriff's deed executed in accordance therewith shall convey to the grantee therein the legal title to such land, all rights of the state and of the original township and of all parties to the suit therein. The auditor of the county may have execution for any balance remaining unsatisfied after such sale but such balance shall be recovered equally from all the lessees, their heirs or assigns, and no person shall be liable for more than his pro rata share thereof. (88 v. 321.) *Sale and incidents thereto.*

SECTION 3229-1. In proceedings commenced under the provisions of section 3213, 3221, 3231 and 3237, notice of the pendency thereof shall be given to the auditor of state thirty days before any order of court may issue therein, and all orders of the court and returns of appraisers under section 3214, 3218, 3219, 3220 and 3222 of the General Code shall be certified to the auditor of state ten days prior to any action or proceedings thereunder. The auditor of state or attorney general may intervene in any such proceedings. (105 v.   .) *Notice of pendency of proceedings to sell before order shall issue.*

SECTION 3230. After payment of all costs and expenses of the action, the proceeds of the sale shall be forthwith paid by the sheriff to the treasurer of the county, and the sheriff shall at the same time certify to the county auditor the fact of such sale and to whom, with a description of the land so sold, the amount for which sold and a statement of the distribution thereof, and the auditor shall make report thereof to the auditor of state at the time, and in the manner provided in case of sale and leases. (88 v. 321.) *Disposition of proceeds.*

Petition and action of auditor.

SECTION 3231. In an action herein provided it shall be sufficient for the auditor to allege in his petition the sale of such land, a proper description thereof, and that there remains due and unpaid the amount claimed with interest, without setting forth in his petition any of the special matter or proceedings had in connection with the sale of such land. The record of the proceedings kept by the auditor, as required by law, shall be proof of the facts of such sale and of the validity thereof, and his record of the amount claimed to be due shall be prima facie evidence of the correctness thereof. The judgment debtor or any one else shall not be entitled to the benefit of the laws for stay of execution or exemption of homestead in the enforcement of any judgment recovered. (88 v. 322.)

Final certificate to purchaser on sale and payment for land; deed.

SECTION 3232. Except when sold under proceedings in civil action, when such lands so sell the purchaser shall pay to the treasurer of the county the amount so bid for such premises. On producing to the auditor the treasurer's receipt for such payment, the auditor shall give him a final certificate, stating the fact of such sale, the name of the purchaser, description of the lands sold, the amount for which sold, the payment thereof, and that the purchaser is entitled to receive from the state a deed in fee simple thereof pursuant to the provisions and conditions of section 3210 of the General Code, on producing to the proper officer such certificate. (105 v. 9.)

Final certificate in other cases.

SECTION 3233. When the purchaser or lessee, his heirs or assigns, has made payment in full, the auditor shall give such person a final certificate, containing, in addition to the former one, the fact of payment in full and that such person is entitled to receive from the state a deed in fee simple pursuant to the provisions and conditions of section 3210 of the General Code, for such premises, on presentation of this certificate to the proper officer. (105 v. 9.)

Deed from state for delinquent lands.

SECTION 3234. Upon the filing of such final certificate in his office, the auditor of state shall prepare a deed for the premises described therein, and deliver it to the governor, together with a certificate, under the seal of his office, that all the papers required by law, and upon which it is based, are on file in his office, and have been examined by him and found to be correct. Such certificate shall contain a brief description of the premises conveyed, and the name of the grantee. When signed by the governor, countersigned by the secretary of state, and sealed with the great seal of the state, such deed shall be returned to the auditor of state, who shall transmit it to the county auditor from whom the final certificate was received, who shall deliver it to the grantee. (79 v. 136.)

Excess of money on delinquent sale.

SECTION 3235. After paying all sums due, and interest and costs, all excess of moneys made on such sale of delinquent lands shall be paid on demand to the delinquent owner, his heirs or assigns, from the county treasury, on the warrant of the auditor, if the demand is made within one year from the time of the sale. If not so demanded, the excess shall be paid into the state treasury and unless it is demanded within one year after it has been paid into the state treasury, it shall be applied for the same uses as the lands are subject to. (70 v. 195.)

SECTION 3236. The fees for services under this chapter relating to sales shall be as follows: The court shall tax such fees on any petition filed therein, as are allowed for similar services on the proceedings for partition; the county auditor shall be allowed one dollar and fifty cents on each sale made by him; for each certificate, fifty cents; for each receipt, six cents, to be paid by the purchaser, and the same fees for recording as are allowed to county recorders, to be paid from the first moneys paid as interest or rents on such sale or surrender. Printer's fees for advertising shall be paid from the county treasury on the warrant of the auditor, and refunded from the first moneys received on the sale as interest or rents. In case of a petition by the trustees, the costs in court shall be paid from the county treasury on the warrant of the county auditor, and refunded from the first moneys received from the sale as interest or rents. If a lessee is petitioner, all costs shall be paid by him. (70 v. 195.) Fees.

SECTION 3237. Lands granted by the congress of the United States for religious purposes, known as section twenty-nine, may be sold, or the permanent leases thereto surrendered, and such sale or surrender shall be regulated by and conducted according to the provisions of this chapter in relation to the sale of school lands and the surrender of permanent leases thereof. (70 v. 195.) Section twenty-nine.

SECTION 3238. The trustees of a township having school lands, whether they lie in such township or elsewhere, may, by action before a proper court in their own names, sue and recover in any existing cause of action arising out of injuries to such lands, or upon any cause of action that may hereafter arise in respect to such lands, as fully as if they had been vested in fee in such trustees from the time such ownership commenced. (54 v. 93 § 1.) Trustees may sue for injuries to school lands.

SECTION 3239. The money paid into the state treasury on account of sales of lands granted by congress for religious purposes, known as section twenty-nine, shall constitute the "ministerial fund," of which the auditor of state shall be the superintendent, and the income therefrom shall be used exclusively for religious purposes. (86 v. 205.) Ministerial fund.

SECTION 3240. The ministerial fund shall constitute an irreducible debt of the state, on which the state shall pay interest annually, to be computed for the calendar year, and the first computation on any payment of principal, hereafter made, shall be from the time of payment to and Account of by auditor of state.

including the thirty-first day of December next succeeding. The auditor of state shall keep an account of the fund and of the interest which accrues thereon, in a book or books to be provided for that purpose, with each original surveyed township or other district to which any part of the fund belongs, crediting each with its share of the fund, and showing the amount of interest thereon which accrues and the amount which is disbursed annually to each. (86 v. 205.)

Statement to be transmitted to county auditor.

SECTION 3241. With each February settlement sheet, the auditor of state shall transmit a certified statement, showing the amount of interest derived from the ministerial fund, payable to each original surveyed township or other district within the county. At the February settlement with the auditor of state, the treasurer of each county shall retain in the county treasury, from the state taxes collected by him, the amount of the funds shown by each certified statement to be due such county. The treasurer of each county shall pay such funds, on the warrant of the county auditor, to the treasurer of the original township in which such lands are located. Such 'warrants shall be drawn for the amount due each original township, as certified by the auditor of state, and the funds shall be apportioned by the trustees thereof in the manner provided for the apportionment of money arising from rents and profits of such lands. (86 v. 205.)

Certain sales of sections sixteen and twenty-nine.

SECTION 3242. Section sixteen, donated and set apart for the support of schools, and section twenty-nine, for the purpose of religion, or lands granted instead of either, by the directors of the Ohio company, on the seventh day of January, seventeen hundred and ninety-six, in the following original surveyed townships within the Ohio company's purchase, to-wit: Township number eight, in range number twelve; township number seven, in range number thirteen; township number eleven, in range number fourteen; township number thirteen, in range number fifteen; townships number eight, nine, eleven, twelve and thirteen, in range number sixteen, and such parts of section twenty-nine, as have not been previously sold, in township number three, in range number fifteen, may be sold or the leases thereto whether permanent or otherwise, surrendered, and such sale or surrender shall be regulated by and conducted according to the provisions of this chapter. The lessees of any such lands holding leases for a term less than ninety-nine years, shall be permitted to surrender their leases in the same manner, and be entitled to the benefit of this chapter, as if their leases were for ninety-nine years. (94 v. 411.)

Error in calculation of purchase money shall be corrected.

SECTION 3243. When in any sale of school or ministerial lands any mistake is made in the calculation of the amount to be paid or in the computation of interest, either inadvertently or designedly by any officer having charge thereof, the auditor of the proper county shall examine into and correct such mistake. Upon being notified of it, a purchaser thereof shall immediately pay the sum he is found to be in default. The auditor shall institute a suit against any purchaser who neglects to pay the amount so found to be unpaid, in the court of common pleas of the county in which such lands are situated, in his own name, for the use of the proper township, and shall prosecute such action to final judgment and execution. If the mistake be by excess of payment, the auditor shall make the correction by paying out of the county treasury the amount overpaid, and charge it to the state or township, as the case requires. (69 v. 76.)

SECTION 2626. The county auditor may also charge and receive fees as follows: For certificate of sale of school land, to be paid by the purchaser, twenty-five cents; for certificate of payment of installment into the treasury on school lands, to be paid by the purchaser, fifteen cents: for final certificate of payment for school lands, to be paid by the purchaser, seventy-five cents; for deeds of lands sold for taxes to be paid by the purchaser, one dollar; for the transfer of an entry of land, lot, or part of lot, to be paid, by the person requiring it, ten cents; but the whole amount of fees for transfers of real estate described in any one deed, plat, or other instrument, shall not exceed one dollar and fifty cents. (102 v. 277.) *Fees for transfers.*

SECTION 3707. When any lot or lots of land lying within the limits of a municipality have been dedicated, given or granted thereto, and set apart for the use and support of schools, on application of the mayor or council thereof, the court of common pleas may authorize an exchange of such lot or lots for such other lot or lots within the limits of such municipality as the interest of the schools therein require. All lots so taken in exchange, shall be held for the same purposes and subject to the same conditions as the original lots. (70 v. 193 § 1.) *Exchange of lots for school purposes.*

SECTION 3708. Each application for such exchange of lots shall be by petition verified by the mayor. The board of education of the municipality and such other persons as the court orders shall be made party defendants. The petition shall set forth an accurate description of each lot proposed to be given or taken in exchange, the specific circumstances which render the exchange necessary, and a prayer for such order as may be required. (70 v. 193 § 2.) *Petition, what shall contain.*

SECTION 3709. Notice of the filing, pendency, and prayer of the petition shall be published for four consecutive weeks, prior to the day of hearing, in a newspaper printed in such municipality, or if there is none, in a newspaper printed in the county and of general circulation in such municipality. (70 v. 193 § 3.) *Notice of petition to be published.*

Hearing and order.

SECTION 3710. If upon the hearing of the petition it appears to the court that notice of the filing, pendency, and prayer thereof has been so given, and that such exchange of lots is necessary and will promote the interests of such schools, and that such an order would not be inconsistent with the terms and conditions of the original grant or devise, the court shall authorize the exchange to be made, and order the mayor of the municipality to execute and deliver such deed or deeds in fee simple, as are necessary to effect the exchange. (70 v. 193 § 4.)

Transfer of property to library trustees.

SECTION 3711. A municipal corporation may transfer by ordinance duly passed, any property, real or personal, acquired or suitable for library purposes, to the trustees of any public library for the school district within which such municipal corporation is situated upon such lawful terms and conditions as are agreed to between the municipal corporation and trustees. (97 v. 133 § 1.)

How school land appropriated.

SECTION 11067. When a railroad company, incorporated in this state, has located its railroad through a part of reserved section twenty-nine or sixteen, or through a part of sections granted by congress instead of section sixteen for school purposes, and such lands remain unsold, or through a town lot or parcels of ground used for or devoted to school purposes, it may appropriate so much of such land or lots as is necessary for its purposes. Service of the summons made on such trustees or school officers, as have possession or control of the lands, shall have the same force and effect as service in other cases on owners of land sought to be appropriated. The money arising from such appropriation must be disposed of by such trustees or school officers in accordance with law. (69 v. 88.)

As the state held in many cases as a trustee sections 29 and 16, and the lands granted in lieu of section 16 for ministerial and school purposes, express authority was given by this section to appropriate a right of way through these lands: State v. Railway, 37 O. S. 157.

Proceedings when land is held without agreement.

SECTION 11084. When a corporation, authorized by law to make appropriation of private property or lands reserved for school purposes, has taken passession of and is occupying or using the land of any person or such school lands for any purpose and the land so occupied or used has not been appropriated and paid for by the corporation, or is not held by an agreement in writing with the owner thereof, or the trustees or school officers having possession or control of such school lands, such owner or owners, or either of them, or such trustees or school officers, may serve written notice upon the corporation in the manner provided for the service of summons against a corporation, to proceed under this chapter to appropriate the lands. On the failure of such corporation for ten days so to proceed, the owner or owners or such trustees or school officers may file a petition in the probate court of the proper county setting forth the fact of such use or occupation by the corporation, that the corporation has no right, legal or equitable thereto and in cases of reserved section sixteen and twenty-nine or any part of sections granted by congress instead of section sixteen for school purposes no right, legal or equitable, derived from the trustees and officers named therein, that such notice has been duly served, that the time of limitation under the notice has elapsed, and such other facts, including a pertinent description of the land so used or occupied, as are proper to a full understanding of the case. (80 v. 114.)

TITLE XIII. PUBLIC SCHOOL DISTRICTS.

CHAPTER I.

CLASSIFICATION OF DISTRICTS.

School districts classified.

SECTION 4679. The school districts of the state shall be styled, respectively, city school districts, village school districts rural school districts and county school districts. (104 v. 133.)

Cited: Christy v. Commissioners, 41 O. S. 711; Toledo v. Railway, 4 O. C. C. 113, 2 O. C. D. 450; State, ex rel., v. Ryland, 7 O. C. C. 1, 396; State, ex rel., v. Board of Elections, 16 O. C. C. 1, 8 O. C. D. 215.

A classification of school districts is held to be valid: State v. Brewster, 39 O. S. 653.

The school act of 1853 was passed in obedience to the mandate of Art. VI. of the Ohio constitution, and the purpose of the statute was to give to the common school system uniformity, harmony, unity and force throughout the state: Finch v. Board of Education, 30 O. S. 37.

In spite of a statutory provision in the school law of May 1, 1873, that school districts were bodies politic and corporate, it was held that they were not corporations within the meaning of Art. XIII, Sec. 1 of the Ohio constitution: State v. Powers, 38 O. S. 54.

The pro isions of this and the following sections relating to the classifications of school districts, were held to be applicable not merely to conditions existing when the statute was passed, but to be prospective in their operation: Eckstein v. Board of Education, 10 O. C. C. 480, 4 O. C. D. 149.

When a newly incorporated village is formed with a tax duplicate of more than $100,000 such village becomes ipso facto a village school district, but when such village fails to elect a board of education when the village officers are elected, a special election for members of such board of education is not authorized by law. Such members can only be elected in the odd numbered years.

When in a township there exists two or more districts unconnected and the village school district and the further special district is organized, the two subdistricts and the part of the township not included in the village district or the special district, will all comprise parts of the township school district and will still remain under the jurisdiction of the township board of education. The village district also will remain under the control of the township board of education until such time as it is properly organized after its members are elected.

Under section 4748, General Code, when three out of five members of a township board of education become disqualified for that office by reason of the formation of a special school district, the two remaining members may fill such vacancies in the township board.

Inasmuch as there are no officers upon whom rests the ministerial duty to organize the village district or to call an election for members of its board of education, such election may not be enforced by mandamus. The organization may be brought about by a sufficient number of electors taking steps to become candidates for the village board of education of the November election and the board of elections would be required to place their names upon the ballots and hold an election therefor. — *Attorney General,* 1913, p. 460.

The county board of education may not, under Section 4736, G. C., 104 O. L., 133, unite two village school districts into one single village district. Sections 4682-1 and 4683, G. C., control in such cases. — *Attorney General,* Opinion No. 36, Jan. 29, 1915.

The county board of education has no authority under Section 4736, G. C., as amended, 104 O. L., 138, to discontinue a rural school district and join it to a rural or village school district contiguous thereto.

A county board having attempted to discontinue a rural school district by resolution of record, a copy of which has been filed with the county auditor, under the provisions of Section 4736, G. C., as amended, should rescind said resolution and furnish a copy of the rescinding resolution to the county auditor. A copy of such rescinding resolution should also be furnished to the clerks of the boards of education of the school districts mentioned in said former resolution.

If the funds of such rural school district have been turned over to the treasurer of the board of education of the rural or village school district contiguous thereto, as a result of the action of the county board of education, upon receipt of the notice as above provided, said funds should be returned to the treasury of the rural school district from which they were transferred.

It is necessary, in order to abolish a rural school district that the question be submitted to a vote of the qualified electors of such district under the provisions of Section 4735, *G. C.* as amended, and supplemented by sections 4735-1 and 4735-2, *G. C.,* 104 O. L., 138.

The question of centralization under provision of Section 4736, G. C., as amended 104 O. L., 139, and the question of issuing bonds under provision of Section 7625, G. C., may be submitted to the qualified electors of a rural school district at one election. — *Attorney General,* Opinion 183, March 29, 1915.

SECTION 4680. Each city together with the territory attached to it for school purposes, and excluding the territory within its corporate limits detached for school purposes, shall constitute a city school district. (97 v. 335.) City school districts.

Cited: Toledo v. Railway, 4 O. C. C. 113, 2 O. C. D. 450.

The village of Loveland is located in three counties and is a part of three special school districts. In order to make the village of Loveland a special school district it will be necessary to get the approval of the three special school districts in the transfer of territory. The statutes provide a method whereby the three special school districts could be abandoned, and then the formation of one special school district would become an easy matter. The problem may be worked out either by abandoning the special school districts and organizing a village district, or by means of transferring the territory of the village from one district to another, so as to get the territory of the village in one school district. — *Attorney General,* 1913, p. 476.

Under Section 4740, General Code, as amended, a village district already employing a superintendent, cannot join with a rural school district which never employed a superintendent and which said districts were never heretofore joined together for supervisory purposes by employing a superintendent in common upon application to the county board of education to be joined and continue as separate districts as authorized by said section.

Under the recently enacted school code, appearing in 104, O. L., 133, school districts formerly designated as "special school districts" now constitute rural school districts, which said rural school districts are a part of the respective county school districts of the state. Part of any county school districts may be transferred to an adjoining school district or city or village school district by the mutual consent of the boards of education having control of such districts. — *Attorney General*, Opinion No. 1054, July 18, 1914.

Village school district.

SECTION 4681. Each village, together with the territory attached to it for school purposes, and excluding the territory within its corporate limits detached for school purposes, and having in the district thus formed a total tax valuation of not less than five hundred thousand dollars, shall constitute a village school district. (103 v. 545.)

An incorporated village which forms part of a township school district, becomes ipso facto a village school district upon the attainment of a tax valuation of one hundred thousand dollars.

Said village may attach territory for school purposes under section 4092, General Code, et seq. — *Attorney General*, 1911-12, p. 537.

By virtue of Section 4681, General Code, when a village attains a tax valuation of one hundred thousand dollars, it constitutes a village school district. When such village attains that valuation in 1911 it must, however, remain a part of the township school district under the jurisdiction of the township board of education until the members of the village district elected in November 1913 can be properly organized.

When, therefore, in 1912 said township board engineered an election for the issuance of $20,000 worth of bonds for the erection of a high school building within the village, in which election; the electors of the entire township voted; held: That the situation has so changed that the board would be justified in declining to act upon the bond issue regardless of the results of the election.

Under Section 4696, General Code, the funds and indebtedness of the township school district should be equitably apportioned between the township and village district as therein provided.

The statutes do not provide specifically for the disposition of the school building situated in the village but the decisions endorse the reasonability of permitting the newly created district to take title to school property within its limits and which was designed for is use, and such is to be deemed the policy of the law. — *Attorney General*, 1912, p. 1282.

When a special school district becomes a village school district, either by the creation of a village having school property to the valuation of $100,000 or by vote of the electors when the valuation is less, the board of education of the special school district shall hold over until the board of education of the village school district is organized.

When the village school district board is elected at a special election, the board shall organize on the second Monday after the special election. — *Attorney General*, 1912, p. 1526.

Under Section 4681, General Code, when a village obtains a valuation of $100,000, it becomes ipso facto a village school district and in view of this statute, any attempt to transfer the village district to the township district would be useless.

Section 4681, General Code, however, contemplates that territory of the township which is contiguous to the village, may be attached to the village school district, and there is no legal objection to making such transfers, under the procedure provided by Sections 4692 et seq., General Code.

In making such transfer, however, its effect upon the right of centralization of schools should be considered. — *Attorney General,* 1912, p. 1349.

Under Section 4740, General Code, as amended, a village district already employing a superintendent, cannot join with a rural school district which never employed a superintendent and which said districts were never heretofore joined together for supervisory purposes by employing a superintendent in common upon application to the county board of education to be joined and continue as separate districts as authorized by said section.

Under the recently enacted school code, appearing in 104, O. L., 133, school districts formerly designated as "special school districts" now constitute rural school districts, which said rural school districts are a part of the respective county school districts of the state. Part of any county school districts may be transferred to an adjoining shool district or city or village school district by the mutual consent of the boards of education having control of such districts. — *Attorney General,* Opinion No. 1054, July 18, 1914.

By force of this section, each incorporated village existing when this section took effect, or since created, "together with the territory attached to it for school purposes and excluding the territory within its corporate limits detached for school purposes and having in the district thus formed a total tax valuation of not less than one hundred thousand dollars," constitutes and is a village school district, no vote of the electors of such village being necessary to the creation or establishment of such district: Buchman v. State, ex rel. 81 O. S. 171.

SECTION 4682. A village, together with the territory attached to it for school purposes, and excluding the territory within its corporate limits detached for school purposes, with a tax valuation of less than five hundred thousand dollars, shall not constitute a village school district, but the proposition to organize the territory thus formed into a village school district may be submitted by the board of education, and shall be submitted by the board of education upon the presentation to it of a written petition for such purpose signed by 25 per cent. of the electors of the territory thus formed, to a vote of the electors of the territory thus formed at any general or a special election called for that purpose, and be so determined by a majority vote of such electors. (103 v. 545.)

Village with less than five hundred thousand valuation not a village district.

Vote to organize village school district.

An incorporated village which forms part of a township school district becomes ipso facto a village school district upon the attainment of a tax valuation of one hundred thousand dollars. Said village may attach territory for school purposes under section 4092, General Code, et seq. — *Attorney General,* 1911-1912, p. 537.

SECTION 4682-1. A village school district containing a population of less than fifteen hundred may vote at any general or special election to dissolve and join any contiguous rural district. After approval by the county board such proposition shall be submitted to the electors by the village board of education on the petition of one-fourth of the electors of such village school district or the village board may submit the proposition on its own motion and the results shall be determined by a majority vote of such electors. (104 v. 133.)

When and how village school district may dissolve and join rural district.

SECTION 4683. When a village school district is dissolved, the territory formerly constituting such village district shall become a part of the contiguous rural district

Title passes to rural district. board of education.

which it votes to join in accordance with section 4682-1, and all school property shall pass to and become vested in the board of education of such rural school district. (104 v. 133.)

By virtue of sections 4723 and 4724, General Code, joint sub-districts are abolished and the territory of such districts situated in the township in which the school house of the joint sub-district is not located is attached for school purposes to the township school district in which said school house is located and shall constitute a part of said township school district.

Pupils of such attached territory, therefore, are entitled to conveyance to the centralized school, when the board abolishes sub-districts; the expense thereof to be paid out of the funds of the township district.

Under the terms of section 7730, General Code, providing such pupils live more than one and one-half miles from such school in accordance with section 7731, General Code, the fact that said officials have failed to make a map of attached territory which is to be made a part of the records of the board of education and a copy of which is to be filed with the auditor of the county in which the territory is situated, as provided by section 4724, General Code, does not operate to prevent the territory included in the joint sub-district and outside of the township becoming a part of the township school district as provided by section 4723, General Code. — *Attorney General*, 1913, p. 1089.

1. Where land is sought to be detached from a village school district, the tenant residing on said land is the proper person to petition for the detachment of the lands from said district. Such petition cannot be made by the owner of the land or by his trustee.

2. No objection can be interposed to the transfer of said territory from the village school district to the township school district on the ground that a bonded indebtedness had been created, which now exists against the first mentioned district. — *Attorney General*, 1913, p. 1392.

County school district defined. SECTION 4684. Each county, exclusive of the territory embraced in any city school district and the territory in any village school district exempted from the supervision of the county board of education by the provisions of sections 4688 and 4688-1, and territory detached for school purposes, and including the territory attached to it for school purposes, shall constitute a county school district. In each case where any village or rural school district is situated in more than one county such district shall become a part of the county school district in which the greatest part of the territory of such village or rural district is situated. (104 v. 133.)

The county commissioners may not lawfully transfer from the general county fund, or from the proceeds of any other county tax levies to supply deficiencies in the county board of education fund, in case there is no money available in the Sheep fund, under Section 5653, General Code, as amended. — *Attorney General*, Opinion No. 1142, September 12, 1914.

The members of the county board of school examiners authorized by Section 7811, General Code, as amended, 104 O. L., 102, are not subject to the civil service law. — *Attorney General*, Opinion No. 1177, Oct. 1, 1914.

Bills for office supplies, stationery, etc., furnished to the county superintendent of schools, should be approved by the county board of education and paid out of the county board of education fund on the warrant of the county auditor. — *Attorney General*, Opinion No. 144, March 17, 1915.

SECTION 4685. The territory included within the boundaries of a city, village or rural school district shall be contiguous except where an island or islands form an integral part of the district. (104 v. 133.)

Territory must be contiguous.

ADVANCEMENT AND REDUCTION.

SECTION 4686. When a village is advanced to a city, the village school district shall thereby become a city school district. When a city is reduced to a village the city school district shall thereby become a village school district. The members of the board of education in village school districts that are advanced to city school districts, and in city school districts that are reduced to village school districts shall continue in office until succeeded by the members of the board of education of the new district, who shall be elected at the next succeeding annual election for school board members. (98 v. 217.)

Change of classification upon advancement or reduction.

When a village advances to a city by reason of the federal census, the village officials remain in office until the city officers elected in the next election have been inducted into office.

The village board of education may determine the number of members to be elected to the city board of education but the power to appoint the city board of examiners resides only in the board elected under the city plan.

The county certificates will be sufficient to carry teachers through the present year but for later periods a certificate must be obtained from the regularly appointed city board of school examiners. — *Attorney General*, 1911-1912, p. 562.

When a village advances to a city by reason of the last federal census, the board of education of the village continues its duties until the induction into office of the city board of education, but with the powers only of a village board of education. Such village board therefore, has the power only to appoint a superintendent for a term of three years as provided for villages under section 7705, General Code.

An appointment by such board of a superintendent for a longer term as provided for cities under section 7702, General Code, is therefore void. — *Attorney General*, 1911-1912, p. 563.

When a village school district, by reason of the last federal census, advances to a city school district, the members of the board of education of the old village district, under sections 4686 and 4700, General Code, shall decide the number of members which shall compose the city board of education.

The successors of the members of the board of education in such instance, shall be elected at the next annual election for school board members.

A superintendent or teacher who had been elected for a legal term of years by said village board, may hold for said term under the city school district regime. — *Attorney General*, 1911-1912, p. 516.

The appropriation and expenditure of taxes levied during the summer of 1910 for which settlement is made August 5, 1911, will be governed by the provisions of section 3797, General Code, and other related sections of the old law.

Taxes collected in December, 1911, however, were levied under the Smith law and appropriations from these collections, must be made in accordance with section 5649-3d, General Code. — *Attorney General*, 1911-1912, p. 1561.

School district
in newly
created vil-
lage.

SECTION 4687. Upon the creation of a village, it shall thereby become a village school district, as herein provided, and, if the territory of such village previous to its creation was included within the boundaries of a rural school district and such rural school district included more territory than is included within the village, such territory shall thereby be attached to such village school district for school purposes, provided such territory has an area of less than sixteen square miles. (104 v. 133.)

If a board of education of a township had established a central or high school under the provisions of former statute (S. & C. 1346; act of March 14, 1853; amended S. & S. 712; act of May 14, 1868) and such board had erected a building in a subdistrict of such township for the use of such school, and by agreement between such board of education and the local directors of such subdistrict, such building was used for the central or high school and also for the school of such subdistrict, and subsequently, prior to the enactment of this statute in its earlier form, the territory included in such subdistrict was formed into an incorporated village after such central or high school had been established, it was held that the property of the central or high school and the management thereof did not pass to the board of education of the incorporated village by virtue of this section in its original form: Board of Education v. Board of Education, 41 O. S. 680.

What village
districts may
become ex-
empt from
supervision of
county board.

SECTION 4688. The board of education of any village school district containing a village which according to the last federal census had a population of three thousand or more, may decide by a majority vote of the full membership thereof not to become a part of the county school district. Such village district by notifying the county board of education of such decision before the third Saturday of July, 1914, shall be exempt from the supervision of the board. (104 v. 133.)

1. If a village school district, containing a village, which according to the last federal census, has a population of 3,000 or more, decides by a majority vote of the full membership thereof, not to become a part of the county school district, and notifies the county board of education of its decision before the third Saturday of July, 1914, as provided by Section 4688, General Code, then such village school district cannot after such date through its board of education rescind its action and become a part of the county school district.

2. If such village school board, by its own action becomes a part of the county school district, because it does not act in accordance with Section 4688, General Code, then such village school district cannot through its board of education, at a later date, withdraw from the county school district, and again become a village school district. — *Attorney General,* Opinion 1015, June 29, 1914.

The term "Supervisor" as employed in Section 7811, 104 O. L., 102, is intended to apply to teachers who have had experience in overseeing or have had charge of schools with authority to direct or regulate matters in connection with the schools, either as an actual superintendent or in a supervisory capacity. The term, "exempted village school district" as employed in said section 7811, applies to village school districts which are exempt from county school districts by virtue of Sections 4688 and 4688-1, General Code, as amended in 104 O. L., 134. — *Attorney General,* Opinion 1341, Dec. 29, 1914.

When a cen-
sus of the
population of
village dis-
trict may be
taken.

SECTION 4688-1. The board of education of a village school district shall upon the petition of one hundred or more electors of such district, or upon its own motion may at any time order a census to be taken of the population of such district. One or more persons may be appointed by the board to take such census. Each person so appointed shall take an oath or affirmation to take such census accurately and to the best of his ability. He shall make his return under oath to the clerk of the board, and certified copies of such return shall be sent to the county auditor and superintendent of public instruction. If the census shows a population of three thousand or more in the village school district, and such census is approved by the superintendent of public instruction, such district shall, upon notification by the board of education of such village school district, be exempted, from the supervision of the county board of education. (104 v. 133.)

The term "Supervisor" as employed in Section 7811, 104 O. L., 102, is intended to apply to teachers who have had experience in overseeing or have had charge of schools with authority to direct or regulate matters in connection with the schools, either as an actual superintendent or in a supervisory capacity. The term "exempted village school district" as employed in said section 7811, applies to village school districts which are exempt from county school districts by virtue of Sections 4688 and 4688-1, General Code, as amended in 104 O. L., 134. — *Attorney General*, Opinion 1341, Dec. 29, 1914.

SECTION 4688-2. All village school districts which are exempted from the supervision of the county board of education as provided in sections 4688 and 4688-1 are thereby rendered ineligible to receive state aid for purposes of supervision and teachers training courses and for the grading of schools as provided in section 7655-5 of the General Code. (104 v. 133.)   *Village district exempt from county supervision ineligible to certain state aid.*

SECTION 4689. The provisions of law relating to the power to settle claims, dispose of property or levy and collect taxes to pay existing obligations of a village that has surrendered its corporate powers, shall also apply to such village school district and the board of education thereof. (104 v. 133.)   *Disposal of property in such cases.*

SECTION 4690. When territory is annexed to a city or village, such territory thereby becomes a part of the city or village school district, and the legal title to school property in such territory for school purposes shall remain vested in the board of education of the school district from which such territory was detached, until such time as may be agreed upon by the several boards of education when such property may be transferred by warranty deed. (104 v. 133.)   *Title to property when territory annexed to city or village.*

By virtue of Section 4681, General Code, when a village attains a tax valuation of one hundred thousand dollars, it constitutes a village school district. When such village attains that valuation in 1911, it must, however, remain a part of the township school district under the jurisdiction of the township board of education until the members of the village district elected in November 1913 can be properly organized.

When, therefore, in 1912, said township board engineered an election for the issuance of $20,000 worth of bonds for the erection of a high school building within the village, in which election, the electors of the entire township voted; held: That the

situation has so changed that the board would be justified in
declining to act upon the bond issue regardless of the results of the
election.

Under Section 4696, General Code, the funds and indebtedness
of the township school district should be equitably apportioned
between the township and village district as therein provided.

The statutes do not provide specifically for the disposition of
the school building situated in the village but the decisions endorse
the reasonability of permitting the newly created district to take
title to school property within its limits and which was designed for
is use, and such is to be deemed the policy of the law. — *Attorney
General*, 1912, p. 1282.

**Attaching vil-
lage territory.** SECTION 4691. When territory located within the corporate limits of a village is attached for school purposes
to a district other than the village school district, and the
boards of education of the districts are unable to agree as
to the transfer of such territory, the board of education of
the village school district may file a petition in the probate
court, asking for the transfer of territory within the corporate limits of the village, and the probate court shall
have the same jurisdiction and powers as are provided by
the preceding section in case of disagreement between
boards. (99 v. 117.)

SECTION 4692. The county board of education may
transfer a part or all of a school district of the county
school district to an adjoining district or districts of the
county school district. Such transfer shall not take effect
until a map is filed with the auditor of the county in which
the transferred territory is situated, showing the boundaries
of the territory transferred, and a notice of such poposed
tansfer has been posted in thee conspicuous places in the
district or districts proposed to be transferred, or printed
in a paper of general circulation in said county, for ten
days; nor shall such transfer take effect if a majority of the
qualified electors residing in the territory to be transferred,
shall, within thirty days after the filing of such map, file
with the county board of education a written remonstrance
against such proposed transfer. If an entire district be
transferred the board of education of such district is
thereby abolished or if a member of the board of education
lives in a part of a school district transferred the member
becomes a non-resident of the school district from which
he was transferred and ceases to be a member of such board
of education. The legal title of the property of the board
of education shall become vested in the board of education
of the school district to which such territory is transferred.
The county board of education is authorized to make an
equitable division of the school funds of the transferred
territory either in the treasury or in the course of collection. And also an equitable division of the indebtedness of
the transferred territory. (106 v. 396.)

When a joint school district prior to the codification of the
school laws, was composed of part of the two townships, P. and
S., the school house of said joint district being located within the
lines of "P" township and the voters of "P" township, under sec-

tion 4726, General Code, have voted for the centralization of schools, held:

That the territory of the entire joint subdistrict becomes a part of the centralized "P" township school district.

That the voters of the part of the joint district territory lying in "S" township are entitled to vote upon the question of a bond issue authorized by section 7625, General Code, and promoted by "P" township, provided that the "S" township school district has not centralized its schools and thereby acquired through section 4725, General Code, jurisdiction of that part of the former joint township school district which lies within "S" township.

Except by fullfillment of the conditions provided for in section 4725, General Code, there is no way that the territory in "S" township attached to the "P" township school district can be detached from the "P" township without the consent of residents and the school board of the "S" township. — *Attorney General*, 1911-12, p. 1400.

Where land is sought to be detached from a village school district, the tenant residing on said land is the proper person to petition for the detachment of the lands from said district. Such petition cannot be made by the owner of the land or by his trustee.

No objection can be interposed to the transfer of said territory from the village school district to the township school district on the ground that a bonded indebtedness had been created, which now exists against the first mentioned district. — *Attorney General*, 1913, p. 1392.

Under Section 4740, General Code, as amended, a village district already employing a superintendent, cannot join with a rural school district which never employed a superintendent and which said districts were never heretofore joined together for supervisory purposes by employing a superintendent in common upon application to the county board of education to be joined and continue as separate districts as authorized by said section.

Under the recently enacted school code, appearing in 104, O. L., 133, school districts formerly designated as "special school districts" now constitute rural school districts, which said rural school districts are a part of the respective county school districts of the state. Part of any county school district may be transferred to an adjoining school district or city or village school district by the mutual consent of the boards of education having control of such districts. — *Attorney General*, Opinion No. 1054, July 18, 1914.

When territory is transferred from one rural or village school district to another, the equitable division of funds or indebtedness required by statute to be made shall be determined upon at the time of the transfer, by the county board of education, which, under Section 4736, General Code, has exclusive power to make such transfer.

The indebtedness apportioned to the transferred district in accordance with the statute becomes a general indebtedness of the whole district, and does not attach only to the transferred territory. — *Attorney General*, Opinion No. 1193, Oct. 8, 1914.

SECTION 4696. A county board of education may transfer a part or all of a school district of the county school district to an adjoining exempted village school district or city school district, or to another county school district, provided at least fifty per centum of the electors of the territory to be transferred petition for such transfer. Provided, however, that if at least seventy-five per cent of the electors of the territory petition for such transfer, the county board of education shall make such transfer. No such transfer shall be in effect until the county board of education and the board of education to which the territory

[margin note: Apportionment of funds or indebtedness when territory is transferred.]

is to be transferred each pass resolutions by a majority vote
of the full membership of each board and until an equitable
· division of the funds or indebtedness be decided upon by
the boards of education acting in the transfer; also a map
· shall be filed with the auditor or auditors of the county or
counties affected by such transfer. (106 v. 396.)

By virtue of Section 4681, General Code, when a village attains a tax valuation of one hundred thousand dollars, it constitutes a village school district. When such village attains that
valuation in 1911 it must, however, remain a part of the township
school district under the jurisdiction of the township board of
education until the members of the village district elected in
November, 1913, can be properly organized.

When, therefore, in 1912 said township board engineered an
election for the issuance of $20,000 worth of bonds for the erection
of a high school building within the village, in which election, the
electors of the entire township voted, held: That the situation has
so changed that the board would be justified in declining to act upon
the bond issue regardless of the results of the election.

Under Section 4696, General Code, the funds and indebtedness of the township school district should be equitably apportioned between the township and village district as therein provided.

The statutes do not provide specifically for the disposition
of the school building situated in the village but the decisions
endorse the reasonability of permitting the newly created district
to take title to school property within its limits and which was
designed for is use, and such is to be deemed the policy of the
law. — *Attorney General*, 1912, p. 1282.

CHAPTER 2.

CITY SCHOOL DISTRICTS.

SECTION 4698. In city school districts containing according to the federal census a population of less than 50,000 persons, the board of education shall consist of not less than three members nor more than five members elected at large by the qualified electors of such district.

In city school districts containing according to the federal census a population of 50,000 persons or more, but less than 150,000 persons, the board of education shall consist of not less than two members nor more than seven members elected at large by the qualified electors of the school district, and of not less than two members nor more than twelve members elected from subdistricts by the qualified electors of their respective subdistricts.

In city school districts containing according to the federal census a population of 150,000 persons or more, the board of education shall consist of not less than five nor more than seven members elected at large by the qualified electors of such district; the office of subdistrict member in boards of education in all such city school districts is hereby abolished and the terms of members elected from subdistricts shall terminate on the day preceding the first Monday in January, 1914. (103 v. 275.)

When a village school district, by reason of the last Federal census advances to a city school district, the members of the board of education of the old village district under Sections 4686 and 4700, General Code, shall decide the number of members which shall compose the city board of education.

The successors of the members of the board of education in such instance, shall be elected at the next annual election for school board members.

A superintendent or teacher' who had been elected for a legal term of years by said village board, may hold for said term under the city school district regime. — *Attorney General*, 1911-12, p. 516.

When the Federal census shows a city to have passed the fifty thousand population mark and the city school district consequently passes from the first to the second class, it is necessary, under Section 4703, General Code, to elect all the members of the board of the second class and the term of the members of the board under the first class regime shall be cut off, upon the induction into office of said board of the second class.

The contrary rule prevails under Section 4707, General Code, when a city school district of the second class is redistricted, and the terms of members shall not be affected thereby. — *Attorney General*, 1911-12, p. 524.

As to boards of education see G. C. Sec. 4745, et seq.
As to female suffrage in school elections see G. C. Sec. 4862.
The uniformity of operation of this and the following section is destroyed by force of the terms of the act, and as amended this act is therefore unconstitutional and void. Previous to its amendment this act was general in character and so far as its terms were concerned, operated uniformly throughout the state, and divested of the amendment the act is unconstitutional: State, ex rel., v. Withrow, 11 O. C. C. (N. S.) 569.

Number of members determined; how.

SECTION 4699. Within thirty days after this act shall take effect, the board of education of each and every city school district in which the number of members does not conform to the provisions of section 4698 shall by resolution determine within the limits prescribed by said sections the number of members of said board of education. Said resolution shall provide for the classification of the terms of members so that they will conform to the provisions of section 4702, General Code, taking into consideration the terms of office of the existing members whose terms do not expire or terminate on the day preceding the first Monday in January, 1914. At the same time such boards of education in city school districts containing according to the federal census a population of 50,000 persons or over, but less than

Division into sub-districts.

150,000 persons shall subdivide such city school district into subdivisions equal in number to the number of members of the board of education in the district, who are to be elected from subdistricts therein so established. Such subdistricts shall be bounded, as far as practicable, by corporation lines, streets, alleys, avenues, public grounds, canals, water courses, ward boundaries, voting precinct boundaries, or present school district boundaries, and shall be as nearly equal in population as possible and be composed of adjacent and as compact territory as practicable. Such subdivision shall be numbered from one up consecutively and the lines thereof so fixed shall not be changed until after each succeeding federal census.

Within three months after the official announcement of the result of each succeeding federal census, the board of education of each city school district which according to such census shall have a population of 50,000 persons or

Redistricting.

over and less than 150,000 persons, shall redistrict such district into subdistricts in accordance with the provisions of this chapter. If the board of education of any such district fails to district or redistrict such city school district, as herein required then the state superintendent of public instruction shall forthwith district or redistrict such city school district, subject to the requirements of this chapter. (103 v. 275.)

A board of education is not liable in its corporate capacity for damages sustained by a pupil while attending the common schools, caused by the negligence of the board in the discharge of its official duty in erecting and maintaining a common school building, in the absence of a statute creating such liability: Finch v. Board of Education, 30 O. S. 37.

Election of additional members, when.

SECTION 4701. Whenever the number of members of the board of education of a city school district, as fixed by the resolution provided for in section 4699, shall be more than the number of members whose terms will not expire or terminate on the day preceding the first Monday in January, 1914, the additional members of such board shall be elected at the general school election in the year 1913 for such terms of two or four years as may be necessary to comply with the two provisions of sections 4698 and 4702.

Whenever the number of members of any such board of education shall by the resolution provided for in said section 4699 be fixed at less than the number of members of said board whose terms do not expire or terminate on the day preceding the first Monday in January, 1914, the member or members to retire shall be determined by lot from among those whose terms would expire on the day preceding the first Monday in January, 1916, lots being cast among members elected at large and among members elected from subdistricts separately, and the terms of office of those on whom the lot falls shall expire on the day preceding the first Monday in January, 1914. (103 v. 275.)

Retiring members determined by lot.

Inasmuch as under Section 4701, General Code, the prosecuting attorney is obliged to prosecute all actions against members of a village board of education for misfeasance or malfeasance in office considerations of public policy will not permit that official to hold a position on such board of education. — *Attorney General,* 1912, p. 1523.

Where in a city of less than 50,000 population three members are elected on the school board when only two should have been elected, the better way to clear up the situation is to declare that the two members receiving the highest number of votes at the November election are elected. If this is not satisfactory to all concerned the dissatisfied party can proceed in court in a proper manner. — *Attorney General,* 1913, p. 1597.

SECTION 4702. The term of office of all members of boards of education in city school districts, except as provided in section 4701, shall be four years. All members in office at the time this act takes effect shall serve the unexpired portions of the terms for which they were respectively elected and until their successors are elected and qualified, unless their terms shall expire or shall have been terminated as provided by sections 4698 and 4701.

Term.

If the number of members of a board of education of any city school district to be elected at large as fixed pursuant to section 4699 be even, one-half thereof shall be elected in the year preceding, and the remaining half in the year following the calendar year divisible by four. If such number be odd, one-half of the remainder after diminishing the number by one shall be elected in the year preceding, and the remaining number shall be elected in the year following the calendar year divisible by four. All members to be elected from odd numbered subdistricts shall be elected at one and the same election, and all members from even numbered subdistricts shall be elected at the alternate election. (103 v. 275.)

When members elected.

Where in a city of less than 50,000 population three members are elected on the school board when only two should have been elected, the better way to clear up the situation is to declare that the two members receiving the highest number of votes at the

November election are elected. If this is not satisfactory to all concerned the dissatisfied party can proceed in court in a proper manner. — *Attorney General,* 1913, p. 1597.

Electors in attached territory entitled to vote.

SECTION 4703. When territory is attached to a city school district for school purposes, the electors residing in said attached territory shall be entitled to vote for school officers and on all school questions in said district. It shall be the duty of the board of education of such city school district to assign such territory to the adjoining election precinct or precincts of said district and to have a map prepared showing such assignment, which shall be made a part of the records of said board. The electors residing in such attached territory shall be entitled to vote in the precincts to which they are assigned, but in case no assignment is made by the board of education, each elector shall vote in the precinct nearest his residence.

An elector residing in a city but not in the city school district of said city shall not be entitled to vote in said city school district. (103 v. 275.)

When the Federal census shows a city to have passed the fifty thousand population mark and the city school district consequently passes from the first to the second class, it is necessary, under Section 4703, General Code, to elect all the members of the board of the second class and the term of the members of the board under the first class regime shall be cut off, upon the induction into office of said board of the second class.

The contrary rule prevails under Section 4707, General Code, when a city school district of the second class is redistricted, and the terms of members shall not be affected thereby. — *Attorney General,* 1911-12, p. 524.

Submission of question of number of members.

SECTION 4704. If, at any time, a petition signed by ten (10%) per cent of the electors in any district shall be filed with the clerk of the board of education of such district asking that the question what shall be the number of members and what the organization of the board of education of such district be submitted to the electors thereof, such board of education shall within thirty days after the filing of such petition provide by resolution for submitting such question to the electors of such district. Such question shall not be submitted to a referendum vote more than once in any period of four years and the percentage of electors required to sign such petition shall be based upon the total vote cast at the last preceding general school election.

Commission to frame plans of organization for submission.

Said resolution shall require that such question shall be submitted at the next regular school election and shall also provide for the appointment of a commission to frame two or more plans of organization for submission as above provided. Said commission shall consist of seven members, three of whom shall be appointed by the president of the board of education of such district, two by the mayor of the city in which such district is embraced and two by the president of the board of sinking fund trustees of such city.

A certified copy of said resolution shall immediately after its passage be transmitted to the mayor and president of the board of sinking fund trustees of said city and such commission shall be appointed and shall organize within sixty days after the passage of said resolution. (103 v. 275.)

The removal from a city school district, indefinitely, of a member of a board of education creates a vacancy in said board. — *Attorney General*, Opinion No. 990, June 19, 1914.

SECTION 4705. Said commission shall prepare and submit to the electors at the next general school election, if one occur not less than one hundred and twenty days after the passage of said resolution, otherwise, at the second general school election, two or more plans for the organization of the board of education in such district, but in no event shall less than two plans be submitted. Each plan shall provide for the number of members, the length of term of the members and the organization of the board; one plan so submitted shall provide for a board of the same number and of the same organization às the board existing in said district at the time of said election. Said plans shall be submitted to the electors of said district on a separate ballot, bearing no party designation and in such form as said commission may determine. A certified copy of the resolution determining such form shall be transmitted by said commission to the proper election authorities à sufficient length of time prior to said election to enable the ballot therefor to be prepared. (103 v. 275.)

When and how plans shall be submitted and for what they shall provide.

The board of education is not vested with any power to refuse admission to pupils who have attained the age of six years, during the session of a school term. — *Attorney General*, 1911-12, p. 1018.

SECTION 4706. Provision shall be made by the board of deputy state supervisors and insepctors of election or other board or officer having charge of elections within any district for the preparation of the ballots for the holding of said election as hereinbefore provided and said election shall be conducted in all respects not herein specifically provided for, in a manner prescribed by general law for school elections.

Election; expense.

The board of education of such district shall make such provision as is necessary for meeting the expense of said commission, but said commissioners shall receive no compensation. (103 v. 275.)

SECTION 4707. If any plan so submitted shall receive a majority of the number of votes cast for all of the plans, it shall thereafter become the law governing the number of members and the organization of the board of education in such district and at the next general school election following the adoption of such plan all of the members of the board of education of such district shall be elected pursuant to such plan.

Adoption of by majority vote.

Expiration of terms.

The terms of all members of the board of education of such district who may have been elected prior to the adoption of such plan, or who may be elected at the general school election at which such plan is adopted, shall expire on the day preceding the first Monday of January following the next general school election thereafter. All members elected at said general school election following the adoption of such plan shall take office on the first Monday of January next following their election and shall hold office during such term or terms as may be provided by such plan adopted by the electors of said district, but no terms shall be for less than two years. (103 v. 275.)

When the Federal census shows a city to have passed the fifty thousand population mark and the city school district consequently passes from the first to the second class, it is necessary, under Section 4703, General Code, to elect all the members of the board of the second class and the term of the members of the board under the first class regime shall be cut off, upon the induction into office of said board of the second class.

The contrary rule prevails under Section 4707, General Code when a city school district of the second class is redistricted, and the terms of members shall not be affected thereby. — *Attorney General*, 1911-12, p. 524.

CHAPTER 3.

VILLAGE SCHOOL DISTRICTS.

SECTION 4708. In village school districts, the board of education shall consist of five members elected at large at the same time as municipal officers are elected and in the manner provided by law. (97 v. 341.)

Board of education in village districts.

When a special school district becomes a village school district, either by the creation of a village having school property to the valuation of $100,000 or by vote of the electors when the valuation is less, the board of education of the special school district shall hold over until the board of education of the village school district is organized.

When the village school district board is elected at a special election, the board shall organize on the second Monday after the special election. — *Attorney General*, 1912, p. 1526.

SECTION 4709. At the first election in such district, a board of education shall be elected, two members to serve for two years and three to serve for four years. At the proper municipal election held thereafter, their successors shall be elected for a term of four years. (97 v. 341.)

Terms of members chosen at first election.

When a special school district becomes a village school district, either by the creation of a village having school property to the valuation of $100,000 or by vote of the electors when the valuation is less, the board of education of the special school district shall hold over until the board of education of the village school district is organized.

When the village school district board is elected at a special election, the board shall organize on the second Monday after the special election. — *Attorney General*, 1912, p. 1526.

When a newly incorporated village is formed with a tax duplicate of more than $100,000, such village becomes ipso facto a village school district, but when such village fails to elect a board of education when the village officers are elected, a special election for members of such board of education is not authorized by law. Such members can only be elected in the odd numbered years.

When in a township there exists two or more districts unconnected and the village school district and the further special district is organized, the two subdistricts and the part of the township not included in the village district or the special district, will all comprise parts of the township school district and will still remain under the jurisdiction of the township board of education. The village district also will remain under the control of the township board.

Under section 4748, General Code, when three out of five members of a township board of education become disqualified for that office by reason of the formation of a special school district, the two remaining members may fill such vacancies in the township board.

Inasmuch as there are no officers upon whom rests the ministerial duty to organize the village district or to call an election for members of its board of education, such election may not be enforced by mandamus. The organization may be brought about by a sufficient number of electors taking steps to become candidates for the village board of education at the November election and the board of elections would be required to place their names upon the ballots and hold an election therefor. — *Attorney General,* 1913, p. 460.

Election in newly created village.

SECTION 4710. In villages hereafter created, a board of education shall be elected as provided in the preceding section. When villages hereafter created, or which have been heretofore created, fail or have failed to elect a board of education as provided in the preceding section, the commissioners of the county to which said district belongs, shall appoint such board, and the members so appointed shall serve until their successors are elected and qualified.

Appointment of board of education on failure to elect.

The successors of the members so appointed, shall be elected at the first election for members of the board of education held in such district after such appointment; two members to serve for two years and three members for four years, and thereafter their successors shall be elected in the manner and for the term as provided by section 4709 of the General Code.

Organization of board.

The board so appointed by the county commissioners shall organize on the second Monday after their appointment. If the members of such board are elected at a special election held in such district the members so elected shall serve for the term indicated in the preceding section, from the first Monday in January after the preceding election for members of the board of education and the board shall organize on the second Monday after such election. (103 v. 166.)

When a special school district becomes a village school district, either by the creation of a village having school property to the valuation of $100,000 or by vote of the electors when the valuation is less, the board of education of the special school district shall hold over until the board of education of the village school district is organized.

When the village school district board is elected at a special election, the board shall organize on the second Monday after the special election. — *Attorney General,* 1912, p. 1526.

By virtue of Section 4681, General Code, when a village attains a tax valuation of one hundred thousand dollars, it constitutes a village school district. When such village attains that valuation in 1911 it must, however, remain a part of the township school district under the jurisdiction of the township board of education until the members of the village district elected in November, 1913, can be properly organized.

When, therefore, in 1912 said township board engineered an election for the issuance of $20,000 worth of bonds for the erection of a high school building within the village, in which election, the electors of the entire township voted, held: That the situation has so changed that the board would be justified in declining to act upon the bond issue regardless of the results of the election.

Under Section 4696. General Code, the funds and indebtedness of the township school district should be equitably apportioned between the township and village district as therein provided.

The statutes do not provide specifically for the disposition of the school building situated in the village but the decisions endorse the reasonableness of permitting the newly created district to take title to school property within its limits and which was designed for is use, and such is to be deemed the policy of the law. — *Attorney General,* 1912, p. 1282.

When a newly incorporated village is formed with a tax duplicate of more than $100,000, such village becomes ipso facto a village school district, but when such village fails to elect a board of education when the village officers are elected, a special election for members of such board of education is not authorized by law. Such members can only be elected in the odd numbered years.

When in a township there exists two or more districts unconnected and the village school district and the further special district is organized, the two subdistricts and the part of the township not included in the village district or the special district, will all comprise parts of the township school district and will still remain under the jurisdiction of the township board of education. The village district also will remain under the control of the township board.

Under section 4748, General Code, when three out of five members of a township board of education become disqualified for that office by reason of the formation of a special school district, the two remaining members may fill such vacancies in the township board.

Inasmuch as there are no officers upon whom rests the ministerial duty to organize the village district or to call an election for members of its board of education, such election may not be enforced by mandamus. The organization may be brought about by a sufficient number of electors taking steps to become candidates for the village board of education at the November election and the board of elections would be required to place their names upon the ballots and hold an election therefor. — *Attorney General,* 1913, p. 460.

Prior to the amendment of 97 v. 341 it was held that the inhabitants of the village district, and not those of the village as such, could vote at the election for members of the board of education; that is, if any territory of the village was attached for school purposes the inhabitants of such territory could not vote for the members of the board of education: State, ex rel., v. Raine, 4 O. C. C. 72.

Where, at the first election of the members of the board of education, under this section, the office and term thereof are not indicated on the ballot, no election is had and the old members of the board for such former districts hold over: State, ex rel., v. Shafer, 18 O. C. C. 525.

SECTION 4711. Electors, residing in territory attached to a village district for school purposes, may vote for school offices and on all school questions at the proper voting place in the village to which the territory is attached. If the village is divided into precincts, the board of education of the village school district shall assign such attached territory to the adjoining precinct or precincts of the village, and have a map prepared showing such assignment, which map shall be made a part of the records of the board. Electors residing in such attached territory may vote in the precinct to which they are assigned, but, if no assignment of territory is made, they shall vote in the precinct nearest their residence. An elector residing in the village but not in the village school district shall not vote in such village school district. (97 v. 341.)

Assignment of electors in attached territory for voting purposes.

CHAPTER 4.

RURAL SCHOOL DISTRICTS.

Board of education in rural school districts.

SECTION 4712. In rural school districts, the board of education shall consist of five members elected at large at the same time township officers are elected and in the manner provided by law, for a term of four years. (104 v. 133.)

In the case of vacancies in a school board filled by appointment Section 10, General Code, provides that a successor shall be elected for the unexpired term at the first general election for such office if such vacancy occurs more than thirty days before any election.

Such appointee, however, has the same right as an elective officer to hold over until his successor is elected and qualified.

Where at an election, five positions were to be filled, two for four years and three for approximately two years and there was no designation upon the ballot to determine who were the candidates for the long term and who were the condidates for the short term, the terms were not definitely settled and there was no valid election. — *Attorney General*, 1912, p. 1102.

Assignment of electors in attached territory for school purposes.

SECTION 4714. Electors residing in a rural school district may vote for school officers and on all school questions at the proper voting place in the township in which such district is located. If the township is divided into different voting precincts, the board of education of such district shall assign the voters thereof to the proper precinct or precincts, and a map shall be prepared showing such assignment, which map shall be made a part of the records of the board. Electors may vote according to such assignment, but, if no assignment of territory is made, they shall vote, in the precinct nearest their residence. (104 v. 133.)

Contrary to the general rule of policy that a member of a board may not hold a salaried position under such board, special provision of statute makes it possible for a member of a board of education to serve as its clerk and receive the salary for both position. — *Attorney General*, 1911-12, p. 1089.

Compensation of members of board.

SECTION 4715. Each member of the board of education of rural school districts, except such districts as contain less than sixteen square miles, shall receive as compensation two dollars for each regular meeting actually attended by such member, but for not more than five meetings in any year. The compensation allowed members of the board shall be paid from the contingent fund. (104 v. 133.)

Members of former township boards of education take their salaries for the year 1914 under the statute prior to amendment. After that they take under the amended statute. — *Attorney General,* Opinion No. 1283, Dec. 8, 1914.

Where there has been no assignment of the voters of a rural school district by the Board of Education under section 4714, G. C., the electors of the rural school district shall vote for school officers and on all school questions in the precinct in which they reside. — *Attorney General,* Opinion 104, 1915.

SECTION 4726. A rural board of education may submit the question of centralization, and, upon the petition of not less than one-fourth of the qualified electors of such rural district, or upon the order of the county board of education, must submit such question to the vote of the qualified electors of such rural district at a general election or a special election called for that purpose. If more votes are cast in favor of centralization than against it, at such election, such rural board of education shall proceed at once to the centralization of the schools of the rural district, and if necessary, purchase a site or sites and erect a suitable building or buildings thereon. If, at such election, more votes are cast against the proposition of centralization than for it, the question shall not again be submitted to the electors of such rural district for a period of two years, except upon the petition of at least forty per cent of the electors of such district. (104 v. 133.)

Question of centralization to be submitted to vote.

It is necessary for a township board of education to submit the question of centralization of schools to a vote, under the provisions of Section 4726, General Code.

All the electors of the township are entitled to vote upon the proposition of the centralization of schools.

The abolishment of all schools in all the subdistricts by virtue of Section 7730 and 7731, General Code, the establishment of new schools and the conveyance of pupils to these schools, operate as the centralization of the schools of the township, provided that no election has been held upon the question of centralization which resulted adversely and provided that no petition may be filed by an election according to law. — *Attorney General,* 1913, p. 1377.

A proposition for the centralization of schools under the provisions of Section 4726, G. C., and a proposition to issue bonds authorized by Section 7625, G. C., may both be submitted to the electors of a rural school district at one election. — *Attorney General,* Opinion No. 41, Jan. 30, 1915.

The provision of Section 4726, G. C., as amended 104 O. L., 139, taken in connection with the provision of Sec. 4839, G. C., authorizes the calling of a special election in a rural school district for the purpose of submitting the question of centralization to the vote of the qualified electors of such district. — *Attorney General,* Opinion No. 184, March 30, 1915.

Where the schools of a township have been centralized, no part of the territory comprising such centralization, is subject to be taken to form a special school district: Fulks v. Wright, 72 O. S. 547.

The centralization of schools is a duty imperatively imposed upon the township board of education under the statutes, but no imperative duty rests upon such board to purchase a site and to erect a building until after a determination by the board of the necessity therefor: State, ex rel., v. Board of Education, 15 O. C. D. 424.

Where upon the submission of the question of centralization a majority voted in favor of centralization, but against the levy of a tax for the purchase of a site and the erection of a building, the board of education is not bound to take any steps toward centralizing the schools: State, ex rel., v. Board of Education, 1 O. C. C. (N. S.) 89.

SECTION 4726-1. In townships in which there are one or more school districts, the qualified electors of such school districts may vote on the question of centralizing the schools of said township districts, or of special school districts therein, without interfering with the existing school district organization until the result of the election shall have been determined. If at such election in any township a majority of all the votes cast shall be in favor of centralizing the schools in said township, the probate judge of the county shall create a new board of education for the said township, without delay, by selecting from the several boards of education thus consolidated, five suitable persons, giving each former district its fair representation in such selection, which such five persons so selected shall constitute the board of education for said township until the first township election thereafter; at such first township election thereafter the electors of such township shall elect two members of the board of education for two years, and three members to serve for three years, and at the proper elections thereafter their successors shall be elected for four years. If a majority of the electors in said township vote against said centralization at the time above designated, then the several school districts in said townships shall proceed as though no election had been held. (106 v. 442.)

Question of decentralization may be submitted after three years.

SECTION 4727. When the schools of a rural school district have been centralized such centralization shall not be discontinued within three years, and then only by petition and election, as provided in section 4726. If at such election more votes are case against centralization than for it, the division into subdistricts as they existed prior to centralization shall thereby be re-established. (104 v. 133.)

CHAPTER 5.

COUNTY SCHOOL DISTRICTS.

SECTION 4728. Each county school district shall be under the supervision and control of a county board of education composed of five members who shall be elected by the presidents of the various village and rural boards of education in such county school district. Each district shall have one vote in the election of members of the county board of education except as is provided in section 4728-1. At least one member of the county board of education shall be a resident of a village school district if such district is located in the county school district and at least three members of such board shall be residents of rural school districts, but not more than one member of the county board of education shall reside in any one village or rural school district within the county school district. (104 v. 133.)

Members of county board of education; election and qualifications.

Where part of a subdistrict of a township school district has been incorporated into a special school district leaving the balance of said township school district unprovided for as to a school house, the board of education of the township school district must either provide a school house in the remaining part of said subdistrict, or transport the pupils to a school. — *Attorney General*, Opinion No. 983, June 17, 1914.

SECTION 4728-1. All school districts other than village and city school districts within a civil township shall be jointly entitled to one vote in the election of members of the county board of education. The presidents of the board of education of all such districts in a civil township shall meet for the purpose of choosing one from their number to cast the vote for members of the county board

How school districts shall cast vote for members of county board.

of education. If no such meeting is held in any year for the purpose of choosing one from their number to cast the vote of such boards, the president of the board having the largest tax valuation shall represent all such districts of the civil township at the election of the county board members. A board of education of a rural district having territory in two or more civil townships shall vote with the boards of education of the districts of the civil township in which the greater part of its taxable property is located. (104 v. 133.)

When members of county board elected and term of office.

SECTION 4729. On the second Saturday in June, 1914, the presidents of the boards of education of the various village and rural school districts in each county school district shall meet and elect the five members of the county board of education, one for one year, one for two years, one for three years, one for four years and one for five years, and until their successors are elected and qualified. The terms of office of such members shall begin on the fifteenth of July, 1914, and each year thereafter on the third Saturday of January. Each year thereafter one member of the county board of education shall be elected in the same manner for a term of five years. The presidents of the various boards of education within the county school district shall be paid their necessary and actual expenses incurred while meeting for the purpose of electing members of the county board of education. Such exepnses shall be allowed by the county auditor and paid out of the county treasury upon the order of the chairman and clerk of the meeting. (104 v. 133.)

Where a part of a subdistrict of a township school district has been incorporated into a special school district leaving the balance of said township school district unprovided for as to a school house, the board of education of the township school district must either provide a school house in the remaining part of said subdistrict, or transport the pupils to a school. — *Attorney General,* Opinion No. 983, June 17, 1914.

Call for meeting, notice, organization.

SECTION 4730. The county auditor of each county shall issue the call for the first meeting, giving at least ten days' notice of the place where such meeting will be held. The call for all future meetings shall be issued by the county superintendent. The meeting shall organize by electing a chairman and a clerk. The vote of a majority of the members present shall be necessary to elect each member of the county board. The members of the county board so elected, may or may not be members or officers of any village or rural board of education. The result of the election of members of the county board of education shall be certified to the county auditor by the chairman and clerk of the meeting. (104 v. 133.)

Where a part of a subdistrict of a township school district has been incorporated into a special school district leaving the balance of said township school district unprovided for as to a school house, the board of education of the township school district must either provide a school house in the remaining part of said subdistrict, or transport the pupils to a school. — *Attorney General*, Opinion No. 983, June 17, 1914.

SECTION 4731. Each member of the county board of education shall within ten days after receiving notice of his election, take an oath that he will perform faithfully the duties of his office. Such oath may be taken before any one authorized by law to administer oaths. If any person so elected shall fail to take such oath within the time prescribed, the office to which he was elected shall be considered vacant. Any vacancy on the board shall be filled in the same manner as is provided in section 4748 of the General Code. (104 v. 133.) Oath; Vacancy.

Where a part of a subdistrict of a township school district has been incorporated into a special school district leaving the balance of said township school district unprovided for as to a school house, the board of education of the township school district must either provide a school house in the remaining part of said subdistrict, or transport the pupils to a school. — *Attorney General*, Opinion No. 983, June 17, 1914.

SECTION 4732. Each county board of education shall meet on the third Saturday of July, 1914, and on the third Saturday of March of each year thereafter, and shall organize by electing one of its members president, and another vice-president, both of whom shall serve for one year. A temporary secretary shall be chosen who shall act until a county superintendent has been elected and thereafter the county superintendent shall act as secretary of the board. The secretary shall keep a full record of the proceedings of the board, properly indexed, in a book provided for that purpose. Each motion, with the name of the person making it and the vote thereon, shall be entered on the record. 104 v. 133.) Meetings of county board; organization; record of proceedings.

Where a part of a subdistrict of a township school district has been incorporated into a special school district leaving the balance of said township school district unprovided for as to a school house, the board of education of the township school district must either provide a school house in the remaining part of said subdistrict, or transport the pupils to a school. — *Attorney General*, Opinion No. 983, June 17, 1914.

SECTION 4733. The regular meetings of the county board of education shall be held at the office of the county superintendent. At the time of the first meeting, the board shall fix the time for holding its regular meetings. Regular meetings shall be held at least every two months and when necessary other meetings may be held at the call of the president, or any two members. A majority of the board shall constitute a quorum at any regular or special meeting. (104 v. 133.) Regular meetings when and where held.

SECTION 4734. Each member of the county board of education shall be paid his actual and necessary expenses incurred during his attendance upon any meeting of the board. Such expenses, and the expenses of the county Payment of expenses.

superintendent, itemized and verified shall be paid from the
county board of education fund upon vouchers signed by
the president of the board. (104 v. 133.)

There are no provisions in the constitution prohibiting a
member of the board of education from serving upon the county
board of education. — *Attorney General*, Opinion 989, June 17, 1914.

The moneys paid into the county board of education fund on
account of the salaries of county and district superintendents,
under Section 4744-3, General Code, as amended, 104 O. L., 143,
are automatically appropriated to the payment of such salaries, and
cannot be used for any other purpose. The expenses of the county
superintendent and his allowance for clerk hire, the expenses of
the members of the board of education and the expenses of the
county institute, which are payable out of this fund, must be paid
from moneys coming into it otherwise than under Section 4744-3,
viz.: examination fees, under Section 7820, as amended, 104 O.
L., 104, and transfers from the dog tax fund, under Section 5653,
General Code, as amended, there being no other source of the
county board of education fund.

If the allowance to the superintendent is made in advance,
such allowance would appropriate moneys in the fund other than
those appropriated to salaries; so that the expenses of conducting
institutes and the expenses of the members of the board of education could be paid unless there were in the fund more than enough
to pay the salaries and superintendent's allowance. — *Attorney
General*, Opinion No. 1143, Sept. 12, 1914.

The county surveyor is not entitled to remuneration for services performed under Section 4736, G. C. — *Attorney General*,
Opinion No. 147, March 18, 1915.

Existing dis-
tricts remain
until changed
by county
board. Officers
continue until
successors
elected.

SECTION 4735. The present existing township and
special school districts shall constitute rural school districts
until changed by the county board of education, and all
officers and members of boards of education of such existing districts shall continue to hold and exercise their respective offices and powers until their terms expire and until their successors are elected and qualified. (104 v. 133.)

The County Board of Education has no authority under section 4736, G. C. as amended 104 O. L. 138, to discontinue a rural
school district and join it to a rural or village school district contiguous thereto.

A County Board having attempted to discontinue a rural
school district by resolution of record, a copy of which has been
filed with the County Auditor under the provisions of 4736, G. C.
as amended, should rescind said resolution and furnish a copy of
the rescinding resolution to the County Auditor. A copy of such
rescinding resolution should also be furnished to the clerks of the
boards of education of the school districts mentioned in said former
resolution.

If the funds of such rural school district have been turned
over to the treasurer of the board of education of the rural or
village school district contiguous thereto, as a result of the action
of the county board of education, upon receipt of the notice as
above provided, said funds should be returned to the treasury of
the rural school district from which they were transferred.

It is necessary, in order to abolish a rural school district, that
the question be submitted to a vote of the qualified electors of
such district under the provision of section 4735, G. C. as amended,
and supplemented by sections 4735-1 and 4735-2, G. C., 104 O.
L. 138.

The question of centralization under the provision of section
4736, G. C., as amended 104, O. L. 139, and the question of issuing
bonds under the provisions of section 7625, G. C. may be submitted

to the qualified electors of a rural school district at one election. — *Attorney General,* Opinion 183, 1915.

Prior existing bonded indebtedness of a school district is a charge upon the property only of the district creating it and may not become a charge upon the property of a district formed by the union of two districts under the provisions of section 4735-1 and 4735-2 of the general code. — *Attorney General,* Opinion 53, 1915.

SECTION 4735-1. When a petition signed by not less than one-fourth of the electors residing within the territory constituting a rural school district, praying that the rural district be dissolved and joined to a contiguous rural or village district, is presented to the board of education of such district; or when such board, by a majority vote of the full membership thereof, shall decide to submit the question to dissolve and join a contiguous rural or village district, the board shall fix the time of holding such election at a special or general election. The clerk of the board of such district shall notify the deputy state supervisors of elections, of the date of such election and the purposes thereof, and such deputy state supervisors shall provide therefor. The clerk of the board of education shall post notices thereof in five public places within the ditsrict. The result shall be determined by a majority vote of such eletcors. (104 v. 133.)

Procedure to dissolve rural district and join to another contiguous thereto.

The sinking fund commissioners of a city school district have no control in the selection of a depository for money subject to their control. — *Attorney General,* Opinion No. 1153, Sept. 14, 1914.

SECTION 4735-2. The legal title of the property of the rural school district, in case such rural district is dissolved and joined to a rural or village district as provided in section 4735-1, shall become vested in the board of education of the rural or village school district to which such district is joined. The school fund of such dissolved rural district shall become a part of the fund of the rural or village school district which it voted to join. The dissolution of such district shall not be complete until the board of education of the district has provided for the payment of any indebtedness that may exist. (104 v. 133.)

Title to property vests in board of education to which it is joined.

The sinking fund commissioners of a city school district have no control in the selection of a depository for money subject to their control. — *Attorney General,* Opinion No. 1153, Sept. 14, 1914.

The County Board of Education has no authority under section 4736, G. C. as amended 104 O. L. 138, to discontinue a rural school district and join it to a rural or village school district contiguous thereto.

A County Board having attempted to discontinue a rural school district by resolution of record, a copy of which has been filed with the County Auditor under the provisions of 4736, G. C. as amended, should rescind said resolution and furnish a copy of the rescinding resolution to the County Auditor. A copy of such rescinding resolution should also be furnished to the clerks of the boards of education of the school districts mentioned in said former resolution.

If the funds of such rural school district have been turned over to the treasurer of the board of education of the rural or village school district contiguous thereto, as a result of the action of the county board of education, upon receipt of the notice as above provided, said funds should be returned to the treasury of the rural school district from which they were transferred.

It is necessary, in order to abolish a rural school district, that the question be submitted to a vote of the qualified electors of such district under the provision of section 4735, G. C. as amended, and supplemented by section 4735-1 and 4735-2, G. C., 104 O. L. 138.

The question of centralization under the provision of section 4736, G. C., as amended 104, O. L. 139, and the question of issuing bonds under the provision of section 7625, G. C. may be submitted to the qualified electors of a rural school district at one election. — *Attorney General*, Opinion 183, 1915.

Prior existing bonded indebtedness of a school. district is a charge upon the property only of the district creating it and may not become a charge upon the property of a district formed by the union of two districts under the provisions of section 4735-1 and 4735-2 of the general code. — *Attorney General*, Opinion 53, 1915.

Powers and duties of county board. SECTION 4736. The county board of education shall arrange the school districts according to topography and population in order that the schools may be most easily accessible to the pupils, and shall file with the board or boards of education in the territory affected, a written notice of such proposed arrangement; which said arrangement shall be carried into effect as proposed unless, within thirty days after the filing of such notice with the board or boards of education, a majority of the qualified electors of the territory affected by such order of the county board, file a written remonstrance with the county board against the arrangement of school districts so proopsed. The county board of education is hereby authorized to create a school district from one or more school districts or parts thereof. The county board of education is authorized to appoint a board of education for such newly created school district and direct an equitable division of the funds or indebtedness belonging to the newly created district. Members of the boards of education of the newly created district shall thereafter be elected at the same time and in the same manner as the boards of education of the village and rural districts. (106 v. 396.)

The sinking fund commissioners of a city school district have no control in the selection of a depository for money subject to their control. — *Attorney General*, Opinion No. 1153, Sept. 14, 1914.

Section 4736, General Code, as amended, 104 O. L., 138, applies to rural or village school districts which go to make up county school districts and does not seem to have application to the internal affairs of the rural school districts, formerly township school districts and village school districts, which go to make up and constitute the respective county school districts of the state.

Local boards of education of rural school districts, formerly township school districts, cannot change boundaries of subdistricts for the reason that such boundaries of such subdistricts no longer exist. However, such boards of education under Section 7684, General Code, have the authority to make such assignment of the youth of their respective districts to the schools established by them as in their opinion will best promote the interests of education in their districts. — *Attorney General*, Opinion No. 1308, Dec. 2, 1914.

When territory is transferred from one rural or village school district to another, the equitable division of funds or indebtedness required by statute to be made shall be determined upon at the time of the transfer, by the county board of education, which, under Section 4736, General Code, has exclusive power to make such transfer.

The indebtedness apportioned to the transferred district in accordance with the statute becomes a general indebtedness of the whole district, and does not attach only to the transferred territory. — *Attorney General*, Opinion No. 1193, Oct. 8, 1914.

Under Section 4736, General Code, the county board of education has the authority to re-arrange boundary lines so as to detach one part of a rural school district and add it to another rural or village district. — *Attorney General*, Opinion 42, January 30, 15.

The county surveyor is not entitled to remuneration for services performed under Section 4736, G. C. — *Attorney General*, Opinion No. 147, March 18, 1915.

Under the provisions of Section 4736, General Code, it is discretionary with the county board of education to determine whether or not there is any real necessity for calling upon the county surveyor for his aid in changing rural district school lines and transferring territory from one rural or village school district to another. If the county board determines that it is necessary to call in the assistance of a surveyor, then such board must call the county surveyor, and it is mandatory that the county surveyor shall make a survey for such board and prepare a map so designating the changes made in the changing of rural district lines and in the transferring of territory from one rural or village school district to another upon receiving a formal request to do so from such board. — *Attorney General*, Opinion 1272, Dec. 2, 1914.

SECTION 4736-1. In rural school districts hereafter created by a county board of education, a board of education shall be elected as provided in section 4712 of the General Code. When rural school districts hereafter so created, or which have been heretofore so created, fail or have failed to elect a board of education as provided in said section 4712, or whenever there exists such school district which for any reason or cause is not provided with a board of education, the commissioners of the county to which such district belongs shall appoint such board of education, and the members so appointed shall serve until their successors are elected and qualified. The successors of the members so appointed shall be elected at the first election for members of the board of education held in such district after such appointment, two members to serve for two years and three members for four years. And thereafter their successors shall be elected in the manner and for the term as provided by section 4712 of the General Code. The board so appointed by the commissioners of the county shall organize on the second Monday after their appointment. (106 v. 550.)

SECTION 4736-2. All appointments of a board of education for such rural school district heretofore made by the commissioners of the county to which such rural school district belongs shall be held to be legal, valid and binding upon such rural school district, and to give such appointed boards the same authority as have other rural school district boards. All proceedings, otherwise legal under the laws applicable to rural school boards, heretofore or hereafter had by such boards so appointed shall be held legal, valid and binding upon such school districts. The bonds heretofore, or hereafter, issued and sold by any such rural school district having a board of education heretofore, or hereafter, appointed by the commissioners of the county to which such district belongs, shall not be declared to be invalid by reason of any want of authority of such board of education of such district to provide for the issuing and sale of such bonds, but, if regularly issued for a lawful purpose and sold for not less than par and accrued interest such bonds shall be held to be legal, valid and binding obligations of such district issuing the same. (106 v. 550.)

Publication of minimum course of study by county board. SECTION 4737. The county board of education shall publish with the advice of the county superintendent a minimum course of study which shall be a guide to local boards of education in prescribing the courses of study for the school under their control. The county board may publish different courses of study for village and rural school districts. (104 v. 133.)

Division of county district into supervision districts. SECTION 4738. The county board of education shall divide the county school district, any year, to take effect the first day of the following September, into supervision districts, each to contain one or more village or rural school districts. The territory of such supervision districts shall be contiguous and compact. In the formation of the supervision districts consideration shall be given to the number of teachers employed, the amount of consolidation and centralization, the condition of the roads and general topography. The territory in the different districts shall be as nearly equal as practicable and the number of teachers employed in any one supervision district shall not be less than thirty. **When county shall be redistricted.** The county board of education shall, upon application of three-fourths of the presidents of the village and rural district boards of the county, redistrict the county into supervision districts. The county board of education may at their discretion require the county superintendent to personally supervise not to exceed forty teachers of the village or rural schools of the county. This shall supersede the necessity of the district supervision of these schools. (106 v. —.)

County Board of Education — Eligibility of district superintendent. — *Attorney General*, Opinion 167, March 25, 1915.

Election of district superintendent. SECTION 4739. Each supervision district shall be under the direction of a district superintendent. Such district superintendent shall be elected by the presidents of the village and rural boards of education within such district, except that where such supervision district contains three or less rural or village school districts the boards of education of such school districts in joint session shall elect such superintendent. The district superintendent shall be employed upon the nomination of the county superintendent but the board electing such district superintendent may by a majority vote elect a district superintendent not so nominated. (104 v. 133.)

'County Board of Education — Eligibility of district superintendent. — *Attorney General*, Opinion 167, March 25, 1915.

SECTION 4740. Any village or rural school district or union of school districts for high school purposes which maintains a first-grade high school and which employs a superintendent shall upon application to the county board of education before September 10, 1915, or before June 1st of any year thereafter, be continued as a separate district under the direct supervision of the county superintendent. Such district shall continue to be under the direct supervision of the county superintendent until the board of education of such district by resolution shall petition to become a part of a supervision district of the county school district. Such superintendents shall perform all the duties prescribed by law for a district superintendent, but shall teach such part of each day as the board of education of the district or districts may direct. Such districts shall receive no state aid for the payment of the salaries of their superintendents, and the salaries shall be paid by the boards employing such superintendents. (106 v. 439.) Supervision of village and rural schools.

The date fixed by Section 4740, General Code, to-wit: July 20, 1914, for officially certifying to the clerk or clerks of the board of education that the village or rural districts or union school districts will employ a superintendent, etc., is mandatory for the reason that on that date it is to be determined by virtue of such certificate or notice what suprevisory districts the respective county districts shall contain.

Where two townships, which never at any time before July 20th, 1914, employed a joint superintendent for supervision purposes, cannot after that date employ a superintendent for supervision purposes and certify the same to the county board of education, the county board of education must attach either all or any portion of said townships to one or more of the other supervision districts of the county, as determined by such board in accordance with the discretion which is vested in said board by Section 4740, General Code. — *Attorney General*, Opinion No. 1128, August 31, 1914.

Under Section 4740, 'General Code, as amended, a village district already employing a superintendent, cannot join with a rural school district which never employed a superintendent and which said districts were never heretofore joined together for supervisory purposes by employing a superintendent in common upon application to the county board of education to be joined and continue as separate districts as authorized by said section.

Under the recently enacted school code, appearing in 104 O. L., 133, school districts formerly designated as "special school districts" now constitute rural school districts, which said rural school districts are a part of the respective county school districts of the state. Part of any county school districts may be transferred to an adjoining school district or city or village school district by the mutual consent of the board of education having control of such districts. — *Attorney General*, Opinion No. 1054, July 18, 1914.

SECTION 4741. The first election of any district superintendent shall be for a term not longer than one year, thereafter he may be re-elected in the same district for a Term of district superintendent.

period not to exceed three years. Whenever for any cause in any district a superintendent has not been appointed by September first, the county board of education shall appoint such superintendent for a term of one year. (104 v. 133.)

Meeting to elect successor to district superintendent.

SECTION 4742. Not less than sixty days before the expiration of the term of any district superintendent, the presidents of the boards of education within such supervision district, or in supervision districts which contain three or less village or rural districts, the boards of education of such districts shall meet and elect his successor. The president of the board in the village or rural district having the largest number of teachers shall issue the call giving at least ten days' notice of the time and place of meeting. He shall also act as chairman and certify the results of such meeting to the county board of education. (104 v. 133.)

Compensation of district superintendent. Amount paid by the state.

SECTION 4743. The compensation of the district superintendent shall be fixed at the same time that the appointment is made and by the same authority which appoints him; such compensation shall be paid out of the county board of education fund on vouchers signed by the president of the county board. The salary of any district superintendent shall in no case be less than one thousand dollars per annum, half of which salary not to exceed seven hundred and fifty dollars shall be paid by the state and half by the supervision district, except where the number of teachers in any supervision district is less than forty in which case the amounts paid by the state shall be such proportion of half the salary as the ratio of the number of teachers employed is to forty. The half paid by the supervision district shall be pro-rated among the village and rural school districts in such district in proportion to the number of teachers employed in each district. (104 v. 133.)

County superintendent; appointment, term, duties.

SECTION 4744. The county board of education at a regular meeting held not later than July 20th, shall appoint a county superintendent for a term not longer than three years commencing on the first day of August. Such county superintendent shall have the educational qualifications mentioned in section 4744-4. He shall be in all respects the executive officer of the county board of education, and shall attend all meetings with the privilege of discussion but not of voting. (104 v. 133.)

The position of county superintendent of schools is not an office, and consequently a member of the General Assembly which created this position of county superintendent of schools would be eligible to appointment as county superintendent of schools during the term for which he was elected or within one year thereafter. — *Attorney General*, Opinion No. 848, April 9, 1914.

Salary of county superintendent; how paid.

SECTION 4744-1. The salary of the county superintendent shall be fixed by the county board of education, to be not less than twelve hundred dollars per year, and shall be paid out of the county board of education fund on vouchers signed by the president of the county board. Half of such salary shall be paid by the state and the balance by the county school ditsrict. In no case shall the amount paid by the state be more than one thousand dollars. The county board may also allow the county superintendent a sum not to exceed three hundred dollars per annum for traveling expenses and clerical help. The half paid by the county school district shall be pro-rated among the village and rural school districts in the county in proportion to the number of teachers employed in each district. (104 v. 133.)

There is nothing in Section 4744-1, General Code, which prohibits a county board of education from fixing the salary of the county superintendent at any amount in excess of $1200.00 per year it may deem proper.

When the board of education fixes the salary of the county superintendent in an amount greater than $2000.00, the county district is to pay the balance remaining after deducting the $1000.00 to be paid by the state and such balance is to be apportioned and certified as provided in Sections 4744-1, 4744-2, and 4744-3, General Code. — *Attorney General,* Opinion No. 1165, September 21, 1914.

The county commissioners may not lawfully transfer from the General county fund, or from the proceeds of any other county tax levies to supply deficiencies in the county board of education fund, in case there is no money available in the Sheep fund, under Section 5653, General Code, as amended. — *Attorney General,* Opinion No. 1142, September 12, 1914.

The position of county superintendent of schools is not an office, and consequently a member of the General Assembly which created this position of county superintendent of school would be eligible to appointment as county superintendent of schools during the term for which he was elected or within one year thereafter. — *Attorney General,* Opinion No. 848, April 9, 1914.

The moneys paid into the county board of education fund on account of the salaries of county and district superintendents, under Section 4744-3, General Code, as amended, 104 O. L., 143, are automatically appropriated to the payment of such salaries, and cannot be used for any other purpose. The expenses of the county superintendent and his allowance for clerk hire, the expenses of the members of the board of education and the expenses of the county institute, which are payable out of this fund, must be paid from moneys coming into it otherwise than under Section 4744-3, viz.: examination fees, under Section 7820, as amended, 104 O. L., 104, and transfers from the dog tax fund, under Section 5653, General Code, as amended, there being no other source of the county board of education fund.

If the allowance to the superintendent is made in advance, such allowance would appropriate moneys in the fund other than those appropriated to salaries; so that the expenses of conducting institutes and the expenses of the members of the board of education could be paid unless there were in the fund more than enough to pay the salaries and superintendent's allowance. — *Attorney General,* Opinion No. 1143, Sept. 12, 1914.

The county surveyor is not entitled to remuneration for services performed under Section 4736, G. C. — *Attorney General,* Opinion No. 147, March 18, 1915.

SECTION 4744-2. On or before the first day of August of each year the county board of education shall certify to the county auditor the number of teachers to be employed for the ensuing year in the various rural and village school districts within the county school district, and also the number of district superintendents employed and their compensation and the compensation of the county superintendent; and such board of education shall also certify

County board shall certify, annually, number of teachers and superintendents employed salaries and amounts apportioned to each district.

to the county auditor the amounts to be apportioned to each district for the payment of its share of the salaries of the county and district superintendents. (104 v. 133.)

There is nothing in Section 4744-1, General Code, which prohibits a county board of education from fixing the salary of the county superintendent at any amount in excess of $1,200.00 per year it may deem proper.

When the board of education fixes the salary of the county superintendent in an amount greater than $2,000.00, the county district is to pay the balance remaining after deducting the $1,000.00 to be paid by the state and such balance is to be apportioned and certified as provided in Sections 4744-1, 4744-2, and 4744-3, General Code. *Attorney General.* Opinion No. 1165, September 21, 1914.

The county commissioners may not lawfully transfer from the General county fund, or from the proceeds of any other county tax levies to supply deficiencies in the county board of education fund, in case there is no money available in the Sheep fund, under Section 5653, General Code, as amended. *Attorney General.* Opinion No. 1142, September 12, 1914.

It is the duty of county auditors to obtain from the distribution of school funds the amounts set apart under Section 4744-3, General Code, for the use of the county board of education fund, regardless of the fact that such retention was not taken into account by the rural boards of education in making their 1913 tax levies. Such retention is to be made out of all the moneys to be distributed to the several districts including the proceeds of local levies, as well as the amount to be apportioned to the district as its portion of the State Common School Fund, and is not to be charged against any one particular fund or levy.

The county auditor cannot make any valid settlement, except on the basis of the certificate required to be made by the county board of education by Section 4474-2, General Code, respecting the number of teachers employed by the various school districts under its jurisdiction, etc. If the county board fails to make proper certification until after the usual period of settlement and the settlement is made, the error should be corrected under Section 2597, General Code, in the next succeeding semi-annual settlement, and in the meantime the county board of education fund must get along without the moneys belonging to it, and the county and district superintendents must serve on one-half pay until the next settlement time, when the arrearages in their respective salaries will be made up. *Attorney General.* Opinion No. 1198, October 8, 1914.

The position of county superintendent of schools is not an office, and consequently a member of the General Assembly which created this position of county superintendent of schools would be eligible to appointment as county superintendent of schools during the term for which he was elected or within one year thereafter. *Attorney General.* Opinion No. 848, April 9, 1914.

County auditor shall retain from apportionment of school funds sum necessary to pay county and district superintendents.

County board shall certify to state auditor amount due from state.

SECTION 4744-3. The county auditor when making his semi-annual apportionment of the school funds to the various village and rural school districts shall retain the amounts necessary to pay such portion of the salaries of the county and district superintendents and for contingent expenses, as may be certified by the county board. Such moneys shall be placed in a separate fund to be known as the "county board of education fund." The county board of education shall certify under oath to the state auditor the amount due from the state as its share of the county and district superintendents of such county school district for the next six months. Upon receipt by the state auditor of such certificate he shall draw his warrant upon the state treasurer in favor of the county treasurer for the required amount; which shall be placed by the county auditor in the county board of educational fund. (106 v. 396.)

There is nothing in Section 4744-1, General Code, which prohibits a county board of education from fixing the salary of the county superintendent at any amount in excess of $1,200.00 per year it may deem proper.

When the board of education fixes the salary of the county superintendent in an amount greater than $2,000.00, the county district is to pay the balance remaining after deducting the $1,000.00 to be paid by the state and such balance is to be apportioned and certified as provided in Sections 4744-1, 4744-2, and 4744-3, General Code. — *Attorney General,* Opinion 1165, September 1, 1914.

The moneys paid into the county board of education fund on account of the salaries of county and district superintendents, under Section 4744-3, General Code, as amended, 104 O. L., 143, are automatically appropriated to the payment of such salaries, and cannot be used for any other purpose. The expenses of the county superintendent and his allowance for clerk hire, the expenses of the members of the board of education and the expenses of the county institute, which are payable out of this fund, must be paid from moneys coming into it otherwise than under Section 4744-3, viz,; examination fees, under Section 7820, as amended, 104 O. L., 104, and transfers from the dog tax fund, under Section 5653, General Code, as amended, there being no other source of the county board of education fund.

If the allowance to the superintendent is made in advance, such allowance would appropriate moneys in the fund other than those appropriated to salaries; so that the expenses of conducting institutes and the expenses of the members of the board of education could be paid unless there were in the fund more than enough to pay the salaries and superintendent's allowance. *Attorney General.* Opinion No. 1143, Sept. 12, 1914.

It is the duty of county auditors to obtain from the distribution of school funds the amounts set apart under Section 4744-3, General Code, for the use of the county board of education fund, regardless of the fact that such retention was not taken into account by the rural boards of education in making their 1913 tax levies. Such retention is to be made out of all the moneys to be distributed to the several districts including the proceeds of local levies, as well as the amount to be apportioned to the district as its portion of the State Common School Fund, and is not to be charged against any one particular fund or levy.

The county auditor cannot make any valid settlement, except on the basis of the certificate required to be made by the county board of education by Section 4744-2, General Code, respecting the number of teachers employed by the various school districts under its jurisdiction, etc. If the county board fails to make proper certification until after the usual period of settlement and the settlement is made, the error should be corrected under Section 2597, General Code, in the next succeeding semi-annual settlement, and in the meantime the county board of education fund must get along without the moneys belonging to it, and the county and district superintendents must serve on one-half pay until the next settlement time, when the arrearages in their respective salaries will be made up. — *Attorney General,* Opinion No. 1198, October 8, 1914.

The county surveyor is not entitled to renumeration for services performed under Section 4736, G. C. *Attorney General.* Opinion No. 147, March 18, 1915.

Distribution of surplus sheep claims fund.

SECTION 5653. After paying all such sheep claims, at the June session of the county commissioners, if there remain more than one thousand dollars of such fund, the excess at such June session, shall be transferred and disposed as follows: in a county in which there is a society for the prevention of cruelty to children and animals, incorporated and organized as provided by law which has one or more agents appointed in pursuance of law, all such excess as the county commissioners deem necessary for the uses and purposes of such society by order of the commissioners and upon the warrant of the county auditor shall be paid to the treasurer of such society, and any surplus not so transferred shall be transferred to the county board of education fund at the direction of the county commissioners. (104 v. 133.)

Disposition of surplus in dog tax fund to humane societies after sheep claims paid, valid: State v. Struble, 24 Dec. 132 (15 N. S. 233).

Who eligible as county superintendents.

SECTION 4744-4. Only such persons shall be eligible as county superintendents who shall have:

(1) Five years' experience as superintendent and a high school life certificate; or

(2) Six years' experience in teaching, two years' additional experience in supervision, and at least a three-year county high school certificate; or

(3) Five years' experience as superintendent and a county high school certificate, and also be a graduate from a recognized institution of college or university rank; or

(4) Five years' teaching experience with one year's professional training in school administration and supervision in a recognized school of college or university rank, and a high school life certificate; or

(5) Five years' teaching experience with one year's professional training in school administration and supervision in a recognized school of college or university rank, and a county high school certificate, and be a graduate from a recognized institution of college or university rank. (104 v. 133.)

Who eligible as district superintendent.

SECTION 4744-5. Only such persons shall be eligible as district superintendents who shall have:

(1) Three years' experience in school supervision, and at least a county high school certificate; or

(2) Four years' experience in teaching, one year's additional experience in supervision or one year's training in supervision in an institution of college or university rank and at least a county high school certificate, or

(3) Three years' experience in teaching, graduation from a first-grade high school or its equivalent, and in addition thereto two years' professional training in a recognized institution of college or normal school rank for the training of teachers and at least a county high school certificate. The county board of education shall ·certify .

to the superintendent of public instruction the qualifications of each county and district superintendent. (104 v. 133.)

County Board of Education — Eligibility of district superintendent. — *Attorney General*, Opinion 167, March 25, 1915.

SECTION 4744-6. The county commissioners of each county shall provide and furnish offices in the county seat for the use of the county superintendent. Such offices shall be the permanent headquarters of the county superintendent and shall be used by the county board of education when in session. (104 v. 133.) *Offices for county superintendent and county board of education.*

Bills for office supplies, stationery, etc., furnished to the county superintendent of schools, should be approved by the county board of education and paid out of the county board of education fund on the warrant of the county auditor. — *Attorney General*, Opinion 144, March 17, 1915.

Section 5653. After paying all such sheep claims, at the June session of the county commissioners, if there remain more than one thousand dollars of such fund, the excess at such June session, shall be transferred and disposed as follows: In a county in which there is a society for the prevention of cruelty to children and animals, incorporated and organized as provided by law, which has one or more agents appointed in pursuance of law, all such excess as the county commissioners deem necessary for the uses and purposes of such society by order of the commissioners and upon the warrant of the county auditor shall be paid to the treasurer of such society, and any surplus not so transferred shall be transferred to the county board of education fund at the direction of the county commissioners. (104 v. 133.) *Distribution of surplus sheep claims fund.*

CHAPTER 6.

BOARDS OF EDUCATION.

Beginning of terms.

SECTION 4745. The terms of office of members of each board of education shall begin on the first Monday in January after their election and each such officer shall hold his office for four years except as may be specifically provided in chapter 2 of this title, and until his successor is elected and qualified. (103 v. 275.)

A member of the board of education whether elected for a full term or appointed to fill a vacancy, holds such office until his successor is elected and qualified.

Where four members are holding an office under equal rights and an elector is chosen at a regular election to succeed any one of them to membership of the board, all four are interlopers and the court has no other alternative but to dismiss all four. The best expedient would be an agreement among themselves in accordance with which one of them should resign to make room for their successor. — Attorney General, 1911-12, p. 1485.

When under Section 7610, General Code, the commissioners have, by reason of the failure of the board of education so to do, made an appointment to fill a vacancy in the board of education, such appointment can be made only "for the unexpired term."

When the county commissioners through a mistaken understanding of their powers, have entered upon their minutes that the appointment is "until the next general election," the fact that the appointment is in reality for the "unexpired term" is not affected, and a 'nunc pro tunc" entry to that effect may be made upon the commissioners' journal as notice of the statutory term. Attorney General, 1912, p. 1146.

In the case of vacancies in the school board filled by appointment Section 10, General Code, provides that a successor shall be elected for the unexpired term at the first general election for such office if such vacancy occurs more than thirty days before any election.

Such appointee, however, has the same right as an elective officer to hold over until his successor is elected and qualified.

Where at an election, five positions were to be filled, two for four years and three for approximately two years and there was no designation upon the ballot to determine who were the candidates for the long term and who were the candidates for the short terms, the terms were not definitely settled and there was no valid election. — Attorney General, 1912, p. 1102.

SECTION 4746. Before entering upon the duties of his office, each person elected or appointed a member of a board of education or elected or appointed to any other office under this title shall take an oath to support the constitution of the United States and the constitution of this state and that he will perform faithfully the duties of his office. Such oath may be administered by the clerk or any member of the board. (71 v. 15.)

Oath of members of board and other officers.

It is said that this section applies to the clerk of the board and that he must take the oath of office to qualify: State, ex rel., v. Coon, 4. O. C. C. (N. S.) 560.

SECTION 5032. The names of candidates for members of the board of education of a school district, however nominated, shall be placed on one independent and separate ballot without any designation whatever, except for members of board of education and the number of members to be elected. (98 v. 116 § 1.)

Ballots for school board.

SECTION 5033. The ballot for members of the board of education shall be prepared and printed as follows: The whole number of ballots to be printed for the school district shall be divided by the number of candidates for member of board of education of the district, and the quotient so obtained shall be the number of ballots in each series of ballots to be printed. The names of candidates shall be arranged in alphabetical order and the first series of ballots printed. Then the first name shall be placed last and the next series printed, and so shall the process be repeated until each name shall have been first. These ballots shall then be combined in tablets with no two of the same order of names together, except when there is but one candidate. (98 v. 116 § 2.)

How ballot for school board printed.

Referred to as showing that voting machines do not allow the rotation of the names of candidates for the board of education: State, ex rel., v. Board, 80 O. S. 471.

SECTION 5034. In city school districts, the ballots for each subdistrict shall contain the names of the candidates for member of the board of education from such subdistrict and also the names of the candidates to be elected at large. (97 v. 354 § 1.)

School districts in cities.

SECTION 4747. The board of education of each city, village and rural school district shall organize on the first Monday of January after the election of members of such board. One member of the board shall be elected president, one as vice-president and a person who may or may not be a member of the board shall be elected clerk. The president and vice-president shall serve for a term of one year and the clerk for a term not to exceed two years. The board shall fix the time of holding its regular meeting. (104 v. 133.)

Date of organization; regular meetings.

Contrary to the general rule of policy that a member of a board may not hold a salaried position under such board, special provision of statute makes it possible for a member of a board of education to serve as its clerk and receive the salary for both positions.

When a sheriff serves several writs, mileage may be charged on each writ regardless of the number of persons thereon or of the fact that said writs, are served at the same time upon several parties residing in the same place. — *Attorney General*, 1911-12, p. 1089.

When a township board of education did not organize as required, on the first Monday in January, and under the board which held over an election to issue bonds was carried, the election is valid as is every action of said board up to the time of the organization as required by section 4747, General Code.

The board may and should, nevertheless, organize as soon as possible, despite their failure to do so within the stipulated time.— *Attorney General*, 1911-12, p. 517.

An attempt by a township board of education, after April 26, 1910 (the date of the amendment making a township clerk the clerk of the school board) to organize and elect other than the township clerk to the office of clerk of the board is void.

After such an organization, an election held to issue bonds, while the illegally appointed clerk is acting without bond, is void.

As the prosecutor is made by statute the legal adviser of both the township clerk and the township board of education, when a controversy arises between these two, he may defend the side which, in his view, appears just. — *Attorney General*, 1911-12, p. 1665.

As there are no compulsory, conflicting duties, the clerk of a township may serve as member of the township board of education. — *Attorney General*, 1911-12, p. 1204.

Under section 4747, General Code, the clerk of the township becomes *ipso facto* the clerk of the school board and no election by the school board is required to authorize him to act as clerk. — *Attorney General*, 1911-12, p. 1099.

From the principles established by the decision in the case of State ex rel. Stolzenbacher vs. Felty, Auditor, No. 9372, decided by the supreme court in 1905, but not recorded.

1. The treasurer of a city, village or township may by failing to qualify as treasurer of the school funds refuse to serve as such treasurer.

2. If the township clerk fails to qualify as clerk of the township board of education, such failure does not affect his status as township clerk.

3. If a township treasurer resigns as treasurer of the school funds the board of education has the right if it chooses to accept his resignation and in such cases may elect a successor to him as treasurer of the school funds.

4. If by reason of the establishment of a depository, the treasurer of the school district is dispensed with according to law, and the clerk gives addition bond required of him as treasurer by virtue of section 4783 G. C., he will then be obliged to perform the duties of the treasurer without extra compensation unless he resigns. He may, however, refuse to qualify as such treasurer and the board may elect a substitute.

5. The refusal of a township clerk to qualify for the duties which devolve upon him by the establishment of a depository under section 4783 G. C., will not in any way affect his status as township clerk, and under such circumstances the board may select a substitute to act as treasurer. — *Attorney General*, 1911-12, p. 289.

By specific provision of Section 4747, General Code, a member of a board of education may at the same time, act as its clerk and receive compensation for both services.

The position of members of the board of education and treasurer of the board are incompatible, however.

Under Section 4782, General Code, when a depository is established, the clerk performs the duties of the treasurer and a member of the school board may, in this case, perform such duties. — *Attorney General,* 1912, p. 1776.

The offices of township clerk and clerk of the board of education though held by the same individual, are distinct and the board may fix its own compensation for services rendered as its clerk by the township clerk. — *Attorney General,* 1912, p. 1152.

Inasmuch as by the provisions of Section 7786, a clerk of the township board of education is obliged to pass on reports of teachers before an order may be drawn by said clerk for the payment of their salaries, the office of said clerk constitutes a check upon the position of teacher, and therefore both positions may not be held at the same time by the same individual. — *Attorney General,* 1913, p. 1097.

Under article 15, section 4 of the constitution, a woman may not be elected to or appointed to any office in this state. Under article 6, section 2 and article 1, section 7, of the constitution, however, through the powers therein conferred upon the general assembly to secure a thorough and efficient system of common schools and to encourage schools and the means of instruction, the provision of section 4862, General Code, permitting a woman to serve as member of the board of education and to vote for members thereof, is held to be valid and constitutional.

Since, therefore, women may serve on the board of education and since, furthermore, section 4747, General Code, provides that in any district other than the township school district, a member of a board of education may be elected clerk of the board, a woman in this district may be so elected clerk, under authority of this statute.

The statutes do not confer the right, however, of a woman to serve as clerk of a township, and since the statutes require such clerk to act as clerk to the school board, a woman may not serve in the latter capacity. The statutes, furthermore, have not made provision for service as treasurer of a school board by a woman and she may, therefore, not serve in that capacity. — *Attorney General,* 1913, p. 466.

Construction of section 7705, General Code, as amended, 104 O. L., 144, also section 4747, General Code, as amended, 104 O. L., 139.

Said sections prohibit a clerk of the board of education from being employed as teacher by the board of which such teacher is the clerk. — *Attorney General,* Opinion 1263, November 27, 1914.

The township clerk remains, ex-officio, the clerk of the township board of education until a board of education has been elected and organized, under the provisions of section 4747, as amended, 104 O. L., 139.

A county board of education may not create a new rural district containing fifteen square miles, from an existing rural district, which leaves the original district containing less than fifteen square miles. — *Attorney General,* Opinion No. 51, February 2, 1915.

A member of the Ohio General Assembly cannot serve as a clerk of the village board of education of which he is a member and receive a salary as such clerk. — *Attorney General,* Opinion 177, March 27, 1915.

The president of a board of education is an officer within the meaning of the statutes which provide for his election, and he continues in offices until his successor is elected and qualified: State, ex rel., v. Withrow, 21 O. C. D. 215.

Under former statutes it was said that one member of the board of education of a special school district could not hold two of the offices of president, clerk and treasurer: State, ex rel., v. Heddleston, 8 Dec. Rep. 77, 5 Bull. 502.

SECTION 4747-1. Once each year all the members of the boards of education of the various village and rural school districts within any county school district shall hold a meeting for the purpose of discussing matters relating to the schools of such county school district. The county

[margin note: Annual meeting of all members for discussion of school matters.]

superintendent shall arrange for the time and place of holding such meeting and shall also act as chairman. (104 v.
133.)

Vacancies in
board, how
filled.

SECTION 4748. A vacancy in any board of education
may be caused by death, non-residence, resignation, removal
from office, failure of a person elected or appointed to
qualify within ten days after the organization of the board
or of his appointment, removal from the district or absence
from meetings of the board for a period of ninety days, if
such absence is caused by reasons declared insufficient by a
two-thirds vote of the remaining members of the board,
which vote must be taken and entered upon the records of
the board not less than thirty days after such absence. Any
such vacancy shall be filled by the board at its next regular
or special meeting, or as soon thereafter as possible, by
election for the unexpired term. A majority vote of all
the remaining members of the board may fill any such
vacancy. (99 v. 51.)

A man who is elected, qualified and acting as a member of
township board of education is ineligible to continue as such
officer after the establishment of a special school district of which
latter district said officer is a resident and a taxpayer. — *Attorney
General*, 1911-12, p. 1477.

Under section 4748, General Code, the vacancy in a board of
education may be filled by the remaining members for the unexpired term only. Where, however, provision is not made for the
election of a successor at the regular election for such officers,
the incumbent will hold over until a successor is elected and qualified. — *Attorney General*, 1913, p. 32.

When a newly incorporated village is formed with a tax
duplicate of more than $100,000, such village becomes ipso facto
a village school district, but when such village fails to elect a
board of education when the village officers are elected, a special
election for members of such board of education is not authorized
ized by law. Such members can only be elected in the odd numbered years.

When in a township there exists two or more districts unconnected and the village school district and the further special
district is organized, the two subdistricts and the part of the township not included in the village district or the special district, will
all comprise parts of the township school district. The village
district also will remain under the control of the township board
of education until such time as it is properly organized after its
members are elected.

Under section 4748, General Code, when three out of five
members of a township board of education become disqualified for
that office by reason of the formation of a special school district,
the two remaining members may fill such vacancies in the township board.

Inasmuch as there are no officers upon whom rests the ministerial duty to organize the village district or to call an election
for members of its board of education, such election may not be
enforced by mandamus. The organization may be brought about
by a sufficient number of electors taking steps to become candidates
for the village board of education at the November election and
the board of elections would be required to place their names upon
the ballots and hold an election therefor. — *Attorney General*, 1913,
p. 460.

When under Section 7610, General Code, the commissioners
have, by reason of the failure of the board of education so to do,

made an appointment to fill a vacancy in the board of education, such appointment can be made only "for the unexpired term."

When the county commissioners through a mistaken understanding of their powers, have entered upon their minutes that the appointment is "until the next general election," the fact that the appointment is in reality "for the unexpired term" is not affected, and a "nunc pro tunc" entry to that effect may be made upon the commissioners' journal as notice of the statutory term. — *Attorney General*, 1912, p. 1146.

The removal from a city school district, indefinitely of a member of a board of education creats a vacancy in said board. — *Attorney General*, Opinion 990, June 19, 1914.

An adjournment of a board of education sine die does not amount to a resignation of the members who participated in such action: State, ex rel., v. Shafer. 18 O. C. C. 525.

By virtue of this section, it was said that if a person elected, qualified within ten days from the organization of the board, his right to his office was not affected by his failure to file a statement required by the corrupt practices act: State, ex rel., v. Jaquis, 11 O. C. D. 91.

SECTION 4749. The board of education of each school district, organized under the provisions of this title, shall be a body politic and corporate, and, as such, capable of suing and being sued, contracting and being contracted with, acquiring, holding possessing and disposing of real and personal property, and taking and holding in trust for the use and benefit of such district any grant or devise of land and any donation or bequest of money or other personal property and of exercising such other powers and privileges as are conferred by this title and the laws relating to the public schools of this state. (85 v. 133.) *[margin: Corporate powers of board of education.]*

Under authority of Sections 4749 and 7620. General Code, boards of education may legally construct a foot bridge upon a strip of land in which a right of way for a walk has been deeded it and a condition in the deed for such right of way providing for its use by the board in common with the grantor would not invalidate the same. — *Attorney General*, 1912, p. 1842.

Section 4750, General Code. providing for the sale of real estate valued in excess of $300.00 at auction does not compel the board of education to dispose of the property to the highest bidder and the board in its notice of sale may reserve the right to reject any and all bids. — *Attorney General*, 1912, p. 493.

Section 4749, General Code. which enumerates the power of the board of education with reference to acquiring, holding, possessing and disposing of real and personal property, does not include any provision for the leasing of such property by the board, and as the statutes nowhere prescribe the manner of executing such a lease. the board cannot be held to possess such power. — *Attorney General*, 1913, p. 1508.

A board of education is a body corporate, capable of suing and being sued, but it is not such a corporation as is contemplated in G. C. Sec. 12304. The courts have no power to do away with a board of education, and while quo warranto would lie against members of a board, it does not lie against the office itself: State, ex rel., v. Board of Education, 7 O. C. C. 152, 3 O. C. D. 703.

A board of education is a body corporate: State, ex rel., v. Liberty Township, 22 O. S. 144.

A board of education is a quasi corporation only, and it is not a public or a municipal corporation: Finch v. Board of Education, 30 O. S. 37.

Under the act of May 1, 1873, for the reorganization and maintenance of common schools, the corporate boards of education therein provided for succeed to all rights of action in relation to the common school property and funds, which were theretofore vested, by previous legislation. in other agencies to whose control such property and funds had been confided: Crofton v. Board of Education, 26 O. S. 571.

Since a board of education is a legal entity endowed with power to sue, it may sue a defaulting treasurer of such board without first resorting to his bond: Board of Education v. Milligan, 51 O. S. 115.

A board of education is not liable in its corporate capacity for damages wherein, in excavating on its own lots for the erection of a school building, it wrongfully and negligently carries the excavation below the statutory depth of nine feet, thereby undermining and injuring the foundation and walls of a building of an adjoining owner: Board of Education v. Volk, 72 O. S. 469.

In the absence of a statute which creates a liability, a board of education is not liable in its corporate capacity for an injury which has been sustained by a pupil while attending the common school, for the negligence of such board in discharging its official duties in erecting and maintaining such common school building: Finch v. Board of Education, 30 O. S. 37.

An agreement by members of a township board of education, acting in their individual capacity, to purchase from another person apparatus for the schools of the township, and to ratify said contract of purchase at the next meeting of the board, is contrary to public policy, and therefore illegal and void: McCortle v. Bates, 29 O. S. 419.

The board of education must act as a body, and not as individuals, and, accordingly, a contract which is signed by the members of the board separately, and which has been delivered by the clerk, but which has been repudiated by the board as a corporate body at a subsequent meeting, is not a valid contract and is not binding on their part: State, ex rel., v. Liberty Township, 22 O. S. 144.

Board may make rules; legal meetings.	**SECTION 4750.** The board of education shall make such rules and regulations as it deems necessary for its government and the government of its employes and the pupils of the schools. No meeting of a board of education, not provided for by its rule or by law, shall be legal unless all the members thereof have been notified, as provided in the next section. (97 v. 356.)

Section 4750, General Code, providing for the sale of real estate valued in excess of $300.00 at auction does not compel the board of education to dispose of the property to the highest bidder and the board in its notice of sale may reserve the right to reject any and all bids. — *Attorney General*, 1912, p. 493.

A rule which provides for the proper examination at the end of the school year of pupils jointly by the teacher of the grade in which such pupils have been students and the superintendent of the schools, and for the promotion of pupils to the next higher grade upon the recommendation of such teacher and superintendent, the same being based on merit, is a reasonable rule: Board of Education v. State, ex rel., 80 O. S. 133.

A board of education is not authorized by this statute to impose upon the clerk the duty of receiving tuition funds belonging to such board or to become the custodian thereof; and if, pursuant to a rule attempting to impose such powers and duties upon the clerk, he receives the tuition funds and the custody thereof, and he fails to account therefore, the sureties upon his bond are not liable therefor: State, ex rel., v. Griffith, 74 O. S. 80.

Under this section a board of education may adopt rules for the election of teachers, but such rules must not be inconsistent with G. C. Sec. 4752; Board of Education v. Best, 52 O. S. 138.

If, under this section, the board of education has adopted a rule to the effect that a resolution which provides for a change of textbooks shall be referred to the textbook committee, and shall not be acted upon for four weeks from its introduction, such rule is held to be reasonable and binding upon the board: State, ex rel., v. Board of Education, 2 O. C. C. 510, 1 O. C. D. 614.

If a board of education has passed a resolution under this section prohibiting the reading of the Bible and prayer or other religious instructions in school, its action is final, and it cannot be reviewed by the courts: Board of Education v. Paul, 7 O. N. P. 58, 10 O. D. (N. P.) 17.

A regulation requiring the reading of the Bible as an opening exercise in school is valid, and the courts have no right to interfere therewith: Nessle v. Hum, 1 O. N. P. 140, 2 O. D. (N. P.) 60.

Special meeting of the board.	**SECTION 4751.** A special meeting of a board of education may be called by the president or clerk thereof or by any two members, by serving a written notice of the time and place of such meeting upon each member of the board either personally or at his residence or usual place of business. Such notice must be signed by the official or members calling the meeting. (97 v. 355.)

The president of a board of education who is also a director and stockholder of a material company, which material company sells its material to the principal contractor dealing with said board of education, has such an interest in said contract as is prohibited by Section 4757, G. C. No criminal penalty is attached to the violation of Section 4857, G. C., but this section does affect the validity of contracts. — *Attorney General,* Opinion 139, March 13, 1915.

SECTION 4752. A majority of the members of a board of. education shall constitute a quorum for the transaction of business. Upon a motion to adopt a resolution authorizing the purchase or sale of real or personal property or to employ a superintendent or teacher, janitor or other employe or to elect or appoint an officer or to pay any debt or claim or to adopt any text book, the clerk of the board shall publicly call the roll of the members composing the board and enter on the record the names of those voting "Aye" and the names of those voting "No." If a majority of all the members of the board vote aye, the president shall declare the motion carried. Upon any motion or resolution, a member of the board may demand the yeas and nays, and thereupon the clerk shall call the roll and record the names of those voting "Aye' 'and those voting "No." Each board may provide for the payment of superintendents, teachers and other employes by pay-roll, if it deems advisable, but in all cases such roll call and record shall be complied with; provided, that boards of education of township school districts may provide for the payment of teachers monthly if deemed advisable upon the presentation, to the clerk, of a certificate from the director of the subdistrict in which the teacher is employed stating that the services have been rendered and that the salary is due; the adoption of a resolution authorizing the clerk to issue warrants for the payment of the teacher's salary on presentation of such certificate shall be held as compliance with the above requirements. (101 v. 316.)

Quorum; yeas and nays in certain cases.

Exception.

A city school district is not authorized to pay for publication in a newspaper of a statement of receipts and expenditures for the year.

When such action is performed,

1. The newspaper cannot be held, as the payment was voluntary:

2. The members of the board of education who voted for the move are guilty of a misfeasance and are subject under the terms of 286, G. C., to civil action by the proper legal officer for a recovery.

3. The president, clerk and treasurer, acting in good faith, in their respective capacities performed merely ministerial acts and are therefore not liable. — *Attorney General,* 1911-12, p. 272.

The position of teacher in public schools is not considered a public office, consequently there is no inhibition against a member of the general assembly being employed as a teacher in the public schools. — *Attorney General,* 1913, p. 52.

Section 4749, General Code. which enumerates the power of the board of education with reference to acquiring, holding, possessing and disposing of real and personal property, does not include any provision for the leasing of such property by the board, and as the statutes nowhere prescribe the manner of executing such a lease, the board cannot be held to possess such power. — *Attorney General,* 1913, p. 1508.

This section is to be construed in connection with G. C. Sec. 4750, and it is not intended that the action provided for in this section may be taken in violation of any reasonable rules which may have been adopted by the board by virtue of G. C. Sec. 4750: State, ex rel., v. Board of Education, 2 O. C. C. 510, 1 O. C. D. 614.

The statutory provision requiring the calling of the roll for an "aye" and "no" vote, and the entering of such vote upon the record, is mandatory; and an election without complying with such provision is a nullity: Board of Education, v. Best, 52 O. S. 138.

Where the minute book, containing a record of the proceedings of a board of education, shows that all the members of the board were present; that a motion to proceed to the election of teachers was carried by a unanimous vote, and that an applicant for the position of teacher was declared elected by a unanimous vote, but that the clerk did not call the roll of the members, and the names of those voting aye were not entered on the record, the requirement of the statute was not sufficiently complied with, and the election was invalid: Board of Education v. Best, 52 O. S. 138.

In order to constitute a legal employment of a teacher by a board of education, a majority of all the members of such board must vote aye on that proposition: Rush v. Board of Education, 20 O. C. C. 361, 11 O. C. D. 181.

A superintendent of schools who has been appointed by a board of education under this section, has been held to be an employe, and not a public officer, within the meaning of the constitutional provision which forbids a change in the salary of a public officer during the term of his office: Ward v. Board of Education, 21 O. C. C. 699, 11 O. C. D. 671.

A contract for sinking a well is included within the provisions of this section, requiring a yea and nay vote, since this amounts to a purchase of a well: Newbauer v. Union Township, 8 O. D. (N. P.) 349.

If the minutes show that there was an aye and nay vote, and they further show how each member voted, such minutes show a sufficient compliance with this section, even if they do not state expressly that the roll was called: Youmans v. Board of Education, 13 O. C. C. 207, 7 O. C. D. 209.

The legal adoption of a resolution by a board of education can only be shown by the entry upon the minutes of the names of the members of the board voting "aye" and the names of the members voting "nay," as required by this section. A statement in the minutes of the board that all the members were present at roll-call, and later on that all voted "aye" on a given question, is not a compliance with this statute: Beck v. Board of Education, 9 O. C. C. (N. S.) 551, 19 O. C. D. 717.

Absence of president or clerk.

SECTION 4753. If the president or clerk is absent at any meeting of the board of education, the members present shall choose one of their number to serve in his place pro tempore. If both the president and clerk are absent, both places shall be filled. On the apprarance of either at the meeting after his place has been so filled, he shall immediately assume the duties of his office. (70 v. 195.)

Record of proceedings and attestation thereof.

SECTION 4754. The clerk of the board of education shall record the proceedings of each meeting in a book to be provided by the board for that purpose, which shall be a public record. The record of proceedings at each meeting of the board shall be read at its next succeeding meeting, corrected, if necessary, and approved, which approval shall be noted in the proceedings. After such approval the president shall sign the record and the clerk attest it. (71 v. 15.)

A board of education can speak only through its records, and these must accordingly be complete, showing just what the board did, and no more. A motion made by a member, seconded by another member, stated by the president, and voted on by the board, is business, and is to be recorded, though not a single member voted for it. Any vote upon it, as to refer, to postpone, or to lay upon the table, is action, and should be recorded. If the board adjourn pending the consideration of the motion, the motion should be recorded. If the mover withdraws the motion, by consent of the board, by general consent it may also be omitted from the records.

The records of a special meeting should state by whom the meeting was called, as the legality of the proceedings depends upon the legality of the call.

If a record is inadequately entered, parol evidences may, it seems, be admitted to show that action was taken which is not found on the records at all. The commissioner of schools of Rhode Island decided, under instruction of Judge Brayton, of the supreme court, that "imperfections in a clerk's record of a resolution do not render invalid a tax properly voted." Yet all these imperfections in the record lead to trouble — some litigation, often to questions which only courts of law can decide, and in which their decision may be such as to defeat what was attempted to be done in the case.

The power to amend the records exists with the clerk while he is in office, but not after his term expires, nor for any purpose other than to make them truthful and complete as to fact: 11 Mass. 477; 17 Maine, 444.

Records of *quasi* corporations are not considered of that absolute verity that parol testimony is inadmissible to show facts upon which the record is silent: 5 Ohio, 136.

Recording of vote in certain cases; see Sec. 4752.

If a contract with a teacher has been made in compliance with statute, and at a regular called meeting, but no record thereof has been made, such teacher may prove the official action of such board by competent oral testimony: Dixon v. Subschool District, 3 O. C. C. 517, 2 O. C. D. 298.

SECTION 4755. By the adoption of a resolution, a board of education may accept any bequest made to it by will of may accept any gift or endowment from any person of corporation upon the conditions and stipulations contained in the will or connected with the gift or endowment. For the purpose of enabling the board to carry out the conditions and limitations upon which a bequest, gift or endowment is made, it may make all rules and regulations required to fully carry them into effect. No such bequest, gift or endowment shall be accepted by the board if the conditions thereof shall remove any portion of the public schools from the control of such board. (97 v. 355.)

> Boards may accept bequests.

A school district which has been created by an invalid special act of the legislature is at least a de facto school district; and the board of education which has been elected therein and acts as a board of education is at least a de facto board, and it may in such capacity accept a bequest for school purposes by virtue of this section: Rockwell v. Blaney, 9 O. N. P. (N. S.) 495.

A bequest to a board of education "for the purpose of erecting a public school building in and for the benefit of said school district," is a bequest in which the beneficiaries are the people of such school district: Rockwell v. Blaney, 9 O. N. P. (N. S.) 495.

A bequest to a board of education for school purposes is a gift in trust for a charitable purpose; and such gift should be construed liberally in order that the intention of the donor may be given effect: Rockwell v. Blaney, 9 O. N. P. (N. S.) 495.

SECTION 4756. When a board of education decides to dispose of real or personal property, held by it in its corporate capacity, exceeding in value three hundred dollars, it shall sell such property at public auction after giving at least thirty days' notice thereof by publication in a newspaper of general circulation or by posting notices thereof in five of the most public places in the district in which such property is situated. When the board has twice so offered a tract of real estate for sale at public auction and it is not sold, the board may sell it at private sale, either as an entire tract or in parcels, as the board deems best. Provided, however, that in case the board of education decides to dispose of such real property, it may sell and convey the same to any municipality or board of trustees of the school district library in which such real estate is situated, upon such terms and conditions as may be agreed upon. The president and secretary of the board shall execute and deliver deeds necessary to complete the sale or transfer provided for by this action. (103 v. 536.)

> How real property may be sold.

Section 4750, General Code, providing for the sale of real estate valued in excess of $300.00 at auction does not compel the board of education to dispose of the property to the highest bidder and the board in its notice of sale may reserve the right to reject any and all bids. — *Attorney General,* 1912, p. 493.

Section 4749, General Code, which enumerates the power of the board of education with reference to acquiring, holding, possessing and disposing of real and personal property, does not include any provision for the leasing of such property by the board, and as the statutes nowhere prescribe the manner of executing such a lease, the board cannot be held to possess such power. — *Attorney General,* 1913, p. 1508.

A dedication of real property for school purposes is a dedication for a specific use, and the board of education acquires thereby no power of alienation so as to extinguish such use: Board of Education v. Edson, 18 O. S. 221.

A board of education has the title to the property on such school district in trust for school purposes; and a lease of a public schoolhouse for the purpose of having a private school conducted therein for a certain period is in violation of such trust, and a resident taxpayer of such district may sue in equity for an injunction to restain such use: Weir v. Day, 35 O. S. 143.

If land has been conveyed to a township board of education, its successors and assigns, for school purposes only, and such land is subsequently sold by such board at public outcry, and the original grantor or his grantee enters upon such land, and to test the title thereto, the grantee of such board of education brings trespass against such original grantor, it was held that such sale was by itself no breach of such condition, it not having been shown that such grantee had diverted such land to other than school purposes: Taylor v. Binford, 37 O. S. 262.

Conveyance and contracts.

SECTION 4757. Conveyances made by a board of education shall be executed by the president and clerk thereof. No member of the board shall have directly or indirectly any pecuniary interest in any contract of the board or be employed in any manner for compensation by the board of which he is a member except as clerk or treasurer. No contract shall be binding upon any board unless it is made or authorized at a regular or special meeting of such board. (70 v. 195.)

Inasmuch as by the provisions of section 7786, a clerk of the township board of education is obliged to pass on reports of teachers before an order may be drawn by said clerk for the payment of their salaries, the office of said clerk constitutes a check upon the position of teacher, and therefore both positions may not be held at the same time by the same individual. — *Attorney General,* 1913, p. 1097.

Section 4749, General Code, which enumerates the power of the board of education with reference to acquiring, holding, possessing and disposing of real and personal property, does not include any provision for the leasing of such property by the board, and as the statutes nowhere prescribe the manner of executing such a lease, the board cannot be held to possess such power. — *Attorney General,* 1913, p. 1508.

As there are no compulsory conflicting duties, the clerk of a township may serve as member of the township board of education. — *Attorney General,* 1911-12. p. 1204.

Inasmuch as it is mandatory upon the board of education to place the deposits in the bank offering the highest rate of interest for the same, members of the board who are stockholders in, or officers of the bank making the best bid, are not criminally liable for ma ing such bank the depository. — *Attorney General,* 1912, p. 1246.k

A bank incorporated under the laws of Ohio cannot be adjudged a bankrupt. A private bank, however, may become bankrupt.

Inasmuch as in order to constitute a preference a transfer must be made to pay a pre-existing debt, a village may receive municipal bonds owned by a private bank as security for the deposit therein of municipal funds. without danger of creation of a preference, or of liability to nullification on the ground of fraud. — *Attorney General.* 1912, p. 1983.

A board of education may enter into a contract with a retired member thereof. — *Attorney General,* 1912, p. 1083.

Board of education can make no contract, appropriation, etc., unless money is in treasury and set apart; exception: G. C. Sec. 5660, et seq.

Columbus — power of school board to convey to city as an addition to public park: 84 v. 108.

This section, together with others which devolve duties upon the president of the board of education, are said to render him an "officer": State, ex rel., y. Withrow, 11 O. C. C. (N. S.) 569, 21 O. C. D. 215 (affirmed, without report, Withrow v. State, ex rel., 81 O. S. 523).

A sale of goods by a partnership to a board of education, the same person being both a member of such partnership and a member of such board, is void: Grant v. Brouse, 1 O. N. P. 145, 2 O. D. (N. P.) 24.

For a former statue invalidating a contract of a board of education unless an appropriation has been made therefor, see American Surety Co. v. Raeder, 15 O. C. C. 47, 8 O. C. D. 684 (affirmed without report, American Surety Co. v. Raeder, 61 O. S. 661).

SECTION 12883. Whoever, being a member of a board of education, accepts or receives for his services as such member any compensation except as clerk or treasurer of such board or as otherwise provided by law, shall be imprisoned in the penitentiary not less than one year nor more than twenty-one years and fined double the amount of money or other property so accepted or received (70 v. 214.)

Member of board of education accepting compensation.

SECTION 12910. Whoever, holding an office of trust or profit by election or appointment, or as agent, servant or employe of such officer or of a board of such officers, is interested in a contract for the purchase of property, supplies or fire insurance for the use of the county, township, city, village, board of education or a public institution with which he is concerned, shall be imprisoned in the penitentiary not less than one year nor more than ten years. (94 v. 391.)

Officer or agent interested in contracts.

This section has been construed as applying to the agents, officers, and employes of towns, villages and cities of the state, and as a prohibition on all contracts between such a municipality and agent or servant interested therein: Findlay v. Pertz, 9 O. F. D. 30.

The penalty is equivalent to prohibiting the act, and if one member of a board of five is interested, the board is in effect reduced to four, and is not then a legal board and its act or contract is Void: Bellaire Goblet Co. v. Findlay, 5 O. C. C. 418.

SECTION 12911. Whoever, holding an office of trust or profit by election or apopintment, or as agent, servant or employe of such officer or of a board of such officers, is interested in a contract for the purchase of property, supplies or fire insurance for the use of the county, township, city, village, board of education or a public institution with which he is not connected, and the amount of such contract exceeds the sum of fifty dollars, unless such contract is let on bids duly advertised as provided by law, shall be imprisoned in the penitentiary not less than one year nor more than ten years. (94 v. 391.)

Same as to other contracts.

SECTION 12932. Whoever, being a local director or member of a board of education, votes for or participates in the making of a contract with a person as a teacher or instructor in a public school to whom he or she is related as father or brother, mother or sister, or acts in a manner in which he or she is pecuniarily interested, shall be fined not less than twenty-five dollars nor more than five hundred dollars or imprisoned not more than six months, or both. (86 v. 207.)

Employing relative as teacher.

Exchange of
real estate.

SECTION 4758. Upon a vote of a majority of the members of a board of education and a concurring vote of the council of a municipal corporation, declaring that an exchange of real estate held by such board for school purposes for real estate held by such municipal corporation for municipal purposes will be mutually beneficial to such school district and municipal corporation, such exchange may be made by conveyances, executed by the mayor and clerk of the corporation and by the president and clerk of the board of education, respectively. (85 v. 133.)

School prop-
erty exempt
from taxa-
tion.

SECTION 4759. Real or personal property vested in any board of education shall be exempt from taxation and from sale on execution or other writ or order in the nature of an execution. (70 v. 195.)

Non-taxation of school property; Sec. 5349.

Provisions relating to taxation of school, ministerial, and other lands; Sec. 5330.

Sidewalk — School property not assessable for: 48 O. S. 87.

Property purchased by a board of education, and upon which there is a mortgage lien, may be sold on foreclosure: 39 B., 76; affirmed by supreme court.

School property cannot be subject to the payment of a claim for damages which have been received by a private person by reason of the negligence of the board of education: Finch v. Board of Education, 30 O. S. 37.

School property is not rendered liable to assessment for a street improvement by reason of the fact that with knowledge that the property was not liable to assessment the school board petitioned for the improvement: Board of Education v. Bowland, 3 O. N. P. (N. S.) 122, 15 O. D. (N. P.) 334.

Where the lien of an assessment for a street improvement has already attached, it will not be defeated by the subsequent purchase of the property by a school board: Board of Education v. Bowland, 3 O. N. P. (N. S.) 122, 15 O. D. (N. P.) 334.

If property upon which there is a mortgage is purchased by a board of education, the lien of such mortgage may be enforced by foreclosure proceedings: Board of Education v. Stephenson (supreme court, not reported), 39 Bull. 75, 1 O. S. U. 743.

If property is conveyed to a board of education for school purposes, the widow of the grantor is not entitled to dower therein; since if dower is adjudged to her, such judgment could not be enforced unless such property were applied to purposes other than school purposes: Steel v. Board of Education, 1 O. D. (N. P.) 276.

School houses,
churches,
colleges, etc.

SECTION 5349. Public school houses and houses used exclusively for public worship, the books and furniture therein and the ground attached to such buildings necessary for the proper occupancy, use and enjoyment thereof and not leased or otherwise used with a view to profit, public colleges and academies and all buildings connected therewith, and all lands connected with public institutions of learning, not used with a view to profit, shall be exempt from taxation. This section shall not extend to leasehold estates or real property held under the authority of a college or university of learning in this state, but leaseholds, or other estates or property, real or personal, the rents, issues, profits and income of which is given to a city, village, school district, or subdistrict in this state, exclusively for the use, endowment or support of schools for the free education of youth without charge, shall be exempt from taxation as long as such property, or the rents, issues, profits or income thereof is used and exclusively applied for the support of free education by such city, village, district or subdistrict. (99 v. 449.)

Land owned by a college and used for a pumping station, from which water is furnished to the college community and is also sold to outsiders at a profit, is taxable so long as the practice of vending water to persons not connected with the college is continued: Kenyon College v. Schnably, 8 O. N. P. (N. S.) 160, 19 O. D. (N. P.) 432.

The exemption from taxation of property belonging to colleges and academies, provided by this section, extends to all buildings and lands that are with reasonable certainty used in furthering or carrying out the necessary objects and purposes of the institution: Kenyon College v. Schnably, 12 O. C. C. (N. S.) 1, 21 O. C. D. 150.

Under this section, residences occupied by the president and professors and janitor of a college are exempt, as also is vacant land from which no revenue is derived; but land used for agricultural purposes or pasturage is not exempt: Kenyon College v. Schnably, 12 O. C. C. (N. S.) 1, 21 O. C. D. 150.

Property leased to parties under an agreement requiring that they conduct therein a grammar school, which is treated as a preparatory department of the college, is not taxable while so used, but becomes taxable upon the burning of the building and the abandonment of the site for grammar school purposes: Kenyon College v. Schnably, 8 O. N. P. (N. S.) 160, 19 O. D. (N. P.) 432.

Under a statute which exempted school property but provided that the buildings, or any land not occupied for literary purposes might be taxed, it was held that the home of a professor upon the grounds of Kenyon college was not exempt from taxation: Kendricks v. Farquhar, 8 O. 189.

That property which is used for college purposes alone is exempt from taxation, see Myers v. Atkins, 8. O. C. C. 228.

A building which is owned by a college and which is used for stores and the like, the income therefrom being applied to college purposes, is not exempt from taxation: Cincinnati College v. State, 19 O. 110.

The exemption of lands belonging to the Ohio university are leased for ninety-nine years, renewable forever, the owner may be exempted from taxation by statute (the statutory exemption in this case was from "all state taxes"): State, ex rel., v. Auditor of State, 15 O. S. 482.

If school land is leased, and the ground rent is used for the support of the school, a building on such land is subject to taxation: State, ex rel., v. Cappeller (Ham. Dist. Court), 8 Dec. Rep. 219, 6 Bull. 339.

SECTION 4760. Process in all suits against a board of education shall be by summons which shall be served by leaving a copy thereof with the clerk or president of the board. (70 v. 195.)

Processes against boards, how served.

In a suit against a board of education process must be served as provided in this section: State, ex rel., v. Coon, 4 O. C. C. (N. S.) 560, 16 O. C. D. 241.

SECTION 4761. Except in city school districts, the prosecuting attorney of the county shall be the legal adviser of all boards of education of the county in which he is serving. He shall prosecute all actions against a member or officer of a board of education for malfeasance or misfeasance in office, and he shall be the legal counsel of such boards or the officers thereof in all civil actions brought by or against them and shall conduct such actions in his official capacity. When such civil action is between two or more boards of education in the same county, the prosecuting attorney shall not be required to act for either of them. In city school districts, the city solicitor shall be the legal adviser and attorney for the board of education thereof, and shall perform the same services for such board as herein required of the prosecuting attorney for other boards of education of the county. (97 v. 355.)

Prosecuting attorney or city solicitor to be counsel of school board.

In a controversy between a board of education of a city school district and the city, the solicitor is at liberty to choose which of the two parties he will represent regardless of a resolution of council ordering him to represent the city. — *Attorney General*, 1912, p. 1771.

The duties of the city solicitor with respect to city school district boards of education, are set out in full in Section 4761, General Code, and as he is made the "legal adviser" of such boards, it is his duty as such to give his opinion upon the legal title to real estate in which the board is interested.

He may formulate his opinion in any reliable legal manner he desires however, and is not compelled to make his advice take the form of an abstract of title. — *Attorney General*, 1912, p. 1841.

Inasmuch as under Section 4701, General Code, the prosecuting attorney is obliged to prosecute all actions against members of a village board of education for misfeasance or malfeasance in office considerations of public policy will not permit that official to hold a position on such board of education. — *Attorney General*, 1912, p. 1523.

Section 4761, General Code, beyond dispute, makes the city solicitor the legal advisor of city school districts. Also, by provision of Section 4761, the prosecuting attorney is made the legal advisor of all school boards within the county with the single exception of boards of education which are engaged in civil actions with one another.

The village solicitor being appointed by contract, fulfilling only contractual duties, serving for an indefinite term and not being obligated to take oath or give bonds, is not an "official" within the meaning of Section 4762, General Code, which stipulates that these duties shall fall upon "any official serving in a similar capacity" to that of prosecuting attorney or city solicitor. This language refers to "county solicitors," "directors of law" and "corporation counsel" (all of which offices existed at the time of the passage of Section 4762, General Code) and to such other similar offices as might be created in the future.

At the present time, therefore, the legal duties necessitated by village board of education also fall upon the prosecuting attorney. — *Attorney General*, 1912, p. 487.

Cited to show that the legislature did not intend the county prosecutor and the county solicitor, where such provision was made for such officer, to have the same duties: State, ex rel., v. Hynicka, 17 O. D. (N. P.) 378.

Unless the city solicitor refuses or fails to act as required by law, the board of education has no power to employ additional counsel. If, however, such solicitor determines to act on behalf of a de facto board, and not on behalf of the de jure board, such latter board may employ other counsel: Caldwell v. Marvin, 8 O. N. P. (N. S.) 387.

This section does not authorize the prosecuting attorney in his official capacity to bring a suit for an injunction to restrain a board of education from applying money which is in its treasury, and which is the proceeds of taxes levied to build a schoolhouse, to refund money which it borrowed in anticipation of such taxes: State, ex rel., v. Van Buren, 11 O. C. C. 41, 5 O. C. D. 447.

When other officers may act; restrictions.

SECTION 4762. The duties prescribed by the preceding section shall devolve upon any official serving in a capacity similar to that of prosecuting attorney or city solicitor for the territory wherein a school district is situated, regardless of his official designation. No prosecuting attorney, city solicitor or other official acting in a similar capacity shall be a member of the board of education. No compensation in addition to such officer's regular salary shall be allowed for such services. (97 v. 355.)

Section 4761, General Code, beyond dispute, makes the city solicitor the legal advisor of city school districts. Also, by provision of Section 4761, the prosecuting attorney is made the legal advisor of all school boards within the county with the single exception of boards of education which are engaged in civil actions with one another.

The village solicitor being appointed by contract, fulfilling only contractual duties, serving for an indefinite term and not being obligated to take oath or give bonds, is not an "official" within the meaning of Section 4762, General Code, which stipulates that these duties shall fall upon "any official serving in a similar capacity" to that of prosecuting attorney or city solicitor. This language refers to "county solicitors," "directors of law" and "cor⸗ poration counsel" (all of which offices existed at the time of the passage of Section 4762, General Code) and to such other similar offices as might be created in the future.

At the present time, therefore, the legal duties necessitated by village board of education also fall upon the prosecuting at⸗ torney. — *Attorney General*, 1912, p. 487.

SECTION 12823. Whoever corruptly gives, promises or offers to a member or officer of the general assembly, or of either house thereof, or to a state, judicial or other officer, public trustee, or an agent or employe of the state of such officer or trustee, either before or after his election, qualification, appointment or employment, any valuable thing, or corruptly offers or promises to do any act bene⸗ ficial to such person to influence him with respect to his official duty, or to influence his action, vote, opinion or judgment, in a matter pending, or that might legally come before him, and whoever, being a member of the general assembly, or a state or other officer, public trustee, agent or employe of the state or of such officer or trustee, either before or after his election, qualification, appointment or employment, solicits or accepts any valuable or beneficial thing to influence him with respect to his official duty, or to influence his action, vote, opinion or judgment, in a matter pending, or that might legally come before him, shall be imprisoned in the penitentiary not less than one year nor more than ten years. (102 v. 129.)

Giving or ac⸗ cepting bribes by officer, etc.

A member of the General Assembly who is convicted of re⸗ ceiving a bribe, is disqualified from holding public office and from the date of his conviction, vouchers due to him as such member must be denied.

Pending an appeal from such conviction, however, the status quo of the payments accruing should be preserved. — *Attorney General*, 1912, p. 114.

EMBEZZLEMENT.

SECTION 12873. Whoever, being charged with the col⸗ lection, receipt, safekeeping, transfer or disbursement of public money or a bequest, or part thereof, belonging to the state, or to a county, township, municipal corporation, board of education, cemetery association or comany, con⸗ verts to his own use, or to the use of any other person, body corporate, association or party, or uses by way of investment in any kind of security, stock, loan, property, land or merchandise, or in any other manner or form, or loans with or without interest to a company, corporation, association or individual, or, except as provided by law, deposits with a company, corporation or individual, public money or other funds, property, bonds, securities, assets or effects received, controlled or held by him for safe⸗ keeping or in trust for a specific purpose, transfer or dis⸗

Embezzlement of public money; de⸗ posit with bank.

bursement, or in any other way or manner, or for any
other purpose, shall be guilty of embezzlement of the money
or other property thus converted, used, invested, loaned,
deposited or paid out, and shall be imprisoned in the penitentiary not less than one year nor more than twnety-one
years and fined double the amount of money or other
property embezzled. (91 v. 338.)

Where a board of education of a township permits its treasurer, by
agreement, to use its funds in his business, and renew this loan after his
term has expired, the treasurer is guilty of embezzlement, and the board of
advising and aiding in the embezzlement, and in an action against the sureties
on the note given for such loan, the illegality of the transaction may be set
up: Board of Education v. Thompson, 33 O. S. 321.

Interest earned upon public moneys becomes a part of the principal
fund as soon as earned, and an appropriation thereof by a state treasurer is
a breach of his official bond for which his sureties are liable: State v.
McKinnon, 9 O. N. P. (N. S.) 513.

A city treasurer is liable for interest received upon the deposit of school
funds: Eshelby v. Board of Education, 66 O. S. 71.

The clerk of the board of education is not authorized, nor is it made
his duty by statute, to become the custodian of tuition funds belonging to
such board, and where, pursuant to a rule of the said board, the clerk received
such funds into his custody and failed to keep them safely, the sureties on
his bond are not liable therefor: State, ex rel., v. Griffith, 74 O. S. 80.

Where an officer of the state, charged by law with the care of public
money, delivers any part of it to another, for use, to be repaid with interest
at a future time, though the bond or other instrument evidencing the obligation to repay may denominate the transaction a "deposit", it is in substance
and legal effect a loan: State v. Buttles, 3 O. S. 309.

A loan by a board of education to its treasurer is within this section:
Board of Education v. Thompson, 33 O. S. 321.

Public money taken by an officer charged with its custody is embezzlement, and not larceny: Brown v. State, 18 O. S. 496.

Although interest received on deposit of public funds may be recovered
from a treasurer of a school district in a civil action, it does not follow that
it was public money within the meaning of this section and that taking it is
embezzlement: State v. Pierson, 83 O. S. 241.

Where one or two partners is a township treasurer, and, with the
knowledge and consent of his partner, the township funds are deposited in
bank to the firm's credit, and drawn upon in payment of the firm's debts,
both parties are guilty of embezzlement: Davis v. Gelhaus, 44 O. S. 69.

It is sufficient to aver that the money embezzled was public money
belonging to the several municipalities, or to one or more of them, without
stating the respective amounts belonging to each: Brown v. State, 18 O. S. 496.

On the trial of a charge of embezzlement, the fact that the money
alleged to have been embezzled by the accused was received in several sums,
at different times, and from different persons, affords no ground for requiring
the prosecutor to elect on which sum he will rely for conviction: Gravatt v.
State, 25 O. S. 162; Campbell v. State, 35 O. S. 70.

The treasurer of a school district, who, under favor of this section,
deposits its funds in a bank which allows interest on the average balance of
the deposit, is required to account to the school district for such interest:
Eshelby v. Board of Education, 66 O. S. 71.

Fine is a judgment against whole estate. SECTION 12874. The fine, provided for in the next
preceding section, shall operate as a judgment at law on
all of the estate of the person sentenced and be enforced
to collection by execution or other process for the use only
of the owner of the property or effects so embezzled, and
such fine shall only be released or entered as satisfied by
the person in interest as aforesaid. (91 v. 338.)

Certain deposits lawful. SECTION 12875. The provisions of section twelve thousand, eight hundred and seventy-three shall not make it un-
lawful for the treasurer of a township, municipal corporation, board of education, or cemetery association, to deposit
public money with a person, firm, company, or corporation
organized to do a banking business under the laws of this
state or the United States, but the deposit of such funds
in such bank shall not release such treasurer from liability

for loss which may occur thereby. Nor shall the provisions of section twelve thousand, eight hundred and seventy-three, make it unlawful for a county auditor, county treasurer, probate judge, sheriff, clerk of courts, or recorder, to deposit fees and trust funds coming into their custody as such officers as above, until such time as said aforesaid officers are required to make payment of the official earnings of their offices, so deposited, into their respective fee funds as required by section twenty-nine hundred and eighty-three, and until such time as the trust funds, so held by them in their official capacities, may be paid to the person, persons, firms, or corporations, entitled to same, and any interest earned and paid upon said deposits shall be apportioned to, and become a part of said fees or trust funds, and shall in no instance accrue to, and be received by, the official making said deposits, for his own use. (106 v. 556.)

SECTION 12876. Whoever, being elected or appointed to an office of public trust or profit, or an agent, clerk, servant or employe of such officer or board thereof, embezzles or converts to his own use, or conceals with such intent, anything of value that shall come into his possession by virtue of such office or employment, is guilty of embezzlement, and, if the total value of the property embezzled in the same continuous employment or term of office, whether embezzld at one time or at different times within three years prior to the inception of the prosecution, is thirty-five dollars or more, shall be imprisoned in the penitentiary not less than one year nor more than ten years, or, if such total value is less than thirty-five dollars, shall be fined not more than two hunlred dollars or imprisoned not more than thirty days, or both. (97 v. 67.)

Embezzlement of public property; fraudulent conversion.

SECTION 12877. Whoever embezzles an evidence of debt, negotiable by delivery only and actually executed but not delivered or issued as a valid instrument, if the total value of the property embezzled in the same continuous employment or term of office, whether embezzled at one time or at different times within three years prior to the inception of the prosecution, is thirty-five dollars or more, shall be imprisoned in the penitentiary not less than one year nor more than ten years, or, if such total value is less than thirty-five dollars, shall be fined not more than two hundred dollars or imprisoned not more than thirty days, or both. (37 v. 74.)

Embezzlement of negotiable instrument before delivery.

SECTION 12878. Whoever, being a member of the council of a municipal corporation, or an officer, agent, clerk or servant of such corporation, or board or department thereof, or an officer, clerk or servant of a board of education, knowingly diverts, appropriates or applies funds, or a part of a fund raised by taxation or otherwise, to any use or purpose other than that for which it was raised or

Embezzlement by municipal and school officers.

appropriated, or knowingly diverts, appropriates or applies money borrowed, or a bond of the corporation or part of the proceeds of such bond, to any use or purpose other than that for which such loan was made, or bond issued, shall be imprisoned in the penitentiary not less than one year nor more than twenty-one years and fined in double the amount of money or other property embezzled. (73 v. 116.)

Fine is judgment on whole estate. SECTION 12879. The fine provided for in the next preceding section, shall be a judgment at law on all of the estate of the person sentenced and be enforced to collection by execution or other process for the use only of the owner of the property or effects so embezzled, and such fine shall only be released or entered as satisfied by the person in interest as aforesaid. (73 v. 116.)

Offering bribe for recommending textbooks. SECTION 12931. Whoever offers or gives a reward or consideration, or makes a present or reduction in price to a person employed in a public school, or to an officer having authority or control over it, for favoring, recommending or advocating the introduction, adoption or use on such school, of a textbook, map, chart, globe or other school supply, or to induce him so to do, or, being an employe or officer of such school accepts, offers or agrees to receive or accept a reward, consideration, present, gift or reduction in price for so doing, shall be fined not less than twenty-five dollars nor more than five hundred dollars or imprisoned not more than six months, or both. (86 v. 207.)

CHAPTER 7.

TREASURER AND CLERK.

SECTION 4763. In each city school district, the treasurer of the city funds shall be the treasurer of the school funds. In all village and rural school districts which do not provide legal depositories as provided in sections 7604 to 7608 inclusive, the county treasurer shall be the treasurer of the school funds of such districts. (104 v. 158.)

<small>Treasurer of the school funds.</small>

Section 4782, General Code, as amended, 104 O. L., 159 provides for creating a depository for the school moneys of the school district, in which even the board of education, by resolution adopted by a vote of a majority of its members, shall dispense with the treasurer of the school moneys belonging to such school district. Said section carries the provision that upon the establishment of such depository, and the dispensation of the treasury on the part of the board of education, thereupon the clerk of the board of education of such district shall perform all the services, discharge all the duties and be subject to all obligation required by law of the treasurer of such school district.

Upon consideration of Section 4763 to 4784, General Code, the clerk of the board of education can receive extra compensation for performing the duties of treasurer of such board, and the board of education has the legal right to fix the compensation of such clerk, when he is required to perform the added duties of treasurer of the board of education, because of the dispensation of said treasurer under Section 4782, General Code. — *Attorney General,* Opinion No. 1141, Sept. 12, 1914.

It is not necessary for school depository banks to give new bonds in order to bind sureties in districts where school treasurers have been dispensed with under section 4782, 104 O. L., 158, in case the bonds held by the respective boards of education bear a date prior to the date of the resolution dispensing with the school treasurer, and the terms of such bonds have not as yet expired.

It is necessary for the clerk of the school board to give a new bond when such clerk assumes the duty of the treasurer of the school funds.

It is not necessary for a county treasurer to give a bond as school treasurer, when he becomes the treasurer of the school funds of village or rural districts.—*Attorney General.* Opinion No. 1382, 1915.

117

From the principles established by the decision in the case of State ex rel. Stolzenbacher vs. Felty, Auditor, No. 9372, decided by the supreme court in 1905, but not reported.

1. The treasurer of a city, village or township may by failing to qualify as treasurer of the school funds refuse to serve as such treasurer.

2. If the township clerk fails to qualify as clerk of the township board of education, such failure does not affect his status as township clerk.

3. If a township treasurer resigns as treasurer of the school funds the board of education has the right if it chooses, to accept his resignation, and in such cases may elect a successor to him as treasurer of the school fund.

4. If by reason of the establishment of a depository, the treasurer of the school district is dispensed with according to law, and the clerk gives the additional bond required of him as treasurer by virtue of section 4783, General Code, he will then be obliged to perform the duties of the treasurer without extra compensation unless he resigns. He may, however, refuse to qualify as such treasurer and the board may elect a substitute.

5. The refusal of a township clerk to qualify for the duties which devolve upon him by the establishment of a depository under section 4783, General Code, will not in any way affect his status as township clerk, and under such circumstances the board may select a substitute to act as treasurer. — *Attorney General,* 1911-12, p. 289.

As the members of the school board must approve the bond of the treasurer and vote upon the question of increasing or changing the same or of requiring additional sureties thereon, the office of member of the board and treasurer of the board are incompatible and may not be held by one individual.

A treasurer of a corporation may refuse to act as treasurere of the school board without thereby affecting his position as treasurer of the corporation. — *Attorney General,* 1912, p. 1160.

Village and township treasurers continued to act as treasurers of the school funds of their respective village and township school districts until they were superseded by the county treasurer by virtue of Section 4763, General Code, as amended, 104 O. L., 159, and such treasurers continued to draw whatever salary they were entitled to until so superseded by the county treasurers at the time said section became effective.

The clerk of the school district, however, would continue to act as the treasurer of such village and township school districts if a depository had been previously provided and the treasurer dispensed with by the respective boards of education. Under said section, 4763, supra, the county treasurers continue to act as the treasurers of the respective village and rural school district funds until such time as a depository is established for such funds, in accordance with Section 4782, General Code, 104 O. L., 159 — *Attorney General,* Opinion 1346, 1914.

When a depository has been provided by a city board of education for its school funds, as authorized by law, the board of education of the district must dispense with the treasurer, and the clerk of the board of the city school district performs all the services and duties of such treasurer. — *Attorney General,* Opinion 45, 1915.

As to release and discharge of treasurer and sureties in certain cases, see G. C. Sec. 2303, et seq.

Township trustees have no authority to discharge a treasurer from liability for any por ion of the township school funds: State v. ex rel., v. Williams, 13 O. 495. t

The same person cannot hold the office of the president of the board of education and treasurer thereof: State, ex rel., v. Heddleston, 8 Dec. Rep. 77, 5 Bull. 502.

The treasurer of a school district who, under favor of the proviso of G. C. Sec. 12875 deposits its funds in a bank which allows interest on the average balance of the deposit is required to account to the school district for such interest: Eshellby v. Board of Education, 66 O. S. 71 (for opinion below, see Eshelby v. Board of Education, 6 O. N. P. 117, 9 O. D. (N. P.) 214).

Since a city treasurer is made by statute the ex officio treasurer of a board of education, he cannot, in the absence of specific statutory provision therefor, have extra compensation for his services in taking charge of such school fund: Board of Education v. Eshelby, 6 O. N. P. 117, 9 O. D. (N. P.) 214; Knorr v. Board of Education, 8 Dec. Rep. 672, 9 Bull. 182.

SECTION 4764. Before entering upon the duties of his **Bond of** office, each school district treasurer shall execute a bond, **treasurer.** with sufficient sureties, in a sum not less than the amount of school funds that may come into his hands, payable to the state, approved by the board of education, and conditioned for the faithful disbursement according to law of all funds which come into his hands, provided that when school moneys have been deposited under the provisions of sections 7604-7608 inclusive, the bond shall be in such amount as the board of education may require. (101 v. 264.)

As there is no statutory authorization for the payment by the board of education of the premium on the clerk's or treasurer's bond, that expense may not be borne by it.

As there is no duty imposed upon the superintendent of schools or the teachers to attend a national educational association, nor upon the members of the board of education or its clerk to attend a meeting of the state association of school boards, and as there is no statutory authorization for the payment of such expenses, the board may not pay the same out of the school funds. —*Attorney General,* 1911-12, p. 430.

Section 7604 of the General Code makes it mandatory upon the board of education of a school district to establish a depository and when it fails so to do, legal proceedings may invoke to compel the same.

When such depository has not been established, however, money may be paid to the treasurer of such school district in accordance with the procedure set out in Sections 4764, 4768 and 4769 of the General Code. — *Attorney General,* 1912, p. 329.

A village treasurer is by law, treasurer of the board of education, and cannot at the same time be a member of the board of education.—*Attorney General,* Opinion No. 862, April 24, 1914.

The treasurer of a school district who deposits money in a bank other than in conformity to the provisions of the depository law, together with the sureties upon his bond, is responsible for losses sustained by failure of the bank. Mere knowledge by the board of education of such deposit does not relieve the treasurer and his sureties of liability.—*Attorney General,* Opinion No. 52, 1915.

From the principles established by the decision in the case of State ex rel Stolzenbacher vs. Felty, Auditor, No. 9372, decided by the supreme court in 1905, but not reported.

1. The treasurer of a city, village or township may by failing to qualify as treasurer of the school funds refuse to serve as such treasurer.

2. If the township clerk fails to qualify as clerk of the township board of education, such failure does not affect his status as township clerk.

3. If a township treasurer resigns as treasurer of the school funds the board of education has the right if it chooses, to accept his resignation, and in such cases may elect a successor to him as treasurer of the school fund.

4. If by reason of the establishment of a depository, the treasurer of the school district is dispensed with according to law, and the clerk gives the additional bond required of him as treasurer by virtue of section 4783, General Code, he will then be obliged to perform the duties of the treasurer without extra compensation unless he resigns. He may, however, refuse to qualify as such treasurer and the board may elect a substitute.

5. The refusal of a township clerk to qualify for the duties which devolve upon him by the establishment of a depository under section 4783, General Code, will not in any way affect his status as township clerk, and under such circumstances the board may select a substitute to act as treasurer. — *Attorney General,* 1911-12, p. 289.

As to release of surety of treasurer of school funds, see G. C. sec. 12200, et seq.

The word "funds" as used in the bond of a school district treasurer includes not merely cash, but also drafts and certificates of deposit which were received and have been paid upon presentation: Reed v. Board of Education, 39 O. S. 635.

If a city treasurer who is ex officio the treasurer of the school funds, by virtue of G. C. Sec. 4763, deposits such funds in a bank in an illegal manner he has violated the conditions of his bond: Board of Education v. Eshelby, 6 O. N. P. 117, 9 O. D. (N. P.) 214.

In an action against the surety upon the bond of a township treasurer given under this section, it is necessary to aver a default as to school funds; and an averment in the petition together with evidence showing a default in the "township funds" in general terms is insufficient: State v. Corey, 16 O. S. 17.

Sureties of treasurer of school fund may apply to be discharged.

SECTION 12200. A surety of the treasurer of school funds, in any lawfully organized school district, may notify the board of education of the district by at least five days' notice, in writing, that he is unwilling to continue as surety for such treasurer, and at a time therein named, will make application to the board to be released from further liability upon his bond. He also shall give at least three days' notice in writing to such treasurer, of the time and place at which the application will be made. (70 v. 195.)

Proceedings by board of education in such case.

SECTION 12201. Upon such notice being given, the board of education shall hear the application, and if in their opinion there is good reason therefor, require the treasurer to give a new bond, conditioned according to law, and to the satisfaction of the board, within such time as they direct. If the treasurer fails to execute such bond the office shall be vacant and shall immediately be filled as are other vacancies therein. (R. S.) (70 v. 195.)

Additional sureties or new bond.

SECTION 4765. Thereafter such treasurer may be required to give additional sureties on his accepted bond, or to execute a new bond with sufficient sureties to the approval of the board of education when such board deems it necessary. If he fails for ten days after service of notice in writing of such requisition, to give such bond or additional sureties, as so required, the office shall be declared vacant and filled as in other cases. (97 v. 367.)

From the principles established by the decision in the case of State ex rel Stolzenbacher vs. Felty, Auditor, No. 9372, decided by the supreme court in 1905, but not reported.

1. The treasurer of a city, village or township may by failing to qualify as treasurer of the school funds refuse to serve as such treasurer.

2. If the township clerk fails to qualify as clerk of the township board of education, such failure does not affect his status as township clerk.

3. If a township treasurer resigns as treasurer of the school funds the board of education has the right if it chooses, to accept

his resignation, and in such cases may elect a successor to him as treasurer of the school fund.

4. If by reason of the establishment of a depository, the treasurer of the school district is dispensed with according to law, and the clerk gives the additional bond required of him as treasurer by virtue of section 4783, General Code, he will then be obliged to perform the duties of the treasurer without extra compensation unless he resigns. He may, however, refuse to qualify as such treasurer and the board may elect a substitute.

5. The refusal of a township clerk to qualify for the duties which devolve upon him by the establishment of a depository under section 4783, General Code, will not in any way affect his status as township clerk, and under such circumstances the board may select a substitute to act as treasurer. — *Attorney General*, 1911-12, p. 289.

As members of the school board must approve the bond of the treasurer and vote upon the question of increasing or changing the same or of requiring additional sureties thereon, the office of member of the board and treasurer of the board are incompatible and may not be held by one individual.

A treasurer of a corporation may refuse to act as treasurere of the school board without thereby affecting his position as treasurer of the corporation. — *Attorney General*, 1912, p. 1160.

SECTION 4766. Each such bond, when so executed and approved, shall be filed with the clerk of the board of education of the district, and recorded. He shall cause a certified copy thereof or the names of additional sureties, to be filed with the county auditor without delay. (97 v. 367.)

Filing and approval of bond.

SECTION 4767. Such board at the time of the approval of any bond or sureties, shall require the treasurer of the school funds to produce all money, bonds or other securities in his hands as such treasurer, and they then must be counted by the board or a committee thereof, in the presence of its clerk, who thereupon shall enter upon the records of the board, a certificate, setting forth the exact amount of money or securities so found in the hands of such treasurer. Such record shall be signed by the president and clerk of the board and be prima facie evidence that the amount therein stated was actually in the treasury at that date. (97 v. 367.)

Counting of funds.

SECTION 4768. No treasurer of a school district shall pay out any school money except on an order signed by the president or vice-president, and countersigned by the clerk of the board of education, and when such school moneys have been deposited as provided by sections 7604-7608 inclusive, no money shall be withdrawn from any such depository, except upon an order signed by the treasurer and by the president or vice-president and countersigned by the clerk of the board of education; and no money shall be paid to the treasurer of the district other than that received from the county treasurer, except upon the order of the clerk of the board, who shall report the amount of such miscellaneous receipts to the county auditor each year immediately preceding such treasurer's settlement with the auditor. (101 v. 264.)

When treasurer may receive or pay money.

A board of education has capacity to sue its treasurer for money received and not accounted for. The remedy is not limited to an action on the bond, but may be for money had and received: 51 O. S. 115.

The treasurer should not pay an order for what he believes to be an illegal object, until he can consult with other members of the board, and have the question fully investigated. A man of discretion is supposed to be chosen to this, as to other offices, that the chances for discovering errors and fraud may be multiplied.

Section 7604 of the General Code makes it mandatory upon the board of education of a school district to establish a depository and when it fails so to do, legal proceedings may invoke to compel the same.

When such depository has not been established, however, money may be paid to the treasurer of such school district in accordance with the procedure set out in Sections 4764, 4768 and 4769 of the General Code. — *Attorney General*, 1912, p. 329.

The treasurer of a school district who deposits money in a bank other than in conformity to the provisions of the depository law, together with the sureties upon his bond, is responsible for losses sustained by failure of the bank. Mere knowledge by the board of education of such deposit does not relieve the treasurer and his sureties of liability. — *Attorney General,* Opinion 52, February 2, 1915.

Under this section orders which are drawn upon the sinking funds of a school district must be drawn by the president and the clerk of the board of education, in favor of the person entitled thereto upon requisition made upon them by the said board therefor: State, ex rel., v. Board of Education, 3 O. N. P. (N. S.) 401, 16 O. C. (N. P.) 386.

This section does not authorize the clerk to receive any miscellaneous funds; but on the contrary upon his order they must be paid directly to the county treasurer: State v. Cottle, 4 O. N. P. (N. S.) 145, 17 O. D. (N. P.) 108.

Since this section requires the action of the president and treasurer, each as a check upon the other, the same person cannot hold both offices: State, ex rel., v. Heddleston, 8 Dec. Rep. 77, 5 Bull. 502.

Maximum amount of funds which treasurer may hold.

SECTION 4769. The clerk of a board of education or the county auditor shall pay no money into the hands of the treasurer of a school district in excess of the amount of his bond. Should any such clerk or auditor violate this provision, he and his bondsmen shall be liable for any loss occasioned thereby. But where depositories for school funds have been created under the provisions of sections 7604-7608 inclusive, all school moneys shall be paid directly into such depository or depositories by the auditor upon the written order of the board of education signed by the president or vice-president and countersigned by the clerk. In case the school funds have been deposited under the provisions of sections 7604-7608 inclusive, the limitation of payment herein contained shall not apply. Before giving such treasurer a warrant or order for school funds, the auditor may require the treasurer to file with him a statement showing the amount of such funds in his possession, signed by the clerk of the board of education. (101 v. 264.)

Section 7604 of the General Code makes it mandatory upon the board of education of a school district to establish a depository and when it fails so to do, legal proceedings may invoke to compel the same.

When such depository has not been established, however, money may be paid to the treasurer of such school district in accordance with the procedure set out in Sections 4764, 4768 and 4769 of the General Code. — *Attorney General*, 1912, p. 329.

SECTION 4770. Within the first ten days of September, each year, the treasurer shall settle with the county auditor for the preceding school year, and for that purpose he shall make a certified statement showing the amount of money received, from whom, and on what account, the amount paid out, and for what purpose. He shall produce vouchers for all payments made. If the auditor, on examination, finds the statement and vouchers to be correct, he shall give the treasurer a certificate of the fact, which shall prima facie be a discharge of the treasurer for the money paid. When the treasurer's term begins on the first day of September, the annual settlement shall be made by the outgoing treasurer. (92 v. 58.)

Annual settlement by treasurer with county auditor.

If it is evident to the county auditor that the school moneys have been illegally paid out, as they would if paid to any member of a board of education on any contract with such board, or as an employe thereof, it is his duty to refuse the treasurer credit for the same. If moneys have been paid from the wrong fund, as from the school fund, when the law says it must be township·fund, the auditor must not allow credit to such orders. He should insist on their correction by the board, or correct them himself by proper debit and credit. No voucher should be received by the auditor which he has reason to believe a court of law would reject. No paper is a voucher for the payment of money to, A, which has not A's receipt on it, or accompanying it. An order properly made out, but merely marked "paid" by the treasurer, is not a receipt.

The county auditor and the township treasurer have no discretion with reference to the common school fund; but the statutory provisions governing the same must be followed strictly: State, ex rel., v. Zeeb, 9 O. C. C. 13, 6 O. C. D. 70.

SECTION 4771. For making such settlement, the treasurer shall be entitled to receive the sum of one dollar, and also five cents per mile for traveling to and from the county seat, to be paid from the county treasury, on the order of the county auditor. (92 v. 58.)

Compensation for making settlement.

SECTION 4772. If the treasurer of any school district wilfully or negligently fails to make such annual settlement within the time so prescribed, he shall forfeit and pay fifty dollars, to be recovered in a civil action in the name of the state, which amount, when collected, shall be paid into the county treasury and applied to the use of the common schools in his district. In case of such failure, the county auditor shall proceed forthwith to recover the forfeiture by suit against the treasurer before a justice of the peace of the county. (71 v. 9.)

Penalty for failure to make settlement.

A board of education may sue its treasurer for money received by him and not accounted for: Board of Education, v. Milligan, 51 O. S. 115.

SECTION 4773. At the expiration of his term of service, each treasurer shall deliver to his successor in office, all books, papers, money, and other property in his hands belonging to the district, and take duplicate receipts of his successor therefor. One of these he shall deposit with the clerk of the board of education within three days thereafter. (85 v. 192.)

Treasurer to deliver funds to successor.

Penalty for failure or refusal to pay over public money; see Section 13674.

The treasurer acquires custody of the money of the district without acquiring title thereto; and if he has deposited such money in a bank which allows interest thereon, he must pay over such interest to the board of educa-

tion as well as the principal of such fund: Eshelby v. Board of Education, 66 O. **S. 71.**
A verbal agreement between the board of education and the treasurer, whereby the money of the township was loaned to the treasurer is a violation of this section: Board of Education v. Thompson, 33 O. S. 321.

Bond of clerk.

SECTION 4774. Before entering upon the duties of his office, the clerk of each board of education shall execute a bond, in an amount and with surety to be approved by the board, payable to the state, conditioned for the faithful performance of all the official duties required of him. Such bond must be deposited with the president of the board, and a copy thereof, certified by him, shall be filed with the county auditor. (70 v. 195.)

Township clerk is authorized to administer oaths connected with school affairs; see Sec. 3303.
Board cannot authorize clerk to become custodian of tuition funds: 74 O. S. 80.
Duties and powers of clerk: 170 D. N. P. 108, 29 O. C. C. 32 (N. S. 120).

As there is no statutory authorization for the payment by the board of education of the premium on the clerk's or treasurer's bond that expense may not be borne by it.
As there is no duty imposed upon the superintendent of schools or the teachers to attend a national education association, nor upon the members of the board of education or its clerk to attend a meeting of the state association of school boards, and as there is no statutory authorization for the payment of such expenses, the board may not pay the same out of the school funds. — *Attorney General*, 1911-12, p. 430.
A member of the Ohio General Assembly cannot serve as a clerk of the village board of education of which he is a member and receive a salary as such clerk. — *Attorney General*, Opinion No. 177, March 27, 1915.

The clerk of a board of education must furnish a bond in order to qualify: State, ex rel., v. Coon, 4 O. C. C. (N. S.) 560.
A bond which is conditioned that the clerk "shall faithfully perform all of the official duties required of him as clerk of such board," is not broken so as to make the sureties liable because of his failure to pay over tuition funds belonging to such board, the receipt and custody of such funds not being as official duty imposed by statute, even if a rule of the board of education requiring him to receive and keep them: State, ex rel., v. Griffith, 74 O. S. 80.
A condition in a bond that he shall "faithfully disburse according to law all such funds as shall from time ot time come into his hands," includes not merely cash received by him, but also drafts and certificates of deposit which he received as cash, and which when received would have been paid upon presentation: Reed v. Board of Education, 39 O. S. 635.

Annual statistical report of board of education.

SECTION 4775. The clerk of each board of education shall prepare the annual report of the receipts and expenditures of school money and the statistical statement in reference to the schools, required by law to be made by the board, and transmit it to the county auditor on or before the first day of September. But in each school district having a superintendent of schools, such report, except the receipts and expenditures of money, shall be made by the superintendent. (97 v. 368.)

Penalty for not making report; see Sec. 7790.
The board of education should see that the reports required by this section are filed before allowing compensation to the clerk for his services.

Publication of statement of receipts and expenditures by clerk.

SECTION 4776. Except city districts, the board of education of each district shall require the clerk of the board annually, ten days prior to the election, to prepare and post at the place or places of holding such elections, or publish in some newspaper of general circulation in the district, an itemized statement of all money received and disbursed by the treasurer of the board, within the school year next preceding. (97 v. 368.)

> The word "publish" as employed in section 7785, General Code, leaves it discretionary with the board of education to publish said annual report in any manner it sees fit, and a publication in a newspaper of such annual report is fully authorized by said section. — *Attorney General*, 1911-12, p. 301.
>
> A city school district is not authorized to pay for publication in a newspaper of a statement of receipts and expenditures for the year.
>
> When such action is performed,
>
> 1. The newspaper cannot be held, as the payment was voluntary.
>
> 2. The members of the board of education who voted for the move are guilty of a misfeasance and are subject under the terms of section 286, General Code, to civil action by the proper legal officer for a recovery.
>
> 3. The president, clerk and treasurer, acting in good faith, in their respective capacities performed merely ministerial acts and are therefore not liable. — *Attorney General*, 1911-12, p. 272.

SECTION 4777. At the expiration of his term of office, each clerk shall deliver to his successor all books and papers in his hands relating to the affairs of his district, including certificates, and copies thereof, and reports of school statistics, filed by teachers. (70 v. 195.) *Clerk to deliver books, etc., to successor.*

SECTION 4778. The auditor of each county shall furnish to the clerk and treasurer of each school district in his county a suitable blank book, made according to the form prescribed by the bureau of inspection and supervision of public offices, in which each must keep an account of the school funds of his district. (97 v. 368.) *How treasurer and clerk to keep accounts.*

SECTION 4779. The clerk's account shall show the amounts certified by the county auditor to be due the district, all sums paid to the treasurer from other sources on his order, and all orders drawn by him on the treasurer, upon what funds and for what purposes drawn. (97 v. 368.) *Clerk's account.*

> This section shows that the clerk is simply an auditing officer to keep a check upon the treasurer; and is not authorized to receive or disburse miscellaneous funds: State v. Cottle, 4 O. N. P. (N. S.) 145, 17 O. D. (N. P.) 108.
>
> Provisions of this section require that all orders issued for money shall show not only out of what fund such payment is to be made, but also the purpose thereof: State, ex rel., v. Board of Education, 3 O. N. P. (N. S.) 401, 16 O. D. (N. P.) 386.

SECTION 284. The bureau of inspection and supervision of public offices, shall examine each public office. Such examination of township, village and school district offices shall be made at least once in every two years and all other examination shall be made at least once a year, except that the offices of justices of the peace shall be examined at such times as the bureau shall determine. On examination, inquiry shall be made into the methods, accuracy and legality of the accounts, records, files and re- *Biennial and annual examinations.*

ports of the office, whether the laws, ordinances and orders pertaining to the office have been observed, and whether the requirements of the bureau have been complied with. (103 v. 506.)

When there is a deficiency in the collection of assessments in anticipation of which bonds have been issued, it is not lawful to issue notes or bonds in anticipation of the subsequent assessment. Such assessments when subsequently collected should be paid out of the sinking fund to supply deficiency created by the payment of the bonds. If the sinking fund has not money enough in it to pay the bonds when due refunding bonds should be issued. — *Attorney General*, Opinion No. 1143, 1914.

There is no statutory authority for the auditor of state to charge back against state institutions the cost of examinations made by examiners from the auditor of state's office, as is done in the examination of taxing districts. Section 288, General Code, refers to taxing districts, and no state institution can be considered a taxing district. — *Attorney General*, 1913, p. 159.

Treasurer's account.

SECTION 4780. The treasurer's accounts shall show the amounts received from the county treasurer, all sums received from other sources on the order of the clerk, the amounts paid out, and from what funds and for what purposes paid. A separate account of each fund must be kept, and each account balanced at the close of the school year, and the balance in the treasurer's hands belonging to each fund shown. (97 v. 368.)

This and the preceding sections show that the county auditor, township clerk and the township treasurer have no discretion with reference to the common school funds, but that the statutes with reference thereto must be complied with strictly: State, ex rel., v. Zeeb, 9 O. C. C. 13, 6 O. C. D. 70.

Certain deposits unlawful.

SECTION 12875. The provisions of section twelve thousand, eight hundred and seventy-three shall not make it unlawful for the treasurer of a township, municipal corporation, board of education, or cemetery association, to deposit public money with a person, firm, company, or corporation organized to do a banking business under the laws of this state or the United States, but the deposit of such funds in such bank shall not release such treasurer from liability for loss which may occur thereby. Nor shall the provisions of section twelve thousand eight hundred and seventy-three, make it unlawful for a county auditor, county treasurer, probate judge, sheriff, clerk of courts, or recorder, to deposit fees and trust funds coming into their custody as such officers as above, until such time as said aforesaid officers are required to make payment of the official earnings of their offices, so deposited into their respective fee funds as required by section twenty-nine hundred and eighty-three, and until such time as the trust funds, so held by them in their official capacities, may be paid to the person, persons, firms, or corporations, entitled to same, and any interest earned and paid upon said deposits shall be apportioned to, and become a part of said fees or trust funds, and shall in no instance accrue to, and be received by, the official making said deposits, for his own use. (106 v. 556.)

SECTION 12878. Whoever, being a member of the council of a municipal corporation, or an officer, agent, clerk or servant of such corporation, or board or department thereof, or an officer, clerk or servant of a board of education, knowingly diverts, appropriates or applies funds, or a part of a fund raised by taxation or otherwise, to any use or purpose other than that for which it was raised or appropriated, or knowingly diverts appropriates or applies money borrowed, or a bond of the corporation or part of the proceeds of such bond, to any use or purpose other than that for which such loan was made, or bond issued, shall be imprisoned in the penitentiary not less than one year nor more than twenty-one years and fined in double the amount of money or other property embezzled. (73 v. 116).

Embezzlement by municipal and school officers.

. The object of this section is to punish as an offense the diversion, appropriation or application of the funds of a municipal corporation, or of a board of education by an officer or agent there named, to a use other than that for which the funds were raised; a conversion of the money to his own use by the officer or agent named in an offense under G. C., Sec. 12873, punishing the embezzlement of public money, and is not within the language or spirit of the above section: State v. Johnson, 53 O. S. 307.

SECTION 4781. The board of education of each school district shall fix the compensation of its clerk and treasurer, which shall be paid from the contingent fund of the district. If they are paid annually, the order for the payment of their salaries shall not be drawn until they present to the board of education a certificate from the county auditor stating that all reports required by law have been filed in his office. If the clerk and treasurer are paid semi-annually, quarterly, or monthly, the last payment on their salaries previous to August thirty-first, must not be made until all reports required by law have been filed with the county auditor and his certificate presented to the board of education as required herein. (97 v 368).

Compensation of treasurer and clerk.

Contrary to the general rule of policy that a member of a board may not hold a salaried position under such board, special provision of statute makes it possible for a member of a board of education to serve as its clerk and receive the salary for both positions. — *Attorney General,* 1911-12, p. 1089.

Though the office of township treasurer is of definite duration, the office of the same individual as treasurer of the school board is of indefinite duration and may be terminated at any time by the school board through the establishment of a depository. — *Attorney General,* 1911-12, p. 519.

A township clerk or a township treasurer may decline to act as clerk and treasurer respectively of the township board of education, and if either does so decline to act, then the board may fill the vacancy by election, and fix the salary of said incumbent.

A township clerk cannot appoint a deputy to do the work of the clerk. — *Attorney General,* 1912, p. 1108.

Section 4782, General Code, as amended, 104 O. L., 159, provides for creating a depository for the school moneys of the school district, in which event the board of education, by resolution adopted by a vote of a majority of its members, shall dispense with the treasurer of the school moneys belonging to such school district. Said section carries the provision that upon the establishment of such depository, and the dispensation of the treasury on the part of the board of education, thereupon the clerk of the board of education of such district shall perform all the services, discharge all the duties and be subject to all obligation required by law of the treasurer of such school district.

Upon consideration of Section 4763 to 4784, General Code, the clerk of the board of education can receive extra compensation for performing the duties of treasurer of such board, and the board of education has the legal right to fix the compensation of such clerk, when he is required to perform the added duties of treasurer of the board of education, because of the dispensation of said treasurer under Section 4782, General Code. — *Attorney General,* Opinion No. 1141, September 12, 1914.

A member of the Ohio General Assembly cannot serve as a clerk of the village board of education of which he is a member and receive a salary as such clerk. — *Attorney General,* Opinion No. 177, March 27, 1915.

An earlier form of this statute was cited in Board of Education v. Eshelby, 6 O. N. P. 117, 9 O. D. (N. P.) 214.

When treasurer of school funds may be dispensed with.

SECTION 4782. When a depository has been provided for the school moneys of a district, as authorized by law, the board of education of the district, by resolution adopted by a vote of a majority of its members, shall dispense with a treasurer of the school moneys, belonging to such school district. In such case, the clerk of the board of education of a district shall perform all the services, discharge all the duties and be subject to all the obligations required by law of the treasurer of such school district. (104 v 158).

From the principles established by the decision in the case of State ex rel. Stolzenbacher vs. Felty, Auditor, No. 9372, decided by the supreme court in 1905, but not reported.

1. The treasurer of a city, village or township may by failing to qualify as treasurer of the school funds refuse to serve as such treasurer.

2. If the township clerk fails to qualify as clerk of the township board of education, such failure does not affect his status as township clerk.

3. If a township treasurer resigns as treasurer of the school funds the board of education has the right if it chooses, to accept his resignation, and in such cases may elect a successor to him as treasurer of the school fund.

4. If by reason of the establishment of a depository, the treasurer of the school district is dispensed with according to law, and the clerk gives the additional bond required of him as treasurer by virtue of section 4783, General Code, he will then be obliged to perform the duties of the treasurer without extra compensation unless he resigns. He may, however, refuse to qualify as such treasurer and the board may elect a substitute.

5. The refusal of a township clerk to qualify for the duties which devolve upon him by the establishment of a depository under section 4783, General Code, will not in any way affect his status as township clerk, and under such circumstances the board may select a substitute to act as treasurer. — *Attorney General,* 1911-12, p. 289.

Though the office of township treasurer is of definite duration, the office of the same individual as treasurer of the school board is of indefinite duration and may be terminated at any time by the school board through the establishment of a depository. — *Attorney General,* 1911-12, p. 519.

By specific provision of Section 4747, General Code, a member of a board of education may at the same time, act as its clerk and receive compensation for both services.

The position of members of the board of education and treasurer of the board are incompatible, however.

Under Section 4782, General Code, when a depository is established, the clerk performs the duties of the treasurer and a member of the school board may, in this case, perform such duties. — *Attorney General*, 1912, p. 1776.

As the members of the school board must approve the bond of the treasurer and vote upon the question of increasing or changing the same or of requiring additional sureties thereon, the office of member of the board and treasurer of the board are incompatible and may not be held by one individual.

A treasurer of a corporation may refuse to act as treasurer of the school board without thereby affecting his position as treasurer of the corporation. — *Attorney General*, 1912, p. 1160.

Section 4782, General Code, as amended, 104 O. L., 159, provides for creating a depository for the school moneys of the school district, in which event the board of education, by resolution adopted by a vote of a majority of its members, shall dispense with the treasurer of the school moneys belonging to such school district. Said section carries the provision that upon the establishment of such depository, and the dispensation of the treasury on the part of the board of education, thereupon the clerk of the board of education of such district shall perform all the services, discharge all the duties and be subject to all obligations required by law of the treasurer of such school district.

Upon consideration of Section 4763 to 4784, General Code, the clerk of the board of education can receive extra compensation for performing the duties of treasurer of such board, and the board of education has the legal right to fix the compensation of such clerk, when he is required to perform the added duties of treasurer of the board of education, because of the dispensation of said treasurer under Section 4782, General Code. — *Attorney General*, Opinion No. 1141, September 12, 1914.

When a depository has been provided by a city board of education for its school funds, as authorized by law, the board of education of the district must dispense with the treasurer, and the clerk of the board of the city school district performs all the services and duties of such treasurer. — *Attorney General*, Opinion No. 45, 1915.

Under the provisions of Section 4782, General Code, it is mandatory upon the board of education to dispense with the office of treasurer of school moneys when a depository has been provided therefor. — *Attorney General*, Opinion No. 1113, 1914.

Village and township treasurers continued to act as treasurers of the school funds of their respective village and township school districts until they were superseded by the county treasurer by virtue of Section 4763, General Code, as amended, 104 O. L., 159, and such treasurers continued to draw whatever salary they were entitled to until so superseded by the county treasurers at the time said section became effective.

The clerk of the school district, however, would continue to act as the treasurer of such village and township school districts if a depository had been previously provided and the treasurer dispensed with by the respective boards of education. Under said section, 4763, supra, the county treasurers continue to act as the treasurers of the respective village and rural school district funds until such time as a depository is established for such funds, in accordance with Section 4782. General Code, 104 O. L., 159. — *Attorney General*, Opinion No. 1346, 1914.

It is not necessary for school depository banks to give new bonds to bind sureties in districts where school treasurers have been dispensed with under Section 4782, 104 O. L., 158, in case the bonds held by the respective boards of education bear a date prior to the date of the resolution dispensing with the school treasurer, and the terms of such bonds have not as yet expired.

It is necessary for the clerk of the school board to give a new bond when such clerk assumes the duty of the treasurer of the school funds.

It is not necessary for a county treasurer to give a bond as school treasurer, when he becomes the treasurer of the school fund of village or rural districts. — *Attorney General*, Opinion No. 1382, 1915.

Construction of Section 4782, General Code, as amended, 104 O. L., 159, relative to the establishment of depositories for school funds of school districts, and the dispensing of the treasurers of the school moneys belonging to such school districts, when such depositories are established. Said section further provides that the clerk of the board of education of such district shall thereupon assume the duties of such treasurers.

If the board of education fails to establish a depository as required by said Section 4782, supra, then an action of mandamus lies against such board to compel such board to comply with the provisions of said section, and any person interested in the schools may bring such action in the name of the state, as provided in Sections 12296 and 12287, General Code. — *Attorney General*, Opinion No. 1261, 1914.

When clerk shall perform the duties of treasurer.

SECTION 4783. When the treasurer is so dispensed with, all the duties and obligations required by law of the county auditor, county treasurer or other officer or person relating to the school moneys of the district shall be complied with by dealing with the clerk of the board of education thereof. Before entering upon such duties, the clerk shall give an additional bond equal in amount and in the same manner prescribed by law for the treasurer of the school district (99 v 206).

From the principles established by the decision in the case of Statae ex. rel. Stolzenbacher vs. Felty, Auditor, No. 9372, decided by the supreme court in 1905, but not recorded.

    1. The treasurer of a city, village or township may by failing to qualify as treasurer of the school funds refuse to serve as such treasurer.

    2. If the township clerk fails to qualify as clerk of the township board of education, such failure does not affect his satus as township clerk.

    3. If a township treasurer resigns as treasurer of the school funds the board of education has the right if it chooses to accept his resignation and in such cases may elect a successor to him as treasurer of the school funds.

    4. If by reason of the establishment of a depository, the treasurer of the school district is dispensed with according to law, and the clerk gives additional bond required of him as treasurer by virtue of section 4783, General Code, he will then be obliged to perform the duties of the treasurer without extra compensation unless he resigns. He may, however, refuse to qualify as such treasurer and the board may elect a substitute.

    5. The refusal of a township clerk to qualify for the duties which devolve upon him by the establishment of a depository under Section 4783, General Code, will not in any way affect his status as township clerk, and under such circumstances the board may select a substitute to act as treasurer. — *Attorney General*, 1911-12, p. 289.

SECTION 4784. If for any reason a depository in such district ceases to act as custodian of the school moneys, they shall be placed in the custody of the treasurer of the city or county in which the school district is located as provided in section 4763. Such moneys shall be held and disbursed by the treasurer in all respects as required by law until another depository is provided for such moneys. Thereupon he shall place such money in the depository and his duties and obligations relating thereto shall then cease. (104 v 158).

Where moneys' placed when depository ceases to act.

TITLE XIV. PUBLIC ELECTIONS.

Election of members of the board of education.

SECTION 4838. All elections for members of boards of education shall be held on the first Tuesday after the first Monday in November in the odd numbered years. (97 v. 40 § 2.)

The statutes do not require or authorize publication of a resolution of a board of education passed for the purpose of submitting to electors the question of issuing bonds for construction of a school building.

Under section 7625, General Code, however, notices of the election shall be given in the manner provided by law for school elections, i. e., under section 4839, General Code, such publication may be made by posting written or printed notices in five public places in the district at least ten days before the holding of the election, or it may be published in a newspaper of general circulation in the district, once at least ten days before holding of the election. — *Attorney General*, 1913, p. 1515.

When a newly incorporated village is formed with a tax duplicate of more than $100,000, such village becomes ipso facto a village school district, but when such village fails to elect a board of education when the village officers are elected, a special election for members of such board of education is not authorized by law. Such members can only be elected in the odd numbered years.

When in a township there exists two or more districts unconnected and the village school district and the further special district is organized, the two subdistricts and the part of the township not included in the village district or the special district, will all comprise parts of the township school district and will still remain under the jurisdiction of the township board of education. The village district also will remain under the control of the township board.

Under section 4748, General Code, when three out of five members of a township board of education become disqualified for that office by reason of the formation of a special school district, the two remaining members may fill such vacancies in the township board.

Inasmuch as there are no officers upon whom rests the ministerial duty to organize the village district or to call an election for members of its board of education, such election may not be enforced by mandamus. The organization may be brought about by a sufficient number of electors taking steps to become candidates for the village board of education at the November election and the board of elections would be required to place their names upon the ballots and hold an election therefor. — *Attorney General*, 1913, p. 460.

For a former special statute with reference to the election of members of a board of education, see Board v. Walker, 71 O. S. 169.

132

SECTION 4839. The clerk of each board of education shall publish a notice of all school elections in a newspaper of general circulation in the district or post written or printed notices thereof in five public places in the district at least ten days before the holding of such election. Such notices shall specify the time and place of the election, the number of members of the board of education to be elected, and the term for which they are to be elected, or the nature of the question to be voted upon. (97 v. 354 § 2.)

Notice of school elections.

The provision of Section 4726, General Code, as amended, 104 O. L., 139, taken in connection with the provision of Section 4839, General Code, authorizes the calling of a special election in a rural school district for the purpose of submitting the question of centralization to the vote of the qualified electors of such district. — *Attorney General,* Opinion No. 184, March 30, 1915.

As the deputy state. supervisor of elections is required by Section 4998 to publish a list of the names of candidates for all school districts it is legal to pay out of the county treasury the expenses of making such publication.

It is not necessary for the clerk of the board of education to be furnished the names of candidates for members of the board. — *Attorney General,* 1911-12, p. 369.

The statutes do not require or authorize publication of a resolution of a board of education passed for the purpose of submitting to electors the question of issuing bonds for construction of a school building.

Under section 7625, General Code, however, notices of the election shall be given in the manner provided by law for school elections, i. e., under section 4839, General Code, such publication may be made by posting written or printed notices in five public places in the district at least ten days before the holding of the election, or it may be published in a newspaper of general circulation in the district, once at least ten days before holding of the election. — *Attorney General,* 1913, p. 1515.

When a newly incorporated village is formed with a tax duplicate of more than $100,000, such village becomes ipso facto a village school district, but when such village fails to elect a board of education when the village officers are elected, a special election for members of such board of education is not authorized by law. Such members can only be elected in the odd numbered years.

When in a township there exists two or more districts unconnected and the village school district and the further special district is organized. the two subdistricts and the part of the township not included in the village district or the special district, will all comprise parts of the township school district and will still remain under the jurisdiction of the township board of education. The village district also will remain under the control of the township board.

Under section 4748, General Code, when three out of five members of a township board of education become disqualified for that office by reason of the formation of a special school district, the two remaining members may fill such vacancies in the township board.

Inasmuch as there are no officers upon whom rests the ministerial duty to organize the village district or to call an election for members of its board of education. such election may not be enforced by mandamus. The organization may be brought about by a sufficient number of electors taking steps to become candidates for the village board of education at the November election and the board of elections would be required to place their names upon the ballots and hold an election therefor. — *Attorney General,* 1913, p. 460.

Qualifications of elector.

SECTION 4861. Every male citizen of the United States, who is of the age of twenty-one years or over, and possesses the qualifications in regard to residence hereinafter provided, shall be entitled to vote at all elections. (Cons. Art. V. § 1.)

Within the meaning of an act creating the office of board of workhouse directors, women are not electors: State, ex. rel., v. Rust, 4 O. C. C. 329, O. C. D. 577.

Only a citizen of the United States is a qualified elector, and as such is eligible to the office of village marshal or village councilman: State, ex rel., v. Collister, 6 O. C. C. (N. S.) 33, 17 O. C. D. 529.

When women may Vote.

SECTION 4862. Every woman, born in the United States or who is the wife or daughter of a citizen of the United States, who is over twenty-one years of age and possesses the necessary qualifications in regard to residence hereinafter provided for men shall be entitled to vote and to be voted for for member of the board of education and upon no other question. (97 v. 354 § 3.)

Under Article 15, Section 4 of the Constitution, a woman may not be elected to or appointed to any office in this state. Under Article 6, Section 2, and Article 1, Section 7 of the Constitution, however, through the powers therein conferred upon the General Assembly to secure a thorough and efficient system of common schools and to encourage schools and the means of instruction, the provision of Section 4862, General Code, permitting a woman to serve as member of the board of education and to vote for members thereof, is held to be valid and constitutional.

Since, therefore, women may serve on the board of education, and since, furthermore, Section 4747, General Code, provides that in any district other than the township school district, a member of a board of education may be elected clerk of the board, a woman in this district may be so elected clerk, under authority of this statute.

The statutes do not confer the right, however, of a woman to serve as clerk of a township, and since the statutes require such clerk to act as clerk to the school board, a woman may not serve in the latter capacity. The statutes, furthermore, have not made provision for service as treasurer of a school board by a woman and she may, therefore, not serve in that capacity. — *Attorney General*, 1913, p. 466.

This statute is valid and constitutional, since it is within the power of the legislature to provide for establishing and maintaining common schools; and not being within the restrictions of Art. V, Sec. 1 of the Ohio constitution; State, ex. rel., v. Columbus, 9 O. C. C. 134.

An alien woman who has married a citizen of the United States and possesses the other requisite qualifications, may vote at a school election: In re Whitehead, 8 O. F. D. 348, 33 Bull. 157.

Registration of women.

SECTION 4940. The provisions of this chapter relating to registration shall apply to women upon whom the right to vote for member of the board of education is conferred by law, but the names of such women may be placed on a separate list. (97 v. 254 § 3.)

Nominations of candidates for board of education.

SECTION 4997. Nominations of candidates for the office of member of the board of education may be made by nomination papers, signed in the aggregate for each candidate by not less than twenty-five qualified electors of either sex of the school district, except in city school districts, such nomination papers shall be signed by petitioners not less in number than one for every one hundred persons who voted at the next preceding general election in such city. (97 v. 340.)

As the deputy state supervisor of elections is required by Section 4998 to publish a list of the names of candidates for all school districts it is legal to pay out of the county treasury the expenses of making such publication.

It is not necessary for the clerk of the board of education to be furnished the names of candidates for members of the board. — *Attorney General*, 1911-12, p. 369.

SECTION 4998. When nominations of candidates for member of the board of education have been made by nomination papers filed with the board of deputy state supervisors, as herein provided, such board of deputy state supervisors shall publish on two different days prior to the election a list of the names of such candidates in two newspapers of opposite politics in the school district, if there is such printed and published therein. If no newspaper is printed in such school district, the board shall post such list in at least five public places therein. (97 v. 340.) *Names of nominees for board published.*

As the deputy state supervisor of elections is required by Section 4998 to publish a list of the names of candidates for all school districts, it is legal to pay out of the county treasury the expenses of making such publication.

It is not necessary for the clerk of the board of education to be furnished the names of candidates for members of the board. — *Attorney General*, 1911-12, p. 369.

SECTION 5016. Except as in this chapter provided, the names of all candidates to be voted for on the first Tuesday after the first Monday in November shall be placed upon the same ballot. (99 v. 399 § 3.) *Names of candidates shall be placed on same ballot.*

SECTION 5029. In election precincts composed of a township or a part thereof, or a municipality or a part thereof, there shall be provided for all elections separate ballots for each precinct, so as to enable electors residing in such precinct to cast their votes for the proper candidates in such precinct; and there shall be provided separate ballots for each district portion of such precinct which shall contain the names of the candidates for members of the board of education for whom electors residing in such district are entitled to vote. (98 v. 234 § 15.) *Separate ballots for each precinct.*

Cited in construing 102 O. I.. 5, State v. Miller, 87 O. S. 12.

SECTION 5032. The names of candidates for members of the board of education of a school district, however nominated, shall be placed on one independent and separate ballot without any designation whatever, except for member of board of education and the number of members to be elected. (98 v. 116 § 1.) *Ballots for school board.*

SECTION 5033. The ballots for members of the board of education shall be prepared and printed as follows: The whole number of ballots to be printed for the school district shall be divided by the number of candidates for mem- *How ballot for school board printed.*

ber of board of education of the district, and the quotient
so obtained shall be the number of ballots in each series
of ballots to be printed. The name of candidates shall be
arranged in alphabetical order and the first series of ballots
printed. Then the first name shall be placed last and the
net series printed, and so shall the process be repeated
until each name shall have been first. These ballots shall
then be combined in tablets with no two of the same
order of names together, except when there is but one
candidate. (98 v. 116 § 2.)

> Referred to as showing that voting machines do not allow the rotation
> of the names of candidates for the board of education: State, ex rel., v.
> Board of Education, 80 O. S. 471.

School districts in cities. SECTION 5034. In city school districts, the ballots for
each subdistrict shall contain the names of the candidates
for member of the board of education from such subdistrict and also the names of the candidates to be elected at
large. (97 v. 354 § 1.)

Poll books and tally sheets for school elections. SECTION 5049. There will be separate poll books and
tally sheets for all elections for school purposes and the
ballots of the electors at such elections shall be deposited
in a separate ballot box. (97 v. 354 § 1.)

Canvass of vote in school elections. SECTION 5120. In school elections, the returns shall
be made by the judges and clerks of each precinct to the
clerk of the board of education of the district, not less
than five days after the election. Such board shall canvass such returns at a meeting to be held on the second
Monday after the election, and the result thereof shall be
entered upon the records of the board. (97 v. 354 § 1.)

> From the language of relative statutory sections, and from
> the fact that the subject is treated under the head of schools, and
> from the further fact that the question is a purely local one,
> affecting only the voters of the school district in which it is held,
> a special election held upon the question of issuing bonds for
> school purposes is to be considered a school election under section
> 5120, and returns thereof should be made to the clerk of the board
> of education of the district, and such board is the authority that
> shall first canvass said returns. — *Attorney General,* 1911-12, p. 507.
> The vote at a special election at which is submitted a proposi-
> tion for the issuance of bonds for the erection of a school house,
> is governed by Section 5120, General Code, and should be can-
> vassed by the Board of Education of the district as therein pro-
> vided. — *Attorney General,* Opinion No. 46, 1915.

How results determined in certain cases. SECTION 5121. In the canvass of the vote for members of the board of education, or assessors of real prop-
erty, the person having the highest number of votes shall
be declared elected, and the next highest, and so on, until
the number required to be elected shall have been selected
from the number having the highest number of votes. If
any number of persons greater than the number to be
elected at such election have the highest and an equal number of votes, the board making the canvass shall determine
by lot which of the persons shall be duly elected. (100
v. 81 § 1.)

PART SECOND

CIVIL.

137

TITLE I. TAXATION.

CHAPTER 12.

LEVYING TAXES.

LIMITATION ON TAX RATE.

SECTION 5649-1. In any taxing district, the taxing authority shall, within the limitations now prescribed by law, levy a tax sufficient to provide for sinking fund and interest purposes for all bonds issued by any political subdivision, which tax shall be placed before and in preference to all other items, and for the full amount thereof. (104 v. 12.)

Levy for sinking fund and interest.

SECTION 5649-1a. All bonds heretofore issued by any political subdivision for a lawful purpose which have been sold for not less than par and accrued interest and the proceeds thereof paid into the treasury, shall be held to be legal, valid and binding obligations of the political sub-division issuing the same. (104 v. 12.)

Former bonds shall be legal.

SECTION 5649-2. Except as otherwise provided in section 5649-4 and section 5649-5 of the General Code, the aggregate amount of taxes that may be levied on the taxable property in any county, township, city, village, school district or other taxing district, shall not in any one year exceed ten mills on each dollar of the tax valuation of the taxable property of such county, township, city, village. school district or other taxing district for that year, and such levies in addition thereto for sinking fund and interest purposes as may be necessary to provide for any indebtedness heretofore incurred or any indebtedness that may hereafter be incurred by a vote of the people. (103 v. 552.)

Tax levy limitation.

Sections 5649-2 et. seq. limit rate of taxation and repeal by implication existing conflicting statutes. Rabe v. Canton Sch. Dist. (Bd. of Ed.) 88 O. S. 403.

Act limiting tax rate not law providing for tax levy and not effective for ninety days. State v. Milroy, 88 O. S. 301.

Limit rate of taxation and repeal by implication existing conflicting statutes. Rabe v. Canton School Dist. (Bd. of Ed.) 88 O. S. 403.

ited in construing Art. 12, Sec. 2. Link v. Karb, 24 Dec. 230 (14 N. S. 244).

Under section 5649-5b, General Code, interest and sinking fund levies to pay for indebtedness created subsequent to June 2, 1911, under authorization of a popular vote, are excluded only from the ten mill limitation of the Smith one per cent. law.

Under section 5649-4, General Code, the taxing authorities are authorized to exceed all limitations for certain emergencies referred to therein.

The destruction of a school house is not such an emergency, however, and therefore when, because of such a casualty, it becomes necessary to borrow money and issue bonds, the amounts authorized by vote of electors on the question of additional taxes and bond issues necessary, must be within the limitation of fifteen mills. — *Attorney General*, 1911-12, p. 1357.

Interest and sinking fund levies, whether for the retirement of bonds issued or for indebtedness incurred prior to the passage of the Smith law by the vote of the people or otherwise, are within the fifteen mill limitation of said law. — *Attorney General*, 1911-12, p. 1377.

The limitation of the Smith law with respect to the amount raised for all purposes in the year 1910 refers to the amount which may be levied by the state, county, school district, township and municipality altogether, and therefore, the only effect of the fact that a municipality had made no levy whatever during the year 1910 would be in allowing the needs of said municipality for 1911, to reduce the amounts allowed to other subdivisions from taxation on the property of said municipality. — *Attorney General*, 1911-12, p. 1451.

A levy of one mill by the board of education imposed annually for the purpose of reimbursing a library association for services to the public in pursuance of a contract between the board and the association, is within the interior limitations of the Smith law and is not a "levy for sinking fund and interest purposes necessary to provide for indebtedness created prior to the passage" of the Smith law.

The obligation which rests upon the board is not an indebtedness within the meaning of the statute nor is there an "impairment of the obligation of contract" in the effect of the Smith law upon such procedures. — *Attorney General*, 1912, p. 1578.

The taxing authorities of a taxing district may levy a tax in addition to that which may be levied within the ten mill levy, now imposed by the amended section as section 5649-2, for the purpose of providing for indebtedness incurred prior to June 2, 1911, or after that date by a vote of the people, and for no other interest and sinking fund levies whatever, except those specifically authorized to be levied by the earlier provision of section 5649-2, General Code. However the budget commission act does not become effective until ninety days after its filing in the office of the secretary of state by the governor.

The action of the budget commission to be taken in the year 1913, is to be governed by the provisions of the original Smith one per cent. law and not by the provisions of House Bill No. 500, and the limitations of section 5649-3, which is repealed by House Bill No. 500, will be operative upon the 1913 levies. — *Attorney General*, 1913, p. 645.

An ordinance authorizing an issue of bonds for extending, enlarging and improving a municipal water works plant, provides for the levy of a sinking fund, and interest tax sufficient to pay the bonds. The fact that the bonds were authorized by vote of the people are together not sufficient to determine whether the issue is to be considered in arriving at the debt limitations of the city under the Longworth Act. — *Attorney General*, Opinion 1033, 1914.

The meaning of the words "heretofore" and "hereafter" occurring in Section 5649-2, General Code, originally enacted on May 31, 1911, and approved on June 2, 1911, but subsequently amended April 16, 1913, by an act which was approved by the governor May 6, 1913, filed in the office of the Secretary of State on May 9, 1913, and which is the case of State ex rel. Schreiber v. Milroy, 88 O. S., is that the original meaning of these words as established as the first enactment of the section was not changed when it was amended, and that the day to which the amended section refers is still June 2, 1909. — *Attorney General,* Opinion No. 900, 1914.

The statutes authorizing the township trustees, under certain circumstances, to levy certain taxes for road improvement purposes, remain in force generally, notwithstanding the enactment of the Smith Law, although the special limitation upon the tax authorized by the original statute has been supplanted by the Smith Law limitations; and in particular that this tax must be levied subject to the ten mill limitation law. — *Attorney General,* Opinion 1222, 1914.

The amendment to Section 5649-2, a part of the so-called Smith law and affecting the ten mill limitation, though subsequent to amendment to Section 5649-5b, imposing the fifteen mill limitation, is to be read together with the letter so that sinking fund and interest levies necessary to provide for previously incurred bonded indebtedness, such indebtedness authorized by vote of the people is still subject to the fifteen mill limitation.—*Attorney General,* Opinion 956, 1914.

The taxing authorities of any taxing district may levy taxes not exceeding the aggregate of ten mills on each dollar of the tax valuation of the property of such taxing district for state, county, township, school and municipal purposes, subject to the further limitation of the paragraphs following.

In addition thereto levies may be made for sinking fund and interest purposes necessary to provide for any indebtedness incurred before the passage of said act, and any indebtedness that may be incurred after the passage of said act by a vote of the people.

In case such levy for the year 1911 shall produce an amount greater than the amount of taxes levied in the year 1910, then such levy of ten mills on the dollar must be reduced to such a rate as will produce no more money than the taxes levied for the year 1910.

A municipal corporation may levy for general purposes, as provided in preceding paragraphs 1, 2, and 3, an aggregate of five mills on the taxable property within such corporation only in the event that such levy of five mills, when added to the levy of state, county, township and school purposes, shall not in the aggregate exceed ten mills on the dollar, and whenever such levies exceed ten mills on the dollar, then it is the duty of the budget commission to scale said levies down in proportion to the amount of each until the total levies so made aggregate ten mills or less.

The right to levy five mills on the taxable property within such corporation is further limited by the provision that if said levy of ten mills for the year 1911 will produce more taxes than were levied in the year 1910, then such levy should again be scaled by the budget commission until the same will produce no larger revenue than the taxes levied in the year 1910.

The five mills which, subject to the qualifications hereinbefore defined, may be levied by a municipal corporation for corporation purposes, are exclusive of such levies for interest and sinking fund purposes as are or may be necessary to provide for any municipal indebtedness incurred prior to the passage of the act of June 2, 1911, and any indebtedness thereafter incurred by a vote of the people.

The supreme court, therefore, found that the relator is entitled to a peremptory writ of mandamus commanding the auditor of Lucas county, defendant herein, to ascertain the rate of taxes necessary to produce the amounts to him certified by the budget commission of Lucas county, provided that the aggregate (exclusive of the levy for the sinking fund and interest purposes, for indebtedness heretofore incurred, and indebtedness that may have been incurred by a vote of the people) shall not exceed the rate of ten mills, and the total fund raised thereby, including the amount necessary for the sinking fund and interest as aforesaid, shall not exceed the amount raised in the year 1910, then to enter the same upon the tax duplicate of Lucas county. Also, that he ascertain the rate of the levy necessary for sinking fund and interest purposes to provide for indebtedness incurred before the passage of said act and any indebtedness that may have been incurred since the passage of the act by a vote of the people, if any, and add such levy to the tax duplicate in addition to said ten mills, but the total of both levies not to exceed the total sum levied in the year 1910.

It was therefore ordered, adjudged and decreed that a peremptory writ of mandamus issue against the defendant, as auditor of Lucas county, commanding him to make levies as provided herein: State, ex rel., v. Sanzenbacher, 84 O. S. 504.

The only change made in the original Section 5649-2, General Code, by the amendment of May 6, 1913 (103 O. L. 552) is the elimination of the part of the original section that is not included in the amendment. The words "heretofore" and "hereafter" found in both refer to the date of the passage of the original act June 2, 1911: State, ex rel., v. Speigel et al., 91 O. S. 12.

SECTION 5649-3a. On or before the first Monday in June, each year, the county commissioners of each county, the council of each municipal corporation, the trustees of each township, each board of education and all other boards or officers authorized by law to levy taxes, within the county, except taxes for state purposes, shall submit or cause to be submitted to the county auditor an annual budget, setting forth in itemized form an estimate stating the amount of money needed for their wants for the incoming year, and for each month thereof. Such annual budgets shall specifically set forth:

(1) The amount to be raised for each and every purpose allowed by law for which it is desired to raise money for the incoming year.

(2) The balance standing to the credit or debit of the several funds at the end of the last fiscal year.

(3) The monthly expenditures from each fund in the twelve months and the monthly expenditures from all funds in the twelve months of the last fiscal year.

(4) The annual expenditures from each fund for each year of the last five fiscal years.

(5) The monthly average of such expenditures from each of the several funds for the last fiscal year, and also the total monthly average of all of them for the last five fiscal years.

(6) The amount of money received from any other source and available for any purpose in each of the last five fiscal years, together with an estimate of the probable amount that may be received during the incoming year, from such source or sources.

(7) The amount of the bonded indebtedness setting out each issue and the purpose for which issued, the date of issue and the date of maturity, the original amount issued and the amount outstanding, the rate of interest, the sum necessary for interest and sinking fund purposes, and the amount required for all interest and sinking fund purposes for the incoming year.

(8) The amount of all indebtedness incurred under authority of section 5649-4 and the amount of such additional taxes as may have been authorized as provided in section 5649-5 of the General Code, setting out each issue in detail as provided in the next preceding paragraph.

(9) Such other facts and information as the tax commission of Ohio or the budget commissioners may require.

The aggregate of all taxes that may be levied by a county, for county purposes, on the taxable property in the county on the tax list, shall not exceed in any one year three mills. The aggregate of all taxes that may be levied by a municipal corporation on the taxable property in the corporation, for corporation purposes, on the tax list, shall not exceed in any one year five mills. The aggregate of
all taxes that may be levied by a township, for township

purposes, on the taxable property in the township on the tax list, shall not exceed in any one year two mills. The local tax levy for all school purposes shall not exceed in any one year five mills on the dollar of valuation of taxable property in any school district. Such limits for county, township, municipal and school levies shall be exclusive of any special levy, provided for by a vote of the electors, special assessments, levies for road taxes that may be worked out by the tax payers, and levies and assessments in special districts created for road or ditch improvements, over which the budget commissioners shall have no control. School.

Such budget shall be made up annually at the time or times now fixed by law when such boards or officers are required to determine the amount in money to be raised or the rate of taxes to be levied in their respective taxing districts. Blanks.

The county auditor shall provide and furnish such boards and officers blank forms and instructions for making up such budgets. (102 v. 266.)

Section 3798, General Code, requiring that unexpended appropriations or balances of appropriations, remaining over at the end of the year, or after a fixed charge has been terminated, shall revert to funds from which they were taken, and section 5649-3e, providing that such funds shall revert to the general fund, have substantially the same meaning and effect.

In view of the provisions of section 3806, General Code, to the effect that sums certified by the auditor to be sufficient for a specific appropriation as a condition precedent to a contract or expenditure, shall not thereafter be considered unappropriated until the obligation is discharged, the word unexpended in these statutes must be construed to mean only such appropriations and balances as have not been certified in accordance with section 3806, General Code, by the auditor to be in the fund. — *Attorney General*, 1913, p. 226.

A levy of taxes made by a board of education for the purpose of providing for the payment of bonds issued in anticipation thereof, under authority of section 7629, General Code, must be made within the limitations of the Smith one per cent law, and also wtihin the five mill limitation, applicable to boards of education as such, and prescribed by section 5649-3a, General Code. — *Attorney General*, 1913, p. 1381.

The county commissioners do not have authority to expend money in the public treasury for the purpose of establishing social centers. If the county commissioners desire to establish such institution they must at the proper time submit to the budget commission an estimate of the amount of money needed for this purpose.

The county commissioners have no authority to pay the salary of a director and other necessary expenses connected with these social centers. — *Attorney General*, 1913, p. 1396.

Levies for interest in sinking fund purposes, not authorized by the electors prior to the enactment of the Smith one per cent. law in special districts, created for road or ditch improvements, are exempted by the terms of section 5649-3a from the limits of county, township, municipal and school levies.

The provision of this statute taking such levy from the control of the budget commissioners merely prevents the budget commissioners from cutting the same down, but does not exempt such levies from the 1910 tax limitations. — *Attorney General*, 1913, p. 1244.

A levy of one mill by the board of education imposed annually for the purpose of reimbursing a library association for services to the public in pursuance of a contract between the board and the association, is within the interior limitations of the Smith law and is not a "levy for sinking fund and interest purposes necessary to provide for indebtedness created prior to the passage" of the Smith law.

The obligation which rests upon the board is not an indebtedness within the meaning of the statute nor is there an "impairment of the obligation of contract" in the effect of the Smith law upon such procedures. — *Attorney General,* 1912, p. 1578.

The statutes authorizing the township trustees, under certain circumstances, to levy certain taxes for road improvement purposes, remain in force generally, notwithstanding the enactment of the Smith Law, although the special limitation upon the tax authorized by the original statute has been supplanted by the Smith Law limitations; and in particular that this tax must be levied subject to the ten mill limitation law. — *Attorney General,* Opinion No. 1222, 1914.

Section 7592, General Code, is no longer in force and no levy outside the five mill limitation of the Smith law can be made thereunder.

Section 7751, General Code, cannot be so interpreted as to permit a levy thereunder outside of the five mill limitation of the Smith Law.

The opinion of the Attorney General to the Auditor of State under date of February 26, 1912, relative to the application of the law for State aid to weak school districts concurred in, but limited to its application to the said law as it then existed.

Opinion of the Attorney General to the Auditor of State relative to the joint operation of the law for State aid to weak school districts and the Smith One Per Cent Law, found in Vol. 1, Annual Report of Attorney General, 1912, p. 89, modified 1b, p. 108, concurred in and followed, subject to the qualification that a board of education which has submitted a budget estimate requiring the levy of taxes to the full extent of any absolute limitation of the Smith Law, such as five mill limitation of Section 5649-3a, General Code, should not be held to have disqualified the district to receive State aid, if such amount is insufficient to operate the schools in accordance with the provisions of the State Aid law. — *Attorney General,* Opinion No 179, March 27, 1915.

Validity of the Smith one per cent law, and application to contracts in force: State v. Sayre, 23 Dec. 319 (12 N. S. 52).
Cited in construing Art. 12, Sec. 2: Link v. Karn, 24 Dec. 229 (14 N. S. 244).

County budget commission, members of, powers and duties.

SECTION 5649-3b. There is hereby created in each county a board for the annual adjustment of the rates of taxation and fixing the amount of taxes to be levied therein, to be known as the budget commissioners. The county auditor, the county treasurer and the prosecuting attorney shall constitute such board. The budget commissioners shall meet at the auditor's office in each county on the first Monday in August annually, and shall complete their work on or before the third Monday in that month, unless for good cause the tax commission of Ohio shall extend the time for completing the work. Each member shall be sworn faithfully and impartially to perform the duties imposed upon him by law. Two members shall constitute a quorum. The auditor shall be the secretary of the board and shall keep a full and accurate record of all proceedings. The auditor shall appoint such messengers and clerks as the board deems necessary, who shall receive

not to exceed three dollars per day for their services for
the time actually employed, which shall be paid out of the
county treasury. The budget commissioners shall be allowed their actual and necessary expenses. Such expenses
shall be itemized and sworn to by the person who incurred
them and paid out of the county treasury when approved
by the board. For the purpose of adjusting the rates of
taxation and fixing the amount of taxes to be levied each
year the county auditor and the budget commissioners shall
be governed by the amount of the taxable property as
shown on the auditor's tax list for the current year; provided, that if the auditor's tax list has not been completed.
the county auditor shall estimate as nearly as practicable the amount of the taxable property for such year
and such officers shall be governed by such estimate. (106
v. 180.)

The amendment to Section 5649-2, a part of the so-called
Smith law and affecting the ten mill limitation, though subsequent
to amendment to Section 5649-5b, imposing the fifteen mill limitation, is to be read together with the latter so that sinking fund
and interest levies necessary to provide for previously incurred
bonded indebtedness, such indebtedness authorized by vote of the
people is still subject to the fifteen mill limitation. — *Attorney
General*, Opinion 956, May 25, 1914.

The statutes authorizing the township trustees, under certain
circumstances, to levy certain taxes for road improvement purposes, remain in force generally, notwithstanding the enactment of
the Smith law, although the special limitation upon the tax authorized by the original statute has been supplanted by the Smith law
limitations; and in particular that this tax must be levied subject
to the ten mill limitation law. — *Attorney General*, Opinion 1222,
November 5, 1914.

SECTION 5649-3c. The auditor shall lay before the Examination
budget commissioners the annual budgets submitted to him of budgets.
by the boards and officers named in section 5649-3a of this
act, together with an estimate to be prepared by the auditor of the amount of money to be raised for state purposes in each taxing district in the county, and such other
information as the budget commissioners may request, or
the tax commission of Ohio may prescribe. The budget
commissioners shall examine such budgets and estimates
perpared by the county auditor, and ascertain the total
amount proposed to be raised in each taxing district
for state, county, township, city, village, school district,
or other taxing district purposes. If the budget commissioners find that the total amount of taxes to be raised
therein does not exceed the amount authorized to be raised
in any township, city, village, school district, or other taxing district in the county, the fact shall be certified to the
county auditor. If such total is found to exceed such
authorized amount in any township, city, village, school
district, or other taxing district in the county, the budget
commissioners shall adjust the various amounts to be raised Adjustment
so that the total amount thereof shall not exceed in any and certifi-
taxing district the sum authorized to be levied therein. In cation.
making such adjustment the budget commissioners may

10 S. L.

revise and change the annual estimates contained in such budgets, and may reduce any or all the items in any such budget, but shall not increase the total of any such budget, or any item therein. The budget commissioners shall reduce the estimates contained in any or all such budgets by such amount or amounts as will bring the total for each township, city, village, school district, or other taxing district, within the limits provided by law.

When the budget commissioners have completed their work they shall certify their action to the county auditor, who shall ascertain the rate of taxes necessary to be levied upon the taxable property therein of such county, and of each township, city village, school district, or other taxing district, returned on the grand duplicate, and place it on the tax list of the county. (102 v. 266.)

> Constitutional: State v. Edmondson, 89 O. S. 000; 59 Bull. Supp. 313.
> Legislature, not budget commission, levies taxes for state purposes: State v. Edmondson, 89 O. S. 000; 59 Bull. Supp. 343.
> Cited in construing Art. 12, Sec. 2: Link v. Karb, 24 Dec. 230 (14 N. S. 244).

Appropriations each fiscal half year.

SECTION 5649-3d. At the beginning of each fiscal half year the various boards mentioned in section 5649-3a of this act shall make appropriations for each of the several objects for which money has to be provided, from the moneys known to be in the treasury from the collection of taxes and all other sources of revenue, and all expenditures within the following six months shall be made from and within such appropriations and balances thereof, but no appropriation shall be made for any purpose not set forth in the annual budget nor for a greater amount for such purpose than the total amount fixed by the budget commissioners, exclusive of receipts and balances. (102 v. 266.)

> The county commissioners do not have authority to expend money in the public treasury for the purpose of establishing social centers. If the county commissioners desire to establish such institution they must at the proper time submit to the budget commission an estimate of the amount of money needed for this purpose.
> The county commissioners have no authority to pay the salary of a director and other necessary expenses connected with these social centers. — Attorney General, 1913, p. 1396.
> The deputies of the budget commission prescribed by Section 5649-3b, General Code, involve the exercise of judgment and discretion, and consequently a deputy cannot exercise the same on behalf of his principal.
> A deputy auditor cannot act for the auditor, nor an assistant city solicitor for the solicitor. The president of council may act on behalf of the mayor for the reason that such president of council is not a deputy of the mayor and in the absence of the mayor becomes acting mayor. — Attorney General, Opinion No. 955, 1914.
> Demands upon the county auditor and treasurer for advance payment of municipal taxes before settlement, may be made only by the city treasurer. No board or officer whatever has authority to control the distribution among the several municipal funds so drawn from the county treasury and placed in the municipal treasury; such moneys belong, pro rata, to the several funds in

the proportion determined by the municipal levies. The county commissioners have no function whatever to discharge with respect to such advance drafts; the trustees of the sinking fund of the city have no authority to make demand upon the county auditor and treasurer for advance payments on account of the city sinking fund levies. — *Attorney General*, Opinion No. 1172, 1914.

SECTION 5649-3e. Unexpected appropriations or balances of appropriations remaining over at the end of the year, and the balances remaining over at any time after a fixed charge shall have been terminated by reason of the object of the appropriation having been satisfied or abandoned, shall revert to the general fund, and shall then be subject to other authorized uses, as such board or officers may determine. (102 v. 266.) Balance unexpended.

SECTION 5649-4. For the emergencies mentioned in sections forty-four hundred and fifty, forty-four hundred and fifty-one, fifty-six hundred and twenty-nine, seventy-four hundred and nineteen and 7630-1 of the General Code, the taxing authorities of any district may levy a tax sufficient to provide therefor irrespective of any of the limitations of this act. (103 v. 527.) Emergencies.

Where the Industrial Commission and its deputy in charge of workshops, factories and public buildings condemn the use of a public school building for school purposes, the order must be complied with, and an emergency is created.

If bonds are issued by the board of education, with the approval of the majority of the electors, at a special election, the tax levies necessary to carry these bonds may be made outside of the limitations of the Smith one per cent law. Such is the effect of the amendment to Section 5649-4. General Code. — *Attorney General*, 1913, p. 1715.

Under section 5649-5b, General Code. interest and sinking fund levies to pay for indebtedness created subsequent to June 2, 1911, under authorization of a popular vote, are excluded only from the ten mill limitation of the Smith one per cent. law.

Under section 5649-4. General Code. the taxing authorities are authorized to exceed all limitations for certain emergencies referred to therein.

The destruction of a school house is not such an emergency, however, and therefore when, because of such a casualty, it becomes necessary to borrow money and issue bonds. the amounts authorized by vote of electors on the question of additional taxes and bond issues necessary, must be within the limitation of fifteen mills. — *Attorney General*, 1911-12, p. 1357.

Where the Inspector of Workshops and Factories prohibits the use of a school house until certain repairs are made, but the board of education decides to erect a new school building instead, and the electors vote for a $25,000 bond issue for the construction thereof, but cannot levy sufficient taxes to pay bonds and maintain school, there would be an emergency within the meaning of Section 5649-4. General Code. and the necessary taxes for the retirement of bonds required for the purpose might be levied outside of all limitations of law. — *Attorney General*, Opinion No. 888, 1914.

In case of the condemnation of a school building by the State Building Inspector, levies for the necessary repairs are not entitled to exemption from all limitations under Sections 7630-1 and 5649-4, General Code. unless bonds are issued by a vote of the people, in which event the interest and sinking fund levies will be exempt from the limitation. Simple repair levies made under these circumstances are subject to all the limitations of law. — *Attorney General*, Opinion No. 1190, October 8, 1914.

Proceedings
when max-
imum rate
insufficient.

SECTION 5649-5. The county commissioners of any county, the council of any municipal corporation, the trustee of any township, or any board of education may, at any time, by a majority vote of all the members elected or appointed thereto, declare by resolution that the amount of taxes that may be raised by the levy of taxes at the maximum rate authorized by sections 5649-2 and 5649-3 of the General Code as herein enacted within its taxing district, will be insufficient and that it is expedient to levy taxes, at a rate, in excess of such rate and cause a copy of such resolution to be certified to the deputy state supervisors of the proper county. Such resolution shall specify the amount of such proposed increase of rate above the maimum rate of taxation and the number of years not exceeding five during which such increased rate may be continued to be levied. (102 v. 266.)

Where the electors of a certain village voted to levy taxes in excess of the Smith law, the amount of five mills for three years and a mistake was made in printing the ballots providing for the levy of two mills for a period of three years. the proceeding is not invalid, and the taxing authorities are authorized to levy two additional mills for municipal purposes during a period of three years. — *Attorney General*, 1913, p. 1442.

Cited in construing Art. 12, Sec. 2: Link v. Karb, 24 Dec. 230 (14 N. S. 244).

Vote.

SECTION 5649-5a. Such proposition shall be submitted to the electors of such taxing district at the November election that occurs more than twenty days after the adoption of such resolution. The deputy state supervisors shall prepare the ballots and make the necessary arrangements for the submission of such question to the electors of such taxing district, and the election shall be conducted, canvassed and certified in like manner, except as otherwise provided by law, as regular elections in such taxing district for the election of officers thereof. Twenty days'

Notice.

notice of the election shall be given in one or more newspapers printed in the taxing districts once a week for four consecutive weeks prior thereto. stating the amount of the additional rate to be levied. the purpose for which it is to be levied. and the number of years during which such increased rate may be continued to be levied, and the time and place of holding the election. If no newspaper is printed therein. the notice shall be posted in a conspicuous place and published once a week for four consecutive weeks in a newspaper of general circulation in such taxing district.

The form of the ballots cast at such election shall be:

"For an additional levy of taxes for the purpose of .... not exceeding .... mills, for not to exceed .... years, Yes."

"For an additional levy of taxes for the purpose of .... not exceeding .... mills, for not to exceed .... years, No." (102 v. 266.)

SECTION 5649-5b. If a majority of the electors voting thereon at such election vote in favor thereof, it shall be lawful to levy taxes within such taxing district at a rate not to exceed such increased rate for and during the period provided for in such resolution, but in no case shall the combined maximum rate for all taxes levied in any year in any county, city, village, school district, or other taxing district, under the provisions of this and the two preceding sections and sections 5649-1, 5649-2 and 5649-3 of the General Code as herein enacted, exceed fifteen mills. (103 v. 57.)

It is necessary for a township board of education to submit the question of centralization of schools to a vote, under the provisions of section 4726, General Code.

All the electors of the township are entitled to vote upon the proposition of the centralization of schools.

The abolishment of all the schools in all the sub-districts, by virtue of sections 7730 and 7731, General Code, the establishment of new schools and the conveyance of pupils to these schools, operate as a centralization of the schools of the township, provided that no election has been held upon the question of centralization which resulted adversely and provided that no petition may be filed for an election according to law. — *Attorney General*, 1913, p. 1377.

Under section 5649-5b, General Code, interest and sinking fund levies to pay for indebtedness created subsequent to June 2, 1911, under authorization of a popular vote, are excluded only from the ten mill limitation of the Smith one per cent. law.

Under section 5649-4, General Code, the taxing authorities are authorized to exceed all limitations for certain emergencies referred to therein.

The destruction of a school house is not such an emergency, however, and therefore when, because of such a casualty, it becomes necessary to borrow money and issue bonds, the amounts authorized by vote of electors on the question of additional taxes and bond issues necessary, must be within the limitation of fifteen mills. — *Attorney General*, 1911-12, p. 1357.

SECTION 5649-6. Whenever two or more taxing districts are consolidated by annexation or otherwise, the aggregate amount of taxes authorized under section 2 of this act, for such consolidated district shall not exceed the sum of the aggregate amount which would have been authorized for all of said taxing districts separately. (101 v. 430.)

SECTION 5054. County commissioners, township trustees, councils, boards of education or other authorities, authorized to levy taxes, shall make the necessary levy to meet such expenses, which levy may be in addition to all other levies authorized or required by law. (99 v. 84 § 14.)

TITLE V. PUBLIC SCHOOLS.

CHAPTER 1.

SCHOOL FUNDS.

Tax levy for state common school fund.

SECTION 7575. For the purpose of affording the advantages of a free education to all the youth of the state, there shall be levied annually a tax of fifty-five thousandths of one mill on the grand list of the taxable property of the state, to be collected as are other state taxes and the proceeds of which shall constitute "the state common school fund," and for the payment of interest on the irreducible or trust fund debt for school purposes, twenty-five ten thousands of one mill, such fund to be styled "the sinking fund". (105 v. 5.)

The county auditor has no authority under the Smith one per cent tax law to place upon the tax duplicate any levies over which the budget commission has control, before that commission has met, organized and performed the duties imposed by section 5649-3c, General Code.

The respective levies for county, township, municipal and school purposes are exclusive of the levy for state purposes; but levies for all these purposes together with the state levy must not exceed, in a given taxing district, the limitations of ten mills, the amount of taxes raised in 1910 and fifteen mills, respectively imposed by different sections of the Smith one per cent. law. — *Attorney General,* 1911-12, p. 1614.

As the tuition fund is in the nature of a trust fund, for the benefit of each individual youth in the state, transfers from said fund, in the treasury of a school district to a building fund cannot be made except under provision and conditions provided for in Section 5655, General Code, for the purpose of reducing tax levy estimates at the annual meeting of the board.

The common pleas court has powers, under Sections 2296-2302, General Code, to permit transfers "when no injury will result therefrom" but in view of the peculiar nature of the tuition fund, such action would be a rare possibility. — *Attorney General,* 1912, p. 1206.

The grammatical construction and the use of the term levy, and the intransitive form "providing for" in the phrase "laws providing for tax levies," section 1-b, article II, of the constitution, compels the conclusion that this section is intended to comprehend only such acts as provide for a specified levy and impose upon some office the mandatory duty of making the same at a defined rate on the grand duplicate of the state or some subdivision thereof.

A law, therefore, such as is House Bill 500, which merely provides for the making of tax levies generally and prescribes the machinery by which such levies are to be carried out, is not subject to the exception provided in this section of the constitution, and is therefore subject to the initiative and referendum. — *Attorney General,* 1913, p. 599.

For limitation upon the tax rate, see G. C. Sec. 5649-2.
For limitations upon the amount to be raised by taxation, see G. C. Sec. 5649-3.
For earlier statutes materially different from those now in force, see Stewart v. Southard, 17 O. 402.

SECTION 251. If the auditor of state ascertains that the money in the state treasury belonging to the state common school fund will probably be insufficient to pay the appropriation payable out of that fund, he shall draw for the amount of the probable deficiency in favor of the treasurer of state on such county treasurers and in such amounts as he deems proper to meet such deficiency, and deliver the drafts to the treasurer of state, take his receipt therefor, and charge the treasurer of state therewith. The treasurer of state shall immediately proceed to collect the drafts, and the county treasurer shall pay them if they have sufficient sums collected for state common school purposes. Drafts so paid shall be evidence of the payment into the state treasury of the sums therein specified, and on delivery to the auditor of state shall be credited to the county

Deficiency in common school fund, how supplied.

treasurers, respectively, in their semi-annual settlement.
The auditor of state shall not issue a draft upon a county
treasurer for a sum in excess of what will be due such
county as its proportion of the state common school fund.
(78 v. 17.)

Treasurer and auditor's duties.

SECTION 6350. A county treasurer receiving such
money shall account for it to the auditor of state and pay
it into the state treasury annually upon the draft of the
state auditor at the time of making his August settlement
with him. The auditor of state shall credit such sum to
the state common school fund. (79 v. 96.)

This section is constitutional: State v. Frame, 39 O. S. 399.

Interest upon proceeds of salt and swamp lands.

SECTION 7577. The state shall pay interest anually,
at the rate of six per cent per annum, upon all money
which has been paid into the state treasury on account of
sales of lands commonly called "salt lands," and upon all
money paid or which may be paid into the state treasury on
account of sales of swamp lands granted to the state by
act of congress. The money received from such sales shall
constitute an irreducible debt of the state; and the interest
shall be apportioned annually on the same basis as the state
common school fund is apportioned, and distributed to the
several counties as hereinafter provided. (70 v. 195.)

As to proceeds of swamp lands under the act of 1894 (91 v. 229), see
appendix, sec. 13917.
As to swamp lands in Paulding county, see 89 v. 232.
For duty of canal commission as to certain swamp lands, etc., see
appendix, Sec. 13916.
If two leases of adjoining tracts of school lands are given to one
person, these two tracts cannot be appraised as one entire tract; and the
trustees are entitled to any enhanced value which arises from the fact that
the tracts are separate, and the lessee or assignee being entitled to any
enhanced value which arise from the fact that the two tracts are used as one:
Trustees of School v. Odlin, 8 O. S. 293.

Proceeds of sale of swamp lands.

SECTION 7578. The net proceeds hereafter paid into
the state treasury, from the sales of swamp lands granted
to the state by act of congress passed September 28, 1850,
is hereby appropriated to the general fund for the support
of common schools; and the state is pledged to pay the
interest annually, on all sums of money paid into the state
treasury, from the sales of such lands, from the receipt of
such money into the treasury. The interest so arising shall
be distributed, annually to the several counties of the
state in proportion to the number of male inhabitants above
the age of twenty-one as the law provides for ascertaining
the apportionment of representatives. The proportion of
interest due to each county shall be distributed for the support for common schools in the respective counties in the
manner prescribed for the distribution of the common
school fund. (80 v. 39 § 1.)

Under a statute which provides for the sale of school lands, and which
directs that interest upon purchase money mortgages should be paid at the
rate of six per cent, until paid, a provision in the mortgage that interest
should be paid annually, at the rate of six per cent. per annum is ultra vires,
and interest cannot be computed with annual rests: Hunter v. Hall, 14 O.
C. C. 425, 6 O. C. D. 366.

SECTION 7579. The money which has been and may be paid into the state treasury on acount of sales of lands granted by congress for the support of public schools in any original surveyed township or other district of country, shall constitute the "common school fund," of which the auditor of state shall be superintendent, and the income of which must be applied exclusively to the support of common schools, in the manner designated in this chapter. (70 v. 195.)

The "common school fund."

1. Under Section 7600, General Code, as amended 104 O. L., 159, requiring state common school funds to be distributed among school districts on the basis of thirty dollars for each teacher employed, each regular member of the teaching force of the district, though employed for part time only, as in the case of music and drawing teachers, is to be counted as a teacher. Substitute teachers elected to fill vacancies in the regular force are not to be counted as additional teachers.

2. Music teachers, etc., regularly employed in more than one district are to be counted as teachers in each district, and each district is entitled to thirty dollars on account of such a teacher.

3. Average daily attendance under Section 7600 as amended, in the distribution of common school funds is to be computed for the time during which the schools are in session during the current year, but in no event less than a legal school year.

4. The interest on common school fund moneys received from the sale of school lands and constituting a part of the irreducible debt of the State is to be distributed by the State to the counties at the February settlement, and by the county treasurer to the districts at the same settlement. In case more than one school district is located within the territorial limits of an original surveyed township, Section 7600, General Code, governs the distribution of such interest, except in parts of such districts located in the original surveyed township, only which are to be taken into consideration. In the event the territory of a school district is co-extensive with that of an original surveyed township, there is no need of applying the rule of Section 7600, because the district will receive all of the interest in such case.

5. Section 7600 requires the distribution of common school funds among the districts of the county, to be made at the August settlement, and it is applicable to the settlement to be made in August 1914, but the succeeding February distribution of such funds is to be made in accordance with the apportionment of the preceding August and need not await distribution until the succeeding August. — *Attorney General*, Opinion No. 1086, 1914.

For the confirmation of the sale of school lands, see appendix, Sec. 13899.
Township trustees have no authority to release a treasurer from his liability for any portion of the school fund belonging to the township, in the absence of some specific statutory provision (see G. C. Sec. 7609): Monroe Township v. Williams, 13 O. 495.
If lands revert to the state, and are afterwards sold again by the state, the payment of the taxes charged thereon may be made out of the proceeds of such second sale, after payment of the balance of the original purchase money: State ex rel., v. Purcel, 31 O. S. 352.
Under the act of April 16, 1852, no action could be brought against the purchaser for the unpaid portion of the purchase price. The only remedy authorized was that by sale or forfeiture: State v. Glidden, 31 O. S. 309.
The act of April 16, 1852, was not restricted to school lands in original surveyed townships, although they would be, of course, included: Seeley v. Thomas, 31 O. S. 301.

SECTION 7580. The common school fund shall constitute an irreducible debt of the state, on which it shall pay interest annually, at the rate of six per cent per annum, to be computed for the calendar year, the first computation on any payment of principal hereafter made to be from the time of payment to and including the thirty-first day

Accounts of common school fund.

of December next succeeding. The auditor of state shall keep an account of the fund, and of the interest which accrues thereon, in a book or books to be provided for the purpose, with each original surveyed township and other district of country to which any part of the fund belongs, crediting each with its share of the fund, and showing the amount of interest thereon which accrues and the amount which is disbursed annually to each. (70 v. 195.)

When a devisor leaves a certain fund for the use of the school fund, such fund must be paid over to the state, and becomes vested in the "common school fund". Through section 7580, General Code, such monies then become a part of "the irreducible debt" of the state upon which shall be paid 6% interest per annum to be applied under section 7581, General Code, according to the intention of the devisor. — *Attorney General*, 1911-12, p. 520.

1. Under Section 7600, General Code, as amended 104 O. L., 159, requiring state common school funds to be distributed among school districts on the basis of thirty dollars for each teacher employed, each regular member of the teaching force of the district, though employed for part time only, as in the case of music and drawing teachers, is to be counted as a teacher. Substitute teachers or teachers elected to fill vacancies in the regular force are not to be counted as additional teachers.

2. Music teachers, etc., regularly employed in more than one district are to be counted as teachers in each district, and each district is entitled to thirty dollars on account of such a teacher.

3. Average daily attendance under Section 7600 as amended, in the distribution of common school funds is to be computed for the time during which the schools are in session during the current year, but in no event less than a legal school year.

4. The interest on common school fund moneys received from the sale of school lands and constituting a part of the irreducible debt of the State is to be distributed by the State to the counties at the February settlement, and by the county treasurer to the districts at the same settlement. In case more than one school district is located within the territorial limits of an original surveyed township, Section 7600, General Code, governs the distribution of such interest, except in parts of such districts located in the original surveyed township, only which are to be taken into consideration. In the event the territory of a school district is co-extensive with that of an original surveyed township, there is no need of applying the rule of Section 7600, because the district will receive all of the interest in such case.

5. Section 7600 requires the distribution of common school funds among the districts of the county, to be made at the August settlement, and it is applicable to the settlement to be made in August 1914, but the succeeding February distribution of such funds is to be made in accordance with the apportionment of the preceding August and need not await distribution until the succeeding August. — *Attorney General*, Opinion No. 1086, 1914.

Bequests, etc. in trust for common school fund. SECTION 7581. When any grant or devise of land, or donation or bequest of money or other personal property, is made to the state, or to any person, or otherwise, in trust for the common school fund, it shall become vested in such fund. When the money arising therefrom is paid into the state treasury, proper accounts thereof must be kept by the auditor of state, and the interest accruing therefrom shall be applied according to the intent of the grantor, donor, or devisor. (70 v. 195.)

When a devisor leaves a certain fund for the use of the common school fund, such fund must be paid over to the state, and become vested in the "common school fund". Through section 7580, General Code, such monies then becomes a part of "the irreducible debt" of the state upon which shall be paid 6% interest per annum to be applied under section 7581, General Code, according to the intention of the devisor. — *Attorney General*, 1911-12, p. 520.

A county may accept a testamentary gift for the use of the schools, and it may apply the same to school purposes in compliance with law: Christy v. Commissioners, 41 O. S. 711.

SECTION 2457. The commissioners of a county may receive bequests, donations, and gifts of real and personal property and money to promote and advance the cause of education in such county. All property and money so received by the commissioners or which has been bequeathed or bestowed upon such commissioners and remains undisposed of, at their discretion, may be paid to any incorporated institution of learning in the county, or a part thereof may be used each year to defray the expenses of the teachers institute, upon such terms and conditions as the commissioners in their discretion prescribe, having reference to the terms of the trust and safety of the fund and its proper application. (84 v. 211 § 1.)

Bequests for educational purposes; application of funds.

SECTION 7582. The auditor of state shall apportion the state common school fund to the several counties of the state semi-annually, upon the basis of the enumeration of youth therein, as shown by the latest abstract of enumeration transmitted to him by the superintendent of public instruction. Before making his February settlement with county treasurers, he shall apportion such amount thereof as he estimates to have been collected up to that time and in the settlement sheet which he transmits to the auditor of each county, shall certify the amount payable to the treasurer of his county. Before making his final settlement with county treasurers each year he shall apportion the remainder of the whole fund collected, as nearly as it can be ascertained, and in the August settlement sheet which he transmits to the auditor of each county shall certify the amount payable to the treasurer of his county. (104 v. 158.)

Apportionment of school funds by auditor of state.

As the tuition fund is in the nature of a trust fund, for the benefit of each individual youth in the state, transfers from said fund, in the treasury of a school district to a building fund cannot be made except under provision and conditions provided for in Section 5655, General Code, for the purpose of reducing tax levy estimates at the annual meeting of the board.

The common pleas court has powers, under Sections 2296-2302, General Code, to permit transfers "when no injury will result therefrom" but in view of the peculiar nature of the tuition fund, such action would be a rare possibility. — *Attorney General*, 1912, p. 1206.

1. Under Section 7600, General Code, as amended 104 O. L., 159, requiring state common school funds to be distributed among school districts on the basis of thirty dollars for each teacher employed, each regular member of the teaching force of the district, though employed for part time only, as in the case of music and drawing teachers, is to be counted as a teacher. Substitute teachers

or teachers elected to fill vacancies in the regular force are not to
be counted as additional teachers.

2. Music teachers, etc., regularly employed in more than one
district are to be counted as teachers in each district, and each
district is entitled to thirty dollars on account of such a teacher.

3. Average daily attendance under Section 7600 as amended,
in the distribution of common school funds is to be computed for
the time during which the schools are in session during the current
year, but in no event less than a legal school year.

4. The interest on common school fund moneys received
from the sale of school lands and constituting a part of the
irreducible debt of the State is to be distributed by the State to
the counties at the February settlement, and by the county treasurer
to the districts at the same settlement. In case more than one
school district is located within the territorial limits of an original
surveyed township, Section 7600, General Code, governs the distribution of such interest, except in parts of such districts located
in the original surveyed township, only which are to be taken into
consideration. In the event the territory of a school district is
co-extensive with that of an original surveyed township, there is
no need of applying the rule of Section 7600, because the district
will receive all of the interest in such case.

5. Section 7600 requires the distribution of common school
funds among the districts of the county, to be made at the August
settlement, and it is applicable to the settlement to be made in
August 1914, but the succeeding February distribution of such
funds is to be made in accordance with the apportionment of the
preceding August and need not await distribution until the succeeding August. — *Attorney General*, Opinion No. 1086, 1914.

If the auditor has not apportioned the school fund, the board of education is not authorized to treat such fund as a contingent fund, and to expend
it according to their discretion: State, ex rel., v. Zeeb, 9 O. C. C. 13, 6 O.
C. D. 70.

Each apportionment is a separate transaction to be complete in itself.
A surplus or a deficit in a former year cannot be considered in determining
the apportionment for the year in question: Saunders v. State, ex rel., 2 O.
C. C. 475, 1 O. C. D. 596.

(HOUSE BILL NO. 343, 1915.)

There is hereby appropriated out of any monies in the
state treasury or that may come into the state treasury to
the credit of the sinking fund or the common school fund;
and to the extent that the monies in such sinking fund or
common school fund are not adequate to satisfy the appropriations made herein, the balances necessary to make
up the sums herein appropriated shall be paid from any
monies in the treasury to the credit of the general revenue
fund not otherwise appropriated:

For interest on the irreducible debt of the state, which
constitutes the school, ministerial, indemnity fund, Ohio
university and Ohio state university funds, falling due

January 1st, 1915, and January 1st, 1916, respectively $645,000.00

For the support of the common schools to be
paid at the rate of two dollars ($2.00)
for each enumerated youth as provided in
sections 7582, 7583, and 7584 of the
General Code, for the fiscal years ending
June 30, 1916, and June 30, 1917, respectively $5,147,866.00

SECTION 7583. In each February settlement sheet the state auditor shall enter the amount of money payable to the county treasurer on the apportionment of interest specified in section seventy-five hundred and seventy-seven, and also enter in each February settlement sheet the amount of money payable to the county treasurer on account of interest for the preceding year on the common school fund, and designate the source or sources from which the interest accrued. With each February settlement sheet he shall transmit a certified statement, showing the amount of interest derived from the common school fund payable to each original surveyed township or other district of country within the county. (70 v. 195.)

1. Under Section 7600, General Code, as amended 104 O. L., 159, requiring state common school funds to be distributed among school districts on the basis of Thirty Dollars for each teacher employed, each regular member of the teaching force of the district, though employed for part time only, as in the case of music and drawing teachers, is to be counted as a teacher. Substitute teachers or teachers elected to fill vacancies in the regular force are not to be counted as additional teachers.

2. Music teachers, etc., regularly employed in more than one district are to be counted as teachers in each district, and each district is entitled to thirty dollars on account of such a teacher.

3. Average daily attendance under Section 7600 as amended, in the distribution of common school funds is to be computed for the time during which the schools are in session during the current year, but in no event less than a legal school year.

4. The interest on common school fund moneys received from the sale of school lands and constituting a part of the irreducible debt of the State is to be distributed by the State to the counties at the February settlement, and by the county treasurer to the districts at the same settlement. In case more than one school district is located within the territorial limits of an original surveyed township, Section 7600, General Code, governs the distribution of such interest, except in parts of such districts located in the original surveyed township, only which are to be taken into consideration. In the event the territory of a school district is co-extensive with that of an original surveyed township, there is no need of applying the rule of Section 7600, because the district will receive all of the interest in such case.

5. Section 7600 requires the distribution of common school funds among the districts of the county, to be made at the August settlement, and it is applicable to the settlement to be made in August 1914, but the succeeding February distribution of such funds is to be made in accordance with the apportionment of the preceding August and need not await distribution until the succeeding August. — *Attorney General*, Opinion No. 1086, 1914.

SECTION 7584. The treasurer of each county, at each semi-annual settlement with the auditor of state, shall retain in the county treasury, from the state taxes collected by him, the amount of the funds herein mentioned shown by the settlement sheet of the auditor of state to be payable to him at that time. If such amount for any county exceeds the amount of state taxes collected therein, the auditor of state shall draw an order on the treasurer of state, in favor of the treasurer of such county, for the balance of school funds due his county, and transmit it to such county treasurer, and the treasurer of the state shall pay such order upon its presentation to him. (70 v. 195.)

The sureties upon the bond of a township treasurer are liable to the successor of such treasurer for school funds which said treasurer has failed to pay over to his successor, even though the order to make such payment is made by the board of education in a manner not authorized by law: Cresswell v. Nesbitt, 16 O. S. 35.

When county line divides township.

SECTION 7585. If parts of an original surveyed township or fractional township are situated in two or more counties, the amount of interest on common school fund due to such township shall be paid in the manner provided in the next two preceding sections to the treasurer of the county wherein the greatest relative portion of such township is situated. But if it be uncertain in which county such portion is situated, the amount of interest due to such township shall be paid to the treasurer of the oldest county in which any part of the township is situated. (70 v. 195.)

Board of education to fix rate of taxation.

SECTION 7586. Each board of education, annually, at a regular or special meeting held between the third Monday in April and the first Monday in June, shall fix the rate of taxation necessary to be levied for all school purposes, after the state funds are exhausted. (98 v. 9.)

As the tuition fund is in the nature of a trust fund, for the benefit of each individual youth in the state, transfers from said fund, in the treasury of a school district to a building fund cannot be made except under provision and conditions provided for in Section 5655, General Code, for the purpose of reducing tax levy estimates at the annual meeting of the board.

The common pleas court has power, under Sections 2296-2302, General Code, to permit transfers "when no injury will result therefrom" but in view of the peculiar nature of the tuition fund, such action would be a rare possibility. — *Attorney General*, 1912, p. 1206.

This and the following sections authorize a levy made by the board of education upon property in the respective school districts, if the state funds are insufficient: Toledo, ex rel., v. Railway, 4 O. C. C. 113, 2 O. C. D. 450.

For a former statute, which exempted the Cincinnati school district from the operation of this and the following sections, see State v. Brewster, 39 O. S. 653.

A board of education is not liable in its corporate capacity for damages, where, in excavating on its own lots for the erection of a school building, it wrongfully and negligently carries the excavation below the statutory depth of nine feet, thereby undermining and injuring the foundation and walls of a building of an adjoining owner: Board of Education v. Volk, 72 O. S. 469.

General Code, Sec. 3782, creating a liability against an "owner" or "possessor" of premises whereon such wrongful and unlawful excavation is made, does not apply to boards of education holding title to the lot or land being excavated, for school and school building purposes: Board of Education v. Volk, 72 O. S. 469.

In the absence of statutory authority, the board of education is not liable in its corporate capacity for an injury which results to a pupil, while attending a public school, although such board of education has been negligent in the discharge of its official duty in the erection and maintenance of a common school building: Finch v. Board of Education, 30 O. S. 37.

A municipal corporation is not liable for the negligence of the board of education in the construction and maintenance of a school building to a pupil attending such school, who is injured by reason of such negligence: Diehm v. Cincinnati, 25 O. S. 305.

See also Sec. 7587.

Levy to be divided into four funds.

SECTION 7587. Such levy shall be divided by the board of education into four funds: First, tuition fund; second, building fund; third, contingent fund; fourth, bonds, interest and sinking fund. A separate levy must be made for each fund. (98 v. 9.)

"A notice, by a clerk of a board of education, of a tax voted by the board, to build a school house, delivered to the auditor on the 11th day of June, is sufficient authority to the auditor for carrying the tax into his duplicate:" II 'Western Law Monthly, 589.

It is a general rule that the statutes, so far as they limit a time for the performance of an act by a public officer, for the public benefit, are merely directory, when *time* is not the *essence* of the thing to be done, unless there are negative words, and the act is valid if done afterwards.

Tuition from non-resident pupils is to be paid to the board of education, and placed in the contingent fund. A teacher has absolutely no authority to retain money received for tuition of non-resident pupils. *Attorney General Opinion.*

Prior to the passage of the present school code (97 O. L. 334), a valid assessment for street-improvement could not be levied against school property. Whether the division of the contingent school fund into separate funds by the present school code will render valid such assessments levied since the enactment of the school code, quaere: 15 O. D. N. P., 334; 48 O. S., 83.

As the tuition fund is in the nature of a trust fund, for the benefit of each individual youth in the state, transfers from said fund, in the treasury of a school district to a building fund cannot be made except under provision and conditions provided for in Section 5655, 'General Code, for the purpose of reducing tax levy estimates at the annual meeting of the board.

The common pleas court has power, under Section 2296-2302, 'General Code, to permit transfers "when no injury will result therefrom" but in view of the peculiar nature of the tuition fund, such action would be a rare possibility. — *Attorney General*, 1912, p. 1206.

SECTION 7591. Except as hereinafter provided, the local tax levy for all school purposes shall not exceed twelve mills on the dollar of valuation of taxable property in any school district, and in city school districts shall not be less than six mills. Such levy shall not include any special levy for a specified purpose, provided for by a vote of the people. (98 v. 127.) Maximum levy.

Repealed by implication: Rabe v. Canton Sch. Dist, 88 O. S. 403.

When a village board of education was authorized by electors under section 7592, 'General Code, to levy an additional tax of five mills for five years, such board may proceed to issue bonds without further authorization of the electors provided that the conditions of 7626 and 7679, 'General Code, with reference to the quality and nature of the bonds and the provisions of section 7629 with reference to the amount of the bonds and the procedure of the board be complied with. — *Attorney General*, 1911-12, p. 534.

Section 7629, 'General Code, still empowers the board of education to issue such amount of bonds without authority of the electors in any one year as does not exceed in the aggregate a tax of two mills for the year next preceding the issue. The limitation of the Smith law must be observed, however. — *Attorney General*, 1911-12. p. 1332.

The decision in the case of Rabe et al. v. Board of Education, does not in any way effect the rights of the Board of Education under Section 5656, 'General Code.—*Attorney General, Opinion* 926, 1914.

Section 5649-2, et seq., limit rate of taxation and repeal by implication existing conflicting statutes: Rabe v. Canton Sch. Dist. (B. of Ed.), 88 O. S. 403.

For limitations upon the tax rate, see G. C. Sec. 5649-2.

For limitations upon the amount to be raised by taxation, see G. C. Sec. 5649-3.

Increase levy for schools at Niles, see 91 v. 451.

If the board of education has made a levy and the county auditor has subsequently placed the school levy upon the duplicate, at a rate less than that certified by the board of education, it will be presumed that the board of education authorized such action; and a taxpayer, who brings suit to compel the auditor by mandamus to place the tax rate at that originally fixed by the board of education, must show that such board of education did not reconsider its action and fix the tax rate at the lower figure: State v. Capperler, 39 O. S. 455.

An earlier form of this statute was so amended as to exclude the Cincinnati school district from its operation: State v. Brewster, 39 O. S. 653.

Greater tax may be levied.

SECTION 7592. A greater or less tax than is authorized above may be levied for any or all school purposes. Any board of education may make an additional annual levy of not more than five mills for any number of consecutive years not exceeding five, if the proposition to make such levy or levies has been submitted by the board, to a vote of the electors of the school district, under a resolution prescribing the time, place and nature of the proposition to be submitted, and approved by a majority of those voting on the proposition. (98 v. 127.)

Repealed by implication: Rabe v. Canton Sch. Dist, 88 O. S. 403.

When a village board of education was authorized by electors under section 7592, General Code, to levy an additional tax of five mills for five years, such board may proceed to issue bonds without further authorization of the electors provided that the conditions of 7626 and 7679, General Code, with reference to the quality and nature of the bonds and the provisions of section 7629 with reference to the amount of the bonds and the procedure of the board be complied with. — *Attorney General*, 1911-12, p. 534.

Section 7629, General Code, still empowers the board of education to issue such amount of bonds without authority of the electors in any one year as does not exceed in the aggregate a tax of two mills for the year next preceding the issue. The limitation of the Smith law must be observed, however. — *Attorney General*, 1911-12, p. 1332.

The decision in the case of Rabe et al. v. Board of Education, does not in any way effect the rights of the Board of Education under Section 5656, General Code. — *Attorney General*, Opinion No. 926, 1914.

For limitations upon the tax rate, see G. C. Sec. 5649-2.
For limitations upon the amount to be raised by taxation, see G. C. Sec. 5649-3.

Notice of election.

SECTION 7593. Notice of such election must be given by publication of the resolution for three consecutive weeks prior thereto in some newspaper published and of general circulation in the district, or by posting copies thereof in five of the most conspicuous places in the district for a like period, if no such paper is published therein. (98 v. 127.)

Repealed by implication: Rabe v. Canton Sch. Dist. 88 O. S. 403.

Amount of levy to be certified to county auditor.

SECTION 7594. The amount of the levy fixed by the boards of education under the next eight preceding sections, shall be certified to the county auditor, in writing, on or before the first Monday in June of each year by the boards of education, and on or before the first Monday in August of each year by the county commissioners when the levy is made by them, who shall assess the entire amount upon all the taxable property of the district, and enter it upon the tax duplicate of the county. The county treasurer shall collect it at the time and in the same manner as state and county taxes are collected, and pay it to treasurer of the district upon the warrant of the county auditor. (102 v. 277.)

The fact that the auditor has not apportioned the school fund does not give authority to the board of education to treat such fund as contingent, and to expend it in accordance with its discretion: State, ex rel., v. Zeeb, 9 O. C. C. 13.

Each apportionment is a separate transaction, and the fact that there was either a surplus or deficit in preceding years, cannot change the apportionment in question: Saunders v. State, ex rel., 2 O. C. C. 475, 1 O. C. D. 596.

If the levy, as fixed by the board of education, exceeds the maximum limit provided for in G. C. Sec. 7591, the auditor cannot be compelled to place such rate on the tax list by proceedings in mandamus: State, ex rel., v. Brewster, 9 Dec. Rep. 357, 12 Bull. 223.

If the board of education has certified the amount of its levy under this section, and if the auditor subsequently enters the school levy upon the tax duplicate at a rate less than that certified, it will be presumed, in the absence of evidence to the contrary, that such action on the part of the auditor was authorized by the board of education; and a taxpayer, in a proceeding in mandamus to compel the auditor to place upon the duplicate the rate originally certified by the board of education, must show that such board has not thereafter reduced such rate: State v. Cappeller, 39. O. S. 455.

For a former amendment excluding the school district of Cincinnati from the operation of this section, see State v. Brewster, 39 O. S. 653.

SECTION 7595. No person shall be employed to teach in any public school in Ohio for less than forty dollars a month. When a school district has not sufficient money to pay its teachers such salaries as are provided in section 7595-1 of the General Code, for eight months of the year, after the board of education of such district has made the maximum legal school levy, at least two-thirds of which shall be for the tuition fund, then such school district may receive from the state treasurer sufficient money to make up the deficit. (106 v. 430.)

Salary of teachers.

State aid to board of education under section 7595, General Code, is to be granted only when the maximum legal levy is insufficient to pay its teachers a minimum salary of $40 per month for eight months of the year, and then only when the number of persons of school age in the district is twenty times the number of teachers therein employed.

Where the shortage arises without these limitations as by reason of inability to comply with contract to pay teachers $50 per month, such indebtedness is a "valid, existing and binding one" and if the board is unable to meet the same by reason of taxation limitations, bonds may be issued and the debts funded under authority of sections 5656, 5658 and 5659, General Code.—*Attorney General*, 1911-12. p. 529.

When a board of education passed a resolution legal in form, employing certain teachers, the effect thereof would be to employ said teachers, though certain provisions of said resolution requiring said teachers to enter into a written contract "to make up for legal holidays and for the time lost in the event of epidemic" would be void because against the statutes and public policy of the state of Ohio.—*Attorney General*, 1911-12. p. 1322.

The provision of section 7595, General Code, stipulating that no teacher shall be employed at less than $40.00 per month may be waived and a contract by a teacher for service for a less sum would be legal.—*Attorney General*, 1911-12. p. 549.

It is the intent of Sections 7644 and 7695, General Code, that a board of education shall maintain a school session of not less than thirty-two weeks in each year as a condition precedent to obtaining State Aid.

It is not the intent to demand the impossible, however, and when, through destruction of the school building by fire, com-

11 S. L.

pliance is absolutely prevented, failure to maintain an eight months' session will not preclude the right to State Aid. — *Attorney General,* 1912, p. 120.

Since repeals by implication are not admitted unless the latter act is clearly inconsistent with the former, and since both constitutional and legislative provision is made for "thorough and efficient schools," the State Aid law for weak school districts has not been repealed by the Smith Law, and the Auditor is still authorized under the proper circumstances to issue his warrant for State Aid as provided in Section 7959, General Code.

Such warrant shall only be issued when the maximum levy for school board purposes, (three-fourths of which has been made for tuition purposes) is insufficient to enable the Board to pay $40 per month for its teachers for eight months of the year.

The "maximum levy" provided for in the State Aid law which was formerly restricted by the twelve mill limitation, is now, by reason of the Smith Law, subject to the four limitations provided for therein. It therefore, follows that what the Budget Commission determines to be the "maximum legal school levy for the district" shall be the maximum levy for the purpose of the State Aid Law.

When, therefore, the Board has properly certified a sufficient sum to the Auditor to provide sufficiently for payment of its teachers, and the Budget Commission has reduced the allowance to such an extent that teachers cannot be paid $40 per month for eight months in the year under the restrictions of Section 7959, General Code, and three-fourths of such allowance is made for tuition purposes, the State Auditor may issue his State Aid Warrant. — *Attorney General,* 1912, p. 89.

Under the weak school district law the proceeds of the August distribution are intended by the law to be used to operate the school for the succeeding half year, and are not available for the use and purpose of the year closing on the 31st of the same month. Such proceeds should not be taken into consideration in determining the existence or amount of a deficiency in the tuition fund when the amount therein available for payment of teachers' salaries during the year ending on August 31st is compared with the needs of the fund for the same period of time under the requirements of Section 7595, General Code. — *Attorney General,* 1913, p. 365.

A weak school district may not only receive enough money in the way of state aid to pay its required number of teachers $40.00 per month for eight months, but it may also pay teachers for attending institutes and also the tuition of high school pupils and the tuition of other pupils, if the same has been paid from the tuition fund and not from the contingent fund.—*Attorney General,* 1913, p. 309.

Minimum salary provision in statute is for benefit of teachers and may be waived: Layne v. Bd. of Ed., 83 O. S. 474 (57 Bull. 237).

School districts eligible to state aid.

SECTION 7595-1. Only such school districts which pay salaries as follows shall be eligible to receive state aid: Elementary teachers without previous teaching experience in the state, forty dollars a month; elementary teachers having at least one year's professional training, forty-five dollars a month; elementary teachers who have completed the full two years' course in any normal school, teachers' college or university approved by the superintendent of public instruction, fifty-five dollars per month; high school teachers not to exceed an average of seventy dollars per month in each high school. (106 v. 430.)

SECTION 7596. Whenever any board of education finds that it will have such a deficit for the current school year, such board shall on the first day of October, or any time prior to the first day of January of said year, make affidavit to the county auditor, who shall send a certified statement of the facts to the state auditor. The state auditor shall issue a voucher on the state treasurer in favor of the treasurer of such school district for the amount of such deficit in the tuition fund. (103 v. 267.)

State aid for weak school districts.

State aid to board of education under section 7595, General Code, is to be granted only when the maximum legal levy is insufficient to pay its teachers a minimum salary of $40 per month for eight months of the year, and then only when the numbers of persons of school age age in the district is twenty times the number of teachers therein employed.

Where the shortage arises without these limitations as by reason of inability to comply with contract to pay teachers $50 per month, such indebtedness is a "valid, existing and binding one" and if the board is unable to meet the same by reason of taxation limitations, bonds may be issued and the debts funded under authority of sections 5656, 5658 and 5659, General Code. — *Attorney General*, 1911-12, p. 529.

Since repeals by implication are not admitted unless the latter act is clearly inconsistent with the former, and since both constitutional and legislative provision is made for "thorough and efficient schools," the State Aid Law for weak school districts has not been repealed by the Smith Law, and the Auditor is still authorized under the proper circumstances to issue his warrant for State Aid as provided in Section 7959, General Code.

Such warrant shall only be issued when the maximum levy for school board purposes, (three-fourths of which has been made for tuition purposes) is insufficient to enable the Board to pay $40 per month for its teachers for eight months of the year.

The "maximum levy" provided for in the State Aid Law which was formerly restricted by the twelve mill limitation, is now, by reason of the Smith Law, subject to the four limitations provided for therein. It therefore, follows that what the Budget Commission determines to be the "maximum legal school levy for district" shall be the maximum levy for the purpose of the State Aid Law.

When, therefore, the Board has properly certified a sufficient sum to the Auditor to provide sufficiently for payment of its teachers, and the Budget Commission has reduced the allowance to such an extent that teachers cannot be paid $40 per month for eight months in the year under the restrictions of Section 7959, General Code, and three-fourths of such allowance is made for tuition purposes, the State Auditor may issue his State Aid Warrant. — *Attorney General*, 1912, p. 89.

The maximum levy necessary to qualify a school district to receive State Aid is any estimate of amount ¾ of which are for tuition purposes made by the board of education to the County Auditor as representing the total amount necessary for all school purposes for the coming year, regardless of reductions made by the Budget Commission providing such reductions are made so as to preserve undisturbed the ¾ proportion for tuition purposes. If a board of education fails to estimate an amount sufficiently large to pay its teachers forty dollars per month, it is not entitled to State Aid. This rule must be qualified, however, to the extent that a board is not disqualified by reason of a mere shrinkage in tax collections.

The statement, therefore, of a former opinion to the effect that a board of education whose estimate had been reduced by the Budget Commission, would be entitled to State Aid to the extent of a difference between the amount allowed by the Budget Commission, and the amount estimated must be overruled. — *Attorney General*, 1912, p. 108.

The auditor of state may legally pay upon application dated after the amendment to section 7596, General Code, became a law, the amounts asked for by boards of education, to make good deficiencies in tuition funds for the past year.

The voucher of the auditor of state, under amended section 7596, must be issued upon the fact and information disclosed by the county auditor's certificate to him for the amount of anticipated deficiency in the tuition fund of a school district for the current year. As soon as the auditor ascertains the amount of such deficiency, he shall issue his voucher for the amount. — *Attorney General*, 1913, p. 340.

Under the weak school district law the proceeds of the August distribution are intended by the law to be used to operate the school for the succeeding half year, and are not available for the use and purpose of the year closing on the 31st of the same month. Such proceeds should not be taken into consideration in determining the existence or amount of a deficiency in the tuition fund when the amount therein available for payment of teachers' salaries during the year ending on August 31st is compared with the needs of the fund for the same period of time under the requirements of Section 7595, General Code. — *Attorney General*, 1913, p. 365.

1. The funds appropriated in House Bill 104 O. L., 196, are not available to pay application for state aid intended to make up deficiency in the tuition fund shown on September 1, 1913, for the year preceding, unless such deficiency existing on said date might lawfully be carried over into the current year then beginning so as to produce a deficiency for that year.

2. The funds so appropriated are available to pay state aid on application for advances on estimated deficiencies for the year ending August 31, 1914, providing the application was made within the time specified in Section 7596, General Code. — *Attorney General*, Opinion No. 885, April 24, 1914.

Number of school age required to entitle district to state aid.

SECTION 7597. No district shall be entitled to state aid as provided in sections 7595, 7595-1 and 7596 unless the number of persons of school age in such district is at least twenty times the number of teachers employed therein, and the schools in such district are maintained at least eight months of the year. (104 v. 165.)

State aid to board of education under section 7595, General Code, is to be granted only when the maximum legal levy is insufficient to pay its teachers a minimum salary of $40 per month for eight months of the year, and then only when the numbers of persons of school age in the district is twenty times the number of teachers therein employed.

Where the shortage arises without these limitations as by reason of inability to comply with contract to pay teachers $50 per month, such indebtedness is a "valid, existing and binding one" and if the board is unable to meet the same by reason of taxation limitations, bonds may be issued and the debts funded under authority of sections 5656, 5658 and 5659, General Code. — *Attorney General*, 1911-12, p. 529.

When district situated in two or more counties.

SECTION 7598. When a school district is composed of territory in two or more counties, the rate of taxation shall be ascertained by the board of education of such district and be certified to the auditors of the several counties, who must place it on the tax duplicate. It shall be collected as provided in section seventy-five hundred and ninety-four. (97 v. 350.)

SECTION 7599. The funds belonging to a district composed of territory in more than one county shall be paid by the treasurers of the other counties to the treasurer of the county having the greatest tax valuation in such district. The auditors of other counties must make settlement on account of such funds with the auditor of the county having the greatest tax valuation; and the treasurer of the district shall make the settlement with such auditor, required by section seventy-six hundred and two. (97 v. 350.)

To whom funds Paid.

SECTION 7600. After each annual settlement with the county treasurer, each county auditor shall immediately apportion school funds for his county. The state common school funds shall be apportioned as follows:

Each school district within the county shall receive thirty dollars for each teacher employed in such district, and the balance of such funds shall be apportioned among the various school districts according to the average daily attendance of pupils in the schools of such districts. If an enumeration of the youth of any district has not been taken and returned for any year and the average daily attendance of such district has not been certified to the county auditor such district shall not be entitled to receive any portion of that fund. The local school tax collected from the several districts shall be paid to the districts from which it was collected. Money received from the state on account of interest on the common school fund shall be apportioned to the school districts and parts of districts within the territory designated by the auditor of state as entitled thereto on the basis of thirty dollars for each teacher employed and the balance according to the average daily attendance. All other money in the county treasury for the support of common schools and not otherwise appropriated by law, shall be apportioned annually in the same manner as the state common school fund. (104 v. 158.)

Apportionment of school funds by county auditor.

District not entitled to funds if enumeration not taken.

As the tuition fund is in the nature of a trust fund, for the benefit of each individual youth in the state, transfers from said fund, in the treasury of a school district to a building fund cannot be made except under provision and conditions provided for in Section 5655, General Code, for the purpose of reducing tax levy estimates at the annual meeting of the board.

The common pleas court has powers, under Sections 2296-2302, General Code, to permit transfers "when no injury will result therefrom" but in view of the peculiar nature of the tuition fund, such action would be a rare possibility. — *Attorney General,* 1912, p. 1206.

1. Under Section 7600, General Code, as amended 104 O. L., 159, requiring state common school funds to be distributed among school districts on the basis of thirty dollars for each teacher employed, each regular member of the teaching force of the district, though employed for part time only, as in the case of music and drawing teachers, is to be counted as a teacher. Substitute teachers or teachers elected to fill vacancies in the regular force are not to be counted as additional teachers. .

2. Music teachers, etc., regularly employed in more than one district are to be counted as teachers in each district, and each district is entitled to thirty dollars on account of such a teacher.

3. Average daily attendance under Section 7600 as amended, in the distribution of common school funds is to be computed for the time during which the schools are in session during the current year, but in no event less than a legal school year.

4. The interest on common school fund moneys received from the sale of school lands and constituting a part of the irreducible debt of the State is to be distributed by the State to the counties at the February settlement, and by the county treasurer to the districts at the same settlement. In case more than one school district is located within the territorial limits of an original surveyed township, Section 7600, General Code, governs the distribution of such interest, except in parts of such districts located in the original surveyed township, only which are to be taken into consideration. In the event the territory of a school district is co-extensive with that of an original surveyed township, there is no need of applying the rule of Section 7600, because the district will receive all of the interest in such case.

5. Section 7600 requires the distirbution of common school funds among the districts of the county, to be made at the August settlement, and it is applicable to the settlement to be made in August 1914, but the succeeding February distribution of such funds is to be made in accordance with the apportionment of the preceding August and need not await distribution until the succeeding August. — *Attorney Geneeral*, Opinion No. 1086, 1914.

It is the duty of county auditors to obtain from the distribution of school funds the amounts set apart under Section 4744-3, General Code, for the use of the county board of education fund, regardless of the fact that such retention was not taken into account by the rural boards of education in making their 1913 tax levies. Such retention is to be made out of all the moneys to be distributed to the several districts including the proceeds of local levies, as well as the amount to be apportioned to the district as its portion of 'the State School Fund, and is not to be charged against any one particular fund or levy.

The county auditor cannot make any valid settlement, except on the basis of the certificate required to be made by the county board of education by Section 4744-2, General Code, respecting the number of teachers employed by the various school districts under its jurisdiction, etc. If the county board fails to make proper certification until after the usual period of settlement and the settlement is made, the error should be corrected under Section 2597, General Code, in the next succeeding semi-annual settlement, and in the meantime the county board of education fund must get along without the moneys belonging to it, and the county and district superintendents must serve on one-half pay until the next settlement time, when the arrearages in their respective salaries will be made up. — *Attorney General*, Opinion No. 1198, 1914.

Distirbution of escheated personal property to schools of a county, collected under Section 8579, General Code, is to be made as provided for the state common school fund under Section 7600, General Code, as said section stands, when the money is paid into the county treasury.

Money received from escheated personal property should be credited to the contingent fund of the school district, when received, under Section 7603, General Code. — *Attorney General*, Opinion No. 48, 1915.

The amounts retained by the county auditor under Section 4744-3, General Code, for the purpose of paying part of the salaries of the county superintendent of schools and the district superintendents should be charged against the apportionment of the state common school fund, and against the tuition fund of the district. — *Attorney General*, Opinion No. 168, March 26, 1915.

SECTION 2602. The auditor shall open an account with each township, city, village, and special school district in the county, in which, immediately after his semi-annual settlement with the treasurer in February and August of each year, he shall credit each with the net amount so collected for its use.

On application of the township, city, village, or school treasurer the auditor shall give him a warrant on the county treasurer, for the amount then due to such treasurer, and charge him with the amount of the warrant but the person so applying for such warrant shall deposit with the auditor a certificate from the clerk of the township, city, village, or district, stating that he is treasurer thereof, was duly elected or appointed, and that he has given bond according to law. (56 v. 128.)

There is no statutory inhibition against an individual holding both the offices of township treasurer and municipal treasurer, and as the offices are not incompatible in their nature, there are no legal objections thereto. — *Attorney General*, 1911-12, p. 1461.

SECTION 2605. If the county auditor fails to make either of the returns required by the preceding section for ten days after the time therein limited, he shall forfeit to the state the sum of fifty dollars, to be recovered by civil action. On being informed of such default by the auditor of state, the prosecuting attorney of the county shall collect such forfeiture and pay it into the state treasury to the credit of the school fund. (66 v. 26.)

SECTION 2689. Immediately after each semi-annual settlement with the county auditor, on demand, and presentation of the warrant of the county auditor therefor, the county treasurer shall pay to the township treasurer, city treasurer, or other proper officer thereof, all moneys in the county teasury belonging to such township, city, village, or school district. (86 v. 168.)

A township treasurer is allowed as compensation, two per cent. on all money paid out by him under the order of the township trustees. Moneys paid out by that official in his capacity as treasurer of the township park funds, are excluded from this provision by reason of the fact that they are paid out upon the order of the park commissioners. As there are no other legal authorizations for compensation to the treasurer for these services, the services are intended to be voluntary and no reimbursement can be allowed for the same.

The township park law, however, providing for park commissioners, is unconstitutional. — *Attorney General*, 1911-12, p. 403.

SECTION 2690. If a township treasurer or other proper officer so requires, or the trustees of a township, the council of a city, village, or the board of education of a school district, respectively, so direct, such moneys shall remain in the county treasury, to be drawn by the proper treasurer on the warrant of the county auditor, in sums of not less than one hundred dollars. (86 v. 168.)

Moneys shall not be held without authority.

SECTION 2691. If a county treasurer retains, or if such local treasurer permits such moneys to remain in the county treasury, in any manner other than herein provided, he shall forfeit and pay for such offense not less than one hundred nor more than one thousand dollars, to be recovered in an action at the suit of the state, for the use of the county. (86 v. 168.)

Advance payments to local authorities.

SECTION 2692. When the local authorities so request, the county auditor may draw, and the county treasurer shall pay on such draft to township, city and village treasurers, and the treasurer of any board of education, from June twentieth and December twentieth to the date of the semi-annual distribution, each year, any sum not eceeding two-thirds of the current collection of taxes for such local authorities, respectively, in advance of the semi-annual settlements. (97 v. 378.)

Sec. 2692 of the General Code makes it mandatory upon the county auditor to draw the draft therein provided for when porperly requested by the proper local authority. — *Attorney General*, 1912, p. 1734.

Moneys to be forwarded to state treasurer.

SECTION 2693. The county treasurer shall remit to the treasurer of state, all moneys received for section sixteen and section twenty-nine, as soon after they are received as practicable, and in no case later than the end of the fiscal quarter in which received. He shall immediately forward one of the receipts returned therefor to the auditor of state. (44 v. 120.)

Distribution of money after apportionment.

SECTION 7601. Immediately after such apportionment is made, the auditor must enter it in a book to be kept for that purpose, and furnish a certified copy of the apportionment to each school treasurer and clerk in his county. He shall give to each of such treasurers an order on the county treasurer for the amount of money payable to him, and take his receipt therefor. (70 v. 195.)

Boards of education can leave school moneys in county treasury and draw the same from time to time in amounts of not less than one hundred dollars: see Sec. 2690.
County auditors shall in no case permit treasurer to have in his hands school funds amounting to more than the amount of his bond; see Sec. 4769.

The amounts retained by the county auditor under Sec. 1744-3, General Code, for the purpose of paying part of the salaries of the county superintendent of schools and the district superintendents should be charged against the apportionment of the state common school fund, and against the tuition fund of the district. — *Attorney General*, Opinion No. 168, March 26, 1915.

Failure of the auditor to enter an apportionment does not render the school funds contingent funds, to be expended at the discretion of the board: State, ex rel., v. Zeeb, 9 O. C. C. 13, 6 O. C. D. 70.

Apportionment when county line divides original surveyed township.

SECTION 7602. When an original surveyed township of fractional township is situated in two or more counties, and the land granted thereto by congress for the support of public schools has been sold, the auditor of the county to whose treasurer the interest on the proceeds of such sale is paid must apportion such interest to the counties in which such township is situated in proportion to the youth of the township enumerated in each. Such auditor shall certify to the auditor of each of the other counties the amount so ascertained to belong to the part of the township situated in his county, and transmit to the treasurer of each of such counties an order on the treasurer of his own county for such amount. The auditor of each county shall apportion the amount of such interest belonging to the part of the township in his county, to the districts or parts or districts entitled thereto as is provided for the apportionment of the state common school funds in section 7600, and certify and pay it to the proper school officers, as provided in section 7601. (104 v. 158.)

SECTION 7603. The certificate of apportionment furnished by the county auditor to the treasurer and clerk of each school district must exhibit the amount of money received by each district from the state, the amount received from any special tax levy made for a particular purpose, and the amount received from local taxation of a general nature. The amount received from the state common school fund and the common school fund shall be designated the "tuition fund" and be appropriated only for the payment of superintendents and teachers. Funds received from special levies must be designated in accordance with the purpose for which the special levy was made and be paid out only for such purpose, except that, when a balance remains in such fund after all expenses incident to the purpose for which it was raised have been paid, such balance will become a part of the contingent fund and the board of education shall make such transfer by resolution. Funds received from the local levy for general purposes must be designated so as to correspond to the particular purpose for which the levy was made. Moneys coming from sources not enumerated herein shall be placed in the contingent fund. (97 v. 350.)

Certificate of apportionment.

As the tuition fund is in the nature of a trust fund, for the benefit of each individual youth in the state, transfers from said fund, in the treasury of a school district to a building fund cannot be made except under the provision and conditions provided for in Section 5655, General Code, for the purpose of reducing tax levy estimates at the annual meeting of the board.

The common pleas court has powers, under Sections 2296-2302, General Code, to permit transfers "when no injury will result therefrom" but in view of the peculiar nature of the tuition fund, such action would be a rare possibility. — *Attorney General.* 1912, p. 1206.

A board of education may not provide that the superintendent of schools shall receive, in addition to a stated salary, all funds received for tuition of non-resident pupils, for the reason that such payment would not be a "fixed" salary as intended by Section 7690, General Code.

Furthermore, such would be in contravention to Section 7603, General Code, which provides special distribution for the respective funds under the control of the board. — *Attorney General,* 1912, p. 491.

The amounts retained by the county auditor under Sec. 4744-3, General Code, for the purpose of paying part of the salaries of the county superintendent of schools and the district superintendents should be charged against the apportionment of the state common school fund, and against the tuition fund of the district. — *Attorney General*, Opinion No. 168, March 26, 1915.

Failure of the auditor to make the apportionment, does not render the funds contingent, to be expended at the discretion of the board of education: State, ex rel., v. Zeeb, 9 O. C. C. 13, 6 O. C. D. 70.

Each apportionment is a separate transaction; and a deficit or surplus in one year does not justify and require a change in the apportionment for another year: Saunders v. State, 2 O. C. C. 475, 1 O. C. D. 596.

Deposit
of school
funds;
limitation.

SECTION 7604. That within thirty days after the first Monday of January, 1916, and every two years thereafter, the board of education of any school district by resolution shall provide for the deposit of any or all moneys coming into the hands of its treasurer. But no bank shall receive a deposit larger than the amount of its paid in capital stock, and in no event to exceed three hundred thousand dollars. (106 v. 328.)

The treasurer of a school district who deposits money in a bank other than in conformity with the provisions of the depository law, together with the sureties upon his bond, is responsible for losses sustained by failure of the bank. Mere knowledge by the board of education of such deposit does not relieve the treasurer and his sureties of liability. — *Attorney General*, Opinion No. 52, Feb. 2, 1915.

The duty of the board of education to deposit the money of the school district on competitive bidding is such an obligation of public interest and right as to permit an individual taxpayer to maintain a mandamus suit for its compulsion. — *Attorney General*, 1911-12, p. 372.

Section 7604 of the General Code makes it mandatory upon the board of education of a school district to establish a depository and when it fails so to do legal proceedings may invoke to compel the same.

When such depository has not been established, however, money may be paid to the treasurer of such school district in accordance with the procedure set out in Sections 4764, 4768 and 4769 of the General Code. — *Attorney General*, 1912, p. 329.

. There is only one limitation in the Smith law upon levies for "specific purposes" such as one for library purposes, and that is found in section 5649-3, which provides that the rate for such purpose shall not exceed such rate as when levied upon all property of the district in 1911 would not exceed the amount which might have been levied for such purpose in 1910.

By the second paragraph of section 5649-3 this limitation may be exceeded, if for another purpose a less amount is levied than was levied for such other purpose in 1910. — *Attorney General*, 1912, p. 1192.

Inasmuch as it is mandatory upon the board of education to place the deposits in a bank offering the highest rate of interest for the same, members of the board who are stockholders in, or officers of the bank making the best bid, are not criminally liable for ma ing such bank the depository. — *Attorney General*, 1912, p. 1246.k

The deposit of a board of education of a village district wherein there is no bank, is governed by section 7607, General Code, which provides for a contract by the board with a conveniently located bank offering the highest interest. Such a contract is within section 4757, General Code, and when made by the board, with a bank whereof a member of the board is both a stockholder and a director, it is therefore void. — *Attorney General*, 1912, p. 254.

Section 2295, General Code, provides that all moneys from both principal and premiums on the sale of bonds (by a board of education) shall be credited to the fund on account of which the bonds are issued and sold. Such premiums and accrued interest must be applied to the fund created by the sale of bonds and not to the sinking fund.

Section 7603, General Code, provides that "moneys coming from sources not enumerated herein shall be placed in the contingent fund." This is the only section in any way bearing upon the distribution of an unexpended surplus in a fund raised by a bond issued by a board of education, and therefore, under the technical construction of the statute, such unexpended surplus must be paid into the contingent fund. Such a procedure, however, is in conflict with sound business principles and with the procedure outlined by the statutes, with reference to the disposition of such funds in other taxable districts, and the better course would be to credit such surplus to the sinking fund, for the purpose of devoting the same to the reduction of the bonded indebtedness upon the theory that specific provision therefor has been mistakenly omitted from the statutes. — *Attorney General,* 1913, p. 1473.

The board of commissioners of the sinking fund of a school district appointed under G. C. Sec. 7614, is entitled to the management and control of said fund for the payment of debts and investment of the surplus without dictation, but is not entitled to the custody or possession thereof: State, ex rel., v. Board of Education, 3 O. N. P. (N. S.) 401, 16 O. D. (N. P.) 386.

Under G. C. Sections 4768, 76[16] and 7617, orders drawn on the sinking funds of a school district must be drawn by the president and clerk of the board of education in favor of the person entitled thereto upon requisition made upon them by the board of education therefor: State, ex rel., v. Board of Education, 3 O. N. P. (N. S.) 401.

The term "capital stock" used in this section means "capital"; and accordingly a partnership bank, as well as one which is incorporated, may be selected as a depository for such funds: State, ex rel., v. Board of Education, 15 O. D. (N. P.) 720.

SECTION 7605. In school districts containing two or more banks such deposit shall be made in the bank or banks, situated therein, that at competitive bidding offer the righest rate of interest which must be at least two per cent for the full time funds or any part thereof are on deposit. Such bank or banks shall give a good and sufficient bond, or shall deposit bonds of the United States, the state of Ohio or county, municipal, township or school bonds issued by the authority of the state of Ohio, at the option of the board of education, in a sum not less than the amount deposited. The treasurer of the school district must see that a greater sum than that contained in the bond is not deposited in such bank or banks and he and his bondsmen shall be liable for any loss occasioned by deposits in excess of such bond. But no contract for the deposit of school funds shall be made for a longer period than two years. (106 v. 328.)

Deposit when district contains two or more banks; bond of depository.

The duty of the board of education to deposit the money of the school district on competitive bidding is such an obligation of public interest and right as to permit an individual taxpayer to maintain a mandamus suit for its compulsion. — *Attorney General,* 1911-12, p. 372.

Section 2295, General Code, provides that all moneys from both principal and premiums on the sale of bonds (by a board of education) shall be credited to the fund on account of which the bonds are issued and sold. Such premiums and accrued interest must be applied to the fund created by the sale of bonds and not to the sinking fund.

Section 7603, General Code, provides that "moneys coming from sources not enumerated herein shall be placed in the contingent fund." This is the only section in any way bearing upon the distribution of an unexpended surplus in a fund raised by a bond issued by a board of education, and therefore, under the technical construction of the statute, such unexpended surplus must be paid into the contingent fund. Such a procedure, however, is in conflict with sound business principles and with the procedure outlined by the statutes, with reference to the disposition of such funds in other taxable districts, and the better course would be to credit such surplus to the sinking fund, for the purpose of devoting the same to the reduction of the bonded indebtedness upon the theory that specific provision therefor has been mistakenly omitted from the statutes. — *Attorney General*, 1913, p. 1473.

The purpose of G. C. Sections 7604 to 7609 is to obtain a revenue from the idle funds of the school board. Accordingly the provision that the depository shall give "a good and sufficient bond of some approved guaranty company" is incidental merely and shows an intention to require a good, sufficient and valid bond, and nothing more: State, ex rel., v. Rehfuss, 7 O. C. C. (N. S.) 179, 19 O. C. D. 62.

The board of education has discretion to keep its funds in the hands of its treasury, or to place them on deposit in a bank; but when it is determined upon the policy of placing its funds on deposit with a bank, and has advertised to receive bids, the statute becomes mandatory in that the deposits must be made with a bank which, at competitive bidding, offers the highest rate of interest: State, ex rel., v. Board of Education, 15 O. D. (N. S.) 720.

Bids.

SECTION 7606. The board shall determine in such resolution the method by which bids shall be received, the authority which is to receive them, the time for which such deposits shall be made and all details for carrying into effect the authority herein given. All proceedings in connection with such competitive bidding and deposits of moneys must be so conducted as to insure full publicity and shall be open at all time to public inspection. If in the opinion of a board of education there has been any collusion between the bidders, it may reject any or all bids and arrange for the deposit of funds in a bank or banks without the district as hereinafter provided for in districts not having two or more banks located therein. (97 v. 351.)

Section 2295, General Code, provides that all moneys from both principal and premiums on the sale of bonds (by a board of education) shall be credited to the fund on account of which the bonds are issued and sold. Such premiums and accrued interest must be applied to the fund created by the sale of bonds and not to the sinking fund.

Section 7603, General Code, provides that "moneys coming from sources not enumerated herein shall be placed in the contingent fund." This is the only section in any way bearing upon the distribution of an unexpended surplus in a fund raised by a bond issued by a board of education, and therefore, under the technical construction of the statute, such unexpended surplus must be paid into the contingent fund. Such a procedure, however, is in conflict with sound business principles and with the procedure outlined by the statutes, with reference to the disposition of such funds in other taxable districts, and the better course would be to credit such surplus to the sinking fund, for the purpose of devoting the same to the reduction of the bonded indebtedness upon the theory that specific provision therefor has been mistakenly omitted from the statutes.—*Attorney General*, 1913, p. 1473.

SECTION 7607. In all school districts containing less than two banks, after the adoption of a resolution providing for the deposit of its funds, the board of education may enter into a contract with one or more banks that are conveniently located and offer the highest rate of interest, which shall not be less than two percent for the full time the funds or any part thereof are on deposit. Such bank or banks shall give good and sufficient bond or shall deposit bonds of United States, the state of Ohio, or county, municipal, township or school bonds issued by the authority of the state of Ohio at the option of the board of education in a sum at least equal to the amount deposited. The treasurer of the school district must see that a greater sum than that contained in the bond is not deposited in such bank or banks, and he and his bondsmen shall be liable for any loss occasioned by deposits in excess of such bond. (101 v. 290.)

Districts containing less than two banks.

This section is constitutional: State, ex rel., v. Rehfuss, 7 O. C. C. (N. S.) 179, 19 O. C. D. 62.

The duty of the board of education to deposit the money of the school district on competitive bidding is such an obligation of public interest and right as to permit an individual taxpayer to maintain a mandamus suit for its compulsion. — *Attorney General,* 1911-12, p. 372.

Section 2295, General Code, provides that all moneys from both principal and premiums on the sale of bonds (by a board of education) shall be credited to the fund on account of which the bonds are issued and sold. Such premiums and accrued interest must be applied to the fund created by the sale of bonds and not to the sinking fund.

Section 7603, General Code, provides that "moneys coming from sources not enumerated herein shall be placed in the contingent fund." This is the only section in any way bearing upon the distribution of an unexpended surplus in a fund raised by a bond issued by a board of education, and therefore, under the technical construction of the statute, such unexpended surplus must be paid into the contingent fund. Such a procedure, however, is in conflict with sound business principles and with the procedure outlined by the statutes, with reference to the disposition of such funds in other taxable districts, and the better course would be to credit such surplus to the sinking fund, for the purpose of devoting the same to the reduction of the bonded indebtedness upon the theory that specific provision therefor has been mistakenly omitted from the statutes. — *Attorney General,* 1913, p. 1473.

The treasurer of a school district who deposits money in a bank other than in conformity to the provisions of the depository law, together with the sureties upon his bond, is responsible for losses sustained by failure of the bank. Mere knowledge by the board of education of such deposit does not relieve the treasurer and his sureties of liability. — *Attorney General,* Opinion No. 52, Feb. 2, 1915.

SECTION 7608. The resolution and contract in the net four precedinxg sections provided for, shall set forth fully all details necessary to carry into effect the authority therein given. All proceeding connected with the adoption of such resolution and the making of such contract must be conducted in such a manner as to insure full publicity and shall be open at all times to public inspection. (97 v. 351.)

What resolution to contain.

Section 2295, General Code, provides that all moneys from both principal and premiums on the sale of bonds (by a board of education) shall be credited to the fund on account of which the bonds are issued and sold. Such premiums and accrued interest must be applied to the fund created by the sale of bonds and not to the sinking fund.

Section 7603, General Code, provides that "moneys coming from sources not enumerated herein shall be placed in the contingent fund." This is the only section in any way bearing upon the distribution of an unexpended surplus in a fund raised by a bond issued by a board of education, and therefore, under the technical construction of the statute, such unexpended surplus must be paid into the contingent fund. Such a procedure, however, is in conflict with sound business principles and with the procedure outlined by the statutes, with reference to the disposition of such funds in other taxable districts, and the better course would be to credit such surplus to the sinking fund, for the purpose of devoting the same to the reduction of the bonded indebtedness upon the theory that specific provision therefor has been mistakenly omitted from the statutes. — *Attorney General*, 1913, p. 1473.

This section is constitutional: State, ex rel., v. Rehfuss, 7 O. C. C. (N. S.) 179, 19 O. C. D. 62.

Liability of treasurer relieved.

SECTION 7609. When a depository is lawfully provided, and the funds are deposited therein, the treasurer of the school district and his bondsmen shall be relieved from any liability occasioned by the failure of the bank or banks of deposit or by the failure of the sureties therefor, or by the failure of either of them, except as above provided in cases of excessive deposits. Upon the failure of the board of education of any school district to provide a depository according to law the members of the board of education shall be liable for any loss occasioned by their failure to provide such depository, and in addition shall pay to the treasurer of the school funds two per cent on the average daily balance on the school funds during the time said school district shall be without a depository. Said moneys may be recovered from the members of the board of education for the use and benefit of the school funds of the district upon the suit of any taxpayer of the school district. (106 v. 328.)

This section is constitutional: State, ex rel., v. Rehfuss, 7 O. C. C. (N. S.) 179, 19 O. C. D. 62.

The duty of the board of education to deposit the money of the school district on competitive bidding is such an obligation of public interest and right as to permit an individual taxpayer to maintain a mandamus suit for its compulsion. — *Attorney General*, 1911-12, p. 372.

Section 2295, General Code, provides that all moneys from both principal and premiums on the sale of bonds (by a board of education) shall be credited to the fund on account of which the bonds are issued and sold. Such premiums and accrued interest must be applied to the fund created by the sale of bonds and not to the sinking fund.

Section 7603, General Code, provides that "moneys coming from sources not enumerated herein shall be placed in the contingent fund." This is the only section in any way bearing upon the distribution of an unexpended surplus in a fund raised by a bond issued by a board of education, and therefore, under the technical construction of the statute, such unexpended surplus must be paid into the contingent fund. Such a procedure, however, is in conflict with sound business principles and with the procedure outlined by the statutes, with reference to the disposition of such funds in other taxable districts, and the better course would be to credit such surplus to the sinking fund, for the purpose of devoting the same to the reduction of the bonded indebtedness upon the theory that specific provision therefor has been mistakenly omitted from the statutes. — *Attorney General*, 1913, p. 1473.

The treasurer of a school district who deposits money in a bank other than in conformity to the provisions of the depository law, together with the sureties upon his bond, is responsible for losses sustained by failure of the bank. Mere knowledge by the board of education of such deposit does not relieve the treasurer and his sureties of liability. — *Attorney General*, Opinion No. 52, 1915.

SECTION 7610. If the board of education in a district fails in any year to estimate and certify the levy for a contingent fund as required by this chapter, or if the amount so certified is deemed insufficient for school purposes, or if it fails to provide sufficient school privileges for all the youth of school age in the district or to provide for the continuance of any school in the district for at least thirty-two weeks in the year, or to provide for each school an equitable share of school advantages as required by this title, or to provide suitable schoolhouses for all the schools under its control, or to elect a superintendent or teachers, or to pay their salaries, or to pay out any other school money needed in school administration, or to fill any vacancies in the board within the period of thirty days after such vacancies occur, the commissioners of the county to which such district belongs, upon being advised and satisfied thereof, shall perform any or all of such duties and acts, in the same manner as the board of education by this title, is authorized to perform them. All salaries and other money so paid by the commissioners of the county, shall be paid out of the county treasury as are other county expenses, but they shall be a charge against the school district for which the money was paid. The amount so paid shall be retained by the county auditor from the proper funds due to such school district, at the time of making the semi-annual distribution of taxes. (99 v. 51.)

Neglect of certain duties by board.

A county commissioner cannot hold the office of member of the board of education of any school district within the county for which he is such commissioner. — *Attorney General*, Opinion.

When under Section 7610, General Code, the commissioners have, by reason of the failure of the board of education so to do, made an appointment to fill a vacancy in the board of education, such appointment can be made only "for the unexpired term."

When the county commissioners through a mistaken understanding of their powers, have entered upon their minutes that the appointment is "until the next general election," the fact that the appointment is in reality for the unexpired term is not affected, and a "nunc pro tunc" entry to that effect may be made upon the commissioners' journal as notice of the statutory term. — *Attorney General*, 1912, p. 1146.

County commissioners can only employ teachers when the township board of education fails to do so; and when they have suspended school in two subdistricts and provided transportation to other districts it is not a failure to make lawful provision for school in such district and the county commissioners cannot interfere: Wayne Tp. (Bd. of Ed.) v. Shaul, 17 Dec. 269 (4 N. S. 433.)

When the county commissoners have wrongfully interferred with the management of township schools the remedy of the township board of education is by injunction: Wayne Tp. (Bd. of Ed.) v. Shaul, 17 Dec. 269 (4 N. S.) 433).

Before a teacher may be entitled to $2.00 per day for attendance at an institute as provided by section 7870 G. C., he must have attended such institute at least for four days, and the rule is the same whether during such attendance school is in session or not.

A teacher cannot be compelled to do janitor work by the board of education unless under the terms of a special contract with said teacher and providing for extra compensation therefor. Section 7610 provides for relief through the county commissioners, where the board fails to provide janitor service.— *Attorney General*, 1911-12, p. 201.

In fixing the school levy, and in determining the number of schools which shall be maintained in a school district, the board of education is exercising official discretion, and the county commissioners have no authority to interfere, unless the policy of the board of education is a gross abuse of the discretion confided in it by law: Board of Education v. Commissioners, 10 O. N. P. (N. S.) 505.

If the levy for school purposes is limited in accordance with the provisions of G. C. Sec. 7591, and if the estimate and certificate of the board of education is insufficient, the remedy is by application to the county commissioners: State, ex rel., v. School District, 20 O. C. D. 657.

If the board of education of a village district fails to elect a superintendent of schools, and the county commissoners appoint a superintendent, he is, in such case, to be paid out of the funds of the school, as he would be if he were elected by the board of education: State, ex rel., v. Board of Education, 3 O. N. P. 236, 4 O. D. (N. P.) 329.

County commissioners denied jurisdiction to reverse township board's action in fixing levy and determining number of schools to be maintained, especiallly where condition requiring more subdistricts is temporary: Washington Tp. (Bd. of Ed.) v. Board of County Commissioners, 24 Dec. 495 (10 N. S. 505).

Personal liability of board members.

SECTION 7611. The members of a board who cause such failure shall be each severally liable, in a penalty not to exceed fifty dollars nor less than twenty-five dollars, to be recovered in a civil action in the name of the state upon complaint of any elector of the district, which sum must be collected by the prosecuting attorney of the county and when collected be paid into the treasury of the county, for the benefit of the school or schools of the district. (99 v. 51.)

Duty of county auditor.

SECTION 7612. The auditor of each county shall collect, or cause to be collected, all fines and other money for the support of common schools in his county, and pay them to the county treasurer. He also must inspect all accounts of interest accruing on account of section sixteen, or other school lands, whether it is payable by the state or by the debtors; and take all proper measures to secure to each school district in his county the full amount of school funds to which it is entitled. (70 v. 195.)

FINES TO BE PAID INTO SCHOOL FUND.

Secs. 2605 and 2606. Penalty against county auditors for failing to report to state auditor.

Sec. 2607. Relating to dog tax.

Sec. 2924. Relating to the disposition of the proceeds of the sale of timber growing on state or school lands, unlawfully cut down.

Secs. 12465 and 12466. Providing for the disposition of the proceeds of the sale of unclaimed property, stolen, embezzled, or obtained under false pretenses.

Sec. 3192. Penalty against township trustees and treasurers who refuse to serve.

Sec. 3304. Penalty against township clerk for failure to make detailed statement.

Sec. 8358. Penalty against assessors for neglecting or refusing to make out and return statistics.

Sec. 3359. Penalty against any person, company, or corporation, refusing to make out and deliver a statement of facts for taxation.

Sec. 8309. Relating to the proceeds of the sale of unclaimed goods by express companies, common carriers, etc.

Sec. 9238. Penalty for avoiding toll on turnpikes or plank road.

Sec. 7611. Penalty against member of board of education who fails to perform certain duties.

Sec. 7802. Penalty against the clerk of a local board for failure to take the school enumeration.

Sec. 4772. Penalty against treasurers of school districts for failure to make annual settlement.

Sec. 7790. Penalty against county auditors and clerks of boards of education for failing to make certain reports.

Sec. 7792. Penalty against county auditors for failure to make einumeration return.

Sec. 7867. Penalty against institute committee for failure to make required report.

Secs. 5808 and 5814. Penalty for allowing certain animals to run at large.

Sec. 6321. Penalty against owners or keepers of wharf boats.

Sec. 6350. Relating to peddlers' license.

Sec. 6497. Penalty against auditors, engineers, commissioners, and probate judges, who fail to perform certain duties relating to county ditches, sinkholes, etc.

The fact that the auditor does not apportion the school funds, as required by G. C. Sec. 7600, does not render such fund contingent; and the board of education cannot expend it at its discretion: State, ex rel., v. Zeeb, 9 O. C. C. 13.

SINKING FUND.

SECTION 7613. In any school district having a bonded indebtedness, for the payment of which, with interest, no provision has been made by a special tax levy for that particular purpose, the board of education of such district annually, on or before the thirty-first day of August, shall set aside from its revenue a sum equal to not less than one-fortieth of such indebtedness together with a sum sufficient to pay the annual interest thereon. (97 v. 352 § 1.)

Board of commissioners of the sinking fund.

Under a statute providing for a board of fund trustees and visitors of common schools in a municipal corporation, such corporation is not liable for an injury suffered by a pupil of such school by reason of the negligence of such board: Diehm v. Cincinnati, 25 O. S. 305.

Boards of education may borrow money for only two purposes:

1. For specific building or improvement enterprises.

2. To fund or refund a valid existing indebtedness of the district.

Inasmuch as no indebtedness may be created except in case of hiring of teachers and other employes, without the issuance of a certificate of the clerk to the effect that the money necessary is in the treasury to the credit of the proper fund and not appropriated for any other purpose, it is clear that a valid existing indebtedness for contingent expenses, could not be created beyond the amount in the treasury to cover the same. There cannot, therefore, exist, so far as contingent expenses are concerned, such a valid existing indebtedness as would permit the funding or refunding of the same.

Sections 7587 and 7613, General Code, provide for the creation of a sinking fund for the payment of bonds and interest out of the board's levy, and Section 7614, General Code, provides for the appointment of commissioners of the sinking fund, through the common pleas court.

These sections are mandatory and the interest on the money borrowed by reason of exhaustion of funds for the payment of teachers should be paid from such sinking fund and such should not be paid from either the tuition or the contingent fund. — *Attorney General*, 1912, p. 1519.

Under Section 7604, General Code, and the following statutes which provide for the deposit of all moneys coming into the hands of the treasurer of the board of education of a school district and the following statutes which provide the mode of procedure for deposit of funds; and under section 4768, which provides that no money shall be withdrawn from depositories except upon an order signed by the treasurer and by the president or vice-president, and counter-signed by the clerk of the board of education; and under section 7613, and related statutes, which require the board of education to set aside and appropriate funds for the use of the sinking fund commission, the custody of such funds must reside with the board and its treasurer, whilst the control of the same is vested in the sinking fund commission.

The commission of the sinking fund may withdraw for its own purpose from such funds, therefore, only by requisition directed to the board. — *Attorney General,* 1913, p. 260.

Under section 7614, General Code, it is the mandatory duty of a board of education having a funded debt, to levy for the retirement of the bond and payment of interest, and to create a sinking fund commission, and even though such commission be not created, a levy specifically made for the payment of bonds and interest must be credited to the sinking and separated from other funds of the district.

The purpose of the sinking fund cannot be considered to have been accomplished until the bonds for which it is intended to provide, have been fully paid, and there is never a surplus in the sinking fund until all bonds and interest outstanding are paid and discharged.

For this reason moneys in the sinking fund may not be appropriated to any other purpose, under section 5649-3e, General Code, which section authorizes balances remaining over after the fixed charges shall have been terminated, to revert to the general fund. Any surplus remaining after all bonds and interest have been paid may be transferred to the contingent fund under section 5655, General Code. — *Attorney General,* 1913, p. 1139.

Who to pro-vide funds. SECTION 7614. The board of education of every district shall provide a sinking fund for the extinguishment of all its bonded indebtedness, which fund shall be managed and controlled by a board of commissioners designated as the "board of comissioners of the sinking fund of ...." (insert the name of the district), which shall be composed of five electors thereof, and be appointed by the common pleas court of the county in which such district is chiefly located, except that, in city or village districts the board of commissioners of the sinking fund of the city or village may be the board of the school district. Such commissioners shall serve without compensation and give such bond as the board of education requires and approves. Any surety company authorized to sign such bonds may be accepted by such board of education as surety. The cost therof, together with all necessary expenses of such commissioners shall be paid by them out of the funds under their control. (97 v. 352 § 1.)

The board of commissioners of the sinking fund of a school district are entitled to its management and control: State, ex rel., v. Board of Education, 3 O. N. P. (N. S.) 401, 16 O. D. (N. P.) 386.

Under Section 7604, General Code, and the following statutes which provide for the deposit of all moneys coming into the hands of the treasurer of the board of education of a school district and the following statutes which provide the mode of procedure for deposit of funds; and under section 4768, which provides that no money shall be withdrawn from depositories except upon an order signed by the treasurer and by the president or vice-president, and counter-signed by the clerk of the board of education; and under section 7613, and related statutes, which require the board of education to set aside and appropriate funds for the use of the sinking fund commission, the custody of such funds must reside with the board and its treasurer, whilst the control of the same is vested in the sinking fund commission.

The commission of the sinking fund may withdraw for its own purpose from such funds, therefore, only by requisition directed to the board. — *Attorney General,* 1913, p. 260.

Under section 7614, General Code, it is the mandatory duty of a board of education having a funded debt, to levy for the retirement of the bond and payment of interest, and to create a sinking fund commission, and even though such commission be not created, a levy specifically made for the payment of bonds and interest must be credited to the sinking and separated from other funds of the district.

The purpose of the sinking fund cannot be considered to have been accomplished until the bonds for which it is intended to provide, have been fully paid, and there is never a surplus in the sinking fund until all bonds and interest outstanding are paid and discharged.

For this reason moneys in the sinking fund may not be appropriated to any other purpose, under section 5649-3e, General Code, which section authorizes balances remaining over after the fixed charges shall have been terminated, to revert to the general fund. Any surplus remaining after all bonds and interest have been paid may be transferred to the contingnet fund under section 5655, General Code. — *Attorney General,* 1913, p. 1139.

SECTION 7615. The board of commissioners of the sinking fund shall invest that fund in bonds of the United States, of the state of Ohio, of any municipal corporation, county, township or school district of any state or in bonds of its own issue. All interest received from such investments shall be deposited as other funds of such sinking fund and reinvested in like manner. For the extinguisment of any bonded indebtedness included in such fund, the board of commissioners may sell or use any of the securities or money of such fund. (98 v. 45 § 2.)

Investment of sinking fund.

The board of commissioners of the sinking fund of a school district, appointed under the preceding section, is entitled to the management and control of said fund for the payment of debts and investment of the surplus without dictation, but is not entitled to the cusody of possession thereof: State, ex rel., v. Board of Education, 3 O. N. P. (N. S.) 401.

Under Section 7604, General Code, and the following statutes which provide for the deposit of all moneys coming into the hands of the treasurer of the board of education of a school district and the following statutes which provide the mode of procedure for deposit of funds; and under section 4768, which provides that no money shall be withdrawn from depositories except upon an order signed by the treasurer and by the president or vice-president, and counter-signed by the clerk of the board' of education; and under section 7613, and related statutes, which require the board of education to set aside and appropriate funds for the use of the sinking fund commission, the custody of such funds must reside with the board and its treasurer, whilst the control of the same is vested in the sinking fund commission.

The commission of the sinking fund may withdraw for its own purpose from such funds, therefore, only by requisition direced to the board. — *Attorney General,* 1913, p. 260.

Under section 7614, General Code, it is the mandatory duty of a board of education having a funded debt, to levy for the retirement of the bond and payment of interest, and to create a sinking fund commission, and even though such commission be not created, a levy specifically made for the payment of bonds and interest must be credited to the sinking and separated from other funds of the district.

The purpose of the sinking fund cannot be considered to have been accomplished until the bonds for which it is intended to provide, have been fully paid, and there is never a surplus in the sinking fund until all bonds and interest outstanding are paid and discharged.

For this reason moneys in the sinking fund may not be appropriated to any other purpose, under section 5649-3e, General Code, which section authorizes balances, remaining over after the fixed charges shall have been terminated, to revert to the general fund. Any surplus remaining after all bonds and interest have been paid may be transferred to the contingent fund under section 5655, General Code. — *Attorney General*, 1913, p. 1139.

Sinking fund commissioners may, issue re-funding bonds.   SECTION 7616. The board of commissioners of the sinking fund may refund, extend or renew the bonded debt of the school district or any part thereof, existing April 25, 1904, by issuing the bonds of such school district for such periods, not exceeding twenty years, in such denomination, payable at such place and at a rate of interest not to exceed the rate previous to such refunding, extension or renewal. But the aggregate amount of the refunding, extending or renewing bonds so issued shall not exceed that of the bonds so refunded, extended or renewed. (97 v. 353 § 3.)

Report of sinking fund commissioners.   SECTION 7617. The board of commissioners of the sinking fund shall make an annual report to the board of education giving a detailed statement of the sinking fund for each year ending with August thirty-first. Such report must be filed with the board of education on or before September thirtieth of each year and other reports may be required by such board of education when deemed necessary. (98 v. 45 § 4.)   ,

Orders upon the sinking fund must be drawn by the president and clerk of the board of education, in favor of the person entitled thereto, upon requisition made upon them by the board of education therefor: State, ex rel., v. Board of Education, 3 O. N. P. (N. S.) 401, 16 O. D. (N. P.) 386.

Payment of bonds and interest.   SECTION 7618. The board of education shall appropriate to the use of such sinking fund any taxes levied for the payment of interest on its bonded indebtedness, together with the sum provided for in sections seventy-six hundred thirteen and seventy-six hundred and fourteen. Sums so apporpriated shall be applied to no other purpose than the payment fo such bonds, interest thereon and necessary expenses of such sinking fund commission. (98 v. 45 § 4.)

Under Section 7604, General Code, and the following statutes which provide for the deposit of all moneys coming into the hands of the treasurer of the board of education of a school district and the following statutes which provide the mode of procedure for deposit of funds; and under section 4768, which provides that no money shall be withdrawn from depositories except upon an order signed by the treasurer and by the president or vice-president, and counter-signed by the clerk of the board of education; and under section 7613, and related statutes, which require the board of education to set aside and appropriate funds for the use of the sinking fund commission, the custody of such funds must reside with the board and its treasurer, whilst the control of the same is vested in the sinking fund commission.

The commission of the sinking fund may withdraw for its own purpose from such funds, therefore. only by requisition directed to the board. — *Attorney General, 1913, p. 260.*

Under section 7614, General Code, it is the mandatory duty of a board of education having a funded debt, to levy for the retirement of the bond and payment of interest, and to create a sinking fund commission, and even though such commission be not created, a levy specifically made for the payment of bonds and interest must be credited to the sinking and separated from other funds of the district.

The purpose of the sinking fund cannot be considered to have been accomplished until the bonds for which it is intended to provide, have been fully paid, and there is never a surplus in the sinking fund until all bonds and interest outstanding are paid and discharged.

For this reason moneys in the sinking fund may not be appropriated to any other purpose, under section 5649-3e, Genreal Code, which section authorizes balances remaining over after the fixed charges shall have been terminated, to revert to the general fund. Any surplus remaining after all bonds and interest have been paid may be transferred to the contingent fund under section 5655, General Code. — *Attorney General, 1915, p. 1139.*

SECTION 7619. When a board of education issues bonds for any purpose, such issue first shall be offered for sale to the board of commissioners of the sinking fund, who may buy any or all of such bonds at par. Within five days of the time when notice is given, the board shall notify the board of education of its action upon the proposed purchase. After that time the board of education shall issue any portion not purchased by such commission according to law. (98 v. 45 § 4.) {Bonds issued by board of education.}

It is necessary to advertise the sale of bonds by a board of education under Section 7626. G. C., and a board of education is not authorized to dispense with competitive bidding in the sale of the same.

A board of education which has advertised the sale of bonds bearing a certain rate of interest, and has received no bids for the same, and which then proceeds by resolution to raise the rate of interest on said bonds, must again offer said bonds to the board of commissioners of the sinking fund of the school district. if such there be, and then to the Industrial Commission of Ohio. prior to again advertising the same for sale. — *Attorney General,* Opinion No. 79, 1915.

Where specific power is given by the legislature authorizing board of education to issue negotiable bonds for school purposes upon certain conditions prescribed,. the regularity of the proceedings of the board cannot be disputed, where the bonds, upon their face, purport to have been issued under the law in question. and where they have been sold by the board and afterward passed into the hands of a bona fide holder: State, ex rel., v. Board of Education, 27 O. S. 96.

For the power of the board of education to borrow money to pay debts. and to issue bonds therefor, see State, ex rel., v. Board of Education, 35 O. S. 519.

SECTION 6510. The board of education of a district interested in land granted by congress for the support of common schools, unless such lands have been permanently leased. and of a district owning or holding other land for school purposes, when an assessment is made upon such land, or part thereof. under the provisions of this chapter, shall pay such assessment out of the contingent fund of {When board of education may levy to pay assessment.}

the district, and, if necessary for that purpose, may increase the levy for such fund otherwise authorized by law. (68 v. 60.)

Disposition of proceeds of sale.

SECTION 8369. From the proceeds of such property, such person, association, or company, shall pay all the necessary costs and expenses of the sale, and all proper charges for freight and storage of the property sold, apportioning such expenses and charges, as near as may be, among the articles sold, to the amount received for each and hold any overplus, subject to the order of the owner thereof, at any time within one year after the sale, upon proof of ownership by affidavit of the claimant or his attorney. After the expiration of one year, all such sums unclaimed shall be paid into the state treasury, to be placed to the credit of the common schools. Any article remaining unsold may be again offered as above provided, until sold. (74 v. 18.)

Accumulations, how invested.

SECTION 9357. A company organized under the laws of this state may invest its accumulations as follows:

1. In United States, state, county, school or city bonds, if their market value at the date of purchase, is at least eighty per cent of their par value.

2. In bonds and mortgages upon unincumbered real estate, the market value of which is at least double the amount loaned thereon, at the date of the investment, and in bonds and mortgages upon leasehold estates on real estate for ninety-nine years renewable forever, unincumbered, except rentals accruing therefrom to the owner of the fee, the market value of which leasehold estate is at least double the amount loaned thereon at the date of investment. If the amount loaned exceeds one-half of the value of the land mortgaged, or one-half the value of the leasehold estate mortgaged, exclusive of structures thereon, such structures must be insured in an authorized fire insurance company or companies, in an amount not less than the difference between one-half the value of such land, or leasehold estate, exclusive of structures, and the amount loaned, and the policy or policies shall be assigned to the mortgagee. The value of such real or leasehold estate, shall be determined by a valuation, made under oath by two real estate owners, residents of the county where the real estate, or leasehold, is located.

3. In loans upon the pledge of such bonds or mortgages, if the current market value of the bonds or mortgages is at least twenty-five per cent more than the amount loaned thereon.

4. In loans upon its own policies, not exceeding the reserve or present value thereof, computed according to the American Experience Table of Mortality with interest at four per cent, or according to such other higher standard or standards as the company has adopted, the reserve be-

ing the amount of debts of life insurance companies by reason of their outstanding policies in gross, and which may be so treated in the returns for taxation made by them. Such companies may sell, change, or reinvest such investments, or any part thereof, at pleasure. (102 v. 356.)

SECTION 9660. To invest any of its idle funds, or any part thereof, in bonds or interest bearing obligations of the United States, or of the District of Columbia, or of the state of Ohio, or of any county, township, school district, or other political division in the state of Ohio, or of any incorporated city or village, in the state of Ohio; and in such other securities as now are or hereafter may be accepted by the United States to secure government deposits in national banks. But such investments at no time shall amount in the aggregate to more than twenty per cent of the assets of such corporation. (99 v. 530 § 16.)

Idle funds, how invested.

CHAPTER 2.

SCHOOL HOUSES AND LIBRARIES.

SCHOOL HOUSES.

Powers and duties of boards of education.

SECTION 7620. The board of education of a district may build, enlarge, repair and furnish the necessary school houses, purchase or lease sites therefor, or rights of way thereto or purchase or lease real estate to be used as playgrounds for children, or rent suitable schoolrooms, provide the necessary apparatus and make all other necessary provisions for the schools under its control. It also, shall provide fuel for schools, build and keep in good repair fences inclosing such school houses, when deemed desirable plant shade and ornamental trees on the school grounds, and make all other provisions necessary for the convenience and prosperity of the schools within the subdistricts. (102 v. 419.)

Courts of common pleas may authorize an exchange of school lots; Sec. 3707.

County commissioners may act as board of education under certain cricumstances; Sec. 7610.

Penalty for destroying plants or trees; Sec. 12490.

Penalty for using school house without certificate of inspector; Sec. 12574.

Under authority of Sections 4749 and 7620, General Code, boards of education may legally construct a foot bridge upon a strip of land in which a right of way for a walk has been deeded it and a condition in the deed for such right of way providing for its use by the board in common with the grantor would not invalidate the same. — *Attorney General*, 1912, 1842.

Section· 7620, General Code, makes it a mandatory duty of the board of education of the district, to build and keep in good repair, fences inclosing school houses. — *Attorney General*, 1911-12, p. 1212.

Board of education may not become a member of a mutual insurance association. There is a broad distinction between "loaning of credit" of a board of education to private business enterprises for the procurance of his immediate needs, such as coal, etc., and the loaning of its credit as a member of a mutual insurance association. The latter is within constitutional inhibition upon the government or any of its subdivisions against becoming a stockholder in, raising money for, or loaning its credit to, a joint stock company, corporation or association. Furthermore, membership in such an associaiton would be inharmonious with the nature of the board of education and with its statutory duties.

Such membership would include a view to gain and an object to further pecuniary interests. — *Attorney General*, 1911-12, p. 1690.

Where a township district school house is located upon a private road, and other lawful means for securing a necessary and convenient approach to the school house being absent, it is proper for the board of education to provide for the construction of a bridge on this road, under the provisions of Section 7620, General Code. — *Attorney General*, Opinion No. 777, 1914.

All persons who deal with a board of education or other public officer or board are charged with knowledge of the powers and authority of such board or officer. Accordingly contracts entered into by such board or officer are unenforceable, if in excess of the authority conferred upon them by law, even if the person dealing with such board or officer was in fact ignorant of such powers: State, ex rel., v. Freed, 10 O. C. C. 294, 6 O. C. D. 550.

A lease of a public schoolhouse for the purpose of having a private or select school taught therein for a term of weeks, is in violation of the trust; and such use of the schoolhouse may be restrained at the suit of a resident taxpayer of the district: Weir v. Day, 35 O. S. 143.

' The incorporated village of Van Wert was laid out in 1835, and the proprietors by plat duly acknowledged and recorded, dedicated two specified lots therein "for school purposes, and on which to erect schoolhouses." By reason of the subsequent construction and continued operation of a railroad, and the location of a depot in connection therewith, in close proximity to these lots, they were rendered unsuitable to be used as sites for schoolhouses, and their use for that purpose became dangerous. A petition was filed by the board of education of the incorporated village, praying, for the reason aforesaid, that the court of common pleas might order the lots to be sold, 'and the proceeds of sale to be applied to the purchase of suitable schoolhouse sites, or to the erection of schoolhouses on suitable grounds to be procured by the board. Upon demurrer to the petition, it was held that the dedication was for a specific use, and conferred no power of alienation so as to extinguish the use.

That if the use created by the dedication were abandoned, or should become impossible of execution, the premises would revert to the dedicators or their representatives, and that, without their consent they could not be divested of their contingent right of reversion by an absolute alienation.

The principle upon which a trust may under certain circumstances, be executed cy pres is not applicable to such a case: Board of Education v. Edson, 18 O. S. 221.

Where a township board of education had resolved to sell the old site of a subdistrict schoolhouse, and had purchased a new site, and notifying the local directors of the subdistrict of their action in the premises, instructed them to sell the former, and to build a new schoolhouse on the latter, and the local directors, disregarding such instructions, proceed to build a new schoolhouse on the old site and keep up a school therein, it was held that the local directors are guilty of such insubordination and neglect as justify the township board of education in exercising the powers and duties which would otherwise devolve on the local directors, and in building a schoolhouse on the new site and employing a teacher therein; and such teacher is entitled to be paid his wages out of the township treasury, on the order of the township board: State, ex rel., v. Lynch, 8 O. S. 347.

Under a former statute authority to determine the place at which a schoolhouse in a subdistrict should be built was conferred upon the township board of education: and the authority of the local directors of the subdistrict was to be exercised in subordination to the paramount authority of the township, board: Hughes v. Board of Education, 13 O. S. 336.

Where a board of education had established a central or high school (compare G. C. Sec. 7665) and directed a building in a subdistrict of the township for the use of such school, and such building was used before for the central or high school and for the school of the subdistrict, by agreement between the board of education and the local directors of such subdistrict, and the territory within such subdistrict was formed into an incorporate village, it was held that such school building did not pass to the board of education of such incorporated village under the statutes then in force: Board of Education v. Board of Education, 41 O. S. 680.

Under a statute which vested in board of education property held at the time of the enactment of such statute by the board of education or the council of any municipal corporation, for the use of public schools in any district (R. S. Sec. 3972; omitted from the General Code as executed), it was held that public school property, whether real or personal, that had been set apart by a township board of education for the purpose of a public school of a grade higher than the primary grade, and for the benefit of the youth of the whole township, did not pass to or vest in the board of education of a special school district, which was organized afterwards out of the territory in which it happened that such public school property was situated, although such section (R. S. 3972) was passed thereafter: Board of Education v. Board of Education, 46 O. S. 595.

Under R. S. Sec. 3972, a board of education succeeded to the rights of former boards of education or councils of municipal corporations, in property held for the use of public schools; and such new board of education accordingly succeeded to the right of a municipal corporation to bring an action for money paid by mistake out of the school funds in the construction of a school building: Crofton v. Board of Education, 26 O. S. 571.

The discretion of a board of education is not an arbitrary and unlimited discretion; and accordingly if the existing school house is adequate and satisfactory, and located near the center of a school district, injunction will issue to prevent such board of education from erecting another schoolhouse in another place in such subdistrict: Watkins v. Hall, 13 O. C. C. 255.

Since a board of education may appropriate real property for school purposes (see G. C. Sec. 7642) a conveyance by the owner of real property to a board of education for school purposes bars the dower of the wife of such owner, although she does not join in such deed: Steel v. Board of Education, 1 O. D. (N. P.) 276.

For the power of commissioners appointed by the probate court to select a site for a schoolhouse, under former statutes since repealed (R. S. Sec. 3946 to 3948), see Moss v. Board of Education, 58 O. S. 354.

A former statute (R. S. Sec. 3995) authorized a board of education to purchase "apparatus," but limited the amount which might be expended thereon; while the amount which might be expended for furniture was within the discretion of the board, as long as the revenues of the school district were not exceeded: Board of Education v. Andrews, 51 O. S. 199; State, ex rel., v. Freed, 10 O. C. C. 294, 6 O. C. D. 550.

For a definition of apparatus, see State, ex rel., v. Freed, 10 O. C. C. 294.

Under this section tellurian globes were held to be apparatus and not furniture: Board of Education v. Andrews, 51 O. S. 199.

The purchase of blocks for teaching, in excess of the statutory amount, was held to be unauthorized: State, ex rel., v. Freed, 10 O. C. C. 294.

School and reading charts were held not to be apparatus; and the amount which might be expended thereon was not limited by such statute: State, ex rel., v. Township Treasurer, 2 O. C. C. 363.

The same view was taken of cabinets, which contained charts or maps which were to be attached to the wall: Bank v. Board of Education, 15 O. C. C. 561.

The power to purchase apparatus was not co-extensive with the power given for furnishing a schoolhouse (see this section and G. C. 7623): State, ex rel., v. Freed, 10 O. C. C. 294.

Neither this section, specifically empowering boards of education, among other designated things, to provide fuel; nor G. C. Sec. 7623, prescribing for bids for certain designated supplies and contracts, but omitting mention of fuel; nor G. C. Sec. 7695, requiring the director of schools where one is chosen, to advertise therefor requires advertising for bids for coal or purchase from the lowest responsible bidder: Gosline v. Board of Education, 11 O. C. C. (N. S.) 195.

Rights and liabilities not affected.

SECTION 3514. Such surrender of corporate powers shall not affect vested rights or accrued liabilities of such village, or the power to settle claims, dispose of property, or levy and collect taxes to pay existing obligations, but after the presentation of such petition, council shall not create any new liability until the result of the election is declared, nor thereafter, if such result is in favor of the surrender of corporate powers. Due and unpaid taxes may thereafter be collected, and all moneys or property remaining after such surrender shall belong to the school district embracing such village. (96 v. 21 § 4.)

Theatrical and other public exhibitions.

SECTION 3657. To regulate, by license or otherwise, restrain or prohibit theatrical exhibitions, public shows and athletic games of whatever name or nature, for which money or other reward is demanded or received; to regulate, by license or otherwise, the business of trafficking in theatrical tickets, or other tickets of licensed amusements, by parties not acting as agents of those issuing them, but public school entertainments, lecture courses and lectures on historic, litereary or scientific subjects, shall not come within the provision of this section. (102 v. 88.)

·By virtue of section 3657, General Code, council is given power to regulate atheltic games by license or otherwise and such authorization extends to baseball playing on Sunday afternoons, within municipal limits. — *Attorney General*, 1911-12, p. 1559.

Section 13049, General Code, makes baseball playing on Sunday forenoon a penal offense. Baseball playing in the afternoon, in the absence of regulation or prohibition by council, under authority of section 3657, General Code, is not unlawful. — *Attorney General*, 1911-12, p. 1670.

SECTION 3963. No charge shall be made by the director of public service in cities, or by the board of trustees of public affairs in villages, for supplying water for extinguishing fires, cleaning fire apparatus, or for furnishing or supplying connections with fire hydrants, and keeping them in repair for fire department purposes, the cleaning of market houses, the use of any public building belonging to the corporation, or any hospital, asylum, or other charitable institutions, devoted to the relief of the poor, aged, infirm, or destitute persons, or orphan or delinquent children, or for the use of public school buildings, but in any case where the said school building or buildings, are situated within a village or cities, and the boundaries of the school districts include territory not within the boundaries of the village or cities in which said building, or buldings, are located, then the directors of such school district snall pay the village or cities for the water furnished for said building or buildings. (102 v. 94.) *Water supply free for certain purposes.*

Under the language of section 3963, General Code, the water furnished to school buildings which are located in cities whose school district is partly in the city and party comprises territory outside of the city, must be paid for by the director of such district to the city. — *Attorney General*, 1911-12, p. 548.

The purposes for which council may supply free water, are enumerated in Section 3963, General Code, and free water for no other purpose is authorized.

A contract, therefore, by the village with a public utility, containing in its provisions a grant of free water and light to said utility, is void. — *Attorney General*, 1912, p. 277.

The director of public service is not authorized to employ day laborers to make a public improvement to be paid for from a bond issue, where such improvement will cost to exceed $500. — *Attorney General*, 1913, p. 1520.

SECTION 4424. The board of health shall abate all nuisances and may remove or correct all conditions detrimental to health or well-being found upon school property by serving an order upon the board of education, school board or other person responsible for such property, for the abatement of such nuisance or condition within a reasonable but fixed time. A person failing to comply with such order, unless good and sufficient reason therefor is *Nuisance or unsanitary conditions on school property may be corrected.*

shown, shall be fined not to exceed one hundred dollars. The board may appoint such number of inspectors of schools and school buildings as it deems necessary to properly carry out these provisions. (95 v. 433.)

Board shall inspect schools and may close them and prohibit public gatherings.

SECTION 4448. Semi-annually, and oftener if in its judgment necessary, the board of health shall inspect the sanitary condition of all schools and school buildings within its jurisdiction, and may disinfect any school building. During an epidemic or threatened epidemic, or when a dangerous communicable disease is unusually prevalent, the board may close any school and prohibit public gatherings for such time as it deems necessary. (95 v. 433.)

Handling explosives regulated; where statement to be filed.

SECTION 5903. A person, partnership or corporation manufacturing, handling, or storing gunpowder, blasting powder, dynamite, nyalite, jovite, masurite, fulminates, nitro-glycerine, any nitro-explosive compound, chlorate of potash explosive compound, picric acid explosive compound, or other explosive substance, shall file with the chief inspector of workshops and factories, upon blanks furnished by him upon application, a complete statement of the location of such factory, storehouse or magazine owned or controlled by such person, partnership or corporation, together with the kind and character of the explosive substance or substances manufactured, handled or stored and intended to be manufactured, handled or stored thereat, the quantity stored or kept on hand, and the quantity intended to be stored or kept on hand, the number of persons employed at each factory, storehouse or magazine and the number of persons intended to be employed thereat, and the distance which such factory, storehouse or magazine is located or will be located from the nearest factory, workshop, mercantile or other establishment, occupied dwelling, church, schoolhouse, building in which people are accustomed to assemble, railroad or public highway. (99 v. 211 § 1.)

Statement submitted to district inspector; certificate of chief inspector.

SECTION 5904. Such statement, when filed, shall be submitted by the chief inspector of workshops and factories, for examination, correction and investigation, to the district inspector of explosives, who shall make a personal examination of each such factory, storehouse or magazine. If it is found to be located at a safe distance from the nearest factory, workshop, mercantile or other establishment, occupied dwelling, church, schoolhouse, building in which people are accustomed to assemble, railroad or public highway, and so planned and managed as to insure as great safety as is consistent with the nature of the business, and if the facts required in such statement are fully set out therein, and found to be true, such chief inspector shall grant a certificate approving the plans and location of such factory, storehouse or magazine as set forth in such statement. (99 v. 211 § 2.)

SECTION 12438. Whoever in the night season maliciously and forcibly breaks and enters, or attempts to break and enter an uninhabited dwelling house, or a kitchen, smokehouse, shop, office, storehouse, warehouse, malthouse, stillhouse, mill, pottery, factory, water craft, schoolhouse, church or meeting house, barn or stable, railroad car, car factory, station house, hall or other building, or attempts to break and enter an inhabited dwelling house with intene to steal property of any value, or with intent to commit a felony, shall be imprisoned in the penitentiary not less than one year nor more than fifteen years. (100 v. 5.) *Burglary in an uninhabited dwelling or other building.*

SECTION 12441. Whoever, by day or night maliciously enters a dwelling house, kitchen, shop, storehouse, malthouse, stillhouse, mill, office, treasury, bank, railroad car, pottery, water craft, schoolhouse, church or meeting house, smokehouse, barn or stable and attempts to commit a felony, shall be imprisoned in the penitentiary not less than one year nor more than two years. (78 v. 28.) *Entering a house by night or day and attempting to commit felony.*

SECTION 12442. Whoever, in the day time, maliciously breaks and enters a dwelling house, kitchen, shop, store, warehouse, malthouse, stillhouse, mill, pottery, water craft, schoolhouse, church or meeting house, smokehouse, barn, stable, railroad car, car factory, depot, station house, hen house, wagon house, sugar house, boat house, grain house or greenhouse with intent to steal, shall be fined not more than three hundred dollars or imprisoned not more than six months, or both. (88 v. 342.) *Breaking into building in day time to steal.*

SECTION 12443. Whoever, in the night season, unlawfully breaks open and enters a dwelling house, shop, store, ship, boat or other water craft, in which a person resides or dwells, and commits or attempts to commit personal violence or abuse, or is so armed with a dangerous weapon as to indicate a violent intention, shall be fined not more than three hundred dollars, and imprisoned not more than thirty days. (29 v. 144.) *Breaking into house, etc., in the night season and commiting or attempting to commit personal violence.*

SECTION 7621. All boards of education are required to display the United States national flag upon all schoolhouses under their control, during all day school sessions in fair weather, which shall be displayed on the inside of the schoolhouse on all other days. Such boards shall make all rules and necessary regulations for the care and keeping of such flags, the expense thereof to be paid out of their contingent funds. (92 v. 86 § 1.) *Display of U. S. flag.*

SECTION 7622. When, in the judgment of a board of education, it will be for the advantage of the children residing in any school district to hold literary societies, school exhibitions, singing schools, religous exercise, select or normal schools, the board of education shall authorize the *Regulating use of school houses.*

opening of the school-houses for such purposes. The board of education of a school district in its discretion may authorize the opening of such schoolhouses for any other lawful purposes. But nothing herein shall authorize a board of education to rent or lease a schoolhouse when such rental or lease in any wise interfers with the public schools in such district, or for any purpose other than is authorized by this chapter. (91 v. 44.)

Powers of boards of education; Sec. 4749.

The board of education has no authority in law to rent a school building, or part thereof, to a secret society for the purpose of holding lodge sessions and such social functions and entertainments of such society as are not open to all persons in the community on equal terms or which will not, in the judgment of the board of education, benefit the people of the community. — *Attorney General*, Opinion No. 197, April 3, 1915.

Schools and other buildings available for educational and recreational purposes.

SECTION 7622-1. That upon application of any responsible organization, or of a group of at least seven citizens, all school grounds and schoolhouses, as well as all other buildings under the supervision and control of the state, or buildings maintained by taxation under the laws of Ohio, shall be available for use as social centers for the entertainment and education of the people, including the adult and youthful population, and for the discussion of all topics tending to the development of personal character and of civic welfare. Such occupation, however, should not seriously infringe upon the original and necessary uses of such properties. The public officials in charge of such buildings shall prescribe such rules and regulations for their occupancy and use as herein provided as will secure a fair, reasonable and impartial use of the same. (106 v. 552.)

Citizens only responsible for damages.

SECTION 7622-2. The organization or group of citizens applying for the use of properties as specified in section 7622-1 of the General Code shall be responsible for any damage done them over and above the ordinary wear, and shall, if required, pay the actual expense incurred for janitor service, light and heat. (106 v. 552.)

Purposes other than school for which houses or rooms may be used.

SECTION 7622-3. The board of education of any school district may, subject to such regulation as may be adopted by such board, permit the use of any schoolhouse and rooms therein and the grounds and other property under its control, when not in actual use for school purposes, for any of the following purposes:

1. For giving instructions in any branch of education, learning or the arts.

2. For holding educational, civic, social or recreational meetings and entertainments, and for such other purposes as may make for the welfare of the community. Such meetings and entertainments shall be non-exclusive and open to the general public.

3. For public library purposes, as a station for a public library, or as reading rooms.

4. For polling places, for holding elections and for the registration of voters, for holding grange or similar meetings. (106 v. 552.)

SECTION 7622-4. Upon the nomination of the super- Supervision
and conduct
of social and
recreational
work.
intendent of any school district the board of education of
such district may employ a person or persons to supervise,
organize, direct and conduct social and recreational work
in such school district. The board of education may employ
competent persons to deliver lectures, or give instruction on
any educational subject, and provide for the further education of adult persons in the community. (106 v. 552.)

SECTION 7622-5. In cities employing a person to di- Use in
cities.
rect and supervise social and recreational work such person may use the school buildings, grounds, and other public
buildings or grounds in such city for the purposes indicated
in section 7622-3 of the General Code subject to the limitations provided in sections 7622-1 to 7622-3 of the General
Code. (106 v. 552.)

SECTION 7622-6. Boards of education may co-operate Co-operation
with other
public
officials.
with commissioners, boards or other public officials having
the custody and management of public parks, libraries,
museums and public buildings and grounds of whatever
kind in providing for education, social, civic and recreational activities, in buildings and upon grounds in the custody and under the management of such commissioners,
boards or other public officials. (106 v. 552.

SECTION 7622-7. The board of, education of any Tax levy
for social
center fund.
school district or a municipality may levy annually upon the
taxable property of such school district or municipality
within the limitations of secton 5649-2 of the General Code.
not to exceed two-tenths of a mill for a social center fund
to be used for social and recreational purposes. (106 v.
552.)

SECTION 7623. When a board of education deter- Directions for
bidding and
for letting
contracts.
mines to build, repair, enlarge or furnish a schoolhouse or
schoolhouses, or make any improvement or repair provided
for in this chapter, the cost of which will exceed in city
districts, fifteen hundred dollars, and in other districts five
hundred dollars, except in cases of urgent necessity, or for
the security and protection of school property, it must proceed as follows:

1. For the period of four weeks. the board shall advertise for bids in some newspaper of general circulation
in the district, and in two such papers, if there are so many.
If no newspaper has a general circulation therein, then by
posting such advertisement in three public places therein.
Such advertisement shall be entered in full by the clerk on
the record of the proceedings of the board.

2. The bids, duly sealed up, must be filed with the clerk by twelve o'clock, noon, of the last day stated in the advertisement.

3. The bids shall be opened at the next meeting of the board, be publicly read by the clerk, and entered in full on the records of the board.

4. Each bid must contain the name of every person interested therein, and, shall be accompanied by a sufficient guarantee of some disinterested person, that if the bid be accepted, a contract will be entered into, and the performance of it properly secured.

5. When both labor and materials are embraced in the work bid for, each must be separately stated in the bid, with the price thereof.

6. None but the lowest responsible bid shall be accepted. The board in its discretion may reject all the bids, or acecpt any bid for both labor and material for such improvement or repair, which is the lowest in the aggregate.

7. Any part of a bid which is lower than the same part of any other bid, shall be accepted, whether the residue of the bid is higher or not; and if it is higher, such residue must be rejected.

8. The contract must be between the board of education and the bidders. The board shall pay the contract price for the work, when it is completed, in cash, and may pay monthly estimates as the work progresses.

9. When two or more bids are equal, in the whole, or in any part thereof, and are lower than any others, either may be accepted, but in no case shall the work be divided between such bidders.

10. When there is reason to believe that there is collusion or combination among the bidders, or any number of them, the bids of those concerned therein shall be rejected. (97 v. 356.)

Section 7623, G. C., requiring that bids for the erection of a school building be "accompanied by a sufficient guarantee of some disinterested person" vests the board of education with a certain discretion, but does not empower it to demand more than the statute intends.

When the board, therefore, has provided that bids be accompanied by a certified check for ten per cent. of the bids and the lowest bidder accompanies his bid by a surety company bond equal to its amount, for its payment, the board cannot reject the bid unless bona fide it does not consider the guarantee sufficient. — *Attorney General*, 1911-12. p. 1195.

Cases of urgent necessity are excepted from the provisions of section 7623, General Code, providing for certain procedure when the cost of repairing or improving a school house in other than city districts exceeds five hnudred dollars.

Inasmuch, therefore, as the board of education is required to provide for at least thirty-two school weeks in a year, and as the mayor may prohibit use of school buildings until compliance has been made with the orders of the chief inspector of workshops and factories, the board of education of a village, upon such order from the chief inspector of workshops and factories, made after the school year has begun, may dispense with the procedure of section 7623 and execute necessary repairs .without advertising for bids. — *Attorney General*, 1911-12. p. 1318.

Inasmuch as the statutes do not prescribe otherwise, when a

board of education sells bonds, the premium and accrued interest must, in accordance with the general rule that all accretions follow a trust fund, be credited to the fund for the purpose of which the bonds were sold.

It is the object of the statutes to maintain a fair competition in the letting of bids, and when a board of education has received bids for the construction of a building, alterations may not be made in the plans and specifications, and the bids let, accommodated, by deductions or increases, to the changes made in the plans and specifications.

The board of education may not expend any moneys derived by it from an issue of bonds, unless the clerk shall first certify that the money is in the treasury and not appropriated to any other purpose. Said board may, therefore, not enter into a contract for the construction of a building, the money for which is furnished by additional bonds, before the funds arising from such issue are in the treasury of the district. — *Attorney General*, 1912, p. 1249.

The board of education submitted to the electors the question of a bond issue, the amount of which, in addition to the amount certified to the auditor, would prove sufficient to improve a certain school building in accordance with an order of the inspector of workshops and factories, but by reason of the reduction of the estimate by the budget commission, the board was unable to proceed with the improvement.

In order to supply the deficiency, the board twice submitted the issue of bonds to the electors, under Section 7625 and received a negative vote in each instance. Held:

That action once having been taken under Section 7625, General Code, recourse could not be had to Section 7629, General Code, for the same purpose, and that the board was without remedy. — *Attorney General,* 1912, p. 1200.

In case the state building inspector orders repairs on a school building to be made by a date certain, the impossibility of completing them by such date without dispensing with competitive bidding, etc., does not create a case of "urgent need", or for "security and protection of school property" within the meaning of Section 7623, General Code, permitting such bidding and other formalities to be dispensed with in such cases.

The interests of the schools themselves, that is, the use of the building by pupils with safety and convenience must be consulted in order to determine whether a case for dispensing with the statutory requirements exists so that if it is anticipated that although the work cannot be completed before the building must be used for school purposes, the part remaining undone can be prosecuted without impairing the safety and usefulness of the schools, the statutory requirements may not be dispensed with; otherwise they may be disregarded. — *Attorney General,* Opinion No. 1087, 1914.

Advertising for bids for public work is not merely directory as to boards of education but is mandatory as to all public boards: Mueller v. Board of Education, 11 O. N. P. (N. S.) 113.

Failure of a board of education to advertise for bids for "extras" which have become necessary for the completion of a high school building under a contract theretofore awarded, renders void a contract for the supplying of such extras, unless an urgent necessity existed for completion of the work without the delay incident to advertising for the submission of bids: Mueller v. Board of Education, 11 O. N. P. (N. S.) 113.

Where failure to comply with the statutory requirement with reference to public work may be excused by "urgent necessity" for an early completion of the work must be determined from the circumstances of the particular case: Mueller v. Board of Education, 11 O. N. P. (N. S.) 113.

The necessity for the completion of a high school building which was already in use by some of the pupils who found ingress to the building without passing through the main corridor where the work in question remained to be done, did not present such a case of "urgent necessity" as to release the parties from the necessity of advertising for bids for the customary period in the statutory manner: Mueller v. Board of Education, 11 O. N. P. (N. S.) 113.

While this section is mandatory as to all the classes of contracts comprised within its terms, it does not require a contract for the supply of coal to be let to the lowest bidder: Gosline v. Board of Education, 11 O. C. C. (N. S.) 195.

The provisions of this section which require advertisement for bids and letting contracts on competitive bidding for building, repairing, enlarging or furnishing a schoolhouse, do not require the board of education to advertise for bids for contracts for fuel, or let such contracts upon competitive bidding: Gosline v. Board of Education, 11 O. C. C. (N. S.) 195.

If advertisement is not necessary for the contract in question, the board may accept or reject such bids as it sees fit: State, ex rel., v. Board of Education, 13 O. C. C. 603.

The provision of this statute that every bid should be accomplished by a sufficient guaranty of some disinterested person, that if the bid be accepted a contract will be entered into, and the performance of it properly secured, is not complied with by writing the word "sureties" at the bottom of the page, followed by the name of the individual who is offered as surety: State, ex rel., v. Board of Education, 42 O. S. 374.

A contract for the building of a schoolhouse, awarded to a contractor who has been permitted to change his bid by omitting various items and thus reducing the aggregate cost to the amount realized from the sale of bonds, is a contract made without notice or competition, and is illegal and void, but public funds paid out on a contract, free from fraud and collusion and completed in good faith, cannot be recovered back at the instance of a taxpayer, notwithstanding the contract was illegal and void: McAlexander v. School District, 7 O. N. P. (N. S.) 590, 19 O. D. (N. P.) 89.

Where a bid is uncertain as to whether it is for parts of a job as well as for the whole, and the bidder induces the board to construe it as for all or none, such bidder cannot afterwards complain that the board awarded the whole job to the lower bidder, although under a different construction, the board would have been bound to award to such bidder a portion of the work: State, ex rel., v. Board of Education, 42 O. S. 374.

The provision of this section which requires labor and materials to be stated separately in the bid with the price thereof, is not complied with by a bid which state the price of each separately, but also contains a provision that such bid if accepted at all is to be accepted as a whole: State, ex rel., v. Board of Education, 4 O. N. P. 44, 6 O. D. (N. P.) 235.

After a bid has been received and opened, the board of education cannot permit the contractor to amend it; and accordingly if the person who, as the lowest bidder refuses to enter into a contract because of an alleged mistake in the scale upon which the plans were drawn, and his estimate based, the board of education cannot permit him to amend his bid, even though as amended it is still lower than any other of the regular bids received; and a contract on such bid is invalid: McGreevy v. Board of Education, 20 O. C. C. 114, 10 O. C. D. 724.

It is not necessary that a bid on a heating and ventilating apparatus should state separately the cost of labor and materials: State, ex rel., v. Board of Education, 14 O. C. C. 15, 7 O. C. D. 338.

The provision of this section which requires "the lowest responsible bid" to be accepted, and gives discretion to the board to reject all bids, does not authorize the board to accept any bid except the lowest responsible bid: State, ex rel., v. Board of Education, 42 O. S. 374.

Under this statute the board of education may in its discretion reject any and all bids: State, ex rel., v. Board of Education, 13 O. C. C. 603.

Subdivisions 6 and 7 are apparently in conflict with each other; and accordingly if the discretion conferred by subdivision 6 is not exercised, thus in the consideration of bids containing two separate items or more any part of a bid which is lower than the same part of any other bid should be accepted: Gilbert v. Board of Education, 21 O. C. C. 416, 11 O. C. D. 552.

Where a bona fide bidder for public work in good faith submits a bid which is based on a mistake in measurements which would involve him in serious financial loss were he to do the work for the amount named, the minds of the parties have not met, and he cannot be compelled to execute the proposed contract, notwithstanding the terms on which the bid was submitted, provided that it should not be withdrawn; and injunction will lie on the petition of the bidder to restrain the board having charge of the contract from accepting the bid and insisting that he execute the contract or subject himself to an action for damages: Construction Co. v. Board of Education, 11 O. N. P. (N. S.) 86.

If bids are received for different systems of heating, the board may determine after such bids are in, which system of heating it will adopt, and it is not necessarily bound to select that which is offered for the lowest bid: State, ex rel., v. Board of Education, 14 O. C. C. 15, 7 O. C. D., 338; see, to the same effect, State, ex rel., v. Board of Education, 10 Dec. Rep. 314, 20 Bull. 156.

A contract for the building of a schoolhouse at a cost in excess of the amount raised for that purpose from an issue of bonds, is not void for want of authority on the part of the board of education to make such a contract after having underestimated the amount of money needed: McAlexander v. School District, 7 O. N. P. (N. S.) 590, 19 O. D. (N. P.) 89.

An unsuccessful bidder, who is not able to show that he himself has complied with the statutory requirements, cannot compel the board of education to award the bid to him, by proceedings in mandamus, even if the bid on which the contract was awarded was so irregular and defective that the board of education should not have accepted it: State, ex rel., v. Board of Education, 42 O. S. 374.

If a board of education has in good faith determined that the lowest bidder is not the lowest responsible, and has awarded the contract to the bidder to whom it has in good faith determined to be the lowest responsible bidder, mandamus will not lie to compel the board of education to award the contract to the lowest bidder; and in such proceedings the court cannot determine the question whether such bidder is in fact responsible: State, ex rel., v. Board of Education, 6 O. N. P. 317, 9 O. D. (N. P.) 336.

If the right to reject any and all bids is conferred by statute or reserved in the advertisement (see division 6 of this section), the lowest bidder cannot compel the board of education by proceedings in mandamus to award the contract to him: State, ex rel., v. Board of Education, 13 O. C. C. 603, 5 O. C. D. 379.

In mandamus proceedings to compel the board of education to award a contract, the relator must show that he is the party with whom the contract should be made, irrespective of the rights of any oher person; and he cannot rely upon the weakness, informality, or irregularity of the bids of others, or upon the proposed irregular action of the board of education, with reference to any one else; nor the fact that the board of education was about to let the contract to a person who had not complied with the law: State, ex rel., v. Board of Education, 14 O. C. C. 15, 7 O. C. D. 338.

Injunction will lie to prevent a board of education from abusing its discretion; as where it orders a new schoolhouse built, although the existing schoolhouse is in good condition and is adequate in size: Watkins v. Hall, 13 O. C. C. 255, 7 O. C. D. 434.

If the board of education is about to award a contract for installing certain devices in a public building upon a bid which is based on terms not contained in the original specifications as advertised, which bid was received subsequent to the time designated in the advertisement for the submission of bids, such action is illegal and unauthorized, and will be restrained by a court of equity by injunction. Mandamus will not lie, however, to compel the board of education to award the bid to the lowest responsible bidder, who submits a bid at the time specified in the advertisement: State, ex rel., v. Board of Education, 6 O. C. C. (N. S.) 345, 17 O. C. D. 832.

SECTION 2362. An officer, board or other authority of the state, a county, township, city, village, school or road district or of any public institution belonging thereto, authorized to contract for the erection, repair, alteration or rebuilding of a public building, institution, bridge, culvert or improvement and required by law to advertise and receive proposals for furnishing of materials and doing the work necessary for the erection thereof, shall require separate and distinct proposals to be made for furnishing such materials or doing such work or both, in their discretion, for each separate and distinct trade or kind of mechanical labor, employment or business entering into the improvement. (85 v. 218.)

Separate bids for work and materials.

The letting of a contract for a schoolhouse is controlled by G. C. Sec. 7623, except as far as the provisions of G. C. Secs. 2362 to 2364, which are not inconsistent with G. C. Sec. 7623 apply: Gilbert v. Board of Education, 21 O. C. C. 416, 11 O. C. D. 552.

If a board of education advertises for bids for heating and ventilating a schoolhouse, bids which offer systems of heating and ventilating, which are covered by patent or proprietory rights, need not state separately the cost of labor and material, but under this section the bid may be for a lump sum: State, ex rel., v. Board of Education, 14 O. C. C. 15, 7 O. C. D. 338.

Cited in construing G. C. 2342; State v. Edmondson, 23 Dec. 91, 12 (N. S.) 577.

A bidder who does not comply with the requirements of the statute, and who does not submit bids in conformity with the specifications cannot compel the public officers in question to award the contract to him: State, ex rel., v. Board of Education 14 O. C. C. 15, 7 O. C. D. 338.

A school board has discretion to determine what system of ventilating and heating apparatus it will install in a schoolhouse; and such discretion can not be controlled by mandamus: State, ex rel., v. Board of Education, 14 O. C. C. 15, 7 O. C. D. 338.

Inasmuch as the statutes do not prescribe otherwise, when a board of education sells bonds, the premium and accrued interest must, in accordance with the general rule that all accretions follow a trust fund, be credited to the fund for the purpose of which the bonds were sold.

It is the object of the statutes to maintain a fair competition in the letting of bids, and when a board of education has received bids for the construction of a building, alterations may not be made in the plans and specifications, and the bids let, accommodated, by deductions or increases, to the changes made in the plans and specifications.

The board of education may not expend any moneys derived by it from an issue of bonds, unless the clerk shall first certify that the money is in the treasury and not appropriated to any other purpose. Said board may, therefore, not enter into a contract for the construction of a building, the money for which is furnished by additional bonds, before the funds arising from such issue are in the treasury of the district. — *Attorney General,* 1912, p. 1249.

A part of the appropriation made for the construction of a building for science and agriculture at the Bowling Green normal school may be used for the construction of a corridor, this corridor to be a part of this building.

When contract shall not be awarded for entire work. All laboratory fixtures that are permanently attached to the science building should be made a part of the plans and specifications for such building. Bids for such furnishings should be asked for as part of the entire bid for construction of the building. — *Attorney General,* 1913, p. 1030.

SECTION 2363. When more than one trade or kind of mechanical labor, employment or business is required no contract for the entire job, or for a greater portion thereof than is embraced in one such trade or kind of mechanical labor shall be awarded, unless the separate bids do not cover all the work and materials required or the bids for the whole or for two or more kinds of work or materials are lower than the separate bids therefor in the aggregate. (85 v. 218.)

A part of the appropriation made for the construction of a building for science and agriculture at the Bowling Green normal school may be used for the construction of a corridor, this corridor to be a part of this building.

All laboratory fixtures that are permanently attached to the science building should be made a part of the plans and specifications for such building. Bids for such furnishings should be asked for as part of the entire bid for construction of the building. — *Attorney General,* 1913, p. 1030.

Power to appropriate land for school purposes. SECTION 7624. When it is necessary to procure or enlarge a school site or to purchase real estate to be used for agricultural purposes, athletic field or play ground for children, and the board of education and the owner of the property needed for such purposes are unable to agree upon the sale and purchase thereof, the board shall make an accurate plat and description of the parcel of land which it desires for such purposes, and file them with the probate judge, or court of insolvency, of the proper county. Thereupon the same proceedings of appropriation shall be had which are provided for the appropriation of private property by municipal corporations. (103 v. 466.)

Municipality may convey real property to board of education. SECTION 7624-1. A municipal corporation may by ordinance duly passed authorize the transfer and conveyance by deed, of any real property owned by it and not needed for municipal purposes, to the board of education of any such municipality, to be used by said board of education as an athletic field, a play ground for children or for school sites, upon such terms and conditions as are agreed to between the municipal corporation and the board of education and when such property is so conveyed, the same shall be under the control and supervision of such board of education. (103 v. 466.)

SECTION 7625. When the board of education of any May issue bonds. school district determines that for the proper accommodation of the schools of such district it is necessary to purchase a site or sites to erect a schoolhouse or houses, to complete a partially built schoolhouse, to enlarge, repair or furnish a schoolhouse, or to purchase real estate for playground for children, or to do any or all of such things, that the funds at its disposal or that can be raised under the provisions of sections seventy-six hundred and twenty-nine and seventy-six hundred and thirty, are not sufficient to accomplish the purpose and that a bond issue is necessary, the board shall make an estimate of the probable amount of money required for such purpose or purposes and at a general election or special election called for that purpose, submit to the electors of the district the question of the issuing of bonds for the amount so estimated. Notices of the election required herein shall be given in the manner provided by law for school elections. (102 v. 419.)

A board of education can purchase a site, erect a school house, complete a partially built school house, etc.

When a proposition for a bond issue for erection or equipment of a school house has been voted down three times, further submission of the proposition may be enjoined as an abuse of discretion and authority on the part of the board. 19 Dec. 80, 7 (N. S.) 590.

From the language of relative statutory sections, and from the fact that the subject is treated under the head of schools, and from the further fact that the question is a purely local one, affecting only the voters of the school district in which it is held, a special election held upon the question of issuing bonds for school purposes is to be considered a school election under section 5120, and returns thereof should be made to the clerk of the board of education of the district, and such board is the authority that shall first canvass said returns. — *Attorney General,* 1911-12, p. 507.

When the electors of a school district have voted favorably upon the necessity of erecting a high school, there is no statutory limit as to the time when the board shall issue the bonds. The fact of the necessity which exists, however, and its recognition by the voters, imposes upon the board the obligation to proceed within a reasonable time. — *Attorney General,* 1911-12, p. 527.

Where by popular vote the electors have authorized the centralization of schools, but have later, by popular vote refused to authorize a bond issue necessary for a proper building for the purpose of such centralization, the centralization is not deemed complete until the voters have also authorized the "means" to carry it out and until such time the board of education may adhere to the old district school arrangement. — *Attorney General,* 1911-12, p. 1145.

When it becomes necessary for a board of education to improve school buildings by reason of an order from the inspector of workshops and factories, and such improvements cannot be made within the ordinary limitations of the Smith tax law, and when furthermore the electors have repeatedly refused to authorize bond issues under sections 7625 and 7628, General Code, the board of education may have recourse to sections 7629 and 7630, General Code.

By these sections, they may issue bonds for this purpose in a sum not to exceed the amount of a tax at the rate of two mills for the year next preceding the issue, and may extend the payment of such bonds over a period of forty years. — *Attorney General,* 1911-1912, p. 1384.

When a village board of education was authorized by electors under section 7592, General Code, to levy an additional tax of five mills for five years such board may proceed to issue bonds without further authorization of the electors, provided that the conditions of 7626 and 7679, General Code, with reference to the quality and nature of the bonds and the provisions of section 7629 with reference to the amount of the bonds and the procedure of the board be complied with. — *Attorney General*, 1911-12, p. 534.

The intention of 7625, General Code, is clearly expressed therein, to comprise within its terms the authority to call for an election upon the question of issuing bonds for the erection of a school house, as well as for the purpose for a site for such purpose. — *Attorney General*, 1911-12, p. 510.

The language of the statutes will not permit of a construction allowing a board of education to erect an eight-room building in place of a four-room building mentioned in the resolution and notice in the bond issue proceedings for said purpose.

Neither has the board power to construct an addition to a school building in another part of the city not mentioned in said notice and resolution. — *Attorney General*, 1911-12, p. 1516.

The statutes do not require or authorize publication of a resolution of a board of education passed for the purpose of submitting to electors the question of issuing bonds for construction of a school building.

Under section 7625, General Code, however, notices of the election shall be given in the manner provided by law for school elections, i. e., under section 4839, General Code, such publication may be made by posting written or printed notices in five public places in the district at least ten days before the holding of the election, or it may be published in a newspaper of general circulation in the district, once at least ten days before holding of the election. — *Attorney General*, 1913, p. 1515.

Written notice of special meeting necessary to render bonds issued thereat valid: Kateman, v. New Knoxville Sch. Dist. (Bd. of Ed.) 34 O. C. C. 306, 15 (N. S.) 232.

Inasmuch as the statutes do not prescribe otherwise, when a board of education sells bonds, the premium and accrued interest must, in accordance with the general rule that all accretions follow a trust fund, be credited to the fund for the purpose of which the bonds were sold.

It is the object of the statutes to maintain a fair competition in the letting of bids, and when a board of education has received bids for the construction of a building, alterations may not be made in the plans and specifications, and the bids let, accommodated, by deductions or increases, to the changes made in the plans and specifications.

The board of education may not expend any moneys derived by it from an issue of bonds, unless the clerk shall first certify that the money is in the treasury and not appropriated to any other purpose. Said board may, therefore, not enter into a contract for the construction of a building, the money for which is furnished by additional bonds, before the funds arising from such issue are in the treasury of the district. — *Attorney General*, 1912, p. 1249.

A proposition for the centralization of schools under the provisions of Section 4726, General Code, and a proposition to issue bonds authorized by Section 7625, General Code, may both be submitted to the electors of a rural school district at one election. — *Attorney General*, Opinion No. 41, 1915.

Dayton board of education may levy two-tenths of a mill for training schools: 91 v. 865.

This and the following sections are construed, in State, ex rel., v. Van Buren, 11 O. C. C. 41, 5 O. C. D. 447.

A contract for the building of a schoolhouse, at a cost in excess of the amount raised for that purpose from an issue of bonds, is not illegal and void for want of authority on the part of the board of education to make such a contract after having underestimated the amount of money needed: McAlexander v. School District, 7 O. N. P. (N. S.) 590, 19 O. D. (N. P.) 89.

The clerk is required to give notice of all school elections: State, ex. rel., v. Coon, 4 O. C. C. (N. S.) 560, 16 O. C. D. 241.

SECTION 5654. The proceeds of a special tax, loan or bond issue shall not be used for any other purpose than that for which the same was levied, issued or made, except as herein provided. When there is in the treasury of any city, village, county, township or school district a surplus of the proceeds of a special tax or of the proceeds of a loan or bond issue which cannot be used, or which is not needed for the purpose for which the tax was levied, or the loan made, or the bonds issued, all of such surplus shall be transferred immediately by the officer, board or council having charge of such surplus, to the sinking fund of such city, village, county, township or school district, and thereafter shall be subject to the uses of such sinking fund. (103 v. 521.)

SECTION 5656. The trustees of a township, the board of education of a school district and the commissioners of a county for the purpose of extending the time of payment of any indebtedness, which from its limits of taxation such township, district or county is unable to pay at maturity, may borrow money or issue the bonds thereof, so as to change, but not increase the indebtedness in the amounts, for the length of time and at the rate of interest that said trustees, board or commissioners deem proper not to exceed the rate of six per cent per annum payable annually or semi-annually. (97 v. 514.)

A board of education may borrow money under Section 5656, General Code, to pay obligations incurred in furnishing the transportation to pupils which the law requires to be furnished, such expense being a charge against the district, regardless of the existence of sufficient funds in the district treasury, and the contract for transportation being at least in the nature of an employment contract.

It is not a condition precedent to the exercise of power under said·section that previously incurred floating or funded indebtedness has been created under the same section, that is, it is not necessary that the one debt shall be extinguished before the time of payment of the other is extended. — *Attorney General,* Opinion No. 1226, 1914.

The decision in the case of Rabe et al. v. Broad of Education, does not in any way affect the rights of the Board of Education under Section 5656, General Code. — *Attorney General,* Opinion No. 926, May 11, 1914.

A board of education may borrow money under Section 5656, General Code, for the purpose of paying unpaid installments of teachers' salaries.

Bonds may not be issued under this section, however, unless within the limitations of the law interest and sinking fund levies sufficient to retire them may be made during the years for which they are to run. Such interest and sinking fund levies being preferred to current levies by the Act found in 104 O. L. 12, the board should anticipate its needs for current purposes and its needs for interest and sinking fund purposes and so apportion its indebtedness as not to impair its future revenues for either purpose. — *Attorney General,* Opinion No. 178, March 27, 1915.

When a board of education has been authorized to issue bonds in the sum of twenty-five thousand dollars for the erection of a building and has so done, and later on order of the inspector of workshops and factories makes necessary a further expenditure of seven thousand dollars which the electors have twice refused the authority to liquidate, the board may fund such indebtedness by issuing bonds under Section 5656 General Code. — *Attorney General*, 1911-12, p. 1339.

The board of education under sections 5656 and 5658, G. C., may fund valid existing and binding indebtedness to meet current binding obligations which they are unable to pay by reason of the limits of taxation.

The salary of a teacher is such a binding obligation as to be within this rule. — *Attorney General*, 1911-12, p. 522.

State aid to board of education under Section 7595, General Code, is to be granted only when the maximum legal levy is insufficient to pay its teachers a minimum salary of forty dollars per month for eight months of the year, and then only when the numbers of persons of school age in the district is twenty times the number of teachers employed therein.

Where the shortage arises without these limitations as by reason of inability to comply with contract to pay teachers fifty dollars per month such indebtedness is a "valid existing and binding one" and if the board is unable to meet the same by reason of taxation limitations bonds may be issued and the debts funded under authority of Sections 5656, 5658 and 5659, General Code. — *Attorney General*, 1911-12, p. 529.

Section 5656, General Code, empowers the board of education when pressed by reason of taxation limitations to issue bonds or borrow money for the purpose of meeting such valid existing and binding indebtedness among its running expenses as are excepted under section 5661, General Code, from the necessity of the Auditor's Certificate to the effect that funds are in the treasury.

The power is extended alone to these enumerated expenses, namely: "Contracts authorized to be made by other provisions of law for the employment of teachers, officers and other school employes of boards of education." — *Attorney General*, 1911-12, p. 551.

It is recommended to proceed under Sections 2296-2302, General Code, to obtain authority of the court to transfer to the sinking fund.

Though bonds levied for the purpose aforesaid are within the limitations of the Smith law, the holders of these bonds may compel the making of such levies as are pledged for their retirement, and therefore the budget commissioners must make the necessary reductions upon the amounts to be levied for other township, county, municipal or educational purposes. — *Attorney General*, 1911-12, p. 1424.

Whether this and the following sections are constitutional or not was discussed but not decided in Bower, v. Board of Education, 8 O. C. C. (N. S.) 305, 18 O. C. D. 624.

Power to exchange bonds. SECTION 5657. When it appears to the trustees of a township, board of education of a school district or commissioners of a county, to be for the best interests of such township, school district or county to renew, refund or extend the time of payment of any bonded indebtedness which has not matured and thereby reduce the rate of interest thereon, they may issue, for that purpose, new bonds, and exchange the bonds with the holder or holders of such outstanding bonds if such holder or holders consent to make such exchange and to such reduction of interest. (97 v. 514.)

The board of education under sections 5656 and 5658 G. C., may fund valid existing and binding indebtedness to meet current binding obligations which they are unable to pay by reason of the limits of taxation.

The salary of a teacher is such a binding obligation as to be within this rule. — *Attorney General*, 1911-12, p. 522.

Section 5656, General Code, empowers the board of education when pressed by reason of taxation limitations to issue bonds or borrow money for the purpose of meeting such valid existing and binding indebtedness among its running expenses as are excepted under section 5661, General Code, from the necessity of the Auditor's Certificate to the effect that funds are in the treasury.

The power is extended alone to these enumerated expenses, namely: "Contracts authorized to be made by other provisions of law for the employment of teachers, officers and other school employes of boards of education." — *Attorney General*, 1911-12, p 551.

It is recommended to proceed under Section 2296-2302, General Code, to obtain authority of the court to transfer to the sinking fund.

Though bonds levied for the purpose aforesaid are within the limitations of the Smith law, the holders of these bonds may compel the making of such levies as are pledged for their retirement, and therefore the budget commission must make the necessary reductions upon the amounts to be levied for other township, county, municipal or educational purposes. — *Attorney General*, 1911-12, p. 1424.

The decision in the case of Rabe et al v. Board of Education, does not in any way affect the rights of the Board of Education under Section 5656, General Code. — *Attorney General*, Opinion 926, May 11, 1914.

County commissioners are authorized by this section to issue new bonds and, to exchange them for outstanding bonds, but they are not authorized to exchange them for the promissory notes or other evidences of the debt of the county: Commissioners, v. State, 78 O. S. 287.

SECTION 5658. No indebtedness of a township, school district or county shall be funded, refunded or extended unless such indebtedness is first determined to be an existing, valid and binding obligation of such township, school district or county by a formal resolution of the trustees, board of education or commissioners thereof, respectively. Such resolution shall state the amount of the existing indebtedness to be funded, refunded or extended, the aggregate amount of bonds to be issued therefor, their number and denomination, the date of their maturity, the rate of interest they shall bear and the place of payment of principal and interest. (97 v. 514.)

Resolution as to such debts.

When a board of education has been authorized to issue bonds in the sum of twenty-five thousand dollars for the erection of a building and has so done, and later on order of the inspector of workshops and factories makes necessary a further expenditure of seven thousand dollars which the electors have twice refused the authority to liquidate, the board may fund such indebtedness by issuing bonds under Section 5656, General Code. — *Attorney General*, 1911-12, p. 1339.

The board of education under sections 5656 and 5658, G. C., may fund valid existing and binding indebtedness to meet current binding obligations which they are unable to pay by reason of the limits of taxation.

The salary of a teacher is such a binding obligation as to be within this rule. — *Attorney General*, 1911-12, p. 522.

State aid to board of education under Section 7595, General Code, is to be granted only when the maximum legal levy is insufficient to pay its teachers a minimum salary of forty dollars per month for eight months of the year, and then only when the numbers of persons of school age in the district is twenty times the number of teachers employed therein.

Where the shortage arises without these limitations as by reason of inability to comply with contract to pay teachers fifty dollars per month such indebtedness is a "valid existing and binding one" and if the board is unable to meet the same by reason of taxation limitations bonds may be issued and the debts funded under authority of Sections 5656, 5658 and 5659, General Code. — *Attorney General*, 1911-12, p. 529.

Section 5656, General Code, empowers the board of education when pressed by reason of taxation limitations to issue bonds or borrow money for the purpose of meeting such valid existing and binding indebtedness among its running expenses as are excepted under section 5661, General Code, from the necessity of the Auditor's Certificate to the effect that funds are in the treasury.

The power is extended alone to these enumerated expenses, namely: "Contracts authorized to be made by other provisions of law for the employmnet of teachers, officers and other school employes of boards of education." — *Attorney General*, 1911-12, p. 551.

The decision in the case of Rabe et al v. Board of Education, does not in any way affect the right of the Board of Education under Section 5656, General Code. — *Attorney General*, Opinion No. 926, May 11, 1914.

Levy to meet payment of bonds.

SECTION 5659. For the payment of the bonds issued under the next three preceding sections, the township trustees, board of education or county commissioners shall levy a tax, in addition to the amount otherwise authorized, each year during the period the bonds have to run sufficient in amount to pay the accruing interest and the bonds as they mature. (97 v. 514.)

When a board of education has been authorized to issue bonds in the sum of twenty-five thousand dollars for the erection of a building and has so done, and later on order of the inspector of workshops and factories makes necessary a further expenditure of seven thousand dollars which the electors have twice refused the authority to liquidate, the board may fund such indebtedness by issuing bonds under Section 5656, General Code. — *Attorney General*, 1911-12, p. 1339.

State aid to board of education under Section 7595, General Code, is to be granted only when a maximum legal levy is insufficient to pay its teachers a minimum salary of forty dollars per month for eight months of the year, and then only when the numbers of persons of school age in the district is twenty times the number of teachers employed therein.

Where the shortage arises without these limitations as by reason of inability to comply with contract to pay teachers fifty dollars per month such indebtedness is a "valid existing and binding one" and if the board is unable to meet the same by reason of taxation limitations bonds may be issued and the debts funded under authority of Sections 5656, 5658 and 5659, General Code. — *Attorney General*, 1911-12, p. 529.

The decision in the case of Rabe et al v. Board of Education, does not in any way affect the rights of the Board of Education under Section 5656, General Code. — *Attorney General*, Opinion No. 926, May 11, 1914.

Taxing districts authorized to issue bonds when 50% of tax collection is enjoined or in litigation.

SECTION 5659-1. All municipal corporations, the board of education of any district and the commissioners of any county, through their proper officers, shall have power to borrow money and to issue bonds in payment therefor, to provide funds, to meet the payment of current expenses and sinking fund indebtedness, when the collection of general taxes aggregating fifty percent (50%) or more of the general tax duplicate, for any fiscal year, of their respective taxing districts, has been enjoined by any court or the collection of which is in litigation. The bonds so issued may be made to run for a term not to exceed ten years and shall not bear a greater rate of interest than six per cent (6%), nor be sold for less than par with accrued interest. All moneys received from the sale of bonds, as herein provided, shall become a part of the general fund of the taxing district wherein bonds are so issued, and shall be used for only such purposes as the enjoined or otherwise litigated collection of taxes were appropriated for. (106 v. 11.)

SECTION 5659-2. All tax collections which are paid into the treasury of any taxing district, which have theretofore been enjoined or the collection of which has been in litigation, and for which deficit bonds have been issued, under authority of the preceding section, shall be turned over to the trustees of the sinking fund of said taxing district, to be applied toward the payment of the principal and interest of the deficit bonds so issued. (106 v. 11.)

Application of money derived from bond issue.

SECTION 5660. The commissioners of a county, the trustees of a township and the board of education of a school district, shall not enter into any contract, agreement or obligation involving the expenditure of money, or pass any resolution or order for the appropriation or expenditure of money, unless the auditor or clerk thereof, respectively, first certifies that the money required for the payment of such obligation or appropriation is in the treasury to the credit of the fund from which it is to be drawn, or has been levied and placed on the duplicate, and in process of collection and not appropriated for any other purpose; money to be derived from lawfully authorized bonds sold and in process of delivery shall, for the purpose of this section, be deemed in the treasury and in the appropriate fund. Such certificate shall be filed and forthwith recorded, and the sums so certified shall not thereafter be considered unappropriated until the county, township or board of education, is fully discharged from the contract, agreement or obligation, or as long as the order or resolution is in force. (101 v. 37.)

Certificate, what to specify.

Filing and recording.

Payment of counsel employed by de jure board of education to test legality of board enjoined for failure to file clerk's certificate of funds available: Caldwell v. Marvin, 20 Dec. 715 (8 N. S. 387).

Township trustees act as a board of health in making provision for infectious diseases: Knauss v. Bader, 22 Dec. 59 (11 N. S. 495).

This section insofar as it applies to boards of education is unconstitutional for lack of uniformity of operation; and failure on the part of a board of education to comply with the requirements of this section in incurring an obligation does not render the obligation void: Bower v. Board of Education, 8 O. C. C. (N. S.) 305.

Failure of the auditor or clerk to first certify that the money necessary to meet the expense of building a new schoolhouse is in the treasury to the credit of the fund from which it is to be drawn, or has been levied and is in process of collection and has not been appropriated for any other purpose, renders the contract void under G. C. Sec. 3806: McAlexander v. Haviland School District, 7 O. N. P. (N. S.) 590.

Exceptions thereto.

SECTION 5661. All contracts, agreements or obligations, and orders or resolutions entered into or passed contrary to the provisions of the next preceding section, shall be void, but such section shall not apply to the contracts authorized to be made by other provisions of law for the employment of teachers, officers, and other school employes of boards of education. (99 v. 520.)

It cannot be too often repeated that a board of education speaks only through its records. Its acts, findings, and determinations are only known by its records. Hence, although the words of the statute may not clearly settle the question, yet it is safest to assume that this *determination* is to be an *official* determination. Purchases of bonds are likely to scrutinize such matters closely, and they will question whether the board acquires jurisdiction to take steps for raising a tax unless it first officially "ascertains" and "determines" all the preliminary facts mentioned in the statute, and makes a record of such finding.

Section 5656, General Code, empowers the board of education when pressed by reason of taxation limitations to issue bonds or borrow money for the purpose of meeting such valid existing and binding indebtedness among its running expenses as are excepted under section 5661, General Code, from the necessity of the Auditor's Certificate to the effect that the funds are in the treasury.

The power is extended alone to these emunerated expenses, namely: "Contracts authorized to be made by other provisions of law for the employment of teachers, officers and other school employes of boards of education." — *Attorney General*, 1911-12, p. 551.

Township trustees are not authorized to loan the township Board of Education surplus funds. — *Attorney General*, Opinion No. 908, 1914.

A board of education may borrow money under Section 5656, General Code, to pay obligations incurred in furnishing the transportaiton to pupils which the law requires to be furnished, such expense being a charge against the district, regardless of the existence of sufficient funds in the district treasury, and the contract for transportaiton being at least the nature of an employment contract.

It is not a condition precedent to the exercise of power under said section that previously incurred floating or funded indebtedness has been created under the same section, that is, it is not necessary that the one debt shall be extinguished before the time of payment of the other is extended. — *Attorney General*, Opinion No. 1226, 1914.

Auditor shall ascertain amount.

SECTION 5699. The county auditor shall carefully ascertain the net amount of taxes collected for each particular purpose. (103 v. 521.)

If question approved, board may issue such bonds.

SECTION 7626. If a majority of the electors, voting on the proposition to issue bonds, vote in favor thereof, the board thereby shall be authorized to issue bonds for the amount indicated by the vote. The issue and sale thereof shall be provided for by a resolution fixing the amount of each bond, the length of time they shall run, the rate of interest they shall bear, and the time of sale. Such bonds shall be sold in the manner provided by law. (106 v. 492.)

Section 7629, General Code, still empowers the board of education to issue such amount of bonds without authority of electors in any one year as does not exceed in the aggregate a tax of two mills for the year next preceding the next issue. The limitaitons of the Smith law must be observed, however. — *Attorney General,* 1911-12, p. 1332.

There is no provision of law other than Secitons 7626, et seq., General Code, whereby boards of education authorized by vote under Section 4726 to centralize schools may borrow money with which to erect a centralized school building. — *Attorney General,* Opinion No. 913, 1914.

When a village board of education was authorized by electors under section 7592, General Code, to levy an additional tax of five mills for five years such board may proceed to issue bonds without further authorization of the electors, provided that the conditions of 7626 and 7679, General Code, with reference to the quality and nature of the bonds and the provisions of section 7629 with reeference to the amount of the bonds and the procedure of the board to be complied with. — *Attorney General,* 1911-12, p. 534.

As to sale of public bonds, see G. C. Sections 2294 and 2295.

SECTION 7627. Such bonds shall bear a rate of inter- *Requisites*
est not to exceed six per cent per annum payable semi-an- *of bonds.*
nually, be made payable within at least forty years from the date thereof, be numbered consecutively, made payable to the bearer, and be signed by the president and clerk of the board of education. The clerk of the board must keep a record of the number, date, amount and the rate of interest of each bond sold, the amount received for it, the name of the person to whom sold, and the time when payable, which record shall be open to the inspection of the public at all reasonable times. Bonds so issued shall in no case be sold for less than their par value and accrued interest. (106 v. 492.)

When it becomes necessary for a board of education to improve school buildings by reason of an order from the inspector of workshops and factories, and such improvements cannot be made within thee ordinary limitations of the Smith tax law, and when furthermore the electors have repeatedly refused to authorize bond issues under sections 7625 and 7628, General Code, the board of education may have recourse to sections 7629 and 7630, General Code.

By these sections, they may issue bonds for this purpose in a sum not to exceed the amount of a tax at the rate of two mills for the year next preceding the issue, and may extend the payment of such bonds over a preiod of forty years. — *Attorney General,* 1911-12, p. 1384.

When a village board of education was authorized by electors under section 7592, General Code, to levy an additional tax of five mills for five years such board may proceed to issue bonds without further authorization of the electors, provided that the conditions of 7626 and 7679, General Code, with reference to the quality and nature of the bonds and the provisions of sections 7629 with reference to the amount of the bonds and the procedure of the board to be complied with. — *Attorney General,* 1911-12, p. 534.

Section 7629, General Code, still empowers the board of education to issue such amount of bonds without authority of electors in any one year as does not exceed in the aggregate a tax

of two mills for the year next preceding the issue. The limitations of the Smith law must be observed, however. — *Attorney
General*, 1911-12, p. 1332.

Tax levy to
pay bonds
thus issued.

SECTION 7628. When an issue of bonds has been provided for under the next three preceding sections, the board
of education, annually, shall certify to the county auditor
or auditors as the case may require, a tax levy sufficient to
pay such bonded indebtedness as it falls due together with
accrued interest thereon. Such county auditor or auditors
must place such levy on the tax duplicate. It shall be collected and paid to the board of education as other taxes
are. Such tax levy shall be in addition to the maximum
levy for school purposes, and must be kept in a separate
fund and applied only to the payment of the bonds and interest for which it was levied. (97 v. 358.)

Mandamus is the proper remedy to compel the board to appropriate
moneys already in their treasury for that purpose, toward the payment of
such bonds, and to levy such tax as may be necessary to complete such
payment: 27 O. S. 96.

When a joint school district is formed for high school purposes by a township school district and an adjoining village district, such district becomes one· district and taxes for the support
of the same must be borne by the respective joined districts in
proportion to the total valuation of the property in each, notwithstanding the fact that the village district sends the most pupils
and has the smallest valuation. — *Attorney General,* 1911-12, p.
1042.

When it becomes necessary for a board of education to improve school buildings by reason of an order from the inspector
of workshops and factories, and such improvements cannot be
made within the ordinary limitations of the Smith tax law, and
when furthermore the electors have repeatedly refused to authorize bond issues under Sections 7625 and 7628, General Code,
the board of education may have recourse to Sections 7629 and
7630, General Code.

By these sections, they may issue bonds for this purpose in
a sum not to exceed the amount of a tax at the rate of two mills
for the year next preceding the issue, and may extend the payment of such bonds over a period of forty years. — *Attorney
General*, 1911-12, p. 1384.

Advertisement
of sale
of public
bonds.

SECTION 2294. All bonds issued by boards of
county commissioners, boards of education, township trustees, or commissioners of free turnpikes, shall be sold to
the highest bidder after being advertised once a week for
three consecutive weeks and on the same day of the week,
in a newspaper having general circulation in the county
where the bonds are issued, and, if, the amount of bonds
to be sold exceeds twenty thousand dollars, like publications shall be made in an additional newspaper having general circulation in the state. The advertisement shall state
the total amount and denomination of bonds to be sold,
how long they are to run, the rate of interest to be paid
thereon, whether annually or semi-annually, the law or

section of law authorizing the issue, the day, hour and place in the county where they are to be sold. (106 v. 492.)

The county commissioners should be able to secure money for their immediate needs for the relief of the poor by issuing notes themselves, conditioned upon the subsequent issue of bonds. Persons lending money on notes of this kind should first see that the county is able to float its bonds when issued. — *Attorney General*, Opinion No. 742, 1914.

It is necessary to adevrtise the sale of bonds by a board of education under Section 7626, G. C., and a board of education is not authorized to dispense with competitive bidding in the sale of the same.

A board of education which has advertised the sale of bonds bearing a certain rate of interest, and has received no bids for the same, and which then proceeds by resolution to raise the rate of interest on said bonds, must again offer said bonds to the board of commissioners of the sinking fund of the school district, if such there be, and then to the Industrial Commission of Ohio, prior to again advertising the same for sale. — *Attorney General*, Opinion No. 79, 1915.

See G. C. Sections 7626, 7627 and 7629 as to sale of bonds by boards of education.

Cleveland school building bond issue subject to this law: 93 v. 459.

As to sale of bonds by boards of educaiton see G. C. Sec. 7626, et seq.

SECTION 2295. None of such bonds shall be sold for less than the face thereof with any interest that may have accrued thereon, and the privilege shall be reserved of rejection of any or all bids. When such bonds have been once advertised and offered at public sale, as provided by law, and they, or any part thereof, remain unsold, those unsold may be sold at private sale at not less than their par value and accrued interest. All moneys from the principal on the sale of such bonds shall be credited to the fund on account of which the bonds are issued and sold, and all moneys from premiums and accrued interest on the sale of such bonds shall be credited to the sinking fund from which said bonds are to be redeemed. (106 v. 492.)

How sold; when bids rejected.

SECTION 2295-1. That all bonds, hereafter issued by any county, city or city school district within this state, except those issues permanently held by the sinking fund trustees of the municipality issuing same, may have, endorsed thereon, a certificate attesting the genuineness of the signatures thereto signed by a registrar legally authorized and qualified to act therein. (101 v. 256.)

Endorsement.

SECTION 2295-2. That every county, city or city school district within this state having the power to issue such bonds, shall have the power to employ such registrar, the compensation of which together with all proper expenses incident to such certification shall be paid on the allowance of such authority out of the county, city or city school district treasury or fund benefited or to be benefited by the sale of such bonds, as the case may be. (101 v. 256.)

Registrar; appointment and compensation.

SECTION 2295-3. That it shall be the duty of the clerk, or other officer having charge of the minutes of the council of any municipal corporation, board of county commissioners, board of education, township trustees, or other district or political subdivisions of this state, that now has or may hereafter have, the power to issue bonds, to furnish to the successful bidder for said bonds, a true transcript certified by him of all ordinances, resolutions, notices and other proceedings had with reference to the issuance of said bonds, including a statement of the character of the meetings at which said proceedings were had, the number of members present, and such other information from the records as may be necessary to determine the regularity and validity of the issuance of said bonds; that it shall be the duty of the auditor or other officer, having charge of the accounts of said corporation or political subdivision, to attach thereto a true and correct statement certified by him of the indebtedness, and, of the amount of the tax duplicate thereof, and such other information as will show whether or not said bond issue is within any debt or tax limitation imposed by law. (103 v. 179.)

Certified transcript of proceedings required to be furnished successful bidder for bonds by certain officers.

Attached statement of indebtedness by auditor.

SECTION 2295-4. Any such clerk or officer, or any deputy or subordinate thereof, who shall knowingly make or certify a false transcript or statement in respect to any of the matters hereinabove set forth, shall be guilty of a misdemeanor and be fined not less than twenty-five ($25.00) dollars, nor more than five hundred ($500.00) dollars, or imprisoned not exceeding one year, or both. (103 v. 179.)

Penalty for certifying false transcript or statement.

SECTION 2295-5. Whenever bonds, notes or certificates of indebtedness, issued by a municipal corporation, school district, county, township, or other political subdivision or taxing district of this state, are lost or destroyed, said corporation, school district, county, township, subdivision or district may reissue to the holder or holders duplicates thereof in the same form and signed as the original obligations were signed, which obligation so issued shall plainly show upon its face as being a duplicate of such lost bond, note or certificate, upon proof of such loss or destruction and upon being furnished with a bond of indemnity against all loss or liability for or on account of the obligations so lost or destroyed. (106 v. 303.)

Re-issue of lost or destroyed bonds or certificates.

SECTION 3924. Sales of bonds, other than to the trustees of the sinking fund of the city or to the board of commissioners of the sinking fund of the city school district as herein authorized, by any municipal corporation, shall be to the highest and best bidder, after publishing notice thereof for four consecutive weeks in two newspapers printed and of general circulation in the county where such municipal corporation is situated, setting forth

Notice of sale; publication.

the nature, amount, rate of interest, and length of time the bonds have to run, with the time and place of sale. Additional notice may be published outside of such county by order of the council, but when such bonds have been once so advertised and offered for public sale, and they, or any part thereof, remain unsold, those unsold may be sold at private sale at not less than their par value, under the directions of the mayor and the officers and agents of the corporation by whom such bonds have been, or may be, prepared, advertised and offered at public sale. (106 v. 492.)

SECTION 7629. The board of education of any school district may issue bonds to obtain or improve public school property, and in anticipation of income from taxes, for such purposes, levied or to be levied, from time to time, as occasion requires, may issue and sell bonds, under the restrictions and bearing a rate of interest specified in sections seventy-six hundred and twenty-six and seventy-six hundred and twenty-seven. The board shall pay such bonds and the interest thereon when due, but provide that no greater amount of bonds be issued in any year than would equal the aggregate of a tax at the rate of two mills, for the year next preceding such issue. The order to issue bonds shall be made only at a regular meeting of the board and by a vote of two-thirds of its full membership, taken by yeas and nays and entered upon its journal. (97 v. 358.)

Issue of bonds by boards of education.

On authority of Rabe v. Board of Education, 88 O. S., 403, Section 7629, General Code, providing for the issuance of bonds under certain circumstances, by boards of education, is still in effect. This opinion discusses the present operation under the Smith Law and Article XII, Section 11 of the Constitution. — *Attorney General,* Opinion No. 1088, 1914.

When it becomes necessary for a board of education to improve school buildings by reason of an order from the inspector of workshops and factories, and such improvements cannot be made within the ordinary limitations of the Smith tax law, and when furthermore the electors have repeatedly refused to authorize bond issues under sections 7625 and 7628, General Code, the board of education may have recourse to section 7629 and 7630, General Code.

By these sections, they may issue bonds for this prurpose in a sum not to exceed the amount of a tax at the rate of two mills for the year next preceding the issue, and may extend the payment of such bonds over a period of forty years. — *Attorney General,* 1911-12, p. 1384.

Section 7629, General Code, still empowers the board of education to issue such amount of bonds without authority of electors in any one year as does not exceed in the aggregate a tax of two mills for the year next preceding the next issue. The limitations of the Smith law must be observed, however. — *Attorney General,* 1911-12, p. 1332.

There is no provision of law other than Sections 7626, et seq., General Code, whereby boards of education authorized by vote under Sections 4726 to centralize schools may borrow money with which to erect a centralized school building. — *Attorney General,* Opinion No. 913, 1914.

In order to obtain or improve school property, a board of education may issue and sell bonds. No greater amount of bonds can be issued in one year than would equal the aggregate of a tax at the rate of two mills for the year next preceding such issue.

The order to issue bonds shall be made only at the regular meeting of the board and by a two-thirds vote of the full membership of the board. — *Attorney General*, 1913, p. 1317.

A levy of taxes made by a board of education for the purpose of providing for the payment of bonds issued in anticipation thereof, under authority of section 7629, General Code, must be made within the limitations of the Smith One Per cent Law, and also within the five mill limitation, applicable to boards of education as such, and prescribed by Section 5649-3a, General Code. — *Attorney General*, 1913, p. 1381.

When it becomes necessary for a board of education to improve school building by reason of an order from the inspector of workshops and factories, and such improvements cannot be made within the ordinary limitations of the Smith tax law, and when furthermore the electors have repeatedly refused to authorize bond issues under Sections 7625 and 7628, General Code, the board of educa ion may have recourse to Sections 7629 and 7630, General Code. t

By these sections, they may issue bonds for this purpose in a sum not to exceed the amount of a tax at the rate of two mills for the year next preceding the issue, and may extend the payment of such bonds over a period of forty years. — *Attorney General*, 1911-12, p. 1384.

A board of education, under the provisions of an act authorizing it to borrow money to pay existing indebtedness, by the issue and sale of bonds bearing interest at a rate not exceeding eight per cent. per annum, payable semi-annually, agreed to borrow a sum of money at an aggregate rate of interest of fifteen per cent. in manner following: For the amount so to be borrowed bonds were to be issued, bearing the authorized rate of interest, and for the excess of interest orders on the treasury were to be issued payable at the same time as the legal interest. The bonds were regularly issued, bearing eight per cent. interest, and sold at par, and the money was received and used as authorized. For the excess of interest orders on the treasury were at the same time issued and delivered to the purchaser, as agreed to by the parties, but were never presented for payment, and after their maturity he offered to return them for cancellation. It was held that this agreement to pay excess of interest is void, and having never been executed in whole or in part, will not avoid a recovery on the bonds.

The fact that such agreement for unlawful interest was made, does not make the purchaser chargeable with notice of prior fraudulent practices of members of the board in incurring the debt for the payment of which the money was barrowed, which had no connection with the sale of the bonds, and of which the purchaser had no knowledge: State, ex rel., v. Board of Education, 35 O. S. 519.

A board of education being authorized by a special act to issue its bonds to an amount not to exceed the sum of $20,000, issued the same to the full extent of its authority, payable to............................, or bearer; and thereafter took up and paid certain of such bonds and left them with its treasurer, who was a member of such board, with instructions to cancel them, which he failed to do, but negotiated them, before maturity to S., as collateral security for a loan made to him by S., who made no inquiry in regard to them. It was held that the payment of the bonds by the board extinguished them, and they were incapable of being reissued. There was no negligence on the part of the board in not seeing that its treasurer complied with its instructions to cancel the bonds. S. was guilty of contributory negligence in taking the bonds without inquiry: Board of Education v. Sinton, 14 O. S. 504.

Sections 5649-2, et seq., limit rate of taxation and repeal by implication existing conflicting statutes: Rabe v. Canton Sch. Dist. (Bd. of Ed.), 88 O. S. 408.

Limit of issue.

SECTION 7630. In no case shall a board of education issue bonds under the provisions of the next preceding section in a greater amount than can be provided for and paid with the tax levy authorized by sections seventy-five hundred and ninety-one and seventy-five hundred and ninety-two, and paid within forty years after the issue on the basis of the tax valuation at the time of issue. (97 v. 358.)

When it becomes necessary for a board of education to improve school buildings by reason of an order from the inspector of workshops and factories, and such improvements cannot be made within the ordinary limitations of the Smith tax law, and when furthermore the electors have repeatedly refused to authorize bond issues under sections 7625 and 7628, General Code, the board of education may have recourse to sections 7629 and 7630, General Code.

By these sections, they may issue bonds for this purpose in a sum not to exceed the amount of a tax at the rate of two mills for the year next preceding the issue, and may extend the payment of such bonds over a period of forty years. — *Attorney General*, 1911-12, p. 1384.

When a village board of education was authorized by electors under section 7592, General Code, to levy an additional tax of five mills for five years such board may proceed to issue bonds without further authorization of the electors, provided that the conditions of 7626 and 7679, General Code, with reference to the quality and nature of the bonds and the provisions of section 7629 with reference to the amount of the bonds and the procedure of the board be complied with. — *Attorney General*, 1911-12, p. 534.

.When the tax duplicate of the preceding year is such that a tax of two mills would raise only $2,600.00 the board of education may not expend for the construction of a school house the sum of $3,300.00 without first submitting the question of expenditure to a vote of the people. — *Attorney General*, 1913, p. 1345.

The decision in the case of Rabe et al. v. Board of Education, does not in any way affect the rights of the Board of Education under Section 5656, General Code. — *Attorney General*, Opinion No. 926, May 11, 1924.

There is no provision of law other than Section 7626, et seq., General Code, whereby boards of education authorized by vote under Section 4726 to centralize schools may borrow money with which to erect a centralized school building. — *Attorney General*, Opinion No. 913, May 4, 1914.

Section 7629, General Code, still empowers the board of education to issue such amount of bonds without authority of the electors in any one year as does not exceed in the aggregate a tax of two mills for the next year preceding the issue. The limitation of the Smith law must be observed, however. — *Attorney General*, 1911-12, p. 1332.

Section 7630-1. If a school house is wholly or partly destroyed by fire or other casualty, or if the use of any schoolhouse for its intended purpose is prohibited by any order of the chief inspector of workshops and factories, and the board of education of the school district is without sufficient funds applicable to the purpose, with which to rebuild or repair such school house or to construct a new schoolhouse for the proper accommodation of the schools of the district, and it is not practicable to secure such funds under any of the six preceding sections because of the limits of taxation applicable to such school district, such board of education may, subject to the provisions of sections seventy-six hundred and twenty-six and seventy-six hundred and twenty-seven, and upon the approval of the electors in the manner provided by sections seventy-six hundred and twenty-five and seventy-six hundred and twenty-six issue bonds for the amount required for such purpose. For the payment of the principal and

Replacement of school houses condemned or destroyed.

interest on such bonds and on bonds heretofore issued
for the purposes herein mentioned and to provide a sinking fund for their final redemption at maturity, such board
of education shall annually levy a tax as provided by law.
(103 v. 527.)

Where the Inspector of Workshops and Factroies prohibits
the use of a school house until certain repairs are made, but the
board of education decides to erect a new school building instead,
and the elections vote for a $25,000 bond issue for the construc-
tion thereof, but cannot levy sufficient taxes to pay bonds and
maintain school, there would be an emergency within the meaning of Section 5649-4, General Code, and the necessary taxes for
the retirement of bonds required, for the purpose might be levied
outside of all limitations of law. — *Attorney General,* Opinion No.
888, 1914.

If a board of education deems it necessary to secure a new
site in order to replace a school house condmened or destroy the
tax levies necessary for the purposes of such site are not within
the exemption of Section 7630-1 and 7630-2, General Code, but
must be made within all the limitations of the Smith one per cent
law. — *Attorney General,* Opinion No. 1110, 1914.

In case of the condemnation of a school buliding by the state
building inspector, levies for the necessary repairs are not entitled
to exemption from all limitations under Sections 7630-1 and 5649-4,
General Code, unless bonds are issued by a vote of the people, in
which event the interest and sinking fund levies will be exempt
from the limitation. Simple repair levies made under these circumstances are subject to all the limitations of law. — *Attorney
General,* Opinion No. 1190, Oct. 8, 1914.

Where the Industrial Commission and its deputy in charge
of workshops, factories and public buildings condemn the use of a
public school building for school purposes, the order must be
complied with, and an emergency is created.

If bonds are issued by the board of education, with the
approval of the majority of the electors, at a special election, the
tax levies necessary to carry these bonds may be made outside of
the limitations of the Smith One Per Cent Law. Such is the effect
of the amendment to Section 5649-4, General Code. — *Attorney
General,* 1913, p. 1715.

When a school building fit for occupancy prior to the flood
has been damaged by the flood as to render the same unfit for
use, the provisions of the Snyder Emergency Act, exempting from
the general limitations of the law upon levies and borrowing
powers may be resorted to.

The question of damage is one of fact, the answer to which
may be assisted by the reports of the Chief Inspector of Workshops and Factories.

Under Section 7630-1, General Code, a school building condemned by the Chief Inspector of Workshops and Factories may
be rebuilt or repaired. The money may be borrowed therefor,
regardless of the Smith law limitation. — *Attorney General,* 1913,
p. 14.

LIBRARIES.

Establishment
of free public
library.

SECTION 7631. The board of education of any city,
village, or rural school district, by resolution, may provide
for the establishment, control and maintenance, in such
district, of a public library, free to all the inhabitants
thereof. For that purpose, by purchase, it may acquire
the necessary real property, and erect thereon a library
building; acquire, by purchase or otherwise, from any
other library association, its library property; receive donations and bequests of money or property for such li-

brary purposes, and maintain and support libraries now in existence and controlled by the board. (104 v. 225.)

For decisions under an earlier form of this statute, in which were found provisions authorizing the board of education to purchase "apparatus", but limiting the amount thereof, see G. C. Sec. 7620, and note thereto.
Board of education may accept bequest for public library and Y. M. C. A. building: Blume v. Thompson, 23 Dec. 512 (15 N. S. 97).

SECTION 7632. Such board of education annually **Taxation.** may make a levy upon the taxable property of such school district, in addition to all other taxes allowed by law, of not to exceed one mill for a library fund, to be expended by the board, for the establishment, support and maintenance of such public library. (98 v. 244 § 1.)

SECTION 7633. But when a donation or bequest of **Libraries jointly owned by two or more school districts.** money or property has been or is made to two or more school districts jointly, or jointly and severally for the purpose of establishing and maintaining such public library, and the money so donated has been or may be expended in the purchase of a site and the erection of a library building thereon, the provisions of this subdivision shall apply. In such case the board of education of each of the districts annually may levy not exceeding one mill, in addition to all other taxes allowed by law, upon the taxable property of such school districts for the establishment, support and maintenance of such public library, and the library building may be located at a convenient place in either district. (98 v. 244 § 1.)

SECTION 7634. The control of such building and library and the expenditure of all moneys for the purchase **Board of trustees, appointment, term.** of books and other purposes and the administration of the library shall be vested in a board of six trustees, three to be appointed by each of the boards of education for the term of five years. They must serve without compensation, and until their successors are appointed. In case of vacancy in the board, from refusal to serve, resignation or otherwise, it shall be filled by the boards of education of such district, for the unexpired term. (98 v. 244 § 1.)

State library commissoners to give advice and attention to free public library officers; see Sec. 793.

SECTION 7635. The board of education may provide **Management and control of library.** for the management and control of such library by a board of trustees to be elected by it as herein provided. (100 v. 16.)

SECTION 7636. Such board of library trustees shall **Library trustees, number and eligibility of.** consist of seven members, who must be residents of the school district. No one shall be eligible to membership on such library board who is or has been for a year previous to his election, a member or officer of the board of education. The term of office shall be seven years, except that at the first election the terms must be such that one member retires each year. Should a vacancy occur in the board, it shall be filled by the board of education for the unexpired term. The members of the library board must serve without compensation and until their successors are elected and qualified. (100 v. 16.)

Powers of board.

SECTION 7637. In its own name, such library board shall hold the title to and have the custody, and control of all libraries, branches, stations, reading rooms, of all library property, real and personal, of such school district, and of the expenditure of all moneys collected or received from any source for library purposes for such district. It may employ a librarian and assistants, but previous to such employment their compensation shall be fixed. (100 v. 16.)

May acquire land.

SECTION 7638. By a two-thirds vote of its members such library board may purchase or lease grounds and buildings, and erect buildings for library purposes. It also may appropriate land for library purposes if the owner and the board cannot agree upon terms, and dispose of land when, in its opinion, it is no longer needed for library purposes. Conveyances made by the board shall be executed in its name by its president and secretary. In the event any balance to the credit of the library fund shall remain in the treasury at the close of any fiscal year, such surplus or any part thereof may be set aside by a two-thirds vote of the members of the board as a

Repair fund.

special building and repair fund. It may accept any gift, devise or bequest for the benefit of such library. No member of the library board shall be interested, directly or indirectly, in any contract made by the board. It shall report annually in writing to the board of education. (101 v. 304.)

Library fund; how provided and maintained.

SECTION 7639. Such board of library trustees annually, during the month of May, shall certify to the board of education the amount of money needed for increasing, maintaining and operating the library during the ensuing year in addition to the funds available therefor from other sources. The board of education annually shall levy on each dollar of taxable property within such school district, in addition to all other levies authorized by law, such assessment not exceeding one and one-half mills, as shall be necessary to realize without reduction, the sum so certified, which must be placed on the tax duplicate and collected as other taxes. (101 v. 304.)

Payments from library fund.

SECTION 7640. The proceeds of such tax will constitute a fund to be known and designated as the library fund. Payments therefrom shall be made only upon the warrant of the library board of trustees, signed by the president and secretary thereof. (96 v. 9 § 4.)

SECTION 7641. · The board of education in any city, village, or rural school district may contract annually with any library corporation or other organization owning and maintaining a library or with any board of trustees appointed by authority of law, having the management and control of a library, for the use of such library by the residents of such district. Such board of education shall require an annual report in writing from such library corporation or other organization or board of trustees. (104 v. 225.)

Tax levy to maintain public library.

A levy of one mill by the board of education imposed annually for the purpose of reimbursing a library association for services to the public in pursuance of a contract between the board and the association, is within the interior limitations of the Smith law and is not a "levy for sinking fund and interest purposes necessary to provide for the indebtedness created prior to the passage" of the Smith law.

The obligation which rests upon the board is not an indebtedness within the meaning of the statute, nor is there an "impairment of the obligation of contract" in the effect of the Smith law upon such procedures. — *Attorney General*, 1912, p. 1578.

•SECTION 7642. The board of education of any school district of the state, in which there is not a public library operated under public authority and free to all the residents of such district annually may appropriate not to exceed two hundred and fifty dollars from its contingent fund for the purchase of books, other than school books, for the use and improvement of the teachers and pupils of such school district. The books so purchased shall constitute a school library, the control and management of which shall be vested in the board of education, which may receive donations and bequests of money or property therefor. (96 v. 9 § 6.)

School library.

SECTION 7643. The board of education of any school district, or board of trustees managing and controlling a library in any school district, may found and maintain a museum in connection with and as an adjunct to such library, and for such purpose may receive bequests and donations of money or other property. (96 v. 9 § 7.)

Museum.

CHAPTER 3.

SCHOOLS AND ATTENDANCE.

SECTION 7644. Each board of education shall establish a sufficient number of elementary schools to provide for the free education of the youth of school age within the district under its control, at such places as will be most convenient for the attendance of the largest number thereof. Every elementary day school so established shall continue not less than thirty-two nor more than forty weeks in each school year. All the elementary schools within the same school district shall be so continued. (99 v. 85.)

Elementary schools; minimum and maximum school weeks.

Cases of urgent necessity are excepted from the provisions of sections 7623, General Code, providing for certain procedure when the cost of repairing or improving a school house in other than city districts exceeds five hundred dollars.

Inasmuch, therefore, as the board of education is required to provide for at least thirty-two school weeks in a year, and as the mayor may prohibit use of school buildings until compliance has been made with the orders of the chief inspector of workshops and factories, the board of education of a village, upon such order from the chief inspector of workshops and factories, made after the school year has begun, may dispense with the procedure of section 7623 and execute necessary repairs without advertising for bids. — *Atorney General*, 1911-12, p. 1318.

When a board of education passed a resolution legal in form, employing certain teachers, the effect thereof would be to employ said teachers, through certain provisions of said resolution requiring said teachers to enter into a written contract "to make up for legal holidays and for the time lost in the event of epidemic" would be void because against the statutes and public policy of the state of Ohio. — *Attorney General*, 1911-12, p. 1322.

It is the intent of Sections 7644 and 7595, General Code, that a Board of Education shall maintain a school session of not less than thirty-two weeks in each year as a condition precedent to obtaining State Aid.

It is not the intent to demand the impossible, however, and when, through destruction of the school building by fire, compliance is absolutely prevented, failure to maintain an eight months' session will not preclude the right to State Aid. — *Attorney General*, 1912, p. 120.

Under section 4750, General Code, a board of education is empowered to make such regulations as it deems necessary for the government of its employes and the pupils of the school. -Under this section, the board may designate what studies such pupils shall be required to take. — *Attorney General*, 1913, p. 1153.

Sections 5649-2, et seq., limit rate of taxation and repeal by implication existing conflicting statutes: Rabe v. Canton Sch. Dist. (Bd. of Ed.), 88 O. S. 403.

Tuberculosis schools.

SECTION 7644-1. The board of education in any city school district may establish such special elementary schools as it deems necessary for youth of school age who are afflicted with tuberculosis, and may cause all youth, within such district, so afflicted, to be excluded from the regular elementary schools, and may provide for and pay from the school funds, the expense of transportation of such youth to and from such special schools. (101 v. 319.)

Graded course of study.

SECTION 7645. Boards of education are required to prescribe a graded course of study for all schools under their control in the branches named in section seventy-six hundred and forty-eight, subject to the approval of the superintendent of public instruction. (104 v. 225.)

Where part of a subdistrict of a township school district has been incorporated into a special school district leaving the balance of said township unprovided for as to a school house, the board of education of the township school district must either provide a school house in the remaining part of said sibdistrict, or transport the pupils to a school. — *Attorney General*, Opinion No. 983, 1914.

Neglect to instruct pupils in fire drills.

SECTION 12900. Whoever, being a principal or person in charge of a public or private school or educational institution having an average daily attendance of fifty or more pupils, wilfully neglects to instruct and train such pupils by means of drills or rapid dismissals at least once a month while such school or institution is in session, so that such pupils, in a sudden emergency may leave the school building in the shortest possible time and without confusion, or willfully neglects to keep the doors and exits of such building unlocked during school hours, shall be fined not less than five dollars, nor more than twenty dollars for each offense. (99 v. 231 §§ 1, 2.)

Same as to dangers of fire.

SECTION 12901. Whoever, being a teacher or instructor in a public, private or parochial school, wilfully neglects to devote less than thirty minutes in each month during which such school is in session to instructing the pupils thereof between the ages of six and fourteen years, as to dangers of fire, shall be fined not less than five dollars nor more than twenty dollars. (99 v. 231 §§ 1, 2.)

Duty of state fire marshal.

SECTION 12902. The state fire marshal shall prepare a book for the purpose of the instruction of pupils provided in the next two preceding sections. Such book shall be conveniently arranged in a sufficient number of chapters or lessons to provide a different one thereof for each week of the maximum school year. One of such chapters or lessons shall be read each week by the teacher in such school. (99 v. 231 § 1.)

SECTION 12903. Such books shall be published at the expense of the state under the direction of the superintendent of public instruction, who shall furnish a copy thereof to each teacher required to give such instruction. (104 v. 225.)

Duty of superintendent.

SECTION 12904. The next four preceding sections shall not apply to college and universities. (99 v. 232 § 4.)

Exceptions to same.

SECTION 12905. The members of the boards of education, school directors, trustees or other body of persons having control of the schools of a township, village or city shall cause a copy of the next five preceding sections to be printed in the manual or handbook prepared for the guidance of teachers, where such manual is in use. (99 v. 232 § 3.)

Manual to be issued.

SECTION 7646. The board of education of each rural school district shall establish and maintain at least one elementary school in each subdistrict under its control, unless transportation is furnished to the pupils thereof as provided by law. (104 v. 225.)

Elementary school shall be maintained.

SECTION 7647. The board of education in any city school district may establish and maintain a normal school within its district, and also establish and maintain such summer or vacation schools, school gardening and play grounds as to it seems desirable. (99 v. 85.)

Normal school.

A normal school which is maintained by the board of education forms a part of the public school system: Brown v. Board of Education, 6 O. N. P. 411.

SECTION 7648. An elementary school is one in which instruction and training are given in spelling, reading, writing, arithmetic, English language, English grammar and composition, geography, history of the United States, including civil government, physiology and hygiene. Nothing herein shall abridge the power of boards of education to cause instruction and training to be given in vocal music, drawing, elementary algebra, the elements of agriculture and other branches which they deem advisable for the best interests of the schools under their charge. (97 v. 359.)

Elementary school defined.

The constitutional guaranty of an efficient system of common schools throughout the state does not, in the absence of specific statutory provision, require township boards of education to pay the tuition of pupils who wish to enjoy the advantages of a high school outside of the township of their residence, either in the same or an adjoining county (compare G. C. Sec. 7750): Board of Education v. Board of Education, 10 O. D. (N. P.) 459.

SECTION 7649. A high school is one of higher grade than an elementary school, in which instruction and training are given in approved courses in the history of the United States and other countries; composition, rhetoric, English and American literature; algebra and geometry; natural science, political or mental science, ancient or mod-

High school defined.

ern foreign languages, or both, commercial and industrial branches, or such of the branches named as the length of its curriculum makes possible. Also such other branches of higher grade than those to be taught in the elementary schools, with such advanced studies and advanced reviews of the common branches as the board of education directs. (95 v. 115.)

A high school diploma is not legal which is granted to a person who was never a member of the high school which granted the diploma and if the person had never performed the work required by the curriculum of the said high school, or any part of it, or its equivalent, and never did any regular school work beyond the grade schools. — *Attorney General,* Opinion No. 1163, Sept. 21, 1914.

The constitutional guaranty of an efficient system of common schools throughout the state does not, in the absence of specific statutory provision, require township boards of education to pay the tuition of pupils who wish to enjoy the advantages of a high school outside of the township of their residence, either in the same or an adjoining county (compare G. C. Sec. 7750): Board of Education v. Board of Education, 10 O. D. (N. P.) 459.

College defined.

SECTION 7650. A college is a school of a higher grade than a high school, in which instruction in the high school branches is carried beyond the scope of the high school and other advanced studies are pursued, or a school in which special, technical or professional studies are pursued, and which, when legally organized, may have the right to confer degrees in agreement with the terms of the law regulating its practices or its charter; or in the absence of legislative direction, in agreement with the practices of the better institutions of learning of their respective kinds in the United States. (95 v. 115.)

High schools classified.

SECTION 7651. The high schools of the state shall be classified into schools of the first, second, and third grades. All courses of study offered in such schools shall be in branches enumerated in section seventy-six hundred and forty-nine. (95 v. 116.)

When a township board of education maintain a third grade high school, such board is in no sense liable for tuition of pupils at other high schools of higher grade, when such pupils are not graduates of the said third grade local high school. — *Attorney General,* 1911-12, p. 1257.

Requisites for admission to examination.

SECTION 1270. The state medical board shall appoint an entrance examiner who shall not be directly or indirectly connected with a medical college and who shall determine the sufficiency of the preliminary education of applicants for admission to the examination. The following preliminary educational credentials shall be sufficient:

A diploma from a reputable college granting the degree of A. B., B. S., or equivalent degree.

A diploma from a legally constituted normal school, high school or seminary, issued after four years of study:

A teacher's permanent or life certificate:

A student's certificate of examination for admission to the freshman class of a reputable literary or scientific college.

In the absence of the foregoing qualifications, the entrance examiner may examine the applicant in such branches as are required for graduation from a first-class high school of this state, and to pass such examination shall be sufficient qualification. If the entrance examiner finds that the preliminary education of the applicant is sufficient, he shall, upon payment to the treasurer of the state medical board of a fee of three dollars, issue a certificate thereof, which shall be attested by the secretary of the state medical board.

The applicant must also produce a certificate issued by the entrance examiner and a diploma from a legally chartered medical institution in the United States, in good standing, as defined by the board, at the time the diploma was issued, and which institution, subsequent to May 1st, 1913, requires for admission for the degree of M. D., to such institution, a preliminary education equal to that required for graduation from a first-grade high school in this state, or a diploma or license approved by the board which conferred the full right to practice all branches of medicine or surgery in a foreign country. (103 v. 438.)

SECTION 7652. A high school of the first grade shall be a school in which the courses offered cover a period of not less than four years, of not less than thirty-two weeks each, in which not less than sixteen courses are required for graduation. (95 v. 116.) *First grade.*

When a township board of education maintains a third grade high school, such board is in no sense liable for tuition of pupils at other high school of higher grade, when such pupils are not graduates of the said third grade local high school. — *Attorney General*, 1911-12, p. 1257.

SECTION 7653. A high school of the second grade shall cover a period of not less than three years, of not less than thirty-two weeks each, in which not less than twelve courses of study are required for graduation. (95 v. 116.) *Second grade.*

When a township board of education maintains a third grade high school, such board is in no sense liable for tuition of pupils at other high schools of higher grade, when such pupils are not graduates of the said third grade local high school. — *Attorney General*, 1911-12, p. 1257.

SECTION 7654. A high school of the third grade shall cover a period of not less than two years, of not less than twenty-eight weeks each, in which not less than eight courses of study are required for graduation. (95 v. 116.) *Third grade.*

When a township board of education maintains a third grade high school, such board is in no sense liable for tuition of pupils at other high schools of higher grade, when such pupils are not graduates of the said third grade local high school. — *Attorney General*, 1911-12, p. 1257.

Rural and village first grade high schools may establish normal departments for training of teachers.

Where and how established.

SECTION 7654-1. Boards of education which maintain first-grade high schools in village or rural districts may establish normal departments in such schools for the training of teachers for village and rural schools. Not more than three such normal schools shall be established in any one county school district, and not more than one such department shall be maintained in any village or rural district. At least one such school in each county shall be located in a rural district or in a village with less than 1,500 population, and not more than one such school in each county shall be located in a village having a population of 1,500 or more. Schools desiring such a department shall make application therefor to the superintendent of public instruction and a copy of such application shall be filed with the county superintendent. The superintendent of public instruction shall examine all applications and shall designate such schools as may establish such departments. (104 v. 155.)

Courses and entrance requirements.

SECTION 7654-2. Each high school normal department shall offer at least a one-year course for the training of teachers. The entrance requirements of such departments shall be fixed by the superintendent of public instruction. Such departments may offer short courses during the school year but shall not offer summer courses unless practice departments are maintained during such courses. (104 v. 155.)

Employment of director and instructors. Salaries.

SECTION 7654-3. Each normal department shall employ a director and such other instructors as the superintendent of public instruction may prescribe. Such director and instructors shall be employed on the nomination of the county superintendent. No director or instructor in any normal training department shall be paid less than seventy-five dollars per month. (104 v. 155.)

Practice division may be maintained.

SECTION 7654-4. Each normal department may maintain a practice division and shall be authorized to arrange with different boards of education for observation and practice teaching privilege in the rural schools under their control. (104 v. 155.)

Board of education shall receive state aid not to exceed $1,000.

SECTION 7654-5. The board of education in any village or rural school district which maintains a normal training department approved by the superintendent of public instruction shall receive from the state, the cost of maintaining such department in a sum not to exceed one thousand dollars per annum for each school so maintained. Such amount shall be allowed by the auditor of state upon the approval of the superintendent of public instruction, but no payment by the state shall be made for work in such schools prior to January 1, 1915. (104 v. 155.)

SECTION 7654-6. There shall be established in the college of education of the Ohio State University and in each of the normal schools and colleges which are maintained either wholly or in part by state funds, a department of efficiency tests and survey. Such departments shall at the request of the superintendent of public instruction assist him in working out efficiency methods in school administration, and in conducting co-operative school surveys. (104 v. 155.)

Department of efficiency tests and survey by O. S. U. and other schools and colleges supported by the state.

SECTION 7654-7. Each of the state normal schools at Athens, Oxford, Bowling Green, and Kent shall be authorized to arrange with the boards of education of not more than six non-centralized rural districts to assume the management of a one one-room rural school in each district and maintain such schools as model one-room rural schools. Each state normal school which complies with the provisions of this section subject to the approval of the superintendent of public instruction shall receive $500 annually from the state for each of such schools when vouchers therefor have been approved by the superintendent of public instruction. (104 v. 155.)

State normal schools authorized to maintain a model one-room rural school in certain districts. State aid.

SECTION 7655. Public schools of a less grade shall be denominated as elementary schools. A course of study shall consist of not less than four recitations a week continued throughout the school year. (95 v. 116.)

Elementary grade.

SECTION 7655-1. Every one-room school in any rural school district where the schoolhouse and outbuildings are kept in proper condition and repair, buildings and yard clean, and separate screened privies are maintained for each sex, shall be considered a rural elementary school of the second grade. (104 v. 125.)

What constitutes elementary rural school of second grade.

SECTION 7655-2. Each one-room school in any rural school district which shall fulfill the requirements of this section shall be considered a rural elementary school of the first grade. Such requirements are as follows:

What constitutes rural elementary school of first grade.

(a) Clean buildings and yard.
(b) Building in good repair.
(c) Separate screened privies for each sex or inside toilets.
(d) Maps of Ohio and United States.
(e) Library of not less than 50 volumes.
(f) 100 square feet of slate or composition blackboard. The lower margin of not less than twelve lineal feet of which board, shall be within two feet of the floor.
(g) A system of heating with ventilation — minimum a jacketed stove.
(h) Buildings hereafter constructed to have in connection with them not less than one acre of land for organized play.
(i) Teacher with at least a three-year certificate.

(j) Agricultural apparatus to a value of at least fifteen dollars. (104 v. 125.)

SECTION 7655-3. Each consolidated school in any village or rural school district which shall fulfill the requirements of this section shall be considered a consolidated elementary school of the second grade. Such requirements are as follows:

(a) Clean building and yard.

(b) Building in good repair.

(c) Separate screened privies for each sex or inside toilets.

(d) Library of not less than 100 volumes.

(e) 100 square feet of slate or composition blackboard. The lower margin of not less than twelve lineal feet of which board, shall be within two feet of the floor.

(f) A system of heating with ventilation — minimum a jacketed stove.

(g) Buildings hereafter constructed to have at least two acres of land for organized play and agricultural experiment.

(h) At least two rooms and two teachers on full time one of whom must have at least a three-year certificate.

(i) One teacher to be employed for ten months each year giving part of his or her time during the school year to the teaching of agriculture or domestic science or both and during part of vacation supervise agricultural work of boys and domestic art work of the girls.

(j) Agricultural apparatus to the value of at least twenty-five dollars.

(k) A case of not less than six maps including a map of Ohio. (104 v. 125.)

SECTION 7655-4. Each consolidated school in any village or rural school district which shall fulfill the requirements of this section shall be considered a consolidated elementary school of the first grade. Such requirements are as follows:

(a) Clean building and yard.

(b) Building in good repair.

(c) Separate screened privies for each sex, or inside toilets.

(d) A case of not less than six maps including a map of Ohio.

(e) Library of not less than 150 volumes.

(f) 100 square feet of slate or composition blackboard. The lower margin of not less than twelve lineal feet of which board, shall be within two feet of the floor.

(f) A system of heating with ventilation — minimum a jacketed stove.

(h) Buildings hereafter constructed to have at least three acres of land in connection with each school one for agriculture and school garden purposes.

(i) Three rooms and three teachers or more on full time, one teacher to have at least a three-year certificate.

(j) A course in domestic science.

(k) Two teachers to be employed for ten months each, one teaching agriculture during the school term and to supervise agriculture during part of the vacation. The other to teach domestic science during the school term and to supervise domestic science instruction during part of the vacation.

(l) Agricultural and domestic science apparatus to the value of at least one hundred dollars. (104 v. 125.)

SECTION 7655-7. After September 1st, 1915, the holder of a certificate of graduation from any one-room rural school of the first grade or of any consolidated rural school which has been recognized shall be entitled to admission to any high school without examination. Graduates of any elementary school shall be admitted to any high school without examination on the certificate of the district superintendent. (104 v. 125.) *Admission to high school from rural school of first grade.*

SECTION 7655-8. The superintendent of public instruction shall furnish the board of education in the village and rural school districts metal placards which shall be placed on the various school buildings showing the grades of such schools. (104 v. 125.) *Metal placard showing grade of rural school.*

SECTION 7656. A diploma must be granted by the board of education to any one completing the curriculum in any high school, which diploma shall state the grade of the high school issuing it as certified by the superintendent of public instruction, be signed by the president and clerk of the board of education, the superintendent and the principal of the high school, if such there be, and shall bear the date of its issue. (104 v. 225.) *Diploma granted to graduates.*

A high school diploma is not legal which is granted to a person who was never a member of the high school which granted the diploma and if the person had never performed the work required by the curriculum of the said high school, or any part of it, or its equivalent, and never did any regular school work beyond the graded schools. — *Attorney General,* Opinion No. 1163, Sept. 21, 1914.

SECTION 7657. A certificate shall also be issued to the holder of each diploma in which shall be stated the grade of the high school, the names and extent of the studies pursued and the length of time given to each study to be certified to in the same manner as set forth for a diploma. (95 v. 116.) *Certificate as to grade of school.*

A high school diploma is not legal which is granted to a person who was never a member of the high school which granted the diploma and if the person had never performed the work required by the curriculum of the said high school, or any part of it, or its equivalent, and never did any regular school work beyond the graded schools. — *Attorney General,* Opinion No. 1163, Sept. 21, 1914.

15 S. L.

Admission to professional school, college or university.

SECTION 7658. A holder of a diploma from a high school of the first grade may be admitted without examination to any college of law, medicine, dentistry, or pharmacy in this state, when the holder thereof has completed such courses in science and language as are prescribed by the legally constituted authorities regulating the entrance requirements of such college; except such institutions privately endowed which may require a higher standard for entrance examinations than herein is provided. After September 1, 1915, the holder of a diploma from a first-grade high school shall be entitled to admission without examination to the academic department of any college or university which is supported wholly or in part by the state. (104 v. 125.)

Who eligible to take examination for admission to bar or to enter professional school; exception.

SECTION 7659. A holder of a diploma from any grade of high school or of a teacher's certificate from a county or city board of teacher's examiners, when he has pursued his studies under private tutorage or in an office, shall be eligible to take the examination for admission to the practice of law or to take the examination prescribed to enter a college of law, medicine, dentistry or pharmacy; except such institutions privately endowed, which may require a higher standard for entrance examinations than herein is provided. (95 v. 116.)

Information to superintendent of public instruction as to high schools.

SECTION 7660. The clerk of the board of education of each district in which a high school is established and maintained shall furnish to the superintendent of public instruction definite and accurate information concerning the length of time necessary for the completion of the high school curriculum or curriculums, the courses of instruction offered therein, and such other information as the superintendent of public instruction requires in relation to the high school work of the district, and in the form and manner he prescribes. Such information shall be filed when high schools are established or any changes made in curriculums. (104 v. 225.)

Certificate as to grade of high school; withholding approval.

SECTION 7661. Upon examination of the information thus filed, or after personal inspection of work done if he deems this advisable, or both, the superintendent of public instruction shall determine the grade of each such high school and, under the seal of his office, certify to the clerk of the board of education his findings as to the grade of the high school maintained by such board. But he may withhold his approval of any curriculum, when it appears to him that it does not comply with legal and reasonable requirements. When it appears that any curriculum, already approved, has been so modified as to change the grade of the high school, either by advancing or reducing its grade, the superintendent of public instruction shall certify his finding and all diplomas issued thereafter shall bear the grade so designated by him. (104 v. 225.)

SECTION 7662. No school shall be considered a high school that has not furnished the information and received a certificate as provided above, nor be entitled to the privileges and exceptions provided by law for high schools. (95 v. 117.)

SECTION 7663. A board of education may establish one or more high schools, whenever it deems the establishment of such school or schools proper or necessary for the convenience or progress of the pupils attending them, or for the conduct and welfare of the educational interests of the district. (95 v. 117.)

This section fully authorizes boards of education to establish high schools without submitting the question to a vote of the electors of the district, unless it should be found necessary to levy a tax in excess of the maximum allowed by law and issue bonds; in which case an election is required; see Sec. 7625.
Sections 5649-2, et seq., limit rate of taxation and repeal by implication existing conflicting statutes: Rabe v. Canton Sch. Dist. (Bd. of Ed.), 88 O. S. 403.

SECTION 7664. Such school or schools, when established, shall not be discontinued under three years from the time of their establishment, except by a vote of three-fourths of all the members of the board of education of the district, at a regular meeting. (95 v. 117.)

SECTION 7665. When a township board of education establishes and maintains a high school or high schools within the district under its control, it shall have the management and control thereof, and may employ and dismiss teachers, and give certificates of such employment, and for services rendered, directed to the township clerk. (95 v. 117.)

SECTION 7666. Such board of education shall build, repair, add to and furnish the necessary schoolhouses, purchase or lease sites therefore, or rent suitable rooms and make all other necessary provisions relative to such schools as may be deemed proper. (95 v. 117.)

SECTION 7667. Such board of education may regulate and control the admission of pupils from the elementary schools under its charge to such high school or high schools, according to age and attainments, may admit adults over twenty-one years of age, and pupils from other districts on such terms and under such rules as it adopts. It shall maintain such high school or high schools not less than twenty-eight nor more than forty weeks in any school year. (95 v. 117.)

SECTION 7668. In rural districts where a high school or high schools are, or may be established, by the rural board of education, it annually shall determine by estimate, as near as practicable, the entire amount of money necessary to be expended in the rural district for school and schoolhouse purposes, including the paying of teachers in such schools the prolonging of the terms of the several elementary schools of the rural district after the state funds have been exhausted, the erecting, repairing and furnishing of schoolhouses, and any other school purposes which amount shall be certified in writing to the county auditor, by such rural board, on or before the first Monday in June of each year. (104 v. 225.)

Union of districts for high school purposes.

SECTION 7669. The boards of education of two or more adjoining rural school districts, or of a rural and village school district by a majority vote of the full membership of each board, may unite such districts for high school purposes. Each board also may submit the question of levying a tax on the property in their respective districts, for the purpose of purchasing a site and erecting a building, and issue bonds, as is provided by law in case of erecting or repairing schoolhouses; but such question of. tax levy must carry in each district before it shall become operative in either. If such boards have sufficient money in the treasury to purchase a site and erect such building, or if there is a suitable building in either district owned by the board of education that can be used for a high school building it will not be necessary to submit the proposition to vote, and the boards may appropriate money from their funds for this purpose. (104 v. 225.)

When a joint school district is formed for high school purposes by a township school district and an adjoining village district, such district becomes one district and taxes for the support of the same must be borne by the respective joined districts in proportion to the total valuation of the property in each, notwithstanding the fact that the village district sends the most pupils and has the smallest valuation. — *Attorney General,* 1911-12, p. 1042.
There is no statutory provision for the uniting of a part or portion of a township school district with another township, village or special school district for high school purposes.
Where a petition asks for the uniting of the north half of Salt Creek Township School District of Pickaway County to the village school district of Tarlton for high school purposes, such petition cannot be granted. — *Attorney General,* 1913, p. 1358.
There is no provision of statute whereby joint high school districts may be dissolved. — *Attorney General,* Opinion No. 1273, 1914.

As to centralized township district, see G. C. Sec. 4726.

High school committee.

SECTION 7670. Any high school so established shall be under the management of a high school committee, consisting of two members of each of the boards creating such joint district, elected by a majority vote of such boards. Their membership of such committee shall be for the same term as their terms on the boards which they respectively represent. Such high school shall be free to all youth of school age within each district, subject to the rules and regulations adopted by the high school committee, in regard to the qualifications in scholarship requisite for admission, such rules and regulations to be of uniform operation throughout each district. (99 v. 462 § 1.)

When a joint school district is formed for high school purposes by a township school district and an adjoining village district, such district becomes one district and taxes for the support of the same must be borne by the respective joined districts in proportion to the total valuation of the property of each, notwithstanding the fact that the village district sends the most pupils and has the smallest valuation. — *Attorney General,* 1911-12, p. 1042.

SECTION 7671. The funds for the maintenance and support of such high school shall be provided by appropriations from the tuition or contingent funds, or both, of each district, in proportion to the total valuation of property in the respective districts, which must be placed in a separate fund in the treasury of the board of education of the district in which the schoolhouse is located, and paid out by action of the high school committee for the maintenance of the school. (99 v. 462 § 1.)

Funds, how provided.

When a joint school district is formed for high school purposes by a township school district and an adjoining village district, such district becomes one district and taxes for the support of the same must be borne by the respective joined districts in proportion to the total valuation of the property in each, notwithstanding the fact that the village district sends the most pupils and has the smallest valuation. — *Attorney General,* 1911-12, p. 1042.

There is no statutory provision for the uniting of a part or portion of a township school district with another township, village or special school district for high school purposes.

Where a petition asks for the uniting of the north half of Salt Creek Township School District of Pickaway County to the village school district of Tarlton for high school purposes, such petition cannot be granted. — *Attorney General,* 1913, p. 1358.

SECTION 7672. Boards of education exercising control for the purpose of taxation over territory within a rural or joint rural high school distict shall determine by estimate the amount necessary for the maintenance of any rural or joint rural high school to which such territory belongs and shall certify such amount to the county auditor in the annual budget as provided in section 5649-3a. All funds derived from levies so made shall be kept separate and be paid out for the maintenance of the school for which they were made. (104 v. 225.)

Estimate to maintain schools certified to county auditor in annual budget.

When a joint school district is formed for high school purposes by a township school district and an adjoining village district, such district becomes one district and taxes for the support of the same must be borne by the respective joined districts in proportion to the total valuation of the property in each, notwithstanding the fact that the village district sends the most pupils and has the smallest valuation. — *Attorney General,* 1911-12, p. 1042.

SECTION 7673. The school board of any village school district in which is located a university, college, or academy organized under the laws of this state, as an institution of learning not for profit, and under the management of a board of trustees, may levy a tax not exceeding two mills annually, upon all taxable property within such district for the support of such university, college or academy. (104 v. 225.)

Tax levy for support of municipal university.

Admission or high school graduates.

SECTION 7674. In the event such levy is made, all holders of a high school diploma obtained from such village district high school shall have the right to attend such university or college for the period of two years, free of tuition. (99 v. 520 § 2.)

Disposition of funds.

SECTION 7675. The funds arising from such tax levy shall be turned over to the board of trustees of such university college or academy by the county treasurer to be exepnded by them in the conduct of the university, college or academy and for no other purpose. (104 v. 225.)

Schools at children's homes and orphans' asylums.

SECTION 7676. The board of education in any dis-. trict in which a children's home or orphans' asylum is established by law, when requested by the board of trustees of such children's home or orphans' asylum when no public school is situated reasonably near such home or asylum, shall establish a separate school in such home or asylum, so as to afford to the children therein, as far as practicable, the advantages and privileges of a common school education. Such schools must be continued in operation for such period as is provided by law for public schools. If the distributive share of school funds to which the school at such home or asylum is entitled by the enumeration of children in the institution is not sufficient to continue the schools for that length of time, the deficiency shall be paid out of the funds of the institution or by the county commissioners: (103 v. 864.)

Sections 3085 and 3088, General Code, vest the control of schools located at county children's homes in the board of trustees of such homes and they maintain control of the same until such time as schools are established by the respective boards of education of the districts wherein such county or orphans' homes are located, upon the request of the board of trustees of such homes to such board of education to so establish such schools. There is no statutory provisions whereby the schools of county homes can be brought uniformly under the supervision of the boards of education of the respective districts, except that it be done in accordance with the provisions of sections 7676 and 7677, General Code, supra.

Schools in county homes may be established and maintained independently of the boards of education of the respective districts wherein such homes are located, until such time as such schools may be brought under the control of the boards of education of such respective districts by the boards of education establishing schools at such homes in accordance with sections 7676 and 7677, General Code, herebefore mentioned.

The phrase "or orphans' asylums established by law," as employed in Section 7676, General Code, does not include an institution incorporated for the purpose of caring for dependent children, and which is not maintained in any manner by funds derived from governmental sources. The phrase "established by law" means those children's homes or orphans' asylums which are established and maintained by the state or some political subdivision thereof, and cannot be said to apply to institutions incorporated for the purpose of caring for dependent children, which are privately managed institutions and which do not derive support from the state. — *Attorney General,* Opinion No. 1296, 1914.

Inmates of a children's home are classed equally with other youth under the meaning of section 7681, General Code, and such inmates may attend a village school not within their own district, if there is no school within their own district within one and one-half miles of the home or at closer proximity than the village schools. The board of education of said village cannot charge tuition for said inmates until they have notified the board of education of the district in which the pupils reside.

The duty of providing for the education of such inmates devolves upon the board of education of the township in which they reside and not upon the trustees of the home. — *Attorney eral*, 1911-12, p. 1480.

There is no statutory authority for the joint building of a school house by the board of education of a school district and the trustees of an orphans' home in the same district for the accommodation of the pupils of the school district and those of the orphans' home. — *Attorney General*, 1911-12, p. 511.

Under the provisions of Section 7676, General Code, the board of education of the respective school districts of the state wherein are located county or children's homes, are required to provide schools and sufficient educational facilities for the inmates of such county or children's home, either by the establishment of special schools located at such county or district children's homes or in the regular schools of the respective districts.

Under Section 7681, General Code, the public schools of the state are free to the inmates of orphans' asylums located in such respective school districts, regardless of whether or not such orphan asylums are private or public institutions. — *Attorney General*, Opinion 1049, 1914.

SECTION 3088. During the two weeks ending on the fourth Saturday in July, the clerk of the board of trustees shall take and return to the county auditor the names and ages of all youth of school age in such home. The state common school fund, not otherwise appropriated by law, shall be apportioned in proportion to the enumeration of youth, to such home and other districts, sub-districts and joint sub-districts within the county. The amount of money due such home under such apportionment shall be set apart by the auditor of the county, and shall become a part of the children's home fund and used to maintain a common school in such home, and shall be paid out on certificate of the trustees, stating in the certificate, the amount and the purposes thereof. Thereupon the county auditor shall issue his warrant on the treasurer for the amount so certified. This section shall not apply to children's homes in counties where such children attend the public schools. When in their judgment advisable, the trustees may employ a teacher to teach the school in any such home, as provided by law, but such teacher must have a "teacher's elementary school certificate" as provided for by section seven thousand eight hundred and twenty-nine of the General Code. (103 v. 864.)

Clerk shall report names and ages to auditor.

Section 3085 and 3088, General Code, vest the control of schools located at county children's homes in the board of trustees of such homes and they maintain control of the same until such time as schools are established by the respective boards of education of the districts wherein such county or orphan's homes are located, upon the request of the board of trustees of such homes to such board of education to so established such schools. There is no statutory provision whereby the schools of county homes can be brought uniformly under the supervision of the boards of education of the respective districts, except that it be done in accordance with the provisions of sections 7676 and 7677, General Code, supra.

Schools in county homes may be established and maintained independently of the boards of education of the respective districts wherein such homes are located, until such time as such schools may be brought under the control of the boards of education of such respective districts by the boards of education establishing schools at such homes in accordance with Sections 7676 and 7677, General Code, here before mentioned.

The phrase "or orphans asylum established by law," as employed in Section 7676, General Code, does not include an institution incorporated for the purpose of caring for dependent children, and which is not maintained in any manner by funds derived from governmental sources. The phrase "established by law" means those children's homes or orphans asylums which are etablished and maintained by the state or some political subdivision thereof, and cannot be said to apply to institutions incorporated for the purpose of caring for dependent children, which are privately managed institutions and which do not derive support from the state. — *Attorney General*, Opinion No. 1296, Dec. 14, 1914.)

Control and management of such schools.

Teachers.

SECTION 7677. All schools so established in any such home or asylum shall be under the control and management of the respective boards of education of the school districts in which such homes and institutions are located, and courses of study, length of school term, and all other school matters shall be uniform in the respective school districts. Teachers employed in such homes or institutions must have a teacher's elementary school certificate as provided by section seven thousand eight hundred and twenty-nine of the General Code. (103 v. 864.)

There is no statutory authority for the joint building of a school house by the board of education of a school district and the trustees of an orphans' home in the same district for the accommodation of the pupils of the school district and those of the orphans' home. — *Attorney General*, 1911-12, p. 511.

Sections 3085 and 3088, General Code, vest the control of schools located at county children's homes in the board of trustees of such homes and they maintain control of the same until such time as schools are established by the respective boards of education of the districts wherein such county or orphans' homes are located, upon the request of the board of trustees of such homes to such board of education to so establish such schools. There is no statutory provision whereby the schools of county homes can be brought uniformly under the supervision of the boards of education of the respective districts, except that it be done in accordance with the provisions of sections 7676 and 7677, General Code, supra.

Schools in county homes may be established and maintained independntly of the boards of education of the respective districts wherein such homes are located, until such time as such schools may be brought under the control of the boards of education of such respective districts by the boards of education establishing schools at such homes in accordance with Sections 7676 and 7677, General Code herebefore mentioned.

The phrase "or orphans' asylums established by law," as employed in Section 7676, General Code, does not include an institution incorporated for the purpose of caring for dependent children, and which is not maintained in any manner by funds derived from governmental sources. The phrase "established by law" means those children's homes or orphans' asylums which are established and maintained by the state or some political subdivision thereof, and cannot be said to apply to institutions incorporated for the purpose of caring for dependent children, which are privately managed institutions and which do not derive support from the state. — *Attorney General*, Opinion 1296, 1914.

SECTION 7678. In the establishment of such schools the commissioners of the county in which such children's home or orphans' asylum is established, shall provide the necessary school room or rooms, furniture, fuel, apparatus and books, the cost of which for such schools must be paid out of the funds provided for such institution. The board of education shall incur no expense in supporting such schools. (103 v. 864.)

Cost; how paid.

Inmates of a children's home are classed equally with other youth under the meaning of section 7681, General Code, and such inmates may attend a village school not within their own district, if there is no school within their own district within one and one-half miles of the home or at closer proximity than the village school. The board of education of said village cannot charge tuition for said inmates until they have notified the board of education of the district in which the pupils reside.
The duty of providing for the education of such inmates devolves upon the board of education of the township in which they reside and not upon the trustees of the home. — *Attorney General*, 1911-12, p. 1480.

SECTION 7679. In any rural, village, or city district, or part thereof, parents or guardians of youth of school age may petition the board of education to organize an evening school. The petition must contain the names of not less than twenty-five youth of school age who will attend such school, and who for reasons satisfactory to the board are prevented from attending day school. Upon receiving such petition the board of education shall furnish a suitable room for the evening school and employ a competent person who holds a regularly issued teacher's certificate, to teach it. Such board may discontinue any such evening school, when the average evening attendance for any month falls below twelve. (104 v. 225.)

Establishment of evening schools.

When a village board of education was authorized by electors under section 7592, General Code, to levy an additional tax of five mills for five years, such board may proceed to issue bonds without further authorization of the electors provided that the conditions of 7626 and 7679, General Code, with reference to the quality and nature of the bonds and the provisions of section 7629 with reference to the amount of the bonds and the procedure of the board be complied with. — *Attorney General*, 1911-12, p. 534.

SECTION 7680. Any person more than twenty-one years old may be permitted to attend evening school upon such terms and upon payment of such tuition as the board of education prescribes. (90 v. 117.)

Attendance by person more than twenty-one years old.

SECTION 12906. Whoever, being a pupil in the public schools, organizes, joins or belongs to a fraternity, sorority or other like society composed of or made up of pupils of the public schools, shall be fined not less than

Pupil joining fraternity; penalty.

ten dollars nor more than twenty-five dollars for each offenses. (99 v. 253 §§ 1, 3.)

If the fraternities, sororities, or societies are composed of or made up of, in whole or in part, of persons other than pupils of the public schools, a pupil joining such a fraternity or society would not be liable for so doing.

The only way in which the penalty can be assessed is by proper prosecution and conviction under the acts relating to criminal procedure. Atty. Gen. Opinion.

Teacher, principal or superintendent failing to give notice of fraternity in schools.

SECTION 12907. Whoever, being a teacher, principal or superintendent, having knowledge or reason to believe that a fraternity, sorority or like society composed or made up of pupils of the public schools, is being organized or maintained in the public schools or that a pupil attending such school is organizing, or is a member of, such fraternity, sorority or like society, fails forthwith to advise the president or secretary of the board of education in charge of such schools thereof, shall be fined not less than ten dollars nor more than twenty-five dollars for each offense. (99 v. 253 §§ 2, 3.)

Board of education to investigate charges of existence of fraternity; notice to members thereof.

SECTION 12908. Whoever, being a board of education in charge of public schools, upon being advised in accordance with the provisions of the next preceding section, within thirty days thereafter, fails to investigate such charges after not less than ten days' written notice to such pupils, their parents or guardians, or being the secretary of such board of education, when such board has found the charges mentioned in the next preceding section to be correct and true, fails forthwith to notify in writing the pupils organizing, joining or belonging to such fraternity, sorority or like society, to disband and discontinue it and to withdraw therefrom within five days from the receipt of such notice, shall be fined not less than ten dollars nor more than twenty-five dollars for each offense. (99 v. 253 §§ 2, 3.)

Suspension of pupil who fails to obey notice.

SECTION 12909. Whoever, being a pupil in the public schools, organizing, joining or belonging to a fraternity, sorority or like society composed or made up of pupils of the public schools, fails to obey the notice provided for in the next preceding section, shall be forthwith suspended from the public schools by the superintendent or principal in charge thereof, until such pupil shall comply with the order of such board of education. (104 v. 225.)

Who may be admitted to school free; children's homes and orphans' asylums.

SECTION 7681. The schools of each district shall be free to all youth between six and twenty-one years of age, who are children, wards or apprentices of actual residents of the district, including children of proper age who are inmates of a county or district or of any public or private children's home or orphans' asylum located in such a school district, but the time in the school year at which beginners may enter upon the first year's work of the elementary schools shall be subject to the rules and regulations of the local boards of education. The board of education in any district in which a public or private children's home or orphans' asylum is located, when requested by the governing body thereof, shall admit the children of school age of such home or asylum to the public schools of the school district. The county commissioners shall pay the tuition of such pupils to the school or schools maintained by the board of education at a per capita rate which shall be ascertained by dividing the total expenses of conducting the elementary schools of the district attended, exclusive of permanent improvement and repairs, by the total enrollment in the elementary schools of the district, such amount to be computed by the month. An attendance any part of the month shall create a liability for the whole month. The distributive share of school funds from the state for the children of such home or asylum shall then be paid to the county commissioners. But all youth of school age living apart from their parents or guardians and who work to support themselves by their own labor, shall be entitled to attend school free in the district in which they are employed. (106 v. 489.)

Under section 4750, General Code, a board of education is empowered to make such regulations as it deems necessary for the governemnt of its employes and the pupils of the school. Under this section, the board may designate what studies such pupil shall be required to take. — *Attorney General*, 1913, p. 1153.

The board of education is not vested with any power to rfeuse admission to pupils who have attained the age of six years, during the session of a school term. — *Attorney General*, 1911-12, p. 1018.

Inmates of a children's home are classed equally with other youth under the meaning of section 7681, General Code, and such inmates may attend a village school not within their own district, if there is not school within their own district within one and one-half miles of the home or at closer proximity than the village school. The board of education of said village cannot charge tuition for said inmates until they have notified the board of education of the district in which the pupils reside.

The duty of providing for the education of such inmates devolves upon the board of education of the township in which they reside and not upon the trustees of the home. — *Attorney General*, 1911-12, p. 1480.

Under the provisions of Section 7676, General Code, the board of education of the respective school districts of the state wherein are located county or children's homes, are required to provide schools and sufficient educational facilities for the inmates of such county or children's home, either by the establishment of special schools located at such county or district children's homes or in the regular schools of the respectve districts.

Under Section 7681, General Code, the public schools of the state are free to the inmates of orphan asylums located in such respective school districts, regardless of whether or not such orphan asylums are private or public institutions. — *Attorney General*, Opinion No. 1049, 2914.

A township board of education not maintaining a high school is not required to pay the tuition of a Boxwell-Patterson graduate who received a diploma from said township board of education, who has moved with his parents into a village school district, provided his parents have an actual residence in such village. The mere fact that the father of the pupil holds a voting residence in the township, if he has an actual residence in the village would not require the township to pay the tuition. — *Attorney General*, Opinion No. 962, 1914.

Non-resident pupils.

SECTION 7682. Each board of education may admit other persons upon such terms or upon the payment of such tuition as it prescribes. (97 v. 360.)

The provisions of Sec. 7683 of the General Code providing for a deduction from the tuition of a non-resident high school pupil, of the amount of school tax paid by such pupil or his parent upon property owned and located within the school district attended, referred to cases where the pupil or parent were themselves chargeable with such tuition.

Said section has no application to Sec. 7747 of the General Code, under which the board of education of such pupil's residence is now made liable for such tuition.

In this case, therefore, the amount of said school tax may not be deducted: Attorney General 1912, p. 1421.

Crediting of school tax on tuition.

SECTION 7683. When a youth between the age of six and twenty-one years or his parent owns property in a school district in which he does not reside; and he attends the schools of such district, the amount of the school tax paid on such property shall be credited on his tuition. (97 v. 360.)

The provisions of section 7683 of the General Code providing for a deduction from the tuition of a non-resident high school pupil, of the amount of school tax paid by such pupil or his parent upon property owned and located within the school district attended, referred to cases where the pupil or parent were themselves chargeable with such tuition.

Said section has no application to section 7747 of the General Code, under which the board of education of such pupil's residence is now made liable for such tuition.

In this case, therefore, the amount of said school tax may not be deducted. — Attorney General, 1912. p. 1421.

If a parent of a non-resident pupil owns stock in a mercantile or other corporation which is taxed in the district no part of the same paid by such corporation under the levy for school purposes may be credited upon the tuition chargeable against such parent in that district. — Attorney General, Opinion No. 767, 1914.

Assignment of pupils.

SECTION 7684. Boards of education may make such an assignment of the youth of their respective districts to the schools established by them as in their opinion best will promote the interests of education in their districts. (97 v. 360.)

School attendance should not be determined under Section 7730, General Code, at a time when there is an epidemic prevailing in the school, or rather in the district wherein such school is located. Such average daily attendance should be determined during the year when the school attendance is normal or not affected by an epidemic.

When the average daily attendance of a school during the preceding year has been below twelve, because of an epidemic and such average daily attendance for the succeeding year would be more than an average of twelve, the board could legally employ a teacher and continue such school, and the payment of such teacher would be legally authorized under the law. — Attorney General, Opinion No. 1370, 1914.

Section 4736, General Code, as amended. 10 O. L., 138, applies to rural or village school districts which go to make up county school districts and does not seem to have application to the internal affairs of the rural school districts. formerly township school districts and village school districts, which go to make up and constitute the respective county school districts of the state.

Local boards of education of rural school districts, formerly township school districts, cannot change boundaries of subdistricts for the reason that such boundaries of such subdistricts no longer exist. However, such boards of education under Section 7684, General Code, have the authority to make such assignment of the youth of their respective districts to the schools established by them as in their opinion will best promote the interests of education in their districts. — *Attorney General*, Opinion No. 1308, 1914.

Under Section 7730, General Code, prior to its amendment, 104 O. L., 139, it was optional with Board of Education of a township school district to suspend the schools when the average daily attendance thereof was less than twelve. If a township board of education entered into a contract with a teacher for teaching a subdistrict under its jurisdiction, and such subdistrict was abolished in accordance with Section 7730, General Code, such act operated as a termination of the contract, provided such act occurred before the termination of the contract because of the lapse of time such contract was to run. Likewise such contract would be terminated if the school should be suspended in accordance with the mandatory provisions of Section 7730, General Code, as amended, 104 O. L., 139. An expenditure of money upon such contract, after being so treminated under the provisions contained in said section as the same existed both prior to its amendment and since its amendment above referred to would be illegal.

By virtue of Section 7684, General Code, a board of education may assign pupils to attend a school which had been previously suspended under Section 7730, supra, because of the attendance being less than twelve for the preceding year and such school may again be continued as such school, provided that this course in the opinion of the board, will best promote the interests of education in the district. — *Attorney General*, Opinion No. 1321, 1914.

A rule which provides for the proper examination at the end of the school year of pupils by the teacher of the grade in which such pupils have been students and the superintendent of the schools, and for the promotion of pupils to the next higher grade upon the recommendation of such teacher and superintendent, the same being based on merit, is a reasonable rule.

A pupil who has favorably passed examination, and been given a proper certificate authorizing him to enter the next higher grade, is without right, in the absence of authority from the board of education, to omit such grade to which he has been promoted and passed to a higher one.

Where by direction of the parent of the pupil thus promoted, the pupil, without authority of the board, enters the room of such higher grade for the purpose of remaining there, it is the right and duty of the superintendent to refuse to allow the pupil to remain and direct him to go to the room of the grade to which he has been promoted.

In the absence of any showing that application had been made to the board for permission to the pupil to enter such higher grade, and in the absence of showing that the board had before it a report of its superintendent recommending the promotion of the pupil to such higher grade, mandamus will not lie to compel the board to order such promotion even though it be shown that the pupil was, at the time of such attempted entry, in fact fitted to enter such grade: Board of Education v. State, ex rel., 80 O. S. 133.

Upon the question of separate schools for colored children, see G. C. 7681.

SECTION 7685. No pupil shall be suspended from school by a superintendent or teacher except for such time as is necessary to convene the board of education, nor shall one be expelled except by a vote of two thirds of such board, and after the parent or guardian of the offending pupil has been notified of the proposed expulsion, and permitted to be heard against it. No pupil shall be suspended or expelled from any school beyond the current term thereof. (89 v. 96.)

Suspension and expulsion of pupils.

The father of a child entitled to the benefits of the public school of the sub-district of his residence may maintain an action against the teacher of the school, and the local directors of the sub-district, for damages for wrongfully expelling the child from school: Roe v. Deming 21 O. S. 666.

A pupil cannot be expelled from school, except in strict compliance with the statutory provisions on that subject: Brown v. Board of Education, 6 O. N. P. 411, 8 O. D. (N. P.) 378.

In case of compliance with statutory provisions, the court will not interfere with the sound discretion of the school authorities: Brown v. Board of Education, 6 O. N. P. 411, 8 O. D. (N. P.) 378.

Vaccination of pupils.

SECTION 7686. The board of each district may make and enforce such rules and regulations to secure the vaccination of, and to prevent the spread of small-pox among the pupils attending or eligible to attend the schools of the district, as in its opinion the safety and interest of the public require. Boards of health, councils of municipal corporations, and the trustees of townships, on application of the board of education of the district, at the public expense, without delay, shall provide the means of vaccination to such pupils as are not provided therewith by their parents or guardians. (69 v. 22.)

This section is constitutional. State ex rel. v. Board of Educaiton, 76 O. S. 297.

This section confers authority on the board of education to make and enforce rules to secure vaccination to prevent the spread of smallpox: State, ex rel., v. Barberton, 19 O. C. D. 375; Carr v. Board of Education, 1 O. N. P. (N. S.) 602.

The fact that it is the policy of the state to encourage education, and to enforce attendance at school (see G. C. Sec. 7762, et seq.) does not render invalid a rule which required vaccination for smallpox as a condition of admission to the public schools: State, ex rel., v. Board of Education, 7 O. C. C. (N. S.) 608.

A parent who sends his child to a public school and is willing to continue so to do, but the child is excluded for failure to comply with a rule of the board of education requiring vaccination, is not liable to conviction under the compulsory education act: State v. Turney, 12 O. C. C. (N. S.) 33, 21 O. C. D. 222.

Dismissal of school on holidays.

SECTION 7687. Teachers in the public schools may dismiss their schools, without forfeiture of pay, on the first day of January, the twenty-second day of February, the thirtieth day of May, the fourth day of July, the first Monday in September, the twenty-fifth day of December, and on any day set apart by proclamation of the president of the United States, or the governor of this state as a day of fast, thanksgiving or mourning. (97 v. 360.)

A teacher is not bound by the provisions of a contract which are in contravention of law.

He may dismiss his school on legal holidays without forfeiture of pay, notwithstanding the clause in his contract providing salary by the day.

Boards of education cannot compel teachers to make up for time lost on the above-mentioned days.

Hiring teachers by the day does not affect their rights under this section. — *Attorney General,* Opinion.

The board of education is not acting illegally in employing a person not possessed of a teacher's certificate to teach in the emergency arising by reason of the illness of a regular teacher.

The action of the board in allowing said regular teacher full pay during said absence is in effect an increase in pay and not illegal. Such action, however, should be scrutinized.

The payment by the absent teacher, of compensation to the aforesaid substitute, is a private arrangement not objectionable. — *Attorney General,* 1912, p. 226.

When a board of education passed a resolution legal in form employing certain teachers, the effect thereof would be to employ said teachers, though certain provisions of said resolution requiring said teachers to enter into a written contract "to make up for legal holidays and for the time lost in the event of epidemic" would be void because against the statutes and public policy of the state of Ohio. — *Attorney General,* 1911-12, p. 1322.

For other holidays, see G. C. Sec. 5976, et seq.

SECTION 8301. The following days, viz: Holidays specified.

1. The first day of January, known as New Year's Day;

2. The twenty-second day of February, known as Washington's Birthday;

3. The thirtieth day of May, known as Decoration or Memorial Day;

4. The fourth day of July, known as Independence Day;

5. The first Monday of September, known as Labor Day;

6. The twelfth day of October, known as Columbus Discovery Day; Columbus discovery day.

7. The twenty-fifth day of December, known as Christmas Day;

8. Any day appointed and recommended by the governor of this state or the president of the United States as a day of fast or tranksgiving; and

9. Any day which may hereafter be made a legal holiday, shall for the purpose of this division, be holidays. But if the first day of January, the twenty-second day of February, the thirtieth day of May, the fourth day of July, or the twenty-fifth day of December be the first day of the week, known as Sunday, the next succeeding secular or business day shall be a holiday. (101 v. 34.)

First Monday of September, Labor Day, a holiday for all purposes: G. C. Sec. 5977.

SECTION 7688. Not later than April the governor of the state shall appoint and set apart one day in the spring season of each year, as a day on which those in charge of the public schools and institutions of learning under state control, or state patronage, for at least two hours must give information to the pupils and students concerning the value and interest of forests, the duty of the public to protect the birds thereof, and also for planting forest trees. Such day shall be known as Arbor Day. (95 v. 38 § 1.) Arbor day.

SECTION 7689. The school year shall begin on the first day of September of each year, and close on the thirty- first day of August of the succeeding year. A school week shall consist of five days, and a school month of four school weeks. (72 v. 181.) School year, month, and week.

Boards of education cannot compel pupils to attend school, or teachers to teach the same, more than five days in any one week, and teachers cannot make up for lost time by teaching six days in a week without express authority from the board of education. — *Attorney General.*

Cases of urgent necessity are excepted from the provisions of section 7623, General Code, providing for certain procedure when the cost of repairing or improving a school house in other than city districts exceeds' five hundred dollars.

Inasmuch, therefore, as the board of education is required to provide for at least thirty-two school weeks in a year, and as the mayor may prohibit use of school buildings until compliance has been made with the orders of the chief inspector of workshops and factories the board of education of a village upon such order from the chief inspector of workshops and factories, made after the school year has begun, may dispense with the procedure of section 7623 and execute necessary repairs without advertising for bids. — *Attorney General*, 1911-12, p. 1318.

Control of
schools vested
in boards.

SECTION 7690. Each board of education shall have the management and control of all of the public schools of whatever name or character in the district. It may appoint a superintendent of the public schools, truant officers, and janitors and fix their salaries. If deemed essential for the best interests of the schools of the district, under proper rules and regulations, the board may appoint a superintendent of buildings, and such other employes as it deems necessary, and fix their salaries. Each board shall fix the salaries of all teachers, which may be increased, but not diminished during the term for which the appointment is made. Teachers must be paid for all time lost when the schools in which they are employed are closed owing to an epidemic or other public calamity. (97 v. 360.)

A board of education may not provide that the superintendent of schools shall receive, in addition to a stated salary, all funds received for tuition of non-resident pupils, for the reason that such payment would not be a "fixed" salary as intended by section 7690, General Code.

Furthermore, such would be in contravention to Section 7603, General Code, which provides special distribution for the respective funds under the control of the board. — *Attorney General*, 1912, p. 491.

When a board of education passed a resolution legal in form employing certain teachers, the effect thereof would be to employ said teachers, though certain provisions of said resolution requiring said teachers to enter into a written contract "to make up for legal holidays and for the time lost in the event of epidemic" would be void because against the statutes and public policy of the state of Ohio. — *Attorney General*, 1911-12, p. 1322.

A special act of the legislature providing for the payment by a board of education of compensation to a teacher who performed teacher's services without a certificate as well as janitor's services at the behest of said board, is not invalid. — *Attorney General*, 1912, p. 1339.

A Board of Education is not to be denied State Aid by reason of the fact that it pays authorized expenses other than teachers' salaries out of the tuition fund, such as Superintendent's salary and institute fees.

The amount of State Aid allowed, however, shall not exceed such sum as is necessary to make teachers' salaries equal to $40.00 per month. — *Attorney General*, 1912, p. 98.

In general, a city or any other taxing district cannot be made to bear more than its proportionate share of a shortage made necessary to bring the total levy for all purposes within the limitations of the Smith one per cent tax law. The abuse of discretion, however, on the part of the budget commissioners must be clearly apparent before the courts will substitute their judgment for that of the budget commission.

The direction of the supreme court in State vs. Sanzenbacher, stating that it is the duty of the budget commission in revising and reducing levies "to have due regard to the proportions of the total amount that each taxing board or taxing officers are authorized to levy" is not to be construed strictly. The words imply a discretionary power on the part of the commission.

A clear, arbitrary and considerable violation of this discretion may be remedied by injunction or mandamus. — *Attorney General,* 1912, p. 1544.

This section is constitutional and valid: Pierce v. Board of Education, 1 O. N. P. 286.

The courts have no power to interfere with the discretion of the board of education in the appointment of teachers, unless such discretion has been abused grossly; and injunction will not lie to control such discretion: Youmans v. Board of Education, 13 O. C. C. 207.

The discretionary power of the board of education cannot be controlled by a writ of mandamus: State, ex rel., v. Board of Education, 19 O. C. C, 574.

The court cannot by injunction prevent the board of education from adopting and enforcing a rule requiring the reading of the Bible as a part of the opening exercises of the school: Nessle v. Hum, 1 O, N. P. 140.

The board of education may, if it deems proper, forbid the reading of the Bible in the public schools; and they may discharge a teacher who refuses to comply with such rule: Board of Education v. Pulse, 7 O. N. P. 58.

By virtue of G. C. Sec. 4752, which provision is mandatory, an election of a teacher by unanimous vote, but without calling the roll of the members and entering upon the record the names of those voting aye, is invalid: Board of Education, v. Best, 52 O. S. 138.

For the election of teachers upon recommendation of the superintendent see G. C. Sec. 7703.

Authority to elect teachers cannot be delegated: State, ex rel., v. Williams, 29 O. S. 161.

Under a provision that a person cannot be employed as a teacher, unless he has the proper certificate (see G. C. Sec. 7830, et seq.), a contract of employment made with a teacher before he obtains the necessary certificate is valid, if such teacher obtains the proper certificate before he enters upon the performance of his duties as teacher: School District v. Dilman, 22 O. S. 194; see also, Youmans v. Board of Education, 13 O. C. C. 207.

A record which shows the yea and nay vote and how each member voted is sufficient, although it does not expressly state that the roll was called: Youmans v. Board of Education, 13 O. C. C. 207.

The courts will interfere with the discretion of a board of education in electing teachers only in case of a gross abuse of its discretionary power: Youmans v. Board of Education, 13 O. C. C. 207.

It is not necessary that a superintendent of schools should have a certificate to teach all the branches which are taught in the schools of which he is elected superintendent; and if there are other teachers in such schools, it will not be presumed, in the absence of evidence, that the superintendent taught any of the branches of which he did not have a certificate: State, ex rel., v. Moser, 12 O. C. C. 247.

A contract is entered into between a teacher or superintendent and a school district when the board of education passes a resolution for the employment of such teacher or superintendent, causes notice thereof to be given to the person elected, and such person accepts such employment and enters upon the performance of his duties: State, ex rel., v. Moser, 12 O. C. C. 247.

A board of education may affirm or reject the report of its committee upon teachers; and it cannot be required by proceedings in mandamus to give a good and sufficient reason for its action in the selection of a teacher: State, ex rel., v. Board of Education, 5 O. N. P. 446.

Under a statute which required the clerk to call the roll of the board, and required each member of the board to announce verbally the name of the candidate who is his choice, the adoption of a written resolution naming the teachers to be employed upon roll call by a yea and nay vote, not in compliance with this section, is invalid: Pierce v. Board of Education, 1 O. N. P. 286.

The fact that the auditor has not apportioned the school funds does not relieve the board of education from liability for the salaries of the teachers who are properly employed: State, ex rel., v. Zeeb, 9 O. C. C. 13, 6 O. C. D. 70.

A promise which a board of education makes to a superintendent who has been elected at a definite salary, whereby after such election they agree to increase his salary to a stated amount, is invalid, as being without consideration, if no new services on the part of such superintendent are provided for, and if no new contract is entered into: Ward v. Board of Education, 21 O. C. C. 699.

The statutes entrust the exclusive management and control of the public schools to the board of education. Each board has the right, if it deems it right, to forbid the reading of the Bible in the public schools, and to discharge a teacher who refuses to comply with such rule: Board of Education v. Pulse, 7 O. N. P. 58, 10 O. D. (N. P.) 17.

The board of education has power to suspend pupils for disobedience of the lawful rules of the board: Sewell v. Board of Education, 29 O. S. 89.

If a pupil has failed to comply with a lawful rule of the board of education, and no excuse for such non-compliance is presented, and such pupil is suspended by the teacher, with the consent of such board, neither the teacher nor the board is liable personally therefor: Sewell v. Board of Education, 29 O. S. 89.

A rule that pupils should be prepared with rhetorical exercises at the time appointed, and in case of failure so to be prepared, such pupil should be suspended immediately from such department, unless excuse on account of sickness or other reasonable cause, was held to be a reasonable and valid rule: Sewell v. Board of Education, 29 O. S. 89.

A board of education has power to adopt the necessary rules and regulations for the government of the schools and for enforcing the rules and regulations thus adopted: Sewell v. Board of Education, 29 O. S. 89.

S. L.

If a pupil is wrongfully suspended from a school by the teacher, with the consent of the directors of the sub-district, such wrongful act does not justify the treasurer in refusing to draw a warrant for the salary of such teacher, if such salary is properly certified by the local directors: State, ex rel., v. Blain, 36 O. S. 429.

The salary which is due a teacher may be reached by garnishee: Belknap v. Pearson, 39 Bull. 140 Editorial.

Terms.

SECTION 7691. No person shall be appointed as a teacher for a term longer than four school years, nor for less than one year, except to fill an unexpired term, the term to begin within four months of the date of the appointment. In making appointments teachers in the actual employ of the board shall be considered before new teachers are chosen in their stead. (97 v. 360.)

A teacher's license is not a contract and is subject to existing reasonable future restrictions.

Section 7830, General Code, was amended so as to require after September 1, 1912, "elementary agriculture" in addition to the subjects formerly required, a certificate issued under the formr law as an "elementary school certificaet" and valid for "all" branches of study required at that time, can now be considered only as a "special certificate" valid as to certain specific studies but not for "all" subjects now required.

The holder of a teacher's elementary certificate which was issued prior to the amendment above stated and which certificate extends beyond Sept. 1, 1912, will be required to take an examination in elementary agriculture, in order to teach after Sept. 1, 1912.

It would not be legal to place "elemnetary agriculture" upon a teacher's elementary certificate issued prior to the amendment aforesaid, after the holder had passed an examination in this subject. A special certificate for the added branch may in such case be issued however.

After the amendment and prior to Sept. 1, 1912, elementary agriculture should be added as a required branch.

Former elementary certificates may be renewed only as "special certificates."

A renewal certificate issued after passage of the amendment may have "elementary agriculture" included therein provided, both the applicant's special certificates which are of the same class, including one for "elementary agriculture" and one for all subjects formerly required, run out of date of contemplated renewal.

As section 7821, General Code, has been amended so as to make all certificates ineffective until the first of September following, holders of certificates which terminate prior to that date, may under section 7826, General Code, be granted temporary certificates extending from said date of termination to the first of September following. — *Attorney General,* 1911-12, p. 555.

The question of the constitutionality of an act being for the courts and it being the custom of the attorney general to withhold judgment except in cases of manifest clearness, it is simply stated in the way of suggestion that in amending section 7691, General Code, relating to the appointment of teachers in the public schools, the question should be borne in mind whether such act, in making a teacher's position permanent after six years service, "promotes the efficiency of the schools" as stipulated in article VI, section 2 of the constitution of Ohio.

The questions also figure as to whether such provision conflicts with the rights of the school boards to contract for teacher's services, and whether such act would be contrary to the best interests of the public. — *Attorney General,* 1911-12, p. 7.

When a board of education passed a resolution legal in form employing certain teachers, the effect thereof would be to employ said teachers, though certain provisions of said resolution requiring said teachers to enter into a written contract "to make un for legal holidays and for the time lost in the event of epidemic" would be void because against the statutes and public policy of the state of Ohio. — *Attorney General*, 1911-12, p. 1322.

SECTION 7692. Each and every board of education in this state may appoint at least one school physician; provided two or more school districts may unite and employ one such physician, whose duties shall be such as are prescribed in this act. Said school physician shall hold a license to practice medicine in Ohio. School physicians may be discharged at any time by the appointing power whether the same be a board of education or of health or health officer, as herein provided. School physicians shall serve one year and until their successors are appointed, and shall receive such compensation as the appointing board may determine. Such boards may also employ trained nurses to aid in such inspection in such ways as may be prescribed by the board. Such board may delegate the duties and powers herein provided for to the board of health or officer performing the functions of a board of health within the school district if such board or officer is willing to assume the same. Boards of education shall co-operate with boards of health in the preventing of epidemics. (103 v. 864.)

School physician, appointment, qualifications.

Nurses.

SECTION 7692-1. School physicians may make examinations and diagnosis of all children referred to them at the beginning of every school year and at other times if deemed desirable. They may make such further examination of teachers, janitors and school buildings as in their opinion the protection of health of the pupils and teachers may require. Whenever a school child, teacher or janitor is found to be ill or suffering from positive open pulmonary tuberculosis or other contagious disease, the school physician shall promptly send such child, teacher, or janitor home, with a note, in the case of the child, to its parents or guardian, briefly setting forth the discovered facts, and advising that the family physician be consulted. School physicians shall keep accurate card index records of all examinations, and said records, that they may be uniform throughout the state shall be according to the form prescribed by the state school commissioner, and the reports shall be made according to the method of said form; provided, however, that if the parent or guardian of any school child or any teacher or janitor after notice from the board of education shall within two weeks thereafter furnish the written certificate of any reputable physician that the child, or teacher or janitor has been examined, in such cases the services of the medical inspector herein provided for shall be dispensed with, and such certificate shall be furnished by such parent or guardian from time to time, as required by the board of education. Such individual records shall not be open to the public and shall be solely for the use of the boards of education and health or other

Examinations and diagnosis of children, teachers and janitors.

Uniform card index records shall be kept.

health officer.　If any teacher or janitor is found to have positive open pulmonary tuberculosis or other communicable disease, his or her employment shall be discontinued upon expiration of the contract therefore, or, at the option of the board, suspended upon such terms as to salary as the board may deem just until the school physician shall have certified to a recovery from such disease. (103 v. 864.)

Publication of rules for enforcement of act.

SECTION 7692-2. The state school commissioner and the state board of health, shall jointly pass rules for the detailed enforcement of the purposes of this act, which rules shall bear the seals of said board and commissioner, the said rules to be printed and promulgated by the state printer; promulgation to consist in supplying a reasonable number of copies to each school superintendent, from whom all that are interested may receive copies. (103 v. 864.)

Who not eligible as physician.

SECTION 7692-3. No member of the board of education in any district in this state shall be eligible to the appointment of school physician during the period for which he or she is elected. (103 v. 86.)

Affidavit of compliance.

SECTION 7692-4. Each board of education by the affidavit of an officer thereof or otherwise shall prove to the satisfaction of the state school commissioner that it has complied with the requirements of section seven thousand six hundred and ninety-two, seven thousand six hundred and ninety- two-one, and seven thousand six hundred and ninety-two-two, of the General Code. (103 v. 864.)

Board may provide additional compensation.

SECTION 7693. The board of education of any school district, may provide and pay compensation to the employes of the board of health in addition to that provided by the city, township or other municipality. (103 v. 864.)

Director of schools.

SECTION 7694. A board of education in a city school district, may elect a director of schools, who shall serve as such for the term of two years, unless earlier removed. A vacancy in this office shall be filled for the unexpired term thereof. (97 v. 360.)

Powers.

SECTION 7695. As director of schools, he shall execute for the board of education, in the name of the school district, its contracts and obligations, except that bonds issued must be signed by the president of the board, and attested by the clerk. He shall see that all contracts made by or with such board are fully and faithfully performed. Except teachers, asistant teachers, supervisors, principals, superintendent of instruction, clerk of the board of education, such director shall have the appointment subject to the approval and confirmation of the board of all employes, and may discharge them. He shall have the care and custody of all property of the school district, real and personal, except moneys, oversee the construction of buildings, in the process of erection, and the repairs thereof; and advertise for bids and purchase all suplies and equipments authorized by the board. (97 v. 360.)

As the tuition fund is in the nature of a trust fund, for the benefit of each individual youth in the state, transfers from said fund, in the treasury of a school district to a building fund cannot be made except under provision and conditions provided for in Section 5655 General Code for the purpose of reducing tax levy estimates at the annual meeting of the board.

The common pleas court has powers, under Sections 2296-2302, General Code, to permit transfers "when no injury will result therefrom" but in view of the peculiar nature of the tuition fund, such action would be a rare possibility. — *Attorney General,* 1912, p. 1206.

A director of schools is not required, under G. C. Sec. 7623 and this section, to go to the expense of advertising for bids for every trivial thing in the way of supplies which may have been ordered by the board to be purchased: Gosline v. Board of Education, 11 O. C. C. (N. S.) 195.

Accordingly this section does not make it necessary that the board of education shall let the contract for the supply of coal to the lowest bidder: Gosline v. Board of Education, 11 O. C. C. (N. S.) 195.

SECTION 7696. Such director shall report to the board monthly, and oftener if required, as to all matters under his supervision, and report to the board a statement of its accounts, exhibiting the revenues, receipts, disbursements, assets and liabilities, the sources from which the revenues and funds are derived, and in what manner they have been disbursed. He shall keep acurate account of taxes levied for school purposes, and of all moneys due to, received and disbursed by the board; also, of all assets and liabilities and all appropriations made by it, and receive and preserve all vouchers for payments and disbursements made to or by the board. He must issue all warrants for the payment of money from the school fund, but no warrant shall be issued for the payment of any claim until it has been approved by the board. The pay roll for teachers, assistant teachers and supervisors must be countersigned by the superintendent of instruction. Such director shall attend all meetings of the board, and perform all of its executive functions not hereinbefore excepted in defining the duties of the director of schools. He must devote such portion of his time to the duties of his office as is required by the board of education at or before his election, and give a bond for the faithful discharge of his duties as director of schools, in such sum as the board determines, his sureties to be approved by it, which bond shall be deposited with the president of the board within ten days after his appointment. (97 v. 360.) — Duties.

SECTION 7697. Such director shall receive such compensation, not exceeding five thousand dollars per annum, as is fixed by the board before his election, which shall not be changed during his term of office. (97 v. 360.) — Compensation.

SECTION 7698. By a two-thirds vote for cause, the board of education at any time may suspend or remove the director of schools, but such suspension or removal shall not be made unless the charges are preferred in writing, and an — May suspend or remove director.

opportunity afforded to bring all offered pertinent testimony in as a defense, which testimony shall be received and considered by the board and made a part of its record. (97 v. 360.)

Appointees; clerk's duty. SECTION 7699. Upon the appointment of any person to any position under the control of the board of education, the clerk promptly must notify such person verbally or in writing of his appointment, the conditions thereof, and request and secure from him within a reasonable time to be determined by the board, his acceptance or rejection of such appointment. An acceptance of it within the time thus determined shall constitute a contract binding both parties thereto until such time as it may be dissolved, expires, or the appointee be dismissed for cause. (97 v. 360.)

Resignations. SECTION 7700. All resignations or requests for release from contract by teachers, superintendents, or employes, must be promptly considered by the board, but no resignation nor release shall become effective except by its consent. (97 v. 360.)

Dismissals. SECTION 7701. Each board may dismiss any appointee or teacher for inefficiency, neglect of duty, immorality, or improper conduct. No teacher shall be dismissed by any board unless the charges are first reduced to writing and an opportunity be given for defense before the board, or a committee thereof, and a majority of the full membership of the board vote upon roll call in favor of such dismissal. (97 v. 360.)

Superintendent. SECTION 7702. The board of education in each city school district at a regular meeting, between May 1st and August 31st, shall appoint a suitable person to act as superintendent of the public schools of the district, for a term not longer than five school years, beginning within four months of such appointment and ending on the 31st day of August.

Vacancy. Provided, that in the event of a vacancy occurring in the office of the superintendent prior to May 1st, the board of education may appoint a superintendent for the unexpired portion of that school year.

Provided, also, that if the vacancy occur through resignation or removal for cause, the superintendent thus resigning or removing shall be ineligible for reappointment to such office until after the reorganization of the board of education following the next general election of members of such board. (102 v. 193.)

When a village advances to a city by reason of the last federal census, the board of education of the village continues its duties until the induction into office of the city board of education, but with the powers only of a village board of education. Such village board therefore, has the power only to appoint a superintendent for a term of three years as provided for villages under section 7705, General Code.

An appointment by such board of a superintendent for a longer term as provided for cities under section 7702, General Code, is therefore void. — *Attorney General*, 1911-12, p. 563.

On April 20, 1911, section 7702, General Code, as it then existed did not provide as it does in its present form, that the appointment of a school superintendent by the board of education in a city school district must be for a term beginning within four months of such appointment, and that such appointment must be made between May 1 and August 31. An appointment made on that date therefor to take effffect on July 1 of that year is valid. — *Attorney General*, 1913, p. 1510.

SECTION 7703. Upon his acceptance of the appointment, such superintendent, subject to the approval and confirmation of the board, may appoint all the teachers, and for cause suspend any person thus appointed until the board or a committee thereof considers such suspension, but no one shall be dismissed by the board except as provided in section seventy-seven hundred and one. But any city board of education, upon a three-fourths vote of its full membership, may re-employ any teacher whom the superintendent refuses to appoint. Such superintendent shall visit the schools under his charge, direct and assist teachers in the performance of their duties, classify and control the promotion of pupils, and perform such other duties as the board determines. He must report to the board annually, and oftener if required, as to all matters under his supervision, and may be required by it to attend any and all of its meetings. He may take part in its deliberations but shall not vote. (97 v. 362.)

Powers and duties.

SECTION 7704. On the third Monday of every January the clerk of the board of education of a city school district shall certify to the board of education of which he is clerk, the number of pupils enrolled in the public schools of that district, whereupon the board of such city school district may by resolution set aside from the contingent fund a sum not to exceed five cents for each child so enrolled, such sum of money to be known as the "service fund" to be used only in paying the expenses of such members actually incurred in the performance of their duties; such payments to be made only on statement of the several members furnished at the last meeting held in each month. (99 v. 322 § 1.)

"Service fund."

SECTION 7705. The board of education of each village, and rural school district shall employ the teachers of the public schools of the district, for the term not longer than three school years, to begin within four months of the date of appointment. The local board shall employ no teacher for any school unless such teacher is nominated therefor by the district superintendent of the supervision district in which such school is located except by a majority vote. In all high schools and consolidated schools one of the teachers shall be designated by the board as principal and shall be the administrative head of such school. (104 v. 133.)

Employment of teachers.

Designation of principal in high and consolidated schools.

When a village advances to a city by reason of the last federal census, the board of education of the village continues its duties until the induction into office of the city board of education, but with the powers only of a village board of education. Such village board therefore, has the power only to appoint a superintendent for a term of three years as provided for villages under section 7705, General 'Code.

An appointment by such board of a superintendent for a longer term as provided for cities under section 7702, General Code, is therefore void. — *Attorney General*, 1911-12, p. 563.

When a village school district, by reason of the last federal census, advances to a city school district, the members of the board of education of the old village district, under sections 4686 and 4700, General Code, shall decide the number of members which shall compose the city board of education.

The successors of the members of the board of education in such instance, shall be elected at the next annual election for school board members.

A superintendent or teacher who has been elected for a legal term of years by said village board, may hold for said term under the city school districts regime. — *Attorney General*, 1911-12, p. 516.

Construction of Section 7705, General Code, as amended, 104 O. L., 144, also Section 4747, General Code, as amended, 104 O. L., 139.

Said sections prohibit a clerk of the board of education from being employed as teacher by the board of which such teacher is the clerk. — *Attorney General*, Opinion No. 1263, 1914.

1. * * * *

2. Teachers who were hired by township board of education before the new law, Section 7705, General 'Code, as amended, went into effect, for a term which extends beyond such time that said section went into effect, were legally hired, and the rural board of education is now bound to respect such contracts. — *Attorney General*, Opinion No. 1271, 1914.

Under Section 4740, General Code, as amended, a village district already employing a superintendent, cannot join with a rural school district which never employed a superintendent and which said districts were never heretofore joined together for supervisory purposes by employing a superintendent in common upon application to the county board of education to be joined and continue as separate districts as authorized by said section.

Under the recently enacted school code, appearing in 104, O. L., 133, school districts formerly designated as "special school districts" now constitute rural school districts, which said rural school districts are a part of the respective county school districts of the state. Part of any county school districts may be transferred to an adjoining school district or city or village school district by the mutual consent of the boards of education having control of such districts. — *Attorney General*, Opinion No. 1054, 1914.

Sexual intercourse with female pupils. SECTION 13030. Whoever, being a male person over twenty-one years of age and superintendent, tutor or teacher in a private, parochial or public school, or a seminary or other public institution, or instructor of a female in music, dancing, roller skating, athletic exercise, or other branch of learning, has sexual intercourse with a female, with her consent, while under his instruction during the term of his engagement as such superintendent, tutor or instructor, shall be imprisoned in the penitentiary not less than two years nor more than ten years. (83 v. 92.)

SECTION 7706. The district superintendent shall visit the schools under his charge, direct and assist teachers in the performance of their duties, classify and control the promotion of pupils, and shall spend not less than three-fourths of his working time in actual class room supervision. He shall report to the county superintendent annually, and oftner if required, as to all matters under his supervision. He shall be the chief executive officer of all boards of education within his district and shall attend any and all meetings. He may take part in their deliberations, but shall not vote. Such time as is not spent in actual supervision shall be used for organization and administrative purposes and in the instruction of teachers. At the request of the county board of education he shall teach in teachers' training courses which may be organized in the county school district. (104 v. 133.)

Duties of district superintendent.

SECTION 7706-1. The district superintendent shall, as often as advisable, assemble the teachers of his district for the purpose of conference on the course of study, discipline, school management and other school work and for the promotion of the general good of all the schools in the district. The county superintendent shall co-operate with the different district superintendents in holding such teachers' meetings and shall attend as many of them as his other duties will permit. (104 v. 133.)

Assemble teachers for conference.

SECTION 7706-2. It shall be the duty of the district superintendent to recommend to the village and rural boards of education within such district, such text books and courses of study as are most suitable for adoption. (104 v. 133.)

Recommend text books and course of study.

SECTION 7706-3. The county superintendent shall hold monthly meetings with the district superintendents and advise with them on matters of school efficiency. He shall visit and inspect the schools under his supervision as often as possible and with the advice of the district superintendent shall outline a schedule of school visitation for the teachers of the county school district. (104 v. 133.)

Duties of county superintendent.

SECTION 7706-4. The county superintendent shall have direct supervision over the training of teachers in any training courses which may be given in any county school district and shall personally teach not less than one hundred nor more than two hundred periods in any one year. It shall be his duty to see that all reports required by law are made out and sent to the county auditor and superintendent of public instruction and make such other reports as the superintendent of public instruction may require. Any county superintendent or district superintendent who becomes connected with or becomes an agent of or financially interested in any book publishing or book selling company or educational journal or magazine, shall become ineligible to hold such office and shall be forthwith

Supervision of training courses; reports.

Superintendent financially interested in book company ineligible to hold such office.

removed by the board having control over such county superintendent or district superintendent. (104 v. 133.)

SECTION 7706-5. The provisions of this act shall apply only to the public schools of the state. (104 v. 133.)

General duties of teachers. SECTION 7707. Teachers must exercise reasonable care in regard to school property, apparatus, and supplies intrusted to their keeping. They shall strive to guard the health and physical welfare of the pupils in their schools, give sufficient instruction in the studies pursued, and endeavor to maintain good discipline over all the pupils under their charge. But no teacher shall be required by any board to do the janitor work of any school room or building, except as mutually agreed by special contract, and for compensation in addition to that received by him for his services as teacher. (97 v. 363.)

Before a teacher may be entitled to $2.00 per day for attendance at an institute as provided by Section 7870 G. C., he must have attended such institute at least for four days, and the rule is the same whether during such attendance school is in session or not.

A teacher cannot be compelled to do janitor work by the board of education unless under the terms of a special contract with said teacher and providing for extra compensation therefor.

Section 7610 provides for relief through the county commissioners, where the board fails to provide janitor service. — *Attorney General,* 1911-12, p. 201.

A teacher who is required by the board of education to do janitor work, without any special contract so to do and without compensation in addition to that received by him for his service as teacher, in violation of this section, may recover reasonable compensation for his services: Reid v. Board of Education, 6 O. N. P. (N. S.) 526.

Teachers dismissed for insufficient cause. SECTION 7708. If the board of education of any district dismisses a teacher for any frivolous or insufficient reason, the teacher may bring suit against such district. If, on trial of the cause a judgment be obtained against the district, the board thereof shall direct the clerk to issue an order upon the treasurer for the sum so found due to the person enttiled thereto, to pay it out of any money in his hands belonging to the district, applicable to the payment of teachers. In such suits process may be served on the clerk of the district, and service upon him shall be sufficient. (97 v. 363.)

Since possession of a certificate is *prima facie* evidence of competency and good character the burden of sustaining a charge against the teacher for inefficiency, neglect of duty, immorality or improper conduct is thrown upon the person or persons preferring such charges. — *Attorney General,* Opinion.

The fact that a teacher has wrongfully suspended a pupil, in doing which he is complying with the orders of the board of education, does not prevent such teacher from recovering the agreed compensation for his services: State, ex rel., v. Blain, 36 O. S. 429.

Referred to as showing that process may be served upon the clerk of a board of education: State, ex rel., v. Coon, 4 O. C. C. (N. S.) 560.

Filing and preservation of copies and price list of school books. SECTION 7709. Any publisher or publishers of school-books in the United States desiring to offer school-books for use by pupils in the common schools of Ohio as hereinafter provided, before such books may be lawfully adopted and purchased by any school board, must file in the office of the superintendent of public instruction, a copy of each book proposed to be so offered, together with the published list wholesale price thereof. No revised edition of any such book shall be used in common schools until a copy of such edition has been filed in the office of the superintendent together with the published list of wholesale price thereof. The superintendent must carefully preserve in his office all such copies of books and the price thereof. (104 v. 225.)

The object of Section 7709, General Code, is to fix certain conditions, compliance with which shall entitled publishers of textbooks to contract with boards of education for the sale of their books.

After fixing the price which the books of a certain publisher may be sold at, 75% of the wholesale price, the state school commissioner cannot within five years reduce such price unless the publisher refiles such book for listing with the commission.

Where a text book company has made a contract for 75% of the wholesale price as fixed by the commission, but which contract extends beyond the five years' time for which such price was listed, and such company refuses to refile such book with the commission after such period has expired, the contract may be treated as terminated for the reasoon that said company's rights to so contract is limited to the five year period for which the price was fixed. — Attorney General, 1911-12, p. 540.

The revision of a school book is the same as the offering of a new book under Sections 7709 and 7710, and therefore, the expiration of the listing of such revised school book expires five years from the date such revised edition is filed. — Attorney General, Opinion No. 1080, 1914.

SECTION 7710. When and so often as any book and the price thereof is filed in the office of the superintendent of public instruction as provided in section 7709 a commission consisting of the governor, secretary of state and superintendent of public instruction, immediately shall fix the maximum price at which such books may be sold to or purchased by boards of education, as hereinafter provided, which price must not exceed seventy-five per cent of the published list wholesale price thereof. The superintendent of public instruction immediately shall notify the publisher of such book so filed, of the maximum price fixed. If the publisher so notified, notifies the superintendent in writing that he accepts the price fixed, and agrees in writing to furnish such book during a period of five years at that price, such written acceptance and agreement shall entitle the publisher to offer the book so filed for sale to such boards of education. (104 v. 225.)

Maximum price; notice to publisher.

The object of Section 7709, General Code, is to fix certain conditions, compliance with which shall entitle publishers of text books to contract with boards of education for the sale of their books.

After fixing the price which the books of a certain publisher may be sold at, 75% of the wholesale price, the state school commissioner cannot within five years reduce such price unless the' publisher refiles such book for listing with the commission.

Where a text book company has made a contract for 75% of the wholesale price as fixed by the commission, but which contract extends beyond the five years' time for which such price was listed, and such company refuses to refile such book with the commission after such period has expired, the contract may be treated as terminated for the reason that said company's rights to so contract is limited to the five year period for which the price was fixed. — *Attorney General*, 1911-12, p. 540.

The revision of a school book is the same as the offering of ' a new book under Sections 7709 and 7710, and therefore, the expiration of the listing of such revised school book expires five years from the date such revised edition is filed. — *Attorney General*, Opinion No. 1080, 1914.

Names and addresses of publishers furnished to boards.

SECTION 7711. Such superintendent, during the first half of the month of June, in each year, must furnish to each board of education the names and addresses of all publishers who during the year ending on the first day of the month of June in each year, agreed in writing to furnish their publications upon the terms above provided. A board of education shall not adopt or cause to be used in the common schools any book whose publisher has not complied, as to such book, with the provisions of law relating thereto. (104 v. 225.)

The object of Section 7709, General Code, is to fix certain conditions, compliance with which shall entitle publishers of text books to contract with boards of education for the sale of their books.

After fixing the price which the books of a certain publisher may be sold at, 75% of the wholesale price, the state school commissioner cannot within five years reduce such price unless the publisher refiles such book for listing with the commission.

Where a text book company has made a contract for 75% of the wholesale price as fixed by the commission, but which contract extends beyond the five years' time for which such price was listed, and such company refuses to refile such book with the commission after such period has expired, the contract may be treated as terminated for the reason that said company's rights to so contract is limited to the five year period for which the price was fixed. — *Attorney General*, 1911-12, p. 540.

Violation of agreement by publisher.

SECTION 7712. If a publisher who agreed in writing to furnish books as above provided, fails or refuses to furnish such books adopted as herein provided to any board of education or its authorized agent upon the terms herein provided, such boards at once must notify such commission of such failure or refusal, and it at once shall cause an investigation of such charge to be made. If it is found to be true the commission at once shall notify such publisher and each board of education in the state that such book shall not thereafter be adopted and purchased by boards of education. Such publisher shall forfeit and pay to the state of Ohio five hundred dollars for each failure, to be recovered in the name of the state, in an action to be brought by the attorney-general, in the court of common pleas of Franklin county, or in any other proper court or in any other place where service can be made. The amount, when collected, must be paid into the state treasury to the credit of the common school fund of the state. (92 v. 283 § 4.)

The object of Section 7709, General Code, is to fix certain conditions, compliance with which shall entitle publishers of text books to contract with boards of education for the sale of their books.

After fixing the price which the books of a certain publisher may be sold at, 75% of the wholesale price, the state school commissioner cannot within five years reduce such price unless the publisher refiles such book for listing with the commission.

Where a text book company has made a contract for 75% of the wholesale price as fixed by the commission, but which contract extends beyond the five years' time for which such price was listed, and such company refuses to refile such book with the commission after such period has expired, the contract may be treated as terminated for the reason that said company's rights to so contract is limited to the five year period for which the price was fixed. — *Attorney General*, 1911-12, p. 540.

SECTION 7713. At a regular meeting, held between the first Monday in February and the first Monday in August, each board of education shall determine by a majority vote of all members elected the studies to be pursued and which of such text-books so filed shall be used in the schools under its control. But no text-books now in use or hereafter adopted shall be changed, nor any part thereof altered or revised, nor any other text-book be substituted therefor for five years after the date of the selection and adoption thereof, as shown by the official records of such boards, except by the consent at a regular meeting, of five-sixths of all members elected thereto. Books so substituted shall be adopted for the full term of five years. (99 v. 460 § 5.)

Text books; how determined; five-year term.

The object of Section 7709, General Code, is to fix certain conditions, compliance with which shall entitle publishers of text books to contract with boards of education for the sale of their books.

After fixing the price which the books of a certain publisher may be sold at, 75% of the wholesale price, the state school commissioner cannot within five years reduce such price unless the publisher refiles such book for listing with the commission.

Where a text book company has made a contract for 75% of the wholesale price as fixed by the commission, but which contract extends beyond the five years' time for which such price was listed, and such company refuses to refile such book with the commission after such period has expired, the contract may be treated as terminated for the reason that said company's rights to so contract is limited to the five year period for which the price was fixed. — *Attorney General*, 1911-12, p. 540.

The stipulation of Section 7713, General Code, to the effect that the adoption of text books shall be made at a regular meeting between "the first Monday in February and the first Monday in August" is directory and not mandatory in accordance with the general principle of construction and in view of the further fact that the duty is a positive one enjoined by law.

Text books shall not be changed within five years except by a vote of five-sixths of the members of the board. After the lapse of five years, however, a majority vote shall be sufficient to make such change. — *Attorney General*, 1911-12, p. 538.

Section 7714, General Code, merely gives the board of education the power to pay for transportation on text books and is not a mandatory direction to the effect that it must always do so. — *Attorney General*, 1911-12, p. 528.

A proposed change in textbooks without authority of the law may be prevented by injunction: Lenhart v. Newton Township, 5 O. N. P. (N. S.) 129.

Text-books, of whom ordered.

SECTION 7714. Each board of education shall cause it to be ascertained, and at a regular meeting determine which, and the number of each of such books the schools under its charge require, and cause an order to be drawn for the amount in favor of the clerk of the board of education, payable out of the contingent fund. Such clerk at once shall order the books so agreed upon by the board, of the publisher, who on the receipt of such order must ship them to the clerk without delay. He forthwith shall examine the books, and, if found right and in accordance with the order, remit the amount to the publisher. The board of education must pay all charges for the transportation of the books, out of the school contingent fund. But if such boards of education at any time can secure of the publishers books at less than such maximum price, they shall do so, and without unnecessary delay may make effort to secure such lower price before adopting any particular text-book. (99 v. 460 § 5.)

A board of education can require by contract that the publishers pay the freight. — *Attorney General*, Opinion.

Board of education, power and duties of.

SECTION 7715. Each board of education shall make all necessary provisions and arrangements to place the books so purchased within easy reach of and accessible to all the pupils in their district. For that purpose it may make such contracts, and take such security as it deems necessary, for the custody, care and sale of such books and accounting for the proceeds; but not to exceed ten per cent of the cost price shall be paid therefor. Such books must be sold to the pupils of school age in the district, at the price paid the publisher, and not to exceed ten per cent therefor added. The proceeds of sales shall be paid into the contingent fund of such district. Boards also may contract with local retail dealers to furnish such books at prices above specified, the board being still responsible to the publishers for all books purchased by it. (99 v. 460 § 5.)

Old books, purchase of.

SECTION 7716. When pupils remove from any district, and have text-books of the kind adopted in such district and not the kind adopted in the district to which they remove, and wish to dispose of them, the board of the district from which they remove, if requested, shall purchase them at the fair value thereof, and resell them as other books. Nothing herein shall prevent the board of education from furnishing free books to pupils as provided by law. (99 v. 460 § 5.)

Who shall not be sales agent.

SECTION 7718. A superintendent, supervisor, principal or teacher employed by any board of education in the state shall not act as sales agent, either directly or indirectly, for any person, firm or corporation whose school text books are filed with the superintendent of public instruction as provided by law, or for school apparatus or equipment of any kind for use in the public schools of the state. A violation of this provision shall work a forfeiture of their certificates to teach in the public schools of Ohio. (106 v. 447.)

SECTION 7720. During the vacations of schools, or when they are not in session such books shall be taken care of in the same manner that maps, globes, dictionaries and other school apparatus are cared for and preserved. (89 v. 241 § 2.)

Care and preservation of books.

SECTION 7721. Physical training shall be included in the branches regularly to be taught in public schools in city school districts, and in all educational institutions supported wholly or in part by money received from the state. Boards of education of city school districts, and boards of such educational institutions must make provisions in the schools and institutions under their jurisdiction for teaching physical training, and adopt such methods as will adapt it to the capacity of pupils in the various grades therein. Other boards may make such provisions. The curriculum in all normal schools of the state shall contain a regular course on physical education. (97 v. 364 § 1.)

Physical culture in schools.

SECTION 7722. Any board of education may establish and maintain manual training, domestic science, and commercial departments; agriculture, industrial, vocational and trades schools, also kindergartens, in connection with the public school system; and pay the expenses of establishing and maintaining such schools from the public school funds, as other school expenses are paid. (100 v. 17 § 1.)

Powers of board of education, as to manual training, etc.

SECTION 7723. The nature of alcoholic drinks and other narcotics, and their effects on the human system, in connection with the various divisions of physiology and hygiene, shall be included in the branches to be regularly taught in the common schools of the state, and in all educational institutions supported wholly, or in part, by money from the state. (94 v. 396 § 1.)

Instruction as to effect of alcoholic drinks on the human system.

SECTION 7724. Boards of education, and boards of such educational institutions shall make suitable provisions for this instruction in the schools and institutions under their respective jurisdictions, giving definite time and place therefor in the regular course of study; adopt such methods as will adapt it to the capacity of pupils in the various grades; and to corresponding classes as found in ungraded schools. The same tests for promotion shall be required in this as in other branches. (94 v. 396 § 1.)

Provision therefor.

SECTION 7724-1. It shall be the duty of each teacher in the public schools of the state to devote not less than thirty minutes in each month, during the time such school is in session, for the purpose of instructing the pupils thereof as to ways and means of preventing accidents. (103 v. 134.)

Instruction in preventing accidents.

Manual of instruction to be provided.

SECTION 7724-2. The superintendent of public instruction shall prepare, publish and distribute, at the expense of the state, a manual conveniently arranged in chapters or lessons for the guidance of teachers in carrying out the prfovisions of this act. (103 v. 134.)

Instruction of teachers.

SECTION 7725. In all teachers' institutes, normal schools and teachers' training classes, hereafter established by the state, adequate time and attention shall be given to instruction in the best methods of teaching such branch. (94 v. 396 § 2.)

Examination of teachers required.

SECTION 7726. No certificates shall be granted to any person to teach in the common schools, or in any educational institution supported by the state who does not pass a satisfactory examination on such subject, and the best methods of teaching it. (94 v. 396 § 2.)

Duties of superintendent.

SECTION 7727. The superintendent of public instruction shall see that the provisions in the next two preceding sections relating to county teachers' institutes, and schools and classes by whatever name hereafter established for training teachers, and the examination of teachers, are carried out. Each year, he must make full report of the enforcement of such sections in connection with his annual report. (104 v. 225.)

Forfeiture for failure to give instruction.

SECTION 7728. Any school official, or employe in any way concerned, in the enforcement of the next five preceding sections who wilfully refuses or neglects to provide for, or to give the instruction as to the nature and effect of alcoholic drinks and other narcotics, hereinbefore required, shall forfeit and pay for each offense the sum of twenty-five dollars. Mayors, justices of the peace and probate judges shall have concurrent jurisdiction with the common pleas court to try all such offenses. All forfeitures collected hereunder must be paid into the general county school fund of the county in which it was collected. (94 v. 397 § 3.)

When German language may be taught.

SECTION 7729. Boards of education may provide for the teaching of the German language in the elementary and high schools of the district over which they have control, but it shall only be taught in addition, and as auxiliary to, the English language. All the common branches in the public schools must be taught in the English language. (97 v. 364.)

Power of board to suspend a school. Conveyance of pupils.

SECTION 7730. The board of education of any rural or village school district may suspend any or all schools in such village or rural school district. Upon such suspension the board in such village school district may provide, and in such rural school district shall provide, for the conveyance of pupils attending such schools, to a public school in the rural or village district, or to a public school in another district. When the average daily attendance of any school for the preceding year has been below ten, such school shall be susepnded and the pupils transferred to another school or schools when directed to do so by the county board of education. No school of any rural district shall be suspended until ten days' notice has been given by the board of education of such district. Such notice shall be posted in five conspicuous places within such village or rural school district; provided, however, that any suspended school as herein provided, may be re-established by the suspending authority upon its own initiative, or upon a petition asking for re-establishment, signed by a majority of the voters of the suspended district, at any time the school enrollment of the said suspended district shows twelve or more pupils of lawful school age. (106 v. 396.)

When a school has been suspended because the average daily attendance during the preceding year was less than twelve in accordance with Section 7730, General Code as amended, 104 O. L. 139, and the territory comprising said district has been annexed to a contiguous district, then the board of education would be compelled to furnish conveyance or transportation to such pupils in accordance with the provisions of Section 7731, and such board will be required to transport or furnish conveyance only to those pupils residing in such suspended district who live more than two miles from the school to which they are assigned. — *Attorney General*, Opinion No. 1355, 1914.

A board of education for a special school district through its truant officer can compel pupils of a special school district who reside more than one and one-half miles from the school in such special district to attend school of such district without providing conveyance therefor, provided that such pupils are within the age limitation fixed by Section 7763 of the General Code, and provided they are not excused from attending school in the manner provided by said section. — *Attorney General*, Opinion No. 744, 1914.

A village board of education is not authorized to make expenditures for the conveyance of its high school pupils to a neighboring district upon abandonment of its high school.

Such board may not include in a tuition contract with neighboring boards of education, a provision for conveyance of high school pupils to and from such district. — *Attorney General*, 1911-12, p. 1246.

When the schools of a township school district are centralized, the board of education must provide a conveyance for all pupils residing at a greater distance than a mile and a half from the school.

Transportation of pupils residing within the distance of a mile and a half is entirely optional with the school board. — *Attorney General*, 1911-12, p. 1415.

In a township in which there is no township board of education and wherein a number of special school districts exist, there are no special statutory provisions for the centralization of schools. However, by means of the election provided for by Section 4743, General Code, a school district may be abandoned and the original township district from which the abandoned school district was taken, may be thereby recreated, and from this revived township district, the centralization may be completed as provided by statute.

When a special school district is abandoned, by vote of the electors or otherwise, such special school district continues to exist for the purpose of paying any and all indebtedness of such special school district, and any taxes levied to pay such indebtedness should be collected upon the property on the duplicate in such school district, even though such district is situated in two or more townships. — *Attorney General*, 1912, p. 1122.

Under Section 7730, of the General Code, when schools in sub-districts have been suspended, a township board of education may pay each patron for conveying his own pupil instead of employing one man to convey all pupils, where funds are insufficient to apply the latter method. — *Attorney General*, 1912, p. 1415.

Under 4716, General Code, a board of education of a township may consolidate two school subdistricts into one and there are no statutory provisions enabling the people of such subdistricts to object to or prevent such action.

When such consolidation is carried out, the board is not required by the statutes to provide transportation for pupils attending the consolidated school. — *Attorney General*, 1912, p. 497.

By virtue of Sections 4723 and 4724, General Code, joint sub-districts are abolished and the territory of such districts situated in the township in which the school house of the joint sub-district is not located, is attached for school purposes to the township school district in which said school house is located and shall constitute a part of said township school district.

Pupils of such attached territory, therefore, are entitled to conveyance to the centralized school, when the board abolishes sub-districts; the expense thereof to be paid out of the funds of the township district.

Under the terms of Section 7730, General Code, providing such pupils live more than one and one-half miles from such school in accordance with Section 7731, General Code, the fact that said officials have failed to make a map of attached territory which is to be made a part of the records of the board of education and a copy of which is to be filed with the auditor of the county in which the territory is situated, as provided by Section 4724, General Code, does not operate to prevent the territory included in the joint sub-district and outside of the township becoming a part of the township school district as provided by Section 4723, General Code. — *Attorney General*, 1913, p. 1089.

It is necessary for a township board of education to submit the question of centralization of schools to a vote, under the provisions of Section 4726, General Code.

All the electors of the township are entitled to vote upon the proposition of the centralization of schools.

The abolishment of all the schools in all the sub-districts by vtriue of Sections 7730 and 7731, General Code, the establishment of new schools and the conveyance of pupils to these schools, operate as a centralization of the schools of the township, provided that no election has been held upon the question of centralization which resulted adversely and provided that no petition may be filed for an election according to law. — *Attorney General*, 1913, p. 1377.

Where part of a subdistrict of a township school district has been incorporated into a special school district leaving the balance of said township district unprovided for as to a school house, the board of education of the township school district must either provide a school house in the remaining part of said subdistrict, or transport the pupils to a school. — *Attorney General*, Opinion No. 983, 1914.

A board of education may borrow money under Section 5656, General Code, to pay obligations incurred in furnishing the transportation to pupils which the law requires to be furnished, such expense being a charge against the district, regardless of the existence of sufficient funds in the district treasury, and the contract for transportation being at least in the nature of an employment contract.

It is not a condition precedent to the exercise of power under said section that previously incurred floating or funded indebtedness has been created under the same section, that is, it is not necessary that the one debt shall be extinguished before the time of payment of the other is extended. — *Attorney General*, Opinion No. 983, 1914.

School attendance should not be determined under Section 7730, General Code, at a time when there is an epidemic prevailing in the school, or rather in the district wherein such school is located. Such average daily attendance should be determined during the year when the school attendance is normal or not affected by an epidemic.

When the average daily attendance of a school during the preceding year has been below twelve, because of an epidemic and such average daily attendance for the succeeding year would be more than an average of twelve, the board could legally employ a teacher and continue such school, and the payment of such teacher would be legally authorized under the law. — *Attorney General,* Opinion No. 1370, 1914.

Under Section 7730, General Code, prior to its amendment, 104 O. L., 139, it was optional with board of education of a township school district to suspend the schools when the average daily attendance thereof was less than twelve. If a township board of education entered into a contract with a teacher for teaching a subdistrict under its jurisdiction, and such subdistrict was abolished in accordance with Section 7730, General Code, such act operated as a termination of the contract, provided such act occurred before the termination of the contract because of the lapse of time such contract was to run. Likewise such contract would be terminated if the school should be suspended in accordance with the mandatory provisions of Section 7730, General Code, as amended, 104 O. L., 139. An expenditure of money upon such contract, after being so terminated under the provisions contained in said section as the same existed both prior to its amendment and since its amendment above referred to would be illegal.

By virtue of Section 7684, General Code, a board of education may assign pupils to attend a school which had been previously suspended under Section 7730, supra, because of the attendance being less than twelve for the preceding year and such school may again be continued as such school, provided that this course in the opinion of the board, will best promote the interests of education in the district. — *Attorney General,* Opinion No. 1321, 1914.

Under the provisions of Section 7730, General Code, the board of education is required to give sixty days' notice provided for therein; in order to suspend a school the procedure set forth in said section should be carried out. — *Attorney General,* Opinion No. 1096, 1914.

SECTION 7731. In all rural and village school districts where pupils live more than two miles from the nearest school the board of education shall provide transportation for such pupils to and from such school. The transportation for pupils living less than two miles from the schoolhouse, by the most direct public highway shall be optional with the board of education. When transportation of pupils is provided, the conveyance must pass within one-half mile of the respective residences of all pupils, except when such residences are situated more than one-half mile from the public road. When local boards of education neglect or refuse to provide transportation for pupils, the county board of education shall provide such transportation and the cost thereof shall be charged against the local school district. (104 v. 133.)

When board shall provide transportation.

A board of education for a special school district through its truant officer can compel pupils of a special school district who reside more than one and one-half miles from the school in such special district to attend school of such district without providing conveyance therefor, provided that such pupils are within the age limitation fixed by Section 7763 of the General Code, and provided they are not excused from attending school in the manner provided by said section. — *Attorney General,* Opinion No. 744, 1914.

A village board of education is not authorized to make expenditures for the conveyance of its high school pupils to a neighboring district upon abandonment of its high school.

Such board may not include in a tuition contract with neighboring boards of education, a provision for conveyance of high school pupils to and from such district. — *Attorney General,* 1911-12, p. 1246.

When the schools of a township school district are centralized, the board of education must provide a conveyance for all pupils residing at a greater distance than a mile and a half from the school.

Transportation of pupils residing within the distance of a mile and a half is entirely optional with the school board. — *Attorney General,* 1911-12, p. 1415.

It is necessary for a township board of education to submit the question of centralization of schools to a vote, under the provisions of Section 4726, General Code.

All the electors of the township are entitled to vote upon the proposition of the centralization of schools.

The abolishment of all the schools in all the subdistricts by virtue of Sections 7730 and 7731, General Code, the establishment of new schools and the conveyance of pupils to those schools, operate as a centralization of the schools of the township, provided that no election has been held upon the question of centralization which resulted adversely and provided that no petition may be filed for an election according to law. — *Attorney General,* 1913, p. 1377.

Section 7731, General Code, providing that, when transportation of pupils is provided for upon the centralization of schools, the conveyance must pass within at least one-half mile from the residence of each pupil, except where the residence is more than one-half mile distant from a public road, is satisfied when a vehicle stops within a half mile of such residence even though good road exists to a nearer distance. — *Attorney General,* 1911-12. p. 1365.

Under the provisions of Sections 7735 and 7736, General Code, a pupil residing in a district and attending schools of another district, under Section 7735, General Code, cannot continue to attend the schools of said latter school district and demand transportation after the schools of the district which such pupils have been attending have been centralized, and transportation provided for. — *Attorney General,* 1913, p. 1415.

A board of education may borrow money under Section 5656, General Cole, to pay obligations incurred in furnishing the transportation to pupils which the law requires to be furnished, such expense being a charge against the district, regardless of the existence of sufficient funds in the district treasury, and the contract for transportation being at least in the nature of an employment contract. — *Attorney General,* Opinion No. 1226, Nov. 5, 1914.

When a school has been suspended because the average daily attendance during the preceding year was less than twelve in accordance with Section 7730, General Code, as amended, 104 O. L., 139, and the territory comprising said district has been annexed to a contiguous district, then the board of education would be compelled to furnish conveyance or transportation to such pupils in accordance with the provisions of Section 7731, and such board will be required to transport or furnish conveyance only to those pupils residing in such suspended district who live more than two miles from the school to which they are assigned. — *Attorney General,* Opinion No. 1355, 1914.

Deposits for shelter of children.

SECTION 7731-1. The boards of education of city, village or rural school districts may by resolution designate certain places as depots from which to gather children for transportation to school, when such districts provide transportation. The places designated as depots shall be provided with a shelter and be made comfortable during cold and stormy weather. Such depots shall in no case be more than one and one-half miles from any home having children within such district. (106 v. 496.)

SECTION 7733. At its option, the board of education in any village school district may provide for the conveyance of the pupils of the district or any adjoining district, to the school or schools of the district, the expense of conveyance to be paid from the school funds of the district in which such pupils reside. But such boards as so provide transportation, shall not be required to transport pupils living less than one mile from the schoolhouse or houses. (101 v. 307.)

Conveyance of pupils in village districts.

Under 4716, General Code, a board of education of a township may consolidate two school subdistricts into one and there are no statutory provisions enabling the people of such subdistricts to object to or prevent such action.

When such consolidation is carried out, the board is not required by the statutes to provide transportation for pupils attending the consolidated school. — *Attorney General,* 1912, p. 497.

A board of education for a special school district through its truant officer can compel pupils of a special school district who reside more than one and one-half miles from the school in such special district to attend school of such district without providing conveyance therefor, provided that such pupils are within the age limitation fixed by Section 7763 of the General Code, and provided they are not excused from attending school in the manner provided by said section. — *Attorney General,* Opinion No. 744, 1914.

SECTION 7734. The board of any district may contract with the board of another district for the admission of pupils into any school in such other district, on terms agreed upon by such boards. The expense so incurred shall be paid out of the school funds of the district sending such pupils. (73 v. 243.)

Pupils may be sent from one district to another.

Who may be admitted to the public schools; See Sec. 7681.
The contract must be express, merely permitting the attendance of a non-resident pupil creates no liability: 50 O. S. 439.

Where a pupil lives less than one and one-half miles from the school house of the district wherein such pupil lives, there is no liability on the part of the board of education of such district to pay the tuition of pupils attending school in another adjoining district, in the absence of any agreement to pay such tuition in accordance with Section 7734, General Code. In the absence of any contract for the payment of tuition, the father of such child may be held for a reasonable amount in payment of such tuition.

The distance between the home of the pupil and the school house of the district wherein such pupil resides, should be determined by the nearest route from such home to such school house as determined by Section 7735, General Code. — *Attorney General.* Opinion No. 1390, 1914.

SECTION 7735. When pupils live more than one and one-half miles from the school to which they are assigned

Attendance at nearest school.

in the district where they reside, they may attend a **nearer** school in the same district, or if there be none **nearer** therein, then the nearest school in another school district, in all grades below the high school. In such cases the board of education of the district in which they reside must pay the tuition of such pupils without an agreement to that effect. But a board of education shall not collect tuition for such attendance until after notice thereof has been given to the board of education of the district where the pupils reside. Nothing herein shall require the consent of the board of education of the district where the pupils reside, to such attendance. (97 v. 364.)

Under Section 7730, of the General Code, when schools in subdistrict have been suspended, a township board of education may pay each patron for conveying his own pupil instead of employing one man to convey all pupils, where funds are insufficient to apply the latter method. — *Attorney General,* 1912, p. 1415.

Where a pupil lives less than one and one-half miles from the school house of the district wherein such pupil lives, there is no liability on the part of the board of education of such district to pay the tuition of pupils attending school in another adjoining district, in the absence of any agreement to pay such tuition in accordance with Section 7734, General Code. In the absence of any contract for the payment of tuition, the father of such child may be held for a reasonable amount in payment of such tuition.

The distance between the home of the pupil and the school house of the district wherein such pupil resides, should be determined by the nearest route from such home to such school house as determined by Section 7735, General Code. — *Attorney General,* Opinion No. 1390, 1914.

When the board of education of Madison township has made no agreement with another board of education for attendance of Madison township pupils at a high school in the same or in an adjoining township, the board of said Madison township can be compelled to pay a "reasonable sum" for the tuition of its pupils to the board whose high school said pupils elect to attend, provided notice is served by said pupils on the Madison board at least five days previous to the date of attendance. — *Attorney General,* 1911-12, p. 1129.

Inmates of a children's home are classed equally with other youth under the meaning of Section 7681, General Code, and such inmates may attend a village school not within their own district, if there is no school within their own district within one and one-half miles of the home or at closer proximity than the village school. The board of education of said village cannot charge tuition for said inmates until they have notified the board of education of the district in which the pupils reside.

The duty of providing for the education of such inmates devolves upon the board of education of the township in which they reside and not upon the trustees of the home. — *Attorney General,* 1911-12, p. 1480.

As no contract is necessary to charge one board of education with the tuition of its resident pupils for attendance at school in another district, the notice provided for in Section 7735, General Code, is intended, not to establish a right, but to fix the time from which said liability for tunition shall accrue. — *Attorney General,* 1912, p. 1273.

A board of education is not to be denied state aid by reason of the fact that it pays authorized expenses other than teachers' salaries out of the tuition fund, such as superintendent's salary and institute fees.

The amount of state aid allowed, however, shall not exceed such sum as is necessary to make teachers' salaries equal to $40.00 per month. — *Attorney General,* 1912, p. 98.

A board of education of a special school district, through its truant officer, can compel pupils of a special school district who reside more than one and one-half miles from the school in such special district to attend school of such district, without providing conveyance therefor, provided that such pupils are within the age limitation fixed by Section 7763 of the General Code, and provided they are not excused from attending school in the manner provided by said section. — *Attorney General,* Opinion No. 744, Feb. 9, 1914.

A board of education is not to be denied state aid by reason of the fact that it pays authorized expenses other than teachers' salaries out of the tuition fund, such as superintendent's salary and institute fees.

The amount of state aid allowed, however, shall not exceed such sum as is necessary to make teachers' salaries equal to $40.00 per month. — *Attorney General,* 1912, p. 98.

When a pupil lives more than one and one-half miles from the school to which he is assigned and has been attending a nearer school in another township, when such other township centralizes its schools, and thus makes the centralized school further than the school to which he has been assigned, the board of education of his township cannot be compelled to pay tuition to the centralized school under the provisions of Section 7735, General Code. — *Attorney General,* Opinion No. 1006, June 26, 1914.
10 O. C. 617.

This section was said to be unconstitutional in Board of Education v. Board of Education, 17 O. C. D. 824, 3 O. L. R. 116 (reversed, without report, Board of Education v. Board of Education, 74 O. S. 477).

In the absence of specific statutory provision, a board of education is not liable for the tuition of pupils living within its district who attend a school in another district, unless there is an express contract therefor: Board of Education v. Board of Education, 50 O. S. 439.

Under this section no contract is necessary. If the board of the school district to which such pupils go, permits them to attend, and the facts come within this section, the permission of the board of the district in which the pupils reside is not necessary: Board of Education v. Board of Education,

The distance of its residence from the school of its district which, under this section, entitles a child of school age to attend the school of another district, is one and a half miles by the most direct public highway from the school to the nearest part of the curtilage of its residence: Board of Education v. Board of Education, 58 O. S. 390.

This section does not require the board of education of a school district to admit children to a school outside of the district in which they reside unless the school in their own district is more than a mile and half from their residence and more remote from their residence than the school to which admission is sought: Boyce v. Board of Education, 76 O. S. 365.

In determining the distance pupils of a public school must travel in going from their home to the schoolhouse, the measurements should begin at the exit from the curtilage and run thence along the most direct established route by lane or path to the nearest highway, and then follow the center line of the highway to the door of the schoolhouse: Board of Education v. Board of Education, 11 O. N. P. (N. S.) 286.

Measurement of distance pupils must travel to school: Concord Spec. Sch. Dist. (Bd. of Sd.) v. Blue Ash Spec. Sch. Dist. (Bd. of Ed.), 34 O. C. C. 213 (15 N. S. 521).

SECTION 7736. Such tuition shall be paid from either the tuition or the contingent funds and the amount per capita must be ascertained by dividing the total exepnse of conducting the elementary schools of the district attended, exclusive of permanent improvements and repairs, by the total enrollment in the elementary schools of the district, such amount to be computed by the month. An attendance any part of a month will create a liability for the whole month. (97 v. 364.

Expense per capita.

Under the provisions of sections 7735 and 7736, General Code, a pupil residing in a district and attending schools of another district, under section 7735, General Code, cannot continue to attend the schools of said latter school district and demand transportation after the schools of the district which such pupils have been attending have been centralized, and transportation provided for. — *Attorney General*, 1913, p. 1415.

Not to apply when schools are centralized.

SECTION 7737. When the schools of a district are centralized or transportation of pupils provided, the provisions of the next two preceding sections shall not apply.` (97 v. 364.)

No contracts between the boards is necessary. If the receiving board give the permission, the sending board must pay, no permission of the sending board is necessary: 10 C. C. 617.

The distance is to be measured by the most direct public highway, from the school house to the nearest portion of the curtilage of the child's residence: 58 O. S. 390.

Under the provisions of sections 7735 and 7736, General Code, a pupil residing in a district and attending schools of another district, under section 7735, General Code, cannot continue to attend the schools of said latter school district and demand transportation after the schools of the district which such pupils have been attending have been centralized, and transporation provided for. — *Attorney General*, 1913, p. 1415·

Measurement of the distance pupils must travel to school along most direct established route: Blue Ash Spec. Dist. (Bd. of Ed.) v. Concord Special Sch. Dist. (Bd. of Ed.), 23 Dec. 698 (11 N. S. 286).

Sufficient school accommodations to be provided.

SECTION 7738. Every board of education in this state must provide sufficient accommodations in the public schools for all children in their districts compelled to attend the public schools under the provisions of this chapter. Authority to levy the tax and raise the money necessary for such purpose, is hereby given the proper officers charged with such duty under the law. (95 v. 622.)

Free school-books.

SECTION 7739. Each board of education may furnish, free of charge, school-books, necessary to enable the parent or guardian, without expense therefor, to comply with the requirements of this chapter, to be paid for out of the contingent fund at its disposal. Such levy each year, in addition if necessary to that otherwise authorized, as may be necessary to furnish such school-books free of charge to all the pupils attending the public schools, is hereby authorized. But pupils wholly or in part supplied with necessary school-books shall be supplied only as other or new books are needed. All school-books furnished as herein provided, shall be the property of the district, and loaned to the pupils on such terms and conditions as each such board prescribes. (91 v. 260.)

Boards of education which furnish free text-books to pupils in the schools under their control may pay the exchange price when making an exchange of text-books; but it is unlawful to do so when the board has not previously adopted the free text-book plan as provided for by law. — *Attorney General*, Opinion.

This section is constitutional, and does not provide for an unauthorized diversion of the public school funds: Mooney v. Bell, 8 O. N. P. 658.

SECTION 7747. The tuition of pupils who are eligible for admission to high school and who reside in rural districts, in which no high school is maintained, shall be paid by the board of education of the school district in which they have legal school residence, such tuition to be computed by the month. An attendance any part of the month shall create a liability for the entire month. No more shall be charged per capita than the amount ascertained by dividing the total exepnses of conducting the high school of the district attended, exclusive of permanent improvements and repair, by the average monthly enrollment in the high school of the district. The district superintendent shall certify to the county superintendent each year the names of all pupils in his supervision district who have completed the elementary school work, and are eligible for admission to high school. The county superintendent shall thereupon issue to each pupil so certified a certificate of promotion which shall entitle the holder to admission to any high school. Such certificates shall be furnished by the superintendent of public instrutcion. (104 v. 125.)

Tuition of pupils eligible to high school shall be paid by district board.

Certificate to pupils eligible to high school.

The provisions of Section 7683 of the General Code, providing for a deduction from the tuition of a non-resident high school pupil, of the amount of school tax paid by such pupil or his parent upon property owned and located within the school district attended, referred to cases where the pupil or parent were themselves chargeable with such tuition.

Said section has no application to Section 7747 of the General Code, under which the board of education of such pupil's residence is now made liable for such tuition.

In this case, therefore, the amount of said school tax may not be deducted. — *Attorney General*, 1912, p. 1421.

Inasmuch as parochial pupils are not pupils of township, special or village districts, they do not come within the terms of sections 7740 and 7744, General Code, providing for the examination of pupils of such district and the presentation of the successful applicants with a diploma which shall entitle its holder to enter any high school in the state.

Under section 7681, General Code, which provides that schools of each district shall be free to all youth of the district, pupils of parochial schools are entitled to admission into the high school of the city in which they live, upon compliance with such examination requirements as the school authorities may provide.— *Attorney General*, 1913, p. 458.

1st. A township board of education is not liable for the tuition of a student who passes a Boxwell examination and receives her grades but did not take part in the county commencement as required by law, and received no diploma.

2d. A township board of education maintaining a third grade high school is not legally liable for the payment of the tuition of a Boxwell-Patterson graduate, holding a diploma as such for a period of two years at a first grade high school, and who is not a graduate from a third grade high school maintained by the township school district wherein such pupil resides. — *Attorney General*, Opinion No. 844, 1914.

Section 7748, General Code, providing for the transportation, by the board of education, of pupils who are required to go to school more than four miles distant from the pupil's residence, in lieu of the payment of tuition at a nearer school in another district, by said board, does not have any application to village and city boards of education, but only to boards of education of rural districts. — *Attorney General*, Opinion No. 1062, 1914.

A township board of education not maintaining a high school is not required to pay the tuition of a Boxwell-Patterson graduate who received a diploma from said township board of education, who has moved with his parents into a village school district, provided his parents have an actual residence in such village. The mere fact that the father of the pupil holds a voting residence in the township, if he has an actual residence in the village would not require the township to pay the tuition. — *Attorney General*, Opinion No. 962, May 28, 1914.

Tuition of graduates of third grade high school.	SECTION 7748. A board of education providing a third grade high school as defined by law shall be required to pay the tuition of graduates from such school residing in the district at any first grade high school for two years, or at a second grade high school for one year. Should pupils residing in the district prefer not to attend such third grade high school the board of education of such district shall be required to pay the tuition of such pupils at any first grade high school for four years, or at any second grade high school for three years and a first grade high school for one year. Such a board providing a second grade high school as defined by law shall pay the tuition of graduates residing in the district at any first grade high
Exception.	school for one year; except that, a board maintaining a second or third grade high school is not required to pay such tuition when the maximum levy permitted by law for such district has been reached and all the funds so raised are necessary for the support of the schools of such district. No board of education is required to pay the tuition of any pupil for more than four school years; except that it must pay the tuition of all successful applicants, who have complied with the further provisions hereof, residing more than four miles by the most direct route of public travel, from the high school provided by the board, when such applicants attend a nearer high school, or in lieu of paying such tuition
Provision for transportation of pupils.	the board of education maintaining a high school may pay for the transportation of the pupils living more than four miles from the said high school, maintained by the said board of education to said high school. Where more than one high school is maintained, by agreement of the board and parent or guardian, pupils may attend either and their transportation shall be so paid. A pupil living in a village
Effect of removal from village or city district.	or city district who has completed the elementary school course and whose legal residence has been transferred to a rural district in this state before he begins or completes a high school course, shall be entitled to all the rights and privileges of a resident pupil of such district. (104 v. 125.)

Under 4716, General Code, a board of education of a township may consolidate two school subdistricts into one and there are no statutory provisions enabling the people of such subdistricts to object to or prevent such action.

When such consolidation is carried out, the board is not required by the statutes to provide transportation for pupils attending the consolidated school. — *Attorney General*, 1912, p. 497.

A Board of Education is not to be denied State Aid by reason of the fact that it pays authorized expenses other than teachers' salaries out of the tuition fund, such as Superintendent's salary and institute fees.

The amount of State Aid allowed, however, shall not exceed such sum as is necessary to make teachers' salaries equal to $40.00 per month. — *Attorney General*, 1912, p. 98.

The provisions of Section 7683 of the General Code, providing for a deduction from the tuition of a non-resident high school pupil, of the amount of school tax paid by such pupil or his parent upon property owned and located within the school district attended, referred to cases where the pupil or parent were themselves chargeable with such tuition.

Said section has no application to Sections 7747 of the General Code, under which the board of education of such pupil's residence is now made liable for such tuition.

In this case, therefore, the amount of said school tax may not be deducted. — *Attorney General*, 1912, p. 1421.

1st. A township board of education is not liable for the tuition of a student who passes a Boxwell examination and receives her grades but did not take part in the county commencement as required by law, and received no diploma.

2d. A township board of education maintaining a third grade high school is not legally liable for the payment of the tuition of a Boxwell-Patterson graduate, holding a diploma as such for a period of two years at a first grade high school, and who is not a graduate from a third grade high school maintained by the township school district wherein such pupil resides. — *Attorney General*, Opinion No. 844, 1914.

When a pupil resides five miles from any high school and has a high school in its district no closer than five miles, and no high school in any district nearer than five miles, free transportation to such high school may be furnished by the board of education when the nearest high school is its own high school. The board of education cannot under any circumstances furnish transportation to such pupil to any high school except its own. — *Attorney General*, Opinion No. 824, 1914.

A board of education of a special school district, through its truant officer, can compel pupils of a special school district who reside more than one and one-half miles from the school in such special district to attend school of such district, without providing conveyance therefor, provided that such pupils are within the age limitation fixed by Section 7763 of the General Code, and provided they are not excused from attending school in the manner provided by said section. — *Attorney General*, Opinion No. 744, 1914.

Section 7748, General Code, providing for the transportation, by the board of education, of pupils who are required to go to school more than four miles distant from the pupil's residence, in lieu of the payment of tuition at a nearer school in another district, by said Board, does not have any application to village and city Boards of Education, but only to Boards of Education of rural districts. — *Attorney General*, Opinion No. 1062, July 20, 1914.

SECTION 7749. When the elementary schools of any rural school district in which a high school is maintained are centralized and transportation of pupils is provided, all pupils resident of the rural school district who have completed the elementary school work shall be entitled to transportation to the high school of such rural district, and the board of education thereof shall be exempt from the pay-

Transportation to high school.

ment of the tuition of such pupils in any other high school for such a portion of four years as the course of study in the high school maintained by the board of education includes. (104 v. 125.)

Under section 4716, General Code, a board of education of a township may consolidate two school subdistricts into one and there are no statutory provisions enabling the people of such subdistricts to object to or prevent such action.

When such consolidation is carried out, the board is not required by the statutes to provide transportation for pupils attending the consolidated school. — *Attorney General,* 1912, p. 497.

A village board of education is not authorized to make expenditures for the conveyance of its high school pupils to a neighobring district upon abandonment of its high school.

Such board may not include, in a tuition contract with neighboring boards of education, a provision for conveyance of high school pupils to and from such district. — *Attorney General,* 1911-12, p. 1246.

When a township board of education maintains a third grade high school, such board is in no sense liable for tuition of pupils at other high schools of higher grade, when such pupils are not graduates of the said third grade local high school — *Attorney General,* 1911-12, p. 1257.

When the board of education of Madison township has made no agreement with another board of education for attendance of Madison township pupils at a high school in the same or an adjoining township, the board of said Madison township can be compelled to pay a "reasonable sum" for the tuition of its pupils to the board whose high school said pupils elect to attend, provided notice is served by said pupils on the Madison board at least five days previous to the date of attendance. — *Attorney General,* 1911-12, p. 1129.

Agreement, effect of, as to tuition.

SECTION 7750. A board of education not having a high school may enter into an agreement with one or more boards of education maintaining such school for the schooling of all its high school pupils. When such agreement is made the board making it shall be exempt from the payment of tuition at other high schools of pupils living within three miles of the school designated in the agreement, if the school or schools selected by the board are located in the same civil township, as that of the board making it, or some adjoining township. In case no such agreement is entered into, the school to be attended can be selected by the pupil holding a diploma, if due notice in writing is given to the clerk of the board of education of the name of the school to be attended and the date the attendance is to begin, such notice to be filed not less than five days previous to the beginning of attendance. (100 v. 74.)

Under section 7750, General Code, a board of education, by entering into a contract for the education of such graduates, may be exempted from paying the tuition of pupils residing within three miles of the school designated in the agreement, when such school is located in the same or some adjoining township. Under the same statute, if no such agreement is made, a pupil selecting his own school is entitled to have his tuition paid only upon his giving notice to the board of education of his residence as therein provided. The terms of such statute, however, do not require such notice of pupils residing outside of three miles of the school designated by a contract agreement made by the board of education. — *Attorney General*, 1913, p. 1205.

When a township board of education maintains a third grade high school, such board is in no sense liable for tuition of pupils at other high schools of higher grade, when such pupils are not graduates of the said third grade local high school. — *Attorney General*, 1911-12, p. 1257.

The constitutional guaranty of an efficient system of common schools throughout the state does not, in the absence of specific statutory provision therefor, require boards of education to pay the tuition of pupils who wish to attend a high school outside of such school district: Ashland Township v. Montgomery Township, 10 O. D. (N. P.) 459.

An action brought under this section to recover tuition may be brought by the school district which such pupils have attended, and it may be against the school district from which such pupils have come: and it is not necessary that the pupils or their parents be made parties to such action: School District v. Harrison Township, 14 O. D. (N. P.) 62.

SECTION 7751. Such tuition shall be paid from either the tuition or contingent funds and when the board of education deems it necessary it may levy a tax of not to exceed two mills on each dollar of taxable property in the district in excess of that allowed by law for school purposes. The proceeds of such levy shall be kept in a separate fund and applied only to the payment of such tuition. (100 v. 74.)

Tuition, how paid.

The board of education has no authority in law to rent a school building, or part thereof, to a secret society for the purpose of holding lodge sessions and such social functions and entertainments of such society as are not open to all persons in the community on equal terms or which will not, in the judgment of the board of education, benefit the people of the community. — *Attorney General*, Opinion No. 197, April 3, 1915.

Section 7592, G. C. is no longer in force and no levy outside the five mill limitation of the Smith Law can be made thereunder.

Section 7751 G. C. cannot be so interpreted as to permit a levy thereunder outside of the five mill limitation of the Smith Law.

The opinion of the Attorney General to the Auditor of State under date of February 26, 1912, relative to the application of the law for state aid to weak school districts concurred in, but limited to its application to the said law as it then existed.

Opinion of the Attorney General to the Auditor of State relative to the joint operation of the law for state aid to weak school districts and the Smith One Per Cent Law, found in Vol. I, Annual Report of the Attorney General, 1912, page 89, modified Ib, p. 108, concurred in and followed, subject to the qualification that a Board of Education which has submitted a budget estimate requiring the levy of taxes to the full extent of any absolute limitation of the Smith law, such as five mill limitation of Section 5649-3a, G. C., should not be held to have disqualified the district to receive state aid, if such amount is insufficient to operate the schools in accordance with the provisions of the State Aid law. — *Attorney General*, Opinion, No. 179, 1915.

SECTION 7752. No board of education shall be entitled to collect tuition under this chapter unless it is maintaining a regularly organized high school with a course of study extending over not less than two years and consisting mainly of branches higher than those in which the pupil is examined. The standing or grade of all public high schools in the state shall be determined by the superintendent of public instruction and his finding in reference thereto shall be final. (104 v. 225.)

What shall constitute a high school.

Appointment of high school inspectors.

SECTION 7753. The superintendent of public instruction shall appoint two competent public high school inspectors, who are connected with no college or university, two public high school inspectors selected from the faculty staff of the college of education of Ohio State University, and one public high school inspector from each of the faculties of the Ohio normal colleges at Oxford and Athens and the Ohio normal schools at Kent and Bowling Green. The inspectors appointed by the superintendent of public instruction from the faculty staffs of the college of education, normal colleges and normal schools shall be nominated by the presidents of their respective institutions. The superintendent of public instruction may also appoint when necessary, competent instructors from any public or private school to inspect such high schools as the superintendent may direct. (104 v. 173.)

Duties of high school inspectors.

SECTION 7753-1. The two public high school inspectors connected with no college or university shall give their entire time to the examination and inspection of public high schools in the state. The inspectors chosen from the faculty staffs shall devote a part of their time, not more than half, to public high school inspection. The superintendent of public instruction shall require all part time inspectors to inspect schools the first half of the year beginning August 1, or the last half of the year beginning February 1, or such other times as may be agreed by the superintendent of public instruction and the president of the institution nominating such inspector. The public high school inspectors shall confer with various authorities and assist the superintendent of public instruction in the classification of schools and in such other ways as he may direct. (104 v. 173.)

Meeting for conference and direction: classification.

SECTION 7753-2. All public high school inspectors shall meet in Columbus at the call of the superintendent of public instruction for the purpose of conference and direction. They shall recommend to the superintendent of public instruction standards and official ratings for all the public high schools of the state, and the decision of the superintendent of public instruction as to the classification of such schools shall be final, but no public high school shall be recommended for rating except on a majority vote of the inspectors at a meeting called by the superintendent of public instruction who shall be ex-officio chairman of their meetings. (104 v. 173.)

Compensation and expenses.

SECTION 7753-3. The high school inspectors giving full time shall be paid an annual salary, the amount of which shall be fixed by the superintendent of public instruction with the approval of the governor, and shall each receive his actual and necessary traveling expenses not to exceed eight hundred dollars per year. The half time inspectors shall receive a compensation, the amount of which shall be fixed by the superintendent of public instruction, and shall also receive their necessary and actual traveling expenses not to exceed four hundred dollars each, for each half year. Both compensation and expenses shall be paid upon vouchers signed by the superintendent of public instruction. (104 v. 173.)

SECTION 7754. All public high school inspectors appointed by the superintendent of public instruction shall furnish reports of all inspection of public high schools made by them. The reports shall be in such form as the superintendent of public instruction may prescribe. Eight copies of the report of each inspection shall be made. Two copies shall be placed on file in the office of the superintendent of public instruction, one copy furnished to each of the institutions from which the half time inspectors are chosen, and one copy furnished to the school inspected. (104 v. 173.)

Reports of inspection.

SECTION 7755. Upon application by a board of education of any school district in Ohio to the superintendent of public instrutcion he shall grant permission to such board and it may thereupon establish and maintain within its limits one or more day schools at an average attendance of not less than three pupils for the instruction of deaf persons, residents of this state, over the age of three, for the instructions of blind persons, residents of this state, over the age of four, and of crippled persons, residents of this state, over the age of five. (103 v. 270.)

Establishment of schools for education of the deaf, blind and crippled.

SECTION 7756. A board of education which maintains one or more day schools for the instruction of the deaf, crippled or blind persons shall report to the superintendent of public instruction annually, and as often as such superintendent directs such facts concerning such school or schools as he requires. (104 v. 225.)

Report of school for deaf, blind, and crippled, to superintendent.

SECTION 7757. At the close of each school year each board of education of the school district in which such schools for the education of the deaf, crippled or blind shall be established and maintained, shall certify to the auditor of state the number of pupils given instructions in said schools during the preceding school year and thereupon the auditor of state shall draw his warrant upon the treasurer of state in favor of such board of education, payable out of the general state fund in an amount equal to $150.00 for each deaf or crippled pupil given instruction in such schools within said district for nine months during said school year, and a proportionate amount for each deaf or crippled pupil given instructions therein for a part of said school year less than nine months, and the sum of $200. for each blind pupil given instruction in such schools within such district for nine months during said school year, and a proportionate

How expense of schools defrayed.

amount for each blind pupil given instruction therein for a part of said school year less than nine months. (103 v. 270.)

A school district receiving permission, prior to 1913, to maintain a school for the deaf, is entitled, without further permission, to maintain such school and to receive from the state treasury the sum of one hundred and fifty ($150.00) dollars for each deaf pupil taught in such school during the year ending August, 1914. — *Attorney General,* Opinion No. 8, 1915.

Payment by state treasurer. SECTION 7758. The sums provided in the next preceding section shall be paid by such state treasurer upon the presentation of such warrant or order upon satisfactory proof made to him by the president or clerk of the board of education maintaining such school, of the number of pupils instructed therein, their residence, and the period of time such pupils were so instructed in such school or schools the preceding school year. (103 v. 270.)

Appointment and qualification of teachers. SECTION 7759. Teachers in such schools shall be appointed and employed as are other public school teachers. They shall possess the usual qualifications required of teachers in the public schools, and in addition thereto such special training and equipment as the board of education may require. The so called oral system shall be taught by such teachers in schools for the deaf. If, after a fair trial of nine months, any of such children in any school for the deaf for any reason is unable to learn such method, then they may be taught the manual method in a separate school, providing however that there are not fewer pupils than provided in Sec. 7755 of the General Code. (103 v. 270.)

Who considered deaf, blind or crippled. SECTION 7760. For the purpose hereof, any person of sound mind who, by reason of defective hearing or defective vision, or so crippled as to be physicially unable to care for himself without assistance, cannot profitably be educated in the public schools as other children, shall be considered as deaf, blind, or crippled and after the establishment of any such school by any school district, may be compelled to attend such school or a state institution. (103 v. 270.)

Inspection of schools for deaf, etc. SECTION 7761. The superintendent of public instruction shall select some competent person to inspect all such day schools established by virture of this act, and cause inspection to be made at least twice a year concerning the methods of instruction, the condition of the buildings in which the same are held, the conditions under which such schools are maintained, and such other matters as may be of interest in the education of such children in such schools; and such persons so appointed shall make full report thereof in writing to the state superintendent of public instruction at the close of each school year. (104 v. 225.)

CHAPTER 3a.

TEACHING OF AGRICULTURE.

SECTION 7761-1. Agriculture shall hereafter be taught in all the common schools of all village and rural school districts of the state of Ohio, which are supported in whole or in part by the state, and may be taught in city school districts at the option of the board of education. Such agricultural instruction in each county district shall be under the 'general supervision of the county superintendent of schools. (106 v. 111.)

Teaching of agriculture in public schools; supervisor.

Branches children must be taught. SECTION 7762. All parents, guardians and other persons who have care of children, shall instruct them, or cause them to be instructed in reading, spelling, writing, English grammar, geopraphy and arithmetic. (95 v. 615.)

It is the duty of all truant officers to use legal procedure if that is necessary to force and compel school attendance on the part of all boys and girls who come within the provisions of Sections 7770 and 7771, General Code, as amended in 103, O. L. 903, regardless of the grade of school that they should attend or would attend if they properly attended school. — *Attorney General*, Opinion No. 721, 1914.

Under Section 7773 of the General Code, it is the duty of every parent, guardian or other person in charge of children between fourteen and sixteen years of age to cause such children to attend some recognized school. If such parent, guardian or other person in charge of such children fail to do this they neglect to perform a duty imposed upon them by law relating to compulsory education, and consequently violate this section. — *Attorney General*, 1913, p. 1588.

Under Section 7766, General Code, the superintendent of schools or the person authorized by him when the parent so demands, is legally bound, if all the conditions imposed by said section are complied with to issue the age and schooling certificate therein provided to a child, upon satisfactory proof that such child is over fourteen years of age and passed a satisfactory fifth grade test in the studies enumerated in Section 7762 and is engaged in some regular employment, unless a "reasonable doubt exists in the mind of the superintendent or the person authorized by him that the child had not reached the normal development of a child of its age and is not in sound health and physically able to perform the work which it intends to do." If such doubt exists, the parent or guardian must be required to procure a certificate from the board of health showing that the child is able to perform the work he is to be employed at. — *Attorney General*, 1912, p. 500.

A parent who sends his child to a public school and is willing to continue to do so, but the child is excluded for failure to comply with a rule of the board of education requiring vaccination, is not liable to conviction under the compulsory education act: State v. Turney, 12 O. C. C. (N. S.) 33.

SECTION 7763. Every parent, guardian or other person **School** having charge of any child between the ages of eight and **attendance.** fifteen years of age if a male, and sixteen years of age, if a female, must send such child to a public, private or parochial school, for the full time that the school attended is in session, which shall in no case be for less than twenty-eight weeks. Such attendance must begin within the first week of the school term, unless the child is excused therefrom by the superintendent of the public schools, or by the principal of the private or parochial school, upon satisfactory showing either that the bodily or mental condition of the child does not permit of its attendance at school, or that the child is being instructed at home by a person qualified, in the opinion of such superintendent or clerk, as the case may be, to teach the branches named in the next preceding section. (104 v. 225.)

It is the duty of all truant officers to use legal procedure if that is necessary to force and compel school attendance on the part of all boys and girls who come within the provisions of Sections 7770 and 7771, General Code, as amended in 103, O. L. 903, regardless of the grade of school that they should attend or would attend if they properly attended school. —*Attorney General,* Opinion No. 721, 1914.

Under Section 7773 of the General Code, it is the duty of every parent, guardian or other person in charge of children between fourteen and sixteen years of age to cause such children to attend some recognized school. If such parent, guardian or other person in charge of such children fail to do this they neglect to perform a duty imposed upon them by law relating to compulsory education, and consequently violate this section. — *Attorney General,* 1913, p. 1588.

By virtue of Section 4750, General Code, the board of education may pass rules and regulations for the government of its pupils, and the right of the board to suspend pupils for violation of such rules, subject to the restrictions of Section 7685, General Code.

When, therefore, a pupil has partaken in a proceeding in which a teacher was hung in effigy, the board may suspend such pupil by a two-thirds vote, for a reasonable time not exceeding the limit of the current school year, after permitting the parent or guardian of the offender to be heard.

The board may further offer to lift said suspension upon the signing of an apology by the culprit.

The board has no control over other than pupils or employes. — *Attorney General,* 1912, p. 1214.

Under Sections 7763, 12977 and 12978 of the General Code, the parent if able so to do is bound to see to the education of his child and must provide the latter with books, or be subjected to the penalty provided by section 1655 of the General Code. — *Attorney General,* 1913, p. 1292.

A board of education of a special school district, through its truant officer, can compel pupils of a special school district who reside more than one and one-half miles from the school in such special district to attend school of such district, without providing conveyance therefor, provided that such pupils are within the age limitation fixed by Section 7763 of the General Code, and provided they are not excused from attending school in the manner provided by said section. — *Attorney General,* Opinion No. 744, 1914.

Appeal in
case of
refusal to
excuse.

SECTION 7764. In case such superintendent, principal or clerk refuses to excuse a child from attendance at school, an appeal may be taken from such decision to the judge of the juvenile court of the county, upon the giving of a bond, within ten days thereafter, to the approval of such judge, to pay the costs of the appeal. His decision in the matter shall be final. All children between the ages of fifteen and sixteen years, not engaged in some regular employment, shall attend school for the full term the schools of the district in which they reside are in session during the school year, unless excused for the reasons above named. (103 v. 864.)

It is the duty of all truant officers to use legal procedure if that is necessary to force and compel school attendance on the part of all boys and girls who come within the provisions of Sections 7770 and 7771, General Code, as amended in 103, O. L. 903, regardless of the grade of school that they should attend or would attend if they properly attended school. — *Attorney General,* Opinion No. 721., 1914.

Under Section 7773 of the General Code, it is the duty of every parent, guardian or other person in charge of children between fourteen and sixteen years of age to cause such children to attend some recognized school. If such parent, guardian or other person in charge of such children fail to do this they neglect to perform a duty imposed upon them by law relating to compulsory education, and consequently violate this section. — *Attorney General,* 1913, p. 1588.

By virtue of Section 4750, General Code, the board of education may pass rules and regulations' for the government of its pupils, and the right of the board to suspend pupils for violation of such rules, subject to the restrictions of Section 7685, General Code.

When, therefore, a pupil has partaken in a proceeding in which a teacher was hung in effigy, the board may suspend such pupil by a two-thirds vote, for a reasonable time not exceeding the limit of the current school year, after permitting the parent or guardian of the offender to be heard.

The board may further offer to lift said suspension upon the signing of an apology by the culprit.

The board has no control over other than pupils or employes. — *Attorney General,* 1912, p. 1214.

Age and
school cer-
tificates of
girls and
boys em-
ployed.

Sec. 7765. No boy under sixteen years of age and no girl under eighteen years of age shall be employed or be in the employment of any person, company or corporation unless such child presents to such person, company or corporation an age and school certificate herein provided for, as a condition of employment. Such employer shall keep the same on file in the establishment where such minor is employed for inspection by the truant officer or officers of the department of workshops and factories. (103 v. 864.)

Under Section 7773 of the General Code, it is the duty of every parent, guardian or other person in charge of children between fourteen and sixteen years of age to cause such children to attend some recognized school. If such parent, guardian or other person in charge of such children fail to do this they neglect to perform a duty imposed upon them by law relating to compulsory education, and consequently violate this section. — *Attorney General,* 1913, p. 1588.

The history of the statute and its process of codification make clear that the words "as provided by law" in Section 12994, General Code, providing a penalty for employing children between fourten and sixteen years of age without schooling certificate "provided by law," refer to Section 7765 and Section 7766, General Code, which require the certificate only for employment during the school term.

Such a construction harmonizes the statutes and is in keeping with the undoubted legislative intent to prevent child labor only insofar as it interferes with schooling. — *Attorney General,* 1912, p. 899.

Under the provisions of the act of April 28th, 103 O. L. 914, girls over sixteen and under eighteen years of age may labor at employments not prohibited by law, providing they can pass a satisfactory educational test. It is not the intention of the legislature to permit them to remain out of school and not labor. The insertion of the words "over eighteen" in section 7766, is a mistake; it was intended that it should be "over sixteen." With this construction the law becomes operative. — *Attorney General,* 1913, p. 938.

It is the duty of the board of education to provide for relief out of its contingent fund for any boy under fifteen years of age and any girl under sixteen years of age, who is unable to attend school because absolutely required to work at home or elsewhere in order to support himself or herself or help to support or care for others who are unable to support or care for themselves, upon the report of the truant officer that he is satisfied of such necessity. — *Attorney General,* Opinion No. 1294, 1914.

SECTION 7766. An age and schooling certificate shall be approved only by the superintendent of schools, or by a person authorized by him, or, in case of vacancy in the office of superintendent, by the clerk of the board of education, upon satisfactory proof that such child, if a male, is over fifteen years of age, or, if a female, is over sixteen years of age and that such child has been examined and passed a satisfactory sixth-grade test, if a male, a seventh-grade test, if a female, in the studies enumerated in section seventy-seven hundred and sixty-two, provided, that residents of other states who work in Ohio must qualify as aforesaid with the proper school authority in the school district in which the establishment is located, as a condition of employment or service, and that the employment contemplated by the child is not prohibited by any law regulating the employment of such children. Every such age and schooling certificate shall be signed in the presence of the offices issuing the same by the child in whose name it is issued.

Approval of certificate.

In order to ascertain whether applicants for such certificates have satisfactorily completed the studies herein prescribed as a condition for the issuance of said certificates the board of education of each city school district may appoint a juvenile examiner who shall receive such compensation as may be fixed by the board of education. No such child residing in a city shall be granted such certificate unless such juvenile examiner shall have previously certified that he has examined such child and that he has passed to his satisfaction the grade test as provided by this section; provided, further, that if a child in the opinion

Juvenile examiner; duties and compensation.

of said juvenile examiner is below the normal in mental development so that he cannot with due industry pass such test, and if the school record shows that such child is below the normal in development, such fact may be certified to by said examiner, and the superintendent or person authorized by him may at his discretion grant such child such age and schooling certificate. Provided, that if said examiner is satisfied that the standard of any school is sufficiently high, he may accept the records thereof as showing that such child has passed such test without further examination.

Form of certificate.

The age and schooling certificate must be formulated by the superintendent of public instruction, and furnished in blank by the clerk of the board of education. It shall show the date of its issue. A record giving all the facts contained on every certificate issued shall be kept on file in the office issuing the same, and also a record of the names and addresses of the children to whom certificates have been refused, together with the names of the schools which such children should attend and the reasons for refusal.

List to whom certificates issued furnished industrial commission.

The superintendent of schools of other persons authorized to issue employment certificates shall transmit between the first and tenth days of each month, to the office of the industrial commission, upon blanks to be furnished by it, a list of the names of the children to whom certificates have been issued, returned or refused. Such lists shall give the name and address of the prospective employer and the nature of the occupation the child intends to engage in.

Child shall be placed in school who ceases to work.

Any child between fifteen and sixteen years of age, who shall cease to work for any cause whatever, shall report the fact and cause at once to the superintendent of schools; or to a person authorized by him or, in case there is a vacancy in the office of superintendent, to the clerk of the board of education; said child shall be required to return to school within two weeks, provided other employment is not secured within such time: provided that, should a child in the opinion of the superintendent or person acting in his stead, lose his employment by reason of persistent, wilful misconduct or continuous inconstancy, he may be placed in school until the close of the current school year.

Papers to be approved and filed before certificate issued.

The superintendent of schools or the person authorized by him to issue age and schooling certificates, shall not issue such certificates until he has received, examined, approved and filed the following papers duly executed.

Pledge of employer.

(1) The written pledge or promise of the person, partnership, or corporation to legally employ the child also the written agreement to return to the superintendent of schools or to the person authorized by him to issue such certificates, the age and schooling certificate of the child within two days from the date of the child's withdrawal or dismissal from the service of the person, partnership, or corporation, giving the reason for such withdrawal or dismissal.

(2 The school record of such child, properly filled out and signed by the principal or other person in charge of the school with such child last attended, giving the name, age, address, standing in studies enumerated in section seven thousand seven hundred and sixty-two, and the number of weeks attendance in school during the school year previous to applying for such school record, and general conduct. School record.

(3) As evidence of age (a) a passport or duly attested transcript of a passport, filed with a register of passports or other officer charged with the duty of registering passports at the several ports of entry to the United States; or duly attested transcript of the certificate of birth or baptism or other religious record, showing the date and place of birth of such child; or (b) a duly attested transcript of the birth certificate filed according to law with a registrar of vital statistics, or other officer charged with the duty of recording births, shall be conclusive evidence of the age of the child. (c) In case none of the above proofs of age can be produced, other documentary evidence of age which shall appear to be satisfactory to the officer issuing the certificate, (aside from the school record of such child or the affidavit of parent, guardian or custodian), may be accepted in lieu thereof. In such case a school census or enumeration record, duly attested, may be used as proof of age in the discretion of the officer issuing the certificate. (d) In case no documentary proof of age of any kind can be procured, the officer issuing the certificate may receive and file an application signed by the parent, guardian or custodian of the child for a physician's certificate. Such application shall contain the name, alleged age, place and date of birth, and present residence of the child, together with such further facts as may be of assistance in determining the age of such child, and shall contain a statement certifying that the parent, guardian or custodian signing such application is unable to produce any of the documentary proofs of age specified in the preceding subdivisions of this section. If the superintendent of officer authorized by him to issue such certificate, is satisfied that a reasonable effort to procure such documentary proof has been made, the certificate of the school physician, or, if there be none, of a physician employed for the purpose by the board of education that such physician has made a physical examination of such child and is satisfied that he is more than fifteen years of age, if a male or that she is more than sixteen years of age, if a female shall be accepted as sufficient proof of the age of such child for the purpose of this act: Birth certificate.

Application in case no documentary proof.

(4) A certificate from the school physician or if there should be none, of the board of health, and if there be no board of health, within the school district in question, from a licensed physician appointed by the board of education showing that the child is physically fit to be employed in any of the occupations permitted by law for Health certificate.

a child between fifteen and sixteen years of age. Provided that if the records of the school physician show such child to have been previously sound in health, no further physician's certificate need be required, but the officer authorized to issue such certificate may at his discretion require such physican's certificate in any case, as a condition to the issuing of an age and schooling certificate.

The superintendent or person authorized by him may issue special vacation certificates to boys under sixteen years of age and girls under eighteen years of age, which shall entitle the holders thereof to be employed during vacation in occupations not forbidden by law to such children even though such child may not have completed the sixth grade, but provided he has complied with all the other requirements for obtaining the certificate hereinbefore described. (104 v. 129.)

Under Section 7766, General Code, the superintendent of schools or the person authorized by him when the parent so demands, is legally bound, if all the conditions imposed by said section are complied with to issue the age and schooling certificate therein provided to a child, upon satisfactory proof that such child is over fourteen years of age and passed a satisfactory fifth grade test in the studies enumerated in Section 7762 and is engaged in some regular employment, unless a "reasonable doubt exists in the mind of the superintendent or the person authorized by him that the child had not reached the normal development of a child of its age and is not in sound health and physically able to perform the work which it intends to do." If such doubt exists, the parent or guardian must be required to procure a certificate from the board of health showing that the child is able to perform the work he is to be employed at. — *Attorney General*, 1912, p. 500.

The history of the statute and its process of codification make clear that the words "as provided by law" in Section 12994, General Code, providing a penalty for employing children between fourteen and sixteen years of age without schooling certificate "provided by law," refer to Section 7765 and Section 7766, General Code, which require the certificate only for employment during the school term.

Such a construction harmonizes the statutes and is in keeping with the undoubted legislative intent to prevent child labor only insofar as it interferes with schooling. — *Attorney General*, 1912, p. 899.

Under the provisions of the act of April 28th, 103 O. L. 914, girls over sixteen and under eighteen years of age may labor at employments not prohibited by law, providing they can pass a satisfactory educational test. It is not the intention of the legislature to permit them to remain out of school and not labor. The insertion of the words "over eighteen" in section 7766, is a mistake; it was intended that it should be "over sixteen." With this construction the law becomes operative. — *Attorney General*, 1913, p. 938.

It is the duty of the board of education to provide for relief out of its contingent fund for any boy under fifteen years of age and any girl under sixteen years of age, who is unable to attend school because absolutely required to work at home or elsewhere in order to support himself or herself or help to support or care for others who are unable to support or care for themselves, upon the report of the truant officer that he is satisfied of such necessity. — *Attorney General*, Opinion No. 1294, 1914.

SECTION 7767. All minors over the age of fifteen and under the age of sixteen years, who have not passed a satisfactory sixth grade test in the studies enumerated in section seventy-seven hundred and sixty-two, shall attend school as provided in section seventy-seven hundred and sixty-three, and all the provisions thereof shall apply to such minors. *Part time day schools.*

In case the board of education of any school district establishes part time day schools for the instruction of youth over fifteen years of age who are engaged in regular employment, such board of education is authorized to require all youth who have not satisfactory completed the eighth grade of the elementary schools, to continue their schooling until. they are sixteen years of age; provided. however, that such youth if they have been granted age and schooling certificates and are regularly employed, shall be required to attend school not to exceed eight hours a week . between the hours of 8 a. m. and 5 p. m. during the school term. All youth between fifteen and sixteen years of age, who are not employed, shall be required to attend school the full time. ·(103 v. 864.)

SECTION 7768. Every child between the ages of eight and fifteen years, if a male, or between the ages of eight and sixteen years, if a female, and every male child between the ages of fifteen and sixteen years not engaged in some regular employment, who is an habitual truant from school, or who absets itself habitually from school, or who, while in attendance at any public private or parochial school, is incorrigible, vicious or immoral in conduct, or who habitually wanders about the streets and public places during school hours having no business or lawful occupation, or violates any of the provisions of this act, shall be deemed a delinquent child, and shall be subject to the provisions of law relating to delinquent children. (103 v. 864.) *Truants.*

Under Section 7773 of the General Code, it is the duty of every parent, guardian or other person in charge of children between fourteen and sixteen years of age to cause such children to attend some recognized school. If such parent, guardian or other person in charge of such children fail to do this they neglect to perform a duty imposed upon them by law relating to compulsory education, and consequently violate this section. — *Attorney General*, 1913, p. 1588.

SECTION 7769. To aid in the enforcement hereof, truant officers shall be appointed as follows: In city districts the board of education must appoint and employ a truant officer, and may employ such assistants to such truant officer as may be deemed advisable; in village and rural districts the board of education shall appoint a constable or other person as truant officer. The compensation of the truant officer and asistants shall be fixed and paid by the board appointing them. (104 v. 225.) *Truant officers: appointment, compensation.*

Powers of truant officers.

SECTION 7770. The truant officer and assistants shall be vested with police powers, and the authority to serve warrants, and have authority to enter workshops, factories, stores and all other places where children are employed, and do whatever may be necessary, in the way of investigation or otherwise, to enforce this act. He also may take into custody any youth between eight and fifteen years of age, or between fifteen and sixteen years of age when not regularly employed who is not attending school, and shall conduct such youth to the school he has been attending, or which he rightfully should attend. (103 v. 864.)

It is the duty of the board of education to provide for relief out of its contingent fund for any boy under fifteen years of age and any girl under sixteen years of age, who is unable to attend school because absolutely required to work at home or elsewhere in order to support himself or herself or help to support or care for others who are unable to support or care for themselves, upon the report of the truant officer that he is satisfied of such necessity. — *Attorney General,* Opinion No. 1294, 1914.

It is the duty of all truant officers to use legal procedure if that is necessary to force and compel school attendance on the part of all boys and girls who come within the provisions of Sections 7770 and 7771, General Code, as amended in 103, O. L. 903, regardless of the grade of school that they should attend or would attend if they properly attended school. — *Attorney General,* Opinion No. 721, 1914.

Authority of inspectors.

SECTION 6250. The chief and all district inspectors shall have like authority as is vested in the truant officer of a school district, to enforce school attendance of a child found violating the school laws, or he shall make complaint of such violation to such truant officer or the clerk of the board of education in said district. (99 v. 32 § 4.)

Duties of truant officer; record.

SECTION 7771. The truant officer shall institute proceedings against any officer, parent, guardian, person, partnership or corporation violating any provisions of this chapter, and otherwise discharge the duties described therein, and perform such other service as the superintendent of schools or the board of education may deem necessary to preserve the morals and secure the good conduct of school children, and to enforce the provisions of this chapter. The truant officer shall keep on file the name, address and record of all children between the ages of fifteen and sixteen to whom age and schooling certificates have been granted who desire employment, and manufacturers, employers or other persons requiring help of legal age shall have access to such files. The truant officer shall co-operate with the industrial comission in enforcing the conditions and requirements of the child labor laws of Ohio, furnishing upon request such data as he has collected in his reports of children from eight to sixteen years of age and also concerning employers, to the industrial commission and to the superintendent of public instruction. He must keep a. record of his transactions for the inspection and information of the superintendent of schools and the board of education; and make daily reports to the superintendent during the school term in districts having them, and to the clerk of the board of education in districts not having superintendents as often as required by him. Suitable blanks for the use of the truant officer shall be provided by the clerk of the board of education. (104 v. 225.)

Under Section 7773 of the General Code, it is the duty of every parent, guardian or other person in charge of children between fourteen and sixteen years of age to cause such children to attend some recognized school. If such parent, guardian or other person in charge of such children fail to do this they neglect to perform a duty imposed upon them by law relating to compulsory education, and consequently violate this section. — *Attorney General*, 1913, p. 1588.

SECTION 7772. Principals and teachers of all schools, public, private and parochial, shall report to the clerk of the board of education of the city, village or rural district in which the schools are situated, the names, ages and residence of all pupils in attendance at their schools, together with such other facts as said clerk may require in order to facilitate the carrying out of the provisions of this chapter. The clerk shall furnish blanks for such purpose, and such report shall be made during the last week of each month from September to June inclusive of each year. Such principals and teachers also must report to the truant officer, the superintendent of public schools, or the clerk of the board of education, all cases of truancy or incorrigibility in their respective schools as soon after these offenses have been committed as practicable. It shall further be within the power of all principals or teachers in charge of schools, wherever a child in school reaches his or her twelfth year and has not completed the fourth grade work in the studies enumerated in section seventy-seven hundred sixty-two, to relieve such child from pursuing the regular course prescribed, and cause such child to give his entire time to reading, writing, spelling, geography, arithmetic and the use of the English language with as much manual training as opportunity and funds will permit. (104 v. 225.)

Report of teachers to clerks.

Special course.

SECTION 7773. On the request of the superintendent of schools or the board of education or when it otherwise comes to his notice, the truant officer shall examine into any case of truancy within his district, and warn the truant and his parents, guardian or other person in charge, in writing, of the final consequence of truancy if persisted in. When any child between the age of eight and fifteen years, or between the ages of fifteen and sixteen years, in violation of the provisions of this chapter is not regularly employed and is not attending school, the truant officer shall notify the parent, guardian or other person in charge of such child, of the fact, and require such parent, guardian or other person in charge, to cause the child to attend some recognized school within two days from the date of the notice; and it shall be the duty of the parent, guardian or other person in

Notice to parent of truancy of child; complaint.

charge of the child so to cause its attendance at some recognized school. Upon failure to do so, the truant officer shall make complaint against the parent, guardian or other person in charge of the child, in any court of competent jurisdiction in the city, village or rural district in which the offense occurred for such failure. (104 v. 225.)

Under Section 7773 of the General Code, it is the duty of every parent, guardian or other person in charge of children between fourteen and sixteen years of age to cause such children to attend some recognized school. If such parent, guardian or other person in charge of such children fail to do this they neglect to perform a duty imposed upon them by law relating to compulsory education, and consequently violate this section. — *Attorney General*, 1913, p. 1588.

Employing minor without school certificate prohibited.

SECTION 12994. No boy under sixteen years of age and no girl under eighteen years of age shall be employed or permitted to work on or in connection with the establishments mentioned in section 12993 of the General Code, or in the distribution or transmission of merchandise or messages unless such employer first procures from the proper authority the age and scholing certificate provided by law. (103 v. 864.)

Under section 12993, General Code, boys under fifteen and girls under sixteen years of age may not be employed at any kind of employment referred to in said section.

Under section 12994, General Code, it will be necessary for minors to secure a new age and schooling certificate when this law goes into effect.

It is necessary for children who speak a foreign language to pass the same test as a native born person.

Boards of education are not authorized to employ interpreters to examine minors who speak a foreign language and those who cannot take the examination because of this fact will be denied the privilege of working until they have passed the age when a certificate is required. — *Attorney General*, 1913, p. 936.

In the employment of minors where a boy over fifteen years old, or a girl over sixteen years old, attends school, then after school has some employment, the child should not be interfered with in performing such work after school hours, nor should the employer under such circumstances be prosecuted. Under these circumstances such children need no schooling certificate to perform their work. — *Attorney General*, 720 A, 1914.

Filing of certificate.

SECTION 12995. The certificate mentioned in the section 12994 shall be filed in the office of such establishment and shall be produced for inspection upon request therefor by the chief or district inspector of workshops and factories or a truant officer and shall be returned forthwith to the superintendent of schools or other persons legally issuing it, by the person in charge or manager of such establishment upon the termination of the employment of such **Damage on failure to return certificate.** minor. Upon failure on the part of the employer so to return said certificate within two days, the child terminating his employments shall be entitled to recover from such employer in a civil action as damages an amount equal to the wages which he would have earned had he continued in said employment for the period between such termination thereof and the time when such certificate is so returned. If such child at any time fails to appear for work without explanation, the employment shall be deemed within the purposes of this section to have terminated upon the expiration of two days after his so failing to appear. (103 v. 864.)

SECTION 13007-7. It shall be the duty of factory inspectors, truant officers and other officers charged with the enforcement of laws relating to the employment of minors, to make complaints against any person violating any of the provisions of this act and to prosecute the same.

Who shall make complaints for violations.

This shall not be construed as a limitation upon the right of other persons to make and prosecute such complaints. (103 v. 864.)

SECTION 7774. If the parent, guardian or other person in charge of any child, upon complaint for a failure to cause the child to attend a recognized school, proves inability to do so, then he or she must be discharged and thereupon the truant officer shall make complaint that the child is a juvenile disorderly person within the meaning of section seventy-seven hundred and sixty-eight. If such complaint be made before a mayor, justice of the peace, or police judge, it must be certified by such magistrate to the judge of the juvenile court who shall hear the complaint and if he determines that the child is a juvenile disorderly person within the meaning of such section, and if under ten years of age, and eligible for admission thereto he shall commit the child to a children's home, or if not eligible, then to a house of refuge, if there be one in the county, or otherwise committed as provided by law. (103 v. 864.)

Proceedings against disorderly juvenile persons.

SECTION 7776. The expense incurred in the transportation of a child to a juvenile reformatory and the costs in the case in which the order of commitment is made, or the child discharged, or in which judgment is suspended, shall be paid by the county where the offense was committed, after the manner provided in case of commitment to a boy's industrial school. But if for any cause the parent, guardian or other person in charge of a juvenile disorderly person as defined in section seventy-seven hundred and sixty-eight fails to cause such person to attend school, then complaint against such person shall be made, heard and determined in like manner as provided in case the parent proves inability to cause such person to attend school. (95 v. 619.)

Costs.

SECTION 7777. When a truant officer is satisfied that a child, compelled to attend school by the provisions of this chapter, is unable to do so because absolutely required to

Relief to enable child to attend school.

work at home or elsewhere in order to support itself or help to support or care for other legally entitled to its services who are unable to support or care for themselves, such officer must report the case to the president of the board of education. Thereupon he shall furnish text books free of charge, and such other relief as may be necessary to enable the child to attend school for the time each year required by law. The expense incident to furnishing books and relief must be paid from the contingent funds of the school district. Such child shall not be considered or declared a pauper by reason of the acceptance of the relief herein provided for. If the child, or its parents or guardian, refuses or neglects to take advantage of the provisions thus made for its instruction, it may be committed to a children's home or a juvenile reformatory, as provided for in the next three preceding sections. (99 v. 477.)

It is the duty of the board of education to provide for relief out of its contingent fund for any boy under fifteen years of age and any girl under sixteen years of age, who is unable to attend school because absolutely required to work at home or elsewhere in order to support himself or herself or help to support or care for others who are unable to support or care for themselves, upon the report of the truant officer that he is satisfied of such necessity. — *Attorney General*, Opinion No. 1294, 1914.

Deaf and dumb or blind instittutions.

SECTION 7778. The provisions of this chapter shall apply to children entitled under existing statues, to attend school at the institution for the deaf and dumb or the institution for the blind, so far as they are properly enforceable. (95 v. 620.)

Report of truant officers to juvenile court.

SECTION 7779. Annually between the first day of July and the first day of August, truant officers must report to the judge of the juvenile court of their respective counties the names, ages and residences of all such children between the ages of eight and eighteen years, with the names and post-office address of their parents, guardians or the person in charge of them; also a statement whether the parents, guardians or persons in charge of each child are able to educate and are educating the child, or whether the interests of the child will be promoted by sending it to one of the state institutions mentioned. (103 v. 864.)

Proceedings in juvenile court.

SECTION 7780. Upon information thus or otherwise obtained, the judge of the juvenile court may fix a time when he will hear the question whether any such child shall be required to be sent for instruction to one of the state institutions mentioned, and thereupon issue a warrant to the proper truant officer or some other suitable person, to bring the child before him, at his office at the time fixed for the hearing. He also shall issue an order on the parents, guardian or person in charge of the child to appear before him at such hearing, a copy of which order, in writing, must be served personally on the proper person by the truant officer or other person ordered to bring the child before the judge. If, on the hearing, the judge of the juvenile court is satisfied that the child is not being properly educated at home, and will be benefited by attendance at one of the state institutions mentioned, and is a suitable person to receive instructions therein, he may send or commit such child as provided by law. (103 v. 864.)

SECTION 7781. The costs of such hearing, and the *Costs.* transportation of the child to such institution shall be paid by the county after the manner provided, when a child is committed to a state reformatory. Nothing in the next two preceding sections shall require the trustees of either of the state institutions mentioned, to receive any child not a suitable subject to be received and instructed therein, under the laws, rules and regulations governing such institutions. (95 v. 620.)

SECTION 7782. In every case of complaint against a *Notice to board of county visitors.* child involving commitment to a children's home or juvenile reformatory, the board of county visitors may be notified and if so notified, it must-attend and protect the interest of the child on the hearing, as provided by law in regard to the commitment to an industrial or reform school. The order of commitment of the child to a state reformatory may show that the county visitors were so notified and attended the hearing. (103 v. 864.)

SECTION 7783. Boards of education are authorized to *Employment of attorney; compensation.* employ legal counsel to prosecute any case arising under the provisions of this chapter when it deems that necessary. The services of such counsel shall be paid for from the contingent fund of the district. (95 v. 621.)

SECTION 12974. Whoever, being a parent, guardian or *Failure to send child to school.* other person having the care of a child between the age of eight and fourteen years, fails to place such child in a public, private or parochial school at the commencement of the annual school term, in accordance with the law relating to compulsory education and within the time prescribed in such law, shall be fined not less than five dollars nor more than twenty dollars. Upon failure or refusal to pay such fine, said parent, guardian, or other person shall be imprisoned in jail not less than ten days nor more than thirty days. (95 v. 615.)

The intent of this section is to secure the trial of parents charged with having failed to cause their children to attend school, within the district where the offense occurs and the court may insert proper punctuation to give that effect to the section: Grahn v. State, 9 O. D. (N. P.) 816.

A parent who sends his child to a public school and is willing to continue to do so, but the child is excluded for failure to comply with a rule of the board of education requiring vaccination, is not liable to conviction under the compulsory education act: State v. Turney, 12 O. C. C. (N. S.) 33, 21 O. C. D. 222.

Employing certain minors during school session.

SECTION 12976. Whoever employs, during the time a public, private or parochial school is in session in the school district in which such minor resides, a minor over the age of fourteen and under the age of sixteen years who cannot read and write the English language as provided by law; or whoever, employing such minor, fails forthwith to cease such employment upon notice from a truant officer as provided by law, shall be fined not less than twenty-five dollars nor more than fifty dollars. (95 v. 617.)

Violation; penalty.

SECTION 12977. Whoever, being the parent or guardian or other person in charge of a minor between eight and fourteen years of age, or a minor between fourteen and sixteen years of age who has not passed a satisfactory fifth grade test in the studies enumerated in section seventy-seven hundred and sixty-two, or is not regularly employed, upon notice from a truant officer as provided by law, fails to cause such minor to attend a public, private, or parochial school, unless such person proves his inability so to do, shall be fined not less than five dollars nor more than twenty dollars, or the court may in its discretion, require the person so convicted to give a bond in the sum of one hundred dollars, with sureties to the approval of the court, conditioned that he or she will cause the child under his or her charge to attend some recognized school within two days thereafter and to remain at such school during the term prescribed by law; and upon the failure or refusal of any such parent, guardian or other person to pay said fine and costs or furnish said bond according to the order of the court, then said parent, guardian or other person shall be imprisoned in the county jail not less than ten days nor more than thirty days. (101 v. 310.)

Imprisonment.

Under sections 7763, 12977 and 12978 of the General Code, the parent if able so to do is bound to see to the education of his child and must provide the latter with books, or be subjected to the penalty provided by section 1655 of the General Code.— *Attorney General*, 1913, p. 1292.

Person so convicted may give bond.

SECTION 12978. The court may require a person violating the next preceding section to give a bond in the sum of one hundred dollars, with sureties to the approval of the court, conditioned that such person will cause such minor to attend such school within two days thereafter, and remain in attendance therein during the term as provided by law. (95 v. 618.)

SECTION 12979. The truant officer upon a violation of either of the next two preceding sections shall make complaint against a person violating it in any court having jurisdiction in the city, village, township or special school dstrict in which such violation occurred. (95 v. 618.) Duty of truant officer.

SECTION 12980. Whoever, being a parent, guardian, or other person convicted of a violation of sections twelve thousand nine hundred and seventy-seven or twelve thousand nine hundred and seventy-eight, fails or refuses to pay the fine and costs, or furnish the bond provided therein, shall be imprisoned in the county jail not less than ten days nor more than thirty days. (95 v. 618.) Failure to pay fine.

SECTION 12981. Whoever, being an officer, principal, teacher, or other person, neglects to perform a duty imposed upon him by the laws relating to compulsory education or employment of minors, for which a specific penalty is not provided by law, shall be fined not less than twenty-five dolars nor more than fifty dollars for each offense. (95 v. 621.) Violating compulsory education laws.

SECTION 12982. Whoever, being an afficer or agent of a corporation, violates any provision of law relating to the compulsory education or employment of minors, or participates or acquiesces in, or is cognizant of such violation, where a specific penalty is not otherwise provided by law, shall be fined not less than twenty-five dollars nor more than fifty dollars. (95 v. 621.) Same.

SECTION 12983. Whoever violates any provision of law relating to the compulsory education or employment of minors, for which a specific penalty is not provided by law, shall be fined not more than fifty dollars. (95 v. 621.) Same.

SECTION 12984. Mayors, justices of the peace. police judges and probate judges shall have final jurisdiction to try the offenses prescribed in the next ten preceding sections. When complaint is made, information filed, or indictment found against a corporation for violating any provision of such sections, summons shall be served. appearance made. or plea entered as provided by law in cases where an indictment is presented against a corporation, except in complaints before magistrates, when service may be made by the constable. In other cases process shall be served and proceedings had as in cases of misdemeanor. (95 v. 621.) Jurisdiction of mayors et. al.

SECTION 12985. Fines collected under the provisions of the next eleven preceding sections shall be paid into the funds of the school district in which the offense was committed. (95 v. 621.) Fines.

19 S. L.

Second violation of compulsory education or employment laws.

SECTION 12986. Whoever, having been convicted of a violation of any provision of law relating to the compulsory education or employment of minors, again violates a provision of such laws, shall be imprisoned not less than ten days nor more than thirty days. (95 v. 622.)

Jury in such case.

SECTION 12987. On complaint before a mayor, justice of the peace or police judge of a second or further violation of the laws relating to the compulsory education or employment of minors, if a trial by jury is not waived, a jury shall be chosen and proceedings had therein as provided by law in cases of a violation of the law for the prevention of cruelty to animals and children. (95 v. 622.)

Costs in certain prosecutions.

SECTION 12988. No person or officer instituting proceedings under the next fourteen preceding sections shall be required to file or give security for costs. If a defendant is acquitted or discharged, or if convicted and committed to jail in default of payment of fine and costs, the justice, mayor, police judge or probate judge before whom such case was brought shall certify such costs to the county auditor, who shall examine the amount and, if necessary, correct it and issue his warrant to the county treasurer in favor of the respective persons to whom such costs are due for the amount due to each. (95 v. 622.)

Certificate as prima facie evidence.

SECTION 13000. Failure to produce for lawful inspection the age and schooling certificate as provided by law, or the record as provided in section twelve thousand nine hundred and ninety-eight, shall be prima facie evidence of the illegal employment or service of the child whose certificate is not so produced of whose record is not so correctly kept. (99 v. 30 § 1.)

REPORTS.

SECTION 7784. Boards of education shall require all teachers and superintendents to keep the school records in such manner that they may be enabled to report annually to the county auditor and superintendent of public instruction as required by the provisions of this title and shall withhold the pay of such teachers and superintendents as fail to file the reports required of them. The records of each school, in addition to all other requirements shall be so kept as to exhibit the names of all pupils enrolled therein, the studies pursued; also, indicate the character of the work done, the standing of each pupil, and must be as near uniform throughout the state as is practicable. (104 v. 225.)

School records shall be kept by superintendents and teachers.

SECTION 7785. Such boards may require superintendents and teachers to report matters the boards deem important or necessary for information in regard to the management and conduct of the schools and to make such suggestions and recommendations as they deem advisable relative to methods of instruction, school management, or other matters of educational interest. The board of education of each city district shall prepare and publish annually a report of the condition and administration of the schools under its charge, and include therein a complete exhibit of the financial affairs of the district. (97 v. 69.)

Special reports by superintendents and teachers.

The word 'publish" as employed in section 7785, General Code, leaves it discretionary with the board of education to publish said annual report in any manner it sees fit, and a publication in a newspaper of such annual report is fully authorized by said section. — *Attorney General*, 1911-12, p. 301.

SECTION 7786. No clerk of a board shall draw an order on the treasurer for the payment of a teacher for services until the teacher files with him such reports as are required by the superintendent of public instruction and the board of education, a legal certificate of qualification, or a true copy thereof, covering the entire time of the service, and a statement of the branches taught. But orders may

When clerk shall draw order for teacher's pay.

be drawn for the payment of special teachers of drawing,
painting, penmanship, music, gymnastics, or a foreign language, on presentation of a certificate to the clerk, signed
by a majority of the examiners, and the filing with him of a
true copy therof, covering the time for which the special
teacher has been employed, and the specialty taught. (104
v. 225.)

Inasmuch as by the provisions of section 7786, a clerk of the
township board of education is obliged to pass on reports of
teachers before an order may be drawn by said clerk for the
payment of their salaries, the office of said clerk constitutes a
check upon the position of teacher, and therefore both positions
may not be held at the same time by the same individual. — Attorney General, 1913, p. 1097.

Under a former statute which provided that a person should not be
employed as a teacher until he had obtained the certificate required by law,
it was held that a contract of employment entered into before the teacher had
obtained the required certificate was not invalid, if such certificate was obtained
before such teacher entered upon the performance of his duties: School District v. Dilman, 22 O. S. 194.

A superintendent is not required to have a certificate to teach all the
subjects taught in the schools of which he is superintendent; and if there are
one or more teachers besides himself, it will be presumed, in the absence of
evidence, that he did not teach any of the subjects in which he had no certificate: State, ex rel., v. Moser, 12 O. C. C. 247.

Mandamus will not issue to compel the treasurer to pay an order for
the compensation of a teacher, if the funds apportioned to the school district
in which such teacher is employed for school purposes for that year have
been exhausted: Saunders v. State, ex rel., 2 O. C. C. 475.

Annual report of board of education; contents.   SECTION 7787. The board of education of each district shall make a report to the county auditor, on or before
the first day of September in each year, containing a statement of the receipts and expenditures of the board, the
number of schools sustained, the length of time they were
sustained, the enrollment of pupils, the average monthly
enrollment, and average daily attendance, the number of
teachers employed, and their salaries, the number of schoolhouses and school rooms, and such other items as the superintendent of public instruction requires. (104 v. 225.)

Report must be made on blanks furnished by superintendent.   SECTION 7788. Such report must be made on blanks
which shall be furnished by the superintendent of public
instruction to the auditor of each county, and by the auditor
to each school clerk in his county. Each board of education, or officers or employee thereof, or other school officer
in any district or county, when the superintendent so requires, shall report to him direct, upon such blanks as he
furnishes any statement or items of information that he
deems important or necessary. (104 v. 225.)

Duty of county auditor as to school statis-tics.   SECTION 7789. On or before the twentieth day of September, annually, the auditor of each county shall prepare,
and transmit to the superintendent of public instruction an
abstract of all the returns of school statistics made to him
from the several districts in his county, according to the
form prescribed by the superintendent, a statement of the
condition of the institute fund, and such other facts relating to schools and school funds as the commissioner requires. He also shall cause to be distributed all such cir-

culars, blanks, and other papers, including school laws and documents, in the several school districts in the county, as the commissioner may lawfully require. (104 v. 225.)

SECTION 7790. If the auditor neglects to prepare and return any of the abstracts or reports herein required, the county commissioners, shall withhold from him all compensation for his services under this title, and he shall also be liable on his bond for any such neglect, in a sum not less than three hundred nor more than one thousand dollars, on complaint of the superintendent of public instruction, and if the clerk of the board of education of any district fails to make the annual returns of school statistics required by this title, to the county auditor, he shall be liable on his bond, in a sum not less than fifty nor more than three hundred dollars, on complaint of the county auditor, or of the board of education, to be recovered in a civil action in the name of the state, and when collected to be paid into the county treasury, and applied to the use of common schools in such district. (104 v. 225.) *Penalty for neglect to make reports.*

SECTION 7791. Upon the neglect or failure of the clerk of the board of education of any district to make thereports required in this title, and by the time specified, the county auditor must appoint some suitable person, resident of the district, to make such reports who shall receive the compensation therefor, allowed by law for like services. (70 v. 195.) *When auditor to appoint person to make reports.*

SECTION 7792. A county auditor who willfully or negligently fails, in any year, to transmit to the superintendent of public instruction the abstract of enumeration by law required of him, or to perform any other duty required of him in this title, shall be liable on his bond to the extent of twice the sum lost to the school districts of his county in consequence of such failure. Such sum shall be recovered in a civil action against him, on his bond, in the name of the state. The money so recovered must be paid into the county treasury, for the benefit of such districts, and apportioned as the school funds so lost would have been apportioned. (104 v. 225.) *Penalty for failure to transmit abstract of enumeration.*

SECTION 7793. The commissioners of each county, annually shall allow the county auditor a reasonable compensation for his services under this title, not to exceed five dollars for each city, village and rural school district in his county, to be paid out of the county treasury. But before such allowance shall be made for any year the auditor must present to the commissioners a statement, officially certified and signed by the superintendent of public instruction, that he has transmitted to him all reports and returns of statistics for that year required by this title. (104 v. 225.) *Compensation of auditor.*

SECTION 173. The secretary of state shall prepare from the reports filed with him or with the governor of the state, accurate statistical tables and practical and analytical *"Ohio General Statistics."*

information regarding the activities and proceedings of the several offices and departments of the state to be known as "Ohio General Statistics." (106 v. 508).

Publication of "Ohio General Statistics." SECTION 173-1. The secretary of state shall annually publish the "Ohio General Statistics," the number of copies thereof to be detrmined by the commissioners of public printing. The first issue of "The General Statistics" shall be for the period from November 15, 1914, to and including June 30, 1915. (106 v. 508).

Approval by printing commission before publication. SECTION 173-2. No officer, board or commission, shall print or cause to be printed at the public expense, any report, bulletin or pamphlet, unless such report, bulletin or pamphlet be first submitted to and the publication thereof approved by the commissioners of public printing. If such commission shall approve the publication thereof, it shall determine the form of such publication and the number of copies thereof, provided that in all cases the commissioners of public printing shall cause their action thereon to be entered upon the minutes of their proceedings.

Where printing may be done. If such approval is given, the commissioners shall cause the same to be printed, and may authorize such printing to be done at any penal, correctional or benevolent institution of the state having a printing department of sufficient equipment therefor; and when printed, such publications, other than the Ohio General Statistics, shall be delivered to such officer, board of commission for distribution by him or it. (106 v. 508.)

Beginning of fiscal year. SECTION 260-1. For all state officers, departments, commissions, boards and institutions of the state the fiscal year shall be and is hereby fixed to begin on the first day of July in each year and to end on the last day of June of the succeeding year. (106 v. 508.)

Correction of proof sheets and preparation of indexes. SECTION 748. Except as otherwise provided by law, the supervisor of public printing shall examine and correct the proof sheets of the printing for the state, see that the work is executed in accordance with law and when necessary prepare indexes for the public documents. The printing for the opinions of the attorney general, "Ohio General Statistics," and all publications approved by the commissioners of public printing, shall be ordered through him, and he shall see that the number of copies ordered is received from the printer and delivered to the proper department. (106 v. 508.)

Official reports shall be made in triplicate; where filed. SECTION 2264-1. Each elective state officer, and the adjutant general, board of pardons, superintendent of public instruction, the state agricultural commission, the superintendent of public works, the public utilities commission, the superintendent of insurance, the state inspector of building and loan associations, the state superintendent of banks, the commissioners of public printing, the supervisor of public printing, the board of library commissioners, the state geologist, the state commissioner of soldier's claims, the state fire marshal, the state inspector of oils, the state industrial commission, the state highway department, the state board of health, the state medical board, the state dental board, the state board of embalming examiners, the state board of charities, the Ohio commission for the blind, the state board of accountancy, the state board of uniform state laws, the state civil service commission, the commissioners of the sinking fund, the state tax commission, the clerk of the supreme court, the state board of administration, the state liquor licensing board, the state armory board, the trustees of the Ohio state university, and every private or quasi-public institution, association, board of ocorporation receiving state money for its use and purpose, shall make annually, at the end of each fiscal year, in triplicate, a report of the transactions and proceedings of his office or department for such fiscal year excepting however receipts and disbursements unless otherwise specifically required by law. Such report shall contain a summary of the official acts of such officer, board or commission, institution, association or corporation, and such suggestions and recommendations as may be proper. On the first day of August of each year, one of said reports shall be filed with the governor of the state, one with the secretary of state, and one shall be kept on file in the office of such officer, board, commission, institution, association or corporation. (106 v. 508.)

SECTION 2264-2. Wherever in the statutes of this state annual reports are required to be made to the governor, or annual reports to the governor are refered to, the words "to the govenor" shall be held to mean annual reports in triplicate as provided in section 2264-1 and the special information required by any such statutes to be included in such annual report to the governor shall be included in such triplicate reports. (106 v. 508.) *Definition of terms.*

SECTION 2266. The governor may at any time require to be filed with him a detailed report from any state officer, board or commission. (106 v. 508.) *Governor's authority as to reports.*

Annual enumeration.

SECTION 7794. An enumeration of all unmarried youth noting sex, between six and twenty-one years of age, resident within the district, and not temporarily there, shall be taken in each district, annually, during the two weeks ending on the fourth Saturday of May, designating also the number between six and eight years of age, the number between eight and fourteen years of age, the number between fourteen and sixteen years of age, the number between sixteen and twenty-one years of age, the number residing in the Western Reserve, the Virginia Military district, the United States Military district, and in any original surveyed township or fractional township to which belongs section sixteen, or other land in lieu thereof, or any other lands for the use of public schools, or any interest in the proceeds of such lands. (99 v. 80.)

Enumeration in children's homes; see Sec. 3088.
At the annual enumeration of school youth as required by the provisions of Sec. 7794, the ages of such youth at the taking of enumeration should be returned and not as of September 1st following. — *Attorney General.*
The youth enumerated must be actual residents of the district, living with parents or guardians or working to support themselves by their own labor; see Sec. 7681 and notes under same.

False enumeration of school children.

SECTION 12929. Whoever, being an officer having supervision over the annual enumeration of unmarried youths between six and twenty-one years of age, taken in conformity to law, increases or diminishes the number enumerated, shall be fined not less than five dollars nor more than one thousand dollars or imprisoned in the county jail not less than ten days nor more than thirty days. (70 v. 195.)

Repor of deaf, dumb,t blind, insane, and idiotic persons.

SECTION 2606. In each year when an enumeration in that behalf is required, as soon as possible after the third Monday of May, the county auditor shall make and forward to the auditor of state a list of all the deaf, dumb, blind, insane, and idiotic persons in the county, with the names and post office addresses of their parents or guardians, as returned to him by the assessors. If he fails to make and forward such report within a reasonable time, he shall forfeit and pay to the state any sum not exceeding one hundred dollars, to be recovered and paid as provided in the preceding section. (58 v. 40.)

SECTION 7795. When taking such enumeration, the person appointed to take it, shall make every effort to ascertain the number of imbeciles or feeble-minded children between the ages of six and twenty-one, resident within the district. He shall keep an accurate list of the names, sex, age and place of residence of all such children, and make it a part of his report to the clerk of the board of education. There also shall be so taken an accurate enumeration of all physically disabled, blind, deaf or mute children, noting sex, between six and twenty-one years of age, resident within the district. (99 v. 80.) *Additional facts to be ascertained.*

SECTION 7796. On or before the second Saturday in May, the board of education of each school district shall appoint one or more persons to take the enumeration provided for in the next two preceding section. Each person appointed shall take an oath or affirmation to take the enumeration accurately and truly to the best of his skill and ability. When making return thereof to the clerk of the board of education, he shall accompany it with a list of the names of all the youth enumerated, noting the age of each, with his affidavit duly certified that he has taken and returned the enumeration accurately and truly to the best of his knowledge and belief, and that such list contains the names of all such youth so enumerated and none others. The clerk of the board of education or any officer authorized to administer oaths, may administer such oath or affirmation, and take and certify such affidavit. (97 v. 365.) *How enumeration taken.*

SECTION 7797. The clerk shall keep such report and the list of names in his office for five years. Each person so taking and returning the enumeration shall be allowed by the proper board of education reasonable compensation for his service. (97 v. 365.) *Report to be kept; compensation.*

SECTION 7798. When a school district including territory attached for school purposes, is situated in two or more counties, persons taking such enumeration must report the number of youth as provided in sections seventy-seven hundred and ninety-four, and seventy-seven hundred and ninety-five, residing in each county. The clerk of the board shall make returns to the auditors of the respective counties in which such youth reside as provided in the next following section. (97 v. 366.) *When district situated in two or more counties.*

SECTION 7799. Annually, on or before the first Saturday in July, the clerk of each board shall make and transmit to the county auditor, an abstract of the enumeration by this chapter required to be returned by him, according to the form prescribed by the superintendent of public in- *Clerk shall transmit to auditor abstract of enumeration.*

struction, with an oath or affirmation endorsed thereon
that it is a correct abstract of the returns made to him
under oath or affirmation. The oath or affirmation of the
clerk may be administered and certified by any member of
the board of education, or by the county auditor. (104 v.
225.)

When the clerk
fails, auditor
to act.

SECTION 7800. If the clerk of any district fails to
transmit such abstract of enumeration on or before the
first Saturday in July, the auditor at once shall demand it
from him. In case the enumeration has not been taken as
required by this chapter, or the abstract required be not
furnished without delay, the auditor shall employ competent persons to take it, who shall be subject to the legal requirements already specified, except that the return must
be made directly to the auditor, who may administer to each
person employed the oath or affirmation required. He shall
allow the person employed by him, a reasonable compensation, to be paid out of the general county fund, and then
proceed to recover the amount so paid in civil action before any court of competent jurisdiction, in the name of
the state, against such clerk on his bond. The amount so
collected shall be paid into the school funds of the district.
(97 v. 366.)

The returns should now be made on or before the first
Saturday in June, as the time of taking the enumeration was
changed from July to May without changing the time fixed for
making returns. — *Attorney General* Opinion.

When county
line divides
original sur-
veyed town-
ship.

SECTION 7801. If parts of an original surveyed township or fractional township are situated in two counties,
the auditor of the county in which the smallest part is situated, so soon as the abstracts of enumeration are received
by him from the clerks of the boards of education, shall certify to the auditor of the county in which the largest part
is situated the enumeration of youth residing in the part of
the township situated in his county. If parts of such township or fractional township are situated in more than two
counties, like certificates of enumeration must be transmitted to the auditor of the county containing the greatest
relative portion of such township, by the auditors of the
other counties containing portions thereof. When it is uncertain which county contains the greatest relative portion
of such township, such certificates shall be transmitted to
the auditor of the oldest county, by the other auditor or
auditors. If the land granted by congress to such township or fractional township for the support of public schools
has been sold, the auditor to whom such certificates are
transmitted must notify the auditor of state, without delay, that such enumeration has been certified. (70 v. 195.)

This section has nothing whatever to do with the enumeration returned by county auditors to the state commissioner of
common schools. — *Attorney General* Opinion.

SECTION 7802. If an enumeration of the youth of a district be not taken and returned in any year, such district shall not be entitled to receive any part of the school funds distributable in that year. If such loss to a district occurs through the failure of the clerk of the board of education of a district to perform the duty required of him under section seventy-seven hundred and ninety-nine, he shall be liable to the district for the loss, which may be recovered in an action in the name of the state. The money so recovered shall be paid into the county treasury, and apportioned as the school funds so lost would have been apportioned. (104 v. 158.)

District not entitled to school funds when enumeration not taken. Liability of clerk.

SECTION 7803. On or before the third Saturday in July in each year, the auditor of each county shall make and transmit to the superintendent of public instruction, on blanks to be furnished by the commissioners, an abstract of the enumeration returns made to him duly certified. (104 v. 225.)

Auditor shall transmit abstract to superintendent.

SECTION 7804. When, on examination of the enumeration returns of any district, the superintendent of public instruction is of the opinion that the enumeration is excessive in number, or in any other way incorrect, he may require it to be re-taken and returned. If he thinks it necessary for this purpose he may appoint persons to perform the service, who shall take the oath, perform the duties, and receive the same compensation, out of the same funds, as the person or persons who took the enumeration in the first instance. The school fund distributable to the counties in proportion to enumeration shall be distributed upon the corrected returns. (104 v. 225.)

Duty of superintendent when enumeration excessive.

CHAPTER 7.

EXAMINERS.

STATE BOARD OF EXAMINERS.

State board; appointment and qualifications.

SECTION 7805. There shall be a state board of school examiners, consisting of five competent persons, resident of the state, to be appointed by the superintendnt of public instruction. Not more than three of them shall belong to the same political party. (104 v. 100.)

A member of a board of school examiners is said in State, ex rel., v. Board of Education, 4 O. C. D. 540, not to be an officer within the meaning of Art. II. Sec. 20, of the Ohio constitution, which forbids a change in the compensation of an officer during his term. Accordingly, the board of education may reduce the compensation of an examiner during his term of office, but such reduction cannot be retroactive.

SECTION 7806. The term of office of such examiners shall be five years. The term of one of the examiners shall expire on the thirty-first day of August each year. When a vacancy occurs in the board, whether from expiration of the term of office, refusal to serve, or other cause, the superintendent of public instruction shall fill it by appointment for the full or unexpired term, as the case demands. (104 v. 100.)

Terms and vacancies.

SECTION 7807. The board thus constituted may issue three grades of life certificates to such persons as are found to possess the requisite scholarship, and who exhibit satisfactory evidence of good moral character and of professional experience and ability. The certificates shall be for different grades of schools according to branches taught and be valid in the schools specified therein. The clerk of the board shall keep a record of the proceedings, showing the number, date and grade of each certificate, to whom granted, and for what branches of study, and report such statistics to the superintendent of public instruction, annually, on or before the thirty-first day of August. (104 v. 100.)

Power to issue certificates; record thereof.

A contract for the employment of a teacher which is made before he obtains the necessary certificate is not invalid if he obtains the necessary certificate before he enters upon the duties of his employment: School District v. Dilman, 22 O. S. 194.

SECTION 7807-1. Applicants for life certificates of any kind shall possess an amount of professional training as follows:

Professional training of applicants required.

1. On and after January first, 1915, not less than a one-year course or its equivalent in summer school work, in a recognized institution of college or normal school rank for the training of teachers or a year's course in an arts college on the recognized list, maintaining a practice department.

2. On and after January first, 1920, not less than a two-year course, or its equivalent in summer school work, in a recognized institution of college or normal school rank for the training of teachers, or two years' work in an arts college on the recognized list maintaining a practice department, not less than one-fourth of which work shall be in educational subjects including observation and practice teaching. (104 v. 100.)

SECTION 7807-2. In addition to the requirements mentioned in section 7807-1, every applicant for a life certificate, if not a graduate of a recognized institution for the training of teachers of college or normal school rank or liberal arts college on the recognized list, shall have had at least fifty months of successful teaching experience and hold a certificate of graduation from a first grade high school or its equivalent. (104 v. 100.)

Additional requirements when applicant not a graduate.

When elementary certificate may be granted without further examination.

SECTION 7807-3. A graduate from any normal school, teachers' college, college or university, who has completed a full two years' academic and professional course in such institution and who also possesses a first grade high school diploma or its equivalent shall upon application to the superintendent of public instruction and the payment of a fee of one dollar be granted without further examination a provisional elementary certificate valid for four years in any school district within the state; provided that such institution has been approved by the superintendent of public instruction. (104 v. 100.)

When high school certificate may be granted without further examination.

SECTION 7807-4. A graduate from any normal school, teachers' college, college or university, who has completed a full four years' academic and professional course in such institution and who also holds a certificate of graduation from a first grade high school or its equivalent shall upon application to the superintendent of public instruction, and the payment of a fee of one dollar, be granted without further examination, a provisional high school certificate valid for four years in any school district within the state: provided that such institution has been approved by the superintendent of public instruction. (104 v. 100.)

When special certificate may be granted.

SECTION 7807-5. A graduate from any normal school, teachers' college, college or university, who has completed a special two year course, with training school experience, in music, drawing, penmanship, manual training, physical culture, domestic science, agriculture, kindergartening, any modern language, or such other studies as are required to be taught by special teachers or supervisors and who also possess a first grade high school diploma or its equivalent, shall upon application to the superintendent of public instruction and the payment of a fee of one dollar, be granted without further examination a provisional special certificate in such subject or subjects valid for four years in any school district within the state; provided that such institution has been approved by the superintendent of public instruction. (104 v. 100.)

When life certificate shall be issued to holder of provisional certificate.

SECTION 7807-6. It shall be the duty of the state board of school examiners to issue without examination to every holder of a state provisional certificate, a life certificate of similar kind upon satisfactory evidence that the holder thereof has completed at least twenty-four months of successful teaching, after receiving such provisional certificate. (104 v. 100.)

When state life high school certificate shall be issued to holder of degree.

SECTION 7807-7. The state board of school examiners shall issue without examination, a state life high school certificate to the holder of a degree from any normal school, teachers' college, or university that has been approved by the superintendent of public instruction, upon satisfactory evidence that the holder thereof has completed at least fifty months of successful teaching. (104 v. 100.)

SECTION 7808. All certificates issued by such board shall be countersigned by the superintendent of public instruction. They shall supersede the necessity of any and all other examinations of the persons holding them, by any board of examiners, and be valid in any school district in the state, unless revoked by the state board for good cause. (104 v. 100.)

Effect thereof; may be revoked for cause.

SECTION 7809. Each applicant for a certificate shall pay to the board of examiners a fee of five dollars. The clerk of the board must pay to the state treasurer, all fees received, and file with the state auditor a written statement of the amount. (85 v. 330.)

Examination fees.

SECTION 7810. Each member of the board shall receive five dollars for each day he is necessarily engaged in official service, and also his actual and necessary expenses, to be paid out of the state treasury on the order of the state auditor. All books, blanks and stationery required by the board shall be furnished by the secretary of state. (104 v. 100.)

Compensation of examiners.

COUNTY BOARD OF EXAMINERS.

SECTION 7811. There shall be a county board of school examiners for each county, consisting of the county superintendent, one district superintendent and one other competent teacher, the latter two to be appointed by the county board of education. The teacher so appointed must have had at least two years' experience as teacher or superintendent, and be a teacher or supervisor in the public schools of the county school district or of an exempted village school district. Should he remove from the county during his term, his office thereby shall be vacated and his successor appointed. (104 v. 100.)

County board; how composed.

Where an examination for the granting of teachers' certificates is not held on the date advertised, school examiners who attend such meeting and issue temporary certificates are not entitled to any compensation therefor. — *Attorney General,* Opinion No. 928, 1914.

The members of the county board of school examiners authorized by Section 7811, General Code, as amended, 104 O. L., 102, are not subject to the civil service law. — *Attorney General,* Opinion, No. 1177, 1914.

The term "Supervisor" as employed in Section 7811, 104 O. L., 102, is intended to apply to teachers who have had experience in-overseeing or have had charge of schools with authority to direct or regulate matters in connection with the schools, either as an actual superintendent or in a supervisory capacity. The term "exempted village school districts" as employed in said section 7811, applies to village school districts which are exempt from county school districts by virtue of Sections 4688 and 4688-1, General Code, as amended in 104 O. L., 134. — *Attorney General,* Opinion No. 1341, 1914.

SECTION 7812. No examiner shall teach in, be connected with, or financially interested in any school which is not supported wholly or in part by the state, or be em-

Who eligible as examiner.

ployed as a paid instructor in any teachers' institute in his own county; nor shall any person be appointed as, or exercise the office of examiner who is agent of or financially interested in any book publishing or book selling firm, company or business, or in any educational journal or magazine. If an examiner becomes connected with or interested in any school not under state control, or is employed in any such institution in his own county, or becomes an agent of or interested in any book company or journal, or fails to hold the necessary teachers' certificate, or removes from the county, the county board of education upon being apprised of such fact, forthwith shall remove such examiner and appoint his successor. (104 v. 100.)

Term; revocation of appointment.

SECTION 7813. The term of office of such appointive school examiners shall be two years. The term of one of the examiners shall expire on the thirty-first day of August, each year. The county board of education shall revoke the appointment of any examiner, upon satisfactory proof that he is inefficient, intemperate, negligent, guilty of immoral conduct, or that he is using his office for personal or private gain. (104 v. 100.)

Vacancies.

SECTION 7814. When a vacancy occurs in the board, whether from expiration of the term of office, refusal to serve, or other cause, the county board of education promptly shall fill it by appointment for the full or unexpired term, and within ten days, report this to the superintendent of public instruction, together with the names of the other members of the board and the date of the expiration of their several terms of office. (104 v. 100.)

Organization of board; duties of officers.

·SECTION 7815. Annually, in the month of September, the board of county school examiners shall organize by choosing from its members a president and a vice president. The county superintendent shall be the clerk of the board. The president shall preside at all the meetings of the board. In his absence the vice president shall preside. The clerk shall keep a full and accurate record of the proceedings of the board, showing the number, date and character of each certificate issued, to whom, for what term and what branches of study, with such other statistics relating to the examination and proceedings of the board as the superintendent of public instruction requires, in the form and manner required by him, and made a report of all such items annually on or before the first day of September. (104 v. 100.)

Rules and regulations.

SECTION 7816. The board shall make all needful rules and regulations for the proper discharge of its duties and the conduct of its work, subject to statutory provisions and the approval of the superintendent of public instruction. (104 v. 100.)

The board of county examiners has no authority to honor a certificate of teachers who have taught in a foreign state, or to issue certificates to them without taking an examination in this state. — *Attorney General,* 1913, p. 1341.

SECTION 7817. Each board shall hold public meetings for the examination of applicants for county teachers' certificates on the first Saturday of September, October, January, March, April, May, and the last Friday of June and August of each year, unless any such day falls on a legal holiday, in which case, it shall be held on the corresponding day of the succeeding week, at such place within the county as, in the opinion of the board, best will accommodate the greatest number of applicants. In no case shall the board hold any private examination or antedate any certificate. (104 v. 100.)

Meetings for examinations; notice.

Where an examination for the granting of teachers' certificates is not held on the date advertised, school examiners who attend such meeting and issue temprary certificates are not entitled to any compensation therefor. — *Attorney General,* Opinion No. 928, 1914.

SECTION 7818. A majority of the board may examine applicants and grant certificates. An applicant for a county teachers' certificate may, if he so elects, take one-half of the subjects in which he is to be examined on one day and the remaining one-half not later than the second regular examination day thereafter. The subjects to be taken the first day by an applicant shall be determined by the board of county examiners. If an applicant electing to take the examination in two days fails to obtain on the first day a grade of seventy-five per cent, or more, in any subject or subjects, such applicant may elect to be re-examined in such subject or subjects on the second day on which such applicant is to be examined. As a condition of an applicant's being admitted to take the examination he shall pay to the board for the use of the county board of education fund a fee of fifty cents. Applicants taking the examination in two parts shall make on the date when each part is taken an application accompanied with a fee of fifty cents. (104 v. 100.)

Power of majority to grant certificates.

Applicant may elect to take one-half the subjects at each of two regular examinations.

SECTION 7819. The questions for all county teachers' examinations shall be prepared and printed under the direction of the superintendent of public instruction. A sufficient number of lists shall be sent, under seal, to the clerks of such boards of examiners not less than five days before each examination, such seal to be broken at the time of the examination at which they are to be used, in the presence of the applicants and a majority of the members of the examining board. (104 v. 100.)

Uniform system of examination.

SECTION 12939. Whoever, being a person connected with the preparation, printing, distribution or handling of questions for county, teachers' examinations, makes public in any manner or gives information in regard to the nature or character of such questions, to an applicant for a cer-

Divulging school examiners' questions.

tificate, or other person, prior to such examination in each branch of study respectively, or whoever is found in possession of any of such questions prior to the distribution thereof for the use of applicants at such examination, shall be fined not less than fifty dollars nor more than one hundred dollars, and imprisoned not less than thirty days nor more than ninety days. (98 v. 228.)

Disposition of fees.

SECTION 7820. The clerk of the board of county school examiners shall promptly collect all fees from applicants at each examination and pay them into the county treasury monthly. He shall file with the county auditor a written statement of the amount and the number of applicants, male and female, examined during the month. All money thus received, shall be set apart by the auditor to the crdit of the county board of education fund. (104 v. 100.)

The moneys paid into the county board of education fund on account of the salaries of county and district superintendents, under Section 4744-3, General Code, as amended, 104 O. L., 143, are automatically appropriated to the payment of such salaries, and cannot be used for any other purpose. The expenses of the county superintendent and his allowance for clerk hire, the expenses of the members of the board of education and the expenses of the county institute, which are payable out of this fund, must be paid from moneys coming into it otherwise than under Section 4744-3, viz.: examination fees, under Section 7820, as amended, 104 O. L., 104, and transfers from the dog tax fund, under Section 5653, General Code, as amended, there being no other source of the county board of education fund.

If the allowance to the superintendent is made in advance, such allowance would appropriate moneys in the fund other than those appropriated to salaries; so that the expenses of conducting institutes and the expenses of the members of the board of education could not be paid unless there were in the fund more than enough to pay the salaries and superintendent's allowance. — *Attorney General*, Opinion No. 1143, 1914.

What and how many certificates may be granted.

SECTION 7821. County boards of school examiners may grant teachers' certificates for one year and three years which shall be valid in all villages, and rural school districts of the county wherein they are issued. Not more than three one-year certificates and not more than one three-year certificate may be issued to any one person. Such three-year certificate may be renewed twice only on proof of successful teaching.

Valid from September following.

Such certificate shall be valid for one year and three years respectively from the first day of September following he day of the examination. (104 v. 100.)

The members of the county board of school examiners authorized by Section 7811, General Code, as amended, 104 O. L., 102, are not subject to the civil service law. — *Attorney General*, Opinion No. 1177, 1914.

Five and eight year certificates; how renewed.

SECTION 7821-1. All five-year and eight-year certificates now granted shall continue in force until the end of their terms and shall be renewed by the superintendent of public instruction upon proof that the holders thereof have taught successfully until the time of each renewal. Each application for renewal shall be accompanied by a fee of fifty cents and shall be filed in the office of the superintendent of public instruction. (104 v. 100.)

SECTION 7821-2. All two-year and three-year primary, elementary and high school certificates now granted shall continue in force until the end of their terms and may be renewed by the county boards of examiners on proof of five years' successful teaching experience. (104 v. 100.)

How certificates in force, renewed.

SECTION 7822. Applicants for a one-year elementary certificate shall be admitted to examination, and if found proficient may be granted a certificate to teach in the public schools in the county in which such certificate is granted for one school year, without previous professional training, but applicants for a one-year or a three-year elementary certificate who have taught in the public schools for one school year previous to the time of such application, unless said applicant is a graduate of a college or university of approved educational standing, shall possess an amount of professional training consisting of class room instruction in a recognized institution for the training of teachers, not less than the following: after January 1, 1916, such applicant shall possess not less than six weeks of such instruction; after January 1, 1917, not less than twelve weeks of such instruction; after January 1, 1918, not less than eighteen weeks of such instruction; after January 1, 1919, not less than twenty-four weeks of such instruction; after January 1, 1920, not less than thirty weeks of such instruction; after January 1, 1921, not less than one year of such class room instruction, in a recognized school for the training of teachers. (106 v. 340.)

Professional training of applicants for teachers' certificate.

SECTION 7823. Applicants for a one-year or a three-year high school or special certificate shall possess qualifications in professional training as follows:

1. On and after January 1st, 1915, not less than six weeks of class room instructiton in a recognized school for the training of teachers.

2. On and after January 1st, 1916, not less than twelve weeks of class room instruction in a recognized school for the training of teachers.

3. On and after January 1st, 1917, not less than eighteen weeks of class room instruction in a recognized school for the training of teachers.

4. On and after January 1st, 1918, not less than twenty-four weeks of class room instruction in a recognized school for the training of teachers.

5. On and after January 1st, 1919, not less than thirty weeks of class room instruction in a recognized school for the training of teachers.

Professional training required of applicants for one-year or three-year high school or special certificate.

6. On and after January 1st, 1920, and thereafter not less than one year of class room instruction in a recognized school for the training of teachers. (104 v. 100.)

Training required after Jan. 1, 1915 and after Jan. 1, 1920.

SECTION 7823-1. On and after January 1st, 1915, all applicants for one-year or a three-year high school or special certificate shall have had at least two years' training in an approved high school, or its equivalent, and on and after January first, 1920, all applicants for high school and special certificates shall have certificates of graduatiton from a first grade high school or its equivalent. (104 v. 100.)

Effect of certificates of other counties.

SECTION 7824. County boards of school examiners at their discretion may issue certificates without formal examinations to holders of certificates granted by other county and city boards of school examiners. (99 v. 350.)

Additional test to written examination. When and by whom made.

SECTION 7825. Every aplicant for a teacher's certificate shall be required to take in addition to the written examination, to test accademic and professional knowledge, a practical test in actual teaching. Such test shall be made at any time during the preceding year or before the applirant receives his certificate, by a member of the board of examiners, a local supervisor, a teacher of method or any other competent person authorized by the county board of school examiners to make such test. Applicants without previous teaching experience may be given such class room test in the practice department of any recognized summer school. The test shall include three subjects of instruction unless the applicant desires a special certificate in which case three separate tests shall be given in the desired subject. Each applicant shall make a satisfactory showing in both written and practical tests. The superintendent of public instruction shall prescribe the forms for such examination. (104 v. 100.)

Temporary certificates.

SECTION 7826. Between regular examinations county boards of school examiners at their discretion may issue temporary certificates which shall be valid only until the next regular examination held by such boards after the issue of such certificate, and at any regular examination such board upon proper application being made, subject to the same rules and regulations as applied to the granting of regular certificates shall issue temporary certificates which shall be valid from the date of issue until the first day of September following. (102 v. 418.)

Temporary certificates shall be valid from the date of taking until the first day of September thereafter.

All regular certificates are to be issued as of date September 1. For instance, if an applicant takes an examination in January, March, April or May, the certificate which is issued to such applicant is to be dated as of the September 1, following the date upon which such examination is taken. — *Attorney General* Opinion.

SECTION 7827. No certificate shall be issued to any person who is less than eighteen years of age. If at any time the recipient of a certificate be found intemperate, immoral, incompetent or negligent, the examiners, or any two of them, may revoke the certificate; but such recovation shall not prevent a teacher from receiving pay for services previously rendered. Before any hearing is had by a board of examiners on the question of the revocation of a teacher's certificate, the charges against the teacher must be reduced to writing and placed upon the records of the board. He shall be notified in writing as to the nature of the charges and the time set for the hearing, such notice to be served personally or at his residence; and be entitled to produce witnesses and defend himself. The examining board may send for witnesses and examine them on oath or affirmation which may be administered by any member of the board touching the matter under investigation. (99 v. 350.)

Minimum age limit.

The action of the board of examiners in revoking a certificate cannot be reviewed by the courts, at least in the absence of a showing of bad faith or improper motives: State, ex rel., v. Board of School Examiners, 1 O. N. P. 151.

SECTION 7828. The fees and the per diem of examiners for conducting such investigation at three dollars a day each and other expenses of such trial shall be certified to the county auditor by the clerk and president of the examining board and be paid out of the county treasury upon the order of the auditor. (99 v. 350.)

Fees for examiners conducting investigation.

No applicant who is not eighteen years of age at the time of the examination can receive a legal certificate.

The revocation of a teacher's certificate by the county school examiners for intemperance and immorality is not reviewable by the courts. Hence that board will not be compelled by mandamus to sign a bill of exceptions setting out the evidence on the trial to revoke: 1 N. P. 151.

The revocation of a certificate is not strictly a judicial proceeding. The law which clothes the boards of examiners with discretionary power, will protect them in the proper use of it. They cannot, of course, be mulcted in damages nor removed from office, for refusing to grant a certificate, nor for revoking a certificate, in the exercise of this discretion. If malice or other undue motive enter into the transaction, however, the candidate has his remedy in the courts, and the probate judge may remove any member for such cause, as a malfeasance in office — an immorality — one of the causes enumerated in the law.

Notice of revocation should at least be given to the boards of education concerned. A person cannot draw pay after his certificate is revoked.

A certificate cannot be antedated; see Sec. 7817.

An official trust cannot be delegated; see III Central Law Journal, p. 472. The board has no authority, therefore, to appoint a substitute to perform the duties of any of its members. A certificate depending on the signature of such substitute for its validity, is worthless. As all citizens are bound to know the law, so candidates and school authorities are bound to know who are legal, or, at least, *de facto* public officers.

SECTION 7829. Three kinds of teachers' certificates only shall be issued by county boards of school examiners, which shall be styled respectively "teacher's elementary school certificate," valid for all branches of study in schools below high school rank, "teacher's high school certificates," valid for all branches of study in recognized high schools and for superintendents and "teacher's special certificate," valid in schools of all grades, but only for the branch or branches of study named therein. (97 v. 372.)

What kind of certificates shall be issued.

SECTION 7830. No person shall be employed or enter upon the performance of his duties as a teacher in any elementary school suported wholly or in part by the state in any village, or rural school district who has not obtained from a board of school examiners having legal jurisdiction a certificate of good moral character; that he or she is qualified to teach orthography, reading, writing, arithmetic, English grammar and composition, geography, history of the United States, physiology, including narcotics, literature and elementary agriculture, and that he or she possess an adequate knowledge of the theory and practice of teaching. (104 v. 100.)

A teacher's license is not a contract and is subject to existing and reasonable future restrictions.

Section 7830, General Code, was amended so as to require after September 1, 1912, "elementary agriculture" in addition to the subjects formerly required, a certificate issued under the former law as an "elementary school certificate" and valid for "all" branches of study required at that time, can now be considered only as a "special certificate" valid as to certain specific studies but not for "all" subjects now required.

The holder of a teacher's elementary certificates which was issued prior to the amendment above stated and which certificate extends beyond Sept. 1, 1912, will be required to take an examination in elementary agriculture, in order to teach after Sept. 1, 1912.

It would not be legal to place "elementary agriculture" upon a teacher's elementary certificate issued prior to the amendment aforesaid, after the holder had passed an examination in this subject. A special certificate for the added branch may in such case be issued however.

After the amendment and prior to Sept. 1, 1912, elementary agriculture should be added as a required branch.

Former elementary certificates may be renewed only as "special certificates."

A renewal certificate issued after passage of the amendment may have "elementary agriculture" included therein provided, both the applicant's special certificates which are of the same class, including one for "elementary agriculture" and one for all subjects formerly required, run out of date of contemplated renewal.

As section 7821, General Code, has been amended so as to make all certificates ineffective until the first of September following, holders of certificates which terminate prior to that date, may under section 7826, General Code, be granted temporary certificates extending from said date of termination to the first of September following. — *Attorney General*, 1911-12, p. 555.

Under this section a contract for the employment of a person as teacher who has not obtained a teachers' certificate is not invalid if such certificate is obtained before such person enters upon the performance of the duties of his employment: School District v. Dilman, 22 O. S. 194.

If more than one teacher is employed in a school, the employment of one as teacher or superintendent is not rendered invalid by the fact that his certificate does not include all the branches which are taught in such school, but in the absence of evidence showing that he is employed to teach the branches not included, in his certificate, it will be presumed that he teaches only the branches included in his certificate: State, ex rel., v. Moser, 12 O. C. C. 247.

SECTION 7831. No person shall be employed or enter upon the performance of his duties as a teacher in any recognized high school supported wholly or in part by the state in any village, or rural school district, or act as a superintendent of schools in such district, who has not obtained from a board of examiners having legal jurisdiction a certificate of good moral character; that he or she is qualified to teach six branches or more selected from the following course of study (three of which branches shall be algebra, rhetoric and physics): Literature, general history, algebra, physics, physiology, including narcotics, Latin, German, rhetoric, civil government, geometry, physical geography, botany and chemistry, and high school agriculture; and that he or she possesses an adequate knowledge of the theory and practice of teaching. (104 v. 100.)

SECTION 7832. No person shall be employed and enter upon the performance of his duties as a special teacher of music, drawing, painting, penmanship, gymnastics, German, French, Spanish, the commercial and industrial branches, or any one of them, in any elementary or high school supported wholly or in part by the state in any city, village, or rural school district. who has not obtained from a board of examiners having legal jurisdiction a certificate of good moral character that he or she is qualified to teach the special branch or branches of study, and, in addition thereto, possesses an adequate knowledge of the theory and practice of teaching. (104 v. 100.) *Teacher's special certificate.*

SECTION 7832-1. A "teacher's emergency certificate" which shall be valid for one year in any village or rural school district in the county may be granted by the county board of school examiners with the approval of the superintendent of public instruction to applicants who have had one year's experience teaching in the public schools whenever for any reason there is a shortage of teachers in such district. (104 v. 100.) *Teacher's emergency certificate.*

SECTION 7832-2. The county board of school examiners may at their discretion grant one-year certificates to teachers who have completed a one year normal course in any high school or normal school which has been approved by the superintendent of public instruction. Such certificates shall be valid in any village or rural school district in the county in which it is granted and may be renewed for one or three years without examination. (104 v. 100.) *Teachers having one year normal course may be granted one-year certificates.*

SECTION 7832-3. The county board of school examiners shall grant one-year certificates to graduates of first grade high schools who have completed in addition to the high schol a one-year professional course in any high school or normal school which has been approved by the superintendent of public instruction. (104 v. 100.) *Graduates of first grade high schools may be granted one-year certificates.*

SECTION 7833. But no person holding a common school life certificate issued by the board of state examiners shall be required to have any other certificate to teach in the elementary schools of the state, nor be required by any board to be examined in any of the branches covered by such certificate in order to be granted the teachers' high school certificate authorized herein. (97 v. 372.) *Recognition or renewal of certificates.*

No money can be legally drawn for teaching a day without a certificate, and to receive public money illegally is a crime under Sections 7786, 7829-7833.

The board of education at G., at a regular meeting, tended C. the election as superintendent of a school in which branches other than those enumerated in the certificate issued to C. by the board of school examiners, were taught. C. accepted the employment tendered, and entered upon its duties. Held, that this constituted a valid contract, and in the absence of proof, other teachers being employed in the school, no presumption arises that C. actually taught branches not enumerated in his certificate: 12 C. C. 247.

As to penalty for bribing or attempting to bribe an officer, see Sec. 12823.

Teachers in schools at children's homes and in kindergarten schools, supported by public funds, must hold certificates.

Compensation of examiners.

SECTION 7834. Each member of the county board of school examiners, except the clerk thereof shall receive ten dollars for each examination of fifty applicants or less, fourteen dollars for each examination of more than fifty applicants and less than one hundred, eighteen dollars for each examination of one hundred applicants and less than one hundred and fifty, twenty-two dollars for each examination of one hundred and fifty applicants and less than two hundred, and four dollars for each additional fifty applicants, or fraction thereof, to be paid out of the county treasury on the order of the county auditor. Books, blanks and stationery required by the board of examiners shall be furnished by the county board of education. (104 v. 100.)

Where an examination for the granting of teachers' certificates is not held on the date advertised, school examiners who attend such meeting and issue temprary certificates are not entitled to any compensation therefor. — *Attorney General*, Opinion No. 928, 1914.

Expenses of board.

SECTION 7835. Such board may contract for the use of suitable rooms in which to conduct examinations, may procure fuel and light, and employ janitors, to take charge of the rooms and keep them in order. Expenses so incurred, shall be paid out of the county treasury on orders of the county auditor, who shall issue them upon the certificate of the president of the board, countersigned by the clerk. (104 v. 100.)

Annual report of clerk; bond.

SECTION 7836. On or before the first day of September in each year, the clerk of such board shall prepare, and forward to the superintendent of public instruction, a statement of the number of examinations held by the board, the number of applicants examined, the total number of certificates granted, and the number for each term mentioned in this chapter, the amount of fees received and paid to the county treasurer, the amounts received from the county treasury by the members of the board for their services, with such other statistics and information in relation to the duties of the board as such superintendent requires. He shall also deposit with the county auditor a bond, with surety to be approved by the auditor, in the sum of three hundred dollars, that he will pay into the county treasury, monthly, the examination fees received by the board, and make the stattistical returns required by this chapter. (104 v. 100.)

SECTION 7837. The county superintendent shall receive no additional compensation for his services as clerk of the county board of school examiners. (104 v. 100.)

CITY BOARD OF SCHOOL EXAMINERS.

SECTION 7838. There shall be a city board of school examiners for each city school district. Such board shall consist of the city superintendent of schools and two other competent teachers serving full time in the day schools of such city to be apointed by the city board of education. The term of office of such examiners shall be two years each, one to be appointed each year; and shall expire on the thirty-first day of August. (104 v. 100.)

SECTION 7839. The board of education may revoke any appointment upon satisfactory proof that the appointee is inefficient, intemperate, negligent, or guilty of immoral conduct. When a vacancy occurs in the board, whether from expiration of term of office, refusal to serve, or other cause, the board shall fill it by appointment for the full or unexpired term, as the case demands. Within ten days after an appointment, the clerk of the board shall report to the superintendent of public instruction the name of the appointee, and whether the appointment is for a full or an unexpired term. (104 v. 100.)

SECTION 7840. Each city board of school examiners shall determine the standard of qualification for teachers, and may examine any school in the district when such examination is deemed necessary to ascertain a teacher's qualifications. But in the examination of applicants and the granting of certificates the board must be governed by the provisions of this chapter relating thereto. (97 v. 374.)

SECTION 7841. To secure a thorough examination of applicants in difficult branches, or special studies, the board may secure the temporary assistance of persons of sufficient knowledge in such branches or studies, who must promise on oath or affirmation, to be administered by the clerk of the board of examiners, to perform the duties of examiner faithfully and impartially. Superintendents of schools shall give to the board all necessary information in reference to branches and special studies to be taught, and the branches of study and grades of school which teachers will be required to teach. (97 v. 374.)

An expert secured by the board to conduct examinations in any particular branch should certify the result of the examination to the board; all certificates should be signed by members of the board and by such members only. — *Attorney General* Opinion.

SECTION 7842. Each city board of school examiners must organize during the month of September each year by choosing from its members a president, vice-president, and clerk. The president shall preside at all the meetings of the board, and in his absence the vice president shall preside. The clerk shall perform all the duties required in this chapter of the clerk of the board of county school examiners in so far as such duties apply. He also must give bond, in the sum of three hundred dollars with surety to be approved by the board of education, conditioned that he will perform faithfully the duties required of him by this chapter, which bond shall be deposited with the clerk of such board. (97 v. 375.)

Meetings for examination; notice.

SECTION 7843. Each board of city school examiners shall hold not less than two meetings each year, notice of which must be published in some newspaper of general circulation in the district. All examinations of applicants shall be conducted at the meetings of the boards thus called. The examination of every applicant must be in the presence of at least two members of the board. .(97 v. 375.)

Certificates for one and three years.

SECTION 7844. Each city board of school examiners may grant teachers' certificates for one year and three years from the first day of September following the examination, which shall be valid within the district wherein they are issued. But certificates granted for one year or three years must be regarded as provisional certificates and shall be renewed only twice each. (104 v. 100.

Certificates for five and eight years; renewals.

SECTION 7845. All five-year and eight-year certificates now granted shall continue in force until the end of their terms and shall be renewed by the superintendent of public instruction upon proof that the holders thereof have taught successfully until the time of each renewal. Each application for renewal shall be accompanied by a fee of fifty cents and shall be filed in the office of the superintendent of public instruction. (104 v. 100.)

Under the provisions of Sections 7845 and 7846, General Code as amended, 104 O. L., 108, constituting a part of the recently adopted school code, the certificates covered by said sections may be renewed more than twice for the reason that there is no limitation in said sections as to the number of times such certificates may be renewed. — *Attorney General*, Opinion 1173, 1914.

Renewal of two and three year certificates.

SECTION 7846. All two-year and three-year primary, elementary and high schol certificates now granted shall continue in force until the end of their terms and may be renewed by the city boards of examiners on proof of five years successful teaching experience. (104 v. 100.)

Under the provisions of Sections 7845 and 7846, General Code, as amended, 104 O. L., 108, constituting a part of the recently adopted school code, the certificates covered by said sections may be renewed more than twice for the reason that there is no limitation in said sections as to the number of times such certificates may be renewed. — *Attorney General*, Opinion No. 1173, 1914.

SECTION 7847. County and city boards of school examiners at their discretion may issue certificates without formal examinations to holders of certificates granted by other city and county boards of school examiners. (104 v. 100.)

SECTION 7849. Between regular examinations, city boards of school examiners, at their discretion, may issue temporary certificates, which shall be valid only until the next regular examination held by the board after the issue thereof. (99 v. 352.)

SECTION 7850. No certificates shall be issued to any person who is less than eighteen years of age, and if at any time the recipient of a certificate be found interperate, immoral, incompetent or negligent, the examiners, or any two of them, may revoke the certificate. But such revocation shall not prevent a teacher from receiving pay for srvices previously rendered. Before any hearing is had by a board of examiners on the question of the revocation of a teacher's certificate, the charges against the teacher must be reduced to writing and placed upon the records of the board. He shall be notified in writing as to the nature of the charges and the time and place set for the hearing. Such notice must be served either personally or at his residence. He shall be entitled to produce witnesses and defend himself. The examining board may send for witnesses and examine them on oath touching the matter under investigation, which oath or affirmation may be administered by any member of the board. (99 v. 352.)

SECTION 7851. The fees and the per diem of examiners for conducting such investigation, at three dollars a day each, and other expenses of such trial shall be certified the city auditor by the clerk and president of the examining board, and be paid out of the city treasury upon the order of the city auditor. (99 v. 352.)

If the board of education of a city district has failed to make a substantial compliance with the provisions of a writ of mandamus which requires such board to fix the compensation to be paid to a member of a board of examiners, and such failure is due to a mistake or misapprehension as to the actual facts; and a compensation which is nominal and wholly insufficient has been fixed, the court will call upon such board to review its action in the light of the facts as found to exist; and the court will see that a fair and bona fide attempt is made to comply with the order of the court: State, ex rel., v. Board of Education, 4 O. C. C. 93.

SECTION 7852. The provisions of this chapter relating to the kinds of certificates authorized to be issued by the county boards of school examiners for teachers in elementary schools, high schools, and for superintendents shall apply to city boards of school examiners; except that city boards, in their discretion, may require teachers in elementary schools to be examined in drawing, music, or German if such subjects are a part of the regular work of such teachers. (97 v. 376.)

Compensation of members and clerk; incidental expenses. SECTION 7853. Each city board of education shall fix the compensation of the members of the city board of school examiners, the additional compensation of the clerk, and the person or persons called to their assistance, furnish the necessary books, blanks and stationery for their use, designate a school building within the district in which they shall conduct examinations and cause such building to be lighted and heated if necessary. Such compensation, and the incidental expenses incurred on account of the board of examiners, shall be paid, by order of the board of education, from the contingent fund of the district. (97 v. 376.)

Duties of clerk of city board of school examiners. SECTION 7854. The clerk of the city board of school examiners shall keep a record of its proceedings, and such statistics as the superintendent of public instruction requires, in the form and manner he requires, and report such statistics to him annually, on or before the first day of September. (104 v. 100.)

Disposition of examination fees. SECTION 7855. Such clerk shall pay the examination fees received by him to the treasurer of the district within ten days after eac meeting, and at the same time file with the board of education a written statement of the amount, also a statement of the number of applicants, male and female, examined, the number of certificates granted, and for what terms. (104 v. 100.)

Consideration of applicants' answers; issue of certificates or notice of failure. SECTION 7856. All manuscripts filed as answers to questions propounded to any applicant appearing before any county or city board of school examiners, shall be promptly considered and passed upon by that board together with the results of oral tests, if any, and such other information as comes to it touching the fitness of any applicant for teaching in the public schools. The board shall promptly issue all certificates granted to successful applicants and send notices of failure to those who fail in the examination, if such there be. (97 v. 377.)

Manuscripts shall be kept on file 60 days; review. SECTION 7857. All manuscripts filed as answers to questions shall be kept on file for sixty days by the members of the examining board. If any applicant has cause to and does believe that he has been discriminated against and his manuscripts unfairly graded, he may review his manuscripts with the member or members of the board having them in charge at any time within sixty days after his returns from the examination. If after such inspection and review, he is still of the opinion that the board will not correct the error, if any, and issue his certificate, he may appeal his case to the superintendent of public instruction for final review. (104 v. 100.)

How appeal may be taken; result. SECTION 7858. Every appeal from the board of examiners shall be in the form of an affidavit setting forth the facts as the applicant believes them and shall be ac-

companied by a fee of one dollars to cover the expenses incident to such appeal. Upon receipt of such affidavit and
fee the superintendent of public instruction shall require
the clerk of such board to procure and forward the manuscripts of such applicant, together with a full explanation
of the reasons for the board's action. If upon examination of the manuscripts, and record the superintendent finds
that the applicant was denied a certificate when one should
have been granted him and has been discriminated against
by the board, the superintendent shall order forthwith a certificate to be issued of the date of the examination attended
by the applicant, and he shall indicate the length of time such
certificate shall be valid. If, upon inspection of the manu-
script and reviewing the facts submitted, the superintendent
of public instruction concludes that no injustice has been
done, he shall so notify the applicant and the clerk of the
board of examiners. (104 v. 100.)

CHAPTER 8.

TEACHERS' INSTITUTES.

COUNTY INSTITUTES.

Organization of county teachers' institutes.

SECTION 7859. A teachers' institute may be organized in any county, by the association of not less than thirty practical teachers of the common schools residing therein, who must declare their intention in writing to attend such institute, the purpose of which shall be the improvement of such teachers in their profession. (95 v. 237.)

There is no provision in the statutes for the payment of a registration fee by teachers who attend a county institute and none can therefore be compelled. Registration may be required by the rule of the institute however, and there is no objection to the payment of a voluntary fee therefore, should teachers desire to contribute the same. — *Attorney General*, 1912, p. 494.

Election of officers; notice; expense.

SECTION 7860. The county teachers' institute, annually, shall elect by ballot, a president and a secretary. Such election of officers shall be held during the session of such institute and at a time fixed by the county board of education. At least three days' notice of the election shall be given the members of such institute by posting conspicuously in the room, where the institute is held, a notice of the time and place of holding it, and of the officers to be voted for. The expenses of conducting such institute shall be paid out of the county board of education fund upon the order of the president of the county board of education. (104 v. 155.)

The county surveyor is not entitled to remuneration for services performed under Section 4736, General Code. — *Attorney General*, Opinion No. 147, 1915.

Report by county superintendent.

SECTION 7865. Within five days after the adjournment of the institute, the county superintendent shall report to the superintendent of public instruction the number of teachers in attendance, the names of instructors and lecturers attending, the amount of money received and disbursed by the county board of education and such other information relating to the institute as the superintendent of public instruction requires. (104 v. 155.)

318

A teacher attending a county institute may receive compensation for acting as secretary, as provided for by Section 7866 of the General Code and for making the report as required by Section 7865. Such teacher is also entitled to the compensation provided for in Section 7870 of the General Code. — *Attorney General,* Opinion No. 850, 1914.

Teachers who are teaching in city school districts are not entitled to compensation when attending county teachers' institutes, when the board of education of the city school district wherein such teachers are teaching provides a city teachers' institute for the teachers of its district.

If a teacher who is teaching in a city school district wherein a city teachers' institute is provided, attends the county institute, and such teacher acts as secretary, then such teacher is entitled to the compensation provided for under Section 7866, General Code. — *Attorney General,* Opinion No. 1084, 1914.

SECTION 7868. The teachers' institutes of each county shall be under the supervision of the county boards of education. Such boards shall decide by formal resolution at any regular or special meeting held prior to February 1st of each year whether a county institute shall be held in the county during the current year. (104 v. 155.)

County boards of education shall determine whether institute shall be held.

SECTION 7868-1. Each village and rural boards of education in counties in which no county institute has been held in any year, shall pay ten dollars to each teacher employed by such board, who has attended for at least six weeks during such year, a recognized summer school for the training of teachers. (104 v. 155.)

When boards of education shall pay teacher who attended summer school.

SECTION 7869. All teachers and superintendents of the public schools within any county in which a county institute is held while the schools are in session may dismiss their schools for the purpose of attending such institute.

Teachers may dismiss school to attend institute.

The county boards of education shall decide the length of time county institutes may remain in session, in no case for longer period than five days. At least one day of such such session shall be under the immediate direction of the county superintendent who shall arrange the program for such day. (104 v. 155.)

Time institutes may remain in session.

SECTION 7870. When a teachers' institute has been authorized by the county board of education the boards of education of all school districts shall pay the teachers and superintendents of their respective districts their regular salary for the week they attend the institute upon the teachers or superintendents presenting certificates of full regular daily attendance, signed by the county superintendent. If the institute is held when the public schools are not in session, such teachers or superintendents shall be paid two dollars a day for actual daily attendance as certified by the county superintendent for not more than five days of actual attendance, to be paid as an addition to the first month's salary after the institute, by the board of education by which such teacher or superintendent is then employed. In case he or she is unemployed at the time of the

Pay for attending institute.

institute, such salary shall be paid by the board next employing such teacher or superintendent, if the term of employment begins within three months after the institute closes. (104 v. 155.)

Before a teacher may be entitled to $2.00 per day for attendance at an institute as provided by section 7870, General Code, he must have attended such institute at least for four days, and the rule is the same whether during such attendance school is in session or not.

A teacher cannot be compelled to do janitor work by the board of education unless under the terms of a special contract with said teacher and providing for extra compensation therefor.

Section 7610 provides for relief through the county commissioners, where the board fails to provide janitor service. — *Attorney General*, 1911-12, p. 201.

Where a teacher entered into a contract with the board of education for forty-five dollars to include compensation for attending teacher's institute, making out reports, etc., he cannot receive extra compensation from the board for attendance at such institute. — *Attorney General*, 1911-12, p. 1063.

There is no provision in the statutes for the payment of a registration fee by teachers who attend a county institute and none can therefore be compelled. Registration may be required by the rule of the institute however, and there is no objection to the payment of a voluntary fee therefore, should teachers desire to contirbute the same. — *Attorney General*, 1912, p. 494.

Section 7870, Geneeral Code, providing for compensation to teachers for attendance at a teachers' institute, requires as a condition precedent to reimbursement, a certificate of actual daily attendance and as such certificate could not be given to a teacher who is in attendance at a summer school while the county institute is in session, he may not receive the institute attendance fee. — *Attorney General*, 1912, p. 1756.

A board of education is not to be denied state aid by reason of the fact that it pays authorized expenses other than teachers' salaries out of the tuition fund, such as Superintendent's salary and institute fees.

The amount of State Aid allowed, however, shall not exceed such sum as is necessary to make teachers' salaries equal to $40.00 per month. — *Attorney* General, 1912, p. 98.

Under the decisions interpreting the same, it is comprehended by section 7870, General Code, that teachers should be allowed payment for attendance at the teachers' institute (1) when such teacher is employed at the time of attendance at such institute, (2) when a teacher, though not employed at such time, is employed within three months subsequent thereto. Therefore, when a board of education of a township school district, prior to the teachers' institute of 1912, hired a teacher then holding a temporary certificate to teach school, and was obliged to dismiss said teacher upon the termination of said certificate, and employ another in the place, under section 7870, General Code, both of said teachers should be allowed compensation therein provided, in addition to their regular salary for attendance at such teachers' institute. — *Attorney General.*, 1913, p. 1082.

Teachers who are teaching in city school districts are not entitled to compensation when attending county teachers' institutes, when the board of education of the city school district wherein such teacheres are teaching provides a city teachers' institute for the teachers of its district.

If a teacher who is teaching in a city school district wherein a city teachers' institute is provided, attends the county institute, and such teacher acts as secretary, then such teacher is entitled to the compensation provided for under Section 7866, General Code. — *Attorney General.*, Opinion No. 1084, 1914.

A teacher attending a county institute may receive com-pensation for acting as secretary, as provided for by Section 7866 of the General Code and for making the report as required by Section 7865. Such teacher is also entitled to the compensation provided for in Section 7870 of the General Code. — *Attorney General*, Opinion No. 850, 1914.

Where a board of education has employed teachers for the public schools of the district for the school year next ensuing thereafter, and such teachers, during vacation and after their employment, attend the county insti-tute during the week it is held in the same county, said board is authorized by the provisions of this section, to pay them for the institute week as an addition to their first month's salary as fixed by the terms of their employ-ment, and at the same rate, on presentation of the certificates prescribed by this section: Beaverstock v. Board of Education, 75 O. S. 144.

In a contract between the board of education and a teacher, under which the teacher was to teach an eight months' term of school at forty-five dollars per month, was included a stipulation that such teacher would not exact, demand or accept pay for attending the teachers' institute. It was held that such stipulation is against public policy and void, and in an action for the purpose the teacher can recover the sum fixed by statute for such attend-ance: Board of Education v. Burton, 11 O. C. C. (N. S.) 103.

A teacher in the public schools may recover compensation for attending the teachers' institute, although it is held in the summer vacation, if such teacher was actually engaged in teaching or began teaching three months after such institute closed: Reid v. Board of Education, 6 O. N. P. (N. S.) 526.

(House Bill No. 687.)

The boards of education of all school districts are hereby authorized to pay teachers who attended the county teachers' institutes during the year 1914 such amounts and in such manner as provided in section 7870 of the General Code prior to its amendment of February 17, 1914, or as amended February 17, 1914.

Payment of teachers who attended institutes.

All payments heretofore made by boards of educa-tion to teachers for such attendance at teachers' institute during the year 1914 are hereby declared to be legal and valid and all boards and officers making such payments are hereby relieved from any liability therefor. (106 v. 558.)

SECTION 7871. The board of education of each city school district may provide for holding an institute yearly for the improvement of the teachers of the common schools therein. General meetings of the teachers of a city dis-trict held upon not less than four days in any year, whether consecutive days or not. for the purpose of instruction, shall constitute a teachers' institute for a city district within the meaning of this section. (97 v. 378.)

Institutes for city districts.

Teachers who are teaching in city school districts are not entitled to compensation when attending county teachers' insti-tutes, when the board of education of the city school district wherein such teachers are teaching provides a city teachers' insti-tute for the teachers of its district.

If a teacher who is teaching in a city school district wherein a city teachers' institute is provided, attends the county institute. and such teacher acts as secretary, then such teacher is entitled to the compensation provided for under Section 7866, General Code. — *Attorney General*, Opinion No. 1084, 1914.

SECTION 7872. The expenses of such institute shall be paid from the city institute fund hereinbefore provided for. In addition to this fund the board of education of any district annually may expend for the instruction of the teachers thereof, in an institute or in such other manner as

Expenses of, how provided for.

it prescribes a sum not to exceed five hundred dollars, to
be paid from its contingent fund. (97 v. 378.)

By virtue of the powers conferred in 7872, General Code, a
board of education may pay the transportation and expenses of
teachers in visiting schools of other cities. — *Attorney General,*
1911-12, p. 275.

The expenses of a teacher, appointed by the board of education as delegate to the educational congress at Columbus, December 5, 1913, may not legally be paid out of the township,
village, or special school district treasury.

When a teacher is appointed by a board of education of a
city district, such expense may not be paid from the school
treasury, nor can the expenses of members of a board of-educa-
tion to such convention be paid out of the city fund. The expenses of persons not members of a board of education or
teachers, incurred in attending the above named congress, may
not be paid from the school fund. Before such expenses can
be paid, an appropriation for this purpose must be made by the
legislature. — *Attorney General,* 1913, p. 416.

When fund in city district to be paid into board of education fund.

SECTION 7873. If the board of a district does not
provide for such institute in any year, it shall cause the
institute fund in the hands of the district treasurer for the
year to be paid to the treasurer of the county wherein the
district is situated, who shall place it to the credit of the
county board of education fund. The teachers of the
schools of such district in such case, shall be entitled to the
advantages of the county institute, subject to the provisions
of sections seventy-eight hundred and sixty-nine, and
seventy-eight hundred and seventy. The clerk of the board
shall make the report of the institute required by section
7874. (104 v. 155.)

Length of session; report of superintendent.

SECTION 7874. All institutes held under the provisions
of this chapter shall continue at least four days. A report
of the institute held in pursuance of the provisions of sections seventy-eight hundred and seventy-one and seventy-
eight hundred and seventy-two shall be made to the superintendent of public instruction within five days after the
adjournment thereof. It must state the number of teachers
in attendance, the names of the instructors and lecturers, the
total expense of the institute, the portion thereof paid from
the institute funds, and such other information relating to
the institute as the superintendent requires. (104 v. 225.)

CHAPTER 9.

TEACHERS' PENSIONS.

The provisions of the statutes providing for exemption from taxation of institutions of purely charity, is intended to apply to private institutions as distinguished from an official or public agency. Inasmuch as the board of trustees of a teachers' pension fund constitutes a public agency rather than a private corporation, pension funds may not be exempted from taxation under this head.

Under article 12, section 2, of the constitution, the legislature would be empowered to exempt such funds under the provisions for the exemption of "public property used exclusively for any public purpose." Not having done so, however, such pension funds must be held to be technically subject to taxation. —*Attorney General*, 1913, p. 470.

SECTION 7875. When the board of education of a school district by resolution, adopted by a majority vote of the members thereof, declares that it is advisable to create a school-teachers' pension fund for that school district, such fund shall be under the management and control of a board to be known as " the board of trustees of the school-teachers' pension fund" for such district. Such board shall be composed of not less than three, nor more than seven members, as the board of education by resolution declares. If composed of less than five a member of the board of trustees of such pension fund shall be elected by the board of education of such school district, and the remaining members by the teachers of the public schools, including the teachers of any high schools, of such district, who have accepted the provisions hereinafter provided. If such board is to be composed of five or more members, two members of the board of trustees of such school district shall be elected by the board of education thereof, and the remaining members by the teachers of the public schools, including the teachers of any high school of such school district, who have accepted such provisions. (95 v. 610.)

Trustees of school teacher's pension fund.

A former statute creating a pension fund in cities of the second grade of the first class, and providing for a compulsory deduction from the compen-

323

sation of the teacher, was held to be unconstitutional as special legislation: State, ex rel., v. Kurtz, 21 O. C. C. 261.

A statute providing for a pension fund for teachers in cities of the third grade of the first class was held to be unconstitutional in State, ex rel., v. Hubbard, 22 O. C. C. 252.

Election of board of trustees.

SECTION 7876. The election of the members of such board by the teachers shall be at a meeting called by the superintendent of schools of such school district, the first election to be at a meeting to be called by the superintendent when one-third of the public school teachers of such school district have accepted the provisions of this chapter. Members of the board of trustees of such pension fund shall be elected for such length of time as the board of education of the school district by resolution declares, to serve not less than one, nor more than three years. They shall serve until their successors are elected and qualified, and without compensation. (95 v. 610.)

Provision for creation of school teachers' pension fund.

SECTION 7877. When the board of education of any school district has declared the advisability of creating a school teachers' pension fund, its clerk shall notify each teacher in the public schools and high schools, if any, of the school district, by notice in writing of the passage of such resolution, and require the teachers to notify the board in writing within thirty days from the date of such notice whether they consent or decline to acecpt the provisions of law for creating such a fund; but teachers who, prior to the first day of July, 1911, were in the employ of a board of education which has created such a fund under this law shall not be denied the right of accepting the provisions hereof before the first day of January, 1912. After the election of the board of trustees herein provided for, two dollars ($2.00) shall be deducted by the proper officers from the monthly salary of each teacher who accepted such provisions, and from the salary of all new teachers such sum to be paid into and applied to the credit of such pension fund; and such sum shall continue so to be deducted during the term of service of such teacher.

All persons employed for the first time as teachers by a board of education which has created such a pension fund shall be deemed new teachers for the purpose of this act, but the term new teachers shall not be construed to include teachers serving under reappointments. New teachers shall by accepting employment as such accept the provisions of this act and thereupon become contributors to said pension fund in accordance with the terms hereof. And the provisions of this act shall become a part of and enter into such contract of employment. (102 v. 445.)

Held to create a mutual contract in the nature of insurance; hence all terms should be given a fair interpretation, without favor, and where one does not come within the express terms there is no reason to strain them to include him: 7 O. C. C. (N. S.) 337.

The teachers' pension act only applies to persons who were teachers at the time of the enactment of the law, or who have taught at some period since its enactment.

A teacher who has rejected the provisions of the pension act may accept the same within sixty days after a new appointment by the board of education. — *Attorney General* Opinion.

A board of education should deduct from the salary of a teeacher only a proportionate part of the $2.00 for a pension fund when such teacher begins her service during the month, or resigns before the entire month's service has been rendered. — *Attorney General,* Opinion No. 106, 1915.

SECTION 7878. All moneys received from donation, legacies, gifts, bequests, or from any other source, shall also be paid into such fund, or into a permanent fund. If paid into a permanent fund, only the interest thereof shall be applied to the payment of pensions. (102 v. 445.)

One who has paid in money to a pension fund, created under unconstitutional legislation, will be restored to his former position by a court of equity: Venable v. Schafer, 7 O. C. C. (N. S.) 337.

SECTION 7879. Such board of trustees may invest such pension fund in the name of the board in bonds of the United States, or of the state of Ohio, or of any county, or municipal corporation, or school district in this state; and may make payments from such fund for pensions granted in pursuance of the laws relating thereto. The board of trustees from time to time also may make and establish such rules and regulations for the administration of the fund as they deem best. (95 v. 610.)

SECTION 7880. Such board of education of such school district, and a union, or other separate board, if any, having the control and management of the high schools of such district; may each by a majority vote of all the members composing the board on account of physical or mental disability, retire any teacher under such board who has taught for a period aggregating twenty years. One-half of such period of service must have been rendered by such beneficiary in the public schools or high schools of such school district, or in the public schools or high schools of the county in which they are located, and the remaining one-half in the public schools of this state or elsewhere. (101 v. 306.)

1st. If a teacher is forced to retire by virtue of the provisions contained in Section 7880, General Code, and comes within the provision of said section as to the length of time such teacher has taught, then such teacher can teach in other public schools of the state than the one from which such teacher has retired, or in the public institutions of the state, and continue to draw her pension. The same rule applies when a teacher voluntarily retires.

2nd. If a teacher requests to be retired under Section 7880, General Code, and after drawing one month's pension, she may marry and still continue to draw her pension the remainder of her natural life. — *Attorney General,* Opinion No. 869, 1914.

For a discussion of the policy of the legislature with reference to teachers' pension fund, see Reid v. Board of Education, 6 O. N. P. (N. S.) 526.

SECTION 7881. The term "teacher" in this chapter shall include all teachers regularly employed by either of such boards in the day schools, including the superintendent of schools, all superintendents of instruction, principals, and special teachers, but in estimating years of service, only service in public day schools or day high schools, supported in whole or in part by public taxation, shall be considered. (98 v. 157.)

In order to be entitled to a pension, a teacher must have served thirty years of actual teaching, and a leave of absence granted to such teacher cannot be counted as service for fixing the amount of pension paid to such teacher under the provisions of Section 7883, General Code, whether the same be granted because of ill health or not. — *Attorney General,* Opinion No. 917, May 6, 1914.

For a discussion of the policy of the legislature with reference to teachers' pension fund, see Reid v. Board of Education, 6 O. N. P. (N. S.) 526.

Voluntary retirement.

SECTION 7882. Any teacher may retire and become a beneficiary under this chapter who has taught for a period aggregating thirty years. But one-half of such term of service must have been rendered in the public schools or in the high schools of such school district, or in the public schools or high schools of the county in which the district is located, and the remaining one-half in the public schools of this state or elsewhere. (101 v. 306.)

1st. If a teacher is forced to retire by virtue of the provisions contained in Section 7880, General Code, and comes within the provision of said section as to the length of time such teacher has taught, then such teacher can teach in other public schools of the state than the one from which such teacher has retired, or in the public institutions of the state, and continue to draw her pension. The same rule applies when a teacher voluntarily retires.

2nd. If a teacher requests to be retired under Section 7880, General Code, and after drawing one month's pension, she may marry and still continue to draw her pension the remainder of her natural life. — *Attorney General,* Opinion 869, 1914.

In order to be entitled to a pension, a teacher must have served thirty years of actual teaching, and a leave of absence granted to such teacher cannot be counted as service for fixing the amount of pension paid to such teacher under the provisions of Section 7883, General Code, whether the same be granted because of ill health or not. — *Attorney General,* Opinion No. 917, May 6, 1914.

Amount of pension.

SECTION 7883. Each teacher so retired or retiring shall be entitled during the remaining of his or her natural life to receive as pension, annually, twelve dollars and fifty cents for each year of service as teacher, except that in no event shall the pension paid to a teacher exceed four hundred and fifty dollars in any one year. Such pensions shall be paid monthly during the school year. (101 v. 306.)

In order to be entitled to a pension, a teacher must have served thirty years of actual teaching, and a leave of absence granted to such teacher cannot be counted as service for fixing the amount of pension paid to such teacher under the provisions of Section 7883, General Code, whether the same be granted because of ill health or not. — *Attorney General,* Opinion No. 917, May 6, 1914.

Who not entitled to pension.

SECTION 7884. No such pension shall be paid until the teachers contributes, or has contributed, to such fund a sum equal to twenty dollars a year for each year of service rendered as teacher, but which sum shall not exceed six hundred dollars. Should any teacher retiring be unable to pay the full amount of this sum before receiving a pension, in paying the annual pension to such retiring teacher, the board of trustees must withhold on each month's payment twenty per cent. thereof, until the amount above provided has been thus contributed to the fund. (98 v. 157.)

It is not compulsory for a teacher, even if financially able, to pay the entire sum of six hundred dollars, before being eligible to receive a pension under the pension act. The wording of this act makes the payment of this fund discretionary with such teacher.

This section seems to equalize the burden between teachers who have paid for the full term of service and those who have not. — *Attorney General* Opinion.

In order to be entitled to a pension, a teacher must have served thirty years of actual teaching, and a leave of absence granted to such teacher cannot be counted as service for fixing the amount of pension paid to such teacher under the provisions of Section 7883, General Code, whether the same be granted because of ill health or not. — *Attorney General,* Opinion 917, May 6, 1914.

SECTION 7885. If such pension fund at any time be insufficient to meet the pensions so provided for, during the period it is insufficient to make such payment, the amount in such fund shall be prorated between the parties entitled thereto. (98 v. 157.)

<small>How, when fund insufficient to pay pensions.</small>

For a discussion of the policy of the legislature with reference to teachers' pension fund, see Reid v. Board of Education, 6 O. N. P. (N. S.) 526.

SECTION 7886. Such board of trustees may use both the principal and income of such fund for the payment of the premiums herein provided for, and the expense thereof, but this shall not apply to the principal of moneys received from donations, legacies, gifts, bequests, or other such sources. (98 v. 158.)

<small>Use of principal and income.</small>

SECTION 7887. Before its distribution and payment by the board of trustees to the beneficiaries, no part of such pension fund shall be liable to be taken or subjected by any writ or legal process against the beneficiary. (98 v. 158.)

<small>Pension exempt.</small>

SECTION 7888. The clerk of the board of education of such school district, and the clerk of the union board of high schools, or other separate board having the control and management of the high schools of the district, if any, each shall certify monthly to such board of trustees all amounts deducted from the salaries of the teachers as above provided, which amounts, as well as all other moneys contributed to such fund, must be set apart as a special fund for the purposes herein specified, subject to the order of the board of trustees. Moneys belonging to such fund shall be paid only on the order of such board, entered upon its minutes on warrants signed by its president and secretary. (95 v. 612.)

<small>Monthly certifications of deductions from salaries.</small>

Who custo-
dian of fund.

SECTION 7889. The treasurer of such school district shall be the custodian of such pension fund, and keep it subject to the order, control and direction of the board of trustees. He must keep books of accounts concerning the fund in such manner as may be prescribed by such board which always shall be subject to the inspection of the board of trustees or of any member thereof. Such treasurer shall execute a bond to the board of trustees with good and sufficient sureties in such sum as the board requires, which bond shall be subject to its approval, and be conditioned for the faithful performance of his duties as custodian and treasurer of the board. (95 v. 612.)

Duties.

SECTION 7890. Such treasurer must keep and truly account for all moneys and profits coming into his hands, belonging to such fund, and at the expiration of his term of office pay over, surrender and deliver to his successor all securities, moneys and other property of whatsover kind, nature and description in his hands or under his control as treasurer. For his services he shall be paid not to exceed one per cent anually of the amount paid into the fund during the year. (95 v. 612.)

Provisions for
refunding.

SECTION 7891. A teacher who resigns, upon application within three (3) months after such resignation takes effect, shall be entitled to receive one-half of the total amount paid by such teacher into such fund. If at any time a teacher who is willing to continue in the service of the board of education is not re-employed or is discharged before his term of service aggregates twenty years, then to such teacher shall be paid back at once all the money he or she may have contributed under this law. But if any teacher who has taught for a period aggregating twenty years is not re-employed by the board of education, such failure to re-employ shall be deemed his retiring, and such teacher shall be entitled to a pension according to the provisions of this act. (102 v. 445.)

Heirs, legatees
or assigns of
deceased
teacher en-
titled to half
amount paid.

SECTION 7892. In case of the death of a teacher, the heirs, legatees or assigns of the deceased, shall be entitled to receive half of the total amount paid by such teacher into such fund upon application therefor, with proof of claim to the satisfaction of the board of trustees. (95 v. 613.)

Rules and
regulations.

SECTION 7893. The board of trustees shall make such rules and regulations as it may deem expedient or necessary for its government; which must be adopted, and when adopted, may be amended, by a vote of not less than two-thirds of all the members of the board. (95 v. 613.)

Monthly pay-
ments to be
made by
board.

SECTION 7894. The board of education in any school district which has created, or shall create, a teachers' pension fund, shall pay monthly into such fund all deductions from the salaries of teachers on account of their tardiness or absence. (95 v. 158.)

SECTION 7895. The board of education in any school district which has created, or shall create, a teachers' pension fund, semi-annually, shall pay from the contingent fund of such school district into such fund, not less than one per cent nor more than two per cent of the gross receipts of the board raised by taxation, which shall be applied to the payment of teachers' pensions, as hereinbefore provided. (98 v. 158.)

Payments from contingent fund.

SECTION 7896. Upon the election and organization of a board of pension trustees under this chapter in any school district, any school teachers' pension fund heretofore created for such district under any former act shall be transferred to the board of trustees created under this chapter by the board or persons having control thereof. Beneficiaries under such transferred fund shall receive pensions under this chapter. (98 v. 613.)

Transfer of existing funds.

CHAPTER 10.

NORMAL SCHOOLS.

State normal schools; location.

SECTION 7897. There are hereby created and established two state normal schools to be located as follows: One in connection with the Ohio university, at Athens, and one in connection with the Miami university, at Oxford. (95 v. 45 § 1.)

Maintenance, control, instruction.

SECTION 7898. Boards of trustees of such universities shall maintain at their respective institutions a normal school which shall be co-ordinate with existing courses of instruction, and be maintained in such a state of efficiency as to provide proper theoretical and practical training for all students desiring to prepare themselves for the work of teaching. Such normal schools, in each case shall be under the general charge and management of the respective boards of trustees of such universities. (95 v. 45 § 2.)

Local tax to aid such school.

SECTION 7899. The trustees of any township in this state, in which a normal school is organized and conducted, annually may levy a tax, not exceeding two mills on the dollar upon all the taxable property of the township for the purpose of aiding in the support of such normal school. (97 v. 389 § 1.)

Questions to be submitted to vote.

SECTION 7900. Before the tax can be levied, the question of making a levy for such purpose, shall be submitted to the qualified electors of the township, at a special or general election to be held therein, due notice of which must be given at least twenty days prior to the election, by publication in some newspaper of general circulation in the township. If a majority of the votes cast at such elction upon the question of tax levy is in favor of levying a tax then the trustees of the township therafter annually shall make the levy and report it to the county auditor for collection as other taxes to be paid over, when collected, to the duly qualified and acting treasurer of the board of trustees of such normal school. (97 v. 389 § 2.)

When another election may be held.

SECTION 7901. At any time after four years from the date of such an election, another election may be petitioned for and shall be ordered by the trustees of the township, if the petition be signed by at least forty per cent of the qualified electors of the township. (97 v. 389 § 3.)

SECTION 7901-1. That the normal school system of the state of Ohio created and established by chapter ten of the General Code, be extended by the creation and establishment of one additional state normal school to be located in eastern Ohio, and to be so located as to afford the best opportunity possible for all the people to obtain the benefits and advantages to be derived from teachers trained both theoretically and practically. Such school shall not be located in any city or village which now has a college located therein. (106 v. 490.)

SECTION 7901-2. Within thirty days after the passage of this act the governor shall appoint a commission composed of five persons, not more than three of whom shall be from any one political party and no one of whom shall ·be personally or financially interested· in any site determined upon by said commission. Said appointees shall constitute a commission with͂ full power and authority to select suitable locations, lands, or lands and buildings and secure options on the same as said commission may find necessary for the establishment of said normal school and upon such terms and conditons as said commission may deem to be for the best interests of the state and submit a report of their proceedings to the governor for his approval on or before the first day of December, 1915. The members of said commission shall serve without compensation but shall be paid their reasonable and necessary expenses while in the discharge· of their official duties and shall serve until the appointment and organization of the boards of trustees, hereinafter provided. (106 v. 490.)

SECTION 7901-3. As soon thereafter as the General Assembly shall appropriate a sufficient amount of money for the purchase of said site and the erection of suitable buildings thereon, the governor shall appoint by and with the advice and consent of the senate five competent persons who shall constitute a board of trustees for the proposed normal school in the eastern portion of Ohio. (106 v. 490.)

SECTION 7901-4. The board of trustees shall organize imediately after its appointment by the election from its members, of a president. a secretary and a treasurer, The treasurer, before entering upon the discharge of his duties shall give bond to the State of Ohio for the faithful performance of his duties and the proper accounting for all moneys coming into his care. The amount of said bond shall be determined by the trustees, but shall not be for less sum than the estimated amount which may come into his control at any time. Said bond shall be approved by the attorney·general.

Before adopting plans for the buildings of said normal school the board shall elect a president of known ability for the school under its control, who shall have advisory power in determining said plans. In planning said buildings, ample provisions shall be made for the establishment of a well-equipped department for the preparation of teachers in the subject of agriculture.

Corps of teachers.

The board of trustees in connection with the president of the normal school shall elect and appoint an able and efficient corps of instructors for the said school, provide a suitable course of study for the theoretical and practical training of students who desire to prepare themselves for the work of teaching, fix rates of tuition and provide proper equipment.

Purchase of site and erection of buildings.

Said board shall proceed without unnecessary delay to purchase said selected sites, lands and buildings, as the case may be, and erect thereon suitable and substantial buildings, or enlarge, reconstruct and properly repair in a suitable and substantial manner such building or buildings, if any there be, and complete said buildings as soon as conditions will permit. And said board of trustees shall do any and all things necessary for the proper maintenance and successful and continuous operation of said normal school and may receive donations of lands and moneys for the purpose of said normal school.

Terms of members.

The governor when appointing said board of trustees shall designate one member of the board to serve one year, one to serve two years, and one to serve three years, one to serve four years and one to serve five years and thereafter one trustee shall be appointed annually for five years for the control and management of said normal school. They shall serve without compensation other than their reasonable and necessay expenses while engaged in the discharge of their official duties. Not more than three members of the board shall be selected from any one political party. (106 v. 490.)

Removals and vacancies.

SECTION 7901-5. The governor shall have power to remove for just cause any appointees herein named, when, in his judgment, he deems it necessary, and shall fill all vacancies that may occur. (106 v. 490.)

CHAPTER 11.

COLLEGES AND UNIVERSITIES.

MUNICIPAL UNIVERSITSIES, ETC.

Powers of board of directors.

SECTION 7902. As to all matters not herein or otherwise provided by law, the board of directors of a municipal university, college or institution, shall have all the authority, power and control vested in or belonging to such municipal corporation as to the sale, lease, management and control of the estate, property and funds, given, transferred, covenanted, or pledged to such corporation for the trusts and purposes relating thereto, and the government, conduct and control of such university, college or institution. It may, unless prohibited by the terms of the trust under which such estate or property is held, sell, or lease perpetually or for any less period and with or without a privilege of purchase, at a fixed price, any part of the whole of any such estate or property, and on sale, or on an election to purchase under a lease containing a privilege to purchase as aforesaid, convey or transfer such estate, or property, and if heretofore any lease with the privilege of purchase at a fixed price shall have been executed and delivered by said board, or any board preceding it in office, for any part or the whole of any such estate or property, said board shall on an election to purchase such lease convey such permises. All instruments affecting real estate shall be executed on behalf of the board by such of its officers as it shall designate by resolution, authorizing the execution of such instrument and all deeds so executed shall convey all the title of said board and of such municipal corporation in and to the real estate so conveyed; it may appoint a clerk and all agents proper and necessary for the care and administration of the trust property, and the collection of the income, rents, and profits thereof; appoint the president, secretaries, professors, tutors, instructors, agents, and servants necessary and proper for such university, college or institution, and fix their compensation; provide all the necessary buildings, books, apparatus, means and appliances, and pass such by-laws, rules and regulations concerning the president, secretaries, professors, tutors, instructors, agents and servants and the admission, government and tuition of students, as it deems wise and proper, and by suitable by-laws, delegate and commit the admission, government, management and control of the students, courses of studies, discipline and other internal affairs of such university, college or institution, to a faculty which the board appoints from among the professors. (101 v. 237.)

Deeds.

By-laws.

This and the following provisions are constitutional: State, ex rel., v. Toledo, 13 O. C. D. 327.

The erection of a house for the president of the university of Cincinnati was held to be a proper exercise of university function: Cincinnati v. Jones, 16 O. D. (N. P.) 343.

The courts cannot control the conduct of the board of directors in matters which are entrusted by law to their discretion, upon the ground that they are acting unwisely: State, ex rel., v. Schauss, 3 O. C. C. (N. S.) 388.

A board of directors which is appointed under this section, or which acts under G. C. Sec. 7921, is not a corporation, but is a legal body upon which certain powers have been conferred by statute. A conveyance to a municipal corporation of trust property for the purposes for which it was ordinarily dedicated does not deprive the board of the powers and interests conferred upon them by the original donation: State, ex rel., v. Toledo, 3 O. C. C. (N. S.) 468.

The city of Cincinnati has power to take and hold property in trust for educational purposes: Perin v. Carey, 24 How. 465.

SECTION 12417. Whoever, being a student or person in attendance at a public, private, parochial, or military school, college or other educational institution conspires to, or engages in hazing or committing an act that injures, frightens, degrades, disgraces, or tends to injure, frighten, degrade or disgrace a fellow student or person attending such institution, shall be fined not more than two hundred dollars or imprisoned in the county jail not more than six months or both, and, in case of fine, the sentence shall be that the defendant be imprisoned until such fine is paid. (98 v. 124 § 1.) *Hazing.*

SECTION 12418. Whoever, being a teacher, superintendent, commandant or other person in charge of a public, private, parochial or military school, college or other educational institution knowingly permits an act of hazing or of attempting to haze, injure, frighten, degrade or disgrace a person attending such institution shall be fined not more than one hundred dollars. 98 v. 124 § 1a.) *Permitting act of hazing, etc.*

SECTION 12419. Whoever in hazing or attempting to haze a person, tattooes or permanently disfigures his body, limbs or features, by the use of nitrate of silver or like substance, shall be imprisoned in the penitentiary not less than three years nor more than thirty years. (90 v. 353 § 2.) *Mayhem.*

SECTION 7903. When requested so to do by resolution of such board, the solicitor of such municipal corporation shall prosecute and defend, as the case may be, for and in behalf of the corporation, all complaints, suits and controversies in which the corporation or such board is a party, and which relate to any property, funds, trusts, rights, claims, estate or affairs under the control or direction of the board, or which, in any manner, relate to the conduct or government of such university, college or institution. (97 v. 542.) *City solicitor to act as attorney.*

SECTION 7904. The board of directors of such university, college or institution upon the recommendation of the faculty thereof, may confer such degrees and honors as are customary in universities and colleges in the United States, and such others as with reference to the course of studies and attainments of the graduates in special departments is deems proper. (97 v. 544.) *When board may confer degrees.*

University
defined.

SECTION 7905. A university supported in whole or in part by municipal taxation, is defined as an assemblage of colleges united, und'r one organization or management, affording instruction in the arts, sciences and the learned professions, and conferring degrees. (97 v. 544.)

The word "university" in G. C. Sec. 4001 is used in its popular and not in its technical sense: Waddick v. Merrill, 5 O. C. C. (N. S.) 103.
The definition of a "university" given in this section can have no bearing on the question of control of a school established by a private donor to carry out his purposes in regard to education, and endowed by his property and the property of others given for the same purpose. The denominating of such a school as a "university" does not deprive it of the protection of the con-stitution of the state and the guaranty that all private property shall ever be held inviolate, notwithstanding it has not yet attained to the full scope of a university: State, ex rel., v. Toledo, 5 O. C. C. (N. S.) 277.
Although not, technically speaking, a "university" within the meaning of this section, the Toledo university is governed by the laws which relate to municipal universities: Waddick v. Merrill, 5 O. C. C. (N. S.) 103.

Council may
provide site
for municipal
university.

SECTION 7906. The council of any such municipal corporation may set apart, or appropriate as a site for the buildings and grounds of such a university, college or insti-tution, public grounds of the city not especially appropri-ated or dedicated by ordinance to any other use, any other law to the contrary notwithstanding; and the board of education of such a municipal corporation also, for a like purpose may set apart, convey or lease for a term of years, any grounds or building owned or controlled by such board. (97 v. 544.)

This section is constitutional: State, ex rel., v. Toledo, 3 O. C. C. (N. S.) 468.
A municipal corporation may set apart public ground for a municipal university which has been created by private endowment, although such ground has been paid for out of the funds raised by general taxation: Cin-cinnati v, McMicken, 6 O. C. C, 188, 3 O. C. D. 409 (affirmed without report, McMicken v. Cincinnati, 29 Bull. 168.)
The word "university" in G. C. Sec. 4001 is used in its popular and not in its technical sense: Waddick v. Merrill, 5 O. C. C. (N. S.) 103.

How such grant
changed.

SECTION 7907. Any grant for the use of such grounds, or buildings heretofore or hereafter made by any council or board of education, may be modified, changed or extended as to the time when it shall take effect and be in force, or otherwise, by agreement between such council, or board of education, and the board of directors of such university, college or institution. Such council shall be taken and held to be the representative of such municipal corporation vested with the title, right of possession and entire control of such property for the purposes of a new grant. (97 v. 544.)

This section is constitutional: State, ex rel., v. Toledo, 3 O. C. C. (N. S.) 468.
Physical culture is included as a necessary university purpose and in-closure of part of the university grounds as an athletic field is a necessary and proper use thereof: University Directors v. Cincinnati, 1 O. N. P. (N. S.) 105.

Tax levies.

SECTION 7908. The council annually may assess and levy taxes on all the taxable property of such municipal cor-poration to the amount of five-tenths of one mill on the dollar valuation thereof, less the amount necessary to be levied to pay the interest and sinking fund on all bonds is-sued for the university subsequent to June 1, 1910, to be applied by such board to the support of such university, college or institution and also levy and assess annually five one-hundredths of one mill on the dollar valuation thereof, for the establishment and maintenance of an astronomical observatory, or for other scientific purposes, to be determined by the board of directors and to be used in connection with such university, college or institution, the proceeds of which shall be applied by the board of directors for such purposes exclusively. But such taxes shall only be levied and assessed when the chief work of such university, college or institution is the maintenance of courses of instruction, in advance of, or supplementary to, the instruction authorized to be maintained in high schools by boards of education.

The above tax levies shall not be subject to any limitations of rates of taxation or maximum rates provided by law, except the limitations herein provided, and the further exception that the combined maximum rate for all taxes levied in any year in any city or other tax district shall not exceed fifteen mills. (103 v. 472.)

SECTION 7909. Such levies shall be made by the council at the time, and in like manner as other levies for other municipal purposes, and must be certified by it and placed upon the tax duplicate as other municipal levies. The funds of any such university, college or institution shall be paid out by the treasurer upon the order of the board of directors and the warrant of the auditor. (98 v. 128.) *When levy to be made.*

SECTION 7910. Any municipal corporation having a university supported in whole or part by municipal taxation, may issue bonds for the erection of additional buildings or the completion of buildings not completed, for such municipal university, and for the equipment thereof. (99 v. 133 § 1.) *Municipal university.*

SECTION 7911. Such bonds may be issued under ordinance of the council of such municipality with the approval of the mayor, but only upon the receipt of a certified resolution from the board of directors of such university of the necessity of such issue. The resolution and ordinance must specify the amount of the issue, the denomination of bonds, their rate of interest, their dates, and the times of their maturity. (99 v. 133 § 2.) *Issue of bonds.*

SECTION 7912. The bonds so issued shall be sold according to the provisions of law for the sale of municipal bonds, and the proceeds thereof, excepting the premiums and accrued interest, shall be placed in the treasury of such municipality and be used only for the purpose of erecting or completing and equipping such additional bulidings as may have been specified in the resolution and ordinance calling for their issue. (99 v. 133 § 3.) *Disposal of bonds.*

Power and control vested in directors.

SECTION 7913. In the use of such fund for such purpose, all power and control shall be vested in the board of directors of the municipal university. Such board shall make any contracts necessary for the erection or completion of the buildings specified, and the equipment thereof; supervise their erection, completion and equipment, and issue proper vouchers for the payment out of such fund of moneys due under such contracts, and for any other expenses connected with the erection, completion, and equipment of such buildings. The amount of premium and accrued interest arising from the sale of the bonds shall be paid into the sinking fund. (99 v. 133 § 3.)

Duties of trustees of sinking fund.

SECTION 7914. The trustees of the sinking fund of any municipality issuing bonds under the above authority, annually shall levy a tax sufficient to pay the interest, and to provide a sinking fund for the final redemption of the bonds at maturity. (99 v. 134 § 4.)

Board of directors of educational institution may accept educational trusts.

SECTION 7915. The board of directors of a university, college or other educational institution of any municipal corporation, in the name and on behalf of such corporation, may accept and take any property or funds heretofore or hereafter given to such corporation for the purpose of founding, maintaining or aiding a university, college or institution for the promotion of education, and upon such terms, conditions and trusts consistent with law as such boards deems expedient and proper for that end. (97 v. 541.)

The term "university" in G. C. Sec. 4001 is used in its popular and not in its technical sense: Waddick v. Merrill, 5 O. C. C. (N. S.) 108.

This section is constitutional: State, ex rel., v. Toledo, 3 O. C. C. (N. S.) 468.

A manual training and polotechnic school which is founded upon private donation accepted under this section, is not a public school in the sense that high schools and grammar schools are public schools: State, ex rel., v. Schauss, 3 O. C. C. (N. S.) 388.

The city of Cincinnati has power to take and hold property in trust for educational purposes: Perin v. Carey, 24 How. 465.

A college of dental surgery has no power to agree to pay interest upon its shares of stock: Ohio College of Dental Surgery v. Rosenthal, 45 O. S. 183.

A college or university which does not come within the letter of the statute will be held to be within its spirit, especially if subscriptions thereto have been made and accepted and liabilities have been incurred thereon: Ohio Wesleyan Female College v. Love's Executor, 16 O. S. 20; Irwin v. Lombard University, 56 O. S. 9.

The property of the Cincinnati college was held to be private property, so that the legislature could not give such property to the university of Cincinnati: State, ex rel., v. Neff, 52 O. S. 376.

If a subscription is made to a college or university, and in reliance thereon, and in order to carry out the object thereof, such college or university incurs liabilities or makes expenditures, such liabilities are expenditures and furnish a sufficient consideration to support such promise: Ohio Wesleyan Female College v. Love's Executor, 16 O. S. 20, Irwin v. Lombard University, 56 O. S. 9.

A subscription which is made for the purpose of paying the pre-existing debts of a college or university is not supported by sufficient consideration, since such college or university cannot have made expenditures or incurred liabilities in reliance thereon: Johnson v. Otterbein University, 41 O. S. 527.

Exemption from taxation.

SECTION 7915-1. All such property, personal or mixed, or real property located within the county in which an university, college or other educational institution of any municipal corporation is located, heretofore or hereafter so given to or received by the board of directors of a university, college or other educational institution of any mu-

nicipal corporation, the rents, issues, profits and income
of which are used exclusively for the use, endowment or
support of a university, college or other educational institution of any municipal corporation, shall be exempted
from taxation so long as such property or the rents, issues,
profits or incomes thereof is used for and exclusively applied to the endowment or support of such university, college or other educational institution of such municipal
corporation. (102 v. 32.)

SECTION 7916. For the further endowment, mainte- How trust
nance and aid of any such university, college or institution funds to be applied.
heretofore or hereafter founded, the board of directors
thereof, in the name and in behalf of such municipal corporation may accept and take as trustee and in trust for
the purposes aforesaid any estate, property or funds which
may have been or may be lawfully transferred to the municipal corporation for such use by any person, persons or
body corporate having them, or any annuity or endowment
in the nature of income which may be covenanted or
pledged to the municipal corporation, towards such use by
any person, persons or body corporate. Any person, persons or body corporate having and holding any estate,
property or funds in trust or applicable for the promotion
of education, or the advancement of any of the arts or
sciences, may convey, assign and deliver these to such municipal corporation as trustees in his, their or its place, or
covenant or pledge its income or any part thereof to it.
Such estate, property, funds or income shall be held and
applied by such municipal corporation in trust for the
further endowment, maintenance and aid of such university, college or institution, in accordance nevertheless with
the terms and true intent of any trust or condition upon
which they originally were given or held. (97 v. 542.)

The term "university" in G. C. Sec. 4001 is used in its popular and not
in its technical meaning: Waddick v. Merrill, 5 O. C. C. (N. S.) 103.
Under this section the board of directors has power to accept or to
reject a gift; but if such board decides to accept a gift, it can accept it only
in accordance with the terms and conditions upon which such gift is offered:
State, ex rel., v. Schauss, 3 O. C. C. (N. S.) 388.

SECTION 7917. Upon such transfer and the accept- Trusteeship
ance thereof the municipal corporation and its successors, to vest in city, etc.
as trustees shall become and be perpetually obligated and
held to observe and execute such trust in all respects according to any other or further terms or conditions lawfully agreed upon at the time of such transfer and acceptance. Any court having jurisdiction of the appointment of
trustees of such trust for educational purposes, in a proceeding therefor, duly instituted and had, may, with the
consent of its council, appoint and constitute such municipal corporation, trustee of the estate. property and funds
so transferred to it, and dispense with bond and surety
upon the part of the municipality for the performance of
such trust, unless that is required by the original terms or
conditions thereof, and upon the due transfer and acept-

ance of such trust, shall release and fully discharge the trustees so transferring it. Any acceptance or acceptances by such municipal corporation of any or all property funds, rights, trust estate or trusts heretofore given, granted, assigned, or otherwise conveyed or transferred to or bestowed upon such a municipal corporation or to or upon such a university, college or institution in good faith, and which are still held and retained by such municipality or such a university, college or institution, shall be held and deemed to be valid and binding as to all parties. (97 v. 542.)

Account of receipts and expenditures of endowment fund.

SECTION 7918. The accounts of such trust estate, property and funds, and of the income and expenditure thereof, shall be kept by the auditor of such municipal corporation entirely distinct from all other accounts or affairs of the municipality and the moneys must be kept by the treasurer of the municipal corporation distinct from other moneys. Such board of directors, at all times, must confine their disbursements for current expenses within the income of the trust, estate, property and funds, and annually shall report to the mayor and council of such municipality a full statement of the accounts of administration of such trust and other funds. (97 v. 543.)

The construction of a dwelling house for the president is a proper expenditure of university funds: Cincinnati v. Jones, 16 O. D. (N. P.) 313.

How funds invested.

SECTION 7919. Such board may invest any part of the funds belonging to, or set apart for the use of such university, college or institution, or to any department thereof, as it from time to time deems proper, in bonds of the United States or of the state of Ohio, or of any municipal corporation of this state, or any county or school district herein, or in any other bonds or first mortgage securities approved by it; and may use any funds including those arising from sales of any property sold under section seventy-nine hundred and two hereof, (provided the terms of the trust do not prohibit such use), in the improvement of any real or leasehold estate belonging either to the particular trust of which the property sold was part or to any other trust under its control or management; or in the improvement of any real or leasehold estate set apart for the use of such university, college or institution. (101 v. 237.)

Citizens not to be charged for admission of children.

SECTION 7920. Citizens of such municipality shall not be charged for instruction in the academic department, except in professional couses therein. Such board of directorm may charge fees to students in other departments and to students in profession courses in the academic department, and from time to time may make such university, college or institution free in any or all of its departments to citizens of the county in which it is located. The board of directors may receive other students on such terms as to tuition or otherwise as they see fit. (97 v. 543.)

For a discussion in detail of the question, who are citizens within the meaning of this section, so as to be entitled to free tuition, see State, ex rel., v. Kuhn, 8 O. N. P. 197.

SECTION 7921. The custody, management and administration of any and all estates or funds, given or transferred in trust to any municipality for the promotion of education, and accepted by the council thereof, and any institution for the promotion of education heretofore or hereafter so founded other than a university as defined in this chapter, shall be committed to, and exerced by, the board of education of the school district including such municipality. Such board of education shall be held the representative and trustee of such municipality in the management and control of such estates and funds so held in trust and in the administration of such institution, excepting always funds and estates held by any municipality which are used to maintain a university as heretofore defined. (97 v. 545.)

Board of education to have control and management of property held in trust for educational purposes.

For the constitutionality of earlier forms of this section see State, ex rel., v. Toledo, 5 O. C. C. (N. S.) 277.
For the validity of this section see State, ex rel., v. Toledo, 3 O. C. C. (N. S.) 468.
This section was held to be unconstitutional insofar as it changes the plans and purpose of the terms of the original trust created by the donors and accepted by the municipal council: Toledo v. Seiders, 56 Bull. 77.

SECTION 7922. For the uses and purposes of such board of education in administering such trusts, the council of such municipality annually may levy taxes on all the taxable property of such municipal corporation to the amount of three-tenths of one mill on the dollar valuation thereof. (97 v. 545.)

Tax levy.

This section is constitutional: State, ex rel., v. Toledo, 3 O. C. C. (N. S.) 468.
The provisions of the municipal code with reference to municipal universities (see G. C. Sec. 4001, et seq.) do not repeal the power of taxation given by this section: Waddick v. Merrill, 5 O. C. C. (N. S.) 103.

STATE UNIVERSITIES GENERALLY.

SECTION 7923. Inasmuch as it is deemed desirable for this state to determine its policy in regard to the support of institutions of higher learning, and further desirable that it adopt a distinct and fixed policy in regard to universites and colleges for all time to come so that the policy of the state with reference to the Ohio State university, the Miami university and the Ohio university shall be determined and made definite and to the end that the state may build up one university worthy of it, as now begun at the Ohio State university, and also to fix such a policy as will provide support for the Miami and Ohio universities, as colleges of liberal arts, but not to include technical or graduate instruction, aside from the usual graduate work for the degree of master of arts, and to determine definitely for all time that the Miami university and the Ohio university shall be no greater charge on the state so far as university purposes

Declaration of policy of state with respect to Ohio state university, Ohio university and Miami university.

are concerned than herein provided for; therefore this sub-division of this chapter is passed to set forth the policy, to-wit: That in the future no representative of the Miami university or of the Ohio university or of the Ohio State university shall violate or attempt to violate this policy herein enacted into law as a policy for the support of higher education and as a guide for future general assemblies of the state of Ohio. (98 v. 309 § 1.)

Tax levy for support of Miami university.
SECTION 7924. For the purpose of affording support to the Miami university, there shall be levied annually a tax on the grand list of the taxable property of the state, which tax shall be collected in the same manner as other state taxes and the proceeds of which shall constitute "the Miami university fund." The rate of such levy shall be eighty-five ten thousandths of one mill upon each dollar of valuation of such property. The sum raised by such levy, or its equivalent in money in case the levy is abolished, shall be the sum total received either from the proceeds of the levy or from appropriations for the support of the college of liberal arts, and shall be used only for the purposes set forth in the next preceding section. This levy shall not hereafter be increased. But this shall not prevent such appropriations from time to time as may be necessary for apparatus for university purposes, exclusive of buildings. (102 v. 266.)

The county auditor has no authority under the Smith one per cent. tax law to place upon the tax duplicate any levies over which the budget commission has control, before that commission has met, organized and performed the duties imposed by section 5649-3c, General Code.

The respective levies for county, township, municipal and school purposes are exclusive of the levy for state purposes; but levies for all these purposes together with the state levy must not exceed, in a given taxing district, the limitations of ten mills, the amount of taxes raised in 1910 and fifteen mills, respectively imposed by different sections of the Smith one per cent. tax law. —*Attorney General*, 1911-12, p. 1614.

The grammatical construction and the use of the term levy, and the intransitive form "providing for" in the phrase "laws providing for tax levies," section 1-b, article II, of the constitution, compel the conclusion that this section is intended to comprehend only such acts as provide for a specified levy and impose upon some office the mandatory duty of making the same at a defined rate on the grand duplicate of the state or some subdivision thereof.

A law, therefore, such as is House Bill 500, which merely provides for the making of tax levies generally and prescribes the machinery by which such levies are to be carried out, is not subject to the exception provided in this section of the constitution, and is therefore subject to the initiative and referendum. —*Attorney General*, 1913, p. 599.

Tax levy for support of Ohio university.
SECTION 7925. For the purpose of affording support to the Ohio university, there shall be levied annually a tax on the grand list of the taxable property of the state which shall be collected in the same manner as other state taxes and the proceeds of which shall constitute "the Ohio university fund." The rate of such levy shall be eighty-five

ten thousands of one mill upon each dollars of valuation
of such taxable property. The sum raised by means of
such levy, or its equivalent in money, in case the levy is
abolished, shall be the sum total received either from the
proceeds of the levy or from appropriations for the support
of the college of libertal arts, and shall be used only for the
purposes set forth in section seventy-nine hundred and
twenty-three. This levy shall not hereafter be increased.
But this shall not prevent such appropriations from time to
time as may be necessary for apparatus for university purposes, exclusive of buildings. (102 v 266.)

The county auditor has no authority under the Smith one
per cent. tax law to place upon the tax duplicate any levies over
which the budget commission has control, before that commission
has met, organizeed and prformed the duties imposed by section
5649-3c, General Code.

The respective levies for county, township, municipal and
school purposees are exclusive of the levy for state purposes;
but levies for all those purposes together with the state levy
must not exceed, in a given taxing district, the limitations of
ten mills, the amount of taxes raised in 1910 and fifteen mills,
respectively imposed by different sections of the Smith one per
cent. tax law. — *Attorney General*, 1911-12, p. 1614.

Money appropriated for the Ohio university by the legislature by House Bill 674, in the sum of $15,000, for the completion
of the electric light plant, comes within the requirements of sections 3216 and 3218, et seq., providing for the advertisement and
reception of proposals or bids, and providing for the execution
of the contract entered into on the bid or proposal accepted. —
Attorney General, 1913, p. 1016.

Under the act of 1804, establishing the Ohio university, and the act of
1805, amendatory thereto, the lands of the university, on lease, are subject to
reValuation: McVey v. Ohio University, 11 O. 134.

The board of trustees of the Ohio university have power to lay out
into lots the portion of land marked as "commons" on the town plat of the
town of Athens, and dispose thereof for the benefit of the uniVersity: Crippen
v. President and Trustees of Ohio University, 12 O. 96.

SSCTION 7926. For the purpose of affording support   Tax levy for
to the state normal school or college, in connection with the support of
Ohio university, there shall be levied annually a tax on the at Ohio uni-
grand list of the taxable property of the state, which shall versity.
be collected in the same manner as other states taxes and
the proceeds of which shall constitute "the Ohio normal
school fund." The rate of such levy shall be five one
thousandths of one mill upon each dollars of valuation of
such taxable property, unless otherwise designated by the
general assembly. Nothing in this section shall prevent
such normal school from securing such additional appropriations as the general assembly sees fit to make from time
to time for the support and equipment of the school. (102
v. 266.)

The county auditor has no authority under the Smith one
per cent. tax law to place upon the tax duplicate any levies over
which the budget commission has control, before that commission
has met, organized and performed the duties imposed by section
5649-3c, General Code.

The respective levies for county, township, municipal and
school purposes are exclusive of the levy for state purposes;
but levies for all these purposes together with the state levy

must not exceed, in a given taxing district, the limitations of ten mills, the amount of taxes raised in 1910 and fifteen mills, respectively imposed by different sections of the Smith one per cent. tax law. — *Attorney General*, 1911-12, p. 1614.

Tax levy for support of normal school at Miami university.

SECTION 7927. For the purpose of affording support to the state normal school or college, in connection with the Miami university, there shall be levied annually a tax on the grand list of the taxable property of this state, which shall be collected in the same manner as other state taxes and the proceeds of which shall constiute "the Miami normal school fund." The rate of such levy shall be thirty-five ten thousandths of one mill upon each dollar of valuation of such taxable property, unless otherwise designated by the general assembly. Nothing in this section shall prevent such normal school from securing such additional appropriations as the general assembly sees fit to make from time to time for the support and equipment of the school. (102 v. 266.)

The county auditor has no authority under the Smith one per cent. tax law to place upon the tax duplicate any levies over which the budget commission has control, before that commission has met, organized and performed the duties imposed by section 5649-3c, General Code.

The respective levies for county, township, municipal and school purposes are exclusive of the levy for state purposes; but levies for all these purposes together with the state levy must not exceed, in a given taxing district, the limitations of ten mills, the amount of taxes raised in 1910 and fifteen mills, respectively imposed by different sections of the Smith one per cent. tax law. — *Attorney General*, 1911-12, p. 1614.

Levy for Bowling Green normal school.

SECTION 7927-a. For the purpose of affording support to the state normal school located at Bowling Green, Ohio, there shall be levied annually a tax on the grand list of the taxable property of the state, which shall be collected in the same manner as other state taxes and the proceeds of which shall constitute "the Bowling Green normal school fund". The rate of such levy shall be five one thousandths of one mill upon each dollar of valuation as such taxable property, unless otherwise designated by the general assembly. Nothing in this section shall prevent such normal school from securing such additional appropriations as the general assembly sees fit to make from time to time for the support and equipment of the school. (103 v. 842.)

Levy for Kent normal school.

SECTION 7927-b. For the purpose of affording support to the state normal school located at Kent, Ohio, there shall be levied annually a tax on the grand list of the taxable property of the state which shall be collected in the same manner as other state taxes and the proceeds of which shall constitute "the Kent normal school fund". The rate of such levy shall be five one thousandths of one mill upon each dollar of valuation as such taxable property, unless otherwise designated by the general assembly. Nothing in this section shall prevent such normal school from securing such additional appropriations as the general assembly sees fit to make from time to time for the support and equipment of the school. (103 v. 842.)

SECTION 7928. No moneys derived under the levies provided for in this subdivision of this chapter shall be expended by the Miami university or by the Ohio university for maintaining or giving instruction in any courses of study other than in liberal arts in the normal school or college branches. (98 v. 311 § 6.)

A decision of a state court on the question of the validity of the state tax which was claimed to be exempt from taxation by reason of state statutes and the state constituion does not present a federal question which can be reviewed by a proceeding in error to the United States supreme court (in this case the effect of the statutes creating Miami university and making provisions for the land belonging thereto were considered): Smith v. Hunter, 48 U. S. (7 How.) 738, 2 O. F. D. 632.

SECTION 7929. For the purpose of affording free the advantages to the youth of the state of a higher, technical, liberal, professional, agricultural, graduate and industrial education, including manual training, there shall be levied annually a tax on the grand list of the taxable property of the state, which shall be collected in the same manner as other state taxes and the proceeds of which shall constitute, "the Ohio State university fund." There shall be levied annually for that purpose five hundred and thirty-five ten thousandths of one mill upon each dollar of valuation of such taxable property, or its equivalent in money should such levy be abolished. Nothing herein shall prevent the Ohio State university from securing any appropriations that the general assembly sees fit to grant for the purposes herein set forth. The Ohio State university never shall maintain a normal school, but may establish a teacher's college of professional grade. Nothing in this section shall prevent the board of trustees from charging incidental expense fees and also reasonable tuition fees for professional education. (102 v. 266.)

The county auditor has no authority under the Smith one per cent. tax law to place upon the tax duplicate any levies over which the budget commission has control, before that commission has met, organized and performed the duties imposed by section 5649-3c, General Code.

The respective levies for county, township. municipal and school purposes are exclusive of the levy for state purposes; but levies for all these purposes together with the state levy must not exceed, in a given taxing district, the limitations of ten mills, the amount of taxes raised in 1910 and fifteen mills, respectively imposed by different sections of the Smith one per cent. tax law. — *Attorney General,* 1911-12, p. 1614.

SECTION 7930. No provision of this sub-division of this chapter shall prevent the boards of trustees of the Ohio State university, the Miami university. the Ohio university or the State Normal school at the Ohio university or at the Miami university from charging reasonable tuition for the attendance of pupils of either of such institutions from students who are non-residents of the state of Ohio. (98 v. 312 § 8.)

Sections 5649-2 et seq. limit rate of taxation and repeal by implication existing conflicting statutes. Rabe v. Canton Sch. Dist. Ed. 23 Dec. 698 (11 N. S. 286).

Inspection of accounts.

SECTION 7931. The expenditure of all moneys under the provisions of this sub-division of this chapter or for the purposes of carrying them out, raised or secured from any source whatsoever, shall be subject to the inspection of the state bureau of public accounting, the cost thereof to be paid by the university or college inspected at the cost as provided by law. (98 v. 312 § 9.)

OHIO UNIVERSITY.

Providing for sale of university lands.

SECTION 7932. The owners of lands or town lots held under leases from the president and trustees of the Ohio university, or held under sale leases or assignments by or under the original lessees, may pay to the treasurer of the university, such sum of money, as, placed at interest at six per cent will yield the amount of rent reserved in the original lease, or in case of a division of the original tract or parcel leased, will equal the proper aliquot part thereof, or the part agreed upon by the several owners. But a person so surrendering and releasing to such corporation must pay the necessary expenses incident to such change of tenure, and procure the services of an agent to perform the necessary labor thereof. Upon payment of such sum and of all rents due upon the land, on demand of such owner, the treasurer shall give him a certificate of such payment. (80 v. 193 § 1.)

The board of trustees of the Ohio university has power to lay out into lots the portion of land marked as "commons" on the town plat of the town of Athens, and dispose thereof for the benefit of the university: Crippen v. Ohio University, 12 O. 96.

Lands sold under the act of 1826 which were held under the act of 1804 were said to be subject to state taxes, in Armstrong v. Athens County, 41 U. S. (16 Pet.) 281, 2 O. F. D. 154 (affirming Armstrong v. Athens County, 10 O. 235).

A lease of land of the Ohio university amounts to a contract between the lessee and the state; and a subsequent act of the legislature imposing a tax upon such land, contrary to the provisions of such lease, is invalid, as impairing the obligations of such contract: Matheny v. Golden, 5 O. S. 361).

The position of trustee of the Ohio university is not vacant unless such trustee dies, resigns, or there is a judicial decree declaring that his position is vacant. The act of the legislature in appointing a successor is not an adjudication of the existence of such vacancy: State, ex rel., v. Bryce, 7 O. 82.

Owner to receive deed; form of.

SECTION 7933. Upon such payment, such owner shall be entitled to receive a deed of conveyance for such land by him owned, to be signed by the president of such corporation, countersigned by its secretary, and sealed with the corporate seal of the university, conveying the premises in fee simple to him, or such owner at his option, may demand and receive a certificate as aforesaid. The governor of Ohio, upon presentation thereof, shall execute and deliver to such owner, a deed conveying the premises in fee simple to him. (80 v. 194 § 2.)

SECTION 7934. Either of such deeds, so made, shall
have the effect in law and in fact to vest in the grantee an
absolute estate in fee simple in the premises, subject, however, to all liens, equities, or rights of third persons in, to
or upon the premises. (80 v. 194 § 3.) Validity of such deed.

SECTION 7935. Such secretary shall keep an accurate registry of all such payments, certificates and deeds,
with an accurate description of the tract or lot of land so
paid for or deeded. Thereafter, the land so deeded shall
be subject to taxation in like manner as other freehold
estates in such county. The original leases therefor, in so
far as regards the land so deeded, shall cease to have force
or effect. (80 v. 194 § 4.) Registry of deed, etc., to be kept.

SECTION 7936. The treasurer of the Ohio university,
on or before the first day of January, next, after such receipt of money, must deposit it in the state treasury upon
the certificate of the state audior. The sums so deposited
shall be added to the irreducible trust funds held by the
state for educational purposes, and interest thereon be paid
semi-annually to the treasurer of such university, upon the
requisition of the state auditor; and the president and trustees of the Ohio university shall have power to receive and
hold in trust, for the use and benefit of the university, any
grant or dvise of land, and any donation or bequest of
money or personal property, to be applied to the general
or special use of the university; all donations or bequests
of money, together with other donations and bequests converted into money, shall be paid to the state treasurer, unless otherwise directed in the donation or bequest, and the
sums so deposited shall be added to the irreducible trust
funds held by the state for educational purposes, and interests thereon shall be paid semi-annually to the treasurer of
said university upon the requisition of the state auditor.
(101 v. 208.) Deposit of money. Power of trustees.

Ohio university, Miami university, Ohio State university and
the combined normal and industrial department of Wilberforce
university are not affected by the provisions of Section 24,
General Code, which provides that state officers, departments,
boards and commissions shall pay to the treasurer of state on or
before Monday of each week all moneys received by them during
the preceding week. — *Attorney General*, Opinion No. 705, Jan. 20,
1914.

SECTION 7937. A state tax or a tax equal to the state
tax upon like property, shall be levied and collected upon
all lands donated to the Ohio university, situated at Athens,
Ohio, and held by lease from it or by deed from the governor or the university, including such parts of such lands
as are or may be owned, occupied or used by railroad companies as road-beds, road-ways, station-houses, or for other
purposes. Such taxes, when collected, shall be paid by the
treasurer of Athens, county, upon the warrant of the Levy and col- lection of state tax upon lands donated to Ohio uni- versity.

auditor of the county, to the treasurer of the Ohio university, for its use. (82 v. 115 § 1.)

Where the state, by an act incorporating the Ohio university vested in that institution two townships of land for the support of the university, and instruction of youth, and in the same act authorized the university to lease said lands for ninety-nine years, renewable forever, and provided that lands thus to be leased should forever thereafter be exempt from all state taxes, it was held that the acceptance of such leases at a fixed rent or rate of purchase by the lessees constitutes a binding contract between the state and the lessees. A subsequent act of the legislature, levying a state tax on such lands, is a "law impairing the obligation of contracts" within the purview of the tenth section of the first article of the constitution of the United States, and is, therefore, pro tanto, null and void: Matheny v. Golden, 5 O. S. 361.

Where one of the lessees of such lands sues as well for himself as for many other lesses of the same lands, holding on like terms with himself, equity will interpose to prevent multiplicity of suits and afford a remedy by injunction: Matheny v. Golden, 5 O. S. 361.

Tax in lieu of rents; tax collected from railroad companies.

SECTION 7938. The tax so collected upon lands so held by lease, shall be in lieu of so much of the rents due to the university. The tax so collected from railroad companies, and paid to the university, shall not include the tax upon rolling stock. (82 v. 115 § 2.)

By the fair construction of the resolutions, no discretion is given to the treasurer of the university to determine the amount of rent to be collected; but he is required to collect such an amount of additional rent as equals the taxes imposed on property of like description by the state: Cable v. Ohio University, 36 O. S. 113.

MIAMI UNIVERSITY.

Appointment of trustees.

SECTION 7939. The government of Miami university shall be vested in twenty-seven trustees, to be appointed by the governor by and with the advice and consent of the senate. Nine trustees shall be appointed every third year, for a term of nine year, beginning on the first day of March in the year of their appointment. Vacancies in the board of trustees shall be filled for the unexpired term in the same manner. (66 v. 73 § 1.)

But seven members of the board of trustees of Miami university are required to transact business legally.

Trustees of Miami university are not entitled to a per diem compensation, but are entitled to actual expenses incurred as trustees. — *Attorney General*, Opinion No. 1352, Dec. 31, 1914.

Annual report.

SECTION 7940. In its annual report the board of trustees shall make a full and accurate report of all receipts and disbursements of the preceding year, the number of students in attendance, studies taught, and such other matters connected with the institution as the board deems important. Such report may be transmitted by the governor to the general assembly. (106 v. 508.)

Duty of standing committee on colleges and universities.

SECTION 7941. The standing committee on colleges and universities of each legislature, shall examine into the condition of Miami university, and report to the legislature such matters as it deems important to the interests of the university. (66 v. 73 § 3.)

Deposit of donations and bequests, when converted.

SECTION 7941-1. The treasurer of Miami university on or before the first day of January next after the receipt of any donations or bequests of money or other property to be converted into money must deposit it in the state treasury upon the certificate of the state auditor. The sum so deposited shall be added to the irreducible trust fund held by the state for educational purposes, and interest thereon be paid semi-annually to the treasurer of such university, upon the requisition of the state auditor; and the president and trustees of Miami university shall have power to receive and hold in trust, for the use and benefit of the university, any grant or devise of land and any donation or bequest of money or personal property, to be applied to the general or special use of the university; all donations or bequests of money, together with other donations and bequests converted into money, shall be paid to the state treasurer, unless otherwise directed in the donation or bequest, and the sum so deposited shall be added to the irreducible trust funds held by the state for educational purposes, and interest thereon shall be paid semi-annually to the treasurer of said university upon the requisition of the state auditor. (103 v. 564.)

OHIO STATE UNIVERSITY.

SECTION 7942. The government of the Ohio state university shall be vested in a board of seven trustees, who shall be appointed by the governor, with the advice and consent of the senate. One trustee shall be appointed each year for a term of seven years from the fourteenth day of May of such year, and serve until his successor is appointed and qualified. A vacancy in the office of trustee shall be filled by an appointment to be made in the same manner as an original appointment, but only for the unexpired term. The trustees shall not receive compensation for their services, but shall be paid their reasonable necessary expenses while engaged in the discharge of their official duties. (75 v. 126 §§ 2, 3.)

Appointment of trustees; term, compensation, etc.

For means to establish agriculture and mechanical college, see appendix, Sec. 13881.

The Ohio State university is a branch of the state of Ohio, and not a corporation; and, accordingly, the statute creating such university. is not a special act conferring corporate powers, and is not in violation of Art. XIII, Sec. 1, of the Ohio constitution: Neil v. Board of Trustees, 31 O. S. 15.

A subscription to the Ohio agricultural and mechanical college in consideration that such college shall be located at a certain place, together with a guaranty of a third person of the performance of such subscription, was delivered to the trustees of such college and was accepted by them, and the college was located in accordance with the provisions of such subscription. Such subscription and guaranty are valid and enforceable instruments, and the board of trustees of such college may bring action thereon: Neil v. Board of Trustees, 31 O. S. 15.

That the board of trustees is not a corporation, see, also, Thomas v. University Trustees, 195 U. S. 207.

SECTION 7943. The trustees and their successors in office shall be styled the "board of trustees of the Ohio state university," with the right as such, of suing and being sued, of contracting and being contracted with, of making and using a common seal, and altering it at pleasure. (67 v. 21 § 4.)

Style and power of trustees.

Under the power vested in the trustees of the Ohio State university to contract, to receive donations of personal property without qualifications as to method, and to control and supervise all buildings and other property belonging to the university, said trustees may enter into an agreement of acceptance with a corporation organized to erect dormitories upon the university campus and ultimately to donate the buildings to the university, when the plans of the buildings are subject to the approval of the trustees and a joint control of expenditures and the entire scholastic management of the buildings vested in the trustees pending completion. — *Attorney General*, 1912, p. 991.

The board of trustees of the Ohio State university is not a corporation: Neil v. Board of Trustees, 195 U. S. 207, 14 O. F. D. 433.

Officers of the board.

SECTION 7944. The board of trustees annually shall elect one of their number chairman, and in the absence of the chairman elect one of their number temporary chairman. It also may appoint a secretary, treasurer, and librarian, and such other officers as the interests of the college require who may be members of the board. Such appointees shall hold their offices for such term as the board may fix, subject to removal by it, and receive such compensation as the board prescribes. (67 v. 21 § 9.)

Bond of treasurer, where filed.

SECTION 7945. Before entering upon the duties of his office the treasurer shall give bond to the state in such sum as the board of trustees determines, but not a less sum than the probable amount that will be under his control in any one year, conditioned for the faithful discharge of his duties and the payment of all moneys coming into his hands, the bond to be approved by the attorney general of the state. Such bond shall be deposited with the secretary of state and kept in his office. (103 v. 528.)

Meetings of board.

SECTION 7946. Meetings of the board of trustees shall be called in such manner, and at such times as the board prescribes. The board shall meet at least three times annually, and at such other times as may be necessary for the best interest of the university. A majority of the board present at any meeting shall constitute a quorum to do business; but a majority of all the board shall be necessary to elect or remove a president or professor. (75 v. 126.)

Annual report of trustees; contents.

SECTION 7947. In its annual report the board of trustees shall state the condition of the university; the amount of receipts and disbursements, and for what the disbursements were made; the number of professors, officers, teachers, and other employes and the position and compensation of each, the number of students in the several departments and classes, and the course of instruction pursued in each; also an estimate of the expenses for the ensuing year; a statement showing the progress of the university, recording any improvements and experiments made, with their costs. and the results, and such other matters as are useful. The president thereof shall transmit by mail one copy respectively to the secretary of the interior and the secretary of agriculture of the United States, and to each of the colleges which are or may be endowed under the provisions of the act of congress of July 2, 1862. (106 v. 508.)

SECTION 7948. The board of trustees may adopt by-laws, rules and regulations for the government of the university. (67 v. 21 § 5.)

SECTION 7949. The board of trustees shall elect, and fix the compensation of and remove, the president and such number of professors, teachers and other employes as may be deemed necessary; but no trustee, or his relation by blood or marriage, shall be eligible to a professorship or position in the university, the compensation for which is payable out of the state treasury or university fund. The board shall fix and regulate the course of instruction and prescribe the extent and character of experiments to be made at the university. (99 v. 602 § 9.)

Professors of the Ohio State university may be employed during the two months' vacation for research work of the experiment station, there being no incompatibility in their work at the university and the work at the experiment station. — *Attorney General,* Opinion No. 874, 1914.

SECTION 7950. The board of trustees shall have general supervision of all lands, buildings, and other property belonging to the university, and the control of all expenses therefor, but shall not contract a debt not previously authorized by the general assembly of the state. (67. v. 21 §8.)

Under the power vested in the trustees of the Ohio State university to contract, to receive donations of personal property without qualifications as to method, and to control and supervise all buildings and other property belonging to the university, said trustees may enter into an agreement of acceptance with a corporation organized to erect dormitories upon the university campus and ultimately to donate the buildings to the university, when the plans of the buildings are subject to the approval of the trustees and a joint control of expenditures and the entire scholastic management of the buildings vested in the trustees pending completion. — *Attorney General,* 1912, p 991.

SECTION 7950-1. The construction of a high school building on the campus of the Ohio state university is hereby authorized upon such terms as may be agreed upon by the trustees of the Ohio state university and the board of education of the city school district of the city of Columbus, Ohio, and such high school shall be used as an observation and practice school by the college of education of the Ohio state university upon the terms and conditions as agreed upon by the said board of trustees and the said board of education.

At no time shall the State of Ohio be called upon to assist in defraying the expenses of conducting or repairing such school. (102 v. 297.)

SECTION 7950-2. The board of trustees of the Ohio state university is hereby authorized to enter into a contract with any incorporated association of alumni of said university whereby such association shall be permitted to erect upon the campus of said university, and upon a site to be designated by said board of trustees, a suitable building or buildings to be used as dormitories for students and members òf the faculty of the university. Such contract may provide that the legal title to such building or buildings shall remain in such association, and that the same shall be subject to mortgage or other encumbrance by such association; that the necessary repairs on such building or buildings shall be made by the trustees of the Ohio state university and paid for out of any appropriation made by the general assembly for such purposes; and that the control and management of such building or buildings shall be vested in such association, subject to such disciplinary regulations as may be provided by said board of trustees. Such contract shall, however, provide that upon the payment of the indebtedness of such association, incurred in the erection and equipment of such building or buildings and the discharge of such building or buildings from liens or encumbrances, the legal title to such building or buildings, and any and all appurtenances thereof, and furniture and equipment therein, shall pass to and be vested in the state. The purpose of this section is to authorize the said trustees to permit the alumni of the Ohio state university to present to the state a building or buildings, and furniture and equipment for the aforesaid purposes, and to adopt such plans and financial arrangements as may be, within the limitations hereinbefore set forth, appropriate therefor. (103 v. 660.)

Board may receive devises of land, etc.

SECTION 7951. The board of trustees may receive, and hold in trust, for the use and benefit of the university, any grant or devise of land, and donation or bequest of money or other personal property, to be applied to the general or special use of the university. All donations or bequests of money shall be paid to the state treasurer, and invested in like manner as the endowment fund of the university, unless otherwise directed in the donation or bequest. (67 v. 22 § 11.)

Under the power vested in the trustees of the Ohio State university to contract, to receive donations of personal property without qualifications as to method, and to control and supervise all buildings and other property belonging to the university, said trustees may enter into an agreement of acceptance with a corporation organized to erect dormitories upon the university campus and ultimately to donate the buildings to the university, when the plans of the buildings are subject to the approval of the trustees and a joint control of expenditures and the entire scholastic management of the buildings vested in the trustees pending completion.— *Attorney General*, 1912, p. 991.

Title of lands to be vested in the state, etc.

SECTION 7952. The title for all lands for the use of the university shall be made in fee simple to the estate of Ohio, with covenants of seizin and warranty, and no title shall be taken to the state for the purpose aforesaid until the attorney-general is satisfied that it is free from all defects and incumbrances. (67 v. 22 § 13.)

Under the power vested in the trustees of the Ohio State university to contract, to receive donations of personal property without qualifications as to method, and to control and supervise all buildings and other property belonging to the university, said trustees may enter into an agreement of acceptance with a corporation organized to erect dormitories upon the university campus and ultimately to donate the buildings to the university, when the plans of the buildings are subject to the approval of the trustees and a joint control of expenditures and the entire scholastic management of the buildings vested in the trustees pending completion. — *Attorney General*, 1912, p. 991.

SECTION 7953. The attorney-general of the state shall be the legal adviser of such board of trustees. He shall institute and prosecute all suits in their behalf and receive like compensation therefor as he is entitled to by law for suits brought in behalf of the asylums of the state. (67 v. 22 § 15.) Attorney-general to be legal adviser of the board.

SECTION 7954. The university shall be open to all persons over fourteen years of age, subject to such rules, regulations and limitations, as to numbers from the several counties of the state, as is prescribed by the board of trustees. But each country shall be entitled to its just proportion, according to its population. The board may provide for courses of lectures, either at the seat of the university or elsewhere in the state, which shall be free to all. (67 v. 20 § 7.) Who admitted as pupils; lectures.

SECTION 7954-1. That for the purpose of advancing and promoting the science and art of medicine and the science and art of dentistry, the board of trustees of the Ohio state university be, and they are hereby authorized and empowered to create, establish, provide for and maintain in said university a college of medicine and a college of dentistry; and to negotiate for and receive conveyances and transfers of property, both real and personal, to be used for the purposes aforesaid; and to accept the students now in attendance at any college of medicine, dentistry or pharmacy whose property is so acquired, with the rank and standing as certified by the proper officers of such college; and to take such steps as may be necessary to protect the professional rights of the alumni of such college or colleges and their predecessors; and to receive from such college or colleges such papers and records as may be necessary for that purpose. (103 v. 344.) Establishment of colleges of medicine and dentistry in Ohio state University.

SECTION 7955. The board of trustees, in connection with the faculty of the university shall provide for the teaching of such branches of learning as are related to agriculture and the mechanic arts, mines and mine engineering and military tactics, and such other scientific and classic studies as the resources of the fund will permit. (77 v. 227 § 10.) Branches prescribed.

SECTION 7955-1. The board of trustees of the Ohio state university is hereby authorized and directed to establish and organize a university extension division for the purpose of carrying on educational extension and correspondence instruction throughout the state. The board of Authority to establish university extension division; purposes.

trustees is authorized to carry on such extension work in connection with any department of the Ohio state university, for the purpose of the development throughout the state of centers for the discussion, consideration and investigation relative to the mining, manufacturing, engineering, social, industrial, economic, medical and civic interests of the state and all other public interests which may be in any way prompted or subserved in the spreading of information throughout the state by any department of the Ohio state university, that now exists or may be hereafter established, pursuant to the grant by virtue of which said university was created and established. (103 v. 662.)

Further purposes.

SECTION 7955-2. The board of trustees of the university, through the university extension division, shall encourage communities to organize for the purpose of social, educational, scientific and recreational advantage, and shall co-operate with them and in every way contribute to the efficiency of the efforts of such communities for these purposes. To this end, as far as practicable, the extension division shall be placed at the service of educational, industrial or civic institutions, organizations and associations, and invite their actve co-operation in matters relating to the civic, scientific, economic and social welfare of the citizens of the state. (103 v. 662.)

Supervise and carry on discussions, investigations, etc., of questions of public interest.

SECTION 7955-3. The board of trustees of the Ohio state university is authorized to carry on, under the supervision of such university extension division, such discussions, investigations, experiments and demonstrations as it may deem advisable for the improvement of the engineering, mining, manufacturing, social, medical, scientific, industrial, economic and civic interests, and such other public interests of the state as may in any way be promoted or subserved by any department of the Ohio state university which now exists or which may hereafter be established, and for such purposes it may provide traveling instructors and conduct correspondence instruction and teaching. It is further provided that any common carrier is authorized and empowered to carry persons employed in such demonstrations, experiments and discussions, and the equipment therefor, and the traveling lecturers and instructors provided for in this act, free, or at reduced rates. (103 v. 662.)

Duties of board as to cereals, etc.

SECTION 7956. The board of trustees shall collect, or cause to be collected, specimens of the various cereals, fruits, and other vegetable products, and have experiments made in their reproduction upon the lands of the university, and make report thereof from year to year, together with such other facts as tend to advance the interests of agriculture. (75 v. 126 § 4.)

SECTION 7957. The board of trustees shall secure and keep in the university a collection of specimens in mineralogy, geology, zoology, botany, and other specimens pertaining to natural history and the sciences. The president of the university shall collect and deposit therein in the manner directed by the trustees, a full and complete set of specimens as collected by him and his assistants, together with a brief description of the character thereof, and where obtained. Such specimens shall be properly classified and kept for the benefit of the university. (75 v. 126 § 5.)

SECTION 7958. The board of trustees of the university shall establish therein a department of ceramics, equipped and designed for the technical education of clay, cement and glassworkers, in all branches of the art which exist in this state, or which profitably can be introduced and maintained herein from the mineral resources thereof, including the manufacture of earthernwares, stonewares, yellowwares, whitewares, china, porcelain and ornamental pottery, the manufacture of sewer-pipe, fire-proofing terracotta, sanitary claywares, electric conduits and specialties, fire-bricks and all refractory materials, glazed an enameled bricks, pressed bricks, vitrified paving material as well as the most economic methods in the production of the coarser forms of bricks used for building purposes; and the manufacture of tiles used for paving, flooring, decorative wall-paneling, roofing and draining purposes; also the manufacture of cement, concrete, artificial stone and all kinds of glass products and all other clay industries, represented in this state. (91 v. 164 § 1.)

SECTION 7959. Such department shall offer special instruction to clay-workers on the origin, composition, properties and testing of clays, the selection of materials for different purposes, the mechanical and chemical preparation of clays, the laws of burning clays, the theory and practice of the formation of clay bodies, slips and glazes, and the laws which control the formation and fusion of silicates. (91 v. 164 § 2.)

SECTION 7960. Such department shall be provided with an efficient laboratory desinged especially for the practical instruction of clay-workers in the list of subjects enumerated in section seventy-nine hundred and fifty-eight, and also be equipped to investigate into the various troubles and defects incident to every form of clay working, which cannot be understood or avoided except by use of such scientific investigation. Such laboratory shall be equipped with apparatus for chemical analysis, with furnaces and kilns for pyrometric and practical trials, with such machinery for the grinding, washing and preparation of clays for manufacture, as is consistent with the character of the department. (91 v. 164 § 3.)

Expert.

SECTION 7961. To conduct this department of ceramics, the board of trustees shall employ a competent expert, who shall unite with the necessary education and scientific acquiremⁿnts, a thorough practical knowledge of clay-working, and not less than two ᵧears' actual experience in some branch of the art. He shall teach the theoretical part of the subject, conduct the laboratory for the instruction of students, prosecute such scientific investigations into the technology of the various clay industries as may be practicable, and from time to time publish the results of his investigation in such form that they will be accessible to the clay-workers of the state for the advancement of the art. (91 v. 164 § 4.)

Establishment of engineering experiment station at O. S. U.

SECTION 7961-1. That the board of trustees of the Ohio state university be, and are hereby authorized and required to establish an organization to be known as the engineering experiment station of the Ohio state university, to be affiliated and operated in connection with the college of engineering. (103 v. 647.)

Purposes of station.

SECTION 7961-2. The purpose of the station shall be to make technical investigations and to supply engineering data which will tend to increase the economy, efficiency and safety of the manufacturing, mineral, transportation and other engineering and industrial enterprises of the state, and to promote the conservation and utilization of its resources. (103 v. 647.)

Board of trustees shall have control; administrative and fiscal officers, terms.

SECTION 7961-3. The station shall be under the control of the board of trustees of the university, through the regular administrative and fiscal officers. The board shall appoint a director on recommendation of the president of the university. There shall be an advisory council of seven members, appointed by the board of trustees, of which council the director shall be ex-officio a member, and chairman, said director and the other six members to be chosen from the faculty of the college of engineering. The terms of these members shall be for three years, except that when first organized, two members shall be appointed for one year, two members for two years, and two for three-year terms respectively. It shall be the duty of the director and advisory council to select suitable subjects for investigation, apportion the available funds, and provide for the dissemination of the results to the people of the state. (103 v. 647.)

Laboratories. and equipment of college aVailable for use.

SECTION 7961-4. The various laboratories of the college of engineering and the equipments shall be available for the use of the engineering experiment station, provided always that their use for instruction and research in the regular work of the college shall take precedence over their use by the station. The director of the station shall have authority to procure for temporary or permanent use such additional equipment as may be needed, and install the same in the laboratories of the college or elsewhere. (103 v. 647.)

SECTION 7961-5. The engineering experiment station shall not be conducted for the private or personal gain of any one connected with it, or for the financial advantage of the Ohio state university as an organization, or for the sole benefit of any individual, firm or corporation.

Any commission, board, bureau or department of the state, or any institution owned by the state, may seek assistance of the engineering experiment station, and such requests shall have precedence over all other outside requests. The advisory council of the engineering experiment station is, however, empowered to decline such requests or to require that the expense of such investigations shall be borne in part or in whole by the commission, board, bureau, or department of state, or institution owned by the state, making such requests.

Any individual, firm, or corporation may seek the assistance of the engineering experiment station; the advisory council of said station is, however, empowered to decline to render such assistance or to require that any expense incidental to such assistance shall be borne in part or in whole by the individual, firm or corporation seeking such assistance, and the advisory council of the engineering experiment station is further authorized at its option to publish the results of such investigations.

Nothing in this bill shall be construed as in any way limiting the powers of the advisory council of the engineering experiment station to carry on lines of investigation upon its own initiative. (103 v. 647.)

SECTION 7962. The board of trustees of the university are required to establish therein, a school of mines and mine engineering, in which shall be provided the means for scientifically and experimentally studying the survey, opening, ventilation, care and working of mines. Such school shall be provided with a collection of drawings, illustrating the manner of opening, working, and ventilating mines; with the necessary instruments for surveying, measuring air, examining and testing the noxious and poisonous gases of mines, and with models of the most improved machinery for ventilating and operating all the various kinds of mines with safety to the lives and health of those engaged therein. Such school also shall be provided with complete mining laboratories for the analysis of coals, ores, fire-clays and other minerals, and with all the necessary apparatus for testing the various coals, ores, fire-clays, oils, gases, and other minerals. (85 v. 155 § 1.)

SECTION 7963. The board of trustees shall employ competent persons to give instruction in the most improved and successful methods of opening, operating, surveying and inspecting mines, including the methods and machinery

employed for extracting coal, ore, fire-clay, oil, gas and
other minerals from the pit's mouth and for facilitating
the ascent and descent of workmen, the draining and free-
ing of mines from water, the causes of the vitiation of air,
the quantities of fresh air required under the various circumstances, natural ventilation, mechanical ventilation by
fiues and fans, and other ventilating machinery, the use of
air-engines, air compressors and coal cutting machinery;
also instruction in the various uses of coals, ores, fire-clays,
oils, gases and other minerals, and the methods of testing,
analyzing and assaying such minerals; and the methods
employed in metallurgical and other processes in the reduction of ores and in determining in the qualities of met-
als, particularly iron and steel as shown by practical and
laboratory tests. There also shall be kept in a cabinent
properly arranged for ready reference and examination,
suitably connected with such school of miners, samples of the
specimens from the various mines in the state, which may
be sent for analysis, together with the names of the mines
and their localities in the counties from which they were
sent, with the analysis and a statement of their properties
attached. Such person shall also furnish an analysis of all
minerals found in the state, and sent to him for that purpose
by residents thereof. (85 v. 155 § 2.)

Written anal-
ysis of fertil-
izers.

SECTION 7964. The professor occupying the chair in
the chemical and mechanical department of the university,
upon application, shall make and give a written analysis of
artificial fertilizers furnished to him for that purpose. (75
v. 91 § 2.)

For an act to establish a state forestry bureau, 82 v. 135, see G. C. Sec.
1166, et seq.

Funds from
sale of land
scrip.

SECTION 7971. All funds derived from the sale of
land scrip issued to this state by the United States, in pursuance of any act of congress, together with the interest
accumulated thereon, shall constitute a part of the irreducible debt of the state, the interest upon which, as provided by law shall be paid to the university by the auditor
of state, upon the requisition of the commissioners of the
sinking fund, issued on the certificate of the secretary of
the board of trustees, that it has been appropriated by such
trustees to the endowment, support, and maintenance of
the university, as provided in such act of congress. (75
v. 126 § 8.)

Investment of
interest of
"scrip fund."

SECTION 7972. On the first days of January and July
in each year, the auditor of state shall invest the interest
arising from the "agricultural college scrip fund" in the
same manner in which the principal thereof is invested.
(67 v. 16 § 2.)   •

For acts authorizing certificates of indebtedness to be issued in
anticipation of the levies under G. C. Sec. 7575; 88 v. 591; 89 v. 321; 92 v. 191,
285; 94 v. 94; 95 v. 545.
Refunding certificates issued under acts of 1891, 1892: 91 v. 62.

SECTION 7973. The College of Agriculture and Domestic Science of the university shall arrange for the extension of its teachings throughout the State, and hold schools in which instructions shall be given in soil fertility, stock raising, crop production, dairying, horticulture, domestic science and kindred subjects. No such school shall exceed one week in length, and not more than one be held in any county during a year. (100 v. 11 § 1.) County schools.

The statutes confer authority upon the Ohio State university to lawfully hold an agricultural extension school upon the campus of the university, provided no other such school is held in Franklin county during the.same year. — *Attorney General*, 1912, p. 994.

SECTION 7974. In addition to the holding of such schools, such college shall give instruction and demonstrations in various lines of agricutlure, at agricultural fairs, institutes, granges, clubs, or in connection with any other organizations, that, in its judgment, may be useful in extending agricultural knowledge. The work in extension may also include instruction by mail in agricultural and mechanical arts, and the publication of bulletins designed to carry the benefits of its teachings to communities remote from the college. Any common carrier is authorized and empowered to carry the persons employed by, and the equipment and exhibits used in such instruction and demonstration, free or at reduced rates. (101 v. 256.) Instructions by mail.

The statutes confer authority upon the Ohio State university to lawfully hold an agricultural extension school upon the campus of the university, provided no other such school is held in Franklin county during the same year. — *Attorney General*, 1912, p. 994.

SECTION 7974-1. There is hereby created and established a state agricultural school to be located at New Lyme, in the county of Ashtabula, to be connected with the Ohio State University, and under the supervision and control of the board of trustees of said university. (106 v. 320.) Establishment of agricultural school at New Lyme; control and supervision.

SECTION 7974-2. Said board of trustees may receive and hold in trust for the special use and benefit of said state agricultural school, any grant, gift or bequest of land or personal property, and also the lands, moneys, notes, mortgages and other personal property now held in trust for educational purposes by the board of trustees of New Lyme Institute located at New Lyme in the county of Ashtabula. (106 v. 320.) Trustees may receive and control certain property.

SECTION 7974-3. The board of trustees of the Ohio State University, in connection with the faculty thereof, shall provide for teaching in said school during a period of at least eight months in each year, such branches of learning as are related to agriculture, the mechanic arts, home economics and such other scientific and classic studies as will prepare students for efficient citizenship, for vocational and industrial pursuits, and for admission to colleges and universities. (106 v. 320.) Branches of learning to be taught.

WILBERFORCE UNIVERSITY.

Normal and industrial department.

SECTION 7975. A combined normal and industrial department shall be established and maintained at Wilberforce university, in Greene county, Ohio. (84 v. 127 § 1.)

Board of trustees.

SECTION 7976. The government of such department shall be vested in a board of nine trustees to be known as "the board of trustees of the combined normal and industrial department of Wilberforce university." Five members of such board shall be appointed by the governor, by and with the consent of the senate, and three members thereof shall be chosen by the board of trustees of the university. The president of the university shall be ex-officio a member of the board. The governor shall appoint one member of such board each year, who shall serve five years, and whose term shall begin upon the first day of July in such year. Such appointment shall be made during the session of the senate next preceding the beginning of such term. (92 v. 275 § 2.)

Choosing of trustees by university board.

SECTION 7977. One member of the board shall be chosen by the board of trustees of the university at a regular meeting in each year, and shall hold office for the term of three years from the thirtieth day of June in such year. (89 v. 368 § 3.)

Vacancies.

SECTION 7978. In case a vacancy in that portion of the board appointed by the governor or chosen by the university board occurs from death, resignation, or other cause, the appointment or selection to fill such vacancy shall be made in the one case by the governor, and in the other by the executive board of the university for the unexpired term. (84 v. 127 § 4.)

Names of trustees to be certified to governor.

SECTION 7979. Forthwith upon a choice by the university board of a trustee, the secretary of the university shall certify to the governor, under the university seal, the name of the persons so chosen as trustees, and shall also in a like manner certify the name of the person chosen by the executive board at any time to fill a vacancy. (84 v. 127 § 5.)

Meetings of trustees; their expenses.

SECTION 7980. The board of trustees so created shall meet in regular session at the university twice a year. The first meeting shall be on the third Thursday in June, and the second on the first Thursday in November of each year. Other meetings may be held at such places and times as a majority of the board determines. The trustees shall receive no compensation, but shall be reimbursed their traveling and other reasonable and necessary expenses out of appropriations under this sub-division of this chapter. (89 v. 368 § 6.)

When a member of the board of trustees of Wilberforce university acts as secretary for the board, he may not receive compensation for such work, although an appropriation has been made by the legislature for the purpose of compensating him for his extra work. — *Attorney General*, 1913, p. 1028.

SECTION 7981. The board of trustees shall take, keep and maintain exclusive authority, directions, supervision and control over the operations and conduct of such normal and industrial department, so as to assure for it the best attainable results with the aid secured to it from the state. The board shall determine the branches of industry to be pursued, purchase through a suitable and disinterested agent, the necessary means and appliances, select a superintendent for the industrial branch of the department, fix his salary and prescribe his duties and authority. The expenditures of all moneys appropriated for carrying out the purposes and provisions of this subdivision of this chapter, shall be made only under such regulations and for such specific purposes not therein provided for, as the board of trustees of such department establish. No money appropriated by the state shall be used for any purpose not in direct furtherance and promotion of the objects of the department. (84 v. 127 § 7.)

Powers and duties of trustees.

SECTIION 7982. No sectarian influence, direction or interference in the management or conduct of the affairs or education of such department shall be permitted by its board; but its benefits shall be open to all applicants of good moral character and within the limitations of age determined by the board. (84 v. 127 § 8.)

Non-sectarian character of department.

SECTION 7983. The treasurer of such department shall give to the state a bond to be approved by the attorney general in the sum of one thousand dollars conditioned that he shall faithfully discharge his duties and account for any money coming into his hands from the state. Such bond shall be deposited with the secretary of state and kept in his office. (106 v. 519.)

Bond of treasurer, where filed.

SECTION 7985. Each senator and representative of the general assembly of the state may designate one or more youth resident of his district who shall be entitled to attend such normal and industrial department free of tuition. (92 v. 275 § 11.)

Designation of pupils by members of general assembly.

SECTION 7986. For the purpose of carrying out the provisions of this subdivision of this chapter, there shall be levied annually a tax on the grand list of taxable property of the state, which shall be collected in a like manner as other state taxes, and the proceeds of which will constitute, "the fund of the combined normal and industrial department at Wilberforce university." The rate of such levy shall be designated by the general assembly at least once in two years. If it fails to designate the rate for any year, for the fund of the "combined normal and industrial department of Wilberforce university" such levy shall be

Levy for Wilberforce university.

thirty-five ten thousandths of one mill upon each dollar
valuation of such taxable property. This shall be paid to
the treasurer of the normal and industrial department at
Wilberforce university in accordance with the provisions
hereof. All revenue arising from tuitions, sales of products
or otherwise under the aforesaid department shall be applied by its board of trustees to defray its expenses, or to
increase its efficiency, a strict account of which shall be kept
by the department board and accompany the report to the
governor. (102 v. 266.)

The county auditor has no authority under the Smith one per
cent. tax law to place upon the tax duplicate any levies over which
the budget commission has control, before that commission has
met, organized and performed the duties imposed by Section
5649-3c, General Code.

The respective levies for county, township, municipal and
school purposes are exclusive of the levy for state purposes; but
levies for all these purposes together with the state levy must not
exceed, in a given taxing district, the limitations of ten mills, the
amount of taxes raised in 1910 and fifteen mills, respectively imposed by different sections of the Smith one per cent. tax law. —
Attorney General, 1911-12, p. 1614.

There is nothing in the Mooney Bill, 104 O. L. 179, which repeals
Section 7986, G. C. However, said section must be read in connection with
said Mooney Bill and the revenues received under the latter part of
Section 7986, G. C., must be paid into the state treasury and appropriated out
of same. Attorney General, Opinion No. 121, March 4, 1915.

CHAPTER 12.

SCHOOLS SPECIALLY ENDOWED.

SECTION 7987. When any person, by deed, devise, gift or otherwise, sets apart any lands, moneys, or effects, as an endowment of a school or academy, not previously established, but does not provide for the management thereof, the common pleas court of the proper county shall appoint five trustees, who shall have the control and management of the property, moneys and effects, so set apart, and of the school or academy thus endowed. They shall hold their offices for five years, and until their successors are elected and qualified. But in making the first appointment the court shall appoint one trustee for one year, one for two years, one for three years, one for four years, and one for five years. The trustees shall be a body corporate, with perpetual succession, and by such name as may be ordered by the court making the first appointment. (53 v. 33 § 1.)

Trustees for schools specially endowed.

The board of trustees of the Toledo university is a legal board vested with certain powers, and not a corporation: State, ex rel., v. Toledo, 3 O. C. C. (N. S.) 468.

For the appointment of trustees of the Toledo university, see State, ex rel., v. Toledo, 3 O. C. C. (N. S.) 468.

The city of Cincinnati, as a corporation, may take any trust, devise and bequest for charitable uses, and it may establish regulations necessary to carry out the objects of the trust, in accordance with the wish of the donor thus expressed in the instrument, whereby such bequest is made: Perin v. Carey, 24 How. 465.

SECTION 7988. Immediately after their appointment the trustees shall organize by appointing a president, secretary and treasurer, from their own number, and severally take and subscribe an oath to faithfully discharge the duties of trustees, and deposit it with the county auditor. Before taking possession of the property, moneys, or effects, constituting the endowment or trust, they severally shall give bond, in such sum as the court requires, with two or more sufficient sureties, to be approved by a judge thereof, whose approval must be indorsed on the bonds, conditioned for the faithful management of the property, moneys, and effects, entrusted to them and accountability therefor in such form as the court or judge may require. From time to time the court may require additional bonds and surety, as appears necessary for the preservation of the trust estate. The bonds required shall be payable to the state, and de-

Organization of board; oath and bond.

posited in the office of the county auditor for safe keeping. (53 v. 33 § 4.)

Filling vacancies; removal.

SECTION 7989. Such court annually shall appoint one trustee, to fill the vacancy then occurring; and at any other time fill vacancies that occur from any cause, for the unexpired term. Upon sufficient cause shown, reasonable notice of the time and place of hearing having been given to the party interested, such court may remove a trustee, and, until a hearing be had, suspend him in the exercise of his office. (53 v. 33 § 2.)

Powers and duties of trustees.

SECTION 7990. From time to time, trustees may establish rules and regulations for the management and safe-keeping of the property, moneys, and effects, belonging to the trust, and the expenditure of the income thereof, and also for the management and govrnment of the school or academy; which must be consistent with the terms of the deed, devise or gift, creating the endowment, and with the laws of this state. They shall not, at any time, or for any cause, incur any debt or liability, beyond the net income of the trust property, moneys, and effects, or use or appropriate it otherwise than to invest for the purposes of income, any part of the principal thereof, unless expressly authorized so to do by the terms of the deed, devise or gift, creating the endowment of trust. (98 v. 206 § 3.)

Contracts with board of education of district in which school is located.

SECTION 7991. The trustees of any school heretofore established under the provisions hereof, and in no way connected with any religious or other sect, and the board of education of the district in which such school is situated, may make contracts whereby such trustees receive into the school pupils from such district, who shall receive such instruction as is, or may be, provided by law for public schools in this state. In consideration of such service by such trustees, such board, under the general restrictions of the law relating to common schools, in so far as they are applicable and not inconsistent herewith, may contribute to the maintenance of such school, and pay such part of the costs of the erection of additional buildings, and upon such conditions, not inconsistent with the deed, devise or gift under which the school is established, as is agreed upon by such board and such trustees. (98 v. 206 § 3.)

Termination of contract if school becomes sectarian.

SECTION 7992. But after the making of such contract if such school becomes sectarian or in way connected with any religious or other sect the contract thereupon shall terminate. When, for such cause, a contract terminates, no right, title, or interest in or to any building toward the cost of which the board of education contributed shall pass to the trustees until full compensation has been made to the board for the contribution made by it to the construction of such building. (98 v. 206 § 3.)

SECTION 7993. On the second Monday of September, Accounts to be rendered. in each year, and at such other times as the court requires, the trustees shall render a full and accurate account, statement, and exhibit, of the condition of the school or academy under their management, and the condition of the trust estate and funds; and cause it to be published in such form as the court directs. Such account, statement, and exhibit, shall be sworn to by the president, secretary, and treasurer, or two of them. (53´v. 34 § 5.)

SECTION 7994. The common pleas court of the proper Visitors. county, annually, at the first session after the second Monday in September, shall appoint three competent and disinterested persons, who may visit any such school or academy, examine it together with the condition of the trust estate or endowment, and shall report thereon to such court. The court shall also authorize such other visitations and examinations as appear to be necessary. (53 v. 34 § 6.)

TITLE IX. PRIVATE CORPORATIONS.

Division 6.

CORPORATIONS NOT FOR PROFIT.

CHAPTER 3.

EDUCATIONAL.

When officers may be appointed and degree conferred. SECTION 9922. When a college, university, or other institution of learning incorporated for the purpose of promoting education, religion, morality, or the fine arts, has acquired real or personal property, of twenty-five thousand dollars in value, has filed in the office of the secretary of state a schedule of the kind and value of such property, verified by the oaths of its trustees, such trustees may appoint a president, professors, tutors, and any other neces-

366

sary agents and officers, fix the compensation of each, and enact such by-laws consistent with the laws of this state and the United States, for the government of the institution, and for conducting the affairs of the corporation, as they deem necessary. On the recommendation of the faculty, the trustees also may confer all the degrees and honors conferred by colleges and universities of the United States, and such others having reference to the course of study, and the accomplishments of the students, as they deem proper. (99 v. 262.)

The board of trustees of the Ohio State university is not a corporation, and it cannot sue or be sued in the United States courts: Thomas v. Ohio State University, 70 O. S. 92.

The board of trustees of the Ohio agricultural and mechanical college is a branch of the state of Ohio, and is not a corporation: Neil v. Trustees, 31 O. S. 15.

A university which has been incorporated by the state, and which is exempt from taxation, but which has received no other state aid, and which has been endowed by private persons, and which charges tuition, is a private corporation; and the courts have no power to regulate or control its internal management as long as its trust funds are not diverted from the purpose for which they were given. Accordingly, the courts can not review the action of such university in dismissing a pupil for a violation of its rules, even though he has paid his tuition: Koblitz v. Western Reserve University, 21 O. C. C. 144, 11 O. C. D. 515.

SECTION 9923. But no college or university shall confer any degree until the president or board of trustees thereof has filed with the secretary of state a certificate issued by the superintendent of public instruction that the course of study in such institution has been filed in his office, and that the equipment as to faculty and other facilities for carrying out such course are proportioned to its property and the number of students in actual attendance so as to warrant the issuing of degrees by the trustees thereof. (104 v. 225.)

Certificate to be filed with secretary of state.

SECTION 9924. A university, college, or academy, or the trustees thereof, may hold in trust any property devised, bequeathed or donated to such institution, upon any specific trust consistent with the objects of the corporations. (50 v. 128.)

May hold donated property in trust.

If a subscription is made to an institution of learning for the purpose of paying future obligations, and liabilities are incurred in reliance upon such subscription, a sufficient consideration exists, and such subscription can be enforced: Wesleyan College v. Love's Executor, 16 O. S. 20; Irwin v. University, 56 O. S. 9 (affirming Irwin v. Webster, 7 O. C. C. 269, 4 O. C. D. 590); Durrell v. Belding, 4 O. C. D. 263; Hooker v. College, 13 Dec. Rep.; 2 C. S. C. R. 353.

A subscription to a fund for paying pre-existing debts of a college is without consideration and cannot be enforced: Johnson v. Otterbein University, 41 O. S. 527.

That a gratuitous subscription cannot be enforced, see Sutton v. University, 7 O. C. C. 343, 4. O. C. D. 627 (affirmed without report University v. Sutton, 54 O. S. 665).

A devise to a university by will executed within a year before the death of the testator, who dies, leaving issue of his body, is invalid by G. C. Sec. 10504; but if the daughter of such testator confirms such devise, the nephews of such testator to whom the property is given in case the daughter does not de ise, cannot attack such gift: Ohio State University v. Folsom, 56 O. S. 701v.

If such daughter has confirmed such devise by deed, her heirs after her death cannot recover the property thus devised: Thomas v. University, 70 O. S. 92.

Property may be devised to the city of Cincinnati in trust for establishing and maintaining colleges for the education of boys and girls; and such city may take such gift in trust: Perin v. Carey, 65 U. S. (24 How.) 465, 3 O. F. D. 634.

SECTION 9925. The president and professors shall constitute the faculty of any incorporated literary college or university, may enforce the rules and regulations enacted by its trustees for the government and discipline of the students, and suspend and expel offenders, as they deem . necessary. (50 v. 128.)

The courts cannot review the expulsion of a student by a private educational corporation: Koblitz v. Western Reserve University, 21 O. C. C. 144, 11 O. C. D. 515.

The faculty of a college or university may regulate matters of discipline, and other matters not so regulated by the board of trustees, as they deem best. The faculty acting as a whole may enforce such regulations, or it may by proper action transfer the power of enforcing such regulation to the president, and may also designate an assistant to the president of a college in the enforcing of such rules, to act in conjunction with the president or in his place when he is absent from the college or university.— *Attorney General*, Opinion No. 845, 1914.

SECTION 9926. Any incorporated university, college, or academy may connect therewith, to be used as part of its course of education, mechanical shops and machinery, or lands for agricultural purposes not exceeding three hundred acres, to which may be attached all necessary buildings for carrying on the mechanical or agricultural operations of such institution. (50 v. 128.)

SECTION 9927. Any company formed in pursuance of this title or which exists by virtue of a sepcial act of incorporation, the property of which, is held as stock, and not derived by donation, gift, devise, or gratuitous subscription may change its capital stock into scholarships when it becomes necessary for the purpose of carrying out the object for which it was formed, in the mode provided in this title for increasing the capital stock of corporations. . (50 v 128.)

A college which is incorporated as a private corporation for educational purposes has power to receive subscriptions to its endowment fund, but in return therefor to give instruction free, either for a limited period or perpetually, according to the amount of the endowment: College v. Carey, 85 O. S. 648.

SECTION 9928. A college, university or other institution of learning, existing by virtue of an act of incorporation, or that hereafter becomes incorporated for any of the purposes specified in this chapter, if three-fourths of the trustees or directors thereof deem it proper, or if the institution is owned in shares, or by stock subscribed or taken, by a vote of the holders of three-fourths of the stock or shares, may change the location of such institution convey its real estate, and transfer the effects thereof, and invest them at the place to which such institution is removed. No such removal shall be ordered, and no vote taken thereon, until after publication in the manner provided by law in case of a sale and distribution of the property of such an institution, in which notice shall be fully set forth the place to which it is proposed to remove the institution. In case of removal, a copy of the proceedings of such meeting shall be filed with the secretary of state. (52 v. 77.)

SECTION 9929. The trustees of a corporation incorporated to create, hold and manage a college endowment fund, the articles of incorporation of which provide that the fund may be applied to any object not inconsistent with the purposes of education different from that particularly specified therein, may apply to the common pleas court in the county where the corporation is located for permission to make such change, designating particularly the purposes to which it is proposed to apply the fund. On being satisfied that such change is not inconsistent with the object of the original creation and institution of the fund, the court shall authorize and sanction it. (51 v. 393.)

The property of a private eleemosynary corporation, although charged with the maintenance of a college, or other "public charity," is private property within the meaning and protection of that clause of Sec. 19, of the constitution of this state, which declares that "private property shall ever be held inviolate": State, ex rel., v. Neff, 52 O. S. 375.

The result of the statute passed April 15, 1892 (89 v. 647), relating to the Cincinnati college, which, in terms, gives absolute control and management of the affairs and property of the Cincinnati college to the directors of the University of Cincinnati, is to take the property of the former and donate it to the latter institution. The statute, therefore, conflicts with Art. 1, Sec. 19, of the constitution of this state, and is void: State, ex rel., v. Neff, 52 O. S. 375.

SECTION 9930. When a vacancy occurs in whole or part, in the board of trustees of an incorporated college, seminary, or academy, by reason of an amendment of the charter thereof, or from other cause, and there is no provision of law for filling it, within three months after receiving information thereof, the governor shall appoint the required number of trustees, one-third thereof to serve for one year, one-third for two years, and one-third for three years. (75 v. 25.)

SECTION 9931. A college, university, academy, seminary, or other institution devoted to the promotion of education, existing by virture of a special act of incorporation, or organized under the provisions of any law, whose property came and is held by donation, gift, purchase, devise, or gratutious subscription, and the amount of which, or the income arising therefrom is limited by such special act, or the articles of association adopted by such institution, may receive, acquire, possess and hold any amount of property, real, personal or mixed, which its board of directors or trustees, for the institution accepts, and by its trustees, sell, dispose of and convey it. But such property shall not be diverted from the express will of the donor, devisor or subscriber. (90 v. 71)

The creation of a fund to pay pre-existing debts of a university is not a consideration for the promise to pay money to such fund: Johnson v. University, 41 O. S. 527.

SECTION 9932. The board of trustees of such a college, university, academy, seminary, or other institution devoted to the promotion of education, in anticipation of donations to be received and collections to be made, for the purpose of constructing, enlarging or adding to college buildings or improvements, may borrow such sum of money as they determine to be necessary therefor, and issue bonds for it and secure them by a mortgage upon the property on which such improvement it to be made, if the property is not held by them under some specific trust. (90 v. 71.)

Statement to be filed.

SECTION 9933. Before such an institution shall be authorized to acquire and hold additional property, the trustees thereof, at a regular meeting of their board, or at a special meeting called for that purpose, from time to time shall make and sign a statement specifying the amount of additional property which they seek to acquire and hold and set forth therein the purposes to which it is to be devoted, which statements shall be entered at large upon the record book of the trustees and be filed in the office of the secretary of state. (90 v. 72.)

How certain boards may be constituted and governed.

SECTION 9934. The board of trustees of any university or college heretofore incorporated, or which may hereafter be incorporated, and operating under the patronage of one or more conferences or other religious bodies of any religious denomination, may accept the provisions of this and succeeding sections 9935, 9936, 9937, 9937-a, 9939, 9941, 9942 and 9943 by resolution adopted at any regular meeting of the board, and entered upon the record of its proceedings. After such acceptance the board in all respects shall be organized, constituted, regulated and perpetuated, pursuant to and under said provisions. No right acquired by any such board, university or college, under its charter or any law of this state, shall in any way be affected thereby. (104 v. 171.)

Trustees to be divided into classes.

SECTION 9935. The president of such university or college shall, ex officio, be a trustee after the acceptance of the provisions of this act by any such university or college. At any meeting of such board after the passage of this act, such board shall divide its number, not including such president, into classes, making one class for each conference or religious body at the time patronizing such university or college, and one class for the alumni of such university or college and one class of trustees at large. No class shall have less than five members nor more than ten. Each conference or other religious body patronizing such university shall have the same number of trustees. The board of trustees of such university or college may designate the number of trustees to be assigned to the alumini association and to the class of trustees at large, but the combined number of trustees apportioned to said patronizing conferences or other religious bodies shall constitute not less than three-fifths of the entire board, not including the president. (104 v. 171.)

Term of office of trustees; vacancies.

SECTION 9936. The regular term of office of such trustees shall be five years, but upon the original formation of classes of trustees one or more trustees may be elected for one, two, three and four-year terms until the regular order can be established. The term of office of an equal number of trustees in each class, as near as may be, shall expire each year. Vacancies which occur in any class of trustees in any manner whatsoever except by expiration of time shall be filled only for the remainder of the term, but the term of office of a trustee shall not expire during any meeting of the board which does not continue for more than two weeks. (104 v. 171.)

SECTION 9937. If the number of conferences or other religious bodies patronizing such university or college shall at any time be increased or decreased, the board of trustees of such university or college may re-classify said trustees of said bodies by an equal reduction of the number in each such class when a new conference or other religious body becomes a patronizing body and by an equal increase of the number in each such class when a conference or other religious body ceases to be a patronizing body. Whenever, by reason of a change in the number of patronizing conferences or religious bodies, it becomes necessary to re-classify the trustees in said board, the board (a lawful quorum being present) shall by appropriate resolution designate the number of trustees apportioned to each class and certify such apportionment to each patronizing conference or other religious body and to such alumni association, and all vacancies in such classes thereafter shall be filled in accordance with such apportionment. (104 v. 171.) *When board may be increased or decreased.*

SECTION 9937-a. The alumni composing the alumni association of such university or college may elect as members of the board of trustees of such university or college, as many members of such alumni association as there are members of the class of alumni trustees assigned or apportioned to said alumni association by the board of trustees of such university or college, this class to constitute not less than one-fifth of the entire board, not including the president. This election shall be held under such regulations as the alumni association may prescribe and the result shall be certified by the proper officials of the amumni association to the board of trustees, which result shall be entered upon the records of said board. Such board of trustees composed of alumni trustees and trustees elected by patronizing conferences or other religious bodies, as provided in section 9935 to section 9937-a inclusive, may increase its own numbers by the election of a class of trustees at large, the number of which class shall be fixed by said board of trustees, under the limitations fixed by sections 9935 and 9937-a. (104 v. 171.) *The alumni association may elect one-fifth of board.*

SECTION 9939. Any conference or other religious body not patronizing any particular university or college may become a patronizing body upon invitation of the board of trustees of such university or college by a majority vote of the whole board. The intention to become such patron- *How a conference may become a patron.*

izing body shall be evidenced by the adoption of an appropriate resolution and certification of the same to the board of trustees of such university or college, and such certified resolution shall be entered upon the minutes of the board of trustees of such university or college thereby completing the right of such conference or religious body to act as a patronizing body. (104 v. 171.)

When right of representation shall cease.

SECTION 9941. If a conference or other religious body patronizing a university or college and having a representation in its board of trustees, ceases to exist, or ceases to patronize such university or college, the right of such conference or other religious body to such representation shall cease, and the board of trustees of such university or college shall apportion or distribute the number of trustees in such class to the remaining patronizing conferences or other religious bodies in order to maintain, as nearly as may be, the established number of trustees and equality of representation from each patronizing body. (104 v. 171.)

Action must be taken by board.

SECTION 9942. Before a conference or other religious body represented in the board of trustees of such university or college shall cease to be represented in said board, the board of trustees shall declare and enter in the rcord of its procedings that the conditions and contingencies terminating such representation have taken place. (104 v. 171.)

Quorum; how constituted.

SECTION 9943. Eleven trustees shall constitute a quorum of the board of any such university or college, whatever the number of trustees if more than twenty is or may become; but when the number is twenty or less, a majority thereof shall constitute a quorum. (65 v. 188.)

Endowment fund corporations.

SECTION 9948. The trustees of a corporation incorporated for the purpose of creating a fund, the income of which is to be applied to the promotion of education, may receive subscriptions for membership in the corporation, and they, or a majority of them, by giving ten days' notice, by publication in the county where the corporation is located, may call a meeting of members to adopt by-laws, and elect not more than nine directors. Each member shall have a vote for every amount by him subscribed equal to that in the articles of incorporation specified as necessary for membership, which may be cast in person or by proxy, but at no subsequent meeting can a member vote for or be eligible as a director who is in arrears to the corporation. The trustees shall control the funds and disburse the income of the corporation as provided by its by-laws. (69 v. 173.)

How certain boards constituted and governed.

SECTION 9949. The board of trustees of a university college or other institution of learning, incorporated, and acting under the patronage of one annual conference or other religious body of a religious denomination, may accept the provisions of this and the succeeding section, by resolution adopted at a meeting of the board, and entered upon the record or journal of its proceedings. After such acceptance the board shall be organized, constituted, regulated, and perpetuated as therein provided. No right acquired by such board, university, or other institution of learning, under its charter, or any law of this state, shall be impaired or affected thereby. (69 v. 180.)

SECTION 9950. The board of trustees of a university or college heretofore incorporated, and now under the patronage of one annual conference, synod or other religious body of a religious denomination, may increase the number of its trustees, not exceeding six. Such additional trustees shall be nominated by the collegiate alumni of the university or college from the collegiate alumni of three years' standing for appointment or election by such patronizing conference or synod, under such regulations as are prescribed by such board, if it determines to increase the number of its trustees and makes such regulations for their nomination, by resolution adopted at a regular meeting of the board and duly entered on the record of its proceedings, and, such patronizing or governing conference or synod consents to the increase and the rules and regulations for their nomination. And after such board is so increased by not exceeding six additional trustees, in all respects it shall be organized, constituted, regulated and perpetuated pursuant to and under its charter, and such provisions. No rights acquired by such a board, university or college, under its charter or any law of this state, shall be affected or impaired thereby. (91 v. 155.) *Increase in number of trustees in certain corporations.*

SECTION 9951. A corporation may be formed for the promotion of acedemic, collegiate or university education, under religious influences, may set forth in its articles or certificate of incorporation, as a part thereof, the name of the religious sect, association or denomination with which it is to be connected, and grant any ecclesiastical body of such religious sect, association or denomination, whether it be a conference, association, presbytery, synod, general assembly, convocation or otherwise, the right to appoint its trustees or directors, or any number thereof. It also may set forth in its articles or certificate such other rights as to the administration of the purpose for which it is organized, consistent with the laws of this state and of the United States, as the incorporation desires to confer upon the ecclesiastical body of such sect, association or denomination, and that body may exercise all rights and powers set forth therein. (94 v. 331.) *Colleges under ecclesiastical patronage.*

SECTION 9952. A corporation formed for the promotion of academic, collegiate or university education, under religious influences, incorporated under the laws of this state, by special act or otherwise, may avail itself of the provisions of the preceding section, as a part of its articles or certificate of incorporation, and may confer on an *How existing corporations may avail themselves of the provisions.*

ecclesiastical body of such religious sect, association or denomination, it is or proposes to be connected with, whether it be a conference, association, presbytery, synod, general assembly, convocation or otherwise, any or all of the rights, powers or privileges by such section allowed to be conferred on corporations hereafter organized, and may accept the provisions by a vote of the majority of its trustees at any regular meeting. (94 v. 331.)

Copy of acceptance to be filed with secretary of state.

SECTION 9953. When so accepted, a copy of the acceptance, certified by the secretary or clerk of its board of trustees or directors, shall be sent to the ecclesiastical body with which it is or proposes to be connected. If such body agrees to accept the powers proposed to be conferred upon it, it shall certify its approval upon the certified copy so sent, and it thereupon shall be filed in the office of the secretary of state. When thus filed it will be a part of the charter of such corporation, and such ecclesiastical body shall exercise all the rights and powers so set forth in the articles or certificate of corporation. (94 v. 331.)

Number of trustees and classes.

SECTION 9954. After such acceptance the board shall certify it to the patronizing conference or other religious body having the right to elect or appoint trustees of such university or other institution of learning, at the next meeting of such conference or other religious body; and thereafter the board shall consist of twenty-one trustees elected or appointed, and the president of such university or other institution of learning, who shall be ex-officio a member thereof. Such elected or appointed trustees shall be divided into three classes of seven members each. (85 v. 140.)

Election; term; vacancies; increase of board.

SECTION 9955. At the first election of appointment after such acceptance, one of such classes shall be elected or appointed for one year, one for two years and one for three years. In subsequent elections or appointments each of the classes of trustees shall be elected or appointed for three years. No term of office of such a trustee shall expire during a meeting of the board which does not continue more than two weeks. Ten mmebers of the board shall constitute a quorum. Vacancies which occur in any class of trustees otherwise than by expiration of the term of office shall be filled only for the remainder of the term. Such a university or other institution of learning which heretofore accepted the provisions of sections ninety-nine hundred and forty-nine, ninety-nine hundred and fifty-four and ninety-nine hundred and fifty-five, may increase its board of trustees by electing or appointing two additional members in each of the classes of trustees herein provided for. (85 v. 140.)

Interchangeable use of the words "academy," "college" and "university."

SECTION 9955-1. A corporation formed for the promotion of academic, collegiate or university education under religious influences, and connected with any religious sect, association, or denomination, and to which, whether it be a conference, association, presbytery, synod, general assembly, convocation, or otherwise, it has granted the right to appoint its trustees or directors, or any number thereof, and which has incorporated into its charter or certificate of incorporation as a part of its corporate name either one or more of the words "academy," "college," or "university," may use one or more of said words not so incorporated therein interchangeably with said word or words which may have been incorporated therein to the same extent and as fully as the word or words so incorporated therein has or have been heretofore used in the name of such corporation, when authorized so to do by a resolution adopted by a majority vote of its trustees, or directors at any regular meeting, or special meeting called for that purpose. Provided that a copy of such resolution certified by the clerk or secretary of such trustees or directors, and accompanied by a resolution of consent passed by such one of such ecclesiastical bodies as aforesaid, with which such corporation is connected, and certified by its clerk or secretary, shall first be filed in the office of the Secretary of State, and a certified copy thereof shall have been issued to and received by said clerk or secretary of such trustees or directors. (104 v. 3.)

SECTION 9955-2. Nothing herein contained, or the interchangeable use of said word or words, as herein provided and authorized, shall be held or construed as abolishing the use of the original corporate name of such corporation, or as affecting the title, right or possession of such corporation to, or of, any gift, grant, devise, or bequest heretofore, or hereafter made to it, whether the same shall have been made or shall be made in the original corporate name, or in one or more of said interchangeable names, or in all of such names: And the use of such original incorporate name, or one or more of such interchangeable names shall be held and construed as vesting in such corporation all gifts, grants, devises, and bequests as fully and to the same extent as if the same had been made in the name of the original incorporated name. (104 v. 3.)

Use of interchangeable words does not affect the right or title to any gift, grant, devise or bequest.

SECTION 9956. The proportion that each stockholder of a college, academy, university, seminary, or other institution for the promotion of education, shall be required to pay to meet the debts and liabilities of the corporation, may be determined and collected in the manner provided by the three succeeding sctions. (58 v. 20.)

Assessments.

SECTION 9957. The trustees of such a corporation desiring to avail themselves of such provisions shall call a meeting of the stockholders for the purpose of determining what amount of its indebtedness shall be paid by each stockholder, and give thirty days' notice to the stockholders in writing or by publication in some newspaper of general circulation in the county where the corporation is located,

Meeting of stockholders; notice.

of the time place, and purpose of the meeting, at which also, the trustees shall submit a detailed statement showing the assets and indebtedness of the corporation. (58 v. 20.)

How amount of assessment fixed. SECTION 9958. A majority in interest of the stockholders present at such meeting may determine what amount of the indebtedness of the corporation is to be paid by each stockholder, and fix the time and mode for the payment of the money assesesd against each stockholder. But these provisions shall not interfere with or abridge the right of a creditor of the corporation to institute any proceedings authorized by law to enforce the liability of stockholders. (58 v. 20.)

Limit of assessment and collection. SECTION 9959. The assessment shall be pro rata upon the stock subscribed or otherwise acquired by each stockholder, and in no case shall exceed the amount for which each stockholder is or may be liable by law. A stockholder who fails to pay the amount so assessed against him, shall be liable in a civil action to be brought in the name of the corporation, for the recovery thereof, as in other cases of indebtedness. (58 v. 20.)

Board of military academies. SECTION 9960. The academic board of an institution incorporated for military and polytechnical education shall consist of the superintendent thereof, the commandant of cadets, and the professors. It may make and enforce rules and regulations for the government of cadets, but they first shall be submitted to and approved by the governor of the state. (64 v. 239.)

Board of visitors. SECTION 9961. The board of visitors of such an institution shall consist of the governor, who shall be ex-officio a member and the president of the board, of two other persons to be named by him, and such other persons as the superintendent of the institution appoints. (64 v. 239.)

Duties of board of visitors. SECTION 9962. The board of vistors shall meet at the institution, on the first day of the annual commencement exercises, and examine into the condition of the classes, quarters, and commons, the discipline, drill, records of standing in study, and conduct of the cadets, and report thereon to the legislature at its next session. The board of visitors, or any member thereof, may visit and inspect the institution at any time. (64 v. 239.)

How term of trustees fixed. SECTION 9963. At a regular meeting for the election of directors or trustees of a college or other institution of learning, the authorized voters may determine by vote. whether the election of directors or trustees shall be held annually, if the term of their election is for a longer period than one year, and also what proportion of the entire board shall be so elected. At the first election hereunder the voters shall designate upon their ballots who shall serve for one year, who for two years, and who for three years. Vacancies caused by expiration of term of office shall be filled by election annually thereafter. (70 v. 125.)

SECTION 9964. The trustees of colleges and other institutions of learning not endowed by voluntary contributions, established under special acts of incorporation, and which, by the provision thereof are located at particular places, may change their location to such other places as they deem proper and erect and maintain academies and other schools auxiliary thereto. (70 v. 248.)

Certain corporations may change location.

SECTION 9965. The trustees of a university, college, or other institution of learning, incorporated by authority of this state under special charter, owned in shares or stock subscribed or taken, may dispose of its property at public sale, on such terms as to payment as the stockholders by a vote of three-fourths of the shares or stock of the institution, direct, after giving public notice thereof, by publication, for six consecutive weeks in some newspaper published in the county where the institution is located. Such notice shall contain a full statement of the terms, time and place of sale, and such action of the trustees. The trustees may close up the corporate existence of such institution, and make an equitable division and distribution of the proceeds of the sale among all the holders of shares or stock, after the payment of its just debts. (67 v. 24.)

Sale and distribution of property of certain corporations.

SECTION 9966. The trustees of any university, college or institution of learning, incorporated under authority of this state, owned in shares of stock subscribed and paid up in full, by a majority of the owners of such stock, for the sole purpose of promoting education, religion and morality, or the fine arts, exclusively among males or females, on the written petition of the owners of a majority of such stock filed before its trustees or on the vote of the owners of the majority of such shares of paid up stock at any general meeting of the stockholders called for such purpose, after thirty days' notice published in some newspaper published and of general circulation in the county, by them, may change the name and enlarge the purposes and objects of such university, college or institution, by amendments to its charter, approved by the owners of the majority of such stock, so that all the educational rights and privileges thereof may be bestowed in the co-equal and co-ordinate education of both sexes. (85 v. 270.)

Certain colleges may file charter and amend.

An incorporated college or university may receive subscriptions to an endowment fund, and in consideration thereof may agree to furnish tuition either for limited periods or perpetually: College v. Carey, 85 O. S. 648.

SECTION 9967. When such amendment is adopted and the original articles of incorporation of such corporation have not been filed and recorded in the office of the secretary of state, a copy of the amendment and of the original articles, with a certificate to each of them thereto affixed,

Copy of amendment to be filed with secretary of state.

signed by the president and secretary of the corporation, and sealed with the corporate seal, if any there be, stating the fact and date of the adoption of such amendment, and that such copy thereof and of the original articles of incorporation are true copies of the originals shall be recorded in such office. When so recorded, such amendment shall be in law the sole articles of incorporation of the corporation. The property, real and personal, corporate franchises, and endowment funds, gifts, bequests, legacies, or mortgage securities, promissory notes, and rights of every kind belonging to, vested in, claimed, or possessed by the original corporation, by such amendment shall pass to, and be enjoyed and exercised by the corporation named, created and organized by such amendment for the promotion of all the objects and purposes of its creation and organization. (85 v. 270.)

Fee of secretary of state. SECTION 9968. For recording such amendments and copies of original articles of incorporation, and furnishing a certified copy or copies thereof, the secretary of state shall receive a fee of twenty cents per hundred words, to be in no case less than five dollars. (85 v. 270.)

Colleges may change name or purpose. SECTION 9969. The board of trustees of a university, college, or institution of learning, incorporated under authority of this state, for the sole purpose of promoting education, religion and morality, or the fine arts, at a regular or special meeting of such board of trustees, called for that purpose, after thirty days' actual notice to each and all such trustees, may change the name and enlarge the purposes and objects of such university, college or institution of learning, by amendment to its charter, approved by a majority of the board ats uch regular or special meeting, so called and so notified, for such change of its name, and the enlargement of its purposes and objects. (87 v. 8.)

Procedure and effect. SECTION 9970. When such amendment is so adopted by the board of trustees of such university, college or institution of learning, a copy thereof with a certificate thereto affixed, signed by the president and secretary of such board and sealed with the corporate seal, if any there be, stating the fact and date of such amendment, and that such copy is a true copy of the original amendment, shall be filed and recorded in the office of the secretary of state, and when so filed and recorded such amendment shall be in law an integral part of the articles of incorporation of such corporation. The property, real and personal, corporate powers and franchises, endowment funds, gifts, bequests, legacies, mortgage securities and promissory notes, belonging to, such original corporation, by such amendment shall pass to, and be enjoyed and exercised by the corporation created and organized by such amendment for the promotion of the objects of its creation and organization. Such new corporation shall be liable for and must perform all the lawful obligations and contracts of the original corporation. (87 v. 8.)

SECTION 9971. For recording such amendment and furnishing a certified copy or copies thereof, the secretary of state shall receive a fee of twenty cents per hundred words, to be in no case les than five dollars. (87 v. 8.) *Fees of secretary of state.*

SECTION 9972. An association incorporated for the purpose of receiving gifts, devises or trust funds to erect, establish, or maintain an academy in any department of fine arts, a gallery for the exhibition of paintings, or sculpture or works of art, a museum of natural or other curiosities, or speciments of art or nature promotive of knowledge, or a law or other library, or courses of lectures upon science, art, philosophy, natural history, or law, and to open it to the public on reasonable terms; or an industrial training school, or a mechanics' institute for advancing the best interests of mechanics, manufacturers and artisans, by the more general diffusion of useful knowledge in those classes of the community, or homes for indigent and aged widows and unmarried women, whose directors or trustees may be of either sex, in its articles of incorporation may prescribe the tenure of office of the trustees or directors, the mode of appointing or electing successors, the administration and management of the property, trust and other funds of the corporation and such other organic rules as are deemed expedient or acceptable to donors, which shall be the permanent organic law of the corporation. (84 v. 31.) *Organic rules may be prescribed in articles of certain corporations.*

SECTION 9973. By certificate duly acknowledged by the trustees or directors, and filed in the office of the secretary of state, such corporations may add to the original objects and purposes thereof, any of the several objects and purposes, mentioned in the preceding section, not provided for by the articles of incorporation. (83 v. 41.) *May add to original objects.*

SECTION 9974. Such corporation heretofore incorporated under the laws of the state, by certificate reciting the organic rules adopted by the corporation as its permanent organic law, duly acknowledged by the trustees or directors, and filed in the office of the secretary of state, may accept the provisions of the second preceding section. (83 v. 41.) *Acceptance of statutory provisions.*

SECTION 9975. The officers of such a corporation charged or intrusted with the receipts and disbursements of its funds or property, shall make and keep acurate and detailed accounts of such funds, and the receipts and disbursements thereof such as are required to be kept by the fund commissioners of the state. On or before the third Monday in January of each year the trustees shall file with the clerk of common pleas court of the county in which the corporation is located an abstract of their account which *Accounts of receipts and disbursements.*

shall correspond in date, amount, person to whom paid, from whom received, and on what account, with the vouchers taken or given on account of such receipts and disbursements. At the same time they annually shall file in such clerk's office a report of the names of the donors, the kind, amount, or value of gifts of each, and a brief statement of the conditions and purposes of the gifts. The filing of such abstract and report, and the supplying of any omission in either, may be enforced by order and attachment of the common pleas court of the proper county, against the trustees, on motion of any respectable citizen. (75 v. 135.)

Trustees ineligible to other office.

SECTION 9976. No trustee of such corporation shall be elegible to any office or agency of the corporation to which a salary or emolument is attached, nor shall the trustees be allowed any salary, emoluments or perquisites, except the right of free ingress to the grounds, rooms, and buildings of the corporation. (75 v. 135.)

Attorney-general may enforce duties of officers.

SECTION 9977. On application to the attorney general by five citizens of the proper county, in writing, verified by the oath or affirmation of one of them, setting forth specific charges against any of the fiscal or other agents or trustees of such a corporation, involving a breach of trust or duty, he shall give notice thereof to the trustees or agents complained of, and inquire into the truth of such charges. For this purpose he may receive affidavits, or enforce, by process from the court of common pleas of Franklin county, the production of papers and the attendance of witnesses before him. If, on testimony or other evidence, he believes the charges or any of them to be true, he shall proceed, by action in that court, in the name of the state, against the delinquent trustee or trustees, fiscal agent or agents, and, on the hearing the court may direct the performance of any duty, or the removal of all or any of the agents or trustees, and decree such other and further relief as is equitable. (75 v. 135.)

May increase number of trustees of certain corporations.

SECTION 9978. The board of trustees of a university or college heretofore incorporated, but not under the patronage of conferences or other ecclesiastical bodies of any religious denomination, may increase the number of such trustees to twenty-four, exclusive of the president, or a less number, and divide such trustees into six classes, each class to serve six years, and one class to be chosen each year, for such term. One trustee of each class may be chosen by the votes of the alumni of such university or college, if the board of trustees so provides by by-law, in which case the board also shall provide by such by-laws, a method of nominating and electing such appointee of the alumni. (87 v. 188.)

Distribution of new members.

SECTION 9979. The president of such university or college shall ex-officio, be a trustee perpetually, and not be included in the classes going out in rotation. If in the first enlargement of the board of trustees, under the preceding section it be necessary to distribute new members to the several classes, whose terms will expire by rotation, the distribution may be made in such manner as the board directs so that no trustee shall be elected for a longer term than six years. (87 v. 188.)

SECTION 9980. The board of trustees of a university or college in this state organized as a stock corporation and not under ecclesiastical patronage, upon the surrender and cancellation of all outstanding shares of its capital stock, may cause a certificate of that fact, sealed with the corporate seal and signed by the president and secretary of such board, to be filed in the office of the secretary of state, which certificate the secretary of state shall record for public use in the records of his office, and certified copy of which he shall return to such board of trustees upon receipt of a fee of twenty cents per one hundred words, to be in no case less than five dollars. Thereupon such university or college shall continue its corporate existence as a corporation not for profit and with the same powers, duties, privileges and immunities as it previously possessed, save such as relate to its capital stock. Such board by resolution may conform the number, tenure and mode of election of its own members to the provisions of the preceding section, except, that trustees not authorized to be elected by the alumni, shall be elected by the board; and that the ex-officio membership thereon of the president of such college or university shall be optional with the board. (99 v. 260.) *Stock corporations may retire stock.*

SECTION 9981. When such a corporation seeking to avail itself of the provisions of the preceding section has procured the surrender for cancellation of not less than sixty per cent of the outstanding shares of its capital stock, any residue thereof standing upon its books in the names of persons, partnerships, societies or corporations that for seven years or more have been deceased, dissolved or of unknown address, and non-participants in the corporate elections, and of whose shares aforesaid no known owner exists, may be cancelled by decree of the court of common pleas of the county wherein such corporation is located, upon its petition, duly certified, being filed therein, making such persons, partnerships, societies and corporations or their legal representatives parties defendant, and on serving such defendants with public notice of the pendency of such petition in the manner provided for service by publication in civil actions, and upon averment and proof by the plaintiff and a finding by the court of the facts as hereinbefore required, and of the further fact that the plaintiff is an eleemosynary corporation. Thereupon the shares of such defendants shall be deemed to be cancelled and surrendered, and the decree shall not be vacated or set aside, on the application of any such defendant, otherwise than as in the case of judgments in civil actions. (99 v. 260.) *Cancellation by decree of court.*

SECTION 9982. A mechanics' institute, incorporated under the laws of this state prior to the year eighteen hundred and fifty-one, may borrow money, issue bonds or notes therefore at no more than the legal rate of interest, and secure them by mortgage upon its real estate. (82 v. 118 § 1.)

SECTION 9983. The directors and trustees of such corporation shall not be personally liable for debts contracted by them, as in the preceding section provided. (82 v. 118 § 2.)

SECTION 9984. Superintendents of city hospitals, directors or superintendents of city or county infirmaries, directors or superintendents, of workhouses, directors or superintendents of asylums for the insane, or other charitable institutions founded and supported in whole or in part at public expense, the directors or warden of the penitentiary, township trustees, sheriffs, or coroners, in possession of bodies not claimed or identified, or which must be buried at the expense of the county or township, before burial, shall hold such bodies not less than thirty-six hours and notify the professor of anatomy in a college which by its charter is empowered to teach anatomy, or the president of a county medical society, of the fact that such bodies are being so held. Before or after burial such superintendent, director, or other officer, on the written application of the professor of anatomy, or the president of a county medical society shall deliver to such professor or president, for the purpose of medical or surgical study or dissection, the body of a person who died in either of such institutions, from any disease, not infectious, if it has not been requested for interment by any person at his own expense. (93 v. 84).

SECTION 9985. If the body of a deceased person so delivered, be subsequently claimed, in writing, by a relative or other person for private interment, at his own expense, it shall be given up to such claimant. (93 v. 84.)

The next of kin of a decedent have the right to determine the place and manner of burial: Smiley v. Bartlett, 6 O. C. C. 234, 3 O. C. D. 432.

SECTION 9986. After such bodies have been subjected to medical or surgical examination or dissection, the remains thereof shall be interred in some suitable place at the expense of the party or parties in whose keeping the corpse was placed. (93 v. 84.)

SECTION 9987. In all cases the officer having such body under his control, must notify or cause to be notified, in writing, the relatives or friends of the deceased person (93 v. 84.)

SECTION 9988. The bodies of strangers or travelers, who die in any of the institutions above named, shall not be delivered for the purpose of dissection unless the stranger or traveler belongs to that class commonly known as tramps. Bodies delivered as herein provided shall be used for medical, surgical and anatomical study only, and within this state. (93 v. 84.)

SECTION 9989. A person, association, or company, having unlawful possession of the body of a deceased person shall be jointly and severally liable with any other persons, associations, and companies that had or have had unlawful possession of such corpse, in any sum not less than five hundred nor more than five thousand dollars, to be recovered at the suit of the personal representative of the deceased in any court of competent jurisdiction, for the benefit of the next of kin of deceased. (Revised Statutes of 1880.)

Liability for having unlawful possession of body.

STATE BUILDING CODE.

Part 2.

SPECIAL REQUIREMENTS.

TITLE 3.

SCHOOL BUILDINGS.

TITLE 3.

SCHOOL BUILDINGS.

CLASSIFICATION.

SECTION 12600-44. Under the classification of school buildings are included all public, parochial and private schools, colleges, academies, seminaries, libraries, museums, and art gallaries, including all buildings or structures containing one or more rooms used for the assembling of persons for the purposes of acquiring knowledge, or for mental training.

GRADE A. Under this grade are included all rooms or buildings appropriated to the use of primary, grammar or high schools, including all rooms or buildings used for school purposes by pupils or students eighteen (18) years old or less.

GRADE B. Under this grade are included all rooms or buildings appropriated to the use of schools, colleges, academies, seminaries, libraries, museums and art gallaries; including all rooms or buildings not included under grade "A". (102 v. 586.)

Class of construction required.

SECTION 12600-45. Class of construction required. Grade A. Where the main first floor line is eight (8) feet or more above the grade line at any entrance to or exit from any story above the basement the basement shall be

384

rated as the first story. Stories over fifteen (15) feet high, measuring from the floor to the ceiling line shall be rated as two stories. All buildings more than two stories high shall be of fireproof construction.

All buildings two stories high and less shall be of fireproof or composite construction.

No school building of grade A shall be built more than three (3) stories high.

Grade B. Where any floor level is more than twenty-six (26) feet above the grade line at any entrance to or exit from the building, the building shall be of fireproof construction.

Where the floor levels are less than twenty-six (26) feet above the grade line at any entrance to or exit from the building, the building shall be of composite or fireproof construction.

No school building of grade B shall be built more than five (5) stories high, nor shall the topmost floor level be more than fifty (50) feet above the grade line at any entrance to or exit from the building.

Provided, however, that this provision as to the number of stories and the height of the topmost floor level, shall not apply to libraries in buildings of fireproof construction throughout.

Grades A and B. Exceptions. All buildings one story high, without basement and with the floor line not more than four (4) feet above the grade line shall be of fireproof, composite or frame construction, providing when built of frame construction the same is erected thirty (30) feet away from any other building structure or lot line, and two hundred (200) feet beyond the city fire limits. (103 v. 860.)

SECTION 12600-45a. None of the provisions of section 12600-45 of the General Code shall prevent the construction of an addition to any school building two stories high or less; such addition to be of the same construction and material as the original building whether it be of fireproof, composite or frame construction. Not more than one addition shall ever be added to any school building under the provisions of this section and the lower floor space of such addition shall in no case exceed twelve hundred square feet. (104 v. 177.)

Addition to school building exempt from provisions of 12600-45.

EXPOSURE AND COURTS.

SECTION 12600-46. EXPOSURE. No building of grade B shall occupy more than ninety-five (95) per cent of a corner lot nor more than ninety (90) per cent of an interior lot or site.

No building of grade A shall occupy more than seventy-five (75) per cent of a corner lot nor more than seventy (70) per cent of an interior lot or site. The measurements being taken at the lowest tier of floor joists.

25 s. l.

No wall of any building coming under this classification containing windows used for lighting school or class rooms shall be placed nearer any opposite building, structure or property line than thirty (30) feet.

COURTS. By inner court is meant an open shaft or court, surrounded on all sides by walls.

By recess court is meant an open air shaft or court, having one side or end opened, and when such opening is on a lot line, it is an inner court.

Recess or inner light courts may be used, providing the least distance between any two opposite walls containing windows for lighting class and school rooms is equal to the height from the lowest window sill to the top of the highest cornice or fire wall. All walls to inner or recess courts shall be of masonary or other fireproof construction (except for buildings of frame construction.)

No inner or recess court shall be covered by a roof, sky-light, or other obstruction.

If area ways are used for lighting basements, the width of the area shall be not less than equal to the height from the lowest window sill to the top of the adjoining grade line. (102 v. 586.)

SUB-DIVISIONS AND FIRE STOPS.

SECTION 12600-47. Buildings of this classification built in connection with a building of a lower grade of construction shall be separated from the other parts of the building by a standard fire wall, and all communicating openings in these walls shall be covered by double standard fire doors, using self closing door on one side of the wall and an automatic fire door or an automatic rolling steel shutter on the other. The automatic shutters or doors for openings used as means of ingress or egress shall be kept open during the occupancy of the building.

All rooms or apartments used for general storage, storing of furniture, carpenter shops, general repairing, paint shops or other equally hazardous purposes shall be constructed with fireproof walls, ceilings and floors, and all openings between these rooms or apartments and the other parts of the building shall be covered by double standard fire doors, using a self closing door on one side of the wall and an automatic fire door or an automatic rolling steel shutter on the other.

No open wells communicating between any two stories shall be used, except the necessary stair and elevator walls.

All exterior and court walls of buildings coming under this classification (except buildings of frame construction) within thirty (30) feet of any other building, structure or lot line shall be provided with the following fire stops, viz:

Walls shall be standard fire walls;

All windows shall be automatic standard fireproof windows, and all door openings shall be covered by standard hinged fire doors without any automatic attachments. (102 v. 586.)

HEATER ROOM.

SECTION 12600-48. Furnaces, hot water heating boilers and low pressure steam boilers may be located in the buildings, providing the heating apparatus, breeching, fuel room and firing room are inclosed in a standard fireproof heater room, and all openings into the same are covered by standard self closing fire doors. *Boilers.*

No boiler or furnace shall be located under any lobby, exit, stairway or corridor.

No cast iron boiler carrying more than 10 pounds pressure or steel boiler carrying more than 35 pounds pressure shall be located within the main walls of any school building. (102 v. 586.)

BASEMENT ROOMS.

SECTION 12600-49. No rooms used for school purposes shall be placed wholly or partly below the grade line. Rooms for domestic science, manual training and recreation may be placed partly below grade, provided the same are properly lighted, heated and ventilated. (102 v. 586.) *Basement rooms.*

DIMENSIONS OF SCHOOL AND CLASS ROOMS.

SECTION 12600-50. FLOOR SPACE. The minimum floor space to be allowed per person, in school and class rooms, shall not be less than the following, viz.: *Dimensions.*

Primary grades sixteen (16) square feet per person.

Grammar grades eighteen (18) square feet per person.

High schools twenty (20) square feet per person.

All other schools and class rooms twenty-four (24) square feet per person.

CUBICAL CONTENTS. The gross cubical contents of each school and class room, shall be of such a size as to provide for each pupil or person not less than the following cubic feet of air space, viz.: Primary grades 200 cubic feet, grammar grades 225 cubic feet, high schools 250 cubic feet and in grade B buildings 300 cubic feet.

HEIGHT OF STORIES. Toilet, play and recreation rooms shall be not less than eight (8) feet high in the clear measuring from the floor to the ceiling line.

The height of all rooms, except toilet, play and recreation rooms shall be not less than one-half the average width of the room, and in no case less than ten (10) feet high.

CAPACITY OF ROOMS. The plans shall be clearly marked showing the maximum number of pupils or persons to be accommodated in each room.

REST ROOMS.

Rest rooms.   SECTION 12600-51. In all school buildings of grade
"A" containing four and not more than eight school or
class rooms, a rest or hospital room shall be provided, and
in all school buildings of grade 'A" containing more than
eight school or class rooms, two such rooms shall be provided.

These rooms shall be provided with a couch and supplies for first aid to the injured, and where water supply
is available shall be provided with water closets and sinks.
(102 v. 586.)

ASSEMBLY HALLS.

Assembly   SECTION 12600-52. A room seating or accommodat-
halls.   ing more than one hundred (100) persons shall be considered as an assembly hall.

No assembly hall in a building of grade A shall be located above the second story in a building of fireproof construction, nor above the first story in a building of composite construction.

Otherwise assembly halls shall be constructed and
equipped as called for under part 2, title 1. (102 v. 586.)

SEATS, DESKS AND AISLES.

Seats, desks   SECTION 12600-53. SECURING SEATS. Seats, chairs
and aisles.   and desks placed in class, recitation, study and high school
rooms seating more than fifteen (15) persons, shall be se-
curely fastened to the floor. Desks and chairs used by the
teachers may be portable.

ASSEMBLY HALL SEATS AND AISLES. Assembly hall
seats and aisles shall be as called for under part2, title 1.

CLASS ROOM SEATS AND AISLES. Class and school
rooms shall have aisles, on all wall sides.

In primary rooms, center aisles shall not be less than
seventeen (17) inches, and wall aisles not less than two feet
four inches (2' 4") wide.

In grammar rooms, center aisles shall not be less than
eighteen (18) inches and wall aisles not less than two feet
six inches (2' 6") wide.

In high school rooms, center aisle shall not be less than
twenty (20) inches and wall aisles not less than three (3)
feet.

In all other class and school rooms, center aisles shall
not be less than twenty-four (24) inches, and wall aisles
not less than three (3) feet. (102 v. 586.)

OPTIC.

Light.   SECTION 12600-54. The proportion of glass surface in
museums, libraries and art galleries, shall be not less than
one (1) square foot of glass to each six (6) square feet of
floor area.

The proportion of glass in each class, study, recitation, high school room and laboratory, shall be not less than

one (1) square foot of glass to each five (5) square feet of floor area. (For glass surface in rooms used for domestic science and manual training, see part 2, title 7, workshops, factories and mercantile establishments.)

The proportion of glass surface in each play, toilet or recreation room, shall be not less than one (1) square foot of glass to each ten (10) square feet of floor area.

Windows shall be placed either at the left, or the left and rear of the pupils when seated.

Tops of windows, except in libraries, museums and art galleries shall not be placed more than eight (8") inches below the minimum ceiling height as established under section 7. *Windows.*

The unit of measurement for the width of a properly lighed room, when lighted from one side only, shall be the height of the window head above the floor.

The width of all class and recitation rooms when lighted from one side only, shall never exceed two and one-half times this unit measured at right angles to the source of light.

All windows shall be placed in the exterior walls of the building, except for halls, corridors, stock and supply closets which may be lighted by ventilated skylights or by windows placed in interior walls or partitions.

Museums, libraries and art galleries may be lighted by skylights, or clear story windows. (102 v. 586.)

MEANS OF EGRESS.

SECTION 12600-55. All means of egress or exist, shall be exit doors unless the same lead to A standard fire escapes, which shall be either exit doors or exit windows. *Entrances and exits.*

Grade A Buildings, of Fireproof Construction. Means of egress from rooms in the basement and superstructure shall be in proportion to three (3) feet in width to each one hundred (100) persons to be accommodated in building accommodating not more than five hundred (500) persons.

When buildings accommodate from five hundred (500) to one thousand (1,000) persons, two (2) feet additional exit width shall be provided for each one hundred (100) persons or fraction thereof in excess of five hundred (500) persons.

When buildings accommodate more than one thousand (1,000) persons, one (1) feet additional exit width shall be provided for each one hundred (100) persons or fraction thereof in excess of one thousand (1,000) persons, but in no case shall an exit be less than three (3) feet or more than six (6) feet wide.

No inclosed standard fireproof stairways or fire escapes will be necessary for buildings of fireproof construction and all exits shall lead to the main corridors.

GRADE A. BUILDINGS OF COMPOSITE CONSTRUCTION. Each room in the superstructure used by pupils as a class or school room, shall have at least two separate and distinct means of egress.

No class, school or high school room shall have more than one door or opening between it and the main halls or corridors of the building.

Communicating door between two class or school rooms shall not be considered as a means of egress.

The proportion of exits to the seating capacity shall not be less than three (3) feet to each one hundred (100) persons to be accommodated.

One-half of the exits shall lead to the main corridors, and the other half to inclosed fireproof stairways, B, C or D standard fire escapes or stone, cement or iron steps leading to the grade line. No exit door shall be less than three (3) feet or more than six feet wide. No fire escape or outside stairway shall be used when the height of the same exceeds eight (8) feet above the grade line.

Each room in the basement used by the pupils shall have a direct exit not less than three (3) feet wide, with stone, cement or iron stairways leading up to the grade line. Stairways shall be not less than three feet six inches (3' 6") wide.

Areaways around such stairways shall have substantial hand and guard rails on both sides.

These exits shall be provided in addition to the usual service stairways and means of ingress.

GRADE B. BUILDING OF FIREPROOF OR COMPOSITE CONSTRUCTION. Each room or apartment used for any purposes other than storage shall have two separate and distinct means of egress.

If the various rooms connect directly with a hallway, means of egress at each end of the hallway will be sufficient; providing however that it is not necessary to pass one means of egress in order to reach the other.

These means of egress shall be either an inside stairway running continuously from the grade line to the topmost story, or from the basement to the grade line; A, B, C or D standard fire escapes; stone, cement or iron steps leading to the grade line; or self-closing doors leading directly to the main corridor of an adjoining section of the same building containing a stairway.

Means of egress shall be at the rate of three (3) feet per hundred persons to be accommodated.

It shall be presumed that half the persons will go to either means of egress.

In libraries, museums, and art galleries, the capacity of the building shall be established by allowing to each person fifteen (15) square feet of floor area in all lobbies, exhibition rooms, toilet rooms, corridors, stairs and other public parts of the building.

GRADE A AND B. BUILDINGS OF FRAME CONSTRUCTION. Each room shall have at least, two three (3) feet exits; one leading to the open with steps to the grade, and the other the usual means of ingress; and all steps shall have hand rails on both sides.

SIGNS. Over each exit door shall be painted a sign indicating the word EXIT in plain block letters not less than six (6) inches high. (102 v. 586.)

STAIRWAYS.

SECTION 12600-56. GRADE A. BUILDINGS OF FIRE-PROOF CONSTRUCTION. Buildings of fireproof construction shall have at least two stairway located as far apart as possible and the same shall be continuous from the grade line to the topmost story.

The basement shall have at least two stairways located as far apart as possible and run from the basement floor level to the grade line, which stairways may be placed under the main stairway. No further means of egress will be necessary.

Stairways shall be enclosed with masonry of fireproof walls with standard self-closing fire doors at each story, and shall be provided with platforms and exit doors not less than three feet (3') wide at the grade line.

GRADE A. BUILDINGS OF COMPOSITE CONSTRUCTION. Basement stairways shall be enclosed with either brick walls not less than nine (9) inches thick, concrete walls six inches (6") thick, or hollow tile walls twelve inches (12) thick.

All openings in these walls shall be provided with standard self-closing fire doors. The width of stairways required under this classification shall be equally divided, one-half being placed in the main service stairways and the other half in the enclosed fireproof stairs or fire escapes. No closet for storage shall be placed under any stairway.

GRADE B. BUILDINGS OF FIREPROOF CONSTRUCTION. Stairways shall be separated from the other parts of the building by masonry or fireproof partitions with standard self-closing fire doors.

Wire glass not less than one-quarter inch ($\frac{1}{4}$") thick, set in stationary metal sash and frames may be used in place of stairway partitions. No wire glass shall be placed in partitions separating stairways from work or storage rooms containing highly combustible material.

Stairways shall be provided with grade line platforms with exit doors not less than three (3) feet wide leading to streets, alleys or open courts.

GRADE B. BUILDINGS OF COMPOSITE CONSTRUCTION. In buildings of composite construction the stairways shall be separated from the other parts of the building by masonry or fireproof walls, with fireproof ceiling at the topmost story, with fireproof floor at the lowermost level, and all openings to these inclosures shall be provided with standard self-closing fire doors.

The above enclosures shall be provided with grade line platforms, and with exit doors not less than three (3) feet wide leading to streets, alleys or open courts.

No closet for storage shall be placed under any stairway.

MONUMENTAL STAIRS. Monumental stairs from the basement to the second story may be used in buildings of grade B, providing they are placed as far distant from the other stairways as posible.

Construction and dimensions of stairways. STAIRWAY CONSTRUCTION. Width of stairways shall be at the rate of three feet per one hundred (100) persons accommodated in buildings accommodating not more than five hundred (500) persons, when building accommodates from five hundred (500) to one thousand (1,000) persons two feet of additional stairway width shall be provided for every one hundred (100) persons or fraction thereof in excess of five hundred (500), when buildings accommodate more than one thousand (1,000) persons, one foot additional stairway width shall be provided for every one hundred (100) persons or fraction thereof in execss of one thousand (1,000) persons.

No stairway shall be less than three feet six inches (3' 6") nor more than six (6) feet wide measuring between the hand rails. Stairways over six (6) feet wide shall have substantial center hand rails with angle and newel posts not less than six (6) feet high. No stairway shall have less than three (3) nor more than sixteen (16) risers in any run.

No stairway shall have winders and all nosing shall be straight.

A uniform width shall be maintained in all stairways and stair platforms by rounding the corners and beveling the angles.

Hand rails shall be provided on both sides of all stairways and steps.

Outside stairways and areaways shall be provided with guard rails not less than two feet six inches (2' 6") high.

Stairways shall have a uniform rise and tread in each run as follows, viz.:

Primary schools shall have not more than a six (6) in rise nor less than eleven (11) inch tread.

Grammar schools shall have not more than a six and one-half (6½) inch rise nor less than eleven (11) inch tread.

All other schools shall have not more than a seven (7) inch rise nor less than ten and one-half (10½) inch tread.

The above dimensions shall be from tread to tread, and from riser to riser.

No door shall open directly upon a stairway, but shall open on a platform or landing equal in length to the width of the door.

In combination primary and grammar school buildings all stairways below the first floor level shall be designed for primary school pupils, and all stairways above the first floor level may be designed for either primary or grammar pupils.

No closet for storage shall be placed under any sttair-way.

All treads shall be covered with rubber or lead mats or equal non-slipping surface. (102 v. 586.)

GRADIENTS.

SECTION 12600-57. To overcome any difference in floor levels which would require less than three risers, gradients shall be employed of not over one (1) inch rise in twelve (12) inch run.

Floors at all exits shall be so designed as to be level and flush with the adjacent floors. (102 v. 586.)

PASSAGEWAYS.

SECTION 12600-58. No hall or passageway leading to a stairway or exit shall be less in width of the stairway or exit, as the case may be.

Halls and pasasgeways shall be so designed and proportioned as to prevent congestion and confusion. (102 v. 586.)

ELEVATORS.

SECTION 12600-59. Elevators shall be enclosed in standard fire walls, or by fireproof walls, ceilings and floors, and all openings to the enclosures shall be covered by standard fire doors for elevators. (102 v. 586.)

EXIT DOORS AND WINDOWS.

SECTION 12600-60. Exit doors shall not be less than Dimensions. three (3) feet wide, nor less than six feet four inches (6' 4") high, level with the floor, swing outward, viz.: toward the open, or towards the natural means of egress, and shall be so hung as not to interfere with passageways or close other openings.

No single door or leaf to a double door shall be more than four (4) feet wide. No two doors hinged together shall be used as a means of ingress or egress. Accordion doors may be used in dividing class rooms, providing the free sections swing outward and give the required amount of exit width.

No double acting, rolling, sliding or revolving exit or entrance doors shall be used.

Exit windows leading to "A" standard fire escapes shall have the lower sash hinged to the side to swing out, or hung on weights to rise. This sash shall be not less than two feet six inces (2' 6") wide, not less than three (3) feet high and not more than two (2) feet above the floor line. (102 v. 586.)

SCUTTLES.

SECTION 12600-61. Every building exceeding twenty-five (25) feet in height shall have in the roof a bulk-head or scuttle not less than two (2) feet wide and not less than three (3) feet long, covered on the outside with metal and provided with a stairway or permanent ladder leading thereto.

Bulk-head and scuttle doors shall never be locked. (102 v. 586.)

SPECIAL CONSTRUCTION.

Floors of toilet rooms. SECTION 12600-62. All floors to toilet rooms, lavatories, water closet compartments, or any enclosure where plumbing fixtures are used within the building, shall have a waterproof floor and base made of non-absorbent indestructible waterproof material, viz.: Asphalt, glass, marble, vitrified or glazed tile or terrazzo, or monolithic composition.

Base shall be not less than six (6) inches high and shall have a sanitary cove at the floor level.

All basement rooms used by the pupils or public shall have a damp or waterproof floor.

All basement ceilings except where concrete or brick is used shall be plastered or be covered with pressed or rolled steel ceiling.

Whenever possible, window and door jambs shall be rounded and plastered, except in museums, libraries and art galleries.

All interior wood finish shall be as small as possible and free from unnecessary dust catchers.

All floors between the finished portions of the building shall be deadened or made sound proof. (102 v. 586.)

FLOOR AND ROOF LOADS.

SECTION 12600-63. In calculating constructing the superimposed load uniformly distributed on the various floors and roofs shall be assumed at not less than the following, viz.:

Class rooms, sixty (60) pounds per square foot.

Halls, assembly halls, stairs and corridors, eighty (80) pounds per square foot.

Museums, libraries and art galleries, one hundred (100) pounds per square foot.

Attics not used for storage, twenty (20) pounds per square foot.

Roofs, forty (40) pounds per square foot. (102 v. 586.)

HEATING AND VENTILATION.

SECTION 12600-64. A heating system shall be installed which will uniformly heat all corridors, hallways, play rooms, toilet rooms, recreation rooms, assembly rooms, gymnasiums and manual training rooms to a uniform temperature of 65 degrees in zero weather; and will uniformly heat all other parts of the building to 70 degrees in zero weather.

EXCEPTIONS. Rooms with one or more open sides used for open air or outdoor treatment.

The heating system shall be combined with a system of ventilation which will change the air in all parts of the building except the corridors, halls, and storage closets not less than six times per hour. *Heating and Ventilation.*

The heating system to be installed where a change of air is required, shall be either standard ventilating stoves, gravity or mechanical furnaces, gravity indirect steam or hot water; or a mechanical indirect steam or hot water system.

Where wardrobes are not separated from the class room they shall be considered as part of the class room and the vent register shall be placed in the wardrobe.

These wardrobes are separated from the class rooms, they shall be separately heated and ventilated the same as the class rooms.

The bottom of warm air registers shall be placed not less than eight (8) feet above the floor line, except foot warmers which may be placed in the floors of the main corridors or lobbies.

Vent registers shall be placed not more than two inches (2″) above the floor line.

The fresh air supply shall be taken from the outside of the building and no vitiated air shall be re-heated. The vitiated air shall be conducted through flues or ducts and be discharged above the roof of the building.

A hood shall be placed over each and every stove in the domestic science room, over each and every compartment desk or demonstration table in the chemical laboratories and chemical laboratory lecture rooms, of such a size as to receive and carry off all offensive odors, fumes and gases.

These ducts shall be connected to vertical ventilating flues placed in the walls and shall be independent of the room ventilation as previously provided for.

Where electric current is available electric exhaust fans shall be placed in the ducts or flues from the stove fixtures in domestic science rooms and chemical laboratories, and where electric current is not available and a steam or hot-water system is used, the main vertical flues from the above ducts shall be provided with accelerating coils of proper size to create sufficient draught to carry away all fumes and offensive odors. (102 v. 586.)

SANITATION.

SECTION 12600-65. Where a water supply and sewerage system are available a sanitary equipment shall be installed as follows:

In the superstructure of the building one sink and one drinking fountain shall be installed on each floor to each six thousand (6000) square feet of floor area or less.

In the basement one sink and one drinking fountain shall be installed on the males' side, and the same on the females' side to each three hundred and fifty (350) pupils, or less.

Sinks shall be the ordinary slop sinks, or in lieu of same. lavatories may be used providing the waste plug or stopper has been removed.

Drinking fountains, sinks, closets, etc.   Sanitary school houses drinking fountains with jet giving a continuous flow of water shall be installed, and no tin cups or tumblers shall be allowed in or about any school building.

In libraries, museums and art galleries there shall be provided the following fixtures, viz.:

One water closet to each one hundred (100) females, or less.

One water closet to each two hundred (200) males, or less.

One urinal to each two hundred (200) males, or less.

The above to be based upon the actual number of persons to be accommodated, the capacity, being established as prescribed under section 12, means of egress.

In all other school buildings there shall be provided the following fixtures, viz.:

On water closet for each fifteen (15) females or less.

One water closet for each twenty-five (25) males or less.

One urinal for each fifteen (15) males or less.

Toilet accommodations for males and females shall be placed in separate rooms, with a traveling distance between the same of not less than twenty (20) feet.

Juvenile or short closets shall be used for primary and grammar grade schools. This does not apply when latrine closets are used.

In buildings accommodating males and females it shall be presumed that the occupants will be equally divided between males and females.

Where water supply and sewerage systems are not available no sanitary equipment shall be installed within the building, but pumps in lieu of drinking fountains, closets and urinals in the above proportions shall be placed upon the school building grounds, and no closets or urinals shall be placed nearer any occupied building than fifty (50) feet.

Where pumps or hydrants are used the outlet shall be inverted.

Buildings more than three stories in height shall be provided with toilet rooms in each story and basement, and in these shall be installed water closets and urinals in the above required ratios in proportion to the number of persons to be accommodated in the various stories.

Toilet rooms for males shall be clearly marked "Boys' toilet" or "Men's toilet" and for female "Girl's toilet" or "Women's toilet." (102 v. 586.)

GAS LIGHTING.

SECTION 12600-66. A system of gas lighting if used shall be installed as follows:

All outlets in class and recitation rooms shall be dropped from the ceiling and be equally distributed so as to uniformly light the room.

The number of burners provided shall not be less than the following: Burners.

In auditoriums one three (3) foot burner to each fifteen (15) square feet of floor area.

In gymnasiums one three (3) foot burner to each fifteen (15) square feet of floor area.

In halls and stairways one three (3) foot burner to each twenty-four (24) square feet of floor area.

In class and recitation rooms one three (3) foot burner to each twelve (12) square feet of floor area.

Enclosed fireproof stairways, service stairways, corridors, passageways and toilet rooms, shall be well lighted by aritificial light and said lights shall be kept burning when the building is occcupied after dark.

Burners shall be placed seven (7) feet above the floor line.

No swinging or movable gas fixtures or brackets shall be used. (102 v. 586.)

ELECTRIC WORK.

SECTION 12600-67. An electric lighting system if used shall be installed as follows:

All wiring shall be done in coduit. All outlets in class and recitation rooms shall be dropped from the ceiling and be equally distributed so as to uniformly light the room. Wiring.

. The candle power of lamps provided shall not be less than the following, viz.: Lighting.

Auditorium one candle power to two and one-half square feet of floor area.

Gymnasium one candle power to two and one-half square feet of floor area.

Halls and stairways one candle power to four square feet of floor area.

Class and recitation rooms one candle power to two square feet of floor area.

Enclosed fireproof stairways, service stairways, corridors, passageways and toilet rooms shall be lighted by artificial light, and said lights shall be kept burning when the building is occupied after dark. (102 v. 586.)

FINISHING HARDWARE.

SECTION 12600-68. All entrance, exit and emergency doors shall be equipped with hardware of such nature as to be always unlockable from within.

Locks, knobs,
levers, etc.

Single outside entrance doors shall have key locks that can be locked from the outside, but can always be opened on the inside, by simply turning the knob or lever, or by pushing against a bar or plate, whether same are locked on the outside or not, the locks being operated by key from the outside only. No night latch attachment shall be placed on face of these locks, or other bolts, hooks, thumb knobs or other locking device shall be placed on these doors.

Outside doors used for exit purposes only, including doors to inclosed fireproof stairways shall have one knob latch or a double extension bolt as hereinafter mentioned, and no bolts, hooks, or other locking device shall be placed on these doors.

Doors from halls to rooms and cloak rooms shall have no locks upon same, but shall be equipped with knob latches only. If locks are desired, the same style locks as above specified for entrance doors shall be used and the same shall be so placed on the door so that they can be locked on the hall side, and can always be opened on the room or cloak room sides, whether locked on hall side or not.

One of each pair of outside or inside double doors shall have a double extension panic bolt on same, bolt to have knob, lever, push bar, push plate, push handle, or device whereby the simple act of turning a knob, or lever, or pushing against the same will release the top and bottom bolts at the same time and allow the doors to open.

Independent top and bottom bolts shall not be used.

The outer door of each pair of outside and inside double doors shall have lock, or latch as above specified.

All bolts, latches, face of locks, working parts of extension bolts, and other exposed working parts about this hardware shall be of cast metal properly protected from corrosion.

Double box windows to A standard fire escapes shall be provided with sash locks and two bar lifts, and hinged sash with either a sash lock, one knob latch or level bolt. (102 v. 586.)

FIRE EXTINGUISHERS.

Hose.

SECTION 12600-69. Standard stand pipe and hose shall be provided in basement of grade A buildings and in each story and basement of grade B buildings with sufficient length of one and one-half (1½) inch hose to reach any part of the story.

Hose lengths shall be not more than seventy-five (75) feet, and where hose of such length will not reach the extreme portions of the story additional standpipes and hose shall be provided.

Where water supply is not available, standard chemical fire extinguishers shall be provided in the proportion of one (1) extinguisher to each two thousand (2,000) square feet of floor area or less.

Standard chemical fire extinguishers shall be provided in each story above the basement of grade A buildings in the proportion of one extinguisher to each two thousand (2,000) square feet of floor area, or less.

All fire extinguishers shall be prominently exposed to view and always accessible. (102 v. 586.)

FIRE ALARM.

SECTION 12600-70. All buildings with basement, and all buildings over one story high shall be provided with eight (8) inch in diameter trip fire gongs with connections enabling the ringing of same from any story or basement.

Gongs.

In semi-detached buildings gongs shall be provided for each section and shall be connected up so as to ring simultaneously from any story or basement of either section.

Gongs shall be centrally located in the main halls, and the operating cords shall be placed so as to be always accessible.

Exceptions. In institutions for the deaf, electric lights with red globes shall be placed near each teacher's desk, and these shall be operated simultaneously by switches placed in each story and basement. (102 v. 586.)

BLOWERS IN WORKSHOPS.

SECTION 12600-71. For blowers in workshops and factories, including rooms for manual training, see General Code state of Ohio section 1027. (102 v. 586.)

GUARDING MACHINERY AND PITS.

SECTION 12600-72. For the necessary devices for guarding machinery and pits, see General Code, state of Ohio, section 1027. (102 v. 586.)

SECTION 12600-274. Sec. 2. It shall be unlawful for any owner or owners, officers, board, committee or other person to construct, erect, build, equip or cause to be constructed, erected, built or equipped any opera house, hall, theater, church, schoolhouse, college, academy, seminary, infirmary, sanitorium, children's home, hospital, medical institute, asylum, memorial building, armory, assembly hall or other building used for the assemblage or betterment of people in any municipal corporation, county or township in this state, or to make any addition thereto or alteration thereof, except in case of repairs for maintenance without affecting the construction, sanitation, safety or other vital feature of said building or structure, without complying with the requirements and provisions relating thereto contained in this act. (102 v. 586.)

Alterations.

SECTION 12600-278. The provisions of this act shall not apply to the construction or erection of any public building or any addition thereto or alteration thereof, the plans and specifications of which have been heretofore submitted to and approved by the chief inspector of workshops and factories; nor shall they apply to the construction, erection

Buildings and structures to which this act does not apply.

or equipment of any public building, addition thereto or alteration thereof, where any lot or land has been purchased for the erection or equipment of such public building or where the contract for the construction, erection or equipping of which has been let or entered into prior to the date at which this act takes effect; nor shall the provisions prescribing the minimum distance at which buildings or structures, or parts thereof, shall be located from any lot line, or the provisions relating to open courts and fireproof passage-ways, apply when the provisions of this act are, or can be, complied with by or with the use of adjoining property, and when such adjoining property affords the widths and areas as prescribed by this act, and is available for the purposes intended, and when such adjoining property is so situated, used, dedicated or deeded, as to preclude the erection of any building or structure or part therof on the widths and areas so used, during the existence of the building or structure erected under the provisions of this act. (106 v. 441.)

Inspection of school-houses and other buildings.

SECTION 1031. The chief inspector of workshops and factories shall cause to be inspected all schoolhouses, colleges and opera houses, halls, theaters, churches, infirmaries, children's homes, hospitals, medical institutes, asylums and other buildings used for the assemblage or betterment of people in the state. Such inspection shall be made with special reference to precautions for the prevention of fires, the provision of fire escapes, exits, emergency exits, hallways, air-space, and such other matters which relate to the health and safety of those occupying, or assembling in, such structures. (99 v. 232 § 1.)

The specifications of such appliances, additions or alterations as are necessary for the proper protection of school children from fire and other dangers, and the requirement that such appliances be installed, is not a provision for the taking of property without due process of law, but is a mere requirement that such property be used in a lawful way, and such a provision is a constitutional and valid enactment. Closing school and other buildings pending the installation of such appliances is within the police power of the state, and the duty of determining what appliances shall be installed may properly be delegated as in this act, leaving the details to be worked out by the officers so delegated. A board of education, however, would have capacity to enjoin oppressive and arbitrary acts whereby schoolhouses are closed and children deprived of the advantages of the public schools: Akron Board of Education v. Sawyer, 7 O. N. P. (N. S.) 401, 19 O. D. (N. P.) 1.

An ordinance of the city of Columbus requiring the issuance to the owner or his agent of a permit for the construction of a building involving installation of sanitary plumbing is not applicable to construction work at the Ohio State University. It is the power and duty of the inspector of buildings in the city of Columbus to approve the plans of buildings of the Ohio State University and to enforce the city building code with respect thereto.

The ordinance of the city of Columbus for licensing the master and journeymen plumbers and prohibiting work at the trade of plumbing in the city of Columbus by unlicensed plumbers is applicable to persons working on the installation of plumbing at the Ohio State University whether employees of the University or not. — *Attorney General,* Opinion No. 1181, 1914.

Written report of district inspector.

SECTION 1032. Upon inspection of such structure, the district inspector of workshops and factories shall file with the chief inspector a written report of the condition thereof. If it is found that necessary precautions for the prevention of fire or other disaster have not been taken or that means for the safe and speedy egress of persons assembled therein have not been provided, such report shall specify what appliances, additions or alterations are necessary therefor. Thereupon the chief inspector shall notify in writing the owner or persons having control of such structure of the necessary appliances, additions or alterations to be added to or made in such structure. (99 v. 232 § 2.)

Where the Inspector of Workshops and Factories prohibits the use of a school house until certain repairs are made, but the Board of Education decides to erect a new school building instead, and the electors vote for a $25,000 bond issue for the construction thereof but cannot levy sufficient taxes to pay bonds and maintain school, there would be an emergency within the meaning of section 5649-4, General Code, and the necessary taxes for the retirement of bonds required for the purpose might be levied outside of all limitations of law. — *Attorney General,* Opinion No. 888, 1914.

SECTION 1033. If such structure is located in a municipality, a copy of such notice shall be mailed to the mayor thereof, otherwise such notice shall be mailed to the prosecuting attorney of such county. Thereupon the mayor with the aid of the police or the prosecuting attorney with the aid of the sheriff, as the case may be, shall prevent the use of such structure for public assemblage until the appliances, additions or alterations required by such notice have been added to or made in such structure. (99 v. 233 § 3.)
<small>Copy of notice to mayor or prosecuting attorney.</small>

SECTION 1034. Upon receipt of such notice, the owner or person in control of such structure shall comply with every detail embodied therein, and upon completion thereof report such fact in writing to the chief inspector of workshops and factories and to such mayor or prosecuting attorney. (99 v. 233 § 4.)
<small>Owner or agent shall comply with notice.</small>

SECTION 1035. The plans for the erection of such structure, and for any alterations in or additions to any such structure, shall be approved by the inspector of workshops and factories, except in municipalities having regularly organized building inspection departments, in which case the plans shall be approved by such department. (99 v. 233 § 5.)
<small>Approval of plans.</small>

SECTION 1036. Whoever, being an architect, builder or other person, alters the plans so approved or fails to construct or alter a building in accordance with such plans without the consent of the department that approved them, shall be fined not less than five hundred dollars nor more than one thousand dollars or imprisoned in the county jail not less than thirty days nor more than one year, or both. (99 v. 233 § 6.)
<small>Penalty.</small>

SECTION 1037. Whoever, being a person, firm or corporations or members of a board, and being the owner or in control of any building mentioned in section ten hundred and thirty-one of this chapter, uses or permits the use of such building in violation of any order prohibiting its use
<small>Penalty.</small>

issued as provided by law, or fails to comply with an order so issued relating to the change, improvement or repair of such building shall be fined not less than ten dollars, nor more than one hundred dollars, and each day that such use or failure continues shall constitute a separate offense. (99 v. 234 § 9.)

Examination of public buildings as to safety in case of fire.

SECTION 4648. On application of the owner or person having control of an opera-house, hall, theater, church, schoolhouse, college, academy, seminary, infirmary, sanitarium, children's home, hospital, medical institute, asylum, or other buildings used for the assemblages or betterment of people in a municipal corporation, the mayor, civil engineer, and chief engineer of the fire department shall carefully make a joint examination thereof to ascertain the means provided for the speedy and safe egress of persons at any time there assembled, and for extinguishing fire at or in such place. If the corporation has no such engineer, the mayor and two members of council shall make such examination. (90 v. 3.)

The act of April 28, 1908 (99 O. L. 232) (G. C. Secs. 1031 and 1032), enlarging the duties of the chief inspector of workshops and factories by requiring inspection of schoolhouses and other places of public assemblage, and authorizing him where means for safe and speedy egress are insufficient to specify such appliances, additions or alterations as are necessary to insure proper protection and require that they be installed, is not a provision for the taking of property without due process of law but is a mere requirement that such property be used in a lawful way and is a constitutional and valid enactment: Board of Education v. Sawyer, 7 O. N. P. (N. S.) 401.

Certificate of safety.

SECTION 4649. Upon such examination, if it is found that such building is abundantly provided with means for speedy and safe egress of such persons; and, if above the first floor, that it is provided therein with water or other equally efficient agency, and proper means to apply it, so that fire at such place can be immediately extinguished, or if the assembly rooms of such church are situated upon the ground floor, with a sufficient number of low windows, in their opinion, provided for, to secure safe and easy means of escape in case of alarm, they or a majority of them, shall issue to such owner or person having control, a certificate of the fact, which shall continue in force one year, unless sooner revoked by council. (62 v. 139.)

Re-examination in case of change in building.

SECTION 4650. If a change or alteration is made in such building, the owner or person having charge of it shall notify the mayor of the fact, who shall cause to be made a re-examination in all respects like that provided for in the preceding section, and if upon such examination such owner, or person having control, is entitled to such certificate, it shall be issued to him, with like effect. (62 v. 39.)

When inspections to be made; inspector to have access to buildings.

SECTION 4657. The chief inspector of workshops and factories, or his district inspectors, shall make inspections of buildings named in the first section of this chapter, as often as he deems necessary, or upon the written demand of the agent or owner of such structures, or upon the written request of five or more citizens of the municipal corporation, county or township in which such structure is located; and they shall have access to such biuldings at any time it is deemed necessary to inspect them. (93 v. 35.)

SECTION 1261-3. It shall be the duty of said inspector ot plumbing, as often as instructed by the state board of health, to inspect any and all public or private institutions, sanitariums, hospitals, schools, prisons, factories, workshops, or places where men women or children are or might be employed and to condemn any and all unsanitary or defective plumbing that may be found in connection therewith and to order such changes in the method of construction of the drainage and ventilation, as well as the arrangement of the plumbing appliances, as may be necessary to insure the safety of the public health. Duties of inspector.

Such inspector shall not exercise any authority in municipalities or other political subdivisions wherein ordinances or resolutions have been adopted by the proper authorities regulating plumbing or prescribing the character thereof. (101 v. 395.)

SECTION 12487. Whoever maliciously injures or defaces a church edifice, schoolhouse, dwelling house or other buildings, its fixtures, books or appurtenances, or commits a nuisance therein, or purposely and maliciously commits a trespass upon the inclosed grounds attached thereto or fixtures placed thereon, or an inclosure or sidewalk about such grounds, shall be fined not more than one hundred dollars. (70 v. 216.) Injuring and committing nuisances in buildings.

SECTION 12536. Whoever manufactures gunpowder, blasting powder, dynamite, nyalite, jovite, dynalite, fulminates, nitro-glycerine, nitro-explosive compounds, chlorate of potash, explosive compounds, or stores more than one hundred pounds thereof within the limits of a municipal corporation, or within sixty rods of a factory, workshop, mercantile or other establishment, occupied dwelling, church, schoolhouse, or building in which people are accustomed to assemble, or manufactures it within ten rods of an adjoining property not owned or leased by such manufacturer, shall be fined not less than one hundred dollars nor more than one thousand dollars. (99 v. 212.) Manufacturing or storing explosives restricted.

SECTION 12537. The distance at which explosives described in the next preceding section, may be stored with relation to the factories, workshops and other buildings owned and used solely for the purpose of manufacturing such explosives, as a part of a manufacturing plant, shall not be governed by the above provision as to distance but shall be determined and regulated by the chief inspector of workshops and factories upon inspection of the district inspector of explosives. (99 v. 212 § 4.) Exception to last section.

Using hall,
theater, etc.,
without certifi-
cate, or
obstructing
aisles.

SECTION 12574.   Whoever, being the owner of a hall, theater, opera house, church or schoolhouse, or having control thereof individually or as agent of a society or corporation, permits it to be used by public assemblies or schools without having the certificate required by law that it is provided with the means of speedy and safe ingress and egress, or blocks up the aisles and hallways thereof by placing chairs or stools therein, or permits them to be occupied by persons standing therein or by any obstruction endangering the safety of persons therein, or cuts off easy escape and egress therefrom, shall be fined not more than one thousand dollars.   (80 v. 28.)

TITLE XV. PUBLIC SCHOOL.

CHAPTER 1.

OHIO STATE UNIVERSITY.

SECTION 14976. The educational institution heretofore designated as the Ohio agricultural and mechanical college shall be known and designated hereafter as "The Ohio State University." (75 v. 126.)

SECTION 14977. A college, to be styled The Ohio Agricultural and Mechanical College, is hereby established in this state, in accordance with the provisions of an act of congress of the United States, passed July 2d, 1862, entitled "an act donating public lands to the several states and territories which may provide colleges for the benefit of agricutlural and mechanic arts," and said college to be located and controlled as hereinafter provided. The leading object shall be, without excluding other scientific and classical studies, and including military tactics, to teach such branches of learning as are related to agricultural and mechanic arts. (67 v. 20.)

SECTION 14978. It shall be the duty of the board of trustees to permanently locate said agricultural and mechanical college upon lands, not less than one hundred acres, which in their judgment is best suited to the wants and purposes of said institution, the same being reasonably central in the state, and accessible by railroad from different parts thereof, having regard to healthiness of location, and also regarding the best interests of the college in the receipt of moneys, lands, or other property donated to said college by any county, town, or individual, in consideration of the location of said college at a given place: provdied, it shall require a three-fifths vote of the trustees to make said location; and, provided further, that said location shall be made on or before the fifteenth day of October, 1870: provided, further, that any person acting as a trustee, who shall accept or receive, directly or indirectly, any sum or amount from any person or persons, to use their influence in favor of the location of said college at any particular point or place, shall be held to be guilty of a misdemeanor, and on conviction thereof by any court of competent jurisdiction, shall be fined in any sum not less than one thousand nor more than ten thousand dollars: provided, further, that in the location of said college the said trustees shall not in any event incur any debt or obligation exceeding forty thousand dollars; and if, in their opinion, the interests of

405

the college cannot be best promoted without a larger expenditure for the location than that sum, then they may delay the permanent location of the same until the third Monday of January, 1871, and report their proceedings and conclusions to the general assembly: provided, further, that said college shall not be located until there are secured thereto for such location, donations in money, or unincumbered lands, at their cash valuation, whereon the college is to be located, or in both money and such lands, a sum equal to at least one hundred thousand dollars. (67 v. 20.)

The act is not in conflict with § 1, Art. XIII, of the Constitution: Neil v. Board of Trustees, etc., 31 O. S. 15, 21.

The act does not constitute the board of trustees a corporation: *Ib.*

R. subscribed $100 and promised to pay the same to the Ohio Agricultural and Mechanical College in consideration that said college should be located at a specified place. N., in writing, at the same time and place, and upon the same consideration, guaranteed the payment of the sum so subscribed. Said subscription, with the guaranty thereto annexed, was delivered to, and accepted by the trustees of the college upon the consideration aforesaid, as one instrument: Held, that the subscriber and guarantor may be jointly sued on said instrument: *Ib.*

SECTION 14979. The unsurveyed and unsold lands ceded to the state of Ohio by a certain act of congress of the United States, approved February 18, 1871, situate and being in the Virginia Military District between the great Scioto and the Little Miami rivers in said state, be and the same are hereby accepted by the state of Ohio, subject to the provisions of said act. (70 v. 107.)

Construction of this act and rights of occupants: Board of Trustees v. Cuppett, 52 O. S. 567.

The cession covered 'all the title the United States had to and in these lands, and all it could convey: State University v. Satterfield, 2 C. C. 86.

The cession covered all unpatented lands held on surveys based on Virginia military *state line* warrants, such warrants not being subject to location in the district, and entries and surveys made thereon, being utterly null and void, and, under § (8430), plaintiff has the title to these lands: *Ib.*

Possession of these lands by defendant, and those under whom he claims, for ninety-two years, will not avail as a defense, as the statute of limitations cannot be pleaded against the United States or the state: *Ib.*

A tax title on these lands does not aid defendant's title, as the lands have never been subject to taxation, and the tax deed is void, and nothing can be claimed under it: *Ib.*

See statement of facts in this case under which it was held that the proviso of the act of Congress of March 2, 1807, extending the time for locating warrants, did not aid defendant's title: *Ib.*

SECTION 14980. That the trustees of the Ohio Agricultural and Mechanical College are hereby authorized to demand from all persons who have destroyed or converted any timber growing upon the lands ceded to the state of Ohio, as stated in the act to which this is supplementary, since the date of said act of congress ceding said lands to the state of Ohio, full compensation for the timber so destroyed or converted, and for all damages, and if payment shall be refused, to institute proper proceedings in the name of said Ohio Agricutlural and Mechanical College, in any court of competent jurisdiction, to recover the same with damages and costs of suit: provided, that the provisions of this section shall not apply to timber taken from the one hundred and sixty acres by any person who shall obtain the title to the same under section *three* [§(4105—21)] of this act. (70 v. 107.)

Section 14981. The title of said lands is hereby vested in the trustees of the Ohio Agricultural and Mechanical College, for the benefit of said college; and said trustees are hereby required to cause a complete survey of said lands to be immediately made, and a correct plat thereof to be returned to said trustees, and to ascertain and set off, in reasonably compact form, by accurate boundaries to each occupant who was in actual possession of and living upon any of said lands at the time of the passage of said act of congress, as provided therein, or their heirs and assigns, a tract not exceeding forty acres; and upon the payment, by the claimant, of the cost of surveying and making the deed, the said trustees shall make and deliver to said claimant a deed for said tract; and if any such occupant shall have been in such actual possession of more than forty acres, and is desirous of holding the same, he shall be entitled to have in addition to said forty acres, any number of acres not exceeding, with said forty acres, the number of one hundred and sixty acres, to be in reasonably compact form, by paying for the said excess over forty acres, the sum of one dollar per acre; and if any claimant under the provisions of this act shall desire to purchase any tract of land adjoining said forty acres, not exceeding, including said forty acres, the amount of one hundred and sixty acres, of which said claimant shall have been in actual possession, but does not desire to purchase the same at one dollar per acre, said trustees, upon notice by said claimant, shall cause said tract or part of tract to be sold separate from other tracts of land at a valuation fixed upon by the appraisers named in this act, payable one-third at the date of the survey, and the residue in two equal annual installments, with interest at six per cent, payable annually, and upon full payment being made with the cost of survey and conveyance, said trustees shall make and deliver to such claimant, his or her heirs or assigns, a deed for said excess over said forty acres: provided, that any person claiming the benefit of the provisions of this section as occupant, shall comply in all respects with, and be subject to the provisions of the thirteenth section of the act of congress, approved September 4, 1841, entitled an act to appropriate the proceeds of the sales of the public lands and to grant pre-emption rights, and to the rules and regulations of the general land office of the United States relating to proof for the establishment of pre-emptor's claims: provided, however, that the affidavit required by said thirteenth section of said act of congress may be made before any justice of the peace or other officer authorized to administer oaths. (70 v. 107.)

Section 14982. All the surveyed and unsold lands in said military district, not occupied as aforesaid, shall be divided by said trustees into such tracts, not exceeding five hundred acres in any one boundary, as will be most advantageous, reference being had to the quality of said

lands and the uses to which they will be applied; the
boundaries to all such tracts and divisions shall be accurately surveyed, and the lines of each tract plainly
marked, and substantial stone monuments firmly placed at
the principal corners. The character of the soil, water-
courses, elevation of hills, timber, ledges, or stratas of the
Waverly building stone, iron ore, fire clay, and limestone,
shall be fully noted by the surveyors on their plats and in
their field-books. All the tracts so divided and surveyed
shall be numbered in consecutive order, commencing with
the tracts in Adams county, and so continuing until all said
lands in said district shall be platted and numbered; which
numbers shall be shown upon the plats, and the said plats
shall correctly indicate all township lines. The said lands,
when so divided, surveyed and numbered, shall be appraised in separate tracts at their true value in money, by
three qualified freehold residents in said state, to be sum-
moned by said trustees, or any committee of theirs. Said
appraisers, before entering upon their duties, shall take
and subscribe an oath before competent authority honestly
and impartially to appraise all such lands, and to perform
all other duties in relation thereto; they shall each be paid
two dollars a day for their services, and their expenses
allowed them; they shall make due return of all their ap-
praisements to said trustees, which, with all said plats and
surveys, shall be delivered by them to the auditor of state,
and the same shall be recorded in the office of said auditor
in suitable books to be provided for such purpose; which,
with all such original plats, surveys, and papers, shall form
a part of the public records of the state in the land department of said office. (70 v. 107.)

The duties of the plaintiff in surveying, dividing, numbering and plat-
ting these lands and reporting them to the land department of the state, are
not conditions precedent to vesting the title in plaintiff: State University
v. Satterfield, 2 C. C. 87.

SECTION 14983. And the said trustees are hereby
authorized and required to sell of said lands at public
or private sale, at a price not less than the appraised value
thereof, on such terms for cash and credit as may be
agreed upon between the purchaser and said trustees, or
any authorized agent of theirs: provided, that the first payment shall, in every case, be not less than one-third of the
appraised value of such tract; all deferred payments shall
bear six per cent interest, to be paid annually, and said
trustees may, in their discretion, extend subsequent annual
payments through a period not exceeding five years. All
public sales of said lands shall be by auction, at the front
door of the court house of the county in which these lands
so offered lie, after having been advertised five consecutive
weeks in a newspaper published and generally circulated
in such county; such notices of sale shall contain a sufficient
description of the premises to clearly identify the same,
with a statement of the terms of payment and the amount
of appraisement, and all such public sales shall be made at

such times as said trustees shall dem expedient; and in case
such land or any tract thereof shall not sell for the amount
of the appraisement at such public sale, then upon the same
being again offered as aforesaid at public sale, the same may
be sold for any sum not less than three-fourths of the appraisement: provided, that no trustee of said college or
appraiser of said land shall be the purchaser of any of
said lands at any such sale or sales, either directly or indirectly. The said trustees shall cause all contracts for the
sale of said lands to be printed or written in a book or
books, stating the consideration and terms of all sales,
which said contracts shall be signed in duplicate by the
said trustees or any authorized agent of theirs, and by the
purchaser or purchasers, one copy of which shall be preserved in said book, and the other shall be delivered to the
purchaser at the time the same shall be signed; and every
purchaser shall execute his promissory note or notes, with
interest, payable as aforesaid, for all deferred payments,
which notes shall be non-negotiable, and payable to said
college at such place or places as may be directed by said
trustees; and upon full payment being made by the purchaser, his heirs, or assigns, for any such land, every such
person shall be entitled to receive a conveyance therefor in
fee simple by deed of said trustees, executed by the president of the board, under the corporate seal of said college;
and all lands disposed of under the provisions of this act,
shall be returned by said trustees to the auditors of the
counties in which they are situate, and by them be placed
on the duplicate for taxation. (70 v. 107.)

SECTION 14984. The proceeds of the sales of such
lands, or so much thereof as may be necessary, after the
payment out of the same of all the necessary expenses of
survey and sale remaining uncertified into the treasury of
said state, may be used by said trustees in building and
maintaining upon the lands of said university a suitable
number of houses, adapted to use as family residences, for
the use of members of the faculty of said university, for
which use a fair and reasonable rent shall be paid to said
university. Said buildings shall be erected under the provisions of title *six* of the revised statutes of Ohio; and the
said trustees shall annually report to the governor a detailed statement of receipts and disbursements in the execution of the trust under the provisions of this act. (70 v.
107.)

SECTION 14985. The act entitled an act to sell lands
ceded to the state of Ohio by the congress of the United
States by act of congress, approved February 18th, 1871,
passed March 26, 1872, and the act supplementary thereto
and amendatory thereof, passed April 29, 1872, be and
they are hereby repealed: provided, that the passage of
this act shall in nowise affect affect the validity of the
transactions of said board of trustees, or rights vested in

any person, under the provisions of said acts; and this act shall take effect and be in force from and after its passage. (70 v. 107.)

SECTION 14986. The auditor of state be and is required to compute the interest which has accrued and will accrue on the agricultural college scrip fund since the same has been sold, to July first, one thousand eight hundred and seventy, compounding the same by semi-annual rests on the first day of January and the first day of July in each year; and on the fifteenth day of June eighteen hundred and seventy to transfer the sum so arising to the said college fund, and invest the same in the interest bearing bonds of the state, in the same manner as the principal of the said fund is now vested. (67 v. 15.)

SECTION 14987. As soon as the board of trustees of the Ohio state university accepts the provisions hereinafter made, it is hereby authorized and required to execute and deliver upon demand, a deed of conveyance to the parties in possession under claim of title of any unpatented survey or part thereof, in said Virginia military district; provvded, however, that all applicants for such deed must furnish said trustees with a certified copy of the deed under which they claim, and if required, a certified copy of the unpatented survey in which their lands are situate, as the necessary evidence to satisfy the board that the same has never been patented, but has been occupied and improved by the said parties in possession or those under whom they claim title, for more than twenty-one years. Provided, also, that each applicant shall pay the board of trustees the sum of two dollars, as the cost of preparing and executing such deed. (86 v. 92.)

SECTION 14988. The auditor of state shall add the sum of one dollar per acre, reckoned by the number of acres of land in each actual survey for all conveyances so made to that part of the irreducible debt of the state, which forms the endowment of said Ohio state university; provided, that in cases where suit has been brought for the recovery of said lands, persons demanding deeds of release, shall pay all court costs of such suits. (86 v. 92.)

WHEREAS, The gnéral assembly of Ohio, on March 14, 1889, passed the following act, to-wit.: [Here follows a repetition of General Code §§ (14987) and 14988)]

And WHEREAS, By said act the state of Ohio allowed certain persons to quiet and perfect the title to their lands for a nominal sum; and

WHEREAS, Other persons in all respects in similar circumstances were compelled to pay large sums of money for the same purpose; and

WHEREAS, It is just and right that the state of Ohio should treat all her citizens with equal justice and liberality; therefore.

SECTION 14989. All persons who were in possession of lands in the Virginia military district under claim of title of an unpatented survey or part thereof, said lands having been occupied and improved by said persons in possession or those under whom they claim title for more than twenty-one years and were compelled by suit, or the fear thereof, to pay the Ohio state university for said lands, are hereby authorized to present a statement of the amount of money so paid by them, together with all the facts relating to the land held by them and their title thereto, to a board composed of the secretary of state, auditor of state and attorney-general, who are hereby authorized and empowered to examine such statements and call for and examine such other testimony as they see fit, and if upon such examination said board are satisfied that said persons are justly entitled to relief as those persons were who have obtained relief under the provisions of the aforesaid act, then said board shall determine how much said party has wrongfully paid and issue an order to the auditor of state directing him to draw his warrant on the treasurer of state for the said amount in behalf of the person filing said statement, provided that where such claims have been heretofore as (or) shall hereafter be allowed by said board, the auditor of state shall add the amount thereof to that part of the irreducible debt of the state which constitutes the endowment fund of said Ohio state university. (91 v. 375.)

SECTION 14990. That there be and is hereby appropriated, out of any money in the state treasury accredited to the fund of the Ohio state university, the sum of twelve hundred and ninety-six ($1,296) dollars to pay said warrants. (90 v. 221.)

SECTION 14991. That persons filing such statements shall pay all the costs incurred in obtaining evidence. (90 v. 221.)

SECTION 14992. Said board shall report all its proceedings to the general assembly. (90 v. 221.)

APPENDIX
FORMS AND INSTRUCTIONS

413

FORMS FOR REPORTS ISSUED BY THE DEPARTMENT OF PUBLIC INSTRUCTION.

Form No.	Report made by.	Report made to.	Statute.	When due.	Reporting.	Copies to be filed in office of.
1	County Board of Education.	County Auditor	474-2	Annually on Aug. 1.	Number of teachers to be employed, etc.	County Auditor and County Superintendent.
2	Dean of Summer School	Supt. of Public Instruction		Annually at the close of summer school	Attendance, courses and all summer school data	Supt. of Public Instruction.
4	School Board	Supt. of Public Instruction	7784	Annually at the close of school	School statistics	Supt. or Clerk of local board.
5	City Superintendent	Supt. of Public Instruction	7787	Annually at the close of school	School statistics	Supt. of Public Instruction and Clerk of local board.
5	Village and District Superintendent	County Superintendent	7706	Annually at the close of school	School statistics	County Superintendent and Clerk of local board.
6	County Superintendent	Supt. of Public Instruction	7706-4	Annually on June 30th	School statistics	Supt. of Public Instruction and County Superintendent.
7	Enumerator	Clerk of Board	7796	Annually fifth Saturday in May.	Enumeration	Clerk of local board.
8	Clerk of local board	County Auditor	7799	Annually first Saturday in June	Enumeration	County Auditor and Clerk of local board.
9	City Auditor	Supt. of Public Instruction	7803	Annually third Saturday in July	Enumeration	Supt of Public Instruction and County Auditor.
10	Clerk of local board	Supt. of Public Instruction	7756	Annually at the close of school	Statistics of school for deaf, blind and crippled children.	Supt. of Public Instruction.
11	High School Inspector / Rural School Inspector / Agricultural Supervisor	Supt. of Public Instruction / Supt. of Public Instruction / Supt. of Public Instruction	7754 / 7761-4 (6)	Monthly	Time sheet and report of activities	Supt. of Public Instruction.
12	High School Inspector	Supt. of Public Instruction	7754		Inspection of high schools	Supt. of Public Instruction and County Superintendent.

No.					
13	Rural School Inspector / Agricultural Supervisor	Supt. of Public Instruction	7761-4		Inspection of elementary schools	Supt. of Public Instruction and County Superintendent.
14	Dean of College	Supt. of Public Instruction	7807-3-4-5		Certificate of graduation and transcript of credits	Supt. of Public Instruction.
14a	Normal Director	Supt. of Public Instruction			Report of credits	Normal Director.
15	District Superintendent	County Superintendent	7747	Annualy at close of year	List of eighth grade graduates.	City Superintendent.
16	District Superintendent	County Superintendent	7706	Monthly	Report of activities	City Superintendent.
17	City and City Board of Examiners	Supt. of Public Instruction	7815, 7864	Annually on September 1st	Record of examinations, certificates issued, etc.	Supt. of Public Instruction and County Superintendent.
18	County Board of Examiners	County Auditor	7820	After each examination	Amount collected from fees, number in examination, etc.	County Auditor and County Superintendent.
19	County Superintendent	Supt. of Public Instruction	7865	Within five days after close of institute	Data concerning county institute	Supt. of Public Instruction and County Superintendent.
20	College and Normal School President	Supt. of Public Instruction	359	Annually at close of academic year.	Data concerning college or private school	Supt. of Public Instruction.
21	County Board of Education	Supt. of Public Instruction	4744-5 (3)		Certificate of qualifications of county and district superintendents	Supt. of Public Instruction.
22	Teacher	Superintendent	7784	Monthly	Teachers' attendance, enrollment, etc.	District Superintendent or Clerk of Board of Education.
23	District Superintendent	County Superintendent	7706	After each visit	Report of class-room instruction — Sample	County Superintendent.
24	Teacher	County Superintendent		Annually during month of September	Professional record — Sample.	County Superintendent.
25	Board of Education	County Auditor	7787, 7788	...ly on September 1st	Financial report	County Auditor and Clerk of local board.
26	County Auditor	Supt. of Public Instruction	7789	Annually on September 20th	Financial report	Supt. of Public Instruction and County Auditor.

FORMS FOR REPORTS ISSUED BY THE DEPARTMENT OF PUBLIC INSTRUCTION—Concluded.

Form No.	Report made by.	Report made to.	Statute.	When due.	Reporting.	Copies to be filed in office of.
27	County Board of Education..	Auditor of State..........	4744-3	Semi-annually	Under 4th, the state's share of the taxes of county and district	Auditor of State.
36	City Board of Education..	County Auditor	7706-4	Annualy on Aug. 31st	Report of taxts and expenditures	City Auditor.
37	Normal Director	Supt. of Public Instruction...	7654-1 to 7654-5	Annually	Statistics	Supt. of Public Instruction.
38	Board of Education.........	City Auditor	7600	August 1st	Report of number of teachers and average daily attendance.	City Auditor.
39	City board of education...	City Auditor	7600	August 1st	Report of number of teachers and average daily attendance.	City Auditor.

FORMS FOR APPLICATIONS ISSUED BY THE DEPARTMENT OF PUBLIC INSTRUCTION.

Form No.	Application made by.	Application made to	Statute.	Applying for.	Copies to be filed in office of.
3	Board of Education	Supt. of Public Instruction	7654-1	Location of normal school	Supt. of Public Instruction.
28	Applicant	Critic Teacher	7825		City Superintendent.
29	Applicant	Board of Examiners	7815		City Superintendent.
30	Board of Education	County Superintendent	7655-6	State aid as standardized school	Supt. of Public Instruction (if approved).
31	Board of Education	Supt. of Public Instruction		Inspection and classification of high school	Supt. of Public Instruction.
32	Teacher	Supt. of Public Instruction	7845, 7821-1	Renewal of five or eight year certificate	Supt. of Public Instruction.
33	Teacher	Supt. of Public Instruction	7807-3-4-5	Provisional certificate	Supt. of Public Instruction.
34	Teacher	State Board of Examiners	7807	State life certificate	Supt. of Public Instruction.
35	Teacher	State Board of Examiners	7807-6-7	State life certificate	Supt. of Public Instruction.

SUGGESTIVE FORMS FOR THE USE OF SCHOOL BOARDS AND OTHER SCHOOL OFFICERS.

No. 1.

SCHOOL BOARD PROCEEDINGS.

(For minutes of board).

..................., ... County, Ohio, ...19....

Upon call of the chairman, the...

Board of Education met in the..at

.............o'clock, ...M., on the.............day of.......................

191...., with the following members present:

....

....

....

                                            Clerk.

After the reading and approval of the minutes of the preceding meeting the following business was transacted:

(Here make complete record of all business of the board. All motions should be recorded whether carried or lost.)

The above is a correct record of the proceedings of the board of education on......................., 19....

....

                                    President.

....

                                    Clerk.

No. 2.   SECTION 7766.

PLEDGE OF EMPLOYER OF YOUTH.

........................., Ohio, ...191....

....

Superintendent of Schools.
Person duly authorized by the Superintendent of Schools.
Clerk of Board of Education.

$\left\{\begin{array}{l} \text{We} \\ \text{I} \end{array}\right\}$ promise to employ...

legally, and to return his age and schooling certificate to you within two days after he ceases to work, giving reasons for his withdrawal or dismissal from $\left\{\begin{array}{l} \text{our} \\ \text{my} \end{array}\right\}$ service.

....

               By...............................

Print here Sec. 12975.

No. 3.   SECTION 7766.

AGE AND SCHOOLING CERTIFICATE.

I, ..., being the

Superintendent of Schools.
Clerk of the Board of Education.
Person duly authorized by the Superintendent of Schools.
(Underscore your official position.)

of the......................School District of........................County,

Ohio, hereby certify that...

was born at........................., in the County of........................

State of...................., on the................day of................19....;

that...........'..has been examined in and has passed a satisfactory............

grade test in reading, spelling, writing, English grammar, geography and arith-

metic; that the papers enumerated and described in Section 7766 of the General

Code have been duly received, examined and filed, and that said.................

......................the description of whom is as follows: height............

feet...............inches; complexion..................; hair................;

eyes................; sex................, is as to............................

development, health and physical fitness, able to perform the labor in which

................is to be employed by..

Approved by me and signed in my presence by the aforesaid.................

....................this............day of....................19....

Signed...
Signature of child.

....
Title of approving officer.

I, ...

Superintendent of Schools.
Clerk of the Board of Education.
Person duly authorized by the Superintendent of Schools.

of........................School District, ...County, Ohio,

hereby certify that I have duly authorized the above named.....................

............................to approve the above Age and Schooling Certificate.

Signed...

Superintendent of Schools.
Clerk of the Board of Education.
Person duly authorized by the Superintendent of Schools.

Of................................School District.

No. 4.   SECTIONS $\begin{cases} 7766 \\ 7773 \\ 12977 \end{cases}$

NOTICE TO PARENT OR GUARDIAN.

State of Ohio, ...*County, ss.*:

      To................................

     You are hereby notified that...................., a child between the ages of............ and............ years, under your charge, is not attending school, that such non-attendance is in direct violation of the law and without legal excuse.

     You are hereby required to cause said child to attend some recognized school within two days from the date of this notice, and you are warned that if the truancy of said child is persisted in the final consequences will be as provided by law, as endorsed hereon.

     Witness my hand this............day of............., 19....

..................................,
Truant Officer.

....................school district, ...county, Ohio.

     Print appropriate selection from Sections 7766, 7773 and 12977 on reverse' of this form.

No. 5.   SECTIONS $\begin{cases} 7766 \\ 7773 \end{cases}$

NOTICE TO TRUANT.

State of Ohio, ...*County, ss.*:

     To............, a child between the ages of .... and .... years.

     You are hereby notified that you are and will be required to attend some recognized school within two days from the date of this notice, and you are hereby warned that if this notice is not complied with the final consequences will be as provided by law as indorsed hereon.

     Witness my hand this .... day of ...., 19....

..................................,
Truant Officer.

...............school district, ...county, Ohio.

     Print sections 7773 and 7766 in full on reverse side of form.

No. 6.   REPORT OF TRUANT OFFICER.   SECTION 7771.

.................., Ohio, ..., 19....

To the { *Clerk of the Board of Education* } of ...., ... *County, Ohio.*
      { *Superintendent of Schools* }

In compliance with your requirements, I hereby submit my report for................, 19...., as shown below.

.... *Truant Officer.*

Name of truant or non-attendant reported.	Age.	Sex.	Warning sent.		Notification of non-attendance sent.		Complaint entered on refusal, failure or neglect.		Complaint entered of juvenile disorderly.	
			Month.	Day.	Month.	Day.	Month.	Day.	Month.	Day.

No. 7.   SECTION 4777.

FINAL RECEIPT OF CLERK.

$.............   ...., Ohio, ..., 19.....

Received of ...., retiring clerk of ...., school district, the sum of .... dollars, the record book, account book, school laws, teachers' certificates and reports, and the other official books and papers in his hands.

............................., Clerk.

No. 8.   SECTION 4774.

CLERK'S BOND.

Know all men by these presents, That we................................ are held and firmly bound unto the state of Ohio, in the sum of.............. dollars, for the payment whereof we jointly and severally bind ourselves.

Whereas, the said .... has been duly chosen and qualified as clerk of the board of education of .... district .... in .... township, ... county, and state of Ohio, for the term of two years from the...............day of January, A. D. 19...., and until his successor is chosen and qualified.

Now, the condition of the above obligation is such, that if the said............ ....shall faithfully perform all the official duties required of him as clerk of said board, then this obligation will be void; otherwise it shall be and remain in full force.

Signed and sealed by us this .... day of ...., A. D. nineteen hundred and ....

....

....

....

The sureties on the above bond, and its amount, approved by said board this .... day of ...., A. D. 19....

............................, President of said Board.

No. 9. SECTION 7836.

BOND OF CLERK OF COUNTY BOARD OF EXAMINERS.

Know All Men by These Presents: That we..........................
...., are held and firmly bound unto the
state of Ohio, in the sum of .... dollars, for the
payment whereof we jointly and severally bind ourselves.

Whereas, the said...has been duly
elected and qualified as county superintendent of schools of......................
.... County, and state of Ohio, for the term of
.... years from the ....day of
.... A. D. 19........ and until his successor
is chosen and qualified, and is therefore clerk of the county board of school examiners of the said county.

Now, if the said .... will
pay into the county treasury monthly the examination fees received by the board,
make the statistical returns required by law and otherwise perform faithfully all
duties required of him as clerk of said board, then this obligation shall be void;
otherwise it shall remain in full force.

Signed and sealed by us this .... day of ....
...................A. D. nineteen hundred and..........

....

....

....

The sureties on the above bond, and its amount, approved by...............
County Auditor of .... County this ....
day of .... A. D. 19..........

....

Auditor.

No. 10.

OATH OF SCHOOL OFFICERS.

This form of oath may be used for school board members, and officers and
may be administered by the clerk or any board member, or any person authorized
to administer oaths:

I, ..., do solemnly swear
(or affirm) that I will support the constitution of the United States, and the
constitution of the State of Ohio; and that I will faithfully and impartially discharge my duties as .... in and for the ....
school district, ... county, Ohio, to the best of my ability,
and in accordance with the laws now in effect and hereafter to be enacted, during
my continuance in said office and until my successor is chosen and qualified.

....

Sworn to and subscribed before me, this .... day
of ...., A. D. 19........

No. 11.   SECTION 4767.

CERTIFICATE OF SCHOOL FUNDS IN TREASURY.

We hereby certify that, as required by law, by a count of all the money, bonds and securities in the hands of .... treasurer of .... school district .... county, Ohio, made this .... day of .... 19...)..., in the presence of the clerk of the board, we find .... dollars (and bonds, etc., in value amounting to .... dollars) of school funds to be in the treasury, and we have directed the clerk to enter upon the records of the board a copy of this report.

....

....

....
                                               Board (or Committee).

Attest:
         .
                ....
                                                    President.

         ....
                                                       Clerk.

No. 12.   SECTION 7587.

CERTIFICATE OF ANNUAL SCHOOL LEVY.

To the Auditor of .... County:

It is hereby certified by the Board of Education of...................... School district, ... County, that the entire amount necessary to be levied upon the property of said school district for school purposes, during the next school year, as directed by Sec. 7587 G. C. is as follows:

For Tuition Fund.......................... ———mills. $————
For Building Fund.......................... ———mills. $————
For Contingent Fund....................... ———mills. $————
For Bonds, Interest and Sinking Fund....... ————mills. $————
For —————— ....'.. ———mills. $————
          By order of the Board of Education.

                ....
                                                       Clerk.

.........................Ohio   .... 19......

No. 13.

COMPLAINT IN REGARD TO SCHOOL FUNDS.

To the Superintendent of Public Instruction:

SIR: I respectfully submit the following state of facts as existing in .... school district, ..., county, Ohio.

(Statement of complaint containing one of the causes mentioned in section 361, G. C.)

In consideration of the above statement I respectfully request the appointment of some competent accountant to investigate the condition of the school funds of said district.

....
Complainant.

State of Ohio, ... County, ss.:

I, ..., ..., and .... do solemnly swear (or affirm) that the statements made in the foregoing complaint are true to the best of my knowledge and belief.

....

....

....

Sworn to by..........................., ..., and ...., and subscribed in my presence this day of ....19......

....
(*Title.*)

I hereby certify that......................., ..., and ...., are taxpayers and residents of ....: school district.

....
County Auditor.

......................., Ohio, ..., 19......

No. 15.

NOTICE OF SPECIAL MEETINGS.

Notice is hereby given that there will be a meeting of the board of education of .... school district, ... County, Ohio, on the .... day of .... at .... o'clock .... M., to consider any business which may be considered necessary.

....
President.

....
Clerk.

...................., 19......

NOTE: — A special meeting may be called by the president, clerk or two **members** of the board. This form may be adapted to the use of county boards **of education.**

No. 16.   SECTION 4692.

TRANSFER OF TERRITORY.

(Form of resolution for minutes of county boards).

Resolved, that the following described territory be and the same is hereby
transferred from .... school district .... County,
Ohio, to..................school district ....County
Ohio, subject to the provisions of section 4692, General Code of Ohio. (Give
description).

Resolved, That the clerk of this board be instructed to notify the board of
education of .... school district of .... County,
Ohio, of the passage of this resolution, and upon similar action being taken by
said board that said clerk file a certified copy hereof with the County Auditors
together with a correct map of the territory described.

NOTE: — A majority of the full membership of the boards is necessary to
carry such a resolution and the yea and nay vote is required.

No. 17.   SECTIONS $\begin{cases} 4682\text{--}1. \\ 4735\text{--}1. \end{cases}$

FORM FOR PETITION TO DISSOLVE SCHOOL DISTRICT AND JOIN CONTIGUOUS SCHOOL DISTRICT.

To the Board of Education of .... School District,

.... County, Ohio.

The undersigned constituting at least one-fourth of the qualified electors
in .... school district, which district contains a population of less
than fifteen hundred persons, respectfully petition your honorable body that the
question of dissolving said school district and joining it to ....
rural school district be submitted to a vote of the qualified electors of said village
school district, as provided in section 4682-1 of the General Code of Ohio.

Signatures.

....

....

....

I hereby certify that the above named electors of ....
school district, ... county, Ohio, are legally qualified electors
and constitute one-fourth of the electors of said school district.

....

The Board of Education upon its own motion may order a special election
for this purpose.

No. 18.

FORM FOR PETITION TO HAVE CENSUS TAKEN.

To the Board of Education of .... *School District,*
.... *County, Ohio.*

The undersigned, constituting at least one hundred of the qualified electors of the .... school district of .... County, Ohio, respectfully petition your honorable body to order a census to be taken of said school district as provided in section 4688-1 of the General Code of Ohio.

Signatures.

....
....
....
....

I hereby certify that this list of petitioners contains the names of one hundred legally qualified electors in .... school district. .... County, Ohio.

....

The Board of Education upon its own motion may order a census of the school district to be taken.

No. 19.

FORM FOR PETITION TO CENTRALIZE SCHOOLS.

To the Board of Education of .... *School District,*
.... *County, Ohio.*

The undersigned, constituting at least one-fourth of the qualified electors in .... school district, respectfully petition your honorable body that the question of centralization of the schools of the .... school district be submitted to a vote of the qualified electors of said school district, and that your body proceed therefore as provided in section 4726, General Code of Ohio.

Signatures.

....
....
....
....

I hereby certify that the above named electors of .... school district .... county, Ohio, are legally qualified electors and constitute one-fourth of the electors of such school district.

....

The Board of Education is also required upon order of the County Board of Education to submit this question to the voters.

If this question is lost at the election thus ordered it may not be submitted again for a period of two years unless a petition is made by at least forty per cent. of the electors of the district.

No. 20.

TEACHER'S CONTRACT.

An agreement entered into between ...., of ....
.... county, Ohio, and the Board of Education of ....
school district in ....,...'..... county, Ohio; the said ....
.... hereby agrees to teach in the public schools of said district
for a term of .... months, and also agrees toabide by and
maintain the rules and regulations adopted by said Board for the government
of said schools of said district. And in consideration of such services, the said
board of education agrees to pay said .... the sum of
.... dollars, payable monthly at the office of the treasurer of
the board of education.

Entered into this .... day of ...., 19......

....
Teacher.

....
President.

....
Clerk.

Any special provisions may be easily inserted.

No. 21.

WEEKLY REPORT OF DISTRICT SUPERINTENDENT.

Month.............

Week | 1 | 2 | 3 | 4 |

(Check V)

Superintendent.............

Supervision District Number.............

Number schools visited.............

Number teachers' meetings held.............

Number board meetings attended.............

	School.	Grade.	Time of entering.	Time spent in room.	Pupils present.	Comment upon		
						Character of instruction.	Discipline.	Any other matters.
Monday.								
Tuesday.								
Wednesday.								
Thursday.								
Friday.								

This form should be printed on thin card board 9″ x 6″. It is suggested for use where County Superintendents desire a report oftener than that made on form 16.

INDEX TO SECTIONS THAT DO NOT COME IN NUMERICAL ORDER.

(431)

Lightning Source UK Ltd.
Milton Keynes UK
UKHW020805271218
334504UK00008B/514/P